THE OBJECT OF
DATA ABSTRACTION
AND STRUCTURES
USING JAVA™

THE OBJECT OF
DATA ABSTRACTION AND STRUCTURES USING JAVA™

David D. Riley

Addison
Wesley

Boston San Francisco New York
London Toronto Sydney Tokyo Singapore Madrid
Mexico City Munich Paris Cape Town Hong Kong Montreal

Executive Editor: *Susan Hartman Sullivan*
Associate Editor: *Galia Shokry*
Executive Marketing Manager: *Michael Hirsch*
Managing Editor: *Pat Mahtani*
Production Supervisor: *Diane Freed*
Text Design: *Susan Carsten Raymond*
Design Manager/Cover Design: *Regina Hagen Kolenda*
Composition: *Gillian Hall, The Aardvark Group*
Copyeditor: *Betsy Hardinger*
Prepress and Manufacturing Coordinator: *Caroline Fell*

Access the latest information about Addison-Wesley titles from our World Wide Web Site: *http://www.aw.com/cs*

Many of the designations used by manufacturers and sellers to distinguish their products are claimed as trademarks. Where those designations appear in this book, and Addison-Wesley was aware of a trademark claim, the designations have been printed in initial caps or all caps.

The programs and the applications presented in this book have been included for their instructional value. They have been tested with care but are not guaranteed for any particular purpose. The publisher does not offer any warranties or representations, nor does it accept any liabilities with respect to the programs or applications.

Library of Congress Cataloging-in-Publication Data
Riley, David D., 1951–
   Data structures and software development in Java / David D. Riley.
     p. cm.
   Includes bibliographical references and index.
   ISBN 0-201-71359-4
     1. Java (Computer program language) 2. Data structures (Computer science)
     3.Computer software--Development. I. Title.

QA76.73.J38 R535 2003
005.13'3--dc21

                         2002026277

ISBN 0-201-71359-4

1 2 3 4 5 6 7 8 9 10—CRW—040302

This book is dedicated to my wife, Sandra, and children, Kasandra and Derek. These three remarkable individuals provided endless assistance, encouragement, and inspiration.

TABLE OF CONTENTS

PART 1 CHAPTERS 1–9

CHAPTER 6 Applying Lists   243

CHAPTER 7 Stacking and Queueing   289

PART 2 CORE CONCEPTS: REVIEW AND REFERENCE

CHAPTER 05 **Files and Streams**   **565**

CHAPTER 06 **Recursion**   **603**

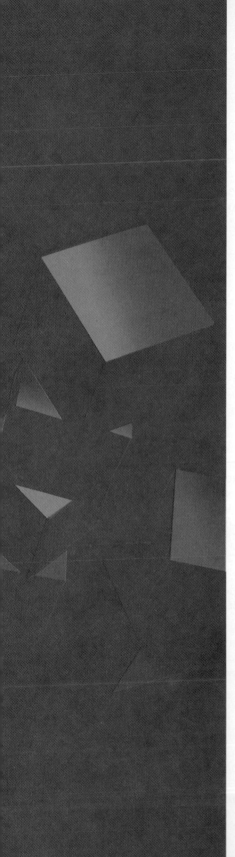

PREFACE

Much of what a software developer needs to know about viewing, organizing, and manipulating data is taught in the second computer science course, often referred to as CS2 or *data structures*. Because object-oriented methodology offers improved approaches for software design and implementation, this study has recently taken on a refreshing new look. This book is written to capture this new perspective on traditional computer science topics. Such a presentation is a natural complement to any CS1 course that takes an early objects approach.

P.1 DESIGN AND ABSTRACTION

CS1 courses necessarily focus on implementation (coding) skills with little time devoted to exploring software design. An examination of data structures provides unique opportunities for illustrating software design techniques, including

- The use of class diagrams to express high-level design
- The choice of where and how to use inheritance in designing classes
- The proper use of abstract classes and the associated template design pattern
- The sharing of data by way of the singleton design pattern
- The design and implementation of interfaces as design tools
- The practice of design by contract in the form of class invariants and method preconditions and postconditions
- The incorporation of exception handling into detailed design as a way to improve robustness
- The use of state diagrams as a technique for both specifying and implementing behavior as a form of table-driven code
- The use of recursion for defining specification functions
- The abstract modeling of containers in terms of set and sequence abstractions
- The consideration of *java.util* conventions as design alternatives
- The application of the iterator design pattern

These software design issues, and many others, are not included in a traditional data structures presentation. However, each of these concepts is a significant tool for the modern software developer that deserves inclusion in early education in computer science. Such topics form a natural second step for those who have taken the first step in mastering object-oriented software development.

All of these object-oriented design (OOD) concepts relate closely to the proper use of data abstraction and data structures in software engineering. For example, knowledge of the template design pattern results in the proper OOD for alternative implementations for a stack. Class specifications can reveal subtle differences between bounded and unbounded structures. Understanding the iterator design pattern gives developers ways to compare and contrast arrays and lists.

This book makes a clear distinction between design and implementation. An abstract data type (ADT) approach emphasizes the importance of the abstract view of the designer/client, and alternative algorithms offer opportunities to explore implementation decisions and their related performance.

P.2 A TWO-PART APPROACH

The presentation is divided into two parts. The first nine chapters represent the central subject matter. Chapter 1 jumps right into three topical threads of the book: abstract data types, specifications, and design patterns. Coverage of Java interfaces, including Comparable and Cloneable, as well as abstract classes introduces these tools, which are used elsewhere for proper ADT design. Chapter 2 introduces another key topical thread: data containers and structures. This chapter covers generic containers, bounded versus unbounded containers, immutable and mutable classes, the `java.util.Collection` interface, and several useful design patterns.

Because software performance issues are a necessary consideration for ADT implementation, Chapter 3 is devoted to an introduction to algorithmic performance. Traditional searching and sorting algorithms are woven into the presentation. This is a lighter treatment of the topic than might be found in a more advanced algorithms course, but the coverage is sufficient to support comparison of the algorithms covered in later chapters.

The remainder of the chapters in the first part (Chapters 4 through 9) focus on common data abstractions and structures: arrays, linked lists, stacks, queues, maps, and trees. The inclusion of arrays (Chapter 4) may seem unusual inasmuch as readers are undoubtedly familiar with arrays. However, we have found this material to be invaluable because it provides a comfortable environment for discussing the relationship between software design and implementation. Furthermore, many array topics tend to get little or no coverage in a first computer science course; these include multidimensional arrays, ragged arrays, `java.util.Vector`, table-driven code, bit vectors, and finite state machines. The topics of lists, stacks, queues, maps, and trees (Chapters 5 through 9) are all viewed from two perspectives: their design and their implementation.

The second part of this book is titled Core Concepts: Review and Reference. These six chapters (numbered Chapter O1 through O6) are a concession to the differences in the way each of us approaches CS1 and CS2 material. Any of these six chapters can be covered like any other chapter; but, as the section name implies, these chapters can also be treated as a review or as reference material.

Most of the Core Concepts section—such as Chapter O1 (Object-Oriented Programming), Chapter O2 (Inheritance), Chapter O3 (Specifications), Chapter O4 (Exceptions), and Chapter O5 (Files and Streams)—may have been covered in the prior course or may not be a topic of some CS2 courses. In such cases, the chapters can be ignored or can be used, as we often do, as a quick refresher. Other faculty will prefer to spend more time with this material. These early Core Concepts chapters, especially Chapters O1 through O3, provide key background for the reader with minimal knowledge of object orientation.

Chapter O6 (Recursion) is unique among the chapters in Part 2. Most CS2 classes include recursion as a major topic. However, there is little agreement on the placement of this material (at the beginning of CS2, the end, or somewhere in between). Because of these different strategies and because recursion is largely outside the mainstream of the main topical threads of CS2, this material has been located in Chapter O6. This arrangement provides maximum flexibility to fit the coverage to the environment.

P.3 ORDER DEPENDENCIES

I've attempted to be mindful that CS2 courses vary widely in topical coverage and in presentation order. Every reasonable effort has been made to minimize topical dependencies.

Although this material is designed to follow the object-centric presentation in my earlier book, *The Object of Java*, allowances are included for other entry paths.

For those individuals who have studied *The Object of Java*, the material in Chapters O1, O2, and O3 is largely a review. In the spirit of spiral pedagogy, these chapters can be read by students at the beginning of the semester and perhaps covered lightly in class. Students with a less object-oriented preparation or who are not familiar with Java will want to spend more time on these topics.

The topical coverage is designed to be inclusive, acknowledging that few CS2 courses will cover all 15 chapters. Some of these topics, such as files (Chapter O5) and maps (Chapter 8), are outside the subject matter range of some CS2 courses; these chapters can be skipped without repercussion. The material from other chapters, such as inheritance (Chapter O3) and arrays (Chapter 4), may have been covered extensively by prerequisite coursework. In these cases it is recommended that the chapters be covered lightly to reinforce understanding and fill in any knowledge gaps.

Figure P.1 diagrams the chapter dependencies. The central chapters are shown in light blue, and the six Core Concepts chapters are shown in white. A solid arrow from Chapter A to Chapter B indicates that Chapter B relies substantially on the material presented in Chapter A. A dashed line indicates a minor dependency that is not essential to order of presentation. For example, if Chapter 3, and the corresponding big-oh material, is ignored, a few scattered references to big-oh performance will be useless, but the associated material can still be presented effectively. (CS2 instructors differ on this issue.) The dashed arrow between Chapter O6 (Recursion) and Chapter 3 (Performance) indicates that Chapter O6 pertains only to two of Chapter 3's topics, quicksort and mergesort.

P.4 SOFTWARE ENGINEERING EMPHASIS

Like good writing, good programming requires skill and discipline. Knowing the guidelines and techniques of software engineering is critical to developing such skill and discipline. Software engineering is a concept integrated throughout the presentation.

You will find "Software Engineering Hint" boxes sprinkled throughout the chapters. These offer a collection of software development best practices. A Software Engineering Hint might, for example, summarize the trade-offs of immutability or offer performance cautions regarding an implementation strategy.

Design by contract is a key aspect of sound software engineering. Method preconditions and postconditions, as well as class invariants, are used consistently throughout program examples. Mathematical models are encouraged as a way to convey abstract definitions.

P.5 UML

To remain true to the software engineering theme, this book restricts diagramming notations to those from the Unified Modeling Language (UML). Using UML diagrams exposes students to the same notations that have now become standard in the software development industry. Two particular UML diagrams are used extensively:

- Class diagrams
- Object diagrams

In addition, the UML notation for state diagrams is used, especially in Chapter 4.

Portions of UML's Object Constraint Language (OCL) notation—particularly for sets and sequences—are used in numerous specifications. OCL expressions are an effective and intuitive way to express abstract properties of ADTs.

Figure P.1 Chapter Dependencies

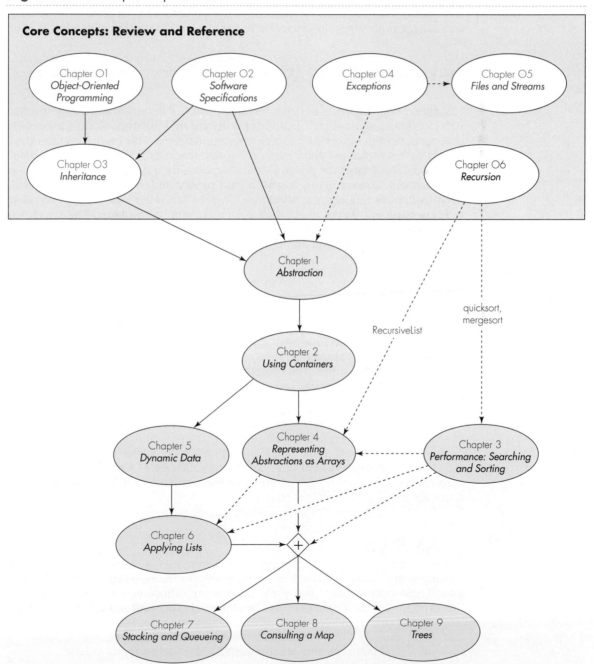

P.6 THE SOFTWARE INSPECTOR

Software engineering studies confirm that the most useful of all testing comes in the form of informal desk checks, design reviews, and walkthroughs. Such practices require fundamental knowledge of what to check, review, and walk through. Every chapter ends with an attempt to provide this information in the form of "The Software Inspector." These sections not only provide a useful review of the chapter's salient points but also couch them in terms of practical how-to ideas.

P.7 DESIGN PATTERNS

CS2 classes help students to begin the transition from concentrating on aspects of software implementation to examining software design issues. A crucial aspect of object-oriented design is the concept of design patterns. This book integrates those design patterns that are good matches for designing data abstractions. Chapter 1 introduces the **template** design pattern, which is used many times in later examples. Similarly, the **adapter**, **iterator**, and **proxy** design patterns, introduced in Chapter 2, have numerous applications. Chapter 4 examines the concept of **table-driven code** and **state machines** as implementation patterns. The **singleton** design pattern is explored in Chapter 5 and used in an example in Chapter 9. Chapter 6 covers the command object pattern.

P.8 JAVA

The Java programming language is used as a vehicle for exploring these topics. It is expected that the reader has written computer programs, ideally in Java. Readers unfamiliar with Java should definitely study Chapters O1 and O2 before proceeding to the central chapters. The central chapters include key Java coverage for topics—such as abstract classes, interfaces, and wrapper classes—that aren't always presented in CS1 classes.

The standard Java libraries contain important tools, especially certain classes in the *java.lang* and *java.util* libraries. Many of the facilities of these libraries are explored in this book. Some of these facilities, such as the java.util.Iterator interface, are compared with other approaches. Strategies for implementing standard classes are often examined. Some of the standard classes with lesser importance are included in optional sections.

P.9 EXAMPLES

I firmly believe that numerous complete examples are essential to effective education. These chapters are filled with the code for complete software components. These programs have been executed, and they are included in digital form among the supplements available with this book. Unlike my prior book, *The Object of Java*, this book does not rely on nonstandard libraries. However, the supplements include several complete implementations of basic data structure classes.

P.10 CLASS TESTED

This work is based on several years of my experience and that of colleagues. I have used manuscripts from this work for two past semesters. During this class testing, I have purposely varied the order of presenting the material to test the flexibility discussed previously. Informal assessment in subsequent courses has reinforced the effectiveness of this approach.

P.11 SUPPLEMENTS

Following is a list of supplementary materials associated with this textbook. These supplements are made available online (*www.aw.com/riley*) for qualified instructors only.

- Copies of the examples included in this book, including the associated data structures classes
- A complete set of solutions to all exercises
- PowerPoint lectures to parallel the chapter presentations
- An instructor's manual
- The source code for software examples

P.12 ACKNOWLEDGMENTS

I want to thank the fine reviewers that Addison-Wesley contracted. These individuals caused me to ponder both content and pedagogy. Clearly, the changes they proposed improved the final work.

Bary W. Pollack, Sierra Nevada College
Bina Ramamurthy, University of New York at Buffalo, SUNY
Robert Moll, University of Massachusetts, Amherst
Parag Doshi, Bell Labs, Lucent Technologies
Richard Pattis, Carnegie Mellon University
Ruben Gonzalez-Rubio, Université de Sherbrooke
Robert Franks, Central College
Jane Turk, La Salle University
Blayne E. Mayfield, Oklahoma State University
Sam Chung, University of Texas of the Permian Basin
Suzanne Westbrook, University of Arizona
Brian Bansenaur, North Seattle Community College
Robert Burton, Brigham Young University
Yenumula B. Reddy, Grambling State University

Last, but certainly not least, are the many good folk who work for Addison-Wesley. Without exception, the following individuals performed outstandingly in their various roles: Susan Hartman Sullivan, Galia Shokry, Diane Freed, Kim Ellwood, Patricia Mahtani, Gillian Hall, Regina Kolenda, Betsy Hardinger, Michael Hirsch, and Jennifer Pelland.

Dave Riley

THE OBJECT OF
DATA ABSTRACTION
AND STRUCTURES
USING JAVA™

PART 1

Chapters 1–9

CHAPTER 1

ABSTRACTION

> "THE ESSENCE OF A SOFTWARE ENTITY IS A CONSTRUCT OF INTERLOCKING CONCEPTS: DATA SETS, RELATIONSHIPS AMONG DATA ITEMS, ALGORITHMS, AND INVOCATIONS OF FUNCTIONS. THIS ESSENCE IS ABSTRACT IN THAT SUCH A CONCEPTUAL CONSTRUCT IS THE SAME UNDER ANY REPRESENTATION. IT IS NONETHELESS HIGHLY PRECISE AND RICHLY DETAILED."
>
> —Fred P. Brooks, Jr., CACM, April 1987

OBJECTIVES

- To explore the concept of an abstract data type (ADT) as an effective tool for software design

- To separate the two views of every ADT: the abstract view and the implementation view

- To emphasize techniques for modeling ADTs abstractly yet precisely

- To examine the Object Constraint Language notations for sets

- To explore ADT design principles

- To introduce the template design pattern and its role in software design

- To examine Java interfaces as purely abstract classes

- To examine how Java interfaces, especially the `Comparable` and `Cloneable` interfaces, can be used to define class properties

- To review the `toString` and `equals` methods as good candidates for inclusion in ADTs

The world is filled with complexity beyond human understanding. When you walk into a new room, you are bombarded with sights, sounds, and smells too varied to perceive and too detailed to assimilate. The visual images, alone, are so intricate that your brain can't keep up with your eyes. You begin to notice the "bigger issues" of the room: the wall color, the floor covering, the ceiling treatments, and the furniture. All these items have other properties that are revealed upon closer inspection. Are the windows open or closed? What are the dimensions of each pane of glass? How dark is the glass? Does it need to be washed? Is there a covering on the window? How is it operated? The list of questions regarding the visual details of the room goes on and on.

The human mind, miraculous as it as, cannot begin to process the complexity of even a simple environment. Fortunately, our minds seem to be equipped with an innate ability to focus on what is important while filtering less significant details and distractions. As you look naturally around a room, try to note the items that your eyes perceive and the items and properties that your brain records. Next, think about the many characteristics of the room that your eyes and brain ignore.

This ability of the brain to focus and filter is often called **abstraction**. Humans use abstraction constantly. Upon sighting a saber-toothed tiger, ancient humans were more likely to scream "Tiger!" than to stand around describing the characteristics of this four-legged, catlike creature with a tail and two curved upper canine teeth approximately 8 inches in length. (Perhaps natural selection shortened the lives of those early humans who were unable to abstract.)

1.1 ABSTRACT DATA TYPES

Because software, especially software built with an object-oriented approach (described in Chapter O1), models real-world entities, it isn't surprising that abstraction is a useful tool for programmers. Every time a programmer names a variable or method, abstraction is at work. The names of these members are abstract labels for the associated data or code.

Perhaps the most useful application of abstraction for the object-oriented programmer is to take an abstract view of a software class. A properly designed class can be viewed from two distinct vantage points. Figure 1.1 illustrates these two perspectives: the implementation view (also called the concrete view) and the abstract view.

Figure 1.1 Implementation and abstract views of a software class

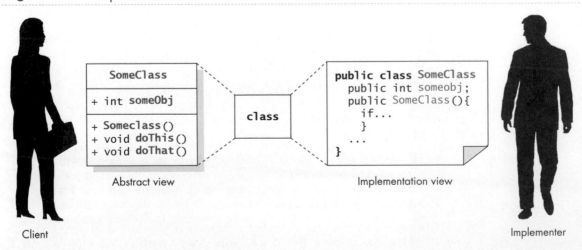

The **abstract view** of a class is an interpretation that is independent of any particular implementation. In other words, an abstract view of a class captures important class features without committing to any specific technique for implementing the class's methods or storing the class's content. For example, you can view a thermometer abstractly as a device to take a reading of the current temperature. You might physically implement this function using a tube full of mercury, a spring that expands and contracts, a strip of plastic with embedded chemicals that activate different temperature numbers along the strip, or by various other technologies. To a design engineer designing a heating system for an office building, the physical implementation of the thermometer is largely unimportant. It is also nonessential to the researcher studying global warming, who is collecting temperature data from around the planet.

The **implementation view** of software, as its name implies, reflects the vantage point of the person who implements the software. The **implementer** must be aware of every local variable, every Java statement, and every algorithm that is part of the class's code. The implementation view of a class is important because the implementer must be fully aware of all such coding details in order to craft correct software.

Abstraction provides the key way to communicate among software developers, and because most software projects involve many developers this communication is crucial to project success. In an object-oriented environment much of the code is classified as **client code**. Any programmer who writes software that uses a class is considered a **client**, and the software is referred to as client code of the **supplier** class. Any of the following situations are included in this definition of client code.

- The client code inherits the supplier class.
- The client code declares a variable belonging to the supplier class.
- The client code declares a parameter with the supplier class as its type.
- The client code includes a method whose type is the supplier class.
- The client code includes an expression that evaluates to the supplier class type.

Every client developer must understand important characteristics of the client code, and it is these characteristics that represent the abstract view needed by the client. When you write software using such library classes as String or JFrame or Object, you are a client of these classes. You need to be knowledgeable about their members and behavior, but you don't need to know (nor should you *want* to know) the details of how String or JFrame or Object was implemented by the Sun Microsystems programmers. It is this level of abstraction—the view of a client, another software developer—that is pursued in this book.

As Figure 1.1 indicates, the view of a supplier class is different for a client than it is for the implementer. The software implementation view exposes several things that are not generally included in the client's abstract view:

- All the class instance variables (discussed in Chapter O1)
- Code for public methods
- Private methods
- Additional private or inner classes

The client's view must be abstract in the sense that it should emphasize key aspects of the class while suppressing unnecessary details of the implementation.

The core of the client's abstract view is the **public interface** of the class. The class's public interface includes all its public instance variables and the signatures of all its public methods. The public interface also includes the behavior of the class methods (abstract specifications), but not the class code. Figure 1.2 summarizes.

Figure 1.2 Elements of the client and implementer views

Entity	*In the Implementer's View?*	*In the Client's view?*
public members	Yes	Yes
private members	Yes	No
protected members	Yes	No (except by an inheriting class)
package scope members	Yes	No (except within the same package)
local variables	Yes	No
class specifications	Yes	Yes
code within class methods	Yes	No

If the class is properly designed, the **public scope** (i.e., the abstract view) is reserved for those members explicitly intended for essential client use. Sometimes the client may require members with other scope. For example, **package scope** members can be used by a client writing another class to be included in the same package, and **protected scope** members can be used when inheriting the class.

The client's view of a class often takes the form of an **abstract data type** (**ADT**). The term "abstract" means that it focuses on the public interface while suppressing the coding details. The term "data type" refers to classes that are used to declare the types for data (objects). Another way to define ADT is as a collection of related data together with their associated operations. ADTs are extremely useful to software designers. In fact, the concept of object-oriented design can be characterized as composing a problem solution from the problem's constituent ADTs.

As an example of how ADTs are useful in software design, consider the task of designing a program to operate an alarm clock. Figure 1.3 pictures the basic kind of alarm clock in question.

Figure 1.3 Alarm clock picture

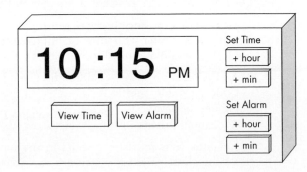

This particular clock displays hours, minutes, and an AM/PM message. The clock can display either the current time or the time to which the alarm has been set, with the two center buttons controlling which time is shown. The buttons on the right are used to set the time and the alarm time. Each +HOUR button advances the corresponding hour setting by 1, and each +MIN button advances the minute setting by 1.

This picture makes it evident that an alarm clock must keep track of two different times: the current time and the alarm setting time. This strongly suggests that the design for the alarm clock can be based on a TimeOfDay ADT. One possible version of a suitable TimeOfDay ADT is specified by the class diagram and class specifications (discussed in Chapter O2) in Figure 1.4.

Figure 1.4   TimeOfDay ADT class diagram and ADT specification

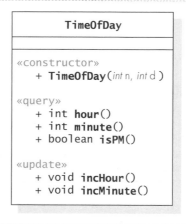

TimeOfDay ADT Specifications

Domain (Every TimeOfDay object has the following components)

    integer **hr**;
    integer **min**;

Invariant

    $0 <= hr <= 23$ (This is a version of military time with midnight at 0.)
    and $0 <= min <= 59$

Constructor Method

public **TimeOfDay** ()

    post: hr == the current clock hour, according to military time
           and min == the current clock minutes

Query Methods

public int **hour** ()

    post: hr < 12 *implies* result == hr
          and hr >= 12 *implies* result == hr − 12

Continued on next page

```
public int minute ()
     post: result == min
public String isPM ()
     post: result == (hr >= 12)
```

Update Methods

```
public void incHour ()
     modifies: hr
     post: hr@pre < 23 implies hr == hr@pre + 1
           and hr@pre == 23 implies hr == 0
public void incMinute ()
     modifies: min
     post: min@pre < 59 implies min == min@pre + 1
           and min@pre == 59 implies min == 0
```

Software Engineering Hint

Both the abstract view and the concrete (implementation) view are important. There are at least three acceptable alternatives for expressing ADTs in software.

- Express abstract specifications on paper with the corresponding class portraying the concrete view.
- Incorporate the abstract specifications into the ADT's class.
- Create a separate abstract class (possibly a Java interface) that incorporates abstract specifications, and inherit from this abstract class to create the concrete class(es).

The ADT specification for TimeOfDay is essentially a class specification with a small, but important, addition. An ADT specification separates into two parts: its data and its operations. The ADT's operations are specified via method signatures, preconditions, and postconditions (discussed in Chapter O2). Sometimes a *modifies* clause is included to indicate the data that potentially will be altered when the operation executes.

A key difference between this ADT specification and most class specifications lies in the data section, called the **domain**. The domain consists of an abstract view of the attributes that contribute to the state of the class. The domain specification in Figure 1.4 portrays TimeOfDay objects as consisting of two parts: an integer called hr, and another integer value called min. Every method postcondition relies on these abstract attributes to define the method's behavior.

As an example of how abstract specifications convey behavior, consider the incMinute method. Here is the postcondition:

> **post:** min@pre < 59 *implies* min == min@pre + 1
> and min@pre == 59 *implies* min == 0

The first line of this assertion states that as long as the value of min is less than 59 at the time incMinute is called, min's value is increased by 1 as a result of executing this method. (The suffix *@pre* denotes a value at the time of the method call; without this notation, a postcondition refers to return time values.) The second line of this postcondition indicates that if the value of min is 59 when incMinute is called, the method resets min to zero. The *modifies* clause further reinforces the fact that calling incMinute modifies the value of min but not hr (something that might not have been clear without the specifications).

To bridge the gap between the abstract ADT view of the client and the concrete view of the implementer, it is common to express ADTs in the form of an abstract class. Such an abstract class should portray the ADT by including the ADT specifications with minimal implementation detail. Figure 1.5 shows TimeOfDayADT, an abstract class version of TimeOfDay.

> ### Software Engineering Hint
>
> A **class invariant** defines a property that is always true for objects of the class. The TimeOfDay class invariant clarifies that hr is always within the range from 0 through 23 and **minute** in the range from 0 through 59.

Figure 1.5 TimeOfDayADT expressed as an abstract class

```
import java.util.*;
/* Domain (every TimeOfDay object has the following two parts)
        integer hr;
        integer min;
    invariant: 0 <= hr <= 23 (a version of military time in which
        midnight is 0) and 0 <= min <= 59 */

public abstract class TimeOfDayADT {
    protected Calendar clock;
    /* post:  hr == the current clock hour for the USA Central
                    Time Zone
                and min == the current clock minutes for the USA
                    Central Time Zone */
    public TimeOfDayADT() {
        clock = now();
    }
    /* post:  result == the current clock time for Central Time in
                    the USA */
    protected Calendar now() {
        final int localTimeOffset = -6; //offset for the Central
            Time Zone, USA
        String[] ids =
            TimeZone.getAvailableIDs(localTimeOffset*60*60*1000);
        SimpleTimeZone localTimeZone = new
            SimpleTimeZone(localTimeOffset*60*60*1000,ids[0]);
        localTimeZone.setStartRule(Calendar.APRIL, 1, Calendar.
            SUNDAY, 2*60*60*1000);
        localTimeZone.setEndRule(Calendar.OCTOBER, -1, Calendar.
            SUNDAY, 2*60*60*1000);
        return new GregorianCalendar(localTimeZone);
    }
    /* post:  hr < 12 implies result == hr
                and hr >= 12
                implies result == hr-12 */
    public abstract int hour();
```

Continued on next page

```
/* post:   result == min */
public abstract int minute();
/* post:   result == (hr >= 12) */
public abstract boolean isPM();
/* modifies:  hr
     post:   hr@pre < 23 implies hr == hr@pre + 1
             and hr@pre == 23 implies hr == 0 */
public abstract void incHour();
/* modifies:  min
     post:   min@pre < 59 implies min == min@pre + 1
             and (min@pre == 59) implies min == 0) */
public abstract void incMinute();
}
```

Software Engineering Hint

The *@pre* suffix, first appearing in `TimeOfDayADT`, denotes the value the expression had at the time of call. This notation should appear only when necessary and only in postconditions.

Software Engineering Hint

Military organizations, and many businesses, use a **need-to-know** policy, which states that individuals should be told only as much as they absolutely need to know. Software engineers are also well advised to adopt this policy. Clients almost never need to know about implementation details. So implementations are best hidden to avoid potential confusion and misuse.

`TimeOfDayADT` illustrates how an abstract class should focus attention on abstract specifications rather than on the code. Many of the public methods—`hour`, `minute`, `isPM`, `incHour`, and `incMinute`—are carefully specified, but all these methods are abstract.

Further evidence of the advantages of abstraction comes from the now method. Apparently, the implementation of `TimeOfDayADT` involves two classes—`Calendar` and `GregorianCalendar`—from the `java.util` package. Although the implementer must be familiar with the use of these two classes, there is no need for the client to know about them. In fact, the clients don't even need to know that `Calendar` and `GregorianCalendar` are used by the implementer.

`TimeOfDayADT` also illustrates that an implementation may use variables in a different way than suggested by the abstract domain. The abstract specifications for `TimeOfDayADT` contain two attributes: an `hr` integer and a `min` integer. However, the implementation appears to maintain both attributes within a `GregorianCalendar` object. This will result in a perfectly acceptable implementation as long as the specifications are properly preserved in the context of the implementation.

Now let's return to the alarm clock object first pictured in Figure 1.3. The class diagram and specification for this ADT are shown in Figure 1.6.

The `AlarmClock` ADT highlights the function, rather than the form, of the alarm clock. Each alarm clock is a visible display that incorporates buttons, but the `AlarmClock` specifications focus on the fact that an alarm clock incorporates two times: the clock's time of day (`clockTime`) and the clock's alarm setting (`alarmTime`). According to the class invariant, one of these two times is displayed on the clock's face (called `alarmClockDisplay`) at all times.

Figure 1.6 AlarmClock ADT class diagram and ADT specification

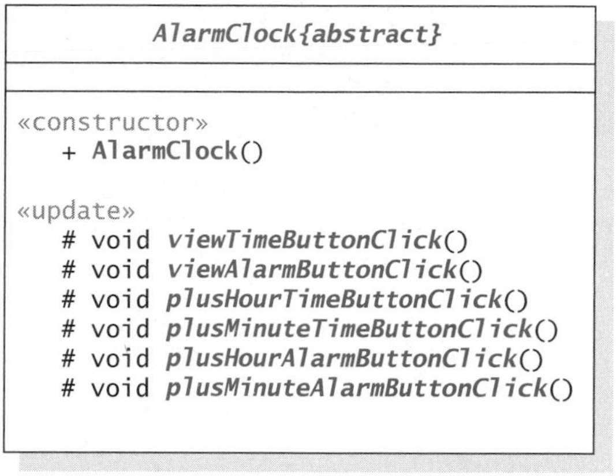

```
┌─────────────────────────────────────────┐
│          AlarmClock{abstract}            │
├─────────────────────────────────────────┤
│                                          │
├─────────────────────────────────────────┤
│  «constructor»                           │
│      + AlarmClock()                      │
│                                          │
│  «update»                                │
│      # void viewTimeButtonClick()        │
│      # void viewAlarmButtonClick()       │
│      # void plusHourTimeButtonClick()    │
│      # void plusMinuteTimeButtonClick()  │
│      # void plusHourAlarmButtonClick()   │
│      # void plusMinuteAlarmButtonClick() │
│                                          │
└─────────────────────────────────────────┘
```

AlarmClock ADT Specifications

Domain (Every AlarmClock object has the following components)

    TimeOfDay clockTime;
    TimeOfDay alarmTime;
    TimeOfDay alarmClockDisplay;

Invariant

alarmClockDisplay == clockTime *or* alarmClockDisplay == alarmTime

Note alarmClockDisplay represents the visible face of the alarm clock object, including six buttons to view the clock time and the alarm time and to increment clock hour, clock minute, alarm hour, and alarm minute.

Constructor Method

public TimeOfDay ()

> **post:** clockTime == current_time() *and* alarmTime == current_time() *and* alarmClockDisplay == clockTime *and* getX() == 0 *and* getY() == 0 *and* getWidth() == 600 *and* getHeight() == 500

Update Methods

protected abstract void viewTimeButtonClick ()

> **post:** alarmClockDisplay == clockTime
> **note:** this method serves as event handler for pressing the View Time button

protected abstract void viewAlarmButtonClick ()

> **post:** alarmClockDisplay == alarmTime
> **note:** this method serves as event handler for pressing the View Alarm button

Continued on next page

```
protected abstract void plusHourTimeButtonClick ()
```
    post: clockTime == clockTime@*pre* plus one hour

    note: this method serves as event handler for pressing the
            Set Time/+hour button

```
protected abstract void plusMinuteTimeButtonClick ()
```
    post: clockTime == clockTime@*pre* plus one minute

    note: this method serves as event handler for pressing the
            Set Time/+min button

```
protected abstract void plusHourAlarmButtonClick ()
```
    post: alarmTime == alarmTime@*pre* plus one hour

    note: this method serves as event handler for pressing the
            Set Alarm/+hour button

```
protected abstract void plusMinuteAlarmButtonClick ()
```
    post: alarmTime == alarmTime@*pre* plus one minute

    note: this method serves as event handler for pressing the
            Set Alarm/+min button

The six AlarmClock update methods describe the event handling behavior of the alarm clock. Each button on the face of the alarm clock corresponds to a separate method. For example, the viewAlarmButtonClick method defines the behavior associated with a click of the View Alarm button. It is unusual to encounter nonpublic methods in an ADT. However, these update methods use a protected scope because, as event handlers, they are not intended for external calls but may be of value to subclasses (described in Chapter O3).

Because TimeOfDay is treated as an abstraction, the AlarmClock class is independent of the particular TimeOfDay implementation. The TimeOfDay class could be implemented using an hour variable and minute variable to store military time. Alternatively, TimeOfDay could maintain time as a single int variable called minutesPastMidnight. Either implementation could be used by AlarmClock. In other words, the AlarmClock class depends on the abstract behavior of TimeOfDay but not on how TimeOfDay is implemented.

1.2   SPECIFICATION AND ABSTRACTION

An ADT has been described as a means to divorce a class design from its implementation. In essence, an ADT defines *what* functions the class performs but not *how* it does so. Each ADT abstractly omits the details of algorithms and nonpublic members that are needed to execute each method.

However, the fact that an ADT is abstract does not make it imprecise. Precision in ADT specifications is at least as important as it is in any other code specification. The implementer uses ADT specifications to define class behavior, and the client uses them to understand the class. How can an implementer properly code an imprecise ADT specification? How can a client rely on the behavior of a poorly specified ADT?

It is always best to define ADT attributes with one of the following two types:

- A well-defined and widely used type
- Another ADT that is precisely defined

The TimeOfDay ADT (Figure 1.4) illustrates an aggregate (discussed in Chapter O3) using the mathematical type Integer because the two attributes (min and hr) are both of type Integer. The AlarmClock ADT bases its definition on another ADT, TimeOfDay, as a type for all its attributes.

Mathematical types that are useful for defining ADTs include the following:

- Integer
- Real
- Boolean
- Set
- Sequence

The following types are not necessarily mathematical but are well defined and widely used:

- Character
- String

The Sequence type may not be as familiar as mathematical types. Sequences are described in Section 2.6. The String and Character types are really borrowed from programming languages, but they are included because of their widespread use in software and because typically they are well understood by software developers.

Figure 1.7 illustrates the use of **set** to define an ADT. The PhoneBook ADT is designed to store the information from typical residential phone listings in a simple telephone book.

Figure 1.7 PhoneBook ADT class diagram and ADT specification

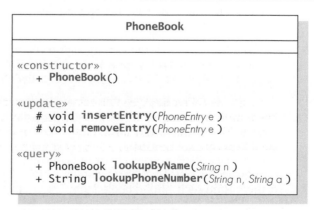

Continued on next page

PhoneBook ADT Specifications

Domain (Every PhoneEntry object has the following type)

    Set of PhoneEntry

Invariant

    forAll (e1, e2: PhoneEntry |
      (this->*includes*(e1) *and* this->*includes*(e2)
      and e1.name() == e2.name() *and* e1.address() == e2.address())
          implies e1.phone() == e2.phone())

Constructor Method

public **PhoneBook** ()

    post: this == *set*{}

Update Methods

public void **insertEntry** (PhoneEntry e)

    pre: *forAll*(x : this->*includes*(x)
            | x.name() != e.name() *or* x.address() != e.address())

    post: this == this@*pre*->*including*(e)

public void **removeEntry** (PhoneEntry e)

    post: this == this@*pre*->*excluding*(e)

Query Method

public PhoneBook **lookupByName** (String n)

    post: result->*forAll*(e | this->*includes*(e) *and* e.name() == n)

public PhoneEntry **lookupPhoneNumber** (String n, String a)

    post: *exists*(e : PhoneEntry | this->*includes*(e)
            and e.name()==n *and* e.address()==a
                implies (this->*includes*(result)
            and result.name()==n *and* result.address()==a)
            and not exists(e : PhoneEntry | this->*includes*(e)
            and e.name()==n *and* e.address()==a)
                implies result == null)

The ADT specification defines PhoneBook as a "*Set* of PhoneEntry." Therefore, a PhoneBook object has the same properties as a mathematical set in which the elements in the set belong to another type, called PhoneEntry.

The class invariant establishes an important characteristic of this particular kind of phone book. According to the invariant, PhoneBooks are not permitted to contain two entries having the same name and address but different phone numbers. The lookupPhoneNumber method is made possible because of this invariant. A call to lookupPhoneNumber either returns the telephone number for the phone book entry with the same name and address as the method's parameters, or it returns null if there is no such phone book entry.

The PhoneBook ADT is another example of how carefully written notations lead to precise specifications. The specification for removeEntry precisely states that attempting to remove a phone entry not found in the phone book has no effect. This conclusion is drawn from the definition of

> this == this@*pre->excluding*(e)

This assertion states that this (i.e., the PhoneBook object) does not change unless e is an element of the set this@*pre*. To understand this, and similar, expressions you must learn the notations of the Object Constraint Language (OCL) as they relate to sets. Figure 1.8 summarizes the more important OCL set notations.

The OCL notations for sets let you express a set literal using a common set enumeration with an additional *set* prefix. For example, the set that is commonly written {1, 3, 5, 7} is properly written as follows in OCL:

> *set*{1, 3, 5, 7}

OCL borrows some symbolism from common mathematical operations, including $==$ [1] (a test for equality), $\neq$ (a test for inequality, and $-$ (set difference).

Several set functions are provided in OCL, among them *union, intersection, including, excluding, includes, excludes,* and *size*. Each of these functions can be applied to a set. The proper OCL notation is, first, the identity of the set, followed by an arrow (->), followed by the function and any parameter. For example, if a set called *s* contained 15 items (a cardinality of 15), the value of the following expression would be 15:

> *s->size*()

Figure 1.8 A digest of set notations

Symbol	Meaning	Example(s)
set{ }	Empty set	
set{e_1, e_2, ..., e_n}	Set enumeration	*set*{1, 2, 3, 4}
s->select(e:*type* | predicate(e))	Set builder notation	*s->select*(e:Integer | 0<e<5) == *set*{1,2,3,4}
==	Equal to	*set*{1, 2} == *set*{2, 1, 2}
$\neq$	Not equal to	*set*{1, 2} $\neq$ *set*{1, 3}
s1->union(s2)	Union	*set*{1,2}*->union*(*set*{1,3}) == *set*{1,2,3}
s1->intersection(s2)	Intersection	*set*{1,2}*->intersection*(*set*{1,3}) == *set*{1}
$-$	Set difference	*set*{1, 2} $-$ *set*{1, 3}== *set*{2}
s->including(e)	Element inclusion	*set*{1,2}*->including*(3) == *set*{1,2,3}
s->excluding(e)	Element removal	*set*{1,2}*->excluding*(2) == *set*{1} *set*{1,2}*->excluding*(3) == *set*{1,2}
s->includes(e)	Test for inclusion	*set*{1,2}*->includes*(2) == TRUE *set*{1,2}*->includes*(3) == FALSE
s->includesAll(s)	Test for subset	*set*{1,2,4}*->includesAll*(*set*{1,4}) == TRUE *set*{1,2,4}*->includesAll*(*set*{1,2,4}) == TRUE *set*{1,2,4}*->includesAll*(*set*{1,3}) == FALSE
s->size()	Cardinality	*set*{1,4}*->size*() == 2

[1]Technically, OCL notation uses a single equal sign (=) to denote set equality. However, in this book the Java notation (==) is used to avoid any potential confusion with the assignment operator.

The union of two sets, *s1* and *s2*, is often written as follows:

s1 ∪ *s2*

This same function is expressed as follows using OCL:

s1->union(s2)

Similarly, the OCL expression for the intersection of two sets, *s1* and *s2*, is as follows:

s1->intersection(s2)

OCL also includes two functions that are somewhat more complicated to express using typical mathematical symbols. The following expression refers to the set that is formed by including element *e* within set *s*:

s->including(e)

Here are two examples of the use of this function, along with the equivalent set for each expression:

set{1,3,5}->including(2) == set{1,3,5,2}
set{1,3,5}->including(3) == set{1,3,5}

An analogous OCL function forms a set by removing an element. Here are two examples of the use of this excluding function:

set{1,3,5}->excluding(2) == set{1,3,5}
set{1,3,5}->excluding(3) == set{1,5}

Two of the Boolean functions that are included in OCL allow for tests of set membership (and nonmembership). The following expression evaluates to *true* exactly when *e* is an element of set *s*:

s->includes(e)

A more common mathematical notation for the preceding expression is ($e \in s$). In the same way, the OCL expression ($e \notin s$) is written as follows:

s->excludes(e)

Another common set function, is-subset-of, is usually symbolized by mathematicians as ⊆. OCL includes a Boolean function, called *includesAll*, to perform this task. For example, the following expression is true exactly when set *s2* is a subset (or equal to) set *s1*:

s1->includesAll(s2)

As Figure 1.7 demonstrates, the OCL set notations are sufficiently expressive to define an ADT, such as PhoneBook. However, the PhoneBook ADT depends upon another ADT, PhoneEntry, so the specification is incomplete without a description of PhoneEntry. Figure 1.9 shows this class diagram and ADT specification.

Taken together, the PhoneBook and PhoneEntry ADTs form a complete abstract specification of the class. These two ADTs are sufficiently precise that implementers can write code to make them behave in this way, clients can write other code that relies on them, and implementers and clients can work at the same time largely independent of one another.

Figure 1.9 PhoneEntry ADT class diagram and ADT specification

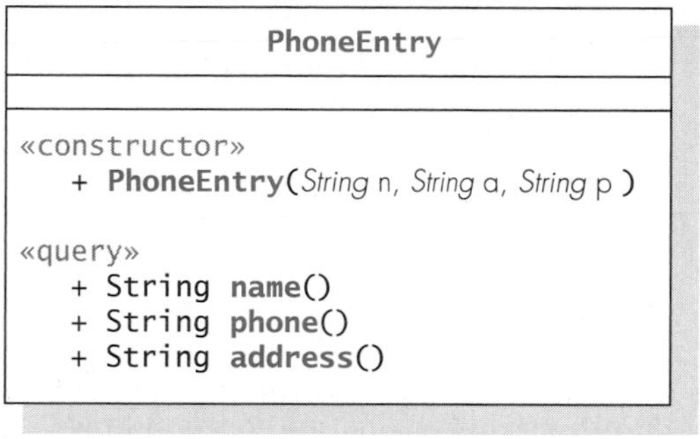

PhoneEntry

«constructor»
    + **PhoneEntry**(*String* n, *String* a, *String* p)
 	
«query»
    + String **name**()
    + String **phone**()
    + String **address**()

PhoneEntry ADT Specifications

Domain (Every PhoneEntry object has the following components)

    String listingName;
    String phoneNumber;
    String streetAddress;

Invariant

    phoneNumber.length() == 7

    and forAll(j : 0<=j<phoneNumber.length()

                | '0' <= phoneNumber.charAt(j) <= '9')

        (i.e., all characters in phoneNumber are digits)

Constructor Method

public PhoneEntry (String n, String a, String p)

    post: listingName == n
        and streetAddress == a
        and (p.length() != 7 *or* some character in p is not a digit)
            implies phone == "0000000"
        and (p.length() == 7 *and* all characters in p are digits)
            implies phone == p

Query Methods

public String name ()

    post: result == listingName

public String number ()

    post: result == phoneNumber

public String address ()

    post: result == streetAddress

1.3   ADT DESIGN PRINCIPLES

Previous sections introduce the basic concept of an ADT and its specification. Now it is time to consider how these concepts can be applied to software development.

Software development involves at least three distinct phases: (1) analysis of the problem to be solved, (2) design of the fundamental components of the software, (3) implementation of the code. The software process is analogous to constructing an office building. Early discussions involve an **analysis** of the project, during which the purpose, requirements, and environment of the new building are assessed. As the project progresses, architects and engineers **design** many models and blueprints to define the building's characteristics. In the end the structure is **implemented** by contractors and their construction workers, who craft the physical edifice.

The larger the project, the more important is the design phase. You may not need blueprints to build a doghouse, but it would be unthinkable to undertake a skyscraper project without blueprints. These design documents allow the customer to make key decisions before construction, allow architects and engineers to examine important structural and aesthetic options, serve as specifications for the construction, and permit the customer to determine whether construction was done properly.

Large software projects are like building projects. The various software developers play a variety of roles; some are designers who create the software architecture, and others craft (implement) the code just as a construction worker crafts parts of a building.

ADTs are arguably the most effective and widely used software design tool. Like a blueprint, an ADT expresses architectural issues in a way that is implementation independent. Ultimately, ADTs are implemented as one or more software classes.

The following three key design principles guide the use of ADTs:

1. Design abstractly.
2. Design precisely.
3. Plan for reuse.

The first principle, *Design abstractly*, refers to the fact that every ADT should be designed to hide implementation details as much as possible. Just as a blueprint often avoids cluttered detail, such as the exact placement of ordinary nail holes or how to string electrical wires, ADTs should also hide the coding statements.

A blueprint may not specify the exact material used to build a wall or the color of the wall, but the blueprint is still likely to provide detailed information on the wall's dimensions and structural strength requirements. In the same way, it is important that ADTs provide precise information regarding the software behavior. The *Design precisely* principle serves as a reminder to express design in carefully prepared documents such as class diagrams, ADT invariants and method pre and post conditions.

The third design principle, *Plan for reuse*, applies to all types of engineering endeavor. Components often can be reused to build other components. An ADT is often a good candidate for such reuse. Nowhere is software reuse more visible than in the standard Java libraries. For example, the `java.lang` package includes a `String` class for textual objects, a `Math` class to provide often-used numerical functions, `Calendar` and `Date` classes to facilitate the storage of calendar data, a `Random` class for instantiating random number generators, and many other library classes. Programmers can use each standard library class without knowledge of the underlying implementation, but they must understand the precise (abstract) behavior of each library class.

To further illustrate these design issues and principles, consider a simple program to let users add "stars" to a display of an image that resembles a night sky. Figure 1.10 shows the desired user interface. This interface contains of a window that is 300 pixels wide and 200 pixels tall with a black background color. The interface contains two buttons; clicking the Make Star button adds one star to the window, and clicking the Remove Star button removes one of the stars selected at random. Each star is a yellow dot with a diameter of 1 to 4 pixels. The star's diameter and position are randomly determined.

Figure 1.10 The bunch of stars user interface

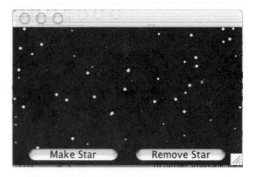

Design often begins by identification of objects and classes. For the night sky program the key objects are as follows:

- The "background" window
- The Make Star button
- The Remove Star button
- A bunch of "stars"

You can implement the first three objects by reuse. The `javax.swing` library includes a class for implementing a display window (`javax.swing.JFrame`) as well as a class to implement a user interface button (`javax.swing.JButton`). A wise designer looks to conserve resources by reusing these `swing` library classes.

For the "bunch of stars" object, however, you don't have an obvious existing design to reuse. Instead, the problem analysis suggests two ADTs: one for the bunch, and one for a star. Figure 1.11 contains a Dot ADT that represents individual stars. It is called Dot, rather than "Star," because Dot is more descriptive of its appearance. If the ADT is ever reused for other programs, the name "Star" could potentially be confusing.

Figure 1.11 Dot ADT class diagram and ADT specification

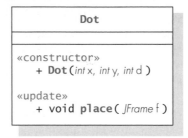

Dot ADT Specifications

Domain (Every Dot object has the following parts)

    `int xPosition` (X coordinate of left edge of the dot)

    `int yPosition` (Y coordinate of top edge of the dot)

    `int diameter`

    `JFrame backgroundFrame`

Invariant

    1 <= diameter <= 4

    and backgroundFrame ≠ `null` *implies* this is drawn as a yellow, filled
       circle appearing upon the background with the given position and
       diameter

Constructor Method

`public Dot (int x, int y, int d)`

    post: xPosition == x *and* yPosition == y *and* diameter == d
         and backgroundFrame == null

Update Methods

`public void place(JFrame f)`

    post: backgroundFrame == f

`public void removeFromDisplay()`

    post: backgroundFrame == null

The size and position of a `Dot` object are specified by parameters to the `Dot` constructor. Two additional methods—`place` and `removeFromDisplay`—are included. The add method causes a dot (star) to be attached (i.e., displayed) on a background window, and `removeFromDisplay` reverses the effect of any prior `place`. The *xPosition*, *yPosition*, *diameter*, and *backgroundFrame* attributes provide a means for precisely expressing various positioning and dimensional characteristics of a `Dot`.

Figure 1.12 contains the class diagram and ADT specifications for the `BunchOfStars` ADT. This ADT is specified to be a set, so the OCL set notation is used to describe method behavior.

Figure 1.12 BunchOfStars ADT class diagram and ADT specification

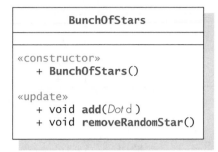

BunchOfStars ADT Specifications

Domain

    Every BunchOfStars set of Dot

Constructor Method

public BunchOfStars()

    post: this == *set{}*

Update Method

public void add (Dot d)

    post: this == this@*pre->including*(d)

public void removeRandomStar ()

    post: *exists*(s : this@*pre->includes*(s) | this == this@*pre->excluding*(s))

               (i.e., some randomly selected item has been removed from this)

Without further knowledge of the Dot and BunchOfStars implementations, it is possible write a client program to solve the starry night problem. Figure 1.13 contains such an application using a main method to initiate program execution.

Figure 1.13 NightSkyApp program

```
import java.awt.Color;
import java.awt.event.*;
import javax.swing.*;
public class NightSkyApp implements ActionListener {
    private JFrame window;
    private JButton addBtn, removeBtn;
    private BunchOfStars stars;
    /* note: This method initiates program execution by
             instantiating this class. */
```

Continued on next page

```
public static void main(String args[]) {
    new NightSkyApp();
}
/*  post:   window has been created in black with two buttons
            upon it and stars == set{} */
public NightSkyApp() {
    stars = new BunchOfStars();
    makeUserInterface();
}
/*  post:   window has been created in black with two buttons
            upon it */
private void makeUserInterface() {
    window = new JFrame();
    window.getContentPane().setLayout(null);
    window.setBounds(10, 10, 300, 200);
    window.getContentPane().setBackground(Color.black);
    addBtn = new JButton("Make Star");
    addBtn.setBounds(20, 155, 120, 20);
    addBtn.addActionListener(this);
    window.getContentPane().add(addBtn);
    removeBtn = new JButton("Remove Star");
    removeBtn.setBounds(160, 155, 120, 20);
    removeBtn.addActionListener(this);
    window.getContentPane().add(removeBtn);
    window.show();
}
/*  pre:    window != null and stars != null
    post:   event e was caused by the add button implies a new
                star is displayed and included in stars
            and event e was caused by the remove button implies
                one random star from stars@pre has been removed
    note:   This method is called in response to all button
            events */
public void actionPerformed(ActionEvent e) {
    if (e.getSource() == addBtn) {
        int xPos = (int)(Math.random()*300);
        int yPos = (int)(Math.random()*155);
        int diameter = (int)(Math.random()*4)+1;
        Dot dot = new Dot(xPos, yPos, diameter);
        dot.place(window);
        stars.add(dot);
    } else { //removeBtn pressed
        stars.removeRandomStar();
    }
    window.repaint();
}
}
```

The NightSkyApp constructor instantiates an empty collection of stars with the following statement:

```
stars = new BunchOfStars();
```

The remainder of this constructor establishes the user interface consisting of window (a JFrame object) and two JButton objects.

The NightSkyApp program is written so that any button click causes the actionPerformed method to be invoked. When the Make Star button is clicked, the following code executes:

```
int xPos = (int)(Math.random()*300);
int yPos = (int)(Math.random()*155);
int diameter = (int)(Math.random()*4)+1;
Dot dot = new Dot(xPos, yPos, diameter);
dot.place(window);
stars.add(dot);
```

Executing these statements causes a new Dot object to be instantiated with random position and size. This object is then placed on window and added to the collection of stars.

When the Remove Star button is clicked, the following statement is executed:

```
stars.removeRandomStar();
```

As is typical for client code, NightSkyApp can be written with an abstract view of the supplier classes (Dot and BunchOfStars). To see why ignoring the implementation of the supplier classes might a wise decision for a client, consider the implementations of Dot and BunchOfStars. Figure 1.14 shows a Dot class implementation.

Figure 1.14 An implementation for the Dot class

```
import javax.swing.*;
import java.awt.*;
public class Dot extends JComponent {
    /* post:   getX() == y and getY() == y
                and getWidth() == d and getHeight() == d */
    public Dot(int x, int y, int d) {
        super();
        setBounds(x, y, d, d);
    }
    /* post:   getParent() == f */
    public void place(JFrame f) {
        if (f != null) {
            f.getContentPane().add(this);
            f.repaint();
        }
    }
```

Continued on next page

```
    /* post:   getParent() == null (i.e., the dot is no longer
               displayed) */
    public void removeFromDisplay() {
        if (getParent() != null) {
            getParent().remove(this);
        }
    }

    /* post:   this is repainted upon its background
       note:   the paint method is invoked by calling repaint() */
    public void paint(Graphics g) {
        g.setColor(Color.yellow);
        g.fillOval(0,0,getWidth(),getHeight());
    }
}
```

Software Engineering Hint

The Dots and BunchOfStars code illustrates that classes often prefer to express preconditions and postconditions in terms of the implementation rather than the abstraction.

To understand the Dot class implementation, you must know that the javax.swing class for building such graphical objects is called JComponent. You must also be familiar with the *swing* mechanism, which calls the paint method every time the object needs to be redrawn. This requires that paint be overridden by any class that is responsible for drawing a screen image. Further important coding detail depends on the behavior of such methods as setBounds, getContentPane, repaint, getParent, remove, setColor, fillOval, getWidth, and getHeight. This Dot class implementation contains a lot of detail, but as long as the Dot code correctly implements the Dot specifications, none of this detail is important for writing client code that utilizes Dot.

Similar implementation details are seen in the BunchOfStars class. Figure 1.15 shows one implementation. Unlike Dot, the BunchOfStars class does not require knowledge of the *swing* library. However, because BunchOfStars implements the set as an array called dots, complications arise whenever the array becomes full of stars. Again, such implementation details are best hidden from other programmers who want to use the BunchOfStars class.

Figure 1.15 An implementation of the BunchOfStars class

```
public class BunchOfStars {
    private Dot[] dots;
    private int dotCount;
    /* post:  dots.length == 1000
              and dotCount == 0 */
    public BunchOfStars() {
        dots = new Dot[1000];
        dotCount = 0;
    }
```

Continued on next page

```
/* post:    dotCount == dotCount@pre + 1
            and dots[dotCount-1] == d
            and dotCount@pre==dots@pre.length
                implies dotCount==dotCount@pre+1000 */
public void add(Dot d) {
    Dot[] newDots;
    if (dotCount == dots.length) {
        newDots = new Dot[dots.length+1000];
        for (int j=0; j<dotCount; j++) {
            newDots[j] = dots[j];
        }
        dots = newDots;
    }
    dots[dotCount] = d;
    dotCount++;
}
/* pre:     dotCount >= 1 (throws IllegalStateException)
   post:    dotCount == dotCount@pre + 1
            and dots[dotCount-1] == d
            and dotCount@pre==dots@pre.length
                implies dotCount==dotCount@pre+1000 */
public void removeRandomStar() {
    int randomPick;
    if (dotCount == 0) {
        throw new IllegalStateException("no stars to remove");
    } else {
        randomPick = (int)(Math.random() * dotCount);
        dots[randomPick].removeFromDisplay();
        dots[randomPick] = dots[dotCount-1];
        dotCount-;
    }
}
}
```

1.4 THE TEMPLATE DESIGN PATTERN

Another reason to divorce the abstract view of an ADT from its implementation is that certain ADTs have not one, but many, implementations. For example, consider an ADT that maintains the name of one person. Figure 1.16 shows a suitable class diagram and ADT specification.

Figure 1.16 Person ADT

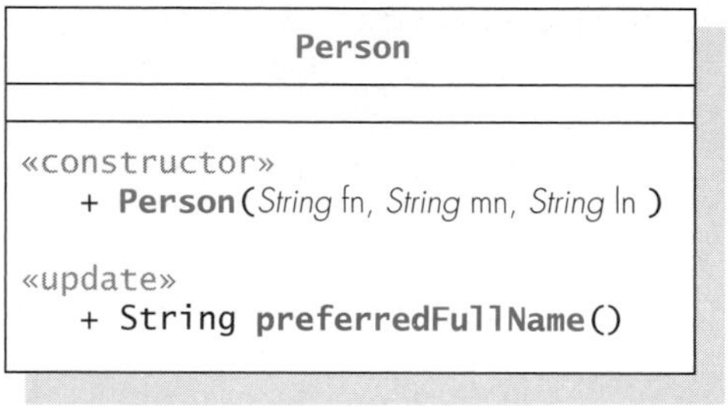

```
┌─────────────────────────────────────────────┐
│                   Person                      │
├─────────────────────────────────────────────┤
│                                               │
├─────────────────────────────────────────────┤
│  «constructor»                                │
│      + Person(String fn, String mn, String ln)│
│                                               │
│  «update»                                     │
│      + String preferredFullName()             │
└─────────────────────────────────────────────┘
```

Person ADT Specifications

Domain (Every Person object has the following parts)

    String firstName
    String middleName
    String lastName

Constructor Method

public Person (String fn, String mn, String ln)

   post: firstName == fn *and* middleName == mn *and* lastName == ln

Query Method

public String preferredFullName ()

   post: result == the preferred name string for this

The important characteristic of the Person ADT is that there are several reasonable alternatives for the value returned by preferredFullName. Some people prefer to be called by their complete name—first, middle and last—as in the following:

Grace Murray Hopper

In other cases, the preferredFullName method should be implemented to list the last name, followed by a comma, and then the first and middle names:

Hopper, Grace Murray

At least six other plausible return values for preferredFullName exist:

Grace M. Hopper
Grace Hopper
G. M. Hopper
Hopper, Grace M.
Hopper, Grace
Hopper, G. M.

Each of these styles for expressing a name results from a different implementation of the ADT. Such ADTs serve as **templates**, which define the important part of the behavior while still permitting variation in behavioral details. Figure 1.17 shows an abstract class that captures the commonality.

Figure 1.17 Person abstract class

```
public abstract class Person {
    protected String firstName;
    protected String middleName;
    protected String lastName;
    /* post:   firstName == fn and middleName == mn
               and lastName == ln */
    public Person(String fn, String mn, String ln) {
        firstName = fn;
        middleName = mn;
        lastName = ln;
    }
    /* post:   result == the preferred name for this */
    public abstract String preferredFullName ();
}
```

Person is an abstract class so it cannot be instantiated. However, it can serve usefully as a parent class (discussed in Chapter O3) for other classes. Figure 1.18 shows two such classes, which inherit Person and supply code for preferredFullName.

Figure 1.18 PersonFirstMiddleLast and PersonLastMiddle classes

```
public class PersonFirstMiddleLast extends Person {
    /* post:   firstName == fn and middleName == mn
               and lastName == ln */
    public PersonFirstMiddleLast(String fn, String mn, String ln) {
        super(fn, mn, ln);
    }
    /* post:   result == firstName + " " + middleName + " " +
               lastName */
    public String preferredFullName() {
        return firstName + " " + middleName + " " + lastName;
    }
}
public class PersonLastFirst extends Person {
    /* post:   firstName == fn and middleName == mn
               and lastName == ln */
    public PersonLastFirst(String fn, String mn, String ln) {
        super(fn, mn, ln);
    }
    /* post:   result == lastName + ", " + firstName */
    public String preferredFullName() {
        return lastName + ", " + firstName;
    }
}
```

Creating a parent class that serves as a template for child classes that supply implementations for selected (template) methods is common in object-oriented design. This **template design pattern** is summarized in Figure 1.19.

Figure 1.19 Template design pattern

Intent   to provide a template (skeleton) method that can be overridden, providing an implementation

Structure (class diagram)

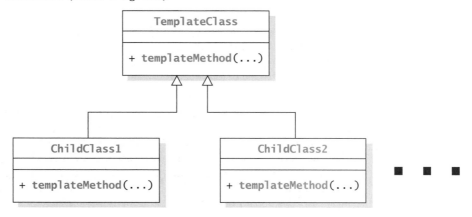

Explanation

Each `ChildClassN` overrides `templateMethod` to provide its own version. Other code can perform `templateMethod` upon `TemplateClass` variables or parameters. Often the template class is an abstract class or an interface.

Example

The `Person` class from Figure 1.17 is a template class, and `preferredFullName` is the template method.

1.5 JAVA INTERFACES

The Java programming language includes a facility, called an **interface**, that plays a special role in the design and implementation of ADTs. A Java interface can be thought of as the ultimate template class—a class in which *every* method is a template method. In a sense, an interface is a purely abstract class.

Syntactically, an interface is similar to an abstract class, with four differences:

Software Engineering Hint

Like an ADT specification, specifications within a Java interface must use abstract notation.

- The word `interface` is used in place of `abstract class`.
- The reserved word `abstract` must not appear anywhere within an `interface`.
- An interface cannot include a constructor.
- An interface cannot contain instance variables (although it is possible to include variables that are `public`, `static`, `final`, and of primitive type).

Figure 1.20 demonstrates an interface called `Solid`. This interface is a template that provides two template methods: `area` and `volume`.

Figure 1.20 Solid interface

```
/*  Domain
        Every object of type solid is a three-dimensional
        geometric solid with a skin surrounding it */
public interface Solid {
    /* post:   result == the total surface area for this solid */
    public double area();
    /* post:   result == the volume enclosed by this solid */
    public double volume();
}
```

Java uses a different notation for the child class of an interface. The child must list the name of its parent interface following the reserved word *implements* rather than the reserved word *extends*. This *implements* clause must follow immediately after the optional *extends* clause. Multiple interfaces can be implemented by a single child, in which case the names of these interfaces are separated by commas within the *implements* clause. Figure 1.21 shows a Cube class that implements both `Solid` and `Cloneable` (from the `java.lang` class package).

Figure 1.21 Cube class

```
public class Cube implements Solid, Cloneable {
        private double side;
        /* post:   side == s */
        public Cube(double s) {
            side = s;
        }
        /* post:   result == 6 * side * side */
        public double area() {
            return 6 * side * side;
        }
        /* post:   result == side * side * side */
        public double volume() {
            return side * side * side;
        }
        /* post:   result.equals(this) and result != this */
        protected Object clone() {
            return new Cube(side);
        }
        . . .
    }
```

The following clause signals that Cube is an implementation of Solid and thereby obligated to include code for the area and volume methods of the interface:

```
... implements Solid ...
```

Cube also implements Cloneable and is the implicit child of the Object parent class, from which it inherits the clone method. The Cube class supplies implementations by overriding all the following template methods: area, volume, and clone.

Unified Modeling Language (UML) notation for class diagrams that involve interfaces is only slightly different from that of other classes. The name of an interface and all its methods are italicized, just as abstract classes and methods are. The notation **<<interface>>** also is included at the top of any interface rectangle. The final difference between class notation and interface notation is that a dashed arrow is used to indicate the implementation of an interface. Figure 1.22 illustrates this class diagram notation for the Cube class relationships.

Figure 1.22 Class diagram for Cube, parent class, and parent interfaces

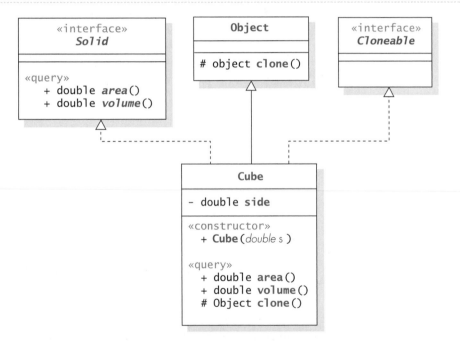

The following code demonstrates how these classes and interfaces can be used to declare and instantiate variables and call methods:

```
Solid solid;
solid = new Cube(43.1);
System.out.println( "Volume is " + solid.volume() );
```

A Java interface is useful for defining whole ADTs. The Solid interface is essentially a Java form for an ADT, called Solid, complete with abstract specifications.

A Java interface can also be used to define a single, abstract property, rather than an entire ADT. Consider an ADT called GroupOfParcels that maintains a collection of parcels to be shipped as freight. This ADT might have an abstract domain such as

> *set* of Parcel

where Parcel is a separate ADT that defines the characteristics of a single shipping parcel. Consider the GroupOfParcels method:

```
/* post:   this->includes(result)
            and forall(p : Parcel and this->includes(p)
                | result ≥ p) */
public Parcel largestParcel()
```

The postcondition states that the value returned is one of the Parcels in this GroupOfParcels and that all other Parcels in the group are less than or equal to this one. Such a method could be useful for loading parcels onto vehicles by loading the largest parcels first, or for distributing large parcels among several vehicles.

There is a subtle difficulty with the design of largestParcel. This method is possible only if the ≥ comparison is possible for two Parcel objects. In other words, Parcel objects must have the property that they can be compared to determine which is greater (>).

Java provides a standard interface for this particular property. The interface, called Comparable (from java.lang.Comparable), is described in the specifications of Figure 1.23.

Figure 1.23 Comparable specifications

Comparable Specifications

Query Method

```
public int compareTo(Object z)
```

> **post:** this less than z *implies* result < 0
> *and* this equal to z *implies* result == 0 (generally equal to
>   means equals)
> *and* this greater than z *implies* result > 0

Because Comparable is an interface, it defines a property. Any class that implements Comparable must have the property that its objects can be compared for greater than and less than (as defined by the compareTo method). Figure 1.24 demonstrates how to turn the Dot class into a child of Comparable.

Figure 1.24 A Comparable version of the Dot class

```
import javax.swing.*;
import java.awt.*;
public class Dot extends JComponent implements Comparable {
    /* post:  getX() == y and getY() == y
            and getWidth() == d and getHeight() == d */
```

Continued on next page

```
public Dot(int x, int y, int d) {
    super();
    setBounds(x, y, d, d);
}
/*  pre:    z instanceof Dot (throws ClassCastException)
    post:   getWidth() < z.getWidth() implies result < 0
            and getWidth() == z.getWidth() implies result == 0
            and getWidth() > z.getWidth() implies result > 0 */
public int compareTo(Object z) {
    if (!(z instanceof Dot)) {
        throw new ClassCastException();
    } else {
        Dot zDot = (Dot)z;
        if (getWidth() < zDot.getWidth())
            return -1;
        else if (getWidth() > zDot.getWidth())
            return 1;
        else
            return 0;
    }
}
/*  post:   getParent() == f */
public void place(JFrame f) {
    if (f != null) {
        f.getContentPane().add(this);
        f.repaint();
    }
}


/*  post:   getParent() == null (i.e., the dot is no longer
            displayed) */
public void removeFromDisplay() {
    if (getParent() != null) {
        getParent().remove(this);
    }
}


/*  post:   this is repainted upon its background
    note:   the paint method is invoked by calling repaint() */
public void paint(Graphics g) {
    g.setColor(Color.yellow);
    g.fillOval(0,0,getWidth(),getHeight());
}
}
```

A second example of a property defined by a standard Java interface is found in
java.lang.Cloneable. A Cloneable object has the capability of being cloned

(copied) by way of the `clone` method. `Cloneable` is unusual because it contains no methods that must be implemented by child classes. Instead, `Cloneable` works in conjunction with the `Object` class, which contains the `clone` method. For any class to acquire the `Cloneable` property, two requirements must be met:

- The class must override the `clone` method to return a copy for which `this.equals` returns true.
- The class must include an `implements Cloneable` clause.

Failure to include the *implements* clause causes the `clone` method to throw runtime exceptions.

1.6 THE OBJECT CLASS

Every Java class implicitly inherits Object. Included with Object are three methods—**toString**, **equals**, and **clone**—that should be considered as candidates for inclusion in each ADT. Figure 1.25 contains the specifications for these methods.

Figure 1.25 Specification for `toString()`, `equals()`, and `clone()`

Specifications (Methods from Object)

Query Methods

`public String toString ()`

> **post:** result is some string representation of this object.

> **note:** This is intended to be a template method available for child classes to override.

`public boolean equals (Object other)`

> **post:** other is the same as this *implies* result == true
> *and* other is different from this *implies* result == false

> **notes:** The default behavior is the same as == .
> This is intended to be a template method available for child classes to override.

`protected Object clone ()`

> **post:** result.equals(this)
> *and* result != this (i.e., result is an exact copy of this object).

> **notes:** Implementing the `Cloneable` interface is required, or the `CloneNotSupportedException` will be thrown for any call to clone. This is intended to be a template method available for child classes to override.

The `toString` method is a standard way to translate any object into a useful String representation. The default implementation for `toString` returns a string that includes the object's class and memory location. For example, the following code uses the Cube class shown previously (Figure 1.21):

```
Cube c;
    c = new Cube(20);
    System.out.println( c.toString() );
```

When the last statement executes, the default implementation of `toString` that was inherited from `Object` outputs a line such as the following:

```
Cube@30c19b
```

This output gives the type of the object `Cube` and an identification code (30c19b) that is unique to this object.

> **Software Engineering Hint**
>
> The implementation of `toString` that is inherited from `Object` is not very useful. Overriding `toString` is almost always a good idea.

Because the default implementation of `toString` isn't particularly useful, many classes will choose to override the method. The `Cube` class can be modified to include a better `toString` method, as shown in Figure 1.26.

Figure 1.26 A suitable `toString` for the `Cube` class

```
public class Cube implements Solid, Cloneable {
    private double side;
    . . .
    /*  post:  result == "Cube" concatenated to the cube's side
               length */
        public String toString() {
            return "Cube (Side length: " + side + ")";
        }
        . . .
    }
```

With a `Cube` class as modified in Figure 1.26, the following code works differently than before:

```
Cube c;
    c = new Cube(20);
    System.out.println( c.toString() );
```

Now when `toString` executes, the `Cube` version of `toString` is used, and the following line is output:

```
Cube (Side length: 20.0)
```

The `print` and `println` methods from the standard `java.io.PrintStream` class call `toString` when passed an arbitrary object. Consider the execution of the following statement:

```
System.out.println( c );
```

The output that results is exactly the same as if the following statement were executed:

```
System.out.println( c.toString() );
```

The equals template method is particularly useful in an object-oriented environment. All **reference types** in Java—types other than the primitive types of `boolean, byte, char, double, float, int, long,` and `short`—support two kinds of equality:

- identity equality
- content equality

In Java the "==" operator tests for **identity equality** because it is true-valued exactly when the compared expressions have identical identity. For example, the following expression is true if and only if `object1` and `object2` have the same identity (i.e., they are bound to the same object) and false otherwise.

```
object1 == object2
```

The default implementation of the `equals` method that is inherited from `Object` also checks for identity equality. This means that if `equals` is not overridden, the expression

```
object1.equals( object2 )
```

will have the same value as the following expression:

```
object1 == object2
```

However, it is intended that `equals` provide a test for **content equality**. Two objects are said to have content equality when their state is equivalent. You check two objects of identical type for content equality by comparing the values of all instance variables. (Less frequently, two objects of different type may also be found to be equivalent. For example, a point stored via Cartesian coordinates can be equivalent to a point stored via polar coordinates, but such a comparison is more complicated than merely checking for equal state.) It is expected that child classes wishing to provide content equality will override `equals`.

Figure 1.27 shows how to include `equals` to test for content equality in the Cube class. Two Cube objects are considered to be (content) equal only when they have identical `side` values.

Figure 1.27 An `equals` method for the Cube class

```
public class Cube implements Solid, Cloneable {
    private double side;
    . . .
    /* post:   result == (z.side == side) */
    public boolean equals(Object z) {
        return z instanceof Cube && side == ((Cube)z).side;
    }
    . . .

}
```

The implementation of `equals` in Figure 1.27 relies on several Java features. Obviously, another object cannot be content equal to a Cube object unless that other object is also of type Cube. However, the z parameter of the overridden `equals` method has a type of Object. The solution is to include the following test before comparing the instance variables:

```
z instanceof Cube
```

This line causes the return statement to short-circuit the Boolean expression and return false whenever it is applied to an argument whose type does not conform to Cube.

The following code illustrates a potential use for the equals method:

```
Cube timsBlock, sarahsBlock;
timsBlock = new Cube(10);
sarahsBlock = new Cube(10);
if ( timsBlock.equals(sarahsBlock) ) {
    System.out.println( "Content Equality" );
} else {
    System.out.println( "Content Inequality" );
}
```

If the Cube class used for the preceding code were redefined to include an equals method as shown in Figure 1.27, then executing the code would output the following message:

```
Content Equality
```

If equals is not overloaded, the Object version of equals is used and the resulting output is

```
Content Inequality
```

Software engineering teaches that the most productive way to improve code quality is to perform frequent and thorough desk checks. A desk check consists of manually scrutinizing various program-related documents, including specifications, design documents, and code. At the end of every chapter, this book includes a section labeled "Software Inspector." These sections offer a checklist of items (related to that chapter) worth considering when you're performing a desk check.

✓ An ADT should be designed abstractly. The public view of a class should therefore hide all implementation details except those that need to be known by clients of the class.

✓ Check every ADT specification to be certain that it maintains precision. It's best to model ADTs from well-formed models, such as those from the UML Object Constraint Language.

✓ Java interfaces can be used as a means of expressing the abstract view of an ADT in programmatic form.

✓ Properties such as Comparable and Cloneable should always be candidates for inclusion in an ADT design.

✓ The toString and equals methods (from the Object class) should be included in an ADT unless there is a good reason not to.

1. Assume that DayTime is a class that implements the TimeOfDay ADT specified in Figure 1.4. Show a segment of code to declare, instantiate, and assign a time that is 2 hours and 13 minutes after the current time to a variable of type DayTime.

2. Assume that TelephoneBook is a class that implements the PhoneBook ADT specified in Figure 1.7. Show a segment of code to declare and instantiate a TelephoneBook variable and to assign this variable the following telephone list:

   Sue Brown, 1018 Main Street, (502) 555-1234

   Sam Green, 987 State Street, (101) 555-4321

   Art Black, 12 Washington Blvd., (831) 555-2222

3. Give the value of each of the following expressions, assuming that all set elements are integers.

   a. *set*{2, 4, 6, 8}->*size*()

   b. *set*{2, 4, 6, 8}->*including*(7)

c. *set{2, 4, 6, 8}->excluding(4)*

d. *set{2, 4, 6, 8}->excluding(7)->including(9)*

e. *set{2, 4, 6, 8}->intersection(set{1, 3, 5, 7, 9})*

f. *(set{1, 2, 3, 4}->union(set{4, 5, 6, 7})->intersection(set{4, 5})*

g. *set{1, 2, 3, 4} - set{4, 5, 6}*

h. *set{2, 4, 6, 8}->intersection({4, 5, 6} - set{2, 5})*

i. *set{2, 4, 6, 8 } - set{1, 3, 5, 7, 9}*

j. *set->select(e | 0<=e<=9)*

k. *set->select(x | x*x=x+x and x > 0 }*

4. What is the value of each of the following Boolean expressions?

   a. *set{2, 4, 6, 8}->includes(4)*

   b. *set{1, 2, 3, 4}->includesAll(set{4, 5, 6, 7})*

   c. *set{1, 2, 3, 4}->includesAll(set{1, 2})*

   d. *set{1, 2, 3, 4}->includesAll(set{1, 2, 3, 4})*

   e. *set{1, 2, 3, 4}->includesAll(set{})*

5. Consider the BunchOfStars class from Figure 1.15.

   a. Modify BunchOfStars so that it is Comparable in the sense that one bunch is greater than another whenever it contains more stars.

   b. Modify BunchOfStars so that it is Cloneable.

   c. Write and test a suitable toString method for BunchOfStars.

6. Consider the Person class from Figure 1.17.

   a. Write and test a suitable equals method for Person.

   b. Write and test a suitable toString method for Person.

7. Inherit the TimeOfDay class (Figure 1.5). Your new subclass must return time in military form (i.e., hours range from 1 through 24 and isPM throws an exception). Your subclass must be fully specified.

1. Design, implement, and test a program that consists of a graphical user interface (GUI) with two buttons (Add Circle and Change Color). Initially this GUI should consist of a white window 300 pixels square, with a red circle centered in the window having a diameter of 250 pixels.

Each click of the Add Circle button must add another red concentric circle that is two-thirds the diameter of the prior circle. Each click of the Change Color button must change the color of all circles (red circles become green, and green circles become red).

Your design must include a `BunchOfCircles` ADT with methods that are appropriate to this problem, along with any other ADTs you believe are needed. See Section 1.3 for examples of how to implement your classes.

2. Design and implement a `StopWatch` ADT. The stopwatch has a Start button, a Stop button, and a Reset button. Clicking the Start button causes time to begin advancing from whatever value is displayed on the watch. (This will "unfreeze" the most recent stop.) Clicking Stop freezes the clock display at its current time. Clicking Reset causes the time to reset to zero. The time of this stopwatch consists of minutes, seconds, and milliseconds.

3. Design, implement, and test a program that serves to prototype a new user interface for a copy machine. This interface contains two buttons (Clear and +1) to specify the number of copies. Clicking the Clear button resets the copy count to zero. Clicking +1 increments the copy count value by 1.

The interface also maintains a darkness value expressed as an integer from 1 (lightest) through 10 (darkest). Two buttons control the darkness; clicking the Darker button increases darkness by 1 (up to its maximum value of 10), and clicking Lighter decreases darkness by 1 (down to a minimum of 1).

Another part of the interface is a Mode button. There are three possible copy modes:

1. front side only

2. two-sided copies from single-sided originals

3. two-sided copies from two-sided originals

Each click of the Mode button toggles the mode to the next option (i.e., Mode 1 becomes Mode 2; Mode 2 becomes Mode 3; Mode 3 becomes Mode 1).

The initial state of the copier should be as follows:

Copy count: 0

Darkness: 5

Mode: Front side only

Your design must include an ADT to keep track of the entire copier interface. Be certain to include a `toString` method that returns a single String value that reflects the complete copier settings (number of copies, darkness value, and mode). Your implementation should provide a user interface with the five user buttons, and it should display the copier state after each button click.

USING CONTAINERS

OBJECTIVES

- To explore the concept of containers that serve as object receptacles

- To propose notations for sequences as ADT models

- To examine generic containers and how they are used

- To introduce the adapter design pattern and related proxy design pattern as techniques for adapting generic containers for other purposes

- To review wrapper classes and explain how to use them to translate between primitive and reference data

- To compare bounded versus unbounded container designs

- To compare mutable versus immutable ADTs

- To introduce the iterator design pattern and Java's Iterator interface

- To introduce the standard Java Collection interface

One common use for an ADT is to serve primarily as a repository, or collection, of other objects. An employee database is a collection of employees. The inventory of a retail store is a collection of merchandise. A ledger sheet is a collection of debits and credits. Another name for an ADT that is designed specifically to serve as a repository (a collection) is a **container**. One of the main topics in this book is the examination of containers: how to define containers abstractly, how to use particular containers to solve common problems, and how to efficiently implement containers.

2.1 INTRODUCTION TO CONTAINERS

The PhoneBook ADT examined in Section 1.2 is a container. A PhoneBook object is a container of PhoneEntry objects. The PhoneBook ADT exhibits many of the methods that are typical among various containers, including the following:

- Methods to construct an initial container (such as PhoneBook)
- Methods to insert additional items into the container (such as insertEntry)
- Methods to remove items from the container (such as removeEntry)
- Methods to test the container for specific content (such as lookupByName and lookupPhoneNumber)

Like many containers, the PhoneBook ADT is defined as a set. In Chapter 1, OCL notations are presented as a means to express abstract specifications for ADTs that exhibit setlike behavior. Figure 2.1 presents another ADT, SetOfInt, which is designed to be a programmatic version of a mathematical set. For this particular set, every element must be of type int.

Figure 2.1 SetOfInt ADT class diagram and ADT specification

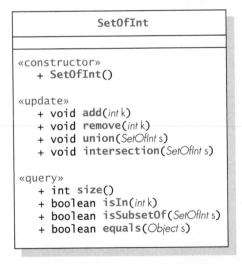

```
                        SetOfInt


«constructor»
    + SetOfInt()

«update»
    + void  add(int k)
    + void  remove(int k)
    + void  union(SetOfInt s)
    + void  intersection(SetOfInt s)

«query»
    + int size()
    + boolean isIn(int k)
    + boolean isSubsetOf(SetOfInt s)
    + boolean equals(Object s)
```

SetOfInt ADT Specifications

Domain Every SetOfInt object is a set in which all elements are of type int.

Constructor Method

public SetOfInt ()

    post: this == *set{}*

Continued on next page

Update Methods

```
public void add ( int k)
    post: this == this@pre->including(k)
public void remove (int k)
    post: this == this@pre->excluding(k)
public void union (SetOfInt s)
    post: this == this@pre->union(s)
public void intersection (SetOfInt s)
    post: this == this@pre->intersection(s)
```

Query Methods

```
public int size ()
    post: result == this->size()
public boolean isIn(int k)
    post: result == this->includes(k)
public boolean isSubsetOf(SetOfInt s)
    post: result == s->includesAll(this)
public boolean equals(Object s)
    post: result == this->includesAll(s) and s->includesAll(this)
```

The methods of SetOfInt closely parallel both mathematical and OCL set operations. The size method returns the set's cardinality. The union method performs a ∪ (*union* in OCL) operation. The intersection operation performs ∩ (*intersection*). The isIn method performs a test for ∈ (*includes*). The isSubsetOf method performs a test for ⊆ (*includesAll*), also known as the **improper subset**.

Software Engineering Hint

A **complete** container is one that includes sufficient methods to construct all the objects described by the domain/invariant. Without the **add** method, **SetOfInt** is incomplete because the only sets that can be built by calling methods would be empty sets.

The SetOfInt constructor and the add method are included to support proper creation of various sets. Calling SetOfInt constructs an empty set, and elements are added to the set one at a time by calling add. The add method is the programmatic counterpart of the OCL *including* function. Following is a sample segment of client code that uses the SetOfInt ADT.

```
SetOfInt setA, setB;
setA = new SetOfInt();
setA.add(1);
setA.add(3);
setA.add(5);
setB = new SetOfInt();
setB.add(3);
setB.add(4);
setA.union(setB);
System.out.println( setA.size() );
```

```
System.out.println( setA.isIn(2) );
System.out.println( setA.isIn(3) );
System.out.println( setA.isIn(4) );
// assert: setA == set{1, 3, 4, 5}
```

When this code segment executes, the following four lines are sent to the standard output device:

```
4
false
true
true
```

Although `SetOfInt` includes many of the common set operations, it lacks one facility that is required by many client algorithms: It has no methods that allow client code to inspect the container content without prior knowledge. In other words, the client code cannot discover set elements without using `isIn`, but `isIn` requires that the client have some knowledge regarding potential elements to test. This limitation of the `SetOfInt` methods makes certain algorithms impractical, if not impossible. For example, without "inside information" it is impractical to craft an algorithm that displays the entire content of a `SetOfInt`.

One way to correct this `SetOfInt` deficiency is to include the following additional method:

```
public double item ()
    pre: this->size() >= 1
    post: this->includes(result)
```

This `item` method returns one of the elements of the set. The precondition ensures that such an element exists, and the postcondition states that whatever value is returned, it must be an element of this set. This particular postcondition specifies only that one set element is returned, but it does not attempt to identify *which* element is returned. This limits the utility of the `item` method. However, you can still use the `item` method to express an algorithm to output all the elements of some set:

```
Double itemValue;
while (setA.size() > 0) {
    itemValue = setA.item();
    setA.remove( itemValue );
    System.out.println( itemValue );

}
```

This algorithm calls `item` repeatedly, and for each call it displays the value that `item` returns. To guarantee that no displayed element is repeated, the algorithm removes each value from `setA` before the subsequent item call. This kind of algorithm is sometimes called **destructive** because it destroys the container content in the sense that all items must be removed in order to accomplish the task.

Methods such as `item` are called **accessor** methods because they permit client code to access or inspect values from inside the container. The particular items that are available via accessor methods differ for different kinds of containers.

2.2   GENERIC CONTAINERS

A SetOfInt object is restricted by the requirement that all its elements be of type int. The set of all prime numbers between 1 and 1,000 could be stored as a SetOfInt, or a SetOfInt could be used to maintain all integers from 0 through 1,000,000 that are perfect squares. However, it is not possible to use SetOfInt to store a dictionary or the collection of landowners in a housing development. You might use a different container, such as SetOfWordAndDefinition, for storing a dictionary, and SetOfPeople is an ADT that is more likely to be of use for storing landowners. This leads to the conclusion that there could be as many SetOf*Thing* classes as there are different kinds of *things*.

Rather than create a separate SetOf*Thing* ADT for each type of set element, intelligent rules of software reuse argue that it is preferable to design a **generic container**. Generic containers are containers that do not restrict the type of the items they contain.

Version 1.4 of the Java Software Development Kit (SDK) does not directly support mechanisms explicitly designed for creating generic containers. However, you can achieve a similar effect by using the Object class. For example, consider the SetOfObject ADT defined in Figure 2.2.

Figure 2.2 SetOfObject ADT class diagram and ADT specification

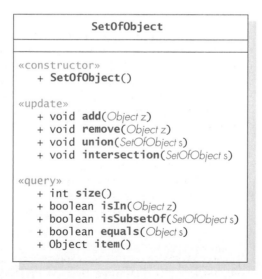

SetOfObject ADT Specifications

Domain Every SetOfObject object is a set in which all elements are of type Object.

Continued on next page

Constructor Method

```
public SetOfObject ()
```
   post: this == *set*{}

Update Methods

```
public void add (Object z)
```
   post: this == this*@pre->including*(z)

```
public void remove (Object z)
```
   post: this == this*@pre->excluding*(z)

```
public void union (SetOfObject s)
```
   post: this == this*@pre->union*(s)

```
public void intersection (SetOfObject s)
```
   post: this == this*@pre->intersection*(s)

Query Methods

```
public int size ()
```
   post: result == this*->size*()

```
public boolean isIn(Object z)
```
   post: result == this*->includes*(z)

```
public boolean isSubsetOf(SetOfObject s)
```
   post: result == s*->includesAll*(this)

```
public boolean equals(Object s)
```
   post: result == this*->includesAll*(s) *and* s*->includesAll*(this)

```
public Object item()
```
   pre: this*->size*() >= 1

   post: this*->includes*(result)

The SetOfObject ADT provides for creating containers that can store items having any Java reference type. For example, a client can use the following code to construct a set called parents with elements of type String:

```
SetOfObject parents = new SetOfObject();
parents.add("Duane");
parents.add("Doris");
/* assert: parents == set{"Duane", "Doris"} */
```

Similarly, SetOfObject can be used to construct a set of elements whose type comes from the Color class (from the package java.awt.Color):

```
SetOfObject primaryColors = new SetOfObject();
primaryColors.add(Color.red);
primaryColors.add(Color.green);
primaryColors.add(Color.blue);
/* assert: primaryColors == set{Color.red, Color,green, Color.blue}
        */
```

You can even mix different reference types within a single set when using SetOfObject. The following code creates a set that contains one String and two Colors:

```
SetOfObject stuff = new SetOfObject();
stuff.add(Color.black);
stuff.add("Wow!");
stuff.add(Color.white);
/* assert: stuff == set{Color.black, "Wow!", Color.white} */
```

Some software developers would argue that the SetOfObject class is "too generic" because of this ability to allow mixtures of data types within the same container. However, a generic class built from Object items is useful because it serves as an excellent parent class on which to base type-specific classes. For example, Figure 2.3 illustrates how to inherit SetOfObject to implement a nongeneric SetOfString class.

Figure 2.3 SetOfString class implemented from SetOfObject

```
/*  Domain
        A SetOfString object is a set in which all elements are of
        type String */
public class SetOfString extends SetOfObject {
    /*  post:   this == set{} */
    public SetOfString() {
        super();
    }
    /*  pre:    z instanceof String
                (throws IllegalArgumentException)
        post:   this == this@pre->including(z) */
    public void add(Object z) {
        if (!(z instanceof String)) {
            throw new IllegalArgumentException();
        } else {
            super.add(z);
        }
    }
    /*  pre:    s instanceof SetOfString
                (throws IllegalArgumentException)
        post:   this == this@pre->union(s) */
    public void union(SetOfObject s) {
        if (!(s instanceof SetOfString)) {
            throw new IllegalArgumentException();
        } else {
            super.union(s);
        }
    }
}
```

Continued on next page

```
    /*  pre:    this->size() > 1
        post:   this->includes(result) */
    public String itemString() {
        return (String)item();
    }
}
```

The SetOfString class overrides the add method, thereby ensuring that no such set will ever contain non-String elements. The overridden version of add uses instanceof to check the type of its argument. Any argument that does not conform to String causes add to throw an exception rather than insert the argument into the set. For a similar reason, the union method also is overridden in SetOfString. Otherwise, it would be possible to pass a set that is not of type SetOfString, thereby permitting non-String elements to be introduced into a SetOfString object.

It is tempting to override replace and intersection, but there is no need to do so because neither method is capable of introducing additional elements in the set. Furthermore, calling remove or intersection with non-String arguments can never alter a SetOfString object because SetOfString objects contain only String elements.

Accessor methods pose a unique challenge when inherited from generic containers. The item method returns a set element, but the returned element has the type Object rather than its actual type. As a result, calls to item often require that the inspected element be cast to its original type. For example, the following statement is a syntactically incorrect attempt to assign an inspected element of setA:

```
String s = setA.item(); // This statement has a syntax error.
```

This statement is properly written as follows:

```
String s = (String)setA.item();
```

The SetOfString class includes an itemString inspector method that avoids the awkwardness of casting inspected set elements. If itemString were eliminated from SetOfString, the class would still be useful but not quite as convenient. Figure 2.4 contains a method that illustrates how convenient it is to use itemString. This display method is the same destructive output algorithm presented in the preceding section.

Figure 2.4 Display method to output SetOfString elements destructively

```
/*post:    Every element of s is displayed, one per line
            and s == set{} */
public void display(SetOfString s) {
    String itemValue;
    while (s.size() > 0) {
        itemValue = s.itemString();
        System.out.println(itemValue);
        s.remove(itemValue);
    }
}
```

2.3 USING OBJECT CONTAINERS

ADTs are often composed from other ADTs. This is a major benefit of a container of Object (a generic container) such as SetOfObject. The SetOfString class shown in Figure 2.4 is easy to implement given SetOfObject. In fact, all the SetOfString methods are simply adapted versions of SetOfObject methods. You can use this technique of implementing one class largely by adapting the methods of another class not only when using containers of Object. In fact, it is used so often that it is given a special name: the **adapter design pattern**. Figure 2.5 describes this technique.

Figure 2.5 Adapter design pattern

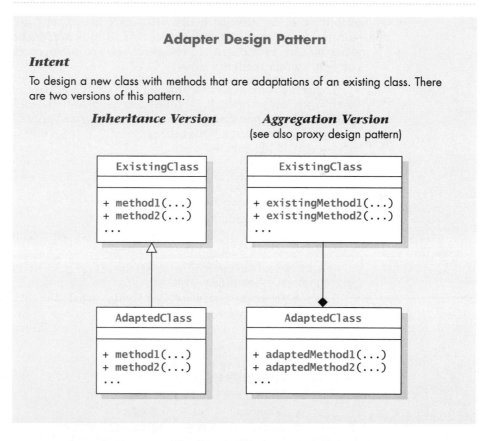

The adapter design pattern has two alternative forms: the inheritance version and the aggregation version. As its name implies, the **inheritance version** is used when the adapted class is implemented by inheriting a parent class. The parent class must have sufficient functionality that its methods can be adapted to serve the needs of the child class. This inheritance version is used to implement SetOfString. Most of the SetOfObject methods that are inherited by SetOfString can be used without adaptation. A couple of the SetOfObject methods (add and union) required adaptation, and some new methods (SetOfString and itemString) are added. Even itemString is largely an adaptation of the inherited item method.

The **aggregation version** of the adapter pattern is implemented using aggregation, not inheritance. In other words, the adapter class will contain an instance variable belonging to the class being adapted. To illustrate this design approach, consider the problem of writing a program to identify Java reserved words in a passage of text.

This task is performed by a component of the Java compiler called the **scanner**, a program that groups contiguous text into logical groups called **tokens**. The type of scanner needed for this program finds tokens that are groupings of alphabetic characters. For example, consider the following text:

This is an example of reserved words like 'if' and 'try'.

The first token is the word *This*, and the remaining tokens from left to right are as follows: *is, an, example, of, reserved, words, like, if, and, and try*. Notice that this scanner "skips" non-alphabetic characters such as punctuation and blanks. These characters can be thought of as **separators**, because they are useful in separating consecutive tokens.

Figure 2.6 contains a Java program that scans a passage of text and prints each token when it is scanned. If the token also happens to be one of the reserved words of the Java programming language, the program prints a message (<--Java reserved word) following that token.

Figure 2.6 ReservedWordScanner application

```
public class ReservedWordScanner {
    private String text
        = "This is an example of reserved words, like 'if' and
            'try'.";
    private ReservedWords javaWords;
    private SetOfChar separators;
    public static void main(String[] args) {
        new ReservedWordScanner();
    }

    public ReservedWordScanner() {
        String token;
        int firstNdx, lastNdx;
        javaWords = new ReservedWords();
        separators = new SetOfChar();
        for (char c=(char)0; c<=64; c++) {
            separators.add(c);
        }
        separators.add('['); separators.add('\\');
        separators.add(']');separators.add('^');
        separators.add('_'); separators.add('`');
        separators.add('{'); separators.add('|');
        separators.add('}');separators.add('~');
```

```
                separators.add('\n'); separators.add('\t');
                lastNdx = 0;
                while (lastNdx != text.length()) {
                    firstNdx = indexOfTokenStart(lastNdx);
                    if (firstNdx == text.length()) {
                        lastNdx = firstNdx;
                    } else {
                        lastNdx = indexOfTokenEnd(firstNdx);
                        token = text.substring(firstNdx, lastNdx);
                        if (javaWords.containsReservedWord(token))
                            System.out.println(token + " <- Java reserved
                            word");
                        else
                            System.out.println(token);
                    }
                }
            }
/*  pre:    0 <= ndx <= text.length() (throws
                IndexOutOfBoundsException)
    post:   exists(c : char | c occurs in text.substring(ndx)
                and c is not an element of separators)
                    implies result is the index of the leftmost such
                    c char
                and (all characters of text.substring(ndx) are
                    elements of separators)
                    implies result == text.length() */
            private int indexOfTokenStart(int ndx) {
                int j = ndx;
                while (j != text.length() && separators.isIn(text.charAt(j)))
                    j++;
                return j;
            }
/*  pre:    0 <= ndx <= text.length() (throws
                IndexOutOfBoundsException)
    post:   exists(c : char | c occurs in text.substring(ndx)
                and c is an element of separators)
                    implies result is the index of the leftmost such
                    c char
                and (no character of text.substring(ndx) is an
                    element of separators)
                    implies result == text.length() */
            private int indexOfTokenEnd(int ndx) {
                int j = ndx;
                while (j!=text.length() && !separators.isIn(text.charAt(j)))
                    j++;
                return j;
            }
        }
```

When the `ReservedWordScanner` program executes as a Java application, the main method instantiates an instance of its own class, effectively creating all instance variables and calling the `ReservedWordScanner` constructor. This constructor scans the text within the `String` variable, `text`. The constructor uses two private methods: `indexOfToken` returns the index of the first character for each new token, and `indexOfTokenEnd` returns the index of the separator character that signals the end of each token.

The `ReservedWordScanner` code relies on two containers: `separators` and `javaWords`. The `separators` variable belongs to a `SetOfChar` class. `SetOfChar`, whose implementation is given in Section 2.4, is analogous to `SetOfString` as a nongeneric class that adapts the `SetOfObject` class to provide similar functionality for set elements of type `char`. The `ReservedWordScanner` constructor initializes `separators` to store a set of those characters that can serve as separator characters within a Java program. Both the `indexOfTokenStart` and the `indexOfTokenEnd` methods call the `isIn` method to check whether characters in the scanned text are separators.

The `javaWords` variable is used to store all the Java reserved words. The type of `javaWords` is a class called `ReservedWords`. This class can also be designed using the adapter design pattern, as shown in Figure 2.7.

Figure 2.7 ReservedWords class

```
/*  Domain
        this is a set of Java reserved words. */
public class ReservedWords {
    private SetOfString words;
    /*  post:   this == set->select(w : String | w is a reserved word
                in Java) */
    public ReservedWords( ) {
        words = new SetOfString(); words.add("abstract");
        words.add("boolean");      words.add("break");
        words.add("byte");         words.add("case");
        words.add("cast");         words.add("catch");
        words.add("char");         words.add("class");
        words.add("const");        words.add("continue");
        words.add("default");      words.add("do");
        words.add("double");       words.add("else");
        words.add("extends");      words.add("false");
        words.add("final");        words.add("finally");
        words.add("float");        words.add("for");
        words.add("generic");      words.add("goto");
        words.add("if");           words.add("implements");
        words.add("import");       words.add("instanceof");
        words.add("int");          words.add("interface");
        words.add("long");         words.add("native");
        words.add("new");          words.add("null");
        words.add("package");      words.add("private");
        words.add("protected");    words.add("public");
        words.add("return");       words.add("short");
```

Continued on next page

```
            words.add("static");        words.add("super");
            words.add("switch");        words.add("synchronized");
            words.add("this");          words.add("throw");
            words.add("throws");        words.add("transient");
            words.add("true");          words.add("try");
            words.add("void");          words.add("volatile");
            words.add("while");
        }
        /* post:   result == words->includes(z) */
        public boolean containsReservedWord(String s) {
            return words.isIn(s);
        }
    }
```

The ReservedWords class adapts its two methods from those of SetOfString. However, this example does not inherit SetOfString. Instead, it is an example of the aggregation version of the adapter design pattern because ReservedWords has an instance variable, called words, that belongs to the SetOfString class.

Two methods must be adapted in ReservedWords. The constructor is adapted from the SetOfString constructor because it initializes the set to contain all the Java reserved words. The containsReservedWord method is also an adaptation, with its behavior adapted from isIn.

The use of the aggregation version of the adapter design pattern often results in another pattern, known as the **proxy design pattern**. The ReservedWords class is an example of the use of the proxy design pattern. Figure 2.8 describes this pattern.

Figure 2.8 Proxy design pattern

Proxy Design Pattern

Intent

To provide a customized interface to another object via a proxy object.

Structure (object diagram)

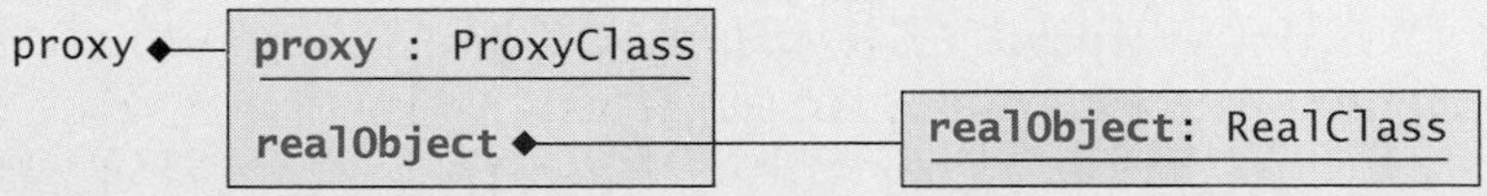

Explanation

The ProxyClass provides different methods to access realObject than would be available from RealClass. Often this pattern is used to provide more specialized or more restricted access to an object.

Example

The ReservedWords class from Figure 2.7 is a proxy class in which the word variable plays the role called realObject above.

There is a slight notational disadvantage when using the proxy design pattern rather than the inheritance version of the adapter design pattern. Suppose that `ReservedWords` had been implemented via the following inheritance:

```
public class ReservedWords extends SetOfString {
```

Such a design would use a constructor that began as follows:

```
public ReservedWords( ) {
    super();
    add("abstract"); add("boolean");
    add("break");
    ...
```

Software Engineering Hint

The inheritance version of the adapter design pattern is best when all inherited members are reusable within the context of the adapted (child) class. When this is not the case, it is preferable to use the proxy design pattern.

Notice that this notation is shorter in the sense that it eliminates references to the `words` variable; the set has been inherited, eliminating the need for the variable. Similarly, consider the following `containsReservedWord` method, repeated from the proxy design pattern version:

```
public boolean containsReservedWord(String s) {
    return words.isIn(s);
}
```

This method would be replaced by the following for the version of `ReservedWords` that uses inheritance.

```
public boolean containsReservedWord(String s) {
    return isIn(s);
}
```

Despite this notational advantage of inheritance, the proxy design pattern has its own advantage that justifies its use in this case. Inheritance applies to *all* methods of the parent class. This is fine as long as these methods are all useful in the context of the adapted class. However, in the case of `ReservedWords`, methods such as `add`, `remove`, `union`, and `intersection` are unnecessary and unwanted. By using the proxy design pattern and a private scope for `words`, the `ReservedWords` class shown in Figure 2.7 prohibits outside code from altering the elements of the set. This is appropriate because the reserved words of Java are fixed.

2.4   WRAPPER CLASSES

Generic classes based on elements of type `Object` work well for content of any reference type. However, primitive types of generic container content require special treatment. For example, the second statement that follows is syntactically unacceptable in Java because the primitive `char` type is incompatible with `Object`.

```
SetOfObject mySet = new SetOfObject();
mySet.add( 'A' ); // This statement has a syntax error.
```

Fortunately, the Java package includes a set of classes to compensate for this inconsistency between the primitive and reference types. These classes are called **wrapper classes** because they provide a way to "wrap up" a single primitive value in the form of a reference object. As shown in Figure 2.8, there is one wrapper class to correspond to every primitive type. A wrapped object maintains a value that is the same as its primitive type counterpart. However, the wrapped object is of reference type, so it conforms to Object.

Wrapper classes generally share the name of their corresponding primitive type, with the first letter of the name capitalized. The two exceptions to this naming convention are for the primitive types int and char. The wrapper class for int is Integer, and the wrapper class for char is Character.

Figure 2.8 Wrapper classes corresponding to primitive types

Primitive Class	*Corresponding Wrapper Class*
boolean	Boolean
byte	Byte
char	Character
double	Double
float	Float
int	Integer
long	Long
short	Short

Each wrapper class includes two key methods:

- A constructor method with a single parameter of its corresponding primitive type. This constructor creates the reference object that stores the value of its argument.
- A query method to return the primitive value stored within the wrapper. These methods are always named with the primitive type followed by the suffix Value, and they are parameterless.

The wrapper class constructor can be thought of as a mechanism for wrapping up a primitive value, and the _Value method is for "unwrapping" the object to retrieve its primitive value. Figure 2.9 illustrates these two methods by supplying the class specifications for the Integer wrapper class.

Like other objects whose type conforms to Object, wrapper class objects can be placed within a SetOfObject. For example, the following statement inserts the Character value 'A' into set mySet:

```
SetOfObject mySet = new SetOfObject();
mySet.add(new Character('A'));
```

The following code converts such a wrapper value from within the container and assigns it to the variable c:

```
if ( mySet.item() instanceof Character) then {
    char c = ((Character)mySet.item()).charValue();
}
```

Figure 2.9 Integer class specifications

Integer Class Specifications

Domain

An Integer object
- Is a wrapper around an embedded value of type int
- Implicitly inherits Object like other classes
- Does not support int operators such as +, -, <, and so on

Constructor Method

public **Integer** (int j)
   post: the embedded value of this == j

Query Method

public int **intValue** ()
   post: result == the embedded value of this

   . . .

The expression `((Character)mySet.item()).charValue()` inspects the wrapped item as a three-step expression:

1. The item method returns the value within a wrapper.
2. A Character cast translates the wrapped item into its proper Character type.
3. The charValue method is applied to the Character object to extract the embedded char value.

Figure 2.10 summarizes the two expression key patterns for using wrapper classes. The first pattern is an expression to return a wrapper object with an embed-

Figure 2.10 Two expression patterns for converting to and from wrapper objects

*To convert from **primitiveExpression** to **WrapperType**:*

```
new WrapperType ( primitiveExpression )
```
Examples:
```
integerVar = new Integer(33);
mySet.insert( new Double(doubleVar) );
```

*To convert from **wrapperExpression** to **primitiveType**:*

```
wrapperExpression.primitiveTypeValue()
```
Examples:
```
intVar = integerVar.intValue();
System.out.println( characterExpression.charValue() );
```

ded primitive value. The second pattern is an expression to return a copy of the primitive value from within the wrapper class object. The variable `intVar` is assumed to be of type `int`; the variable `integerVar` is of type `Integer`; and the variable `doubleVar` is of type `double`.

These two patterns are used in `SetOfChar`, a type-specific subset of `SetOfObject` for char values. Figure 2.11 shows the code for `SetOfChar`.

Figure 2.11 SetOfChar class

```
/*  Domain
        A SetOfChar object is a set in which all elements are of
        type char */
public class SetOfChar extends SetOfObject {
    /*  post:   this == set{} */
    public SetOfChar( ) {
        super();
    }
    /*  pre:    z instanceof Character
                    (throws IllegalArgumentException)
        post:   this == this@pre->including(z)
        note:   Set membership must be unique according to the defi-
                nition of content equality (as tested by the equals
                operation) rather than identity equality (==) */
    public void add(Object z) {
        if (!(z instanceof Character)) {
            throw new IllegalArgumentException();
        } else {
            super.add(z);
        }
    }
    /*  post:   this == this@pre->including(new Character(z)) */
    public void add(char z) {
        add(new Character(z));
    }
    /*  pre:    s instanceof SetOfChar
                    (throws IllegalArgumentException)
        post:   this == this@pre->union(s) */
    public void union(SetOfObject s) {
        if (!(s instanceof SetOfChar)) {
            throw new IllegalArgumentException();
        } else {
            super.union(s);
        }
    }
    /*  pre:    this->size() > 1
        post:   this->includes(result) */
```

Continued on next page

```
        public char itemChar() {
            return ((Character)item()).charValue();
        }
        /* post:    result == this->includes(Character(c)) */
        public boolean isIn(char c){
            return isIn(new Character(c));
        }
    }
```

SetOfChar is another sample application of the adapter design pattern. The inheritance version of the pattern is used because all the methods of the parent class (SetOfObject) are useful or can be adapted via overriding. For example, SetOfObject overrides the add method (the first of the two add methods) to provide a version of add that prohibits non-Character data from being inserted into the set.

SetOfChar also overloads the add method by including a second version with a char parameter. Thus, client code need not deal with wrapper classes when inserting char values. This second add method wraps its parameter's char value within a Character object and then inserts this value within the set. SetOfChar also includes a new itemChar method that unwraps a Character item from the set and returns the embedded char value.

The SetOfChar class stores all objects within Character wrappers, but this fact is largely transparent to client code. The following client code inserts seven char values into a SetOfChar and then outputs one of the items from the set.

```
SetOfChar vowels = new SetOfChar();
vowels.add('a');
vowels.add('e');
vowels.add('i');
vowels.add('o');
vowels.add('u');
vowels.add('y');
vowels.add('w');
System.out.println( vowels.itemChar() );
```

One caution: Although wrapper classes provide a technique for storing primitive values within full-fledged objects, they have many limitations. The arithmetic operations, such as + and −, that are supported for many of the numeric primitive data types are *not* permitted on wrapper objects. None of the relational operators, such as < and >=, or the logical operators (!, && and ||) is supported for wrapper objects. Furthermore, the wrapper classes have no built-in syntax for constants, and Java does not let you assign primitive constants directly to variables belonging to wrapper classes. All these restrictions mean that wrapper classes are really useful only when you must treat primitives like reference objects.

2.5 BOUNDED CONTAINERS

The specifications for the PhoneBook ADT permit each container of this type to store a virtually limitless collection of PhoneEntry objects. Similarly, the SetOfObject

ADT does not restrict the cardinality of the abstract set that it represents. In fact, all the containers examined thus far are known as **unbounded containers** because they impose no special limitations on the quantity of contained items.

Just because a container is unbounded, however, does not mean that there are absolutely no limits on its size. The cardinality of any SetOfChar object will never exceed $2^{16} == 65,536$ (the total number of values of type char) because a set cannot contain an element more than once. Even SetOfString is limited by the fact that an executing program cannot occupy more data space than is available on the computer on which it executes. Such restrictions—inherent to the properties of the container's content type or the run-time system—are not considered to alter the unbounded status of a container.

To be considered as a **bounded container**, an explicit limitation must be imposed on the number of items in the container's collection. For example, a bounded version of the PhoneBook ADT—call it PhoneBookUnder1000—might incorporate the restriction of storing no more than 1000 PhoneEntry items.

Bounded containers deserve attention because certain implementations, most notably array implementations, do not conveniently support unbounded containers. Suppose that an array is used to store the content of a SetOfString so that each cell of the array stores one String from the set. Such an implementation limits the cardinality of the implemented set to the number of cells in the array, making this a bounded container.

There is nothing wrong with the use of bounded containers as long as the client is aware of their limitations. This means that ADT specifications must clearly include all bounding limitations, typically expressed by the ADT invariant. Figure 2.12 shows an example of how to specify a bounded container called BoundedSetOfObject.

Figure 2.12 BoundedSetOfObject ADT class diagram and ADT specification

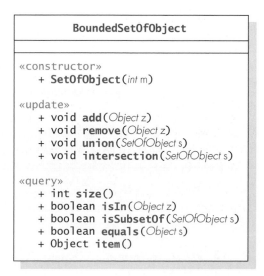

Continued on next page

Bounded SetOfObject ADT Specifications

Domain (Every SetOfObject object has the following parts)

Set of Object theSet;

int maxSize;

Invariant

theSet->size() <= maxSize

Constructor Method

public SetOfObject (int m)

    post: theSet == *set*{}
          and maxSize == m

Update Methods

public void add (Object z)

    pre: theSet->*including*(z)->*size*() <= maxSize
         (throws IllegalStateException)

    post: theSet == theSet@*pre*->*including*(z)

public void remove (Object z)

    post: theSet == theSet@*pre*->*excluding*(z)

public void union (BoundedSetOfObject s)

    pre: theSet->*union*(s)->*size*() <= maxSize
         (throws IllegalStateException)

    post: theSet == theSet@*pre*->*union*(s)

public void intersection (BoundedSetOfObject s)

    post: theSet == theSet@*pre*->*intersection*(s)

Query Methods

public int size ()

    post: result == this->*size*()

public boolean isIn(Object z)

    post: result == this->*includes*(z)

public boolean isSubsetOf(BoundedSetOfObject s)

    post: result == s->*includesAll*(this)

public boolean equals(Object s)

    post: result == this->*includesAll*(s) *and* s->*includesAll*(this)

public Object item ()

    pre: this->*size*() >= 1

    post: this->*includes*(result)

      The BoundedSetOfObject domain is separated into two parts: the content of the set, called theSet, and an int attribute that defines the bounding limitation, called maxSize. The ADT invariant states the bounding limitation—namely, that the cardinality of the abstract set will never exceed the value of maxSize.

Working with bounded containers raises two questions that don't apply to unbounded containers:

- How is the boundary value (maxSize) established?
- Are the methods that increase container size prohibited from overflowing the maximum size?

The BoundedSetOfObject constructor method includes an int parameter that is not present in SetOfObject. At the time of instantiation, the value of this parameter is used to establish the set's maximum cardinality. Calling new BoundedSetOfObject(10) results in a set that cannot exceed a cardinality of 10, and calling new BoundedSetOfObject(99) results in a set that is limited to no more than 99 elements.

Software Engineering Hint

A bounded container limits the container size. A good design strategy is to throw exceptions in response to an attempt to exceed the size limit. The add and union methods from BoundedSetOfObject demonstrate such behavior.

The only other significant difference between BoundedSetOfObject and SetOfObject is that you must take care to ensure that none of the methods is permitted to violate the bounding limitation. In this case, the two methods that can increase the size of the set are add and union. Both methods are designed to throw an exception if client code attempts to make a set that is too large.

2.6   SEQUENCES

The containers examined in previous sections share a property of mathematical sets: They are unordered. A set is **unordered** in the sense that there is no notion of a "first" or "last" set item. For example, *set*{1, 2, 3} has identical content to *set*{3, 2, 1} and *set*{1, 3, 2}. A byproduct of this lack of ordering is that sets are incapable of **element multiplicity**. In other words, a value cannot be an element of a set multiple times. For example, *set*{1, 3, 2, 1} is the same as *set*{1, 2, 3}, which is the same as *set*{1, 2, 2, 2, 2, 3}.

On the other hand, the world is filled with examples of containers in which order or multiplicity (or both) *is* important. The order matters in a dictionary of alphabetized words. A ticket booth at a sporting event can be viewed as a container of fans who are ordered by the time that they arrive in line. An airline reservation system is likely to treat an airplane as a container of passengers ordered by seat number and row. When the contents include multiple indistinguishable items, element multiplicity doesn't matter, such as when a single individual purchases multiple tickets for a movie or when a single pack of jelly beans contains several candies of the same color and flavor.

Just as mathematical sets are effective models for specifying the properties of unordered containers, the concept of a **sequence** is an effective model for specifying many kinds of ordered containers. Furthermore, ordered sequences also support element multiplicity. OCL includes *sequence* as a basic data type, along with a collection of notations that is analogous to sets. For example, the following OCL expression defines a sequence in which the first and third items are 3, the second item is 2, and the fourth item is 5:

sequence{3, 2, 3, 5}

Note that this notation is the same as that for sets except for the ***sequence*** prefix. Figure 2.13 summarizes this and other OCL notations involving sequences.

Figure 2.13   A digest of sequence notations

Symbol	*Meaning*	*Example(s)*
sequence{ }	Empty sequence	
sequence{e_1, e_2, ..., e_n}	Sequence enumeration	sequence{1,2, 3,4}
==[1]	Equal to	sequence{1,2} == sequence{1,2}
≠	Not equal to	sequence{1,2} ≠ sequence{1,3}
s–>includes(e)	Test for inclusion	sequence{1,2}–>includes(2) == TRUE
		sequence{1,2}-> includes(3) == FALSE
s–>size()	Cardinality	sequence{1,2}–>size() == 2
s1–>union(s2)	Concatenation	sequence{1,2}–> union(sequence{1,3}) == sequence{1,2,1,3}
s–>prepend(e)	Insert in front	sequence{1,2,3,4}–>prepend(3) == sequence{3,1,2,3,4}
s–>append(e)	Insert in back	sequence{1,2,3,4}–>append(3) == sequence{1,2,3,4,3}
s–>first()	First item	sequence{1,2,3,4}–>first() == 1
s–>last()	Last item	sequence{1,2,3,4}–>last() == 4
s–>at(j)	jth item	sequence{1,2,3,4}–>at(3) == 3
s–>subSequence(lo,hi)	Sub-sequence	sequence{1,2,3,4} – subSequence(2,3) == sequence{2,3}

---

[1]Technically, OCL notation uses a single equal sign (=) to denote set equality. However, in this book the Java notation of (==) is used to avoid any potential confusion with the assignment operator.

A sequence differs from a set in two ways:

- A sequence has a linear order from beginning to end.
- An individual item may occur more than once within a sequence.

The sequence *sequence*{a,x,b,d,x,e} contains six items. The first item is a, and the second and fifth items are both x. The third item is b; the fourth item is d; and the sixth item is e.

The ==, ≠, *includes*, and *size* functions have a meaning in sequences that is analogous to their set semantics. Two sequences are equal (==) exactly when they have the same length and equivalent items in all corresponding positions.

Four functions—*first, last, at,* and *subSequence*—provide various ways to access portions of their object. The *first* and *last* functions access the beginning and ending item in the sequence, respectively. The *at* function allows any item to be inspected, given that item's position within the sequence. (Positions are numbered with consecutive integers beginning with 1.) For example, the expression *sequence*{a,b,c,d}–>*at*(2) has a value of b.

The *subSequence* function evaluates to another sequence, using two arguments given the first and last position of the items. For example, the expression *sequence*{a,b,c,d,e,f}–>*subSequence*(2,4) has a value of *sequence*{b,c,d}.

Three additional sequence methods—*prepend*, *append*, and *union*—are used to compose sequences. The *prepend* and *append* methods compose by joining an additional item to the front (*prepend*) or the rear (*append*) of a sequence. For example, *sequence*{a,b,c,d}–>*prepend*(z) evaluates to *sequence*{z,a,b,c,d}, and *sequence*{a,b,c,d} –>*append*(z) evaluates to *sequence*{a,b,c,d,z}.

The *union* function, which shares its name with a function from sets, behaves a bit differently than for sets. When *union* is applied to two sequences, the result is a sequence formed by joining the content of the two sequences end to end. This function is analogous to the Java + operator when applied to String data. Such ways to join linear containers are commonly called **concatenation**, and the operation of **concatenating** means to join end to end. The following example uses concatenation via the *union* function, with the value of the function given after the "==":

sequence{a,b,c,d}–>*union*(*sequence*{z,a,x}) == *sequence*{a,b,c,d,z,a,x}

Figure 2.14 uses this OCL *sequence* notation to define an AudioSelection ADT and a related AudioPlayer ADT. The AudioPlayer ADT is designed to model a list of audio recordings and their associated player.

Figure 2.14 AudioSelection and AudioPlayer ADTs

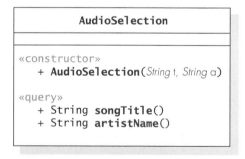

AudioSelection ADT Specifications

Domain

(Every AudioSelection object has the following parts)

String **title**;

String **artist**;

Constructor Method

public **AudioSelection**(String t, String a)

   post: title == t *and* artist == a

Continued on next page

Query Methods

public String **songTitle**( )

    post: result == title

public String **artistName**( )

    post: result == artist

AudioPlayer

«constructor»
   + **AudioPlayer**( )

«update»
   + void **append**(*AudioSelection* a)
   + void **removeFirstSong**( )
   + void **dontPlay**( )
   + void **playFirst**( )
   + void **playNext**( )

«query»
   + int **size**( )
   + AudioSelection **songFromPosition**(*int* p)
   + int **sequenceNumber**(*AudioSelection* ns)

AudioPlayer ADT Specifications

Domain

(Every AudioPlayer object has the following parts)

Sequence of AudioSelection **songs**;

int **currentlyPlaying**;

Invariant

songs->*size*() <= 100
and 0 <= currentlyPlaying <= *songs->size*()

Note currentlyPlaying indicates the sequence number of the song that is currently playing. A currentlyPlaying value of zero indicates that no song is being played.

Constructor Method

public **AudioPlayer**()

    post: songs == *sequence*{}
       and currentlyPlaying == 0

Update Methods

public void **addSong**(AudioSelection ns)

  pre: songs->*size*() < 100 (throws IllegalStateException)

  post: songs == songs@*pre->append*(ns)

Continued on next page

```
public void removeFirstSong()
```
    pre: songs->*size*() >= 1 (throws IllegalStateException)

    post: songs == songs@*pre*->*subSequence*(2,songs@*pre*->*size*())

```
public void dontPlay()
```
    post: currentlyPlaying == 0

```
public void playFirst()
```
    pre: songs->*size*() >= 1 (throws IllegalStateException)

    post: currentlyPlaying == 1

```
public void playNext()
```
    pre: songs->*size*() >= 1 (throws IllegalStateException)

    post: (currentlyPlaying@*pre* <= songs->*size*()
         implies currentlyPlaying == currentlyPlaying@*pre* + 1)
       and (currentlyPlaying@*pre* == songs->*size*()
         implies currentlyPlaying == 1)

Query Methods

```
public int size ()
```
    post: result == songs->*size*()

```
public audioSelection songFromPosition(int p)
```
    post: (1<=p<=songs->*size*()) *implies* result == songs->*at*(p)
         and (p<1 *or* p>songs->*size*()) *implies* result == null

```
public int sequenceNumber(AudioSelection a)
```
    post: songs->*includes*(a) *implies* songs->*at*(result) == a
         and not songs->*includes*(a) *implies* result == 0

As the ADT specifications for AudioPlayer point out, this is a bounded container because the invariant states that the object cannot contain more than 100 songs. Songs are added to an AudioPlayer by calling addSong. The postcondition for addSong, shown next, makes it clear that each newly added song will be placed at the rear of the preceding list of songs. (Note that ns refers to an AudioSelection parameter—i.e., the song to be appended.)

    songs == songs@*pre*->*append*(ns)

The specifications also show that the only way to remove a song from an AudioPlayer is from the front of the list. The removeFirst method has the following postcondition, and it indicates that the song list following a call to this method is the same as the prior song list with the first song removed.

    songs == songs@*pre*->*subSequence*(2,songs@*pre*->*size*())

The playFirst method causes an AudioPlayer object to begin playing music, starting with the first song. A call to playNext advances the player to the song following the one being played. If playNext is called while the last song is playing, the

AudioPlayer returns to the first song in the list. This "return to the first song" behavior is specified by the following clause of the playNext postcondition:

currentlyPlaying@*pre* == songs->*size*() *implies* currentlyPlaying == 1

The first clause of the postcondition from the songFromPosition method illustrates the usefulness of the *at* function. Here is the postcondition for this method for int parameter p:

(1<=p<=songs->*size*()) *implies* result == songs->*at*(p)

This subassertion indicates that this method returns the pth song as long as p is a valid song number.

The same subscript notation is used in a slightly more complex manner for the sequenceNumber method. The first clause of this postcondition is as follows:

songs->*includes*(a) *implies* songs->*at*(result) == a

This assertion states that if an AudioSelection called a is present somewhere in the sequence of songs, then the return value will give the position at which a occurs. (Note that this particular postcondition does not guarantee *which* position is returned if a occurs multiple times within the sequence.)

2.7   STRING

As a second illustration of the utility of the sequence for expressing abstract specifications, this section examines the String data type and several of its methods. The String class is included in the java.lang package. Figure 2.15 contains a partial class diagram and abstract specifications.

Figure 2.15 Partial String class diagram and specification

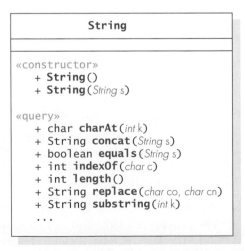

Continued on next page

String Specifications

Domain A String object can be thought of as a sequence in which all elements are of type char.

Constructor Methods

```
public String()
```
 post: this == *sequence{}*

```
public String(String s)
```
 post: this == *sequence{s->at(1), s->at(2), ..., s->at(s->size())}*

Other Methods

```
public char charAt(int k)
```
 pre: 0 <= k <= this->*size*() - 1 (throws IndexOutOfBoundsException)

 post: result == this->*at*(k-1)

```
public String concat(String s)
```
 pre: s != null (throws NullPointerException)

 post: result == this->*union*(s)

```
public boolean equals(String s)
```
 post: result == (this is the same sequence as s)

```
public int indexOf(char c)
```
 post: this->*includes*(c)
   implies (this->*at*(result) == c
  and not this->*subSequence*(1,result-1)->*includes*(c))
  and not this->*includes*(c) *implies* result == -1

```
public int length()
```
 post: result == this->*size*()

```
public String replace(char co, char cn)
```
 post: result == this with all occurrences of co replaced by cn

```
public String substring(int k)
```
 pre: 0 <= k < this->*size*() (throws IndexOutOfBoundsException)

 post: result == this->*subsequence*(k+1,this->*size*())

```
public String substring(int k, int m)
```
 pre: 0 <= k < m < this->*size*() (throws IndexOutOfBoundsException)

 post: result == this->*subsequence*(k+1,m)

  The parameterless String constructor method is defined to create an empty sequence of characters, that is, an empty string. The second String constructor includes a parameter that is also of type String. This constructor is defined by a postcondition that describes how each consecutive character of the original (this) String is used to form the newly instantiated result.

The charAt method returns a single character from within a String. The position of this return character is supplied via the charAt parameter. The charAt specifications clearly show that this argument indexes a String with a value that is 1 less than the corresponding sequence position. For example, str.charAt(0) returns the first character of str, and str.charAt(1) returns its second character. (This numbering convention is consistent with array indexing in Java.) The charAt precondition specifies that an exception will be thrown for an invalid index parameter.

The concat method is a concatenation method for String objects. The behavior of concat is analogous to that of the OCL *union* function.

The indexOf method is designed to locate the position of a character within a String. The following portion of the postcondition states that the returned position that is returned is 1 less than the actual position and that no position of lesser value contains the same character. In other words, indexOf locates the *leftmost* position of its parameter character.

> this->*includes*(c)
>   *implies* (this->*at*(result+1) == c
>   *and not* this->subSequence(1,result)->*includes*(c))

The complete indexOf postcondition clarifies that this position is returned whenever the character is present, and -1 is returned when the character is not present.

The postcondition for the replace method illustrates a situation in which OCL notation seems cumbersome for something that can be stated clearly in English. Therefore, the postcondition is expressed as follows:

> result == this with all occurrences of co replaced by cn

2.8 MUTABILITY

The String class differs from all the containers we've looked at in the sense that String includes no update methods. Objects from such a class have a fixed state because it is impossible to alter the object after it has been instantiated. Classes, such as String and the wrapper classes, that provide no update behavior are known as **immutable**.

The word "immutable" comes from the root word "mutate," which refers to change. Therefore, a **mutable object** is one that can change state dynamically during program execution. Correspondingly, an **immutable object** cannot change state.

Another standard Java class, StringBuffer, illustrates the differences between mutable and immutable classes. Figure 2.16 contains a partial class diagram and abstract specifications for StringBuffer. As with the String class, every object of type StringBuffer stores a single sequence of characters. The most significant difference between String and StringBuffer is that String is immutable and StringBuffer is mutable.

Figure 2.16 Partial `StringBuffer` class diagram and ADT specification

```
StringBuffer
------------------------------------------
------------------------------------------
«constructor»
   + StringBuffer()
   + StringBuffer(String s)

«query»
   + char charAt(int k)
   + boolean equals(String s)
   + int length()
   + String toString()

«update»
   + StringBuffer append(String s)
   + StringBuffer delete(int s, int f)
   ...
```

StringBuffer ADT Specifications

Domain

A `StringBuffer` object can be thought of as a sequence in which all elements are of type `char`.

Constructor Methods

`public` **`StringBuffer()`**

  post: `this` == *sequence*{}

`public` **`StringBuffer`**`(String s)`

  post: `this` == *sequence*{`s->`*at*(1), `s->`*at*(2), ..., `s->`*at*(`s->`size())}

Query Methods

`public int` **`charAt`**`(int k)`

  pre: 0 <= k <= `this->`*size*() – 1 (throws `IndexOutOfBoundsException`)

  post: result == `this->`*at*(k–1)

`public boolean` **`equals`**`(StringBuffer s)`

  post: result == (`this` is the same sequence as `s`)

`public int` **`length()`**

  post: result == `this->`*size*()

`public String` **`toString()`**

  post: result == `this`

Update Methods

`public StringBuffer` **`append`**`(String s)`

  pre: `s` != `null` (throws `NullPointerException`)

Continued on next page

> **post:** this == s->*union*(this@*pre*)
>   *and* result == this
>
> public StringBuffer **delete**(int b, int f)
>
>   **pre:** 0 <= b <= f <= this->*size*() − 1
>   (throws StringIndexOutOfBoundsException)
>
>   **post:** this == this@*pre*->*subSequence*(1,b)
>   ->*union*(this@*pre*->*subSequence*(f+1,this@*pre*->*size*()))
>   *and* result == this
>
> public StringBuffer **insert**(int b, String s)
>
>   **pre:** 0 <= b <= this->*size*() − 1
>   (throws StringIndexOutOfBoundsException)
>
>   **post:** this == this@*pre*->*subSequence*(1,b)
>   ->*union*(s)
>   ->*union*(this@*pre*->*subSequence*(b+1,this@*pre*->*size*()))
>   *and* result == this

StringBuffer contains several methods—such as charAt, equals, and length—that have the same abstract behavior as String methods with the same names. On the other hand, StringBuffer includes methods such as append, insert, and delete that allow for updating (mutating) its string content. These update methods are sometimes called **mutators**.

To illustrate the difference between using mutable and immutable classes, let's compare the append mutator method (from StringBuffer) with the concat method (from String). Both methods are designed to concatenate one sequence of characters to another. The following segment of code concatenates "the end" onto the String variable called str.

```
str = str.concat("the end");
```

When this statement executes, the concat method instantiates and returns a new String object that replaces the prior String referenced by str. The following statement accomplishes an analogous task on a StringBuffer variable called sBuf:

```
sBuf.append("the end");
```

This statement does not instantiate any new objects. Instead, it mutates the existing object referenced by sBuf.

Mutable classes sometimes eliminate the need for additional assignment operations, as shown by this comparison. Another advantage of mutability is that it tends to create fewer objects at run-time. (The concat method always creates a new String object, whereas the append method does not create any new object.)

One advantage of immutable classes is that nonvoid methods can be composed from one another, much as mathematicians compose functions from other functions. For example, the following code segment assigns the string "FINI" to str.

```
String str = "";
str = str.concat("F").concat("I").concat("N").concat("I").
```

Methods that are void cannot be composed consecutively, in this way.

StringBuffer, however, circumvents this issue by designing mutator methods that alter this as well as return a reference to it. Therefore, the following code is possible:

```
StringBuffer sBuff = new StringBuffer("");
sBuf = sBuf.append("F").append("I").append("N").append("I").
```

As a second example of mutable and immutable classes, Figure 2.17 contains class diagrams for two versions of the unbounded generic sets MutableSet and ImmSet. MutableSet is identical to the SetOfObject ADT examined in Section 2.5. ImmSet consists of an analogous collection of operations that are designed in an immutable way.

Figure 2.17 MutableSet and ImmSet class diagrams

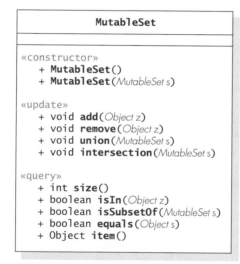
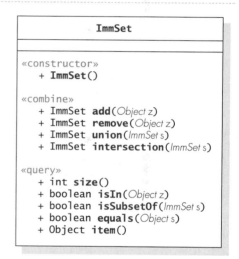

Every void (update) method from MutableSet has a corresponding nonvoid method in the «combine» section of ImmSet. The ImmSet version of each method returns a new ImmSet that has the same content that would result from the corresponding update method of MutableSet. For example, the union method from MutableSet updates an existing (this) set by forming the union from its prior value and the method's parameter. Given two previously assigned MutableSet variables—call them mSet1 and mSet2—the following statements assign the union of these two to mSet1:

```
mSet1.union(mSet2);
```

The execution of this statement causes the value of mSet1 to be altered. If you want mSet1 to remain unchanged, you must create a duplicate set. For such situations, mutable sets should be designed with clone methods. A common way to provide a clone method is through a constructor method that copies its parameter. The second constructor method from `MutableSet` is such a constructor. Using this constructor, you can assign `mSet3` the union of `mSet1` and `mSet2` without disturbing the two union operands.

```
MutableSet mSet3 = new MutableSet( mSet1 );
mSet3.union(mSet2);
```

Immutable classes never allow their objects to be mutated, so executing the following statement does not alter `iSet1`. This statement forms the union of `iSet1` and `iSet2`, assuming that they are nonnull `ImmSet` type variables:

```
ImmSet iSet3 = iSet1.union(iSet2);
```

The following example illustrates how the methods of the immutable `ImmSet` class can be composed. Executing this statement causes `iSet4` to be assigned the union of `iSet1` and `iSet2`, and then the intersection of this union with `iSet3`. The objects referenced by `iSet1`, `iSet2`, and `iSet3` are not altered by this statement.

```
ImmSet iSet4 = iSet1.union(iSet2).intersection(iSet3);
```

2.9 ITERATORS

Whether the container is setlike or sequencelike, mutable or immutable, you often need to examine its content. Accessor methods such as the `item` method from `SetOfObject` provide limited access to the individual container items. However, the `item` method cannot support selective access.

An algorithm to **visit** every item is among the most common container algorithms, but such algorithms are impossible with the item method shown thus far. Visiting an item consists of examining and perhaps altering the item's state. Here are some examples:

- An algorithm to calculate the monthly interest fee for every item in a container of credit-card balances
- An algorithm to print paychecks for every item in a container of employees
- An algorithm to total the annual rainfall from a container of daily rainfall amounts

This need to visit container items is so common that an **iterator design pattern** has been identified as a way to accomplish such algorithms. Figure 2.18 describes the iterator design pattern in a form consistent with the java.util package.

The iterator design pattern relies upon an interface such as `Iterator` that is part of the java.util package. Figure 2.19 describes `Iterator` as an ADT.

Figure 2.18 Iterator design pattern

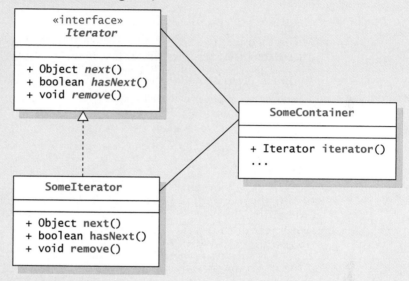

Iterator Design Pattern

Intent

to provide a consistent collection of methods for visiting all items of a container one after another

Structure (class diagram)

Explanation

A container class, such as SomeContainer, includes an iterator method to instantiate a new iterator (of type SomeIterator) positioned at the front of the container. Assuming that variable sc is of type SomeContainer, the following algorithm will visit all items.

```
Iterator it = sc.iterator();
while (it.hasNext()) {
    //visit it.next()
}
```

Example

SetOfObjectIt from Figure 2.19 is a container ADT class that incorporates such an iterator.

Figure 2.19 Iterator interface ADT class diagram and ADT specification

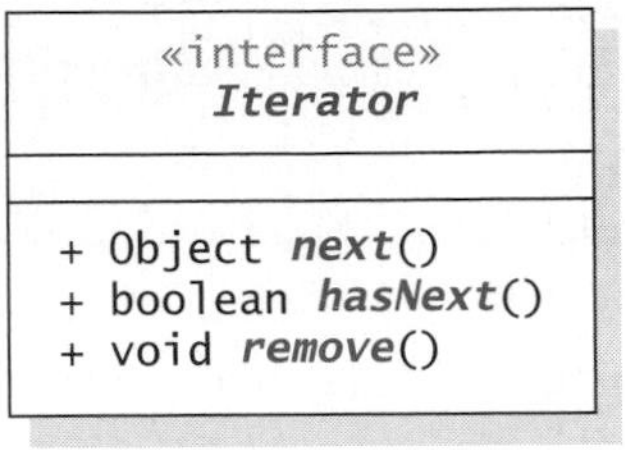

```
              «interface»
               Iterator

        + Object next()
        + boolean hasNext()
        + void remove()
```

Iterator ADT Specifications

Domain (Every Iterator object has the following fields)

Sequence of Object `underlyingSeq`;
`int position`;
`boolean removeIsValid`;

Note Initially, `position == 0` *and* `removeIsValid == false`

Methods

`public Object next( )`

pre: position < underlyingSeq->*size*()
(throws `NoSuchElementException`)

post: position == position@*pre* + 1
and result == underlyingSeq->*at*(position)
and removeIsValid == true

`public boolean hasNext( )`

post: result == (position < underlyingSeq->*size*())

`public void remove( )`

pre: removeIsValid == true (throws `IllegalStateException`)

post: underlyingSeq == underlyingSeq@*pre* with the item at position
removed
and removeIsValid == false

note: Implementing the `remove` method is considered optional. If not
implemented, this method throws
`UnsupportedOperationException`.

An `Iterator` is designed to move through a container from one item to the
next. To perform such a container traversal, three methods are required.

- The `next` method is used to move "forward," with each call to `next` returning a different item from the container.
- The `hasNext` method tests whether or not there are more items as yet unvis-
ited by this iterator. If `hasNext` is true, further calls to `next` are possible; if
`hasNext` is false, then the iterator has visited all items.

- A constructor method is used to instantiate a new iterator that has not visited any of the container's items. (This method, usually called `iterator`, doesn't appear in the class diagram in Figure 2.19.)

Figure 2.20 illustrates how to incorporate `Iterator` into a container class. The `SetOfObjectIt` ADT is the same ADT as `SetOfObject` (from Figure 2.2), with the item method replaced by an `iterator` method.

Figure 2.20 `SetOfObjectIt` ADT class diagram and ADT specification

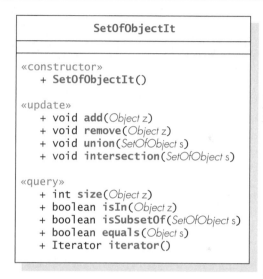

```
                    SetOfObjectIt


«constructor»
    + SetOfObjectIt()

«update»
    + void add(Object z)
    + void remove(Object z)
    + void union(SetOfObject s)
    + void intersection(SetOfObject s)

«query»
    + int size(Object z)
    + boolean isIn(Object z)
    + boolean isSubsetOf(SetOfObject s)
    + boolean equals(Object s)
    + Iterator iterator()
```

SetOfObjectIt ADT

Domain

Every SetOfObjectIt object is a set in which all elements are of type `Object`

Constructor Method

public `SetOfObjectIt` ( )

    post: this == set{}

Update Methods

public void **add** (Object z)

    post: this == this@pre->*including*(z)

public void **remove** (Object z)

    post: this == this@pre->*excluding*(z)

public void **union** (SetOfObjectIt s)

    post: this == this@pre->*union*(s)

public void **intersection** (SetOfObjectIt s)

    post: this == this@pre->*intersection*(s)

Continued on next page

Query Methods
```
public int size ()
    post: result == this->size()
public boolean isIn(Object z)
    post: result == this->includes(z)
public boolean isSubsetOf(SetOfObjectIt s)
    post: result == s->includesAll(this)
public boolean equals(Object s)
    post: result == this->includesAll(s) and s->includesAll(this)
public Iterator iterator ()
    post: result.position == 0 and result.removeIsValid == false
```

The most common client algorithm involving iterators is a loop that visits every item in the container. The general form of this loop for a container called sc is as follows:

```
Iterator it = sc.iterator();
while (it.hasNext()) {
    // visit it.next()
}
```

Figure 2.21 shows an example of this loop. The PrintAllElements method outputs every element from a SetOfObjectIt parameter called s without altering the state of s. This method relies on the iterator method to return a fresh iterator; then it uses the hasNext and next methods defined by the Iterator interface.

Figure 2.21 PrintAllElements method

```
/* post: Each element of s has been output on a separate line */
public void PrintAllElements(SetOfObjectIt s) {
    Iterator it = s.iterator();
    while (it.hasNext()) {
        System.out.println( it.next() );
    }
}
```

Incorporating an iterator into a set ADT may seem unusual. Sets are inherently unordered collections, and iterators impose an ordering of content. However, as the PrintAllElements method illustrates, certain useful algorithms are made possible by the inclusion of iterators.

There is an implementation cost associated with using iterators. Because Iterator is an interface, it must be implemented by some class before it can be used. Therefore, ADTs such as SetOfObjectIt must include an implementation of Iterator. Future chapters include examples that illustrate how to implement such iterators.

The standard Java packages include `java.util.Enumeration`, a second interface that is very similar to Iterator. The Enumeration interface has only two methods:

- `hasMoreElements` has the same behavior as Iterator's hasNext method.
- `nextElement` has the same behavior as Iterator's next method.

2.10 THE JAVA.UTIL.COLLECTION INTERFACE

Well-chosen names for classes and their members can be an asset to any software library or collection of libraries. Poorly chosen names can waste programmer time. One of the most important aspects of effective naming is consistency. Suppose one library includes three kinds of containers, each with its own method to insert a new container item. It is more difficult for library clients if all three methods have different names—such as insert, put, and include—rather than all three methods sharing the same name.

One of the benefits of a Java library interface is that it encourages consistent naming. For example, the Iterator and Enumeration interfaces permit standard method names, such as next and hasNext. At the same time these interfaces permit clients to use identical algorithms on different containers.

Another widely used Java interface that is closely associated with containers is `java.util.Collection`. This interface provides a consistent group of methods that are applicable to virtually all container classes. Figure 2.22 describes Collection interface in the form of a class diagram and an ADT specification.

Figure 2.22 `java.util.Collection` interface diagram and ADT specification

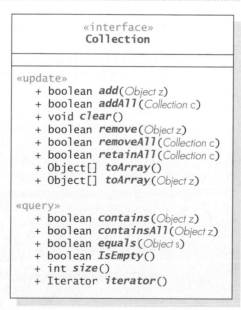

```
        «interface»
        Collection


«update»
    + boolean add(Object z)
    + boolean addAll(Collection c)
    + void clear()
    + boolean remove(Object z)
    + boolean removeAll(Collection c)
    + boolean retainAll(Collection c)
    + Object[] toArray()
    + Object[] toArray(Object z)

«query»
    + boolean contains(Object z)
    + boolean containsAll(Object z)
    + boolean equals(Object s)
    + boolean IsEmpty()
    + int size()
    + Iterator iterator()
```

Continued on next page

Collection ADT Specifications

Domain (Every Collection object has the following type)

Either *Set* of Object Or *Sequence* of Object (The choice is up to the implementation.)

Update Methods

public boolean **add** (Object z)

> **post:** this == this@pre->*including*(z)
> *and* result == (this ≠ this@pre)

> **note:** • If a *sequence* implementation is used, an additional z item is inserted into this@pre. The positioning of the item varies according to the implementation.
>
> • This method is optional; when not supported, UnsupportedOperationException is thrown.
>
> • Implementations may throw ClassCastException or IllegalArgumentException for unacceptable arguments.

public boolean **addAll** (Collection c)

> **post:** this == this@pre->*union*(c)
> *and* result == (this ≠ this@pre)

> **note:** • If a sequence implementation is used, additional c items are inserted into this@pre. The positioning of the items varies according to the implementation.
>
> • This method is optional; when not supported, UnsupportedOperationException is thrown.
>
> • Implementations may throw ClassCastException or IllegalArgumentException for unacceptable arguments.

public void **clear** ()

> **post:** this == {}

> **note:** This method is optional; when not supported, UnsupportedOperationException is thrown.

public boolean **remove** (Object z)

> **post:** this == this@pre->*excluding*(z)
> *and* result == (this ≠ this@pre)

> **note:** • If a sequence implementation is used, only one z item is removed from this@pre. The choice of which z item to remove varies according to the implementation.
>
> • This method is optional; when not supported, UnsupportedOperationException is thrown.

public boolean **removeAll** (Collection c)

> **post:** this == this@pre - c
> *and* result == (this ≠ this@pre)

> **note:** • If a sequence implementation is used, only one instance of each c item is removed from this@pre. The choice of which items to remove is up to the implementation.

Continued on next page

- This method is optional; when not supported, UnsupportedOperationException is thrown.

public boolean **retainAll** (Collection c)

post: this == this@pre->*intersection*(c)
and result == (*this* ≠ this@pre)

note: • If a sequence implementation is used, all items not in c are removed from this@pre.

- This method is optional; when not supported, UnsupportedOperationException is thrown.

public Object[] **toArray** ( )

post: result == the collection of all items from this one per cell

public Object[] **toArray** (Object z)

post: result == the collection of all items that conform to the actual type of z from this one per cell

Query Methods

public boolean **contains**(Object z)

post: result == this->*includes*(z)

public boolean **containsAll**(Collection c)

post: result == this->*includesAll*(c)

public boolean **equals**(Object s)

post: result == (this->*includesAll*(s) and s->*includesAll*(this))

public boolean **isEmpty**( )

post: result == (this == {})

public int size ()

post: result == (this->*size*())

public Iterator **iterator**()

post: result is a new Iterator (result.position==0 *and* result.removeIsValid==false)

The Collection interface is designed to capture the common features of mutable containers, whether the containers are setlike, sequencelike, or structured in some other manner. The most widely used methods from this interface include the following.

add: to insert a new item into the collection
remove: to remove an item from the collection
clear: to reset the collection to empty
contains: to check whether an object is an item of the collection
size: to query the count of items in the collection
equals: to test whether two collections have the same content
iterator: to create a new iterator over the collection

The Collection interface also includes methods to add, remove, and test for the inclusion of other Collections, and toArray methods to convert a Collection into an array of Object. The following Collection methods are optional: add, addAll, clear, remove, removeAll, and retainAll.

The Collection interface permits sufficient flexibility to allow for differences in containers. For example, the add method's implementation for a setlike container would not allow duplicates within the container, whereas each call to add for a sequencelike container should insert another instance of a duplicated item. The add, addAll, remove, removeAll, and retainAll methods return a boolean value to indicate whether or not the container's content is changed by each method call.

Realizing that the Collection interface might be cumbersome to implement with its many methods, the designers of the java.util package also included an abstract class, AbstractCollection, that implements Collection, as shown in Figure 2.23.

Figure 2.23 Class diagram for java.util.AbstractCollection

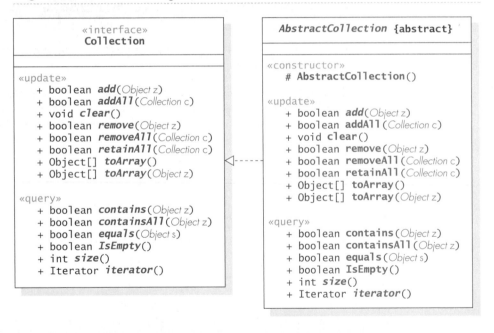

The AbstractCollection class is a minimal implementation of Collection and includes an AbstractCollection constructor. This method has protected scope. When called, AbstractCollection instantiates an empty container.

The key difference between AbstractCollection and Collection is the implementation of several methods. In fact a subclass of AbstractCollection need implement only three methods (add, size, and iterator), along with the three Iterator methods (next, hasNext, and remove), for a fully functional container. Such containers are implemented in later chapters.

THE SOFTWARE INSPECTOR

J̄ava

Following is a collection of hints on what to check when you perform desk checks that involve the concepts of this chapter.

✓ An ADT should be designed abstractly. The public view of a class should therefore hide all implementation details except those that need to be known by clients of the class.

✓ Check every ADT specification to be certain that it maintains precision. It's best to model ADTs from mathematical types, such as Integers and Boolean, as well as from OCL models, such as sets and sequences, or from other properly defined ADTs.

✓ The designer of a container must always consider the options of bounded versus unbounded containers.

✓ When examining an ADT, consider whether an immutable or a mutable ADT provides the best solution for the problem at hand.

✓ A design review of a container must consider whether adequate inspector methods are included.

✓ Knowing the standard Java interfaces can make your design work more convenient and result in designs that are more readily understood by others. The `Iterator`, `Enumeration`, and `Collection` interfaces are particularly useful for container design.

EXERCISES

1. Enumerate the content of each of the following sequences.

 a. *sequence*{1, 2, 3, 4, 3, 1, 5, 8}->*first*()

 b. *sequence*{1, 2, 3, 4, 3, 1, 5, 8}->*last*()

 c. *sequence*{1, 2, 3, 4, 3, 1, 5, 8}->*size*()

 d. *sequence*{1, 2, 3, 4, 3, 1, 5, 8}->at(1)

 e. *sequence*{1, 2, 3, 4, 3, 1, 5, 8}->*at*(6)

 f. *sequence*{1, 2, 3, 4, 3, 1, 5, 8}->*subSequence*(2,5)

 g. *sequence*{1, 2, 3, 4, 3, 1, 5, 8}->*subSequence*(1,7)

 h. *sequence*{2, 4, 6, 8} ->*union*(*sequence*{1, 2, 3, 4})

 i. *sequence*{1, 2, 3, 4, 3, 1, 5, 8}->*append*(9)

 j. *sequence*{1, 2, 3, 4, 3, 1, 5, 8}->*prepend*(9) ->*append*(7) ->*append*(6)

 k. *sequence*{1, 2, 3, 4, 3, 1, 5, 8}->*includes*(3)

 l. *sequence*{1, 2, 3, 4, 3, 1, 5, 8}->*includes*(9)

2. Assume that ObjectSet is a class that implements the SetOfObject ADT specified in Figure 2.2. Show a segment of code to declare and instantiate an ObjectSet variable and to assign this variable the following set:

   set{ "Bo", "Flo", "Joe", "Moe", "So" }

3. Assume that ObjectSet is a class that implements the SetOfObject ADT specified in Figure 2.2. Show a segment of code to declare and instantiate an ObjectSet variable and to assign this variable the following set:

   set{1, 8, 2, 3, 7}

4. Complete the code to implement each of the following methods so that it is correct with respect to the given specifications. (SetOfObject is specified in Figure 2.2, and ObjectSet is explained in Exercise 3.)

   a. /* **pre:**   s1 != null *and* s2 != null
         post: s1 == s1@*pre->union*(s2) */
      public void **combine**(SetOfObject s1, SetOfObject s2)

   b. /* **pre:**   s1 != null *and* s2 != null
         post: result == s1@*pre->intersection*(s2) */
      public ObjectSet **overlap**(SetOfObject s1, SetOfObject s2)

   c. /* **pre:**   s != null
         post: s == s@*pre->including*(0) */
      public void **includeZero**(SetOfObject s)

   d. /* **pre:**   s != null
         post: boolean == s->*includes*(0) */
      public boolean **zeroIsInThere**(SetOfObject s)

   e. /* **pre:**   s != null
         post: boolean == (s == *set*{2}) */
      public boolean **isEvenPrimeSet**(SetOfObject s)

5. Complete the code to implement each of the following methods so that it is correct with respect to the given specifications. (Note that these specifications describe String as a sequence of char.)

   a. /* **pre:**   s->size() > 0
         post: result == s->*last*() */
      public char **lastChar**(String s)

   b. /* **pre:**   s1 != null AND s2 != null
         post: result == s1->*union*(s2) */
      public String **join**(String s1, String s2)

6. Write the specifications for a mutable class similar to String. Your class must include methods to concatenate, return the string length, and assign a substring.

7. Complete the implementation of the class that you designed in the Exercise 6.

1. Design, implement, and test a program that implements the PhoneBook ADT (Figure 1.7). You should express the original PhoneBook specifications in the form of a Java interface. Use the adapter design pattern to implement your PhoneBook class from SetOfObjectIt. (You must decide whether to use the aggregation version or inheritance version of the adapter design pattern.) You are expected to include a test driver class of your own choosing, but be certain that it allows for extensive testing of new insertions into the PhoneBook, look-ups, and removals.

2. Write the same program as in Programming Exercise 1, but use the adapter design pattern to adapt java.util.Collection. Hint: You can use java.util.LinkedList as a non-abstract implementation of java.util. Collection.

3. Design, implement, and test a program that allows the user to simulate a variation on the Pick-3 lottery game. To play the Pick-3 lottery game the player selects a sequence of three digits (0–9). Each day the lottery game, is played using a device that selects at random one ball from each of three ball containers. Each of these containers contains 10 balls numbered 0 through 9. The game is won if the numbers on the three balls that are drawn match the three-digit sequence chosen by the player.

   Simulating the actual game isn't particularly interesting because the odds of winning are small. Instead, your program should simulate only the machine drawing part of the game, using it to estimate how many days typically pass before any prior outcome repeats. You must store each winning number as a SequenceOfInt, representing each chosen digit as a separate sequence item. Use a SetOfObject container to store all the winning sequences, and reset it to empty each time a winning sequence repeats a second time. Write the program so that it tries 100 times to count the length of time until a winning sequence repeats and then reports the average number of days.

4. Another container that is used by mathematicians, but lesser known than a set, is a bag. A **bag** can be thought of as a set, with the added characteristic that a bag allows for elements to be included multiple times (and the multiplicity of each element is maintained). Another way to define a bag is that it is a sequence in which the order of the items doesn't matter. This exercise requires that you design and implement a BagOfInt class using the adapter design pattern to adapt SequenceOfObject, representing each bag item as a separate integer in the sequence.

   Using this BagOfInt class, design, implement, and test a program that simulates rolling a pair of six-sided dice 1,000 times. Assuming that the sides of the dice are numbered in the usual way (from 1 through 6), your program must report the number of times each total occurs out of the 1,000 rolls.

5. Another way to design a bag container (discussed in Programming Exercise 4) is to adapt it from `SetOfObjectIt`. This requires another class to serve as the type of set elements so that each element stores both the integer element from the bag and its bag multiplicity.

Using this `BagOfInt` class, implement a program that simulates drawing pairs of playing cards and counting their blackjack value. A deck of playing cards consists of 52 individual cards, with four suits and 13 cards per suit. The cards in each suit are numbered 2 through 10, along with jack, queen, king, and ace. For the game of blackjack, the suit of each card is immaterial. The value of each card from 2 through 10 is the same as its number. The value of jacks, queens, and kings is 10. The value of an ace is either 11 or 1. (For this exercise use only an ace value of 11.) Your program is to adapt `SequenceOfInt` in order to build a `DeckOfCards` ADT that is sufficient for a blackjack deck.

Design, implement, and test a program that inserts all 52 cards into the deck in random order and then draws cards in pairs. For each pair of cards your program must record the combined value of the two cards. These combined values should be maintained by your `BagOfInt` class, and the number of occurrences of each potential combined value (from 4 through 21) reported when the program completes.

6. Design and implement an immutable version of `SequenceOfObject`, and use it to solve one of the previous exercises.

PERFORMANCE: SEARCHING AND SORTING

OBJECTIVES

- To introduce the idea of using counting and cost functions to measure algorithm performance

- To define big-oh cost

- To explore the various aspects of big-oh arithmetic

- To define and compare the behavior of two basic types of performance: polynomial (which falls into various categories) and exponential

- To introduce methods for measuring the performance of typical control structures

- To explore and compare linear and binary search algorithms

- To explore and compare several N^2 sorting algorithms, including selection sort, linear insertion sort, and bubble sort

- To examine more efficient sorting algorithms, including mergesort, quicksort, and radix sort

- To illustrate some shortcomings of big-oh analysis

- To consider the trade-offs in sorting and searching algorithms between time, space, and intellectual complexity

Correctness is the highest priority of every programmer. A program that isn't correct with respect to its specifications isn't of any value. However, as is demonstrated time and again, there are many correct software solutions to any problem, and some of them are clearly better than others. So it takes more than merely crafting correct code to be a software engineer. Among the most significant characteristics that determine the "better" software are reusability, adaptability, and maintainability.

This chapter explores another significant characteristic of software quality: **performance**. Animated game programs that use fast-moving smooth graphics are preferred over slow, jerkier alternatives. Web search engine algorithms that can locate the most page hits in the shortest time have a big advantage over slower software. Users are much happier with an application that is capable of a speedier translation of the audio from a CD track into MP3 format.

The run-time performance of software has two main ingredients: space and time. **Space** refers to the amount of computer storage that is required to execute a program. Every computer has a fixed amount of available space that is determined by the computer's memory size, its hard disk capacity, and the way the run-time environment utilizes memory and hard disk. The program that uses less space to accomplish a task is considered to be more space efficient. The importance of space efficiency, as a measure of run-time performance, has diminished in recent years because of rapid decreases in the cost of computer storage hardware.

The **time** efficiency of software is measured in the length of time that is required for executing a task. This chapter focuses on time efficiency issues, although most of what is presented has a corresponding analog for space efficiency.

3.1 ALGORITHMS AND COUNTING

The actual time required to execute a program depends on many factors. Among them are the speed of the computer hardware, the intricacies of the operating system or virtual machine that assists program execution, and the supplied user input. More importantly, it is possible to analyze software performance independent of these physical factors.

The method that is most often used as a course measure of run-time performance is based on counting: It is possible to count the number of method calls, the number of times a method body is repeated, the number of assignment statements that execute, and many other run-time occurrences. Any of these counts can serve as a measure of run-time performance. However, counting some things produces more accurate measures than counting others.

Figure 3.1 contains two algorithms that traverse the stuff array in search of an array cell that contains searchValue. If searchValue is equal to one or more cells of the stuff array, then either algorithm will cause the location variable to store the smallest index for which stuff[location] equals searchValue. If the stuff array does not contain searchValue, then executing either loop causes location to be assigned stuff.length.

Figure 3.1 Two loops to find searchValue within the stuff array

Search Algorithm 1

```
int location = stuff.length;
for (int j=0; j!=stuff.length; j++) {
    if (location==stuff.length && searchValue.equals(stuff[j])){
        location = j;
    }
}
```

Search Algorithm 2

```
int location;
while (location!=stuff.length &&
        !searchValue.equals(stuff[location])){
    location++;
}
```

A good measure of the comparative performance of search algorithm 1 and search algorithm 2 is the count of the number of times that each loop body is executed. This is because most of the execution time of each algorithm can be expected to occur within the loops, and the number of loop executions is proportional to the execution time of the loop. Consider, for example, an **unsuccessful search**— a search for which searchValue does not occur within any cell of stuff. For an unsuccessful search, the count of loop body executions for both of the Figure 3.1 algorithms is exactly stuff.length.

Successful searches produce different results. For search algorithm 1, the *for* loop body is executed stuff.length times even for a successful search. On the other hand, the *while* loop of search algorithm 2 is executed fewer times for a successful search. However, without knowing the content of the stuff array you cannot get an exact count of the *while* loop repetitions. If stuff[0] happens to store searchValue, the *while* loop body never executes (the count is zero); but if the only occurrence of searchValue is the last cell of stuff, the count of *while* loop body executions is stuff.length-1.

From the count of loop body executions it would appear that search algorithm 2 performs better for successful searches than search algorithm 1. A careful analysis of the work within the loops tends to confirm this fact. For example, here is the count of the total number of various operations for these two algorithms:

	Search Algorithm 1	*Search Algorithm 2*
Count of ++ executions	1 * loopBodyCount	1 * loopBodyCount
Count of comparisons (==, !=, and/or equals operations)	3 * loopBodyCount[1]	2 * loopBodyCount[1]
Count of array cell inspections	1 * loopBodyCount	1* loopBodyCount

---

[1]The final loop execution makes one fewer comparisons because of conditional evaluation of the && operator.

The example of these two search algorithms points out that you have many choices in what to count, even for simple algorithms. Software developers have only a limited amount of time that can be devoted to consider run-time performance, and that makes it important to count things that explore the major differences between two algorithms. In this case, counting either the total number of ++ operations, the total number of comparisons, or the total number of array cell inspections reveals a similar advantage for search algorithm 2. Counting the number of loop body executions appears to be sufficient.

> ### Software Engineering Hint
>
> Exact measures of performance are impractical, if not impossible, for most nontrivial code, in part because execution time is sensitive to subtle differences. For example, the loop body of search algorithm 2 performs less computation (any a single autoincrement statement) than the loop body of search algorithm 1. However, further investigation reveals that the loop condition of search algorithm 2 requires more execution time than that of search algorithm 1 because the *while* loop condition essentially duplicates the computation of the *if* statement.

This example also shows that run-time performance often depends on the amount of data that is processed. The loop body repetition count is determined by the number of cells in the `stuff` array. The count of loop body executions and the corresponding run-time increases in direct proportion to the length of `stuff`.

This dependence on the amount of data lets you express the count of loop body executions as a function that depends on array size:

LoopBodyExecutionCount(N), for N equal to the data size (i.e., `stuff.length`)

LoopBodyExecutionCount is an example of a **cost function** because it describes an execution "cost." In this case, the cost is a measure of the algorithm's run-time performance in the form of the count of loop body repetitions. You can determine the actual run-time of this code by multiplying *LoopBodyExecutionCount* times the length of time required for each loop iteration (call it *TimePerOneIteration*), including the amount of time for the loop to set up and complete (call it *loopOverhead*). The following formula determines the loop's actual execution time:

$$TotalLoopRuntime == LoopBodyExecutionCount(N) * TimePerOneIteration + loopOverhead$$

3.2   BIG-OH NOTATION

The *LoopBodyExecutionCount* function is an estimate of the actual run-time performance of an algorithm. Computer scientists use such estimates to categorize algorithms into groups according to performance. The so-called **order** of an algorithm is defined by the performance group to which it belongs.

The concept of algorithmic order is based on the mathematical notion of **functional dominance**. Informally stated, one function—call it g(N)—**dominates** (formally called **asymptotically dominates**) another function—call it f(N)—whenever $g(N) \geq f(N)$ for all large values of N.

For example, suppose that the following method gives the actual time required to execute an algorithm in terms of the length of an array, N:

executionTime(N) = $N^2 + 5*N + 100$

The following *estimate1* function can be shown to dominate *executionTime*:

estimate1(N) = $1.1*N^2$

The *estimate1* function dominates *executionTime* because for all "large" values of N, *estimate1*(N) is greater than *executionTime*(N). Figure 3.2 proves this dominance claim. The table demonstrates that whenever N has a value of 66 or greater, the value of *estimate1*(N) exceeds *executionTime*(N). (For values of N that are less than 66, *estimate1*(N) may be smaller, but this is irrelevant for functional dominance.)

Figure 3.2 Table of *executionTime* and *estimate1* functions

N	*executionTime(N)*	*estimate1(N)*
1	106	1.1
2	114	4.4
...	...	...
10	250	101
...	...	...
50	2,850	2,750
...	...	...
65	4,650	4,647.5
66	4,786	4,791.6
67	4,924	4,937.9
...	...	...
100	10,600	11,000
...	...	...

Figure 3.3 plots the values of these two functions. The *executionTime* function is shown as a solid line, and *estimate1* is depicted as a dashed line. The *estimate1* function clearly dominates as the graph extends to the right.

The *estimate1* function is not the only function that dominates *executionTime*. Any function that for large enough N has a functional value that exceeds *executionTime* is said to dominate. Here are a few sample functions that dominate *executionTime*, in increasing order of dominanc:

    estimate2(N) = 1.01 * N^2
    estimate3(N) = 2 * N^2
    estimate4(N) = N^3

The concept of functional dominance is the basis for determining the order of cost functions. Two functions—f(N) and g(N)—have the same order of performance (belong to the same performance category) if and only if c_1*f(N) dominates g(N) and c_2*g(N) dominates f(N) for some two numeric constants c_1 and c_2. Of the preceding functions, *estimate1*, *estimate2*, and *estimate3* all have the same order.

An argument to prove that *estimate1*(N) = 1.1*N^2 and *estimate2*(N) = 1.01*N^2 have the same order proceeds as follows.

Figure 3.3 Plot of *executionTime* and *estimate1* functions

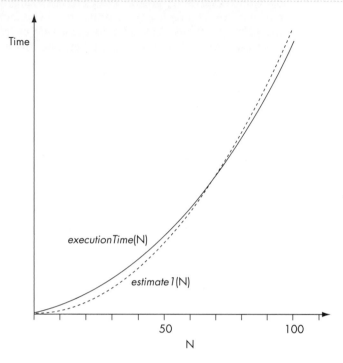

Let $c_1 = 1$, then the following is true.

c_1 * *estimate1*(N) = 1.1*N^2 dominates *estimate2*(N) = 1.01*N^2

Let $c_2 = 2$, then the following is true.

c_2 * *estimate2*(N) = 2.2*N^2 dominates *estimate1*(N) = 1.1*N^2

Therefore

estimate1(N) and *estimate2*(N) have the same order of performance.

The *executionTime* function also belongs to the same performance category as *estimate1*, *estimate2*, and *estimate3*. The algorithm described by *executionTime*, therefore, has the same order as these functions.

By convention each performance order is named by the "simplest" function that belongs to the category. The simplest cost function with the same order as *executionTime* is N^2. The inclusion of N^2 in this category is argued as follows.

Let $c_1 = 1$, then the following is true.

c_1 * *executionTime*(N) = N^2 + 5*N + 100 dominates N^2

Let $c_2 = 2$, then the following is true.

c_2 * N^2 dominates *executionTime*(N) = N^2 + 5*N + 100

Therefore

executionTime (N) and N^2 have the same order of performance.

The most common symbolism for expressing the order of an algorithm is big-oh notation. **Big-oh notation** uses the capital letter O as though it were a function and uses a cost function as the function's argument. It is proper to use an equal sign between this functionlike notation and any other cost function of the same order. For example, the following line is proper because *executionTime* and N2 have the same order.

executionTime(N) = O(N^2)

Alternative phrases also are used to describe this big-oh relationship:

- "The order of *executionTime*(N) is N^2."
- "Big-oh of *executionTime*(N) is N^2."
- "The performance *executionTime*(N) is O(N^2)."

Big-oh notation expresses the relative speed of an algorithm dependent on variables such as N. An algorithm that has O(N) performance has performance speed that is inversely proportional to the value of N. Big-oh is only a crude estimate, and it does not translate into precise execution times. Two algorithms with identical big-oh order may very well have different execution times for the same value of N.

Big-oh is a useful measure because it captures two aspects of performance:

- The basic shape of the plot of the cost function
- The performance cost for large variable (N) values

The shape of a cost function plot reflects the basic growth relationship between a function and its variable(s). A function that grows faster will eventually overtake (dominate) any slower-growing function.

The functional dominance of big-oh order relies upon large variable values because differences in software performance are typically most important when large amounts of data are processed. The performance difference between two algorithms processing the same array of 3 cells is most likely insignificant compared with their performance when processing an array of 100,000 cells. Big-oh is an invalid analysis for comparing algorithms when they are applied to small amounts of data.

Software Engineering Hint

Big-oh analysis is based on the assumption that the most important differences occur when algorithms are slowest (i.e., when they need to process a great deal of data).

As stated earlier, big-oh categories are generally identified by a cost function in its simplest form. Figure 3.4 summarizes three rules that can be helpful for simplifying cost functions.

Figure 3.4 Simplification equalities for big-oh expressions

Constant Factor Rule

O(k * f) = O(f) for any constant k and function f

Multiplicative Rule

O(f) * O(g) = O(f * g) for any functions f and g
or
O(f) / O(g) = O(f / g) for any functions f and g

Additive Rule

O(f + g) = O(f) for any functions f and g such that f dominates g

The first rule (the Constant Factor rule) indicates that constant multipliers have no effect on the order of a function. This rule is a direct consequence of the definition of asymptotic dominance. The Constant Factor rule can be used to conclude that all of the following expressions are $O(N^3)$.

$$cost1(N) = 1.5 * N^3$$
$$cost2(N) = 10 * N^3$$
$$cost3(N) = 9431752 * N^3$$

The second rule (the Multiplicative rule) states that the product of two order functions is the same as the order of the product of the cost functions of each order. This Multiplicative rule is useful in analyzing the performance of a loop such as this one:

```
for (int j=0; j!=N; j++) {
    // Assume that the run-time performance of this body is O(N²)
}
```

This loop is executed N times. Therefore, the performance of this loop can be described as

$$O(N) * O(loopBodyCost())$$

Assuming that the loop body is an $O(N^2)$ algorithm, the preceding expression can be rewritten as

$$O(N) * O(N^2)$$

and this can be simplified as follows by using the Multiplicative rule.

$$O(N) * O(N^2) = O(N^3)$$

The third rule (the Additive rule) in Figure 3.4 indicates that the order of the sum of cost functions is the same as the order of the dominant of the functions. This rule supports the following simplification:

$$O(N^5 + N^2 + 17) = O(\text{dominant of } N^5, N^2, \text{ and } 17)$$
$$= O(N^5)$$

To apply the Additive rule you must understand differences in function domination. Figure 3.5 contains several function expressions that occur frequently in cost functions and their domination relationships.

Figure 3.5 Functional dominance of common cost function expressions

N^M	dominates	$N!$ (N factorial)
$N!$	dominates	a^N
a^N	dominates	b^N when $a > b$
a^N	dominates	N^a
N^a	dominates	N^b when $a > b$
N	dominates	$\log_a(N)$
$\log_a(N)$	dominates	$\log_b(N)$ when $a < b$
$\log_a(N)$	dominates	1

NOTE: These expressions are positive-valued and assume that a and b are positive numeric constants and M and N are variables.

The rules in Figure 3.4 and relationships in Figure 3.5 are useful for simplifying big-oh expressions. For example, the following simplification lists the reasons for each step to the right.

$$O(3*N^4 + 17*N^2 + 175) = O(3*N^4)$$ Additive rule ($3*N^4$ dominates both $17*N^2$ and 175)

$$= O(N^4)$$ Constant Factor rule

Special names are sometimes given to big-oh performance categories that occur often in software algorithms. Algorithms that have a fixed execution time, no matter how long the time, have $O(1)$ performance, also known as **constant** order. An algorithm with performance of $O(N)$ is said to be a **linear** algorithm. **Polynomial** algorithms are those with performance of $O(N^a)$ or better. **Logarithmic** algorithms have a big-oh order of $O(\log_a N)$. The logarithmic algorithms are sufficiently similar in performance that the base (a) is often eliminated, as follows: $O(\log N)$.

Most computer algorithms belong to the polynomial performance category. Other algorithms are sometimes referred to **exponential** algorithms. The growth rate for exponential algorithms is so great that they are useful only in specialized cases. Figure 3.6 illustrates how fast exponential cost functions grow by comparing three polynomial functions (N, $\log_2 N$, $N*\log_2 N$, N^2 and N^3) with two exponential functions (2^N and 3^N).

Figure 3.6 Comparison of polynomial and exponential functions

N	$\log_2 N$	$N*\log_2 N$	N^2	N^3	2^N	3^N
1	0	1	1	1	2	3
2	1	2	4	8	4	9
4	2	8	16	64	16	81
8	3	24	64	512	256	6,561
16	4	64	256	4,096	65,536	43,046,721
32	5	160	1,024	32,768	4,294,967,296	...
64	6	384	4,096	262,144	(Note 1)	
128	7	896	16,384	2,097,152	(Note 2)	
256	8	2,048	65,536	16,777,216	...	

Note 1: This is approximately the number of instructions executed by a 1 Gigaflop computer in 5,000 years.

Note 2: This is approximately 500 billion times the age of the universe (assuming a universe age of 20 billion years).

The importance of the difference between polynomial and exponential algorithms is further illustrated in Figure 3.7. This table shows how much an algorithm improves if it is executed on a computer that is 1000 times faster. The left column lists a cost function and the right column shows the improvement as a factor. For example, a cost function of $N*\log_2 N$ executes 140.2 times faster on the faster computer. Notice that the exponential cost functions (2^N and $N!$) improve their performance by only 100% and 20%, respectively, even though the computer is 1,000 times faster. This demonstrates that faster hardware cannot correct an inefficient algorithm.

Software Engineering Hint

As a general rule, you are best advised to avoid exponential algorithms. The performance of exponential algorithms can be so slow that they are impractical for execution on any computer.

Figure 3.7 The effect of increasing processor speed by 1,000-fold

Cost Function	Speed Increase for a 1,000-fold processor Performance Improvement
N	1000.
$N*\log_2 N$	140.2
N^2	31.6
N^3	10.
2^N	2.0
N!	1.2

3.3 RUN-TIME PERFORMANCE OF CONTROL STRUCTURES

Software developers often analyze code to determine performance. Big-oh performance can often be extracted directly from the control structures of an algorithm. Figure 3.8 shows selected control structures and their corresponding big-oh performance.

Figure 3.8 Control structures and their big-oh performance

Control Structure Pattern	Corresponding Big-oh Performance
Any statement with fixed length execution time	O(1)
statement1; statement2;	dominant of • big-oh for statement1 • big-oh for statement2

if (condition) {
    thenClause;
} else {
    elseClause;
}
	dominant of these three
	• big-oh for condition
	• big-oh for thenClause
	• big-oh for elseClause

for (int j=a; j!=N; j++) {
    loopBody;
}
// Assume that j is not altered within loopBody
// nor does loopBody contain a break.
// Also assume that a is some constant.
	O(N) * big-oh for loopBody

Software without loops or recursion has constant order—O(1). Therefore, determining the big-oh performance of a segment of code is primarily based on identifying loops and recursion that repeats variably. For example, the following loop visits every array item once, assigning each item the value `null`.

```
for (int k=0; k!=size; k++) {
    myArray[k] = null;
}
```

By itself, this assignment statement is O(1). Therefore, the performance of the entire loop is O(size) * O(1) or O(size). This big-oh performance is consistent with the fact that the count of loop repetitions depends upon the value of `size`.

Any loop (or recursion) in which the extent of repetition depends solely on `size`, and the cost of each repetition O(1) has order O(size). In this loop the initial value of k can be any other constant value without altering this performance order. Similarly, the type of loop (*for*, *while*, or *do*) is not important in determining performance order.

As a second example, consider the following nested loop structure for printing the content of a two-dimensional array with equal numbers of rows and columns (i.e., `myArray2.length == myArray2[k].length`).

```
for (int r=0; r!=last; r++) {
    for (int c=0; c!=last; c++) {
        System.out.println( myArray2[r][c] );
    }
}
```

In this case the big-oh performance of the outer loop is O(last) * big-oh of the inner loop. Furthermore, the big-oh order of the inner loop, using reasoning similar to the preceding example, is O(last). Therefore, the performance of the entire group of two nested loops is O(last^2).

These techniques for analyzing algorithm performance also can be applied to larger pieces of software. Consider the `printPythagoreanTriples` method in Figure 3.9. This method outputs Pythagorean triples (i.e., three integers a, b, and c, such that a^2 + b^2 == c^2). The method prints only those triples for which a, b, and c are all less than or equal to the parameter `smallSideMax`, and the triples are always printed in increasing order.

Figure 3.9 printPythagoreanTriples method

```
private void printPythagoreanTriples( int smallSideMax ) {
    int small, next, last;
    small = 1;
    while (small <= smallSideMax) {
        next = small;
        while (next <= smallSideMax) {
            last = next;
            while (last <= smallSideMax) {
```

Continued on next page

```
                    if (last <= small*2 && next <= small*2
                            && last*last == small*small + next*next) {
                        System.out.println( small + ", " + next +", " +
                            last );
                    }
                    last++;
                }
                next++;
            }
            small++;
        }
    }
```

A careful analysis of the print method might begin by dividing the algorithm into separate parts and labeling the parts for identification, as shown in Figure 3.10.

Figure 3.10 printPythagoreanTriples body with labels

You can analyze the big-oh performance of printPythagoreanTriples by working from the outermost loops inward or from the innermost loops outward. This presentation does the latter.

The *if* statement labeled H is analyzed as follows.

big-oh of **H**   = dominant of big-oh of the condition and big-oh of the
                       then clause
                     = dominant of $O(1)$ and $O(1)$
                     = $O(1)$

Next, the performance of G is analyzed.

big-oh of **G**   = $O(smallSideMax)$ * big-oh of the body of G
                     = $O(smallSideMax)$ * (dominant of big-oh of H and
                       big-oh of I)
                     = $O(smallSideMax)$ * (dominant of $O(1)$ and $O(1)$)
                     = $O(smallSideMax)$ * $O(1)$
                     = $O(smallSideMax)$

The order of F is determined as follows:

big-oh of **F**   = $O(smallSideMax)$ * big-oh of the body of F
                     = $O(smallSideMax)$ * (dominant of big-oh of C, big-oh
                       of G, and big-oh of J)
                     = $O(smallSideMax)$ * (dominant of $O(1)$,
                       $O(smallSideMax)$, and $O(1)$)
                     = $O(smallSideMax)$ * $O(smallSideMax)$
                     = $O(smallSideMax^2)$

The analysis of E proceeds in similar fashion.

big-oh of **E**   = $O(smallSideMax)$ * big-oh of the body of E
                     = $O(smallSideMax)$ * (dominant of big-oh of B, big-oh of
                       F, and big-oh of K)
                     = $O(smallSideMax)$ * (dominant of $O(1)$,
                       $O(smallSideMax^2)$, and $O(1)$)
                     = $O(smallSideMax)$ * $O(smallSideMax^2)$
                     = $O(smallSideMax^3)$

Finally, the big-oh performance for the complete method is calculated as follows.

big-oh of **D**   = dominant of big-oh of A and big-oh of E
                     = dominant of $O(1)$ and $O(smallSideMax^3)$
                     = $O(smallSideMax^3)$

This analysis does not refer to any of the loop conditions or to parameter passage because all of these are $O(1)$ for this particular code. However, you must not overlook these parts of the code in circumstances where they have greater order. The loop condition should normally be considered as part of the loop body. Parameter passage can be considered as a separate statement to be executed at the time of the method call.

Software Engineering Hint

It has been said that about 90% of execution time is spent within 10% of the code. The code that is executed most often occurs in the most deeply nested repetition. These are the places to examine in order to improve performance. A software tool, called a **profiler**, is designed to help locate these "hot spots" where most execution time takes place.

3.4 SEARCHING ALGORITHMS

Searching a container for a specific value is one of the most commonly used of all computer algorithms. A typical searching algorithm peruses the content of a container until it locates an item that matches the search value. A search algorithm usually returns enough information to locate the item within the container; an array search returns an index, and a Collection might position an iterator. Figure 3.11 shows two search algorithms: one for searching an array of int, and a second one for searching a java.util.AbstractCollection. In addition to the two kinds of containers, these searches also illustrate two kinds of return values. indexFromSearch returns an integer for the index of an array cell that contains the search value, and iteratorFromLinearSearch returns a java.util.Iterator object that is positioned immediately after the first call to next that returns a search valued item. (Both searches return special values for unsuccessful searches; indexFromSearch returns –1, and iteratorFromLinearSearch returns null.)

Figure 3.11 Linear searches of an array and a Collection

```
/*  pre:    a != null
    post:   exists(j : 0<=j<a.length and a[j] == v | result == j)
            and not exists (j : 0<=j<a.length and a[j] == v
                | result == a.length ) */
private int indexFromSearch(int[] a, int v) {
    int location=0;
    while (location!=a.length && v!=a[location]) {
        location++;
    }
    return location;
}
/*  pre:    collection != null
    post:   exists(c : a cell within list such that s.equals(c)
                | result is positioned immediately beyond
                a result.next() value equal to c
            and not exists(c : a cell within list such that
                s.equals(c) | result == null )
    note:   AbstractCollection and Iterator are found in java.util */
private Iterator iteratorFromSearch(AbstractCollection collection,
                                    Object z)
{
    Iterator it = collection.iterator();
    boolean found = false;
    while (it.hasNext() && !found) {
        found = (it.next().equals(z));
    }
```

Continued on next page

```
        if (found)
            return it;
        else
            return null;
    }
```

Both of the search algorithms shown in Figure 3.11 can be called **linear searches**. In part, the name "linear" results from the sequential (linear) fashion in which each algorithm inspects each container item. The first loop body execution inspects the first container item, and each subsequent loop repetition inspects the next container item. The search loops terminate on one of two conditions: the search value (v or z) has been located, or all the items in the container have been inspected without a match.

A second reason for calling these algorithms linear searches is that both have linear big-oh performance. You can analyze the performance of the indexFromSearch and iteratorFromSearch methods by counting the number of loop body iterations. However, it is more common to analyze a search algorithm by counting the number of **container probes**. A container probe (or "probe" for short) occurs every time one of the container's items is inspected. The probe in the indexFromSearch method occurs when v!=a[location] executes. A probe takes place within iteratorFromSearch whenever it.next() returns an item.

Using the probe count as a basis, the indexFromSearch method is of order O(a.length), and the iteratorFromSearch method is of order O(collection.size()). You can see this performance by observing that the maximum probe count occurs for an unsuccessful search. In such a worst case, the number of probes equals the number of container items, resulting in linear big-oh performance.

Linear searches similar to those of Figure 3.11 are widely used on many kinds of containers. Their linear performance is often the most efficient alternative.

In certain circumstances you can use a **binary search** whose performance is better than that of linear searches. A binary search algorithm requires that the container being searched have two characteristics.

- It must be a direct access container, like an array.
- It must be sorted in either ascending or descending order.

Figure 3.12 shows a binary search algorithm for an array that is sorted in ascending order.

Software Engineering Hint

The big-oh performance of code depends on *all* parts of the code. The locationFromBinary-Search method executes in O(logN). However, checking the precondition would require an O(N) algorithm. Therefore, if the code attempts to check its precondition, the performance gains of the binary search are lost.

This binary search uses of three index variables: lo, mid, and hi. For each loop iteration, the portion of the array that remains to be searched is a[lo] through a[hi]. Each loop body execution begins by calculating the index midway between lo and hi via the following statement:

```
mid = (lo + hi) / 2;
```

Figure 3.12 Binary search of an array

```
/*  pre:     forAll(k : 0<k<a.length | a[k-1] < a[k])
    post:    exists(j : 0<=j<a.length and a[j] == v | result == j)
             and not exists(j : 0<=j<a.length and a[j] == v
                              | result == a.length) */
private int locationFromBinarySearch(Comparable[] a, Comparable z){
    int lo, mid, hi;
    lo = 0;
    hi = a.length-1;
    while (lo < hi) {
        mid = (lo + hi) / 2;
        if ( z.compareTo(a[mid]) > 0 ) {
            lo = mid + 1;
        } else {
            hi = mid;
        }
    }
    if (z.compareTo(a[lo]) == 0) {
        return lo;
    } else {
        return a.length;
    }
}
```

If the search value (z) is greater than a[mid], then lo is updated to mid+1. Otherwise, if z is less than or equal to a[mid], then hi is updated to mid. The search loop terminates when lo == hi because this means that the only possible location for the search value is a[lo].

Figure 3.13 shows a sample trace of the execution of a binary search. In this trace the portion of the array that has yet to be searched (i.e., the region from a[lo] through a[hi]) is shaded. The particular search value is the string "G".

Counting the number of container probes is not so simple as for a counting loop, such as those of linear searches. The binary search in Figure 3.11 has two statements that cause probes in the form of z.compareTo(a[lo]). One way to study performance is to consider probe counts for arrays of various lengths. For example, if a.length == 1, then the count of loop body executions is 1. If a.length is 2, then the count of loop body executions is 2. This discussion is extended in the table at the end of this section.

This demonstrates that the count of loop iterations is $\log_2($a.length$) + 1$. Therefore, the performance of the binary search is O(logN), where N denotes the number of cells to be searched.

Very few container processing algorithms have performance as good as O(logN). Those algorithms that do exhibit such behavior accomplished half of the remaining "work" for each probe (loop iteration). For example, the binary search eliminates roughly half of the cells to be searched for each loop repetition.

Figure 3.13 Sample trace of the `locationFromBinarySearch` method

Search Value

   z == "G"

Initial Array, a

	[0]	[1]	[2]	[3]	[4]	[5]	[6]	[7]
	"A"	"C"	"D"	"G"	"J"	"M"	"P"	"S"

Prior to the first execution of *if* statement

lo == 0   hi == 7   mid == 3

	[0]	[1]	[2]	[3]	[4]	[5]	[6]	[7]
	"A"	"C"	"D"	"G"	"J"	"M"	"P"	"S"

Prior to the second execution of *if* statement

lo == 0   hi == 3   mid == 1

	[0]	[1]	[2]	[3]	[4]	[5]	[6]	[7]
	"A"	"C"	"D"	"G"	"J"	"M"	"P"	"S"

Prior to the third execution of *if* statement

lo == 2   hi == 3   mid == 2

	[0]	[1]	[2]	[3]	[4]	[5]	[6]	[7]
	"A"	"C"	"D"	"G"	"J"	"M"	"P"	"S"

Prior to the third execution of the loop body

lo == 3   hi == 3

	[0]	[1]	[2]	[3]	[4]	[5]	[6]	[7]
	"A"	"C"	"D"	"G"	"J"	"M"	"P"	"S"

a.length	Count of Loop Body Iterations
1	1
2	2
4	3
8	4
16	5
32	6

3.5 N² SORTING

One of the most common algorithms for container processing is to rearrange the container's content to achieve a specific ordering of items. A **sorting** algorithm is any algorithm that rearranges container content so that it is ordered by value. An **ascending sort** leaves the content in increasing order (i.e., each item is less than or equal to every item that follows it). A **descending sort** leaves the content in decreasing order. The terms **strictly ascending** and **strictly descending** refer to ordering that does not permit any duplicate items in the container content.

There are hundreds of sorting algorithms. This section examines two well-known general-purpose sorts. They are called *general-purpose* because they do not rely on any unusual container properties. To illustrate, each algorithm is applied to an array container of double values and performs an ascending sort.

Suppose you present someone with a stack of examination papers, each marked on top with a score. If that person is asked to sort the examinations from worst to best (i.e., an ascending sort), the person might perform the following steps.

1. Find the lowest score in the examinations and place it face down in a new pile.
2. Find the lowest score in the remaining examinations and place it face down on the pile.
3. Repeat step 2 until all examinations have been placed on the pile.

The procedure just outlined is known as a **selection sort** because the algorithm proceeds by repeatedly selecting the smallest (or largest for a descending sort) value among those that remain. Figure 3.14 contains a selection sort method.

The procedure for sorting examination papers uses two separate groups of values: the remaining group of examination papers and the pile where examinations are placed face down. By contrast, the doSelectionSort method keeps all content within a single array. This is referred to as an **in-place sort** because, except for a few variables, no data structures beyond the container (array) are required by the sort.

Even though selection sort is an in-place sort, the algorithm treats the array as though it were two separate containers, corresponding to the *remaining examinations* and the *pile of examinations*. The front portion of the doSelectionSort array is analogous to the *pile of examinations* because it stores those values that are smaller than the "remaining" values in the rear of the array. Furthermore, this front part of the array will be ordered in ascending order. Figure 3.15 illustrates by tracing array content for a particular array each time the outer loop's exit condition is evaluated.

Figure 3.14 doSelectionSort method

```
/*  pre:     a != null
    post:    forAll(j : 0<=j<a.length-1 | a[j] <= a[j+1])
             and a has the same content as a@pre possibly permuted */
private void doSelectionSort( double[] a ) {
    int smallestNdx;
    double temp;
    for (int lastSorted=-1; lastSorted < a.length-2; lastSorted++)
    {
        smallestNdx = lastSorted+1;
        for (int ndx = lastSorted+2; ndx != a.length; ndx++) {
            if (a[ndx] < a[smallestNdx]) {
                smallestNdx = ndx;
            }
        }
        temp = a[lastSorted+1];
        a[lastSorted+1] = a[smallestNdx];
        a[smallestNdx] = temp;
    }
}
```

Figure 3.15 distinguishes the front (sorted) region of the array from the rear (unsorted) region by highlighting the sorted region in gray. As the trace shows, the algorithm uses a variable called lastSorted to store the index of the last cell of the sorted region. Each time the outer loop is executed, one more value is moved from the unsorted region to the sorted region.

The code inside the outer loop consists of two consecutive subalgorithms.

- A linear search to find the smallest value within the unsorted region (smallestNdx stores its index)
- A swap to interchange this smallest value with the cell indexed by lastSorted+1

Analyzing sort algorithms involves slightly more complicated counting than for searching algorithms. Sort algorithms also probe array cells, so counting the number of container probes is one useful measure of performance. However, probe count by itself isn't always an accurate way to determine sort performance. Because sort algorithms must rearrange container content, it also is instructive to count **data movement**. One data movement occurs every time one container item is moved (assigned) to a different location within the container.

It's easy to count the number of data movements for selection sort because it depends only on the number of swaps, with one swap per outer loop execution. Therefore, the data movement count is O(a.length).

Figure 3.15 Sample trace of the doSelectionSort method

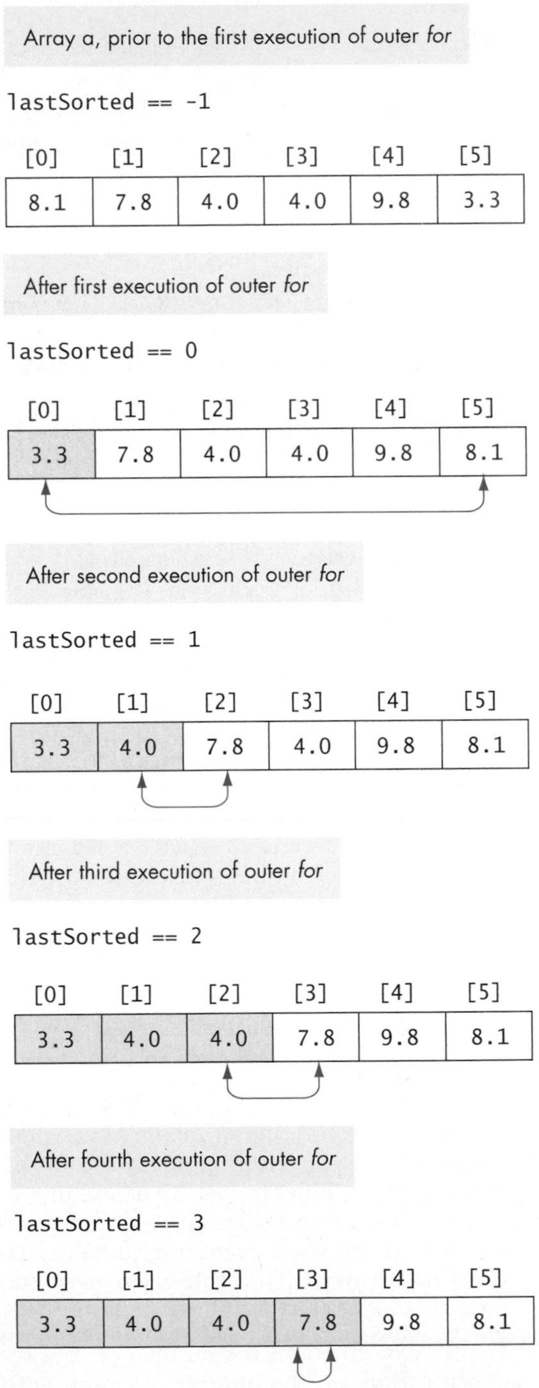

Array a, prior to the first execution of outer *for*

lastSorted == -1

[0]	[1]	[2]	[3]	[4]	[5]
8.1	7.8	4.0	4.0	9.8	3.3

After first execution of outer *for*

lastSorted == 0

[0]	[1]	[2]	[3]	[4]	[5]
3.3	7.8	4.0	4.0	9.8	8.1

After second execution of outer *for*

lastSorted == 1

[0]	[1]	[2]	[3]	[4]	[5]
3.3	4.0	7.8	4.0	9.8	8.1

After third execution of outer *for*

lastSorted == 2

[0]	[1]	[2]	[3]	[4]	[5]
3.3	4.0	4.0	7.8	9.8	8.1

After fourth execution of outer *for*

lastSorted == 3

[0]	[1]	[2]	[3]	[4]	[5]
3.3	4.0	4.0	7.8	9.8	8.1

Continued on next page

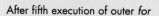

After fifth execution of outer *for*

lastSorted == 4

[0]	[1]	[2]	[3]	[4]	[5]
3.3	4.0	4.0	7.8	8.1	9.8

Counting probes for a selection sort is more difficult than counting data movements. The outer loop is executed a.length -1 times, and each time it searches for the smallest value in the unsorted region. Each successive search performs fewer probes because the unsorted region grows smaller. Because the unsorted region shrinks in a linear fashion, the overall average number of probes per search is roughly half of the array size. You calculate the total count of probes by multiplying the number of searches times the number of probes per search: (a.length − 1) * (a.length / 2). This results in a probe count of O(a.length2).

The final performance calculation for a sorting algorithm relies on the observation that the work of a sort is estimated to be the probe count plus the data movement count. For the selection sort method, its performance is O(a.length) + O(a.length²), which simplifies, using the rules of big-oh, to O(a.length2). Substituting the variable N for the array length in the big-oh performance explains why selection sort belongs to a group of sorts known as the **N² sorts**.

A second member of the N² family of sorts is the **linear insertion sort**. Figure 3.16 shows a method that performs a linear insertion sort on an array of double.

Figure 3.16 doInsertionSort method

```
/* pre:    a != null
   post:   forAll(j : 0<=j<a.length-1 | a[j] <= a[j+1]) */
private void doInsertionSort( double[] a ) {
   int ndx;
   double toBeInserted;
   for (int lastSorted=0; lastSorted < a.length-1; lastSorted++) {
      toBeInserted = a[lastSorted+1];
      ndx = lastSorted;
      while (ndx>=0 && toBeInserted<a[ndx]) {
         a[ndx+1] = a[ndx];
         ndx-;
      }
      a[ndx+1] = toBeInserted;
   }
}
```

As with a selection sort, the linear insertion sort algorithm is an in-place sort that partitions the array into a sorted and an unsorted region. However, whereas selection sort moves data from smallest to largest value, insertion sort moves data in the order it is stored within the array. In the doInsertionSort method, the next item to be moved is assigned to a variable called toBeInserted. The inner loop of doInsertionSort shifts the larger values within the sorted portion of the array to their neighboring cells (the value from a[j] is shifted to a[j+1]) until the proper location for the toBeInserted is identified. The name of the sort comes from the fact that the shift inserts the toBeInserted value in its proper place. Another way to summarize the insertion sort algorithm is that it repeatedly inserts the next unsorted value into its proper place within the sorted region. Figure 3.17 traces the behavior of doInsertionSort for a particular array. The gray arrows indicate cell content shifts, and the blue arrows identify the location of the newly inserted value.

Figure 3.17 Sample trace of the doInsertionSort method

Array a, prior to the first execution of outer *while*

lastSorted == 0

[0]	[1]	[2]	[3]	[4]	[5]
8.1	7.8	4.0	4.0	9.8	3.3

After first execution of outer *while*

lastSorted == 1

[0]	[1]	[2]	[3]	[4]	[5]
7.8	8.1	4.0	4.0	9.8	3.3

After second execution of outer *while*

lastSorted == 2

[0]	[1]	[2]	[3]	[4]	[5]
4.0	7.8	8.1	4.0	9.8	3.3

Continued on next page

After third execution of outer *while*

`lastSorted == 3`

[0]	[1]	[2]	[3]	[4]	[5]
4.0	4.0	7.8	8.1	9.8	3.3

After fourth execution of outer *while*

`lastSorted == 4`

[0]	[1]	[2]	[3]	[4]	[5]
4.0	4.0	7.8	8.1	9.8	3.3

After fifth execution of outer *while*

`lastSorted == 5`

[0]	[1]	[2]	[3]	[4]	[5]
3.3	4.0	4.0	7.8	8.1	9.8

The `doInsertionSort` method generally performs fewer probes than `doSelectionSort` because not every outer loop iteration must probe every item in the sorted region. However, in the worst possible data arrangements, the count of probes is no different for the two algorithms. Therefore, the `doInsertionSort` probe count is O(a.length²).

The count of data movements for `doInsertionSort` is also O(a.length²). This data movement performance results from the fact that there are a.length–1 items to insert, and each item has the potential to require the movement of every item in the sorted region. Therefore, the total count of data movements is roughly (a.length – 1) * (a.length / 2), which is O(a.length²).

Like selection sort, linear insertion sort has an overall performance of O(a.length²). Examining the individual counts reveals that selection sort can be expected to perform fewer data movements than linear insertion sort, whereas linear insertion sort performs fewer probes.

3.6   MERGESORT

Like selection sort and linear insertion sort, N^2 sorts are suitable for sorting relatively small amounts of data, but for large containers more efficient sorting algorithms are recommended. One such algorithm is **mergesort**.

Mergesort is based on a process that repeatedly merges two containers that are already sorted. Figure 3.18 pictures the way in which a mergesort proceeds for a particular collection of eight values.

Figure 3.18 A mergesort for eight values

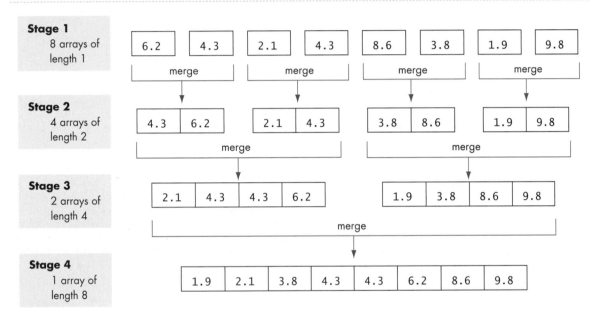

The algorithm begins by breaking down the container of the eight values into eight separate containers (arrays), each one cell long. At Stage 2, each of the single-cell containers has been paired with a neighbor, and the pair has been merged into a sorted container of two items. The resulting four dual-cell arrays are shown. Stage 3 consists of two merge operations: one to merge the two two-cell arrays on the left, and another one to merge the two two-cell arrays on the right. Stage 4 is a single merge of two four-cell sorted containers.

The performance of mergesort can be deduced from further consideration of Figure 3.18, along with the assumption that a single merge can be performed in O(*numberOfItemsToMerge*). The performance of a mergesort results from multiplying the number of merges times the performance of each individual merge. Figure 3.18 shows a situation in which the count of merge operations is 1 less than the number of items being merged. The number of merges isn't always exactly the item count less 1, but it is always roughly the same as the item count.

Even though the performance of each merge operation is O(*numberOfItemsToMerge*), further investigation is required to calculate the "average" performance over all of the merge operations. Notice in Figure 3.18 that more than half (four) of the merge operations involve only two items, and only one operation involves eight items. If the merge cost is measured in terms of items per merge, then the cost of merging two items is 2, and the cost of the large merger is 8. Using this measure, the total cost of all seven mergers of the four stages in this figure is 2+2+2+2+4+4+8 = 24 units. If the number of data items to be sorted is doubled to 16, there will be 15 merge operations and the total merge cost will be 24+24+16 = 64 units. The following table shows these values plus the average cost/merge.

Items	Merge Operations	Cost	Cost/Merge
4	3	8	2.67
8	7	24	3.43
16	15	64	4.27
32	31	160	5.17

This table depicts a logarithmic growth for the cost/merge; as the number of items doubles, the cost/merge increases only by roughly 1. This leads to the conclusion that mergesort performance is the number of merges times the average cost per merge or O(N) * O(logN) == O(NlogN), assuming that N refers to the number of items to be sorted.

Mergesort is often expressed in recursive form, such as the doMergesort of Figure 3.19. This algorithm accepts an array, along with a lower (lo) index and an upper (hi) index that bracket the region of the array to be sorted. The doMergesort method breaks large arrays into smaller ones, and then merges the smaller ones. This is accomplished by calculating a midpoint index (mid) and calling doMergesort twice recursively; one call is for the array region a[lo] through a[mid], and the other call is for the region a[mid+1] through a[hi]. A separate method called merge is called to perform the merge operation.

Figure 3.19 doMergesort method

```
/*     pre:    a != null
       post:   forAll(j : lo<=j<hi | a[j] <= a[j+1]) */
private void doMergesort ( double[] a, int lo, int hi ) {
    if (lo < hi) {
        int mid = (lo + hi) / 2;
        doMergesort(a, lo, mid);
        doMergesort(a, mid+1, hi);
        merge(a, lo, hi);
    }
}
```

The doMergesort method has O(NlogN) performance if the merge algorithm is O(N). Figure 3.20 shows such a merge. As is indicated by its precondition, the merge method requires that it be passed an array that has two regions: a[lo] through a[(lo+hi)/2], and a[(lo+hi)/2+1] through a[hi]. Furthermore, these regions must already be arranged in ascending order. The method's algorithm is designed to merge the values from these two regions into a single sorted group from a[lo] though a[hi].

Figure 3.20 merge method

```
/* pre:    a != null
           and forAll(j : lo<=j<(lo+hi)/2 | a[j] <= a[j+1])
           and forAll(k : (lo+hi)/2<k<hi | a[k] <= a[k+1])
   post:   forAll(m : lo<=<hi | a[j] <= a[j+1]) */
private void merge( double[] a, int lo, int hi ) {
    int mid = (lo + hi) /2;
    int leftNdx = lo;
    int rightNdx = mid+1;
    double[] tmp = new double[hi-lo+1];
    int tmpNdx = 0;
    while (leftNdx <= mid && rightNdx <= hi) {
        if (a[leftNdx] < a[rightNdx]) {
            tmp[tmpNdx] = a[leftNdx];
            leftNdx++;
        } else {
            tmp[tmpNdx] = a[rightNdx];
            rightNdx++;
        }
        tmpNdx++;
    }
    // Copy remaining values from left array into tmp
    for (int j= leftNdx; j<=mid; j++) {
        tmp[tmpNdx] = a[j];
        tmpNdx++;
    }
    // Copy remaining values from right array into tmp
    for (int j= rightNdx; j<=hi; j++) {
        tmp[tmpNdx] = a[j];
        tmpNdx++;
    }
    // Copy tmp back into a
    for (int j=lo; j<=hi; j++) {
        a[j] = tmp[j-lo];
    }
}
```

The merge method is not an in-place sort because it requires a separate array, tmp. The tmp array is used to store the merged collection of values. The keys to the merge algorithm are the leftNdx and rightNdx variables. Each of these variables maintains a position (index) within one of the two sorted regions. The left region (a[lo] through a[mid]) uses `leftNdx`, and the right region (a[mid+1] through a[hi]) uses `rightNdx`. The index variables (`leftNdx` and `rightNdx`) are initially positioned at the first cell of their respective regions because these cells must contain the smallest value of the region.

Within the *while* loop the a[leftNdx] cell is compared to a[rightNdx]. The smaller of these two cells is copied into the next available position of the `tmp` array. Each time through the *while* loop, the index (`leftNdx` or `rightNdx`) of the cell copied to `tmp` is incremented by 1 to the next array region position. Therefore, every *while* loop iteration copies one more cell to `tmp`. The linear performance of the `merge` method is based on this movement of one data cell per loop iteration.

The *while* loop terminates when one of the two regions has been completely merged into `tmp`. The first two *for* loops are included to ensure that all remaining region items are copied into the end of `tmp`. The final *for* loop copies the entire `tmp` array back into the a[lo] through a[hi] region, replacing the two separate regions with a single sorted merge of their content.

3.7 QUICKSORT

Another efficient sorting algorithm, called **quicksort**, is the invention of C.A.R. Hoare. The quicksort algorithm depends on a process of partitioning a container into two smaller subcontainers so that every value in first subcontainer is smaller than any value in the second subcontainer. This partitioning is applied recursively by treating each subcontainer as a separate container. The repeated recursion partitions the subcontainers into smaller and smaller groups. If the containers/subcontainers are represented as array regions, the repeated partitioning will ultimately sort the entire array. This algorithm is summarized informally as follows.

```
if (region to be sorted is 2 cells) {
    Sort the two cells.
} else if (region to be sorted is greater than 2 cells) {
    Select a pivot value from the region.
    Partition the values into a front region with values ≤ pivot and rear
    region with values > pivot.
    Move the pivot to a position between the front and rear regions.
    Apply this algorithm recursively to the front region.
    Apply this algorithm recursively to the rear region.
} else {
    In this case the region is either zero or one cell, so no action is taken.
}
```

Figure 3.21 pictures how such partitioning is used to sort a particular array. Each highlighted group of cells in the figure indicates an array region that requires further rearrangement. The top three regions are rearranged via the partitioning algorithm. The solid arrows point to the results of a partitioning. The dashed arrows associate each partitioned item with its associated array location.

Partitioning a region begins with the selection of a **pivot**. The pivot is one of the values within the region. The other (nonpivot) values of the region are then rearranged into two subregions: a subregion for values less than or equal to the pivot, and a subregion for values greater than the pivot. For example, the initial

Figure 3.21 A quicksort for eight values

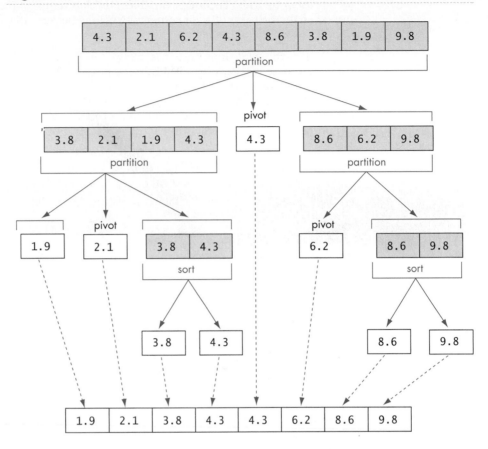

array in Figure 3.21 is partitioned into a <3.8, 2.1, 1.9, 4.3> subregion and a <8.6, 6.2, 9.8> sub-region separated by the 4.3 pivot. Similarly, the four-cell region is partitioned into a <1.9> subregion and a <3.8, 4.3> subregion using a pivot of 2.1. When all the values being partitioned are less than, or all are greater than, the pivot, the result is that one of the two resulting regions is empty. This occurs in the figure when the three-cell region is partitioned and all values are greater than the pivot of 6.2.

Figure 3.22 shows a complete doQuicksort method. This figure also includes an associated swap method. Like the doMergesort method, this method uses three parameters. The first parameter passes the array to be sorted, and the other two parameters indicate the region to be sorted by giving the smallest (lo) and greatest (hi) indices of the region.

Figure 3.22 doQuicksort and swap methods

```
/* pre:    a != null
           and 0 <= lo <= hi <= a.length-1
   post:   forAll(j : lo<=j<hi | a[j] <= a[j+1])
           and the content of a is permuted from a@pre */
```

Continued on next page

```
private void doQuicksort( double[] a, int lo, int hi ) {
    double pivot, temp;
    int leftNdx, rightNdx, pivotNdx;
    if (hi-lo == 1) {
        if (a[hi] < a[lo]) {
            swap(a, lo, hi);
        }
    } else if (hi-lo > 1) {
        // Partition the a[lo] ... a[hi] region
        pivotNdx = (lo+hi) / 2;
        //This line is improved in Figure 3.22
        pivot = a[pivotNdx];
        swap(a, lo, pivotNdx);
        leftNdx = lo + 1;
        rightNdx = hi;
        do {
            while (leftNdx <= rightNdx && a[leftNdx] <= pivot)
                leftNdx++;
            while (a[rightNdx] > pivot)
                rightNdx-;
            if (leftNdx < rightNdx)
                swap(a, leftNdx, rightNdx);
        } while (leftNdx < rightNdx);
        swap(a, lo, leftNdx-1);
        doQuicksort(a, lo, leftNdx-2);
        doQuicksort(a, leftNdx, hi);
    }
}
/*  pre:    a != null
            and 0 <= j, k <= a.length-1
    post:   a[j] == a@pre[k] and a[k] == a@pre[j] */
private void swap(double[] a, int j, int k) {
    double temp = a[j];
    a[j] = a[k];
    a[k] = temp;
}
```

The *then* clause of doQuickSort is executed when the array region is two cells long; in this case the array is sorted with a single *if* statement. The *else if* clause handles all array regions that are three cells or more in length. The partitioning algorithm begins by selecting a pivot; in this case the pivot is the one with an index of (lo+hi)/2. Here is a sample array region in which lo==5 and hi==13.

lo == 5				pivotNbx == 9				hi == 13
[5]	[6]	[7]	[8]	[9]	[10]	[11]	[12]	[13]
7.2	2.3	8.8	3.8	6.2	0.3	9.2	1.4	4.1

After the pivot is selected, it is swapped to the front of the region (a[lo]) so that a[lo+1] ... a[hi] can be partitioned, as pictured next.

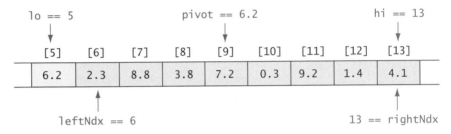

Next, the a[lo+1] ... a[hi] region is partitioned. This partitioning happens inside the *do loop* and uses the index variables leftNdx and rightNdx. Immediately before the *do loop*, these two variables are initialized to bracket the region to be partitioned, as shown next.

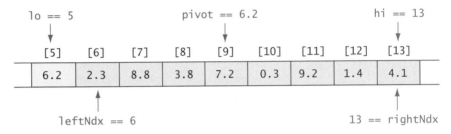

Next, the partitioning algorithm rearranges the region's cell values so that values less than or equal to the pivot are placed on the left and all values greater than the pivot are placed on the right. This is done by repeatedly locating pairs of cells that are out of order and swapping their content. The leftNdx and rightNdx variables are used to search for the cells to be swapped.

The first nested *while* loop (nested inside the *do loop*) repeatedly increments leftNdx either until it indexes a cell greater than pivot or until leftNdx is greater than rightNdx. Note that a cell with a value greater than pivot is on the "wrong side" of the partition region. The second nested *while* loop repeatedly decrements rightNdx until it indexes a cell with a value less than or equal to pivot. For the preceding example, leftNdx is advanced to cell 7 (because 8.8 > 6.2) and rightNdx remains at cell 13 (because 4.1 ≤ 6.2).

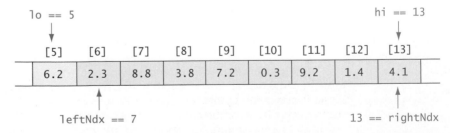

After leftNdx and rightNdx have been positioned at two cells that are out of order, the values of the two cells are swapped, as shown next.

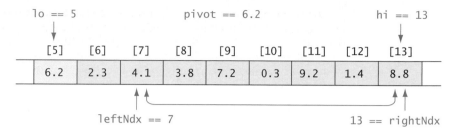

Continuing this example, `leftNdx` and `rightNdx` are advanced to the next two cells that are out of order, and they, too, are swapped. The result is shown next.

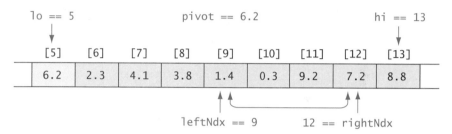

Eventually, this process of incrementing `leftNdx` followed by decrementing `rightNdx` results in a situation in which `leftNdx >= rightNdx`. When this happens the region has been properly partitioned.

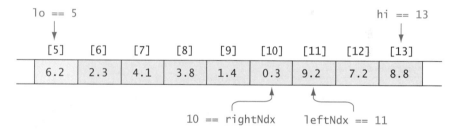

The final action of the partitioning algorithm is the swap call immediately after the *do* loop. This interchanges the pivot (stored in `a[lo]`) with cell `a[leftNdx-1]`. This locates the pivot exactly between the two halves of the partition where it need not be considered further.

The final two statements of `doQuicksort` call the method recursively—once to partition `a[lo]` through `a[leftNdx-2]` and again to partition `a[leftNdx]` through `a[hi]`.

Under ideal circumstances an analysis of the run-time performance of quicksort is similar to that of mergesort. The ideal situation for a quicksort is when every partitioning results in two regions of equal size. In this ideal case the average size of a partition region is O(logN), where N represents the array size. Furthermore, the number of partition algorithms to be performed is O(N), so the best possible performance of quicksort is O(NlogN).

The preceding analysis considers only ideal circumstances. If the partitioning algorithm frequently results in regions of considerable difference in length, then quicksort's performance is not so good. The worst-case performance for quicksort occurs when every partitioning results in one region that is empty (i.e., there are no values less than the pivot or no values greater than the pivot). This worst case results in O(N²) performance.

Software Engineering Hint

"Sweating the details" often pays off in performance gains. For example, somewhat more complicated pivot selection algorithms, such as `medianIndex`, can substantively improve quicksort performance.

The worst-case potential of quicksort makes it imperative that the pivot be selected carefully. The ideal pivot is the median value of the region, but finding the median takes too long. One effective way to approximate the median is to select three values (the first, the last, and the center cell values) from the region and use their median as the pivot. Figure 3.23 shows a method to return the index of the median of a[lo], a[hi], and a[(lo+hi)/2].

Figure 3.23 `medianIndex` methods

```
/*  pre:    a.length >= 1 and 0 <= lo, hi <= a.length-1
    post:   (result == l or result == h or result == (h+l)/2)
            and a[result] is between the other two values
                (i.e., the values of a[l], a[h[ and a[(h+l)/2] */
private int medianIndex( double[] a, int lo, int hi ) {
    int m = (lo + hi) / 2;
    if (a[lo] <= a[hi]) {
        if ( a[m] <= a[lo]) {
            return lo;
        } else if (a[hi] <= a[m]) {
            return hi;
        } else {
            return m;
        }
    } else {
        if ( a[m] <= a[hi]) {
            return hi;
        } else if (a[lo] <= a[m]) {
            return lo;
        } else {
            return m;
        }
    }
}
```

To use `medianIndex`, the following `doQuicksort` statement

```
pivotNdx = (lo+hi) / 2;
```

must be replaced as follows.

```
pivotNdx = medianNdx(a, lo, hi);
```

A quicksort algorithm that uses this technique for selecting a pivot typically performs like an O(NlogN) sort. In fact, quicksort is often among the fastest of the general-purpose NlogN sorting algorithms.

3.8   THE LIMITATIONS OF BIG-OH

Big-oh analysis is widely regarded as an effective way to formulate an initial approximation of performance. However, it is important to recognize the limitations of this approach.

- For complicated algorithms, big-oh analysis is sometimes difficult to perform.
- Big-oh performance sometimes depends on data characteristics other than data quantity. In such cases it can be difficult to predict the expected performance.
- Big-oh is a coarse measure that does not always capture small differences in algorithms.
- Big-oh performance does not apply when you're processing small amounts of data.

Determining the big-oh performance of an algorithm is a nontrivial task. It is often difficult to determine *what* to count, and finding an expression that accurately describes the count isn't easy. Even when the big-oh measure is consistent with the algorithm, the actual performance may be altered dramatically by other factors, such as compiler optimizations and computer hardware mechanisms that permit overlapping multiple simultaneous threads of execution.

A second difficulty with big-oh is determining "expected" behavior. Sometimes an algorithm is only a small portion of a large and complicated program. As a program continues to be used, and modified, over many years, its behavior and performance are likely to change.

One area in which expected behavior is particularly unpredictable is general-purpose library software. One approach is to write library code that can select alternative algorithms based on the application. For example, a general-purpose sorting algorithm might include a parameter that allows the caller to select which sorting algorithm is to be used. A slightly different approach is to permit the algorithm to self-select an algorithm. For example, a general-purpose sorting algorithm might use selection sort for arrays of length 10 or fewer, and quicksort for larger arrays. An even more sophisticated algorithm might analyze the data and use the results to "guess" which sorting algorithm to use for subsequent calls.

Determining an expected case is important because many algorithms have distinctly different performance in the ideal and worst possible cases. Quicksort, for example, is O(NlogN) for ideal partitioning results, but O(N^2) in its worst case.

Whether quicksort generally performs more like its best case or more like its worst case is a question of expected case.

Another sorting algorithm whose performance is highly dependent on data characteristics is **bubble sort**. The bubble sort algorithm consists of repeated passes through the data array. Each pass proceeds from lowest index toward higher indices. During one pass, each neighboring pair of cells is compared, and if their values are found to be out of order, they are swapped. Figure 3.24 contains a bubble sort method.

Figure 3.24 doBubbleSort method

```
/*  pre:     != null
    post:    forAll(j : 0<=j<a.length-1 | a[j] <= a[j+1]) */
private void doBubbleSort( double[] a ) {
    int lastUnsorted = a.length-1;
    int lastSwapNdx;
    while (lastUnsorted != 0) {
        lastSwapNdx = 0;
        for (int k=0; k!=lastUnsorted; k++) {
            if (a[k] > a[k+1]) {
                swap(a, k, k+1); //See Figure 3.21 for swap method
                lastSwapNdx = k;
            }
        }
        lastUnsorted = lastSwapNdx;
    }
}
```

The outer loop of the doBubbleSort method repeats the passes until the array is sorted. The variable lastUnsorted maintains the maximum index of the array region that remains to be sorted. lastUnsorted is initialized to a.length-1 to signify that the entire array must be considered unsorted.

Each execution of the inner (*for*) loop makes a single pass through the array. Each pass needs only to process the portion of the array from an index of 0 to an index of lastUnsorted. The body of the *for* loop compares a[k] to a[k+1] and swaps these two cells if they aren't in ascending order. The name "bubble" comes from the behavior of a single pass, which effectively moves (or bubbles) the largest-valued item in the unsorted region to the rightmost cell of the unsorted region. Figure 3.25 demonstrates this behavior by tracing doBubbleSort for a particular array.

The trace of doBubbleSort shows the resulting array after each pass. Notice that the first three passes bubble one more value into the rightmost position of the unsorted part of the array—first 9.8, then 8.1, and then 7.8. This bubble effect happens because as each consecutive pair of cells is examined, the larger value is always assigned to the cell on the right. Therefore, one pass shifts the value of every cell to its right until it encounters a cell with greater value or the pass is complete.

Figure 3.25 Sample trace of the doBubbleSort method

Array a, prior to the first execution of *while*

lastUnsorted == 5

[0]	[1]	[2]	[3]	[4]	[5]
8.1	7.8	4.0	3.3	9.8	4.0

After first execution of outer *while* (after the first pass)

lastUnsorted == 4

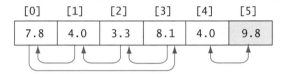

[0]	[1]	[2]	[3]	[4]	[5]
7.8	4.0	3.3	8.1	4.0	9.8

After second execution of outer *while* (after the second

lastUnsorted == 3

[0]	[1]	[2]	[3]	[4]	[5]
4.0	3.3	7.8	4.0	8.1	9.8

After third execution of outer *while* (after the third pass)

lastUnsorted == 2

[0]	[1]	[2]	[3]	[4]	[5]
3.3	4.0	4.0	7.8	8.1	9.8

After fourth execution of outer *while* (after the fourth pa

lastUnsorted == 0

[0]	[1]	[2]	[3]	[4]	[5]
3.3	4.0	4.0	7.8	8.1	9.8

The effect of this bubble rearrangement is to add one more cell to the sorted region of the array (the right end of the array) for each pass. Some bubble sort algorithms use this fact and decrease lastUnsorted by 1 for each pass. The doBubbleSort method uses the slightly more efficient technique of maintaining the index of the rightmost position where a swap was necessary during the pass; the index is stored in a variable called lastSwapNdx. When the pass is completed, lastUnsorted can be assigned the value of lastSwapNdx because no cell with greater index was found to be out of order. This is the reason that the fourth pass of Figure 3.25 is the last.

The bubble sort has notoriously bad performance in its worst case. The worst case for doBubbleSort occurs when the array is initially arranged in descending order. In this case, the algorithm must make O(a.length) passes and O(a.length) swaps per pass for an overall performance of O(a.length^2). Bubble sort tends to be a poor choice even within its family of O(N^2) sorts because it performs O(N^2) comparison/probes as well as O(N^2) data movements.

Despite its poor reputation for general-purpose sorting, bubble sort can be very efficient for sorting an array that is nearly sorted. This is significant because many applications involve nearly sorted data. Consider, for example, applying bubble sort to an array that is completely sorted. The bubble sort algorithm will execute only one pass in this case. Because the performance of a single pass is O(N), where N is the array length, bubble sort outperforms either quicksort or mergesort for processing a sorted array.

> ### Software Engineering Hint
>
> Big-oh performance sometimes varies based on characteristics of the data. In such cases it is often safest to take the Murphy's law approach and assume the worst possible case.

Similarly, bubble sort has performance O(N) for adding one new value to an already sorted array. This requires that the new item be placed in the cell with index 0 so that it is "bubbled" into its proper position in a single pass. The fact that large values bubble up efficiently but small values fail to bubble down with the same efficiency leads to a variation of the bubble sort algorithm in which the odd-numbered passes bubble up (proceed left to right) and the even-numbered passes bubble down (proceed right to left). Such a variation of bubble sort can be quite efficient for many kinds of nearly sorted arrays.

The bubble sort algorithm points out that big-oh performance can't be trusted unless it is understood in the context of certain data characteristics. However, an even more significant shortcoming of big-oh is the coarseness of its measure.

Consider two algorithms. Algorithm A has an execution time of precisely 0.001*N seconds, and algorithm B has an execution time of 1,000*N seconds. Both algorithms have an identical big-oh performance of O(N), but algorithm A is one million times faster than algorithm B!

> ### Software Engineering Hint
>
> A benchmark shows how an algorithm actually performs in one circumstance. Because this is *actual*, not approximated, performance, it is tempting to overestimate the importance of a benchmark. However, the great disadvantage of a benchmark is that it reflects only a single situation. A different benchmark might reveal substantially different results.

Related to the problem of big-oh coarseness is the problem of applying this measure to small amounts of data. Many algorithms do not exhibit their performance advantage except for large amounts of data. To illustrate this fact, a simple experiment was conducted using the sorting methods presented in this chapter. The performance of each algorithm was compared for the same randomly initialized arrays of different lengths. Figure 3.26 contains a table of the resulting execution time in milliseconds.

Figure 3.26 Benchmarks of sorting algorithms for random data

	N = 64	*N = 512*	*N = 8192*	*N = 32768*
doSelectionSort	0 msec.	12 msec.	3,097 msec.	46,794 msec.
doInsertionSort	2 msec.	12 msec.	1,720 msec.	25,804 msec.
doBubbleSort	5 msec.	45 msec.	6,217 msec.	89,735msec.
doMergesort	3 msec.	10 msec.	107 msec.	233 msec.
doQuicksort	2 msec.	6 msec.	40 msec.	157 msec.

Each entry in this table represents a **benchmark**: one particular execution of an algorithm. For these benchmarks, arrays of length 64 and 512 exhibit only a small difference between the performance of O(NlogN) sorts and O(N^2) sorts. Indeed, for arrays of length 64, the O(N^2) sorts often outperform the supposedly faster algorithms. Of course, the advantages of O(NlogN) sorting become apparent in the benchmark data for arrays of length 8,192 and greater.

You can use these benchmarks to approximate formulas for actual sorting time by observing the following relationship for some constant c:

actualExecutionTime(N) == c * big-Oh(N)

Substituting observed values for *actualExecutionTime* allows the value of constant c to be approximated. (Larger data sets are likely to produce a more accurate estimate.) For example, consider the run-time of doSelectionSort. The following analysis results from using observed run-time for a data size of 32,768.

actualExecutionTime(N) == c * big-Oh(N)
actualExecutionTime(N) == c * N^2
$46794 == c * 32768^2$
c ≈ .000044

This leads to the following equation for describing the run-time performance of doSelectionSort:

actualExecutionTime(N) ≈ .000044 * N^2

With this formula you can predict the execution time when this sorting algorithm is applied to arrays of other sizes. Such a predicted time for sorting 1,000 items is $0.000044 * 1000^2 == 44$ msec. Constants for the remaining four sorting algorithms can be similarly approximated.

3.9   PERFORMANCE TRADE-OFFS: RADIX SORT

Most of this chapter is devoted to analysis of time efficiency. However, there are two other kinds of efficiency that must not be forgotten: space and intellectual. Space efficiency, mentioned at the outset of this chapter, is an analysis of the amount of computer storage that is required by an algorithm. **Intellectual efficiency** refers to how complicated the algorithm is to design and to understand.

Algorithms typically exhibit trade-offs among the three types of efficiency. To design an algorithm with better run-time performance, you must often sacrifice space or intellectual efficiency or both. For example, mergesort can be expected to execute faster than insertion sort for large arrays, but mergesort requires more computer storage than an in-place sort such as insertion sort. Similarly, quicksort has better run-time performance than selection sort, but quicksort is generally considered to be more complicated to understand.

A gain in one type of efficiency does not always come at the expense of another. Selection sort is generally considered to be more efficient than bubble sort, but the space and intellectual efficiency of the two algorithms is comparable. In fact it can be argued that selection sort is intellectually simpler because it tends to be more intuitive and takes less time to code.

The **radix sort** is an example of a sorting algorithm with an excellent big-oh performance that results from trade-offs. One form of radix sort arranges positive numbers based on their digits. For example, imagine that all values in a particular container are integers within the range of 0 through 999. A radix sort would begin by assigning each integer to one of ten subcontainers based on the value of its hundreds digit. The algorithm would continue to process each of the ten subcontainers and assign their content values to one of ten subsubcontainers based on their tens digit. Similarly, each subsubcontainer would be processed and assigned according to the ones digits. Suppose this sort is applied to the following sequence of values:

sequence{ 572, 017, 586, 064, 103, 012, 006, 045, 204, 212, 521 }

The radix sort processes these 11 values, assigning each to one of 10 subcontainers according to its hundreds (leftmost) digit. This results in the following 10 containers:

Subcontainer 0 is *sequence*{ 017, 064, 012, 006, 045 }
Subcontainer 1 is *sequence*{ 103 }
Subcontainer 2 is *sequence*{ 204, 212 }
Subcontainer 3 is *sequence*{ }
Subcontainer 4 is *sequence*{ }
Subcontainer 5 is *sequence*{ 572, 586, 521 }
Subcontainer 6 is *sequence*{ }
Subcontainer 7 is *sequence*{ }
Subcontainer 8 is *sequence*{ }
Subcontainer 9 is *sequence*{ }

Seven of these subcontainers either are empty or contain one item and therefore need not be considered further. The remaining four containers are further categorized according to their tens digit, as shown next. (Note that only nonempty containers are shown.)

Subcontainer 0 is reassigned as follows.
  Subsubcontainer 0 is *sequence*{ 006 }
  Subsubcontainer 1 is *sequence*{ 017, 012 }
  Subsubcontainer 4 is *sequence*{ 045 }
  Subsubcontainer 6 is *sequence*{ 064 }
Subcontainer 1 is *sequence*{ 103 }

Continued on next page

Subcontainer 2 is reassigned as follows.
  Subsubcontainer 0 is *sequence*{ 204 }
  Subsubcontainer 2 is sequence{ 212 }
Subcontainer 5 is reassigned as follows.
  Subsubcontainer 2 is sequence{ 521 }
  Subsubcontainer 7 is sequence{ 572 }
  Subsubcontainer 8 is sequence{ 586 }

At this stage, only one subsubcontainer contains more than one item. The content of this container must be assigned to subsubsubcontainers according to the ones digit. The result is as follows.

Subcontainer 0 is reassigned as follows.
  Subsubcontainer 0 is *sequence*{ 006 }
  Subsubcontainer 1 is reassigned as follows.
    Subsubsubcontainer 2 is *sequence*{ 012 }
    Subsubsubcontainer 7 is *sequence*{ 017 }
  Subsubcontainer 4 is *sequence*{ 045 }
  Subsubcontainer 6 is *sequence*{ 064 }
Subcontainer 1 is *sequence*{ 103 }
Subcontainer 2 is reassigned as follows.
  Subsubcontainer 0 is *sequence*{ 204 }
  Subsubcontainer 2 is *sequence*{ 212 }
Subcontainer 5 is reassigned as follows.
  Subsubcontainer 2 is *sequence*{ 521 }
  Subsubcontainer 7 is *sequence*{ 572 }
  Subsubcontainer 8 is *sequence*{ 586 }

This repeated partitioning into more refined containers eventually sorts the data. Note that the values in the sequences shown are sorted in ascending order from top to bottom.

Assuming that there are N items in the original container to be sorted, the runtime performance of a radix sort is O(N). This conclusion is based on the observation that each of the N items will be processed (probed and moved) no more than some fixed number of times. In the preceding example, each value can be processed no more than three times (once for its hundreds digit, once for its tens digit, and once for its ones digit).

One method for coding a radix sort is to use a multidimensional array of integers. The number of dimensions in the array should match the fixed number of dividing elements. For example, sorting three-digit positive integers, as in the preceding example, uses an array such as this one:

```
int [][][] count = new int[10][10][10];
```

Each of the dimensions of the count array is used to represent one position within an item. So count[5][9][1] == 2 would represent a state in which the value 591 occurs twice in the original container.

This technique is shown in the doRadixSort3 method in Figure 3.27. The first *for* loop of this method demonstrates the linear performance of a radix sort by processing the entire array without the need for nested loops. This first *for* loop records each value from the original array by adding 1 to the appropriate cell of the count array.

Figure 3.27 doRadixSort3 method

```
/*  pre:     a != null
             and forAll(j : 0<=j<a.length | 0 <= a[j] <= 999)
     post:    forAll(j : 0<=j<a.length | a[j] <= a[j+1]) */
private void doRadixSort3( int[] a ) {
    int[][][] count = new int[10][10][10];
    int hundreds, tens, ones;
    for (int k=0; k != a.length; k++) {
        hundreds = a[k] / 100;
        tens = (a[k]-hundreds*100) / 10;
        ones = a[k] - hundreds*100 - tens*10;
        count[hundreds][tens][ones]++;
    }
    int ndx = 0;
    for(hundreds =0; hundreds!= 10; hundreds ++) {
        for(tens =0; tens!= 10; tens ++) {
            for(ones =0; ones!= 10; ones ++) {
                while (count[hundreds][tens][ones] != 0) {
                    a[ndx] = hundreds*100 + tens*10 + ones;
                    ndx++;
                    count[hundreds][tens][ones]-;
                }
            }
        }
    }
}
```

The collection of nested loops in the doRadixSort3 method copies the information in the count array back into the container being sorted. For each nonzero count cell, another item is placed into the array. The loops are nested so that the count cells are examined in ascending order with respect to their represented values.

Radix sort algorithms provide a good illustration of the interdependencies of different kinds of efficiency. The cost of linear run-time performance appears to be a sizable amount of storage devoted to the count array. For doRadixSort3, this array is 10*10*10 == 1000 cells. However, if a radix sort were to use a similar approach to sort double cells with a full 16 digits of accuracy, then count would require 10^{16} cells, an impractical size for today's computers. Furthermore, as the data structures become larger, the algorithm becomes slower, because additional time is required to instantiate, initialize, and visit all the additional array cells. Other variations on the radix sort algorithm reduce the size of the additional storage somewhat, but these come at the expense of increased intellectual complexity.

These space and intellectual complexities result in a much larger constant multiplier for radix sort and make it a lesser-used general-purpose sorting technique. Except in specialized cases, such as the example in which all values to be sorted are within the range of 0 through 999, radix sort is probably not a good choice, even though its big-oh performance is better than the preferred alternatives.

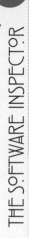

THE SOFTWARE INSPECTOR

Following is a collection of hints on what to check when you examine a design or code that involves the concepts of this chapter.

✓ Performance matters only if the program works! Always make certain that the code works correctly before expending too much energy on optimizing its performance.

✓ To improve the performance of a code segment, it is always a good idea to examine the innermost loops (or nested recursion) to look for code that is unnecessary or can be moved outside the nesting.

✓ Small things can make a big difference in code performance. For example, wise selection of a pivot can substantially improve quicksort performance, and early detection of sorting completion enhances a bubble sort.

✓ For small amounts of data, it is often best to use a simple algorithm, even if it has a mediocre big-oh performance.

✓ Don't forget to analyze *all* code when determining performance. Sometimes an efficient loop body can be overshadowed by a loop condition that requires too long to evaluate.

✓ If an array is sorted, a binary search is a more efficient technique. But binary searches don't work for unsorted arrays or most other containers even when they are sorted.

✓ N^2 sorting algorithms are acceptable for as many as a few hundred items, but NlogN sorts are preferable for larger amounts of data.

EXERCISES

1. For each of the following cost functions, give the big-oh estimate in simplest form (i.e., using performance classes such as those shown in Figure 3.5). You should assume that N and M are both variables.

   a. $9*N^2 + 3*N^5 + 1026$

   b. $*N + 2*log_2N$

   c. $7 * N^2 + 2*log_2N$

   d. $5*N^2 + 6*Nlog_2N$

   e. $3*N^2 + 5*Nlog_2N + 7*(2^N) + 9*log_2N$

   f. $8*N^2 * (2*N + 4*N^2 + 8*N^3)$

   g. $2*N * M * (7*N^3 + 5*N^2)$

   h. $6*N^3 + 4*M^2$

2. Fill in values of a table, like the one shown here, for the expressions N, $\log_3N$, $N\log_3N$, N^2, and 3^N and the following values of N: 0, 3, 9, 27, 81.

N	$\log_3N$	$N*\log_3N$	N^3	3^N
0				
3				
9				
27				
81				

3. Plot the four functions from Exercise 2, creating a graph in the style of Figure 3.3.

4. For each pair of the following big-oh expressions, either pick the dominant or indicate that neither is dominant or indicate that both belong to the same big-oh category. (Assume that N and M are both variables.)

   a. $O(N^3)$ *and* $O(N^2)$

   b. $O(N^2\log N)$ *and* $O(N^3)$

   c. $O(\log N)$ *and* $O(1)$

   d. $O(1)$ *and* $O(256)$

   e. $O(\log N)$ *and* $O(N)$

   f. $O(N^5)$ *and* $O(2^N)$

   g. $O(2*N*N^3)$ *and* $O(N^4 + N^2)$

   h. $O(2^N)$ *and* $O(N!)$

   i. $O(M)$ *and* $O(N^2)$

5. Give the big-oh performance for a single execution of each of the following methods. (Treat each parameter as a variable.)

   a.
   ```
   private int sum1ThruW( int w ) {
       int sum = 1;
       int k = 1;
       while (sum <= w) {
         sum = sum + k;
         k++;
       }
       return sum;
   }
   ```

   b.
   ```
   private int sumRecursively( int w ) {
       if (w <= 0) {
         return 0;
       } else {
         return w + sumrecursively(w-1);
       }
   }
   ```

c.
```
private int sum1Thru1000( ) {
    int sum = 1;
    int k = 1;
    while (sum <= 1000) {
        sum = sum + k;
        k++;
    }
    return sum;
}
```

d.
```
/* pre: arr != null and arr.length == w
        and forAll(k : 0<=k<=arr.length-1 | arr[k].length == w)
*/
private int zeroArray( double[][] arr, int w ) {
    for (int r=0; r!=w; r++) {
        for (int c=0; c!=w; c++) {
            arr[r][c] = 0;
        }
    }
}
```

e.
```
private int countFromWtoZero( int w ) {
    int counter = w;
    while (counter > 0) {
        System.out.println(counter);
        counter-;
    }
}
```

f.
```
private int divideFromWtoZero( int w ) {
    int divider = w;
    while (divider > 0) {
        System.out.println(divider);
        divider = divider / 2;
    }
}
```

g.
```
private int countFrom1000toZero() {
    int counter = 1000;
    while (counter > 0) {
        System.out.println(counter);
        counter-;
    }
}
```

6. How do your answers to Exercise 5 change for a segment of code that consists of a loop calling the method w times?

7. What is the big-oh performance of the following segment of code? (The methods used in this code refer to those shown in Exercise 5, and r is a program variable.)

```
if (r < 0) {
    countFromWtoZero(r);
} else if ( sum1thruW(r) > 300 ) {
    countFrom1000toZero();
} else {
    divideFromWtoZero(r);
}
```

8. Using the benchmark table from Figure 3.26, determine an approximate constant and use this constant in a proper formula to describe the *actualExecutionTime*(N) for each of the following algorithms.

   a. doInsertionSort

   b. doBubblesSrt

   c. doMergesort

   d. doQuicksort (You may estimate doQuicksort as O(NlogN).)

9. Using the formulas derived in Exercise 8, estimate the execution time required to sort an array of 1,000,000 items for each of the different sorting algorithms.

10. For each part, list all the applicable sorting algorithms from the following list.

    bubble sort

    linear insertion sort

    mergesort

    quicksort

    radix sort

    selection sort

    a. List all of these sorts that are typically implemented as in-place sorts.

    b. List all of these sorts that are typically implemented recursively.

    c. Which one of these sorts has the best big-oh performance?

    d. Which one of these sorts is likely to perform best in its ideal case? (An ideal case occurs when the content is arranged in a particular order for fast sorting.)

11. Give the big-oh performance for each of the following algorithms.

    a. Sort an array of length R using selection sort;
       Look up 10 values from the array using a linear search;

b. Sort an array of length R using mergesort;

```
for (int j=0; j!=R; j++) {
    Look up one value from the array using a linear search;
}
```

c. Sort an array of length R using mergesort;

```
for (int j=0; j!=R; j++) {
    Look up one value from the array using a binary search;
}
```

PROGRAMMING EXERCISES

1. The binary search concept can be applied to other algorithms. Parts (a) and (b) represent two such algorithms. Design, implement, and test a program that implements each of these.

    a. The square root of any real number can be approximated by repeatedly guessing its value and then checking the guess (i.e., squaring the guess) to see whether it is greater or less than the actual value. A binary search strategy can be used to select the guesses. Using this method, write a program that allows the user to input a real number and then approximates the square root of the number. Your estimate is close enough if it is within 0.01% of the user's real number. (For example, if the user inputs *100*, your estimate should be closer than 0.01 to the actual square root of 100.)

    b. Polynomial functions, such as fun(x) = x^2 + 2x – 15, are often solved for values of x, called roots or **zeros**, for which fun(x) == 0. For the sample polynomial, the roots happen to be 3 and –5; in other words, fun(3)==0 and fun(–5)==0.

       Write a collection of methods that will find the roots of an arbitrary function—call it *fun*. One way to allow *fun* to change is to write it as a nonvoid method that returns the function's value, such as the one shown next, and expect the body of fun to be altered and recompiled in order to apply the program to different functions.

```
private double fun(double x) {
    return x*x + 2*x - 15;
}
```

       The program should begin searching for roots by traversing the x axis from, say, –1,000,000.5 through 1,000,000.5 in one-unit increments (i.e., it should check fun(–1000000.5) then fun(–999999.5), then fun(–999998.5), ..., through fun(1000000.5)). Note that a root occurs between any two consecutive checks for which one fun value is positive and the other negative. When a root has been found to occur between consecutive checks, a binary search strategy must be employed to estimate the actual root (x) value within 0.001 units.

2. Figure 3.26 contains a table of benchmarks that compare the performance of several sorting algorithms on randomly arranged data. (The Java program that produced this data is included in the programs that accompany this book.) Modify the benchmark program to collect the following additional benchmarks, each for arrays of size 10,000.

   a. the sort times for an array that is already properly sorted

   b. the sort times for an array that is initially sorted in reverse

3. Modify the doBubblesort algorithm from Figure 3.24 so that it bubbles toward higher indices on odd-numbered passes through the outer loop, and toward lower indices on even-numbered passes. Write the program so that it executes both the doBubblesort method from Figure 3.24 and your modified version to sort the same array of randomly selected values and compares the actual run-time of each algorithm. (The java.util.Date class contains a getTime method that can be used as a rough measure of execution time.)

   Create a table of benchmarks for the two versions of bubble sort that includes the following:

   a. sorting 10,000 integers selected at random

   b. sorting 10,000 integers that are already sorted

   c. sorting 10,000 integers that are sorted except for the middle value

   d. sorting 10,000 integers that are sorted except for two cells

   e. sorting 10,000 integers that are sorted except for five cells

4. Modify any or all of the sorting algorithms given in this chapter so that they maintain two counts: (a) the count of how many data movements were needed for a complete sort and (b) the count of how many probes or comparisons were needed for a complete sort. Create a table of each count for different algorithms and array sizes of 1,000.

5. Quicksort is not very efficient at sorting small arrays. Rewrite the quicksort algorithm so that partitioned regions of eight cells or fewer are sorted by a selection sort algorithm. Benchmark your version of quicksort against the one from the chapter.

CHAPTER 4

REPRESENTING ABSTRACTIONS AS ARRAYS

"...PEOPLE HAVE FOR A LONG TIME APPRECIATED THE SIMPLICITY AND APPROPRIATENESS OF THE STATE/EVENT APPROACH...."

—David Harel

OBJECTIVES

- To review one-dimensional arrays

- To introduce the concept of a representation and to examine how representation selection is the first step of implementation

- To point out that implementation specifications are expressed in the language of the program, rather than the abstract models used in abstract specifications

- To propose an array implementation for the Iterator and Collection interfaces, including the use of inner classes

- To examine the Vector class as a facility for creating extensible arrays

- To examine multidimensional arrays

- To explore the array of arrays visualization, including ragged arrays

- To examine table-driven code as an efficient alternative to many control-centered algorithms

- To introduce bit vectors as a representation technique

- To introduce state machines and demonstrate a table-driven implementation

This chapter begins the exploration of implementation tools and techniques by examining the data structure that arguably is the most widely used by programmers: the **array**. Arrays are built into most modern programming languages, including Java. In fact, the array is given special stature in Java as the only container mechanism that does not require a separate class.

4.1 REVIEW OF ONE-DIMENSIONAL ARRAYS

Every array is a container having three key propertie:.

- Each item in the container must conform to the cell type that is specified in the array's declaration.
- An array consists of a group of cells, and each cell is referenced by its subscript(s), also known as an **index** (indices).
- The size of the array (i.e., its cell count) is fixed at the time the array is instantiated.

Like other reference variables, arrays must first be declared and then instantiated before they can be assigned or their contents inspected. Syntactically, a Java array type is specified by its cell type, often called its **base type**, followed by sets of empty square brackets (one set of brackets for each dimension in the array cell grid).

The simplest of all arrays is the **one-dimensional array**. As its name implies, a one-dimensional array is a single linear collection (a sequence) of cells. Here is a declaration of a one-dimensional array:

```
String[] words;
```

This declaration specifies that the name of array is words, that each cell of the array belongs to the String type, and that the array is one-dimensional. However, this declaration does not actually create the array, nor does it determine its size. These two things are established by **instantiating** the array. For example, the following statement instantiates the array and fixes its cell count at 4:

```
words = new String[4];
```

Following the execution of this statement, the words object is created with four cells. Java automatically numbers cells with integers beginning from zero. So the proper object diagram for the result of the preceding statement is as follows.

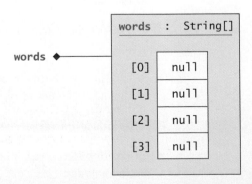

Following the array's instantiation, its cells behave like variables. Their values can be inspected or assigned. For example, the following code segment might follow the instantiation of the words array.

```
words[3] = "Now";
words[2] = "Is";
words[1] = "Time";
words[5-5] = "The";
```

The result of executing these four statements is to assign a string to each cell of the words array. This result is depicted in the following object diagram.

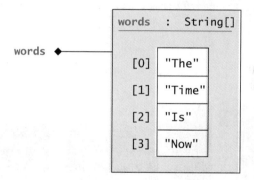

You access individual cells of an array by giving the array name and cell index. For example, an expression such as words[2] refers to the third cell of the array. You can also treat a Java array in the aggregate as a single reference object, conforming to java.lang.Object. For example, executing the following assignment statement assigns the entire array to the sentence variable, creating two bindings to the same array:

```
String[] sentence = words;
```

The result is depicted as follows.

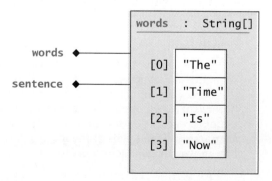

Java also supports the use of the length identifier as an implicit final instance variable of every array. The value of length is the number of cells in the array. For example, the swapFirstWithLast method from Figure 4.1 shows how to use length to test the size of a parameter.

Figure 4.1 The `swapFirstWithLast` method

```
/*  pre:    a != null (throws NullPointerException)
            and a.length>0 (throws IllegalArgumentException)
    post:   a[0] == a@pre[a.length-1]
            and a[a.length-1] == a@pre[0]
            and forAll(j: 1<=j<=a.length-2 | a[j] == a@pre[j]) */
private void swapFirstWithLast(String[] a) {
    if (a.length == 0) {
        throw new IllegalArgumentException();
    } else {
        String temp;
        temp = a[0];
        a[0] = a[a.length-1];
        a[a.length-1] = temp;
    }
}
```

The `swapFirstWithLast` method illustrates that aggregate array parameters are declared syntactically in the same way as array variables: the name of the parameter's type is followed by empty bracket pairs, as many bracket pairs as array dimensions. The name of a corresponding array serves as a valid argument for such an aggregate array parameter. For example, the following statement is a valid call to this method:

```
swapFirstWithLast( words );
```

4.2   IMPLEMENTING BOUNDEDSET

When faced with the task of implementing a container ADT, many developers use an array. In such an implementation it is said that the array **represents** the abstract container.

For example, an ADT called `MembershipList` can be described abstractly as a sequence of members. The client's view of the domain and the methods would therefore be in terms of *sequence* properties and operations. This same `MembershipList` might be implemented as a one-dimensional array in which each member occupies a separate cell. This array serves as the **representation** of the abstraction. The details of the implementer's choice of representation are purposely hidden by the abstraction because it is unnecessary information for the client.

As a first example of using an array to represent an ADT, consider `BoundedSetADT`, whose class diagram is shown in Figure 4.2. This is a slightly abbreviated version of a similar ADT, `BoundedSetOfObject`, introduced in Chapter 2.

Figure 4.3 contains the abstract class code for `BoundedSetADT`. This class portrays the abstract view of the class, including the abstract specifications.

Figure 4.2 BoundedSetADT class diagram

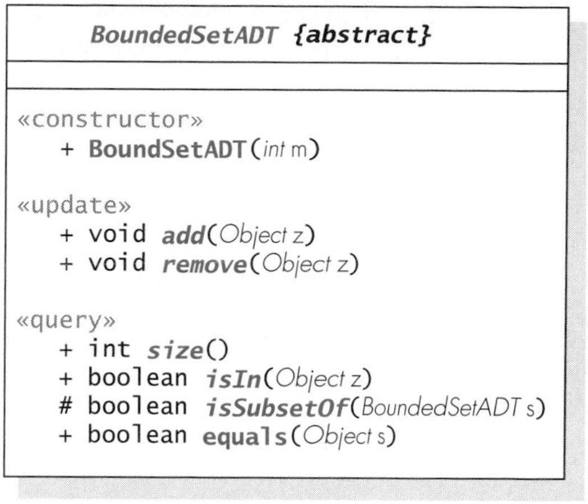

```
┌─────────────────────────────────────────────┐
│          BoundedSetADT  {abstract}           │
├─────────────────────────────────────────────┤
│                                               │
├─────────────────────────────────────────────┤
│ «constructor»                                 │
│     + BoundSetADT(int m)                      │
│                                               │
│ «update»                                      │
│     + void add(Object z)                      │
│     + void remove(Object z)                   │
│                                               │
│ «query»                                       │
│     + int size()                              │
│     + boolean isIn(Object z)                  │
│     # boolean isSubsetOf(BoundedSetADT s)     │
│     + boolean equals(Object s)                │
│                                               │
└─────────────────────────────────────────────┘
```

Figure 4.3 BoundedSetADT abstract class

```
/*  Domain (every BoundedSetADT object has two parts)
        Set of Object theSet
        int maxSize
invariant:
        theSet->size() <= maxSize */
public abstract class BoundedSetADT {
    /*  pre:    m > 0
        post:   theSet == set{}
                and maxSize == m */
    public BoundedSetADT (int m ) {
    }
    /*  pre:    theSet->including(z)->size() <= maxSize
                    (throws IllegalStateException)
        post:   theSet == theSet@pre->including(z) */
    public abstract void add( Object z);
    /*  post:   theSet == theSet@pre->excluding(z) */
    public abstract void remove(Object z);
    /*  post:   result == theSet->size() */
    public abstract int size();
    /*  post:   result == theSet->includes(z) */
    public abstract boolean isIn(Object z);
    /*  post:   result == s->includesAll(this) */
    protected abstract boolean isSubsetOf(BoundedSetADT s);
```

Continued on next page

```
    /* post:   this->includesAll(s) and s->includesAll(this) */
    public boolean equals(Object s) {
        return ((BoundedSetADT)s).isSubsetOf(this)
            && isSubsetOf((BoundedSetADT)s);
    }

}
```

The equals method is the only significant non-abstract method in BoundedSetADT. The equals method is implemented by calling an abstract method called isSubset. In fact, a good reason for including isSubset in BoundedSetADT is to provide a convenient implementation of equals.

A reasonable representation of BoundedSetADT consists of storing each set element in a separate array cell beginning from the cell with index zero and avoiding any duplicates. Figure 4.4 shows BoundedSetArray, the resulting array implementation.

Figure 4.4 BoundedSetArray class

```
/* invariant: forAll(j,k: 0<=j, k<=lastUsed
                    | j!=k implies setContent[j] != setContent[k])
*/
public class BoundedSetArray extends BoundedSetADT {
    private int lastUsed ;
    private Object[] setContent ;
    /* pre:    m > 0
       post:   setContent.length == m
               and lastUsed == -1 */
    public BoundedSetArray (int m ) {
        super(m);
        setContent = new Object[m];
        lastUsed = -1;
    }
    /* pre:    lastUsed+1 < setContent.length
                    (throws IllegalStateException)
       post:   isIn(z) */
    public void add ( Object z) {
        if (!isIn(z)) {
            if (lastUsed+1 == setContent.length) {
                throw new IllegalStateException();
            } else {
                lastUsed++;
                setContent[lastUsed] = z;
            }
        }
    }
```

Continued on next page

```
    /*  post:    !isIn(z)
                 and all other items of this@pre remain in this */
    public void remove(Object z) {
        int zPosition = indexOf(z);
        if (zPosition != -1) {
            setContent[zPosition] = setContent[lastUsed];
            lastUsed-;
        }
    }
    /*  post:   result == lastUsed + 1 */
    public int size() {
        return lastUsed + 1;
    }
    /*  post:   result == exists(j:0<=j<=lastUsed |
                    z.equals(SetContent[j])) */
    public boolean isIn(Object z) {
        return (indexOf(z) != -1);
    }
    /*  post:   result == forAll(j: 0<=j<=lastUsed
                    | exists(js: 0<=js<=lastUsed |
                    setContent[j].equals(s.setContent[js]))) */
    protected boolean isImproperSubsetOf(BoundedSetADT s) {
        for (int j = 0; j != lastUsed+1; j++) {
            if (!s.isIn(setContent[j])) {
                return false;
            }
        }
        return true;
    }
    /*  post:   isIn(z) implies setContent[result].equals(z)
                 and not isIn(z) implies result == -1 */
    private int indexOf(Object z) {
        int pos = 0;
        while (pos<= lastUsed && !setContent[pos].equals(z))
        {
            pos++;
        }
        if (pos > lastUsed) pos = -1;
        return pos;
    }
}
```

BoundedSetArray inherits BoundedSetADT, providing implementations for the methods that are abstract in BoundedSetADT. Because BoundedSetArray is an implementation, you need not write specifications in abstract OCL terminology. Instead, you write the specifications in the implementation class in terms of the instance variables and methods of the class. These specifications show in detail how the abstraction is represented.

The `BoundedSetArray` class represents `BoundedSetADT` with an array called `setContent`, and an `int` variable called `lastUsed`. The cells from `setContent[0]` through `setContent[lastUsed]` represent the set elements. The class invariant makes it clear that there are no duplicate values in this portion of the array.

The `maxSize` attribute, which is used in the abstract class, does not appear in `BoundedSetArray`. In place of `maxSize`, the array `length` serves as the upper bound on the cardinality of the set. This bound can always be tested via `setContent.length`.

The algorithms for methods `isIn` and `remove` share the need to search for object z (passed as a parameter) in the `setContent` array. This common algorithm has been captured by a private method called `indexOf`. The `indexOf` method is another linear search algorithm that probes array cells in order, one-by-one, until it finds a cell that satisfies some condition. If the linear search cannot locate z within the array, then `indexOf` returns –1; otherwise, `indexOf` returns the index of the cell containing z.

A call to `isIn(z)` returns `true` as long as the call to `indexOf(z)` returns something other than –1. The `isIn` method returns false when `indexOf(z)` returns –1.

Implementers must be aware of the need for algorithm efficiency. The designer specifies that the `remove` method must remove the indicated element from the set, but it's up to the implementer to select a good algorithm to do so. At least two alternative removal algorithms are worth considering for this array representation. Both algorithms begin with a linear search to find the index of the element to be removed, and both return immediately if there is no such element.

If the linear search from `indexOf` discovers the index of the cell value to be removed, the array can be visualized as containing a "hole" (i.e., the cell containing the value to be removed). The differences between the two removal algorithms is based on the way in which they "fill" this hole. One alternative is to fill this hole by shifting all the cells with greater index to their next lower-numbered neighboring cell, and then decrement `lastUsed` by 1. This alternative is pictured under "Shift Algorithm" in Figure 4.5.

The second alternative algorithm is to assign `setContent[lastUsed]` to the hole and then decrement `lastUsed` by 1. This alternative is pictured under "Assign Algorithm" in Figure 4.5. This algorithm, unlike the shift algorithm, fails to maintain the prior relative ordering of array cell content. However, the set implementation does not rely on order, and this second algorithm is more efficient: O(1) instead of O(lastUsed).

`BoundedSetADT`, along with its `BoundedSetArray` implementation, is an example of the key activities involved in design and implementation and their correspondence. (See Figure 4.6.) The designer must select a domain that is appropriate for crafting precise and complete abstract specifications. Correspondingly, the implementer must choose how to represent the abstraction in terms of data structures. The designer also composes public methods and defines their abstract behavior, whereas the implementer assembles algorithms to efficiently accomplish the necessary behavior.

Figure 4.5 Two algorithms for BoundedSetArray remove

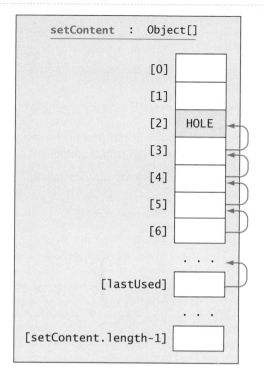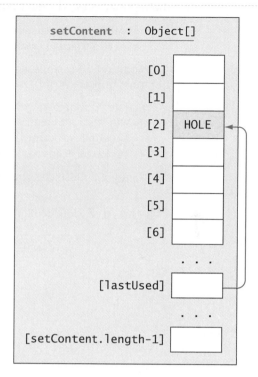

Figure 4.6 Primary activities of design and implementation

Design Activities	**Implementation Activities**
• Select domain and abstract invariant.	• Select representation (data structure with concrete invariant).
• Select public methods and specify them abstractly.	• Select algorithms that are correct and efficient.

4.3 REPRESENTATIONS

The selection of a suitable representation is a crucial part of crafting a good implementation. Furthermore, decisions about how to represent an ADT are usually the first step in an implementation. Choosing a representation involves two major decisions:

Software Engineering Hint

An implementer needs a clear view of the representation—the instance variables or types as well as how they will be used—before proceeding to implement methods.

- *What* instance variables (along with their types) will be used?
- *How* will these variables be used?

For example, the implementer who wrote `BoundedSetArray` first decided to base the representation on the following two variables:

```
private int lastUsed;
private Object[] setContent;
```

Additional decisions were made regarding *how* these variables are used. Here are the most important of these decisions:

- The "initial part" of the array (setContent[0] ... setContent[lastUsed]) will store set elements.
- No duplicate values are permitted within the initial part of the array.
- lastUsed stores the index of the last item of the initial part of the array.

Figure 4.7 illustrates these decisions and the resulting representation.

Figure 4.7 BoundedSetArray representation of BoundedSetADT

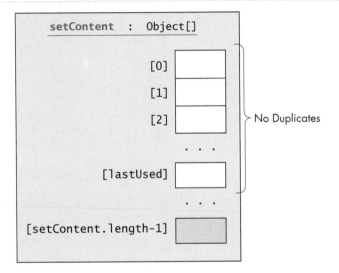

A slightly different representation results if you use a variable—call it cardinality—in place of lastUsed. The cardinality variable stores the count of elements in the set rather than the maximum index of the initial part of the array. It is easily concluded that cardinality == lastUsed + 1. Figure 4.8 pictures this second representation.

The representation shown in Figure 4.8 is nearly the same as BoundedSetArray, but even a change so small has numerous ramifications. To substitute the correct expression involving cardinality in place of lastUsed, you must alter every one of the BoundedSetArray methods.

A third representation—and one that has an even greater impact on method implementation—uses the "final part" of the array instead of the initial part. In other words, set elements are inserted first in those cells with greatest index. This representation, using the cardinality variable, is pictured in Figure 4.9.

Figure 4.8 A representation of BoundedSetADT using cardinality

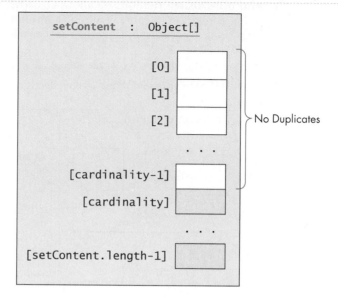

Figure 4.9 A representation of BoundedSetADT using the final array part

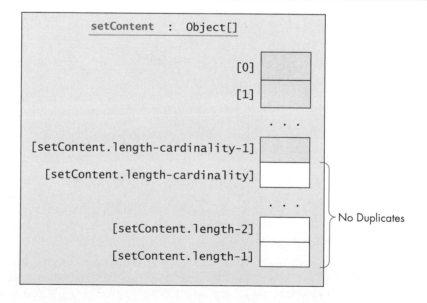

These second and third representations have identical instance variables, but the setContent variable is used in a different way in each. The second representation fills the array beginning with low-numbered indices, and the third implementation fills the array beginning with high-numbered indices. Although the second representation seems more intuitive for most programmers, both representations are valid.

From the three representations of BoundedSetADT shown thus far, you can create three other representations by allowing, rather than prohibiting, duplicates. In such a representation, a value would be considered to be part of the abstract set as long as it occurred *at least* once within setContent. These three representations are illustrated in Figure 4.10.

Figure 4.10 Representations of BoundedSetADT allowing duplicates

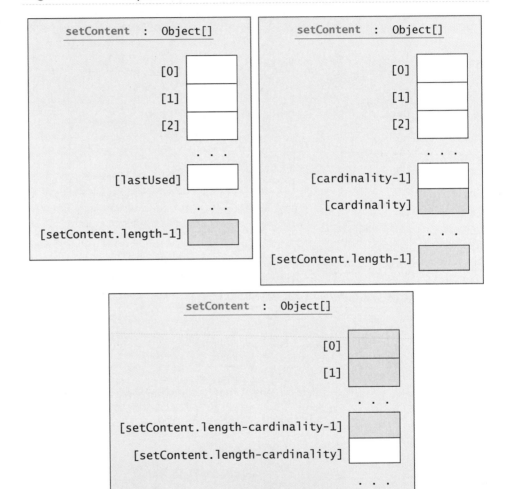

The representations that allow duplicates underscore the importance of choosing a representation before you select algorithms for implementing methods. You implement the remove and add methods differently for representations allowing duplicates than for representations prohibiting duplicates. For example, when removing from a representation allowing duplicates, you must delete *all* duplicates from the array. The `remove` algorithm when duplicates are allowed is slightly less efficient than the `remove` without duplicates, although it remains a linear algorithm.

The `add` method is potentially more efficient (best case is O(1)) when duplicates are allowed because there is no need to search for existing cells that will be duplicated. However, the `add` method for a representation allowing duplicates is complicated by the potential for the array to "fill" prematurely. When every array cell stores a set element, the `add` algorithm must eliminate one or more duplicate entries to make space for a new insertion into the set. The algorithm to search and eliminate duplicates introduces potential inefficiency into the `add` method.

4.4 IMPLEMENTING ITERATORS

Chapter 2 introduces the concept of an iterator to be used in probing the content of a container. The implementation of an iterator is a part of any container that uses the iterator. Just as the choice of representation affects the algorithms required by an implementation, the choice of container representation also affects the way that its iterator is implemented.

To illustrate an iterator implementation for an array representation, let's look at a new ADT container called `SimpleSequenceADT`. Figure 4.11 contains the class diagram for this ADT. (Note that it might be preferable to name `concatItem` as `add`. See Section 4.5 for an explanation.)

Figure 4.11 `SimpleSequenceADT` class diagram

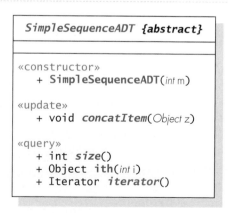

As its name suggests, `SimpleSequenceADT` is a container that exhibits some of the properties of an abstract sequence. `SimpleSequenceADT` is a bounded, generic container. A `SimpleSequenceADT` object is considered to be an empty sequence when it is first instantiated. The `concatItem` method is used to append a new item onto the end of the sequence, and the `ith` method returns an item at a given position. (For example, the value returned by seq.ith(k) is seq->*at*(k).) Figure 4.12 contains the complete abstract class for SimpleSequenceADT.

Figure 4.12 SimpleSequenceADT abstract class

```
/*  Domain (every SimpleSequenceADT object has two parts)
        Sequence of Object theSeq
        int maxLength
    invariant:  theSeq->size() <= maxLength */
import java.util.*;
public abstract class SimpleSequenceADT {
    /*  pre:    m > 0
        post:   theSeq == sequence{}
                and maxLength == m */
    public SimpleSequenceADT (int m ) {
    }
    /*  post:   result == theSeq->size() */
    public int size() {
        Object temp;
        int result = 0;
        Iterator it = iterator();
        while (it.hasNext()) {
            temp = it.next();
            result++;
        }
        return result;
    }
    /*  pre:    1 <= i and i <= theSeq->size()
                    (throws NoSuchElementException)
        post:   result == theSeq->at(i) */
    public Object ith(int i) {
        if (i < 1) {
            throw new NoSuchElementException();
        }
        Object result = null;
        Iterator it = iterator();
        for (int j=i; j!=0; j-) {
            result = it.next();
        }
        return result;
    }
    /*  pre:    theSeq->size() < maxLength
                    (throws IllegalStateException)
        post:   theSeq == theSeq@pre->append(z)*/
    public abstract void concatItem( Object z);
```

Continued on next page

```
        /* post:   result is an iterator over theSeq
                   and result.position == 0
                   and result.removeIsValid==false */
        public abstract Iterator iterator();
}
```

SimpleSequenceADT includes an `iterator` method that returns an iterator conforming to the `java.util.Iterator` interface. Even though the `iterator` method is abstract within SimpleSequenceADT, you can still implement `size` and `ith` within this abstract class by using the iterator.

In addition to iterator, SimpleSequenceADT includes one abstract method: `concatItem`. Figure 4.13 shows an array implementation for SimpleSequenceADT that supplies the remaining implementation details.

Figure 4.13 SimpleSequenceArray class

```
import java.util.*;
public class SimpleSequenceArray extends SimpleSequenceADT {
    private int count;
    private Object[] seqItems;
    /* pre:    m > 0
       post:   seqItems.length == m
               and count == 0 */
    public SimpleSequenceArray(int m ) {
        super(m);
        seqItems = new Object[m];
        count = 0;
    }
    /* post:   result == count */
    public int size() {
        return count;
    }
    /* pre:    1 <= i AND i <= count
            (throws NoSuchElementException)
       post:   result == seqItems[i-1] */
    public Object ith(int i) {
        return seqItems[i-1];
    }
    /* pre:    count < seqItems.length
            (throws IllegalStateException)
       post:   count == count@pre + 1
               and seqItems[count-1] == z */
    public void concatItem( Object z) {
        if (count == seqItems.length) {
            throw new IllegalStateException();
```

Continued on next page

```
            } else {
                seqItems[count] = z;
                count++;
            }
        }
    /*  post:    result is an iterator over seqItems
                 and result.position == 0
                 and result.removeIsValid==false */
    public Iterator iterator() {
        return new SimpleSequenceIterator();
    }
    /*  invariant: 0 <= itemsProbed <= count */
    private class SimpleSequenceIterator implements Iterator {
        private int itemsProbed;
        /*  post:    itemsProbed == 0 */
        public SimpleSequenceIterator() {
            itemsProbed = 0;
        }
        /*  pre:     itemsProbed < count
                        (throws NoSuchElementException)
            post:    itemsProbed == itemsProbed@pre + 1
                     and result == seqItems[itemsProbed-1] */
        public Object next() {
            if (itemsProbed == count) {
                throw new NoSuchElementException();
            } else {
                itemsProbed++;
                return seqItems[itemsProbed-1];
            }
        }
        /*  post:    result == itemsProbed < count */
        public boolean hasNext() {
            return itemsProbed < count;
        }
        /*  post:    throws UnsupportedOperationException */
        public void remove() {
            throw new UnsupportedOperationException();
        }
    }
}
```

The SimpleSequenceArray class represents SimpleSeqenceADT as a one-dimensional array called seqItems and a count variable. This representation uses s.seqItems[0] to store s->*at*(1), uses s.seqItems[1] to store s->*at*(2), and so forth. The representation uses count to maintain the number of items in the abstract sequence.

The SimpleSequenceArray constructor creates an empty sequence by assigning zero to count. The constructor method also instantiates the seqItems array in preparation for manipulation by other methods.

SimpleSequenceArray overrides the size and ith methods, which were previously implemented by the parent (abstract) class. These overrides improve efficiency. The parent version of size uses an iterator to traverse the sequence, counting its content—an O(N) algorithm. The array implementation eliminates the need for such a traversal, because the count variable stores the needed information. The result is that size is implemented by an O(1) algorithm. Similarly, an iterator traversal in the superclass version of ith is eliminated by using the index to directly access the appropriate array cell.

The implementation of the Iterator interface is a kind of "implementation within an implementation." The iterator method must return an object that conforms to Iterator, but because Iterator is an interface, there must be an implementation of Iterator in order for the iterator method to instantiate. Furthermore, iterator can't simply return anything that conforms to Iterator; rather, it must return an iterator that can probe this particular array implementation.

Figure 4.13 shows a way to implement the iterator method by including an **inner** class called SimpleSequenceIterator. This inner class is declared to be private, although its methods must be public because they implement existing public methods from the Iterator interface. Figure 4.14 is a class diagram that shows the unique associations among the various classes involved in implementing SimpleSequenceADT.

Three significant characteristics result from making SimpleSequenceIterator an inner class of SimpleSequenceArray:

1. SimpleSequenceIterator has access to the private instance variables (and methods) of SimpleSequenceArray by virtue of its status as a local class.
2. SimpleSequenceArray can conveniently call any of the methods of SimpleSequenceIterator using the same syntax as if they were part of the outer class.
3. SimpleSequenceIterator is encapsulated, so the implementation, and even the name, of this class is hidden and inaccessible to external classes.

The first characteristic is essential to a proper Iterator implementation. Any implementation of a proper iterator for SimpleSequenceArray must be able to access the key variables and methods that define the representation, even when they are private.

The second characteristic of the inner class approach is that the container class can use the iterator. Such convenient access to an iterator can be useful for many container implementations. However, as SimpleSequenceArray illustrates, this access isn't always essential.

The third characteristic is consistent with the concepts of good information hiding and abstraction. By making the inner class a private class, its innards are completely hidden from any class except SimpleSequenceArray.

Figure 4.14 Class diagram for SimpleSequenceArray and associated classes

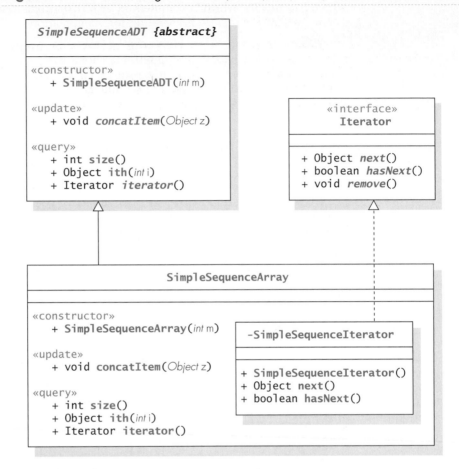

The SimpleSequenceIterator class represents an iterator as a single int variable called itemsProbed. The itemsProbed variable maintains the number of sequence items that have been visited (probed) by calls to the next method. Instantiating a new iterator results in assigning zero to itemsProbed for the new iterator. The hasNext method implementation compares the value of itemsProbed to count. (Note the need for hasNext to access the private count variable.) The next method is implemented by incrementing itemsProbed and returning the appropriate item from the seqItems array cell. Because remove is an optional Iterator method, this example does not provide an implementation, except to throw the appropriate exception for the missing implementation.

4.5 REPRESENTING JAVA.UTIL.COLLECTION (OPTIONAL)

Section 2.10 examines the java.util.Collection interface for providing a standard public interface to container classes. This section shows how to include a

Collection implementation within a container class. In particular, the SimpleSequenceArray implementation is modified to incorporate an implementation of Collection.

To implement the new class—call it SimpleSequenceCollection—you must first decide which classes and interfaces should be inherited or implemented. Because Java does not support multiple inheritance, SimpleSequenceCollection cannot inherit both SimpleSequenceADT and AbstractCollection. Therefore, there seem to be two other alternatives, as pictured in Figure 4.15.

Figure 4.15 Two design alternatives for SimpleSequenceCollection superclasses

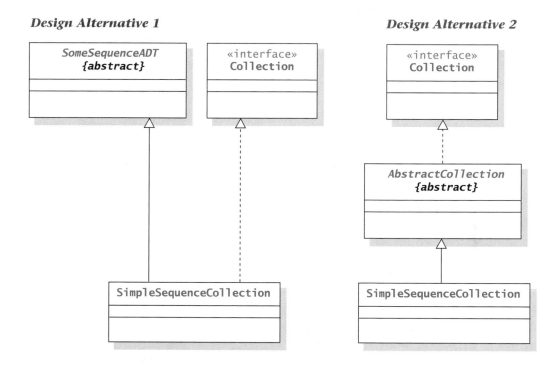

Design Alternative 1

Design Alternative 2

Design alternative 1 is to implement SimpleSequenceCollection by inheriting SimpleSequenceADT and also implementing Collection. The difficulty with this approach is that you must implement a large number of methods from Collection. Design alternative 2 requires that fewer methods be implemented, but it means that SimpleSequenceCollection will not conform to the type of SimpleSequenceADT. Unless such type conformance is required, design alternative 2 seems preferable based on the required programming effort.

Figure 4.16 shows a complete implementation of the SimpleSequenceCollection class using alternative design 2. Those lines of the class that differ from SimpleSequenceArray are highlighted, while lines of code that remain unchanged are shown in light gray.

Software Engineering Hint

In a software industry with a shortage of good developers, the amount of time required to develop a particular design weighs heavily on the design's value. For example, design alternative 2 is selected primarily because it takes less of the developer's time to implement.

Figure 4.16 SimpleSequenceCollection class

```java
import java.util.*;
public class SimpleSequenceCollection extends AbstractCollection {
    private int count;
    private Object[] seqItems;
    /*  pre:    m > 0
        post:   seqItems.length == m
                and count == 0 */
    public SimpleSequenceCollection(int m ) {
        super();
        seqItems = new Object[m];
        count = 0;
    }
    /*  post:   result == count */
    public int size() {
        return count;
    }
    /*  pre:    1 <= i AND i <= count (throws NoSuchElementException)
        post:   result == seqItems[i-1] */
    public Object ith(int i) {
        return seqItems[i-1];
    }
    /*  pre:    count <= seqItems.length
                    (throws IllegalStateException)
        post:   count == count@pre + 1
                and seqItems[count-1] == z */
    public void concatItem( Object z) {
        if (count == seqItems.length) {
            throw new IllegalStateException();
        } else {
            seqItems[count] = z;
            count++;
        }
    }
    /*  post:   result is an iterator over seqItems
                and result.position == 1
                and result.removeIsValid==false */
    public Iterator iterator() {
        return new SimpleSequenceIterator();
    }
    /*  pre:    count < seqItems.length
                    (throws IllegalStateException)
        post:   count == count@pre + 1
                and seqItems[count-1] == z */
    public boolean add( Object z) {
        concatItem(z);
        return true;
    }
```

Continued on next page

```
/*  invariant: 0 <= itemsProbed <= count */
private class SimpleSequenceIterator implements Iterator {
    private int itemsProbed;
    private boolean removeIsValid;
    /*  post:   itemsProbed == 0 */
    public SimpleSequenceIterator() {
        itemsProbed = 0;
        removeIsValid = false;
    }
    /*  pre:    itemsProbed < count
                (throws NoSuchElementException)
        post:   itemsProbed == itemsProbed@pre + 1
                and result == seqItems[itemsProbed-1] */
    public Object next() {
        if (itemsProbed == count) {
            throw new NoSuchElementException();
        } else {
            itemsProbed++;
            removeIsValid = true;
            return seqItems[itemsProbed-1];
        }
    }
    /*  post:   result == itemsProbed < count */
    public boolean hasNext() {
        return itemsProbed < count;
    }
    /*  pre:    removeIsValid == true
                (throws IllegalStateException)
        post:   forAll(j: itemsProbed@pre <= j <= count-1
                | seqItems[j-1] == seqItems@pre[j]]
                and itemsProbed == itemsProbed@pre - 1
                and count == count@pre - 1
                and removeIsValid == false */
    public void remove() {
        if (!removeIsValid) {
            throw new IllegalStateException();
        } else {
            for (int j=itemsProbed; j!=count; j++) {
                seqItems[j-1] = seqItems[j];
            }
            count-;
            itemsProbed-;
            removeIsValid = false;
        }
    }
}
}
```

The required implementations for the three abstract methods from AbstractCollection—add, size, and iterator—are those that are in SimpleSequenceCollection. The iterator and size implementations are the same as those in SimpleSequenceArray. The add method is almost the same as concatItem; the only difference is that add must return a boolean value to indicate whether the method alters the container's content. Because a valid call to add always changes the underlying sequence, this implementation always returns true.

SimpleSequenceCollection provides another example of how consistency in member naming can reduce programming effort and can simplify design. If SimpleSequenceADT had used the more standard add method, the nonstandard concatItem method could be eliminated.

The other requirement needed to properly implement AbstractCollection is for the iterator method to return a complete implementation of the Iterator interface. This includes an implementation of the optional remove method, which wasn't implemented in SimpleSequenceArray. The SimpleSequenceCollection class illustrates a proper implementation of an Iterator remove method. Notice that this remove implementation properly deletes the collection item that was most recently returned by next.

4.6 THE VECTOR CLASS

Once a Java array has been instantiated, its size is fixed. You cannot add any additional cells or remove cells, short of instantiating another array. The standard Java packages—specifically, the java.util package—provide a separate class that has many of the characteristics of a one-dimensional array while overcoming the limitation of a fixed size. Figure 4.17 contains a partial class diagram for this Vector class.

Several of the Vector methods are similar to features that are available for arrays. For example, the size method from Vector, like the length variable of an array, yields the count of cells in the container. Unlike arrays, the Vector notation for inspecting a container cell is separate from the notation for assigning cells. You inspect Vector cells by calling elementAt and assign them by calling setElementAt. Figure 4.18 explains the behavior of these Vector methods by giving the corresponding array notation.

A key difference between Vectors and arrays is that the count of Vector cells is not fixed but rather can change during a program's execution. The Vector constructor establishes the initial size of a Vector, but other methods can alter this size. One such method is setSize. A call to setSize reestablishes the cell count to match the method's argument. If a call to setSize increases the cell count, the new cells are assigned default values (null for reference types), and the prior cells remain unaltered. If a call to setSize decreases the cell count, the content of cells with higher-numbered indices is lost.

The setSize method is a powerful facility because it permits a bounded container to change its bounds. Containers, such as Vector, that are permitted to change size dynamically are known as **extensible containers**.

Figure 4.17 java.util.Vector class diagram

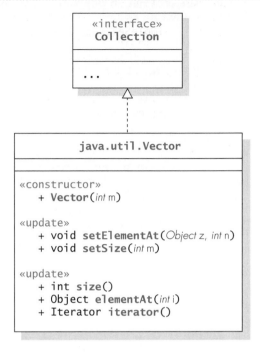

Figure 4.18 Common Vector operations and their array equivalents

Vector Expression	*Corresponding Array Notation*
To instantiate a container	
myVector = new Vector(10);	myArray = new Object[10];
To assign a cell value	
myVector.setElementAt(someObj,3);	myArray[3] = someObj;
To inspect a cell value	
someObj = myVector.elementAt(0);	someObj = myArray[0];
To access container cell count	
System.out.print(myVector.size());	System.out.print(myArray.length);

The Vector class has a second significant advantage compared with arrays because arrays are not full-fledged classes. Two limitations are imposed by the Java implementation of arrays.

- It is impossible to inherit a Java array.
- Arrays do not inherit Object.

There is no Java notation for inheriting an array. However, inheriting the `Vector` class provides an alternative that lets you accomplish essentially the same thing as inheriting an array.

The Java relationship between arrays and the `Object` class is unique. A Java array conforms to `Object`, making it possible to use aggregate array arguments for parameters of `Object` type. On the other hand, a Java array does not implicitly inherit the `Object` class. This means that arrays do not support methods such as `equals` or `toString`. The `Vector` class provides this implicit inheritance of `Object` for arraylike containers.

Because the `Vector` class provides extensibility, implicit inheritance of `Object` and inheritability, all of which are impossible with arrays—why does Java include arrays? The primary answer to the preceding question has to do with software performance. The lack of extensibility permits language implementations to use a single contiguous block of memory space for an array. This contiguous storage allows rapid access to individual cells. As a result, an algorithm that uses an array should be expected to perform as well or better than the same algorithm using a `Vector`.

> ### Software Engineering Hint
>
> Vectors and arrays have many similar properties. Because arrays tend to perform better and because their notation is generally more readable, the default container should be array. However, a need for any of the following might suggest a preference for **Vector** over array: container extensibility, specialization (inheritance) of the container, or compatibility with **Object** facilities such as `equals` or `toString`.

A second, but less important, reason that some programmers prefer an array to a `Vector` is the simplicity of array notation. The constructor notation, indexing notation, and even the `length` variable are slightly abbreviated syntax compared with those of the corresponding `Vector` method calls. Furthermore, for experienced software developers, the square bracket symbolism is more consistent with older, non-object-oriented programming languages.

4.7 MULTIDIMENSIONAL ARRAYS

The earlier examples in this chapter have used one-dimensional arrays, but Java supports arrays of greater dimension. Figure 4.19 demonstrates conventional ways to visualize one-dimensional through four-dimensional arrays.

A two-dimensional array is like a two-dimensional grid of cells. Each cell of the grid resides in a particular row and column, and the cell is identified by two indices: one index for its row number, and one for its column. In Java the numbering of rows and columns, like the index numbering of a one-dimensional array, begins with the number zero (0).

A three-dimensional array is depicted as a small cube. This array's cells (cubes) can be arranged into a regular 3-D structure of row, column, and depth slices. Three indices (corresponding to row, column, and depth) are needed to identify the location of any particular cell. The pattern of additional indices forming arrays with more dimensions continues, even though it is often difficult to visualize dimensions beyond three.

Figure 4.19 One-dimensional through four-dimensional arrays

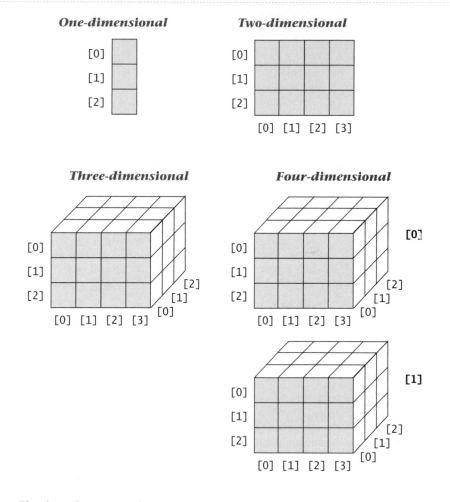

The four-dimensional array in Figure 4.19 attempts to picture a four-dimensional array with its four indices: one index to select one of the two cubes, and the other three indices used as for a three-dimensional array.

You specify the number of dimensions in a Java array in the array declaration by the number of empty brackets following the array type (or name). For example, the following three statements declare, respectively, three-, two- and four-dimensional arrays.

```
ChessPiece[][][] chessBoard3D;
AuditoriumSeat[][] reservation;
Double[][][][] temperatureReading;
```

Similarly, you can instantiate a multidimensional array by specifying the length of each dimension within consecutive brackets in an instantiation statement. For example, a 3-D chess board that consists of three levels of eight-by-eight chess boards is instantiated as follows:

```
chessBoard3D = new ChessPiece[8][8][3];
```

It is customary to treat the first index as a row number and the second as a column. Therefore, an auditorium with a rectangular layout of seats, consisting of 50 rows and 100 seats per row, is instantiated by the following statement:

```
reservation = new AuditoriumSeat[50][100];
```

As an example of the need for more than three dimensions, consider the problem of weather forecasting. Temperature data for a forecast can be maintained in an array in which temperature readings are recorded in a rectangular grid of latitude and longitude and at predetermined altitudes. Suppose the array must store such temperature data for five different latitudes, ten longitudes, and three altitudes. This information could be stored in a single three-dimensional array in which latitude corresponds to the row index, longitude to the column index, and altitude to the depth index. However, if a single array is to be used to maintain these data for a period of one week (one reading per day), a fourth dimension is required. The following array instantiation would be appropriate.

```
double[][][][] temperatureReading = new double[5][10][3][7];
```

Each cell of a multidimensional array is addressed using the same number of indices in the identical order of the array instantiation. For example, the following statement assigns 17.2 to the cell with latitude with index of 1, longitude with index of 4, the greatest possible altitude (index of 2), and the fourth day (index of 3).

```
temperatureReading[1][4][2][3] = 17.2;
```

As a second example, the statement in Figure 4.20 outputs the value of the cell from row 3, column 5 of the middle chess board. This particular chess board cell is highlighted below the statement.

Arrays of dimension greater than one are not linear structures because their cells are not naturally arranged in a line. The solitary loop that forms a convenient foundation for an algorithm to visit every cell of a one-dimensional array or to iterate over every item in a linear container is not suitable for visiting all the cells of a multidimensional array. The multidimensional alternative is a collection of nested loops—one loop for each loop dimension that traverses every index of the dimension. For example, here is a collection of nested loops that assigns a zero to every cell of the temperatureReading array:

```
for (int latitude=0; latitude != 5; latitude++) {
    for (int longitude=0; longitude != 10; longitude++) {
        for (int altitude=0; altitude != 3; altitude++) {
            for (int day=0; day != 7; day++) {
                temperatureReading[latitude][longitude]
                [altitude][day] = 0;
            }
        }
    }
}
```

The order in which these loops are nested does not affect the final outcome of the algorithm, but nesting order does have an impact on the order in which cells are visited. For example, Figure 4.21 shows two nesting orders for the same algorithm and depicts the array content.

Figure 4.20 Reference to a cell of a 3-D chess board

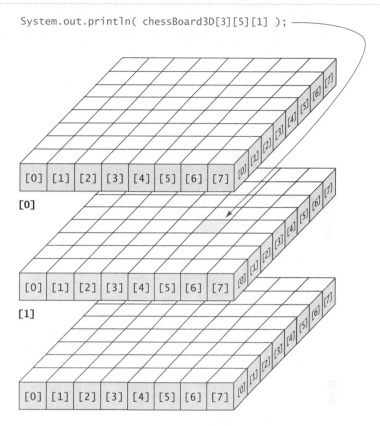

```
System.out.println( chessBoard3D[3][5][1] );
```

Figure 4.21 Different nested loops ordering and the resulting behavior

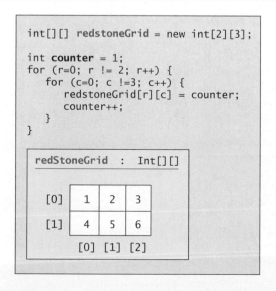

```
int[][] redstoneGrid = new int[2][3];

int counter = 1;
for (r=0; r != 2; r++) {
    for (c=0; c !=3; c++) {
        redstoneGrid[r][c] = counter;
        counter++;
    }
}
```

redStoneGrid : Int[][]

	[0]	[1]	[2]
[0]	1	2	3
[1]	4	5	6

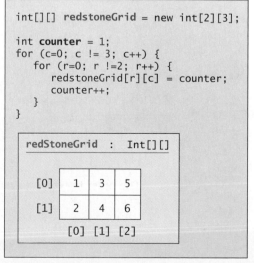

```
int[][] redstoneGrid = new int[2][3];

int counter = 1;
for (c=0; c != 3; c++) {
    for (r=0; r !=2; r++) {
        redstoneGrid[r][c] = counter;
        counter++;
    }
}
```

redStoneGrid : Int[][]

	[0]	[1]	[2]
[0]	1	3	5
[1]	2	4	6

The algorithm on the left side of Figure 4.21 is commonly called a **row major traversal** because it visits cells across one row before progressing to the next. The algorithm on the right side of the figure visits cells in a column-by-column order, so it is called a **column major traversal**. One way to remember the differences in ordering is to observe that the inner loop alters its index value most frequently. Correspondingly, the outer loop alters its index variable with the least frequency.

4.8   ARRAY OF ARRAYS

It is instructive to visualize a two-dimensional array as a rectangular grid of cells. However, a more comprehensive understanding of multidimensional arrays requires a different mental picture: an **array of arrays**. For example, a two-dimensional array should be thought of as a one-dimensional array in which every item is itself a one-dimensional array. Figure 4.22 shows these two ways to visualize a two-dimensional array.

Figure 4.22 A 2-D array visualized as a grid (left) and as an array of arrays

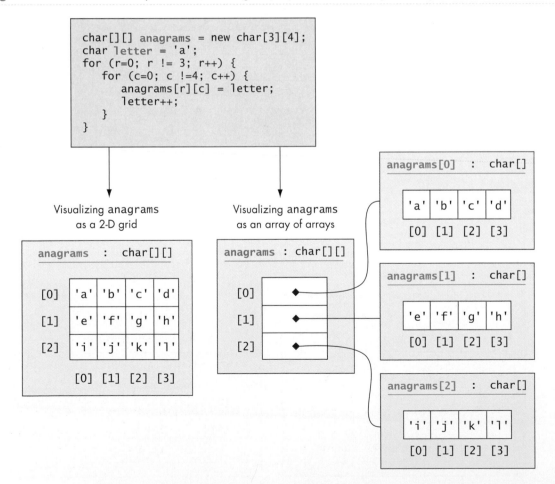

The left side of Figure 4.22 pictures the anagrams array as a grid of char cells. This grid consists of three rows, each with four columns. The right side of the figure visualizes the same array as an array of arrays. In this view, anagrams is thought of as a one-dimensional array with three items (one item for each row). Each of these three items is a one-dimensional array of four items (one item for each column).

Java supports both ways to visualize multidimensional arrays. For example, the following expression refers to a single item (the item from row 2 and column 1):

```
anagrams[2][1]
```

The two alternative visualizations are really only two different abstract views of the same data structure. Sometimes it is more instructive to view an array as a grid, and other times the array of arrays view is the preferred abstraction. Java supports the array of arrays view by permitting expressions that refer to a row in the aggregate, also called a **slice**. For example, the following expression references the entire anagrams row (slice) with index 2:

```
anagrams[2]
```

Furthermore, you can reference the entire array with all rows and columns in the aggregate using the following syntax:

```
anagrams
```

You cannot, however, slice an array into columns as aggregate parts.

To further illustrate these different ways to manipulate arrays in Java, consider the following method for displaying the content of an array.

```
/* post:   all items of a have been displayed across one line */
private void print2D( char[][] a ) {
    for (int r=0; r != a.length; r++) {
        for (int c=0; c != a[r].length; c++) {
            System.out.print( a[r][c] );
        }
    }
    System.out.println();
}
```

The print2D method requires an argument that is a two-dimensional array of char. A proper call to this method is shown in the following statement, where anagrams is passed in the aggregate.

```
print2D( anagrams );
```

Calling the print2D method causes all the characters in the anagrams array to be displayed across a single line. The algorithm uses nested loops to accomplish the task. The length attribute of the entire two-dimensional array, such as a.length, refers to the length of the initial array (the number of rows). Every item in the initial array also has a length attribute, so the expression a[r].length refers to the length (number of columns) for the row of the array having a subscript of r.

Following are two additional methods that print two-dimensional arrays in a slightly different manner.

```
/* post:    all items of a have been displayed with each row across
             a separate line */
private void printByRow(char[][] a) {
    for (int r=0; r != a.length; r++) {
        printOneRow( a[r] );
    }
}


/* post:    all items of a have been output on the same line */
private void printOneRow(char[] a) {
    for (int j=0; j != a.length; j++) {
        System.out.print( a[j] );
    }
    System.out.println();
}
```

You can call the printByRow method using the following statement:

```
printByRow( anagrams );
```

Executing this call causes the single loop within the body of printByRow to execute. Each repetition of this loop causes a different slice (the row with index r) of the anagrams array to be passed as an argument to the printOneRow method. Here is the statement from the code that produces this secondary call:

```
printOneRow( a[r] );
```

The printOneRow method is designed to print a one-dimensional array of char. Because a row slice from anagrams constitutes a one-dimensional array, the preceding statement is a valid call. For this call, the variable j refers to a column index.

The array of arrays view of multidimensional arrays leads to the question, Must all rows have the same length? In Java, the answer to this question is no. A special name is given to arrays in which not all rows have the same length: such structures are known as **ragged arrays**.

Instantiating a ragged array takes in two steps. In the first step, the initial array size is specified, but not the size of the individual slices. The Java notation for this first step is to substitute empty brackets for the unspecified lengths.

The second instantiating step for a ragged array requires the separate instantiation of all slices. Figure 4.23 shows a sample declaration and instantiation of a two-dimensional ragged array, along with pictures of the resulting abstract views as a grid and as an array of arrays.

The array of arrays abstraction is common in real life. For example, consider a hotel chain. The chain consists of several (an array of) hotels. Each hotel consists of one or more (an array of) floors, and each floor is an array of rooms. This situation suggests the following three-dimensional array.

```
HotelRoom[][][] room = new
HotelRoom[hotelsInChain][floorCount][roomCount];
```

This structure is naturally thought of as an array of arrays of arrays, but it would be unnatural to visualize it as a 3-D cubic structure. Furthermore, the HotelRoom

Figure 4.23 A ragged array example

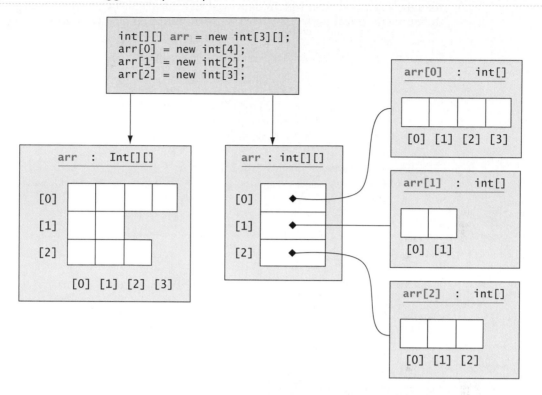

structure is a likely ragged array candidate because not all hotels need to have the same number of floors, and not all floors have the same number of rooms.

4.9   TABLES

The possibility for **direct access** of any item is a key characteristic that distinguishes arrays from other containers. Direct access means that any cell of an array is directly identified by its index (or indices). Direct access often leads to algorithms with better performance. For example, using an iterator to inspect the value of the 100th item in a container requires an algorithm that visits the 99 preceding items (an O(N) algorithm for array size N). However, the 100th array cell can be inspected without visiting any other array items—an O(1) algorithm.

Direct access makes it possible for an array to serve as a **table** for translating from an index (or indices) to some other value (given by the content of an array cell). An algorithm that looks up a table value (i.e., inspects an array cell) is generally more efficient than an algorithm based on control structures. The name **table-driven code** refers to algorithms designed around table look-up operations.

As an example of table-driven code, consider the task of translating the sequence number for a month into the number of days in that month for a non–

leap year. January has a sequence number of 1, and 31 days; the sequence number for February is 2, and it has 28 days; and so forth. Figure 4.24 shows a non-table-driven method that performs such a translation from sequence number to days.

Figure 4.24 daysPerMonthFromIf method using if statements

```
/*  pre:     1 <= m <= 12 (throws IllegalArgumentException)
    post:    result == number of days in month m
                (for a non-leap year)
    note:    the table look up version in Figure 4.24
             is more efficient. */
private int daysPerMonthFromIf( int m ) {
    if (m==1 || m==3 || m==5 || m==7 || m==8 || m==10 || m==12)
    {
        return 31;
    } else if (m==4 || m==6 || m==9 || m==11) {
        return 30;
    } else if (m==2) {
        return 28;
    } else {
        throw new IllegalArgumentException();
    }
}
```

The daysPerMonthFromIf method requires a number of Boolean tests. Each of these tests consumes execution time. If daysPerMonthFromIf is to be used frequently, it is more efficient to construct a table and use a table look-up (array cell inspection) in place of the Boolean tests. Figure 4.25 shows this table-driven alternative.

Figure 4.25 daysPerMonth method using an array

Array (table) Declaration

```
private final int[] monthLength
        = {31, 28, 31, 30, 31, 30, 31, 31, 30, 31, 30, 31};
```

Method Using the Table

```
/*  pre:     1 <= m <= 12 (throws ArrayIndexOutOfBoundsException)
    post:    result == number of days in month m
             (for a non-leap year) */
private int daysPerMonth( int m ) {
    return monthLength[m-1];
}
```

The monthLength array is declared as a final array because it is a table with static values. A small amount of execution time is associated with instantiating the monthLength array, but thereafter, direct access to this array is an extremely efficient way to translate month number into month length.

Calculating factorial values is a second example in which a table-driven approach can improve the performance of an algorithm. Figure 4.26 illustrates how to construct and use such a table.

Figure 4.26 Factorial method using a table

Array (Table) Declaration

```
private final int[] factorialTable
    = {1, 1, 2, 6, 24, 120, 720, 5040, 40320, 362880,
    3628800, 39916800, 479001600 };
```

Method Using the Table

```
/*  pre:    n >= 0 (throws ArrayIndexOutOfBoundsException)
    post:   result == n! (n factorial)
private int factorial( int n ) {
    return factorialTable[n];
}
```

The mathematical factorial function grows so fast that the largest factorial that can be calculated within the bounds of the Java int data type is 12!. factorialTable uses this fact to store the values of 0! through 12! in its 13 cells. The factorial method in Figure 4.26, which calculates factorial by table look-up, is faster for most computations than using a loop or a recursive method to compute factorial values.

Software Engineering Hint

Software developers often use tables to improve the performance of an implementation. It is always wise to examine frequently executed code for ways to replace control structures with tables.

A table commonly associated with maps is a distance table, showing the distance between two locations. Figure 4.27 contains a sample distance table. All the rows and columns are labeled with cities, and the cell at the intersection of any two cities gives the mileage that separates them.

Figure 4.27 Table of distances between selected U.S. cities

	Atlanta	Chicago	Dallas	Los Angeles	New York City
Atlanta	0	722	2,244	800	896
Chicago	722	0	1,047	2,113	831
Dallas	2,244	1,047	0	1,425	1,576
Los Angeles	800	2,113	1,425	0	2,849
New York City	896	831	1,576	2,849	0

The distance table is two-dimensional, so a two-dimensional array is an obvious representation. Figure 4.28 shows this implementation strategy.

Figure 4.28 distanceBetweenCities method

Array (Table) Declaration

```
private final int[] mileage = {  {0, 722, 2244, 800, 896},
                                 {722, 0, 1047, 2113, 831},
                                 {2244, 1047, 0, 1425, 1576},
                                 {800, 2113, 1425, 0, 2849},
                                 {896, 831, 1576, 2849, 0} };
private final int atlanta = 0;
private final int chicago = 1;
private final int dallas = 2;
private final int losAngeles = 3;
private final int newYorkCity = 4;
```

Method Using the Table

```
/* pre:    atlanta <= c1 <= newYorkCity
           and atlanta <= c2 <= newYorkCity
               (throws ArrayIndexOutOfBoundsException)
   post:   result == distance (in miles) between city c1 and c2
private int distanceBetweenCities( int c1, int c2 ) {
    return mileage[c1][c2];
}
```

Software Engineering Hint

Many times the indices of a table have some other meaning than their **int** value. Because Java array indices must be of type **int**, using **final int** variables with meaningful index names can enhance software readability.

The distanceBetweenCities method not only illustrates that two-dimensional arrays can be useful tables but also demonstrates a technique for improving readability by using final int variables as names for indices. By defining atlanta, chicago, dallas, losAngeles, and newYorkCity to be variables with fixed values equal to their corresponding array indices, you can use the following method call:

```
distanceBetweenCities(Chicago, newYorkCity);
```

This statement is much easier to read than the following equivalent:

```
distanceBetweenCities(1, 4);
```

4.10 BIT VECTORS

The performance advantages of using arrays as tables motivate a specialized implementation strategy for certain kinds of setlike containers. This strategy is based on an implementation structure known as a **bit vector**. A bit vector is actually a one-dimensional array of boolean. (The history of the name "bit vector" comes from the fact that "bit" is short for "binary digit." A binary digit has one of two values—0 or 1—just like a boolean value, which can be either false or true.)

The bit vector strategy devotes one cell of the boolean array to each potential set element. For any particular set, if the potential element is a set element, its corresponding cell is assigned true; if the potential element is not in the set, its corresponding cell is assigned false. Figure 4.29 shows three possible sets of decimal digits and their bit vector representations.

Figure 4.29 Three sets of decimal digits and their bit vector representations

Abstract Set	Abstract Set	Abstract Set
{2, 3, 5, 7}	{0, 1, 8, 9}	{ }

Bit Vector		Bit Vector		Bit Vector	
: boolean[]		**: boolean[]**		**: boolean[]**	
[0]	false	[0]	**true**	[0]	false
[1]	false	[1]	**true**	[1]	false
[2]	**true**	[2]	false	[2]	false
[3]	**true**	[3]	false	[3]	false
[4]	false	[4]	false	[4]	false
[5]	**true**	[5]	false	[5]	false
[6]	false	[6]	false	[6]	false
[7]	**true**	[7]	false	[7]	false
[8]	false	[8]	**true**	[8]	false
[9]	false	[9]	**true**	[9]	false

The boolean arrays shown in Figure 4.29 can store any set as long as the elements of the set are restricted to decimal digits (0 through 9). Another good candidate for the bit vector implementation is a set of alphabetic letters. Unicode encodes all alphabetic letters in two consecutive groups: one for uppercase letters, and a second one for lowercase letters. A bit vector implementation of any set of uppercase alphabetic letters can map the letter "A" to an index of zero, the letter "B" to an index of 1, the letter "C" to an index of 2, and so forth. Figure 4.30 shows a portion of the implementation of a set of uppercase letters.

Figure 4.30 UpperAlphaSet a bit vector implementation

```
public class UpperAlphaSet {
    private boolean[] isElement;
    /* post:  isElement.length == 26
              and forAll(j: 0<=j<=25 | isElement[j] == false) */
    public UpperAlphaSet() {
        isElement = new boolean[26];
        for (int k=0; k != 26; k++) {
            isElement[k] = false;
        }
    }
    /* pre:   'A' <= c <= 'Z' (throws IllegalArgumentException)
       post:  isElement[c - 'A'] == true */
    public void add(char c) {
        if ('A' <= c && c <= 'Z') {
            isElement[c - 'A'] = true;
        } else {
            throw new IllegalArgumentException();
        }
    }
    /* post:  'A'<=c<='Z' implies result == isElement[c - 'A']
              and (c<'A' OR c>'Z') implies result == false */
    public boolean isIn(char c) {
        if ('A' <= c && c <= 'Z') {
            return isElement[c - 'A'];
        } else {
            return false;
        }
    }
    // ADDITIONAL METHODS OMITTED.
}
```

The UpperAlphaSet constructor method instantiates the boolean array, called isElement, with 26 cells: one cell for each uppercase letter from "A" through "Z." To create an empty set, this constructor also assigns all array cells the value false.

The add method uses the array's direct access facility with a simple expression (c – 'A') to translate an uppercase letter into its corresponding bit vector index. The isIn method uses the same expression to test for set membership in a single probe of an array cell.

A bit vector set implementation results in O(1) run-time performance for set operations such as add, remove, and isIn. However, this excellent performance comes at a cost. A bit vector implementation is viable only if the collection of potential set elements is a relatively small group that can be efficiently mapped onto array indices. (In Java, array indices must be consecutive integers counting from zero.) If all potential set elements are decimal digits, the consecutive indices from 0 through 9 match the potential elements exactly. If all the potential set elements are odd integers from 1 through 101, the int expression ((j–1)/2) converts any potential set element into an index within the range 0 through 50. If all the potential set elements are lowercase letters, the expression (c – 'a') converts any lowercase letter of char type into an index within the range 0 through 25.

Bit vectors impose a different kind of restriction than does a bounded container with restricted size. Not only does a bit vector restrict the cardinality of the implemented set, but it also places restrictions on the potential elements that can be included in the set. This restriction limits the applicability of bit vectors for various containers.

4.11   FINITE STATE MACHINES

Some of the best known of all table-driven algorithms are based on a model known as a **finite state machine** (FSM). A finite state machine has five parts:

- A set of **states**
- A **start state** (which is an element of the set of states)
- A set of potential **conditions** (and/or events)
- A **transition function** that defines how to progress from one state to the next
- An **action function** that associates an action with each transition

State machines are typically pictured in **state diagram** form as a group of bubbles (one for each state) and arcs (one for each transition and associated action). Following is a portion of a state machine containing two states (*Before Fill* and *Overflow*) and a transition (the arrow connecting the two states).

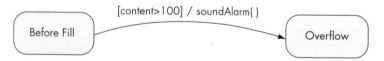

The transition arrow is labeled with a condition or event (or both) under which such a transition occurs. This condition or event is the first part of any transition label (to the left of a forward slash, "/", symbol). The picture indicates that a transition occurs from state *BeforeFill* to state *Overflow* exactly when the "content > 100" condition is satisfied. Optionally, transition labels can include an associated action. The proper UML notation for conditions and actions is to place the forward slash symbol after the condition and before the action. The diagram associates the soundAlarm() action with the transition between states.

State diagrams are useful for describing the run-time behavior of a program. The preceding state diagram means that when the program is in the *BeforeFill* state and content is greater than 100, the result will be to sound an alarm and transition to the *Overflow* state.

As an example of using a state diagram to model a more comprehensive system, consider a refrigerator with a built-in water dispenser. This particular dispenser, pictured in Figure 4.31, has three buttons to select between water, ice cubes, and crushed ice. Pressing any of the three buttons lights the LED lamp directly above the button and inserting a glass in the dispenser causes the device to dispense a predetermined amount of the most recently selected item.

Figure 4.31 Ice and water dispenser in refrigerator door

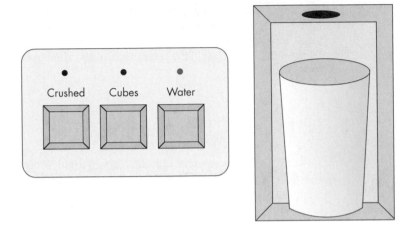

The behavior of the ice and water dispenser can be explained in the form of the state diagram shown in Figure 4.32. This diagram shows three states, corresponding to the three items that can be dispensed. In any state, four events can occur:

- A glass can be inserted into the dispenser (symbolized as event "G").
- The Crushed button can be pressed (symbolized as event "CR").
- The Cubes button can be pressed (symbolized as event "CU").
- The Water button can be pressed (symbolized as event "W").

Because it is possible for any of the four events to occur at any time, each state has four outgoing transitions. Only three arcs are drawn per state arc because three arcs combine two transitions.

Figure 4.32 also illustrates that an arc can connect one state to itself. This occurs from the *ReadyforWater* state when either the Water button is pressed or a glass is inserted into the dispenser. Such so-called **self-loops** are included because the associated events do not change state, but they do result in an action.

One of the states in Figure 4.32, *ReadyforWater*, has an unlabeled incoming arc connected to a black dot. This arrow is not really an arc; instead, this black-dot notation points to the start state. A start state is the state in which behavior begins. Presumably, when the refrigerator is first plugged in to electricity, it will be in the *ReadyforWater* state.

As a second complete state machine example, consider a user interface for selecting colors. This particular interface consists of three buttons (Red, Green, and Blue) and always selects one of six possible colors. The particular color that is selected results from mixing the last two buttons that were pressed. Therefore, pressing Red followed by Blue (or Blue followed by Red) sets the color to magenta, and pressing Green followed by Green sets the color to green. Figure 4.33 contains a state diagram for this behavior.

Figure 4.32 State machine for ice and water dispenser

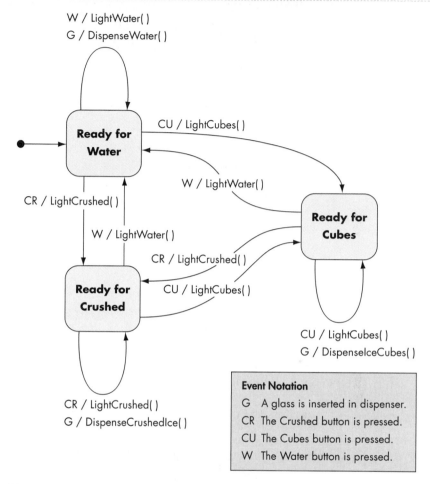

The states in Figure 4.33 do not maintain the selected color; instead, they retain the color of the last button pressed. For example, if the Blue button is pressed from any state, the transition will arrive at the *Blue* state. This use of states allows for proper modeling of behavior that wouldn't be possible if the states maintained the selected color.

State machines are good for clarifying run-time behavior that might otherwise be unclear. For example, the three-button color selector state diagram makes it clear that when the program begins to execute, the first button pressed selects the color to match the button.

As a third sample state machine, consider a cipher lock system, such as those sometimes employed on the car doors. This particular cipher lock has three buttons, labeled A through E. The cipher lock waits for the user to enter a four-key sequence. If the key sequence is correct, the door opens; otherwise, an alarm buzzer sounds. Figure 4.34 shows a state diagram for the particular cipher lock that has the combination "BAAD".

Figure 4.33 State machine for three-button color selector

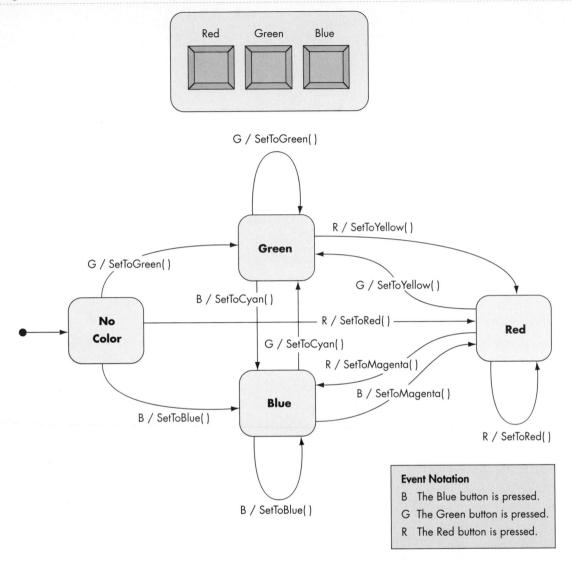

The cipher lock state diagram points out two frequently used abbreviations for events. The "any" notation signifies the occurrence of any possible event. The only events of concern for this state machine result from pressing one of the five cipher lock keys. It is less cluttered to use the term "any" than to list all five keys individually.

The second abbreviation is the word "other," which means any event except those listed explicitly. The "other" notation applies to the outgoing transitions from a state. Therefore, the *other* transition for the arc from *NoKeysEntered* to *FailAfter1* means that either A or C or D or E was pressed, and the other transition from *OKAfter2* to *FailAfter3* means that either B or C or D or E was pressed.

Figure 4.34 State machine for "BAAD" combination on cipher lock

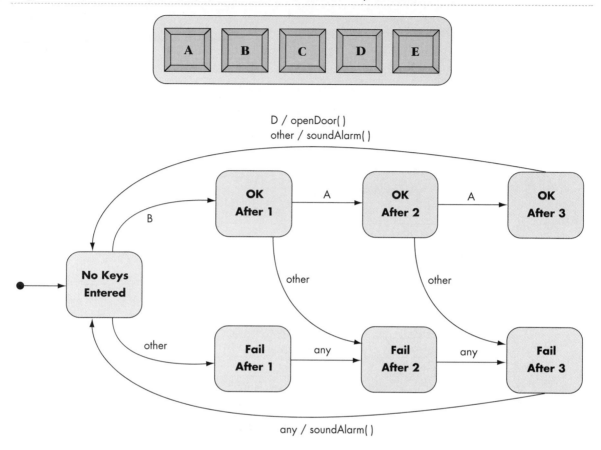

Many state machines can be directly translated into highly efficient table-driven algorithms. Such algorithms are based on the insight that transitions and actions can be characterized as two tables. One of these tables, often called the **transition table**, stores the transition function of the state machine. The other table, sometimes called the **action table**, stores the action associated with all transitions. Figure 4.35 illustrates the transition and action tables for the cipher lock state diagram.

The transition table and the action table have an identical number of rows and columns. Each table has a separate row for each state and a separate column for each possible event or condition from the state machine. The entries in the transition table indicate the state following the transition, sometimes called the *next state*. In other words, the entry in the *OK After 1* row and the column labeled B indicates that from state *OK After 1* a B event (pressing the B key) should make a transition into the *Fail After 2* state.

The action table also contains entries that are appropriate for the outgoing transition from a state and an event or condition. The entries in the action table are actions. The action table in Figure 4.35 contains many empty entries to represent transitions that have no associated action.

Figure 4.35 Transition and action tables for cipher lock state machine

Transition Table

	A	B	C	D	E
No Keys Entered	Fail After 1	OK After 1	Fail After 1	Fail After 1	Fail After 1
OK After 1	OK After 2	Fail After 2	Fail After 2	Fail After 2	Fail After 2
OK After 2	OK After 3	Fail After 3	Fail After 3	Fail After 3	Fail After 3
OK After 3	No Keys Entered	No Keys Entered	No Keys Entered	No Keys Entered	No Keys Entered
Fail After 1	Fail After 2	Fail After 2	Fail After 2	Fail After 2	Fail After 2
Fail After 2	Fail After 3	Fail After 3	Fail After 3	Fail After 3	Fail After 3
Fail After 3	No Keys Entered	No Keys Entered	No Keys Entered	No Keys Entered	No Keys Entered

Action Table

	A	B	C	D	E
No Keys Entered					
OK After 1					
OK After 2					
OK After 3	soundAlarm()	soundAlarm()	soundAlarm()	openDoor()	soundAlarm()
Fail After 1					
Fail After 2					
Fail After 3	soundAlarm()	soundAlarm()	soundAlarm()	soundAlarm()	soundAlarm()

The graphical form of a state diagram makes it possible to overlook possible transitions. The transition and action tables avoid this potential pitfall by including a row for every state and a column for every event or condition. Therefore, the tables exhaust every potential situation. In addition, the "any" and "all" state diagram transitions are enumerated by individual table columns.

To translate transition and action tables into two-dimensional arrays, you begin by mapping the rows and columns onto integers. Because rows are numbered with `int` values, the transition table entries also should be of type `int`. For the cipher lock problem, the corresponding Java code can be written as follows. Note that the transition table is called `nextState`.

```
private int noKeysEntered = 0;
private int okAfter1 = 1;
private int okAfter2 = 2;
private int okAfter3 = 3;
private int failAfter1 = 4;
private int failAfter2 = 5;
private int failAfter3 = 6;
private int[][] nextState =
    {  {failAfter1, okAfter1, failAfter1, failAfter1, failAfter1},
       {okAfter2, failAfter2, failAfter2, failAfter2, failAfter2},
```

```
    {okAfter3, failAfter3, failAfter3, failAfter3, failAfter3},
    {noKeysEntered, noKeysEntered, noKeysEntered, noKeysEntered,
        noKeysEntered},
    {failAfter2, failAfter2, failAfter2, failAfter2,
        failAfter2},
    {failAfter3, failAfter3, failAfter3, failAfter3,
        failAfter3},
    {noKeysEntered, noKeysEntered, noKeysEntered, noKeysEntered,
        noKeysEntered}};
```

Representing the action table in Java is slightly more complicated because Java does not allow arrays to store methods. One solution uses the template design pattern in the form of a StateAction interface with a performAction method and separate subclasses that provide their own unique implementations of performAction(), corresponding to the different actions of the state machine. Figure 4.36 illustrates.

Figure 4.36 StateAction interface and implementations

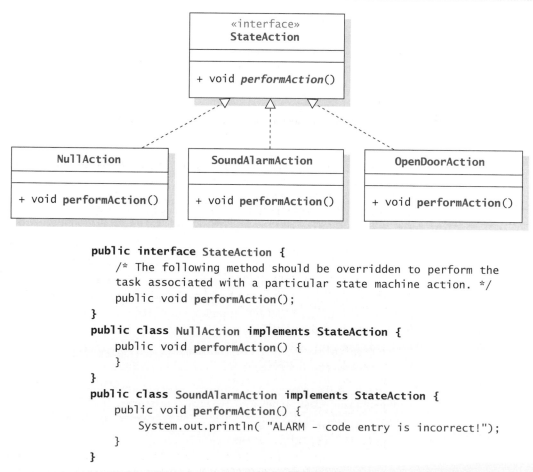

```
public interface StateAction {
    /* The following method should be overridden to perform the
    task associated with a particular state machine action. */
    public void performAction();
}
public class NullAction implements StateAction {
    public void performAction() {
    }
}
public class SoundAlarmAction implements StateAction {
    public void performAction() {
        System.out.println( "ALARM - code entry is incorrect!");
    }
}
```

Continued on next page

```
public class OpenDoorAction implements StateAction {
    public void performAction() {
        System.out.println( "Correct code. The door opens.");
    }
}
```

The action table can be represented as an array of StateAction in which the objects of the array belong to the appropriate StateAction implementations. One object for each kind of action is sufficient. Using this technique, you can create the action table for the cipher lock problem with the following code:

```
private StateAction nullAction = new NullAction();
private StateAction soundAlarm = new SoundAlarmAction();
private StateAction openDoor = new OpenDoorAction();
private StateAction[][] actionTable =
    {   {nullAction, nullAction, nullAction, nullAction, nullAction},
        {nullAction, nullAction, nullAction, nullAction, nullAction},
        {nullAction, nullAction, nullAction, nullAction, nullAction},
        {soundAlarm, soundAlarm, soundAlarm, openDoor, soundAlarm},
        {nullAction, nullAction, nullAction, nullAction, nullAction},
        {nullAction, nullAction, nullAction, nullAction, nullAction},
        {soundAlarm, soundAlarm, soundAlarm, soundAlarm, soundAlarm}
    };
```

Given properly initialized transition and action tables, you can emulate a state machine with two short code segments. The first segment declares a variable to maintain the state throughout the emulation and to assign this variable the value of the start state. The following statement accomplishes these two tasks for the cipher lock problem:

Software Engineering Hint

Emulating a state machine by using table-driven code based on the transition and action tables can be a highly efficient solution for expressing an algorithm. This solution is worth considering, especially when the number of states and conditions is relatively small.

```
private int currentState = noKeysEntered;
```

The second code segment handles each event or condition that corresponds to a state machine transition. This code must cause the action associated with the transition to be performed and must assign currentState the state following the transition. The following code accomplishes these two tasks, assuming that buttonInt stores the integer of the column associated with the transition and action tables (buttonInt==0 for column A, buttonInt==1 for column B, and so forth).

```
actionTable[currentState][buttonInt].performAction();
currentState = nextState[currentState][buttonInt];
```

Figure 4.37 shows a complete FsmEmulator class and the associated CipherButton class. The FsmEmulator class initializes the actionTable and nextState arrays and constructs a window (javax.swing.JFrame) that contains five

CipherButton objects. The actual emulation of the finite state machine occurs in an event-driven fashion. Each time the user clicks one of the buttons, the actionPerformed method is called. Using the button's title (A , B, C, D, or E) and the current state, this method calls the performAction method of the proper object (either nullAction, soundAlarm, or openDoor). Each button click also causes the current state to be updated using the button's title and prior state.

Figure 4.37 FsmEmulator and CipherButton classes

```java
import javax.swing.*;
import java.awt.event.*;
public class FsmEmulator implements ActionListener {
    private CipherButton[] buttons;
    private int noKeysEntered = 0;
    private int okAfter1 = 1;
    private int okAfter2 = 2;
    private int okAfter3 = 3;
    private int failAfter1 = 4;
    private int failAfter2 = 5;
    private int failAfter3 = 6;
    private int[][] NextState = {
        {failAfter1, okAfter1, failAfter1, failAfter1, failAfter1},
        {okAfter2, failAfter2, failAfter2, failAfter2, failAfter2},
        {okAfter3, failAfter3, failAfter3, failAfter3, failAfter3},
        {noKeysEntered, noKeysEntered, noKeysEntered, noKeysEntered,
            noKeysEntered},
        {failAfter2, failAfter2, failAfter2, failAfter2, failAfter2},
        {failAfter3, failAfter3, failAfter3, failAfter3, failAfter3},
        {noKeysEntered, noKeysEntered, noKeysEntered, noKeysEntered,
            noKeysEntered}
    };
    private StateAction nullAction = new NullAction();
    private StateAction soundAlarm = new SoundAlarmAction();
    private StateAction openDoor = new OpenDoorAction();
    private StateAction[][] actionTable = {
        {nullAction, nullAction, nullAction, nullAction, nullAction},
        {nullAction, nullAction, nullAction, nullAction, nullAction},
        {nullAction, nullAction, nullAction, nullAction, nullAction},
        {soundAlarm, soundAlarm, soundAlarm, openDoor, soundAlarm},
        {nullAction, nullAction, nullAction, nullAction, nullAction},
        {nullAction, nullAction, nullAction, nullAction, nullAction},
        {soundAlarm, soundAlarm, soundAlarm, soundAlarm, soundAlarm}
    };
```

Continued on next page

```
        private int currentState;
    /* post:   A JFrame has been instantiated that contains five
                buttons titled 'A' through 'E'.
       note:   this.ActionPerformed is the event handler for all
                five buttons */
    public FsmEmulator() {
        JFrame window = new JFrame();
        window.setBounds(10, 10, 270, 90);
        window.getContentPane().setLayout(null);
        buttons = new CipherButton[5];
        for (int j=0; j != 5; j++) {
            buttons[j] = new CipherButton(10+j*50, 10, 50,
            (char)(j+'A'));
            buttons[j].addActionListener(this);
            window.getContentPane().add(buttons[j]);
        }
        currentState = noKeysEntered;
        window.show();
    }
    /* pre:    noKeysEntered <= currentState <= failAfter3
                and 'A' <= {integerValOfEventButton} <= 'E'
       post:   the action from actionTable[currentState@pre]
                    [integerValOfEventButton]
                    has been performed
                and currentState nextState[currentState@pre]
                    [integerValOfEventButton] */
    public void actionPerformed(ActionEvent e) {
        int buttonInt = intValueOfButton(e.getSource());
        actionTable[currentState][buttonInt].performAction();
        currentState = NextState[currentState][buttonInt];
    }
    /* post:   result == the int equivalent of the title on btn
                (result== 0 for 'A', ==1 for 'B', ..., =4 for 'E')
                */
    private int intValueOfButton(Object btn) {
        return ((CipherButton)btn).getText().charAt(0) - 'A';
    }
}
import javax.swing.JButton;
/* invariant: 'A' <= getText() <= 'E' */
public class CipherButton extends JButton {
    private char symbol;
    /* pre:    'A' <= c <= 'E' (throws IllegalArgumentException)
       post:   this button has upper left corner at (x, y)
                and getWidth() == getHeight() == s
                and getText() == c */
```

Continued on next page

```
public CipherButton(int x, int y, int s, char c) {
    super();
    if (c < 'A' || c > 'E') {
        throw new IllegalArgumentException();
    } else {
        setBounds(x, y, s, s);
        setText(c+"");
    }
}
```
}

One of the strengths of a finite state machine emulator, such as the one shown in Figure 4.37, is that it produces a highly efficient algorithm. Each click of a button uses an array look-up in the nextState array to find the state transition and uses another array look-up in the actionTable array to find the associated action. These array look-ups eliminate a potentially lengthy collection of *if* instructions to test for various situations.

Another advantage of the FSM emulator is that you can easily adapt it to work for virtually any algorithm that can be described by a finite state machine. You must properly initialize the actionTable and nextState arrays for the particular finite state machine, and you must alter the action objects and possibly the event generating objects (buttons in this case). However, the crux of the finite state machine emulator found in the actionPerformed method does not change.

THE SOFTWARE INSPECTOR

Following is a collection of hints on what to check when you perform desk checks that involve the concepts of this chapter.

✓ The first step in the transition from abstraction to implementation is to select a representation. You should always review a class to ensure that the representation is adequately explained. This includes not only *what* data structures will be used but also *how* they are used.

✓ Using an inner class to implement the Iterator interface is a good alternative and not only for arrays.

✓ For any of the following three conditions, you may prefer using the Vector class over an array. (Otherwise, arrays tend to lead to faster algorithms and cleaner notation.)
  • The array size is extremely unpredictable.
  • You need to apply equals or toString on the array.
  • The array class should be subclassed.

✓ When reviewing code with multidimensional arrays, remember that they can be viewed as a grid or as an array of arrays. Sometimes one of these two views is far more useful than the other.

✓ You should examine code to identify occasions when table-driven code might be a suitable alternative. Table-driven code often has performance advantages and sometimes adds flexibility.

✓ State machines are a good tool for diagramming run-time behavior as a part of any code or design review.

✓ Certain algorithms are conveniently implemented by way of a state machine emulator. Generally, the number of states and the sizes of the transition and action tables must be relatively small for this alternative to be viable.

EXERCISES

1. Show the output that results from executing each of the following segments of code.

   a.
```java
double[] wallaby, kangaroo;
wallaby = new double[4];
kangaroo = new double[4];
for (int j = 0; j != 4; j++) {
   wallaby[j] = j;
}
```

```
      for (int j = 0; j != 4; j++) {
        kangaroo[j] = wallaby[j];
      }
      for (int j = 0; j != 4; j++) {
        kangaroo[j] = j*2;
      }
      for (int j = 0; j != 4; j++) {
        System.out.println(wallaby[j] );
        System.out.println(kangaroo[j] );
      }
b. double[] snow, ice;
   snow = new double[5];
   for (int j = 0; j != 5; j++) {
     snow[j] = j;
   }
   ice = snow;
   ice[0] = ice[0] * 10;
   for (int j = 0; j != 5; j++) {
     System.out.println( ice[j] );
     System.out.println( snow[j] );
   }
c. int[][] grid;
   int counter = 1;
   grid = new int[3][2];
   for (int row = 0; row != grid.length; row++) {
     for (int col=0; col != grid[0].length; col++) {
       grid[row][col] = counter;
       counter++;
     }
   }
   for (int col = 0; col != grid[0].length; col++) {
     for (int row=0; row != grid.length; row++) {
       System.out.println( grid[row][col] );
     }
   }
d. double[][] values = { {1.2, 3.4, 5.6},
                         {7.8, 9.0},
                         {3.3},
                         {9.9, 8.8, 7.7, 6.6, 5.5} };
   for (int row = 0; row != values.length; row++) {
     for (int col=0; col != values[0].length; col++) {
       System.out.println( values[row][col] );
       counter++;
     }
   }
```

2. Use the following class to complete parts (a) through (c).

```
public class GameScore {
    protected int homeTeam;
protected int visitingTeam;
    /* post:   homeTeam == h
               and visitingTeam == v */
    public GameScore(int h, int v) {
        homeTeam = h;
        visitingTeam = v;
    }
    /* post:   result == homeTeam */
    public int pointsForHomeTeam() {
        return homeTeam;
    }
    /* post:   result == visitingTeam */
    public int pointsForVisitingTeam() {
        return visitingTeam;
    }
}
```

a. Draw an object diagram that pictures the result of executing the following statement.

```
GameScore[] twoGames = new GameScore[2];
```

b. Show the code for declaring an array and assigning it the following collection of game scores. (Be certain to use a separate assignment statement to assign each game to an array cell.)

Home Team Score	Visiting Team Score
8	3
2	6
0	3

c. Show how to accomplish the same task as in part (b) using a single statement.

3. Complete the code to implement each of the following methods to be correct with respect to the given specifications.

a.
```
/* pre: a != null
   post: result == value of first cell of a */
public char firstChar(char[] a)
```

b.
```
/* pre: a != null
   post: result == value of last cell of a */
public char lastChar(char[] a)
```

c.
```
/* pre: a != null
   post: forAll(j: 0<=j<=a.length-2 | a[j+1] == a@pre[j]) */
public void shiftRight(char[] a)
```

d.   /* **post:** result.length = 5
            and *forAll*(j: 0<=j<=4 | result[j] == null) */
       public String[] emptyCells()

4.   How many total cells are there in each of the following arrays?

a. char[][] letters = new char[4][5];

b. char[][] letters = { {'a', 'b', 'c'},
                        {'c', 'd'},
                        {'e', 'f', 'g', 'h'},
                        {'i', 'j'}
                        {'k', 'l', 'm'} };

c. char[][] letters = new char[3];
   letters[0] = new char[2];
   letters[1] = new char[3];
   letters[2] = new char[4];

d. char[][][][] letters = new char[4][5][6][7];

5.   Show the code for an equals method that could be added to the BoundedSetArray class from Figure 4.4 and the representation without duplicates that is pictured by Figure 4.8. Your method must accept a second BoundedSetArray as a parameter and must return true exactly when the two BoundedSetArray objects represent the same abstract set.

6.   Repeat Exercise 5 using the Figure 4.10 representation that permits duplicates.

7.   Show how to modify the SimpleSequenceArray class from Figure 4.13 to support an iterator that can move *both* forward and backward. Specifically, use ListIterator, instead of Iterator, including an implementation of the following two additional methods: **hasPrevious**() and **previous**().

8.   Assume that an office has four employees and uses an intercom to communicate. The employee and their intercom numbers are as follows.

Employee	*Intercom Number*
Tim	1
Jennifer	2
Sara	3
Joe	4

Using the style of Figures 4.25 and 4.26, show how to initialize an array table and write a method to retrieve the name (a String value) given the intercom number of an employee.

9. Consider the following method and explain how it can be rewritten as table-driven code. (You may assume that the method is called only when $0 \le c \le 7$.)

```java
public double cowsMilk( int c ) {
    double milkAmt = 0.0;
    if ( c == 1 ) {
        milkAmt = 1.0;
    } else if ( c == 0 || c == 2 ) {
        milkAmt =1.1;
    } else if ( c == 3 ) {
        milkAmt =1.2;
    } else if ( c >= 4 && c <= 6 ) {
        milkAmt =1.3;
    } else if ( c == 7 ) {
        milkAmt =1.4;
    }
    return milkAmt;
}
```

10. Draw a picture of the bit vector content for the following set: {1, 4, 9}

11. Use the following finite state machine to complete parts (a) through (c).
    a. Show the precise output that results from the following input: *xywwxw*
    b. Draw a picture of the transition table for this FSM.
    c. Draw a picture of the action table for this FSM.

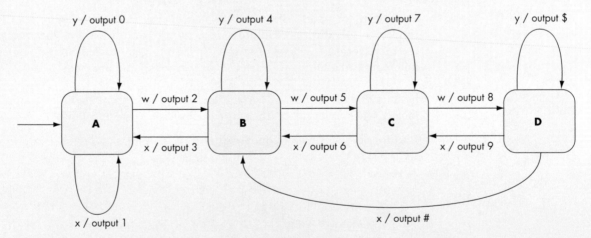

12. Draw the picture of a finite state machine that accepts an input alphabet of only the capital letter A and the capital B and produces output in the following way. The FSM counts consecutive A's (up to three A's in length). After the first A in a consecutive sequence, a "1" is output. After the second A, a "2" is output. After the third A a "3" is output. A fourth consecutive A causes the counting restart at "1". Any input of B results in the output of "X".

Following is some sample input with the corresponding output.

input →   B A B A A B A A A B A A A A A B A
output →   X 1 X 1 2 X 1 2 3 X 1 2 3 1 2 X 1

13. Create a finite state machine to model the following situation: An automobile cruise control system has three buttons:

- An On/off button to activate the system
- A Set button to set the cruise control at the current speed
- A Resume button to reset the cruise control a previously set speed

The cruise control is inactive when the On/off button is set to Off, and it has no memory of prior use. While the system is on, the auto's speed can be set by pressing the Set button. This speed is maintained until the brake pedal is pressed, the Set button is pressed again, or the On/off button deactivates the system. As long as the cruise control is active, the most recent set speed is "remembered" so that pressing the Resume button returns the vehicle to the speed that is remembered. There is no remembered speed at the time the cruise control is turned on, so pressing Resume has no effect.

PROGRAMMING EXERCISES

1. Use an array to implement the `SequenceOfObject` ADT as defined in Chapter 2, and use your implementation to solve the Pick-3 simulation as described in Programming Exercise 3 of Chapter 2.

2. Programming Exercise 4 of Chapter 2 describes a bag ADT. Provide an array implementation for the `BagOfInt` class described in this exercise, and use it to complete the associated programming assignment.

3. Write array implementations for the `BagOfInt` and `SequenceOfInt` ADTs described in Programming Exercise 5 of Chapter 2, and use these two classes to complete the associated programming assignment.

4. Complete any of Programming Exercises 1–3 using `Vector` implementations.

5. Design, implement, and test a program to simulate a robot randomly moving about a grid. You should assume that the grid is nine by nine cells, with walls around the outside. The robot starts in the center grid cell, and every second it moves to a different cell. The robot can turn only in 90-degree increments and has limited speed, so the only choices for the next move are the four neighboring cells (above, below, left, and right). The robot has a visual sensor, so it won't attempt to move into any wall. Your program should simulate the robot's movements for 1,000 seconds and then report how many times the robot occupies each grid cell. It is best to start this exercise by designing an ADT or two.

6. The bit vector concept can be extended to multidimensional tables. For example, you can store a set of four-letter words by using a four-dimensional

array of Boolean and using the first dimension to represent the first letter of the word, the second dimension as the second letter, the third dimension as the third letter, and the fourth dimension as the fourth letter.

Use this technique to design and implement a `SetOfFOURLetterWords` class. Use this set to design, implement, and test a program that accepts user input strings and reports all the four-letter words from this string that happen to be Java reserved words. The list of all Java reserved words that are four letters long is as follows:

```
byte, case, cast, char, else, goto, long, null, rest, this,
true, void
```

7. A Cambridge mathematician, John Conway, created a puzzle that has fascinated thousands following its original publication in the October 1970 issue of *Scientific American*. The puzzle is called simply "the game of life," and it is played on a two-dimensional grid of squares. The game simulates a population in which each square is either alive or dead, and squares can be born or die as the game proceeds. The grid of squares must be initialized to contain initial ("first generation") cells consisting of a mixture of live and dead cells. Thereafter, each "next generation" is calculated from the preceding generation. The rules are based on the concept of a "neighborhood." Each cell has a neighborhood of no more than eight cells and consists of those cells that are adjacent to it (including diagonal adjacency). If the neighborhood of cell c has zero, one, four or more live cells, then cell c will be dead in the next generation. If the neighborhood of cell c has exactly three live neighbors, then cell c will be alive in the next generation. If the cell's neighborhood has exactly two live neighbors, then it does not change state (it remains dead or alive in the next generation).

Design, implement, and test a program to play this game of life, simulating no fewer than 100 generations. You may display the generations using `javax.swing` graphics (with colored squares for live cells and white squares for dead cells) or in the form of nine lines of text per generation ("X" characters are output for live cells, and blanks for dead cells).

8. Design, implement, and test a program to simulate a simple vending machine. This assignment is really a two-part project: (1) Write the code for a general-purpose finite state machine emulator, and (2) use your FSM emulator to simulate the actions of a beverage vending machine.

The particulars of an FSM are to be read from either a file or input lines. The format of this input is as follows:

1. A single `int` value is the number of states in the FSM.

2. A single `int` value is the size of the input alphabet.

3. A sequence of `char` values (the exact number is given by the second input `int`). These `char` values are the potential input symbols for the FSM. (No duplicates are permitted.)

4. A sequence of `int` values to indicate the transition table. (The exact number of these `int` values was given by the first `int` times the second `int`.)

Each of these values indicates the next state for one entry in the transition table. The table is given row by row (row == state), and states are numbered from 0 up to 1 less that the first input int.)

5. A sequence of String values to indicate the output table. (The exact number of these String values was given by the first int times the second int.) Each of these values indicates the output symbol for one entry in the transition table. The table is given row by row (row == state). (Note: State 0 is assumed to be the start state.)

INPUT:
2
2
'0' '1'
1 1
0 0
"X" "X"
"Z" "N"

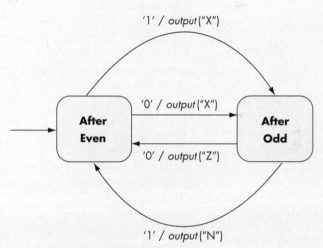

The second part of the assignment is to use your FSM emulator to emulate the following beverage vending machine:

The beverage machine accepts nickels, dimes, and quarters and has a selection button for tea and another for coffee. The FSM should model this machine using these input symbols:

Input Symbol	*Meaning*
N	Nickel inserted
D	Dime inserted
Q	Quarter inserted
T	Tea button pressed
C	Coffee button pressed

(The machine rejects any coin that causes the total inserted to exceed 30¢; otherwise, the inserted coin's value is added to the total.) Tea costs 20¢ and coffee costs 25¢. If the machine total is the exact amount for a selected beverage, then the machine dispenses the beverage upon request. If the total exceeds the cost of the selected beverage, then the overage is returned. (After dispensing a beverage, the machine's total always returns to 0¢.) If the total is insufficient for a selected beverage, the machine emits a buzz. The FSM models these actions with the following output symbols.

Output symbol	Meaning
–	Accept coin
N	Reject nickel
D	Reject dime
Q	Reject quarter
T	Dispense tea and return no change
C	Dispense coffee and return no change
T5	Dispense tea and return 5¢
T10	Dispense tea and return 10¢
C5	Dispense coffee and return 5¢
Z	Buzz

CHAPTER 5

DYNAMIC DATA

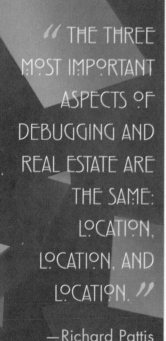

" THE THREE MOST IMPORTANT ASPECTS OF DEBUGGING AND REAL ESTATE ARE THE SAME: LOCATION, LOCATION, AND LOCATION. "

—Richard Pattis

OBJECTIVES

• To review the concept of variables of reference type, focusing on a two-part representation in memory (variable memory and object memory)

• To present three kinds of data lifetime: static, automatic, and dynamic

• To examine the singleton design pattern as a technique for sharing objects among other objects

• To review Java dynamic memory instantiation and object memory orphans

• To explore the concept of encapsulating a variable within a class of the same type, as a means of linking objects to one another

• To examine a singly linked list ADT with built-in iterator

• To present a linked implementation for the singly linked list ADT

• To examine specialized strategies for implementing linked lists, including header cells and prepointers

One common children's toy is a collection of snap-together blocks, such as those manufactured by Lego. These blocks can be connected in various three-dimensional geometries. A new block can be connected to the outside of a group, or a block from the group can be removed. Snapping and unsnapping blocks in the middle of a structure lets you expand or contract the overall size of the structure.

The flexibility of these tiny blocks contrasts with fundamental limitations of arrays. Arrays can be efficient data structures, but this efficiency comes at a cost. An array occupies contiguous space inside the computer's memory. Once an array is instantiated, it has a fixed size. This makes the array analogous to a fixed number of toy blocks connected in one particular geometry. You cannot append new cells to the end of an array without creating another, larger array. You cannot insert or remove cells from the middle of an array, and inserting new content into an array often requires you to shift existing content to make space.

This chapter focuses on some of the details of the data storage options in Java, especially the concept of dynamic data. The chapter culminates with an examination of how to use dynamic data to implement linear structures. These dynamic data structures present the same kind of flexibility exhibited by the toy blocks.

5.1   DATA LIFETIME

At the heart of an understanding of how computer data is manipulated is the concept of **data lifetime**. To appreciate lifetime issues, it is important to understand the actual form and presence of data at run-time. During program execution every piece of data (every variable, every parameter, every referenced object) must occupy a certain amount of the computer's memory space. The Java virtual machine, together with the computer's operating system, manages this memory space.

Different kinds of data occupy different amounts of memory space. An int variable occupies four bytes of memory space, a char variable occupies two bytes, and a double occupies eight bytes.

Primitive variables use their memory space in a somewhat different manner than reference variables. The memory allocated to an int variable stores the actual integer value of the variable. However, a reference variable, such as a variable belonging to the Integer wrapper class, stores a **reference** to an object. For example, consider the execution of the following two statements.

```
int intVar = 3;
Integer integerVar = new Integer(3);
```

This code involves two variables: a primitive variable called intVar, and a reference variable called integerVar. Following the execution of the two statements, both variables will occupy a certain amount of memory space, but they will use that space in different ways. Figure 5.1 illustrates.

The object diagram in Figure 5.1 shows the result of executing the code segment. The intVar variable has been assigned the value 3, and the integerVar variable is bound to an object that contains the value 4. The memory space portion of this figure approximates how computer memory might reflect the object diagram.

The memory of a computer consists of a large array of electronic storage cells, each pictured in Figure 5.1 as a small rectangle. Each memory cell, more properly called a **word**, stores an item of data. Each memory word also has a unique **address**. A memory address is used by computer hardware to identify the related word of memory.

Figure 5.1 Example object diagram and memory space for reference and primitive data

Code

```
int intVar = 3;
Integer integerVar = new Integer(4);
```

Object Diagram (following execution of the code)

intVar == 3

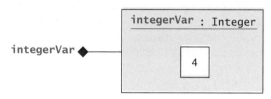

Computer Memory Space (following execution of the code)

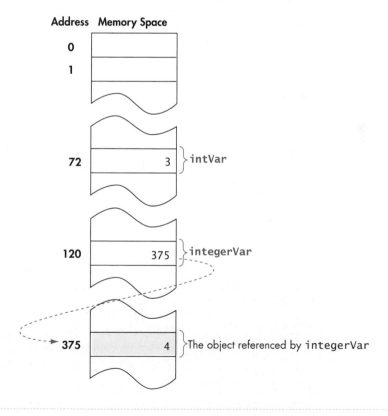

At run-time, each primitive variable is associated with its own word(s) of memory space. Figure 5.1 shows that the address of memory space that happens to be associated with `intVar` is at address 72. The value of `intVar` is stored in this same memory space (i.e., in word 72).

Reference variables involve two pieces of memory space. The reference variable itself occupies a memory word(s) of sufficient size to reference the second portion of memory that stores the object. The object diagram depicts the `integerVar` address as a diamond-headed line connected to the object containing the wrapper integer 4. The memory space picture reveals that `integerVar` is associated with memory address 120, and the content of the reference is another address—namely, the address of the object to which `integerVar` is bound. The address in this case is 375, which is the location in memory where the wrapper object containing 4 is stored. A nonnull reference variable always occupies two such separate portions of memory space: one for the variable that stores the address of the object, and a second one for the object.

To examine data it is helpful to think of two kinds of data storage:

- variable memory
- object memory

Variable memory is the memory space that is directly associated with the variable. The variable memory for a variable of primitive type stores the value of the variable. The variable memory for a variable of reference type stores an address.

Object memory is used to store any nonprimitive object. A variable that references such an object stores the object's address within its variable memory. In Figure 5.1 the variable memory for `intVar` has an address of 72, and the variable memory for `integerVar` has an address of 120. The object memory associated with `integerVar` has the address 375. Reference variables are sometimes called **pointers** because their variable memory can be thought of as pointing to their object memory.

The memory space required for program execution changes as the program executes. Every time the `new` keyword is executed, a new object is instantiated, and therefore additional object memory is required. When a method completes executing and returns, the variable memory for the method's local variables is no longer needed. These comings and goings of data, and their associated memory space, are called the **lifetime** of the data.

Every piece of data has a lifetime corresponding to the length of execution time during which that datum must occupy memory space. A variable's lifetime begins when words of memory are set aside (**allocated**). The lifetime of a variable ends when its variable memory is **deallocated**. Deallocated memory space does not generally remain unused. Instead, it is usually repurposed for some other variable or object memory required by future code execution.

There are three basic lifetime classifications:

- static data
- automatic data
- dynamic data

Data with **static** lifetime is allocated when the program begins executing, and it isn't deallocated until the program completes. The name "static" is appropriate because this memory space remains in use throughout program execution. Section 5.2 examines a particular type of static memory using Java's `static` modifier.

Automatic lifetime results from executing certain statements that automatically allocate or deallocate memory space. In Java, three kinds of data result in automatic lifetime.

- The variable memory for any local variable of a method
- The variable memory for any method parameter
- The variable memory for any variable declared within a *for* loop

Whenever a method is called, the variable memory for all its local variables and its formal parameters is automatically allocated. Whenever the method returns, all this variable memory is automatically deallocated. Similarly, the variable memory for a variable that is declared within the initialization clause of a *for* loop has a lifetime that is the same as the loop's execution time.

Automatic lifetime in Java applies only to variable memory, whereas **dynamic** lifetime applies only to object memory. Furthermore, all object memory exhibits dynamic lifetime. The name "dynamic" stems from the fact that this type of data allocation and deallocation occurs during program execution and depends on the particular statements that execute. Java uses the keyword `new` to denote instantiation, and each instantiation results in the allocation of object memory. Section 5.3 examines dynamic lifetime in more detail.

As an example of the relationship between automatic memory and dynamic memory, consider the partial class shown in Figure 5.2.

Figure 5.2 LifetimeSample class

```java
public class LifetimeSample {
    private Integer instanceInteger;
    public LifetimeSample() {
    }
    // The following method is including solely to illustrate data
    // lifetime
    public void manipulateVars {
        Integer localInteger;
        instanceInteger = new Integer(1);
        localInteger = new Integer(2);
    }
    . . .
}
```

The `LifetimeSample` class contains two variables of interest: an instance variable called `instanceInteger`, and a local variable of the `manipulateVars` method, called `localInteger`. The lifetime of the variable memory for `instanceInteger` is the same as the lifetime of the associated `LifetimeSample` object. For example, executing the following instruction creates a `LifetimeSample` object, necessarily allocating variable memory for the enclosed `instanceInteger`.

```
LifetimeSample oneLifetimeSample = new LifetimeSample();
```

Such variable memory for an instance variable remains intact as long as its object is viable. However, if the following instruction is subsequently executed, the `instanceInteger` variable memory may be deallocated.

```
oneLifetimeSample = null;
```

The deallocation of `instanceInteger` happens when `oneLifetimeSample` is the only remaining reference to its object. When no references to object memory remain, that memory is inaccessible to the program. It is proper to say that the lifetime of `instanceInteger` object ends when all its references are gone.

Executing the `manipulateVars` method demonstrates other potential lifetimes. The execution of the three statements in this method is described in the comments that follow.

```
Integer localInteger;
    //the variable memory for localInteger was allocated
instanceInteger = new Integer(1);
    //a new object (variable memory) was allocated
    //and is referenced by instanceInteger
localInteger = new Integer(2);
    //a new object (variable memory) was allocated
    //and is referenced by localInteger
```

When the `manipulateVars` method completes execution and returns, the variable memory for `localInteger` is automatically deallocated. This deallocation causes the associated object to be left without a reference, also ending its lifetime. The lifetimes of both the variable and the object memory for `instanceInteger` are not affected by returning from `manipulateVars`.

5.2 THE SINGLETON DESIGN PATTERN

Java permits the use of **static variables**. Static variables are declared within a class, as are instance variables, except that a `static` modifier is inserted before the data type. The `static` modifier changes the lifetime of a variable.

Each `static` variable has variable memory with static lifetime. This means that a variable declared to be `static` exists even though its enclosing object has not yet been instantiated. This is made possible by another characteristic of static variables: There is only *one* instance of a particular static variable, regardless of the number of objects that are instantiated. In other words, each static variable is implemented by a single unit of variable memory with static lifetime. This characteristic of a single shared variable per class, as opposed to one variable instance per object, is the reason that static variables are sometimes called **class variables** in Java. A class variable can be named either with a class or an object prefix, followed by a period and the variable name.

Figure 5.3 contains two classes that illustrate the differences between instance variables and class variables. The only significant difference between them is that NonStaticThing (on the left) has a String instance variable called thing, whereas StaticThing (on the right) has a class variable called sThing.

To demonstrate the different behavior of these two classes, consider the following code segment.

```
NonStaticThing ns1, ns2;
ns1 = new NonStaticThing("A");
ns2 = new NonStaticThing("Z");
```

Figure 5.3 NonStaticThing and StaticThing classes

```
public class NonStaticThing {
    public String thing;
    public NonStaticThing(String s) {
        if (thing == null)
            thing = new String(s);
    }
}
```

```
public class StaticThing {
    public static String sThing;
    public StaticThing(String s) {
        if (sThing == null)
            sThing = new String(s);
    }
}
```

Figure 5.4 contains three object diagrams that show the state of computation following each statement's execution.

Before instantiation, Java reference variables are initialized to null. Therefore, the execution of the following statement executes the *then* clause within NonStaticThing to construct a new object with a thing instance variable that references a copy of the String argument "A":

```
ns1 = new NonStaticThing("A");
```

The second statement instantiates ns2 in the same way. Because the instance variable ns2 is null, ns2 will be initialized so that ns.thing references a copy of the String "Z".

Figure 5.4 A trace of NonStaticThing calls using object diagrams

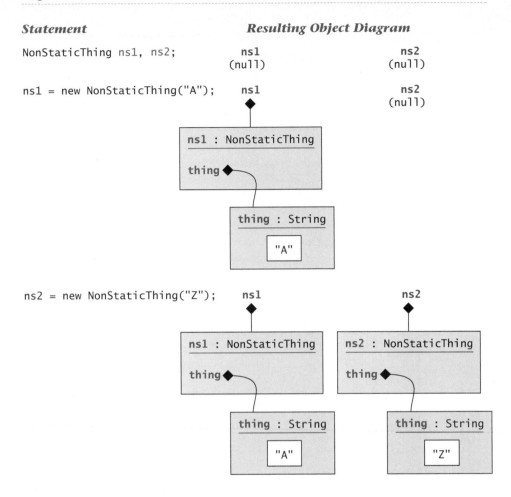

Next, consider an analogous code segment using StaticThing objects, instead of NonStaticThing objects. Figure 5.5 shows this code and the associated trace.

The trace of the code segment involving StaticThing begins with three separate units of allocated variable memory. The s1 and s2 variables are each associated with variable memory following their declaration. The third unit of variable memory is associated with the static (class) variable called sThing. Because sThing is declared to be a class variable, its variable memory is allocated statically once, and only once, for any program using the StaticThing class. Figure 5.5 illustrates this static variable memory by using the StaticThing.sThing notation. The top object diagram shows that StaticThing.sThing is null initially.

When the following statement executes, the StaticThing method is called to instantiate the s1 object:

```
s1 = new StaticThing("A");
```

Figure 5.5 A trace of StaticThing calls using object diagrams

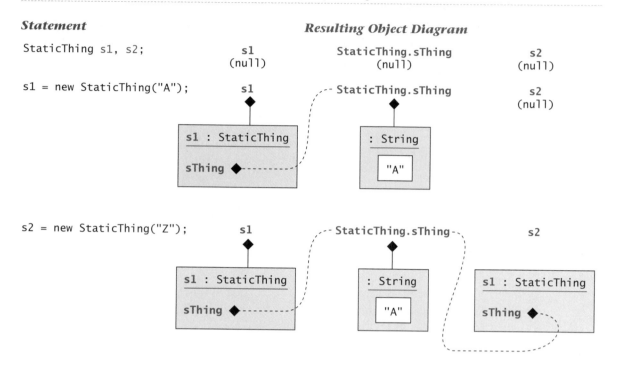

This newly created object is not permitted to have its own copy of sThing because sThing is static. Therefore, the s1 object must use variable memory that is assigned to StaticThing.sThing. The middle object diagram in Figure 5.5 depicts this situation by way of the dashed line, which denotes that s1.sThing is nothing more than a synonym for StaticThing.sThing.

The impact of declaring thing as static is further demonstrated by executing the third statement:

```
s2 = new StaticThing("A");
```

The s2 variable is obligated to share the same sThing variable as s1. In fact, there are now three names for this same variable: s1.sThing, s2.sThing, and StaticThing.sThing. When the s2 constructor method executes, sThing is non-null, having been assigned an object by the previous constructor call for object s1.

Class variables have static variable memory, but they may be assigned differing values throughout program execution, so any associated object memory cannot have static lifetime. Figure 5.5 shows an example for which each call to the StaticThing constructor instantiates a new object and assigns that object to StaticThing.sThing.

Class variables do not follow the usual Java mechanisms of encapsulating data within objects. However, class variables are still a useful part of the object-oriented approach because they provide a tool for solving the occasional problem that requires an approach other than the use of independent objects.

For example, suppose that a program involves objects known as `Tribbles`. Each `Tribble` object is to be numbered with the sequence number of its instantiation. (The first `Tribble` to be instantiated is numbered 1, the second is numbered 2, and so forth.) Further suppose that `Tribble` objects can be created in many ways by different parts of the program, so there is no central location where it is convenient to maintain a `Tribble` count. The use of a `Tribble` class variable allows `Tribbles` to "count themselves." Figure 5.6 contains the relevant parts of such a `Tribble` class.

> **Software Engineering Hint**
>
> Just because Java calls them "static" doesn't mean that everything about static variables is fixed. In fact, the variable memory has static lifetime, but the object memory is dynamic, unless the final modifier is also included in the declaration.

Figure 5.6 Tribble class

```java
public class Tribble {
    private static int totalTribbleCount;
    private int tribbleID;
    /* post:   totalTribbleCount == totalTribbleCount@pre + 1
               and tribbleID == totalTribbleCount */
    public Tribble() {
        totalTribbleCount++;
        tribbleID = totalTribbleCount;
    }
    . . .

}
```

The `Tribble` class maintains a count of the total number of `Tribble` objects that have been created in the form of the class variable called `totalTribbleCount`. Because it is declared as `static`, the `totalTribbleCount` variable is shared by all `Tribble` objects. Like all int variables, `totalTribbleCount` has a default initial value of zero. Therefore, the first instantiation of a `Tribble` object will cause `totalTribbleCount` to be incremented to 1; the second instantiated `Tribble` will increment `totalTribbleCount` to 2; the third instantiation increments to 3; and so forth.

> **Software Engineering Hint**
>
> Class variables should be considered as a last resort. Often it is possible to use an instance variable of a shared object in place of a class variable, and such an alternative tends to be easier to read.

By itself, the `totalTribbleCount` variable is insufficient to maintain the particular number of any one `Tribble`. Whenever a new `Tribble` object is instantiated, the value of `totalTribbleCount` changes, not only for the newly instantiated `Tribble` but also for every other `Tribble`. The `Tribble` class solves the problem of maintaining unique ID numbers by including a second variable called `tribbleID`. The `tribbleID` variable is an instance variable, so each `Tribble` object maintains its own copy of this variable. Having just incremented the `totalTribbleCount` class variable, the `Tribble` constructor immediately assigns a copy of this new value in the `tribbleID` variable. The `tribbleID` variable reliably maintains a different number for each individual `Tribble` object.

Using a class variable to provide a single, shared variable occurs so often that it is recognized as a design pattern: the singleton design pattern. Figure 5.7 describes this pattern in more detail.

Figure 5.7 Singleton design pattern

Intent

to provide a variable that can be shared among many different objects

Structure (class diagram)

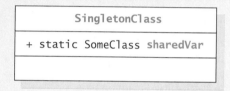

Explanation

Some class, here called `SingletonClass`, includes a static variable. Any object can access this same shared variable using the notation

   `SingletonClass.sharedVar`

Inside `SingletonClass` the same variable can alternatively be referenced as follows:

   `sharedVar`

The same variable can be referenced using a reference to any instantiated object (`singletonRef`) belonging to `SingletonClass` and the following notation:

   `singletonRef.sharedVar`

The *public* declaration of `sharedVar`, shown above, is not an essential part of this pattern. Often, the shared variable is private and shared only among objects of like type.

Example

The `Tribble` class in Figure 5.6 demonstrates the singleton design pattern with `totalTribbleCount` as a shared variable.

The singleton design pattern, as described in Figure 5.7, is designed to share a single piece of variable memory among various parts of a program. Java also provides a mechanism for sharing a single piece of object memory in singleton fashion. Such data is declared to be *both* `static` and `final`. Two rules are associated with any variable that is final.

1. The variable must be assigned a value either in its declaration statement or once within the class constructor.
2. The variable cannot be assigned a value except as described in Rule 1.

These two rules ensure that a static final variable is fixed (constant). If it is of primitive type, the static final variable has a fixed value (i.e., the value assigned within the declaration or by the first constructor call) for the duration of the program execution. If it is of reference type, the static final variable will be bound to the same object throughout program execution. Effectively, such object memory exhibits a kind of static lifetime (although its allocation may be delayed until the constructor call).

The java.lang.Math class includes a static final variable called PI that is declared as follows:

```
public static final double PI = 3.141592653589793;
```

Any class that wishes to use this value of the mathematical constant known as π need only reference Math.PI to access the single copy of this variable. The following statements are examples.

```
double area = radius * radius * Math.PI;
double circumference = radius * 2 * Math.PI;
```

The utility of static final variables is further evident in the java.awt.Color class. This class includes the following 13 static final variables that represent the corresponding Color objects.

```
Color.black
Color.blue
Color.cyan
Color.darkGray
Color.gray
Color.green
Color.lightGray
Color.magenta
Color.orange
Color.pink
Color.red
Color.white
Color.yellow
```

Each of these colors is a reference variable that is assigned to an object within its declaration. Therefore, every object that uses Color.blue is referencing the same Color.blue object. In this way, you can compare colors by way of identity equality checks such as the following that would otherwise be impossible.

```
if (myRectangle.getForeground() == Color.blue) ...
```

Software Engineering Hint

The use of "==" to test for a **Color** value is a bit risky because the **Color** class also provides ways to create the same colors without using the static final names.

Figure 5.8 illustrates this concept by extending the Color class to include two new colors: purple and brown. Both variables are static and final, and both are assigned values within their declaration statements.

Figure 5.8 MoreColor Class

```java
import java.awt.Color;
public class MoreColor extends Color {
    public final static Color purple = new Color(128, 0, 128);
    public final static Color brown = new Color(128, 96, 64);

    /* post:   this color is black */
    public MoreColor() {
        super(0, 0, 0);
    }
}
```

The `Color` constructor method, used to instantiate `purple` and `brown`, gives color values in terms of redness, greenness, and blueness, respectively. The amount of intensity for each color is an integer within the range 0 through 255, with 255 denoting maximum intensity. Therefore, the expression

```java
new Color(0, 0, 0)
```

creates a `Color` object representing the color black, and the expression

```java
new Color(255, 255, 255)
```

creates a `Color` object representing the color white.

The `MoreColor` class inherits all 13 of the `Color` class variables. Therefore, you can assign a foreground color to a `javax.swing.JFrame` window—call it `win`—via the following statement:

```java
win.setForeground( MoreColor.yellow );
```

You can also use the two new colors in the same way:

```java
win.setForeground( MoreColor.brown );
win.setBackground( MoreColor.purple );
```

5.3 DYNAMIC DATA ALLOCATION AND DEALLOCATION

Object memory—except for that of a `final static` variable—exhibits dynamic lifetime. This means that executing statements determine when memory for Java objects is allocated and deallocated.

Object allocation is overt. Every time the `new` keyword executes, another object is instantiated, resulting in the allocation of additional object memory to the executing program.

Although the `new` notation signals allocation, there is no explicit Java notation for deallocation. Instead, Java deallocates object memory whenever the object becomes an **orphan**: an object for which no references remain. In other words, whenever no part of the program's memory space stores the address of a particular unit of object memory, the associated object has been orphaned. An orphan is no longer accessible to the program, so its object memory is dispensable.

An orphan occurs from one of two actions:

- The only remaining reference to the object is assigned a different address.
- The only remaining reference to the object is deallocated (orphaned).

Figure 5.9 traces a sequence of statements that exhibits how orphans result from executing assignment statements.

The four statements begin by instantiating two Double objects and assigning them to the variables d1 and d2. This program has no other reference to either of these two objects. The execution of the d1=null; assignment statement causes the object previously bound to d1 (the object containing 3.7) to be orphaned. The execution of the statement d2=new Double(9.5); binds the d2 variable to a new object, thereby orphaning its prior object binding (to the object containing 6.8).

The second way that an object can be orphaned is for its only reference to be deallocated (orphaned). Such an orphan results when the following method returns:

```
private void orphanMaker() {
    Double d = new Double( 0.1 );
}
```

This orphanMaker method has a local variable, d, that is instantiated by its declaration statement. When this method returns, the d variable is deallocated because it has automatic lifetime. When d is deallocated, the only reference to its object is

Figure 5.9 A trace of the creation of orphans by assignment statements

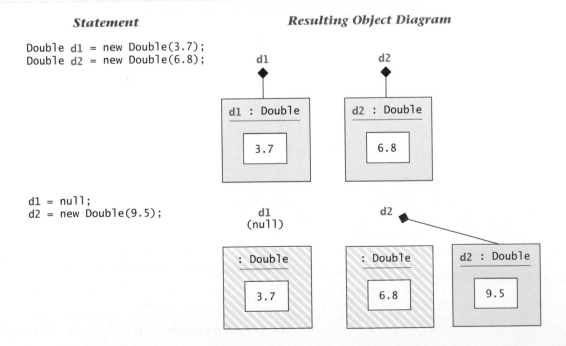

lost, so the object is orphaned. This same kind of orphaning occurs to an object—call it A—when some other object is orphaned and the newly orphaned object contains the only remaining reference(s) to A.

> **Software Engineering Hint**
>
> Orphans are essentially harmless in a language, such as Java, that incorporates garbage collection. However, allocating and deallocating objects still consumes time, so it is a good habit to avoid unnecessary orphan creation.

Orphans are of concern to every programmer. An orphan occupies memory space for no purpose, because the orphan is useless to the executing program. In some programming languages orphans are called **memory leaks** because these language systems cannot recover the orphaned object memory. Memory leaks become particularly problematic if they recur; the program continues to waste increasing amounts of memory space, sometimes resulting in program failure.

Fortunately, Java is among those languages that do not permit orphans to turn into memory leaks. In Java, orphans are automatically recovered by a technique known as **garbage collection**. The Java virtual machine includes a garbage collection mechanism that periodically searches out orphans and recovers all orphaned memory so that it can be repurposed. A Java programmer need not worry that an orphan is wasting memory.

5.4   OBJECTS REFERENCING LIKE OBJECTS

It might seem a bit unusual, but there is nothing to prohibit an object from including references to objects that belong to its own class. In fact, this technique is used to create many widely used data structures. Figure 5.10 contains an example of such a class, called `WithPublicLink`.

Figure 5.10 `WithPublicLink` Class

```
/*  note
        This class is used to illustrate linking, but is not
        recommended for general use because of the use of public
        instance variables. */
public class WithPublicLink {
    public int content;
    public WithPublicLink another;

    /*  post:   content == 0
                and another == null */
    public WithPublicLink() {
        content = 0;
        another = null;
    }
}
```

The key portion of `WithPublicLink` is the variable `another`, which has a type of `WithPublicLink` (i.e., the class containing `another` is the class to which `another` belongs). Such variables are sometimes called **links** because they can be used to link objects that belong to the same class. To illustrate this kind of linking, consider the following statement:

```
WithPublicLink stuff = new WithPublicLink();
```

The object diagram that describes the result of executing this statement looks like this:

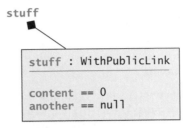

Suppose that the following statement is executed next.

```
stuff.content = 1;
```

The object diagram is altered to appear as follows.

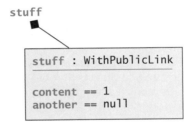

The another attribute of stuff also can be assigned a value by executing the following statement:

```
stuff.another = new WithPublicLink();
```

This statement instantiates a new object and assigns its reference to stuff.another. The following object diagram illustrates.

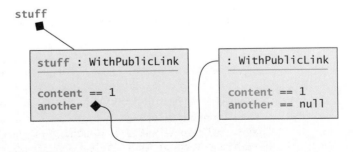

At this stage of program execution, one object is referenced by stuff and the second object is referenced by the another attribute of the first object. An acceptable Java notation for referencing the second object is stuff.another:

```
stuff.another.content = 2;
```

Executing this statement alters the object diagram as follows.

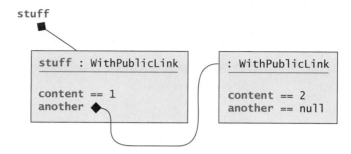

Suppose the program continues to execute the following two statements:

```
stuff.another.another = new WithPublicLink();
stuff.another.another.content = 3;
```

Here is the resulting state.

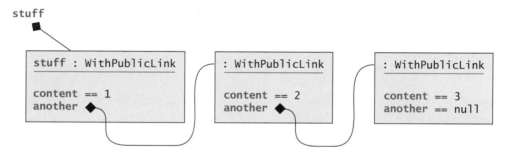

The preceding sample statements illustrate how appending a suffix of .another to a WithPublicLink object reference results in an expression for the linked object. Note that the lifetime of objects referenced only by links is seemingly tenuous. For example, the execution of the following statement would orphan the rightmost two objects shown earlier.

```
stuff.another = null;
```

Furthermore, if the stuff variable is deallocated, all the WithPublicLink cells, whether they are directly referenced or indirectly linked, are orphaned.

5.5 A DYNAMIC APPLICATION

The linear arrangement of linked dynamic cells constructed in Section 5.4 can be used directly to represent abstract data types. The structure is particularly effective for representing an ordered container that changes in size or requires that items be inserted or removed from within. One good candidate for such an implementation is a deck of playing cards. Programs that use a deck of cards need to do things such as shuffle the deck, draw one card, and insert a card within the deck.

Figure 5.11 contains the Java code for a PlayingCard class. Each PlayingCard object represents a single playing card. This class implements an ADT, including abstract PlayingCard specifications.

Figure 5.11 PlayingCard class

```
/* domain: Every playing card has a value and a suit
   invariant: 2 <= value <= ace
              and spades <= suit <= hearts */
public class PlayingCard {
    private int value;
    public static final int jack = 11;
    public static final int queen = 12;
    public static final int king = 13;
    public static final int ace = 14;

    private int suit;
    public static final int spades = 0;
    public static final int clubs = 1;
    public static final int diamonds = 2;
    public static final int hearts = 3;
    public static final char[] suitChar = {'S', 'C', 'D', 'H'};
    public static final String[] valueStr
    = {"0","1","2","3","4","5","6","7","8","9","10","J","Q","K","A"};

    /* pre:   2<=v<=ace and spades<=s<=hearts
                 (throws IllegalArgumentException)
       post:  value == v and suit == s */
    public PlayingCard(int v, int s) {
        if (v<2 || v>ace || s<spades || s>hearts) {
            throw new
                IllegalArgumentException("invalid playing card");
        } else {
            value = v;
            suit = s;
        }
    }

    /* post:   result == suit */
    public int cardSuit() {
        return suit;
    }

    /* post:   result == value */
    public int cardValue() {
        return value;
    }

    /* post:   result == value == z.value and suit== z.suit */
    public boolean equals(Object z) {
        if (!(z instanceof PlayingCard))
            return false;
```

Continued on next page

```
        else
            return value == ((PlayingCard)z).value
                        && suit == ((PlayingCard)z).suit;
    }


    /*  post:   result == the card value followed by a suit char */
    public String toString() {
        return valueStr[value] + suitChar[suit];
    }
}
```

PlayingCard includes two variables, called `value` and `suit`, that are used to store the card's numeric value and its suit. The class also includes `static final` variables to make it more convenient to express the four suits and nonnumeric card values (i.e., jack, queen, king, and ace). Declaring these variables to be `static` is sensible because the same values will be used by all playing cards. If they were not declared as `static`, a deck of 52 playing cards would require memory for 52 separate `jack` variables, 52 separate `queen` variables, and so forth. Similarly, the `suitChar` and `valueStr` arrays are `static final` tables for translating a suit or value into a printable form. These two arrays assist in the implementation of `toString`.

The `PlayingCard` ADT is useful for describing the more complex `DeckOfCards` ADT. Figure 5.12 offers a class diagram and specifications for `DeckOfCards`.

Figure 5.12 DeckOfCards class diagram and specifications

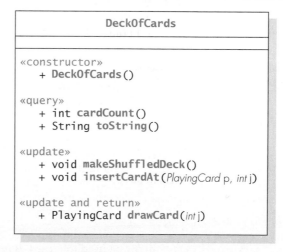

DeckOfCards ADT Specifications

Domain

Every `DeckOfCards` object consists of a *sequence* of `PlayingCard`

Continued on next page

Constructor Method

```
public DeckOfCards( )
```
   post: theSeq == *sequence*{}

Query Methods

```
public int cardCount( )
```
   post: result == this->*size*()

```
public String toString( )
```
   post: result == all sequence items in order and separated by commas

Update Methods

```
public void makeShuffledDeck( )
```
   post: cardCount() == 52
      and this == a sequence of all 52 different playing cards in a
      random order

```
public void insertCardAt(PlayingCard p, int j)
```
   pre: 1 <=j<=cardCount()+1 (throws IllegalArgumentException)
   post: this == this@*pre* with p inserted at position j

Update and Return Method

```
public PlayingCard drawCardFrom(int j)
```
   pre: 1 <=j<=cardCount() (throws IllegalArgumentException)
   post: this == this@*pre* with the item removed from position j
      and result == this@*pre*->*at*(j)

The DeckOfCards class includes methods to inspect the number of cards in a deck (cardCount), to create a complete and shuffled deck of 52 cards (makeShuffled-Deck), to insert a card into the deck at any given position (insertCardAt), and to draw a card from any specified location in the deck (drawCardFrom).

> ### Software Engineering Hint
>
> Generally, it is best for methods to be *either* non-void or mutators. However, sometimes it is acceptable for a method to do both. The **drawCard** method is an example of such a dual-purpose method. The justification in this case is that such behavior is more consistent with the way humans use a deck of cards.

The drawCardFrom method is consistent with the way card decks are used, but it is a bit unusual for a method because it is *both* a query method and an update method. A call to drawCardFrom returns one of the cards from the deck and simultaneously removes this card from the deck.

Figure 5.13 shows an example of how the DeckOfCards class might be used in a card playing program. This program performs the following tasks.

- Creates a complete and shuffled deck of 52 cards
- "Deals" five cards from the top of the deck, displaying each card
- Removes and displays the 10th card from the deck
- Reinserts the 10th card at a random position in the deck
- Displays the resulting deck

Figure 5.13 A sample class for playing cards

```
public class Driver {
    public static void main(String[] args) {
        DeckOfCards deck = new DeckOfCards();
        PlayingCard oneCard;
        deck.makeShuffledDeck();
        for (int k=1; k!=6; k++) {
            oneCard = deck.drawCardFrom(1);
            System.out.println( oneCard );
        }
        oneCard = deck.drawCardFrom(10);
        System.out.println( oneCard );
        deck.insertCardAt(oneCard,
            (int)(Math.random()*(deck.cardCount()+1))+1);
        System.out.println("---");
        System.out.println(deck);
    }
}
```

The DeckOfCards class makes a good candidate for a linked implementation because the number of cards in a deck varies and because cards can be inserted and removed (dealt) from anywhere within the deck. Figure 5.14 demonstrates such a DeckOfCards implementation.

Figure 5.14 DeckOfCards implementation

```
/* invariant:  firstCell links to a linear linked list of playing
               card cells */
public class DeckOfCards {
    private CardCell firstCell;
    private int cellCount;
    private class CardCell {
        public CardCell nextCell;
        public PlayingCard card;
        /* post:   card == p and nextCell == null */
        public CardCell(PlayingCard p) {
            card = p;
            nextCell = null;
        }
    }

    /* post:   firstCell == null and cellCount == 0 */
    public DeckOfCards() {
        firstCell = null;
        cellCount = 0;
    }
```

Continued on next page

```java
/*  post:   result == cellCount */
public int cardCount() {
    return cellCount;
}


/*  post:   result == all sequence items in order and separated
                     by commas */
public String toString() {
    String result;
    if (cellCount == 0)
        result = "(This deck contains no cards.)";
    else {
        result = firstCell.card.toString();
        CardCell cellLink = firstCell;
        for (int j = 1; j!=cellCount; j++) {
            cellLink = cellLink.nextCell;
            result = result + ", " + cellLink.card.toString();
        }
    }
    return result;
}


/*  post:   firstCell links to a list of 52 cards that repesent
            a randomly sorted complete deck. */
public void makeShuffledDeck() {
    PlayingCard aCard;
    for (int v=2; v!=PlayingCard.ace+1; v++) {
        for (int s=PlayingCard.spades;
                 s!=PlayingCard.hearts+1; s++) {
            aCard = new PlayingCard(v, s);
            insertCardAt(aCard,
                (int)(Math.random()*(cellCount+1))+1);
        }
    }
}


/*  pre:    1<=j<=cellCount+1 (throw IllegalArgumentException)
    post:   firstCell links to a list of 52 cards that represent
            a randomly sorted complete deck.
            and cellCount == cellCount@pre + 1 */
public void insertCardAt(PlayingCard p, int j) {
    if (j < 1 || j > cellCount+1) {
        throw new
            IllegalArgumentException("invalid position in card
            deck");
    } else {
        CardCell newCell = new CardCell(p);
```

Continued on next page

```
            if (j==1) {
                newCell.nextCell = firstCell;
                firstCell = newCell;
            } else {
                CardCell cell = firstCell;
                for (int k=1; k!=j-1; k++)
                    cell = cell.nextCell;
                newCell.nextCell = cell.nextCell;
                cell.nextCell = newCell;
            }
            cellCount++;
        }
    }


    /*  pre:    1<=j<=cellCount (throw IllegalArgumentException)
        post:   the structure from firstCell == the structure
                    from firstCell@pre with the jth cell removed
                and cellCount == cellCount@pre - 1 */
    public PlayingCard drawCardFrom(int j) {
        CardCell resultCell;
        if (j < 1 || j > cellCount) {
            throw new
                IllegalArgumentException("invalid position in card
                deck");
        } else {
            if (j==1) {
                resultCell = firstCell;
                firstCell = firstCell.nextCell;
            } else {
                CardCell cell = firstCell;
                for (int k=1; k!=j-1; k++)
                    cell = cell.nextCell;
                resultCell = cell.nextCell;
                cell.nextCell = cell.nextCell.nextCell;
            }
        }
        cellCount-;
        return resultCell.card;
    }
}
```

The ADT specifications define DeckOfCards in terms of an OCL *sequence*. However, the DeckOfCards class in Figure 5.14 uses a collection of cells (a list of cells) that are linked in much the same way as the dynamic data cells presented in Section 5.4. For example, Figure 5.15 shows a particular deck of three cards defined as an abstract sequence, along with the list data structure used by DeckOfCards to implement this collection. The linked structure is pictured as an object diagram.

Figure 5.15 DeckOfCards abstract view and object diagram

Abtract view of one particular DeckOfCards (as a sequence)

sequence{ KingOfHearts, 2ofClubs, 7ofSpades }

Object diagram corresponding to above abstraction

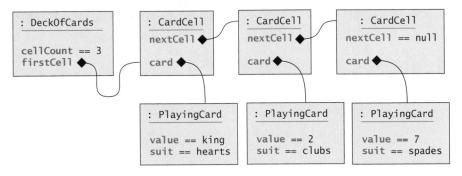

As pictured in Figure 5.16, DeckOfCards contains two instance variables: cellCount and firstCell. The cellCount variable is used to maintain the number of cards in the deck. For the Figure 5.15 example, the deck contains three playing cards, so cellCount == 3.

Figure 5.16 DeckOfCards class diagram showing inner class

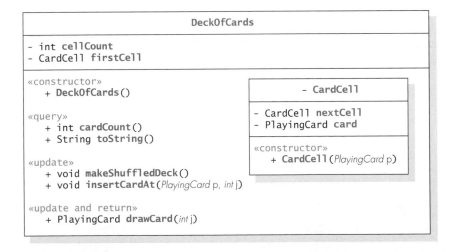

As its name implies, the firstCell variable stores a reference to the first cell in a linked structure. This structure contains a separate cell for each card in the deck, and each cell, except the last, links to the next cell. The order of the cells matches the order of the playing cards.

The DeckOfCards implementation uses an inner class to declare the type of the dynamic cells used in the list. In this case, the inner class, called CardCell, is declared with a private scope so as to encapsulate cell access within the DeckOfCards class. This inner class structure is pictured in the class diagram in Figure 5.16.

Each CardCell object contains two variables: nextCell and card. The nextCell variable serves to link each cell (except the last) with its successor. The last cell is identifiable as the only cell in the list for which nextCell==null. The card variable of CardCell is used as a reference to the particular PlayingCard object in this position of the deck.

The DeckOfCards methods illustrate typical algorithms for manipulating linked list structures. The DeckOfCards constructor uses the following two statements to initialize the list to contain zero playing cards:

```
firstCell = null;
cellCount = 0;
```

Notice that firstCell == null is a signal that the list (deck of cards) is empty.

The makeShuffledDeck method consists of two loops to generate all 52 possible playing cards. Each playing card is generated by its face value (from 2 through ace) and its suit (from spades through hearts). For a face value, v, and a suit, s, the following two statements insert the card into the deck:

```
aCard = new PlayingCard(v, s);
insertCardAt(aCard, (int)(Math.random()*(cellCount+1))+1);
```

This card insertion selects a random location from 1 through the number of cards (cellCount) plus 1. The insertCardAt method does the actual insertion.

The insertCardAt method is called to insert a new card, given by the p parameter, into the list so that it becomes the jth cell. The key portion of the code for this method is as follows:

```
// error case omitted
CardCell newCell = new CardCell(p);
if (j==1) {
    newCell.nextCell = firstCell;
    firstCell = newCell;
} else {
    CardCell cell = firstCell;
    for (int k=1; k!=j-1; k++)
        cell = cell.nextCell;
    newCell.nextCell = cell.nextCell;
    cell.nextCell = newCell;
}
cellCount++;
```

This code begins by creating a new cell for the list, referenced by newCell. The *else* clause is selected when inserting anywhere except the first position. This algorithm begins with a loop to position the cell variable so that it references the (j−1)st cell. The key assignment statement is

```
cell = cell.nextCell;
```

Each execution of this statement advances the cell variable to reference the successor of the cell it previously referenced.

Figure 5.17 demonstrates the behavior of `insertCardAt` for all cases except an insertion at position 1 (i.e., this figure shows the *else* clause behavior). The value of the `cell` variable following the *for* loop is included in the picture.

Calling `insertCardAt` to insert at the front of the deck (j == 1) is a special case that must be handled differently from other insertions. Inserting at the front of the list is the only time that an insertion changes `firstCell`. The behavior of this insertion is shown in Figure 5.18.

The `drawCardFrom` method also has two separate cases to be considered. The non-error portion of this method's code is as follows:

```
CardCell resultCell;
//error case omitted
if (j==1) {
    resultCell = firstCell;
    firstCell = firstCell.nextCell;
} else {
    CardCell cell = firstCell;
    for (int k=1; k!=j-1; k++)
        cell = cell.nextCell;
    resultCell = cell.nextCell;
    cell.nextCell = cell.nextCell.nextCell;
}
cellCount--;
return resultCell.card;
```

Figure 5.17 Behavior of `insertCardAt( QueenOfHearts, 3)`

Behavior of insertCardAt(p, j) for p == *QueenOfHearts* and j == 3

Before

sequence{ *KingOfHearts, 2ofClubs, 7ofSpades* }

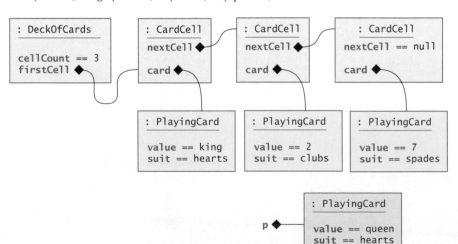

Continued on next page

After

   sequence{ *KingOfHearts, 2ofClubs, QueenOfHearts, 7ofSpades* }

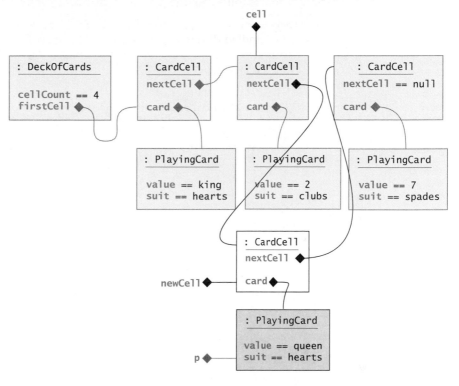

Figure 5.18 Behavior of insertCardAt(QueenOfHearts, 1)

Behavior of insertCardAt(p, j) for p == *QueenOfHearts* and j == 1

Before

   sequence{ *KingOfHearts, 2ofClubs, 7ofSpades* }

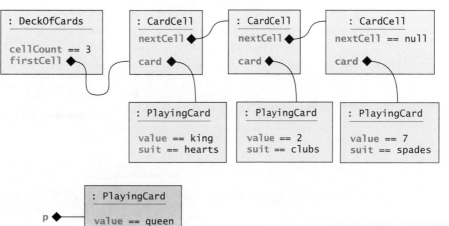

Continued on next page

After

   sequence{ QueenOfHearts, KingOfHearts, 2ofClubs, 7ofSpades }

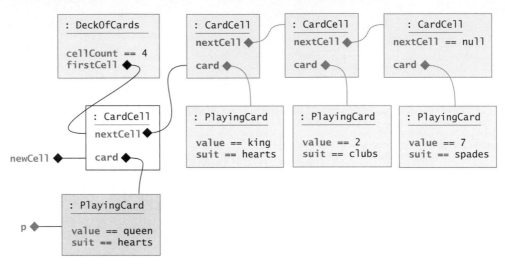

The *else* clause is used for any playing card except the first. The *else* clause begins by setting the cell variable to reference the (j−1)st cell. Next, resultCell is assigned a reference to the jth cell, also identified as cell.nextCell. The list is restructured to eliminate the jth cell with the following single statement.

```
cell.nextCell = cell.nextCell.nextCell;
```

Figure 5.19 shows the behavior for drawing the second playing card (j==2). This picture includes the value of cell and resultCell and the value returned by the method (result) at the time that drawCardFrom(2) returns.

Figure 5.19 Behavior of drawCardFrom(2)

Behavior of drawCardFrom(j) for j == 2

Before

   sequence{ KingOfHearts, 2ofClubs, 7ofSpades }

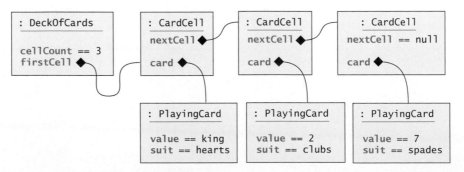

Continued on next page

After

sequence{ *KingOfHearts, 7ofSpades* }

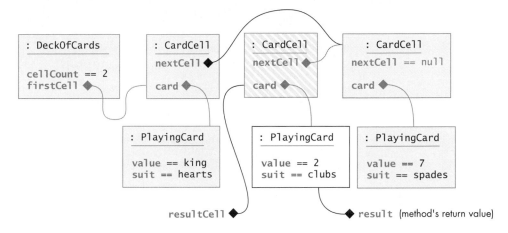

Like `insertCardAt`, the `dealCardFrom` method treats the first card of the deck as a special case. Calling `dealCardFrom(1)` executes the *then* clause. This behavior is pictured in Figure 5.20.

Figure 5.20 Behavior of `drawCardFrom(1)`

Behavior of drawCardFrom(j) for j == 1

Before

sequence{ *KingOfHearts, 2ofClubs, 7ofSpades* }

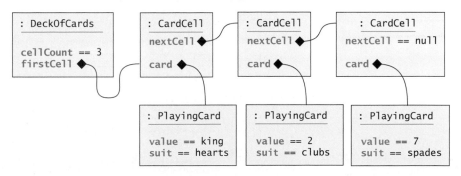

Continued on next page

After

sequence{ 2ofclubs, 7ofSpades }

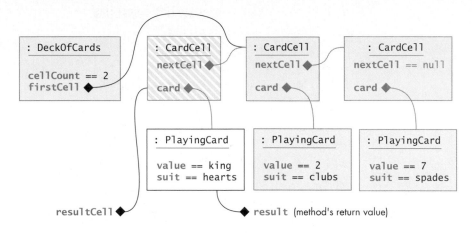

5.6 SINGLY LINKED LIST ADT

The data structure used in the DeckOfCards implementation in Section 5.5 is known as a **singly linked list** because each object (cell) of the structure contains a single link variable (nextCell), and collectively the structure forms a linear list of cells. Before investigating this structure further, it is instructive to suggest the ADT that captures the abstract form of a singly linked list. Figure 5.21 describes such an ADT, SimpleSingleList.

Figure 5.21 SimpleSingleList Specifications

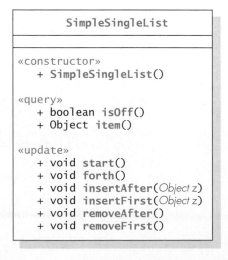

Continued on next page

SimpleSingleList Specifications

Domain (Every SimpleSingleList object has the following components)

    sequence of Object `theSeq`;
    integer `iteratorPos`;

Invariant

    `1 <= iteratorPos <=` `theSeq->`*size()* `+ 1`

Constructor Method

`public SimpleSingleList( )`

    post: `theSeq ==` *sequence*{}
        and `iteratorPos == 1`

Query Methods

`public boolean isOff( )`

    post: `result == (iteratorPos >` `theSeq->`*size())*

`public Object item( )`

    pre: `!isOff()` (throws `java.util.NoSuchElementException`)

    post: `result ==` `theSeq->`*at*`(iteratorPos)`

Update Methods

`public void start( )`

    post: `iteratorPos == 1`

`public void forth( )`

    post: `!isOff()`*@pre implies* `iteratorPos == iteratorPos`*@pre* `+ 1)`
        and `isOff()`*@pre implies* `iteratorPos == iteratorPos`*@pre*

`public void insertAfter( Object z )`

    pre: `!isOff()` (throws `java.util.NoSuchElementException`)

    post: `theSeq ==` `theSeq`*@pre* with z inserted immediately after
        `iteratorPos`

`public void insertFirst( Object z )`

    post: `theSeq ==` `theSeq`*@pre->prepend*`(z)`
        and `iteratorPos == 1`

`public void removeAfter( )`

    post: `iteratorPos <` `theSeq`*@pre->size*`()`
        implies `theSeq ==` `theSeq`*@pre* with the item deleted from
            `iteratorPos+1`
            and `iteratorPos >=` `theSeq`*@pre->size*`()`
        implies `theSeq ==` `theSeq`*@pre*

`public void removeFirst( )`

    pre: `theSeq`*@pre->size*`() > 0` (throws `IllegalStateException`)

    post: `theSeq ==` `theSeq`*@pre with* the first item removed
        and `iteratorPos == 1`

SimpleSingleList defines a list ADT having three major characteristics:

- SimpleSingleList objects contain zero or more items (cells).
- SimpleSingleList is generic in the sense that each item within the list is of type Object.
- A SimpleSingleList incorporates a built-in iterator (a somewhat different type of iterator from those examined in previous chapters).

Like all singly linked lists, SimpleSingleList is best viewed abstractly as a *sequence*. This particular singly linked list includes nine methods: the SimpleSingleList constructor, isOff, item, start, forth, insertAfter, insertFirst, removeAfter, and removeFirst.

The built-in iterator of SimpleSingleList is defined in terms of an integer attribute called iteratorPos. The iteratorPos attribute serves as a useful device for explaining the iterator's position. When iteratorPos == 1, the iterator is positioned at the first item in the list, when iteratorPos == 2, the iterator is positioned at the second item in the list, and so forth. When the iterator has been advanced past all list items, iteratorPos is greater than the list's length.

The behavior of the built-in iterator is defined largely by four parameterless methods: start, forth, isOff, and item. A call to the start method positions the iterator to the first item in the list. Calling forth advances the iterator from one list cell to its subsequent neighboring cell. The isOff query returns false whenever the iterator continues to be positioned within the list, and isOff returns true if the iterator has been positioned past all items.

The item method permits the inspection of one of the SimpleSingleList cells, in particular the cell identified by the iterator's position. This means that a call to item immediately after calling start returns the value of the first item in the list. Subsequent list items can be visited by advancing the iterator by calling forth. The precondition to item specifies that this method will throw an exception if it is called when the iterator is beyond the list's end (i.e., isOff is true).

Four additional methods are included in SimpleSingleList to alter the content of the container. A call to insertAfter inserts the method's argument into the list. The newly inserted item is located immediately beyond the cell at which the iterator is positioned. A call to the insertFirst method is included to insert new items in front of all others because insertAfter cannot insert at this position. Note that any prior list content is not disturbed by a call to insertAfter or insertFirst.

The removeAfter method deletes the item *following* the iterator's position, collapsing the remaining list. Calling removeFirst is similar except that the item deleted is the first one in the list. Both insertFirst and removeFirst reposition the iterator to the front of the list.

To illustrate the use of this built-in iterator, Figure 5.22 shows a segment of Java code. To the right of each statement is the abstract view (as a sequence) of the state of the list variable immediately after the statement's execution. The iterator is pictured as a shaded block covering the item where it is positioned.

The SimpleSingleList iterator, like the java.util.Iterator interface (see Section 5.10), provides a mechanism to visit every item in a container in a linear sequence. However, there are important differences between these two styles of iterators:

- The iterator from `SimpleSingleList` is incorporated within the container. A `java.util.Iterator` is an object that is separate from the container, typically returned by calling an `iterator` method on the associated container.
- Because of its built-in nature, each `SimpleSingleList` object has only one iterator, whereas several `java.util.Iterator` objects per container are permitted.
- A `SimpleSingleList` iterator can be repositioned to the beginning of the list at any time, whereas `java.util.Iterator` objects cannot be repositioned to items visited earlier.
- The `item` method of `SimpleSingleList` does not advance the iterator, as does the `next` method of `java.util.Iterator`. The `item` method often eliminates the need for a variable to "hold onto" a `next()` item that is used more than once, but a separate method (`forth`) is needed.
- The `isOff` method of `SimpleSingleList` returns true when the iterator has been positioned past the last item, and it returns false otherwise. The `hasNext` method of `java.util.Iterator` returns false when all items have been visited by `next`, and it returns true otherwise.

Figure 5.22 Trace of `SimpleSingleList` manipulation

Statement	*State of list*
`SimpleSingleList list = new SimpleSingleList();`	*sequence*{ }
`list.insertFirst( "Pigs" );`	*sequence*{ "Pigs" }
`list.insertAfter( "fly." );`	*sequence*{ "Pigs", "fly." }
`list.insertAfter( "can" );`	*sequence*{ "Pigs", "can", "fly." }
`list.forth();`	*sequence*{ "Pigs", "can", "fly." }
`list.start();`	*sequence*{ "Pigs", "can", "fly." }
`System.out.println( (String)(list.item()) );` `  // assert: "Pigs" was output`	*sequence*{ "Pigs", "can", "fly." }
`list.removeAfter();`	*sequence*{ "Pigs", "fly." }
`list.forth();` `  // assert: isOff() == false`	*sequence*{ "Pigs", "fly." }
`list.start();`	*sequence*{ "Pigs", "fly." }

Software Engineering Hint

There are many variations on the iterator design pattern. `SimpleSingleList` illustrates a style that contrasts with **`java.util.Iterator`** in many ways. Competent software engineers are familiar with various such alternatives because each approach has advantages and disadvantages.

To illustrate this difference, the following loop can be used to output all the items of a `SimpleSingleList` variable called `list`.

```
//assert: list != null
list.start();
while ( !(list.isOff()) ) {
      System.out.println( list.item() );
      list.forth();
}
```

By comparison, the following loop performs the same task using a `java.util.Iterator` variable called `stdIterator`.

```
//assert:  stdIterator != null and stdIterator is positioned
//            at the front of the list
while (stdIterator.hasNext()) {
    System.out.println( stdIterator.next() );
}
```

5.7   IMPLEMENTING A SIMPLE SINGLY LINKED LIST

The implementation of `SimpleSingleList` uses techniques that are similar to those from the `DeckOfCards` implementation. A `SimpleSingleList` is built from dynamic data cells that are linked in a linear order. Figure 5.23 shows the skeleton of such an implementation of `SimpleSingleList`.

Figure 5.23   `SimpleSingleList` including `ListCell`

```
public class SimpleSingleList {
    private class ListCell {
        public Object content;
        public ListCell link;
        /* post: content == z and link == null */
        public ListCell(Object z) {
            content = z;
            link = null;
        }
    }
    private ListCell anchor;
    private ListCell iteratorCell;
    // Methods are shown in Figures 5.25 through 5.28
}
```

Software Engineering Hint

The `ListCell` class is declared private to protect the structure from corruption by code from other classes. The instance variables of `SimpleSingleList` are declared private for the same reason.

As its name implies, a `ListCell` object represents one storage cell from a `SimpleSingleList`. These cells will have dynamic lifetime. Each `ListCell` contains two variables:

- The `content` variable references the cell's value.
- The `link` variable binds to the next cell in the linked list.

The characteristic that distinguishes a singly linked list from other data structures is a form constructed from dynamic cells that are chained together by one link per cell. The `link` attribute of each cell, except the last, of a singly linked list references the subsequent cell. The `link` attribute of the last cell is `null`. Figure 5.24 illustrates this singly linked list structure by showing the object diagram for a `SimpleSingleList` called `list` and its corresponding abstract sequence.

Figure 5.24 Sample object diagram of a `SimpleSingleList`

Abtract view of one particular list (as a sequence)

sequence{**"Cows"**, "do", "not", "tango"}

Object diagram for list (corresponding to above abstraction)

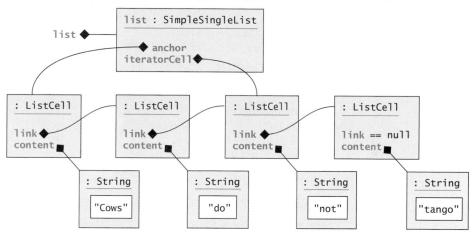

Singly linked lists require only one variable to "hold onto" the list. Each `SimpleSingleList` object contains an anchor variable for this purpose. The anchor variable is a reference to the first cell in the chain. Because all other cells are linked, this lone anchor variable is sufficient to permit access to the entire list structure.

Figure 5.24 also demonstrates how `SimpleSingleList` uses an `iteratorCell` instance variable to keep track of the list's built-in iterator. The cell that is referenced by `iteratorCell` is the one at which the iterator is positioned. Figure 5.24 depicts the state in which the iterator is positioned at the third list item.

To write code for methods, you must have a firm understanding of an implementation's representation strategy. The `SimpleSingleList` representation strategy is summarized as follows:

- A singly linked list of `ListCell` objects
- An anchor variable to reference the first `ListCell` in the list
- An `iteratorCell` variable to reference the cell at the iterator position

The `SimpleSingleList` constructor is designed to create a singly linked list that is empty. This is accomplished by assigning anchor the value `null`. This method also assigns `null` to the iterator. Figure 5.25 contains the appropriate code.

Software Engineering Hint

`SimpleSingleList` specifications are written in terms of the implementation structures to communicate with implementing programmers.

`SimpleSingleList` specifications are abstractly written (using sequences) to communicate with both clients and implementers.

Figure 5.25 SimpleSingleList constructor method

```
public class SimpleSingleList {
    ...

    /* post:   anchor == null
                and iteratorCell == anchor */
    public SimpleSingleList() {
        anchor = null;
        iteratorCell = anchor;
    }
    . . .

}
```

To examine the effect of the SimpleSingleList constructor, consider the following Java statement:

SimpleSingleList list = new SimpleSingleList();

The state following the execution of this statement is pictured in the following object diagram.

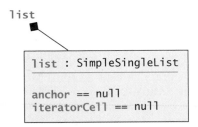

Figure 5.26 shows the implementations of the three primary methods for iterator manipulation: start, isOff, and forth.

Figure 5.26 start, isOff, and forth methods for SimpleSingleList

```
public class SimpleSingleList extends SimpleSingleList {
    ...

    /* post:   iteratorCell == anchor */
    public void start() {
        iteratorCell = anchor;
    }

    /* post:   result == (iteratorCell == null) */
    public boolean isOff() {
        return (iteratorCell == null);
    }
```

Continued on next page

```
/*  post:   !isOff()@pre
                 implies iteratorCell == iteratorCell@pre.link */
public void forth() {
    if (!isOff())
        iteratorCell = iteratorCell.link;
}
    . . .

}
```

Because the anchor variable always references the first cell in the singly linked list, the start method need only assign anchor to the iteratorCell variable in order to reset an iterator to the front of the list. The isOff method also is implemented with a single statement. The iteratorCell variable either will reference one of the ListCell objects of the list, or it will be assigned null to signify that it is positioned off the end of the list. Therefore, isOff need only compare iteratorCell to null.

The abstract view of the forth method is that it advances the iterator from one list item to the next. Because the ListCell referenced by iteratorCell contains a link variable that references the next cell in the list, you can use the following assignment to properly advance the SimpleSingleList iterator:

```
iteratorCell = iteratorCell.link;
```

This statement advances a SimpleSingleList iterator in a way that is analogous to the statement

```
ndx++;
```

for advancing an array index called ndx. Because the link attribute of the last cell is null, the forth method also assigns iteratorCell the proper value (null) when it advances beyond the end of the list.

Before advancing the iterator, the forth method must check to see whether the iterator has already been advanced beyond the end of the list. The *if* statement accomplishes the necessary check by calling isOff. Notice that omission of the if statement in the forth method is likely to lead to null pointer exceptions.

The item method also must avoid undesired run-time errors when the iterator has been positioned off the end of the list. Figure 5.27 shows this method.

One of the greatest benefits of a singly linked list is the ease with which items can be inserted and removed from the structure without the need to rearrange other items. Inserting a new value into the middle of an array of values requires an algorithm for shifting prior array content to "make space" for the new value. Removing a value from the middle of an array leaves an "unused hole" in the array. A linked list avoids the work of rearranging prior container content by updating its links to accommodate each insertion or deletion. Figure 5.28

Software Engineering Hint

The most common run-time error associated with dynamic data structures is the null pointer exception. Programmers must always search their code for potential null pointer exceptions.

Software Engineering Hint

Lists have two primary advantages over arrays:

- It is easier to insert and remove items from the middle of a list.
- Lists do not have a maximum number of cells.

The greatest advantage of the array over a list is the ability it gives you to directly access any cell (using its index) without the need to visit additional cells.

shows the code for the insertAfter, insertFirst, removeAfter, and removeFirst methods of SimpleSingleList.

Figure 5.27 item method for SimpleSingleList

```
public class SimpleSingleList {
   ...

   /* pre:    !isOff() (throws java.util.NoSuchElementException)
      post:   result == iteratorCell.content */
   public Object item() {
      if (isOff()) {
         throw new java.util.NoSuchElementException();
      } else {
         return iteratorCell.content;
      }
   }
   . . .
}
```

Figure 5.28 insertAfter and removeAfter methods for SimpleSingleList

```
public class SimpleSingleList {
   ...

   /* pre:    !isOff() (throws java.util.NoSuchElementException)
      post:   iteratorCell.link == a newly instantiated cell
              and iteratorCell.link.content == z
              and iteratorCell.link.link == iteratorCell.link@pre
              */
   public void insertAfter( Object z ) {
      if (isOff()) {
         throw new java.util.NoSuchElementException();
      } else {
         ListCell newCell = new ListCell(z);
         newCell.link = iteratorCell.link;
         iteratorCell.link = newCell;
      }
   }

   /* post:   anchor == a newly instantiated cell
              and anchor.content == z
              and anchor.link == anchor@pre
              and iterator == anchor */
   public void insertFirst( Object z ) {
      ListCell newCell = new ListCell(z);
```

Continued on next page

```
                newCell.link = anchor;
                anchor = newCell;
                iterator = anchor;
            }
            /* post:   iteratorCell.link != null
                           implies
                               iteratorCell.link == iteratorCell.link@pre.link */
            public void removeAfter( ) {
                if (!isOff() && iteratorCell.link != null) {
                    iteratorCell.link = iteratorCell.link.link;
                }
            }
            /* pre:    anchor!=null (throws IllegalStateException)
               post:   anchor == anchor@pre.link
                           and iterator == anchor */
            public void removeFirst( ) {
                if (anchor == null) {
                    throw new IllegalStateException();
                } else {
                    anchor = anchor.link;
                    iterator = anchor;
                }
            }
            . . .
        }
```

Like other methods for manipulating singly linked lists, insertAfter is composed in a few short lines of code. However, implementing this method can be deceptively complicated, so let's examine the statements one by one. Consider a situation in which the prior state of a list is given by the following object diagram. (Note that the String values for content variables are pictured within each list cell to simplify this diagram.)

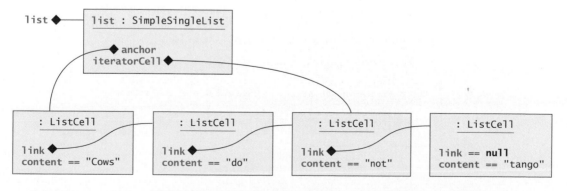

Given this initial state, assume that the following statement executes:

```
        list.insertAfter( "necessarily" );
```

The resulting call to `insertAfter` executes the following statement:

```
ListCell newCell = new ListCell(z);
```

This causes a new cell to be instantiated and assigned content. The following object diagram illustrates.

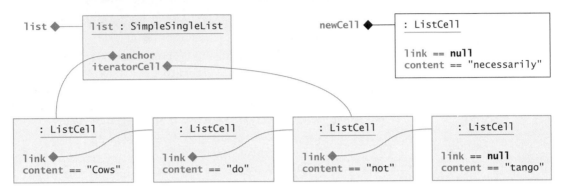

The `insertAfter` statement assigns the `link` variable within the newly instantiated cell. This statement is repeated next, followed by the resulting picture.

```
newCell.link = iteratorCell.link;
```

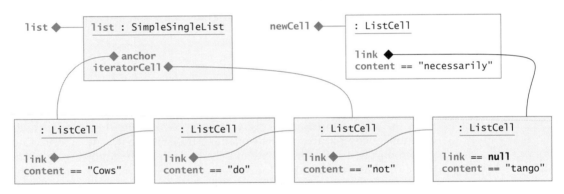

Executing the final `insertAfter` statement causes the `link` attribute of the cell referenced by `iteratorCell` to be attached the newly instantiated cell. This statement and the resulting object diagram are as follows.

```
iteratorCell.link = newCell;
```

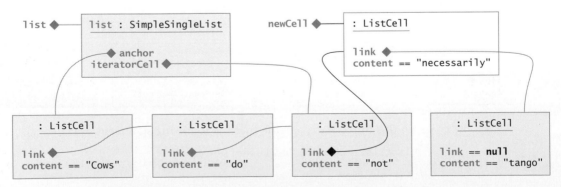

The structure that results from this complete execution of insertAfter has properly inserted the "necessarily" as the content of the fourth cell in a list that is now five cells in length. This new list is the representation of the abstract *sequence*{"Cows", "do", "not", "necessarily", "tango"}.

Inserting into any linked data structure is a three-step process:

1. Instantiate a new cell to be inserted, and assign it the proper content.
2. Assign the link(s) within the cell instantiated in Step 1.
3. Update link(s) from previously existing parts of the structure to incorporate the new cell.

These three steps occur, respectively, as the three assignment statements of insertAfter. The subtle nature of list insertion algorithms is reflected in the fact that any reordering of these three steps will cause insertAfter to fail.

Removing cells from a singly linked list is essentially like Step 3 of list insertion. In other words, all that is required to remove a cell is to properly relink the structure. The following statement from removeAfter performs such relinking:

```
iteratorCell.link = iteratorCell.link.link;
```

Following is an object diagram for a possible SimpleSingleList *before* relinking.

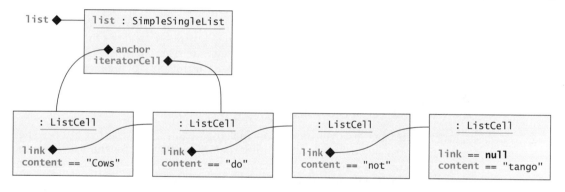

Following the execution of the relinking statement, the state changes as shown next.

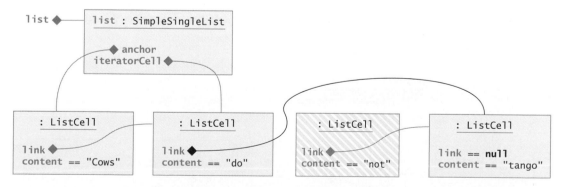

This picture shows that the prior third cell of the list has been removed. This cell has become an orphan. (Do not be misled into thinking that the link attribute of the "not" cell can save it from being orphaned. The cell is an orphan because there is no longer any way to reference it.)

When the iterator is positioned at the last cell in the list, it is impossible to remove the cell *after* the last one. The *if* statement of removeAfter ensures that the list is unaltered when the iterator is either off the list or positioned at the last list item.

5.8 IMPLEMENTATION STRATEGIES: HEADERS AND PREPOINTERS

The SimpleSingleList class takes a straightforward approach to implementing the sequence abstraction in the following two ways:

1. Each cell of the linked list represents one item from the abstract sequence.
2. The iterator is implemented as a reference to the exact cell where it is positioned.

It turns out that a minor change to each of these two implementation decisions enhances the implementation.

Consider first the decision to represent each sequence item with one linked list cell. One of the ramifications of this approach is that the first item requires special treatment. The DeckOfCards class from Section 5.5 contains two methods—insertCardAt and drawCardFrom—that are forced to treat the first position in the list using an algorithm (the *then* clause) separate from all other list positions (handled by the *else* clause). Similarly, SimpleSingleList includes separate methods—insertFirst and removeFirst—to handle insertions and deletions from the front of the list, whereas all other list insertion or deletion is accomplished by calling insertAfter or removeAfter.

You can discover the reason that the beginning of a list is often a special case for many algorithms by examining the object diagram for the list. The top portion of Figure 5.29 (labeled, "Implementation without header cell") shows a typical object diagram for the SimpleSingleList implementation.

Figure 5.29 Sample singly linked list without and with a header cell

Implementation without header cell for sequence{"Sheep", "can", "sing"}

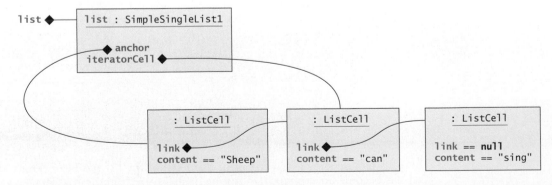

Continued on next page

Implementation with header cell for sequence{"Sheep", "can", "sing"}

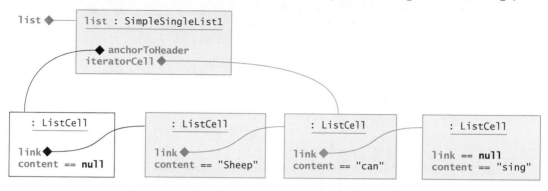

As you can see, inserting (or deleting) at the front of the list is a special case. Any insertion—except a new first cell—requires a new value to be assigned to the link attribute of some list cell. However, an insertion of a new first cell requires that anchor, and not a link attribute, be updated. The informal algorithm for insertion is therefore split into two cases:

```
if (inserting new first cell) {
    // insert new cell by updating anchor (i.e., the special case)
} else {
    // insert new cell by updating link attribute of the cell
    // preceding the insertion
}
```

Software Engineering Hint

Sometimes a fairly minor change to a data structure makes it easier to code algorithms for the structure. The inclusion of a header cell is such a situation.

You can eliminate the special cases for both inserting and removing from the front of a list by adopting an implementation strategy that includes one extra cell at the front of every singly linked list. This extra cell is sometimes called a **header cell** (or **sentinel cell**) because its position is frozen in front of all the other cells of the list. The bottom object diagram in Figure 5.29 shows the same list as the top one with the inclusion of a header cell. The header cell is indicated by solid shading. Note that because the content of the header cell doesn't matter, it is pictured with content equal to null.

A list implementation that incorporates a header cell can *ensure* that anchorToHeader will never be changed, because the header cell is created when the list is instantiated and never replaced or removed. All insertion and removal operations occur beyond the header cell. The special cases are eliminated because there is always some cell (either a cell representing an actual item or a header cell) preceding the point of insertion or removal.

The second implementation decision that is questioned at the beginning of this section is to represent an iterator as a reference to the cell that represents the abstract position. This decision is not problematic for DeckOfCards nor SimpleSingleList because both classes were designed with methods that avoid potential implementation difficulties. However, suppose that the two methods shown in Figure 5.30 were to be added to SimpleSingleList.

Figure 5.30 insertBefore and removeAt Specifications

> **SimpleSingleListPlus Specifications**
>
> *Potential Additional Methods*
>
> public void insertBefore(Object z)
>
> > **pre:** isOff() (throws java.util.NoSuchElementException)
> >
> > **post:** theSeq == theSeq@*pre* with z inserted immediately *before*
> > iteratorPos *and* iteratorPos == iteratorPos@*pre* + 1
>
> public void removeAt( )
>
> > **post:** iteratorPos <= theSeq@*pre*->size() *implies*
> > theSeq == theSeq@*pre* with the item deleted from iteratorPos
> > *and* iteratorPos > theSeq@*pre*->size()
> > *implies* theSeq == theSeq@*pre*

A singly linked list structure is a kind of "one-way" structure because all the links lead in the same direction (toward the later cells of the list). This one-way nature makes an operation such as insertAfter more natural than insertBefore. Similarly, removeAfter is more natural than removeAt. Consider insertBefore:

```
// assert: list == sequence{"Sheep", "can", "sing"}
list.insertBefore( "not" );
// assert: list == sequence{"Sheep", "can", "not", "sing"}
```

This code demonstrates, abstractly, a situation in which insertBefore is inserting in front of the iterator that is positioned at the third item ("sing") in a list. Figure 5.31 uses object diagrams to show the state before and the state after the call to insertBefore.

Figure 5.31 demonstrates that the link attribute of the second nonheader cell (the cell with content of "can") must be updated to reference the newly inserted cell. The problem is how to locate this cell, because it *precedes* the cell referenced by iteratorCell. One general solution is to search for the previous cell using a linear search that begins with the anchor reference and visits all cells until it locates a cell with a link attribute equal to iteratorCell. However, searching for the previous cell is inefficient (an O(*listLength*) algorithm), whereas the entire insertAfter performance is O(1).

Once again, a small change in the representation structure can avoid difficulties with the algorithms. Because insertBefore and removeAt need access to the cell that precedes iteratorCell, it seems better to maintain such a reference. In other words, instead of representing the iterator at the precise cell where the iterator is positioned, it is preferable to represent an iterator as a reference to the cell preceding the iterator position. Figure 5.32 pictures these two alternatives.

The preIteratorCell variable shown in Figure 5.32 is sometimes called a **pre-pointer** because it references ("points to") the cell preceding the cell where the iterator is actually positioned. Maintaining preIteratorCell requires no more effort than maintaining iteratorCell, and slight modifications to the prior methods accommodate the change.

Figure 5.31 Sample relinking of `insertBefore`

Before executing the statement

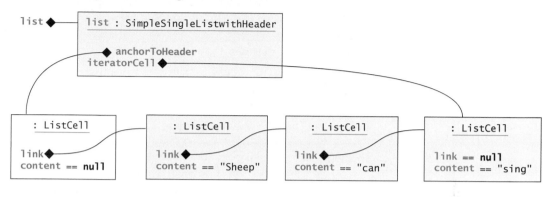

After executing list.insertBefore("not");

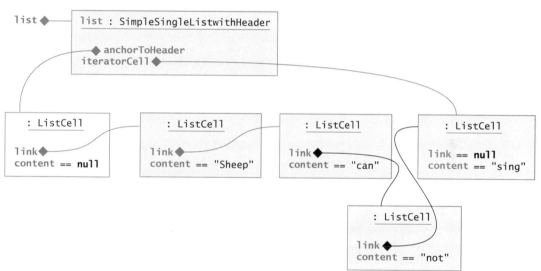

The prepointer implementation strategy provides a secondary reason for including a header cell. The header cell provides a site for the prepointer to representing an iterator positioned at the front of the list.

You can combine the strategies of a header cell and a prepointer to implement `SimpleSingleListPlus`, shown in Figure 5.33. `SimpleSingleListPlus` includes a single insertion method, `insertBefore`, and a single removal method, `removeAt`. These two methods are sufficient to insert or remove any list cell because the iterator is allowed to range, abstractly, from position 1 through *size*()+1. The corresponding `preIteratorCell` representation references the header cell through the final list cell.

Figure 5.32 List representation alternatives (iteratorCell and preIteratorCell)

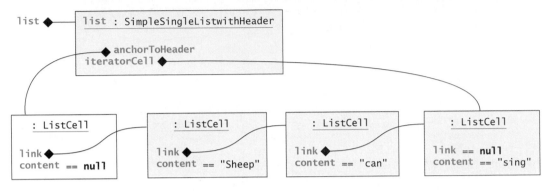

Using iteratorCell to represent sequence{"Sheep", "can", "sing"}

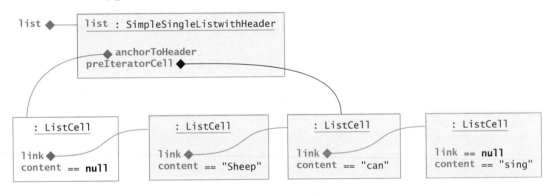

Using preIteratorCell to represent sequence{"Sheep", "can", "sing"}

Figure 5.33 insertBefore and removeAt methods for SimpleSingleListPlus

```java
public class SimpleSingleListPlus {
    private class ListCell {
        public Object content;
        public ListCell link;
        /* post:   content == z and link == null */
        public ListCell(Object z) {
            content = z;
            link = null;
        }
    }
    private ListCell anchorToHeader;
```

Continued on next page

```
    private ListCell preIteratorCell;
    /* post:    anchorToHeader == a newly instantiated cell
                and anchorToHeader.link == null
                and preIteratorCell == anchorToHeader */
    public SimpleSingleListPlus() {
        anchorToHeader = new ListCell(null);
        preIteratorCell = anchorToHeader;
    }


    /* post:   preIteratorCell == anchorToHeader */
    public void start() {
        preIteratorCell = anchorToHeader;
    }


    /* post:   result == (preIteratorCell.link == null) */
    public boolean isOff() {
        return (preIteratorCell.link == null);
    }


    /* post:   !isOff()@pre implies
                    preIteratorCell == preIteratorCell@pre.link */
    public void forth() {
        if (!isOff())
            preIteratorCell = preIteratorCell.link;
    }


    /* pre:    !isOff()
                    (throws java.util.NoSuchElementException)
       post:    result == preIteratorCell.link.content */
    public Object item() {
        if (isOff()) {
            throw new java.util.NoSuchElementException();
        } else {
            return preIteratorCell.link.content;
        }
    }


    /* post:   preIteratorCell == a newly instantiated cell
                and preIteratorCell@pre.link == preIteratorCell
                and preIteratorCell.content == z
                and preIteratorCell.link ==
                    preIteratorCell@pre.link@pre */
    public void insertBefore( Object z ) {
        ListCell newCell = new ListCell(z);
        newCell.link = preIteratorCell.link;
        preIteratorCell.link = newCell;
        preIteratorCell = newCell;
    }
```

Continued on next page

```
/* post:    !isOff()@pre implies
              preIteratorCell.link == preIteratorCell.link@pre.link
              */
public void removeAt( ) {
    if (!isOff()) {
        preIteratorCell.link = preIteratorCell.link.link;
    }
}
}
```

To illustrate this insertBefore algorithm, consider the following SimpleLinkedListPlus, called list, as shown in object diagram form.

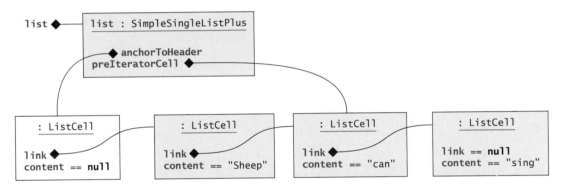

Notice that this picture shows a state in which the iterator is positioned at the last item (the "sing" item) in the list because preIteratorCell references the cell prior to the last. Given this initial state, assume that the following statement executes:

```
list.insertBefore( "barely" );
```

Following the method call, the insertBefore method executes the following statement:

```
ListCell newCell = new ListCell(z);
```

This statement instantiates the new cell for future insertion and assigns this cell its content. The following object diagram pictures the resulting state.

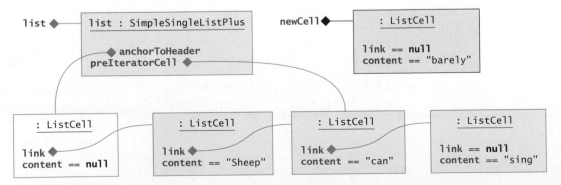

The next `insertBefore` statement to execute assigns the `link` variable within the newly instantiated cell. This statement is repeated next, followed by the state that results when it executes.

```
newCell.link = preIteratorCell.link;
```

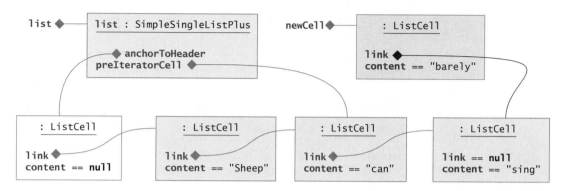

Executing the final two `insertBefore` statements cause the `link` attribute of the cell referenced by `preIteratorCell` to be updated to reference the newly instantiated cell and the iterator to be properly updated. The statements and resulting object diagram are as follows.

```
preIteratorCell.link = newCell;
preIteratorCell = newCell;
```

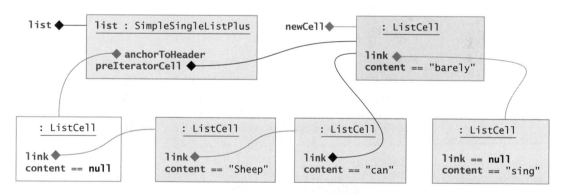

The structure that results from this complete execution of `insertBefore` has properly inserted the `"barely"` `String` as the value of the third cell in a list that is now four cells in length. This new list is the representation for the abstract *sequence*{"Sheep", "can", "barely", "sing"}.

Following is a collection of hints on what to check when you examine a design or code that involves the concepts of this chapter.

✓ A variable of reference type is associated with variable memory and a separate memory space called object memory. To avoid null pointer exceptions, be certain that the object memory is instantiated.

✓ When using reference data, you should be conscious of aliases for the same object memory. Sometimes an unexpected change to the object occurs via a different reference.

✓ Static variables should be scrutinized, especially when they are located within a class that is instantiated multiple times. A commonly programmer error is to assume that there can be multiple occurrences of a static variable.

✓ When you're using linked structures it's often helpful to draw careful object diagrams, particularly for tracing run-time behavior.

✓ It is wise to know where and when orphans are created. An orphan isn't harmful in a language that has garbage collection, such as Java. However, reducing the number of orphans can be expected to improve code performance. Furthermore, many O-O software bugs result from unexpected orphans.

✓ Reading a dereferencing expression (i.e., an expression that follows links) can be simplified if the period expression separators are interpreted as "following a connection (i.e., a line in an object diagram)." For example, the expression

```
stuff.another.content
```

can be interpreted as starting from the stuff variable, following the connection, using the another attribute, following a second connection, and accessing the content attribute.

✓ Inserting into a singly linked list requires assigning two link attributes: the one within the new cell, and the one from the predecessor to the new cell's location. Removing an item from a singly linked list requires assigning only one link.

✓ When you use code involving linked lists, it is generally a good idea to pay special attention to the front and rear of the list. Sometimes operations that occur at one end or the other must be handled (as special cases).

✓ Many list implementations involve the use of header cells or prepointers. When you examine list implementation code, it is important to know such representation details.

1. Consider the following class.

    ```
    public class InnerInt {
            private int theInt;
        public InnerInt() {
            theInt = 100;
        }
        public void decAndPrint() {
            theInt--;
            System.out.println(theInt);
        }
    }
    ```

    a. Show the exact output that results from executing the following segment of code.

    ```
    InnerInt oneVar, twoVar;
    oneVar = new InnerInt();
    oneVar.decAndPrint();
    twoVar = new InnerInt();
    twoVar.decAndPrint();
    oneVar.decAndPrint();
    oneVar = twoVar;
    oneVar.decAndPrint();
    twoVar.decAndPrint();
    oneVar = null;
    twoVar = new InnerInt();
    twoVar.decAndPrint();
    ```

    b. Which statement(s) from part (a) produce an orphan at execution time?

    c. Show the exact output that results from executing the code in part (a), assuming that the declaration of theInt is changed so that it is a static variable.

2. For each of the following statements, specify whether or not the statement has the potential for creating orphans when it executes. If your answer is yes, explain the precise set of circumstances that causes orphans to be created. (You should assume that thePrimitive1 and thePrimitive2 are of type double, and theReference1 and theReference2 are of type Object.)

    a. theReference1 = null;

    b. theReference1 = new Object();

    c. theReference1 = theReference2;

    d. thePrimitive1 = 3;

    e. thePrimitive1 = thePrimitive1 + 3;

    f. thePrimitive1 = thePrimitive2;

g. Any `return` statement

3. Identify each part as either static, automatic, or dynamic memory.

   a. The variable memory associated with a parameter of type `Object`

   b. The object memory associated with a parameter of type `Object`

   c. The memory associated with a parameter of type `char`

   d. The variable memory associated with a local variable of type `Object`

   e. The object memory associated with a local variable of type `Object`

   f. The memory associated with a local variable of type `char`

   g. The variable memory associated with an instance variable of type `Object`

   h. The object memory associated with an instance variable of type `Object`

   i. The memory associated with an instance variable of type `char`

   j. The memory that is created by executing an expression involving the keyword `new`

4. For each part assume that the initial configuration of a `SimpleSingleList`, called `list` is indicated by the initial assertion. Show the content of the container following the code's execution.

   a. ```
   // assert: list == sequence{"aaa", "bbb", "ccc" }
   list.start();
   list.insertFirst("www");
   list.start();
   list.insertAfter("yyy");
   list.forth();
   list.forth();
   list.insertAfter("zzz");
   ```

   b. ```
   // assert: list == sequence{"aaa", "bbb", "ccc" }
   list.start();
   list.forth();
   list.removeAfter();
   list.start();
   list.insertAfter( "rrr" );
   list.start();
   list.forth();
   list.removeAfter();
   ```

   c. ```
   // assert: list == sequence{"aaa", "bbb", "ccc" }
   list.start();
   while (!list.isOff()) {
      list.insertAfter("more");
      list.forth();
      list.forth();
   }
   ```

5. For each part, assume that the initial configuration of a `SimpleSingleList`, called `list`, is indicated by the initial assertion. Show the output that results
   ```

from the code's execution.

a.
```
// assert: list == sequence{"aaa", "bbb", "ccc" }
list.start();
list.forth();
System.out.println( list.item() );
list.forth();
System.out.println( list.item() );
```

b.
```
// assert: list == sequence{"aaa", "bbb", "ccc", "ddd", "eee" }
list.start();
while (!list.isOff()) {
   System.out.println( list.item() );
   list.insertAfter( "more" );
   list.forth();
   list.forth();
}
```

6. The following two methods are not included in `SimpleSingleList` because their implementations are less efficient and convenient without the use of sentinel cells and prepointers. Write a complete implementation of each method *without* the use of these strategies.

a. insertBefore

b. removeAt

7. It is possible to implement an `insertBefore` method for `SimpleSingleList` by altering the content of the current cell and performing an insert after with the previous cell value. Show the code for this method, making certain to properly position the iterator.

8. For each part, assume that the initial configuration of one or two `SimpleSingleListPlus`, called `list1` and `list2`, is indicated by the initial assertion. Show the content of the container following the code's execution.

a.
```
// assert: list1 == sequence{"cat", "dog", "ant"}
list1.start();
list1.insertBefore( "pig" );
list1.forth();
list1.removeAt();
list1.forth();
list1.insertBefore( "bug" );
```

b.
```
// assert: list1 == sequence{"cat", "dog", "ant"}
// assert: list2 == sequence{"bat", "frog", "gnat"}
list1.start();
list2.start();
while (!list1.isOff()) {
   list2.insertBefore( list1.item() );
   list1.forth();
   list1.removeAt();
}
```

9. Write code for each of the following methods so that they could be included in SimpleSingleList.

   a. Method name: **secondItem**

      pre: this->*size*() >= 2 (throws IllegalStateException)

      post: result is the second object in this

   b. Method name: **lastItem**

      pre: this->*size*() >= 0 (throws IllegalStateException)

      post: result is the last object in this

   c. Method name: **moveFirstToLast**

      pre: this->*size*() >= 1 (throws IllegalStateException)

      post: this == this@*pre* with the first item removed and appended to the end

   d. Method name: **concatList**

      Parameter: a SimpleSingleList parameter called **list**

      post: this == this@*pre*->*union*(list)

PROGRAMMING EXERCISES

1. Use DeckOfCards from Section 5.5 to deal two five-card poker hands and determine which hand is better.

2. Design, implement, and test the DeckOfCards class from Section 5.5 by adapting it from the SimpleSingleList class given in Section 5.7.

3. The primitive data types in Java are bounded in the sense that their range of potential values is limited by their fixed size. For example, an int variable can store positive and negative integers no larger than ten digits in magnitude. The standard java.Math package provides two classes to alleviate the limitation: java.Math.BigInteger and java.Math.BigDecimal.

   Write and test a partial implementation of BigInteger. Your representation should be a directly implemented linked list representation that uses one cell per decimal digit and permits BigInteger values to be as short as a single digit or arbitrarily long. Include implementations for all the following methods.

   ```
   public BigInteger(String s)
   public BigInteger add(BigInteger b)
   public int compareTo(BigInteger b)
   public boolean equals(Object z)
   public BigInteger not()
   public BigInteger max(BigInteger b)
   ```

4. Design, implement, and test a program that reads a file of e-mail addresses, sorts the addresses, and stores them back in the same file. The program must be designed to read from a text file named *emailList.txt*. (Your code should assume that this file is located in the same folder as your executable (*.class*) files.)

The *email.txt* file consists of one or more e-mail addresses. Each e-mail address consists of two lines. The first line consists of the e-mail address (something like *riley@cs.uwlax.edu*). The second line consists of the individual's name. This name will contain either two or three parts, with one or more blanks separating the parts. A two-part name consists of the first name and the last name (perhaps *George Washington*). The three-part name also begins with a first name and ends with a last name. The middle part of a three-part name is either a middle name or a middle initial.

Your program *must* use a linked structure to store the e-mail addresses. Write your own cell class that stores the information for a single e-mail address, and design proper methods to manipulate the e-mail list. The file format that results from executing your program should be the same as that of the input file. (This permits the use of a text editor to add new e-mail addresses to the end of the list.) (Hint: An efficient and convenient way to sort a list is to insert items in sorted order while the list is being constructed.)

5. Design, implement, and test a program to process baseball pitcher statistics. One of the requirements of this assignment is that a linked implementation be designed to represent the data. Input for your program comes from a text file called *rawstats.txt*. This file contains data about one or more pitchers in the following form:

The first line of input consists of the pitcher's name. Following the name are zero or more lines of pitching information (one line for every game pitched). Each pitching info line contains four consecutive decimal digits; the first two digits are the number of innings pitched, and the second two digits are the number of earned runs given up. Following the lines for the pitcher's games is a line containing four consecutive zeros (0). For example, suppose Smith pitched two games (one for 9 innings, giving up 10 earned runs; and one for 7 innings, giving up 2 earned runs); Jones pitched one game of 5 innings, giving up 3 runs; and Brown pitched no games. The corresponding file would contain the following lines.

```
Smith
0910
0702
0000
Jones
0503
0000
Brown
0000
```

Your program must read all the input and then print (to the standard output stream) a sorted list of pitchers who pitched one or more games. The list must be sorted by ERA (earned run average), with the lower overall ERA preceding higher overall ERAs. For each pitcher the program must output the name followed by the overall ERA on the first line and the ERAs for each individual game on a second line and separated by blanks. The given data would result in the following output:

```
Jones Overall ERA: 5.4
    5.4
Smith Overall ERA: 6.75
    10.0    2.5714
```

The ERA for an individual game is calculated by multiplying the earned runs by 9 and then dividing by the innings pitched. The overall ERA is the total earned runs times 9 divided by the total innings pitched. (Don't try to average the game ERAs.)

6. Take any one of the programs solving Programming Exercises 3 through 5 and implement it as an adaptation of SimpleSingleListPlus. (See Section 5.8 for a discussion of SimpleSingleListPlus.)

7. Properties of gravity ensure that a group of blocks with horizontal surfaces stacked in a single file remains standing as long as the center of gravity of each contiguous group remains within the range of its underlying block. For example, the following stack of blocks should not topple over.

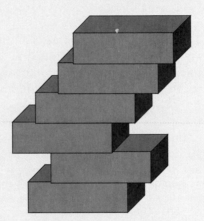

Assuming the weight of a block to be equally distributed, one block will stay atop another as long as the center of the top block is between the edges of the underlying block. In other words, for the following picture the value of C must be between A and B or else the top block will fall off the one underneath.

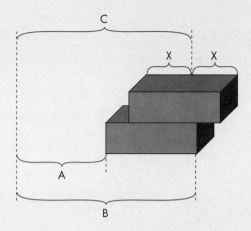

This center of gravity principle can be extended to a collection of several blocks on top. That is to say, the center of gravity of the whole group must lie within the edges of the block on which the group is placed.

Design, implement, and test a program that stores a linear stack of blocks. You may assume that all blocks are of the same size and weight and that the weight within each block is equally distributed. Your program must allow new blocks to be placed on the top block, one at a time. It must also allow the user to slide any of the blocks to the right or the left by some small distance. (Note that sliding one block causes all the blocks on top of it to be carried along.) Each of these slides must be checked for proper centers of gravity. The correct group must topple when the laws of gravity are violated.

APPLYING LISTS

OBJECTIVES

- To explore the basic ways in which linked-list classes can be used to compose other containers

- To illustrate how to build a general-purpose sorted list container

- To examine a linked-list implementation with iterators decoupled from the list class

- To consider the potential for one iterator to corrupt another

- To present circular and doubly linked lists

- To examine the `java.util.ListIterator` class

- To explore an array representation for a singly linked list

- To examine the possibilities for abstracting and implementing lists as recursive structures

The world is filled with linear collections. The automobiles at a busy intersection lined up one after another awaiting a traffic light; the string of beads on a necklace; the row of trees the serve as a windbreak in a country field—all these are linear collections of objects.

In Chapter 5 you learned about the concept of a linked list. This chapter concentrates on these linear data structures by examining several of the common list processing algorithms, a variety of list abstractions, and various list applications.

6.1   A SORTED LIST

The `SimpleSingleListPlus` class discussed in Section 5.8 includes the fundamental methods of a basic singly linked list class. `SimpleSingleListPlus` includes a method for inserting new items (`insertBefore`), a method for removing items (`removeAt`), an accessor method for inspecting items (`item`), and methods to move the iterator about the list (`start`, `forth`, and `isOff`). Figure 6.1 shows the class diagram summarizing these `SimpleSingleListPlus` facilities.

Figure 6.1 `SimpleSingleListPlus` class

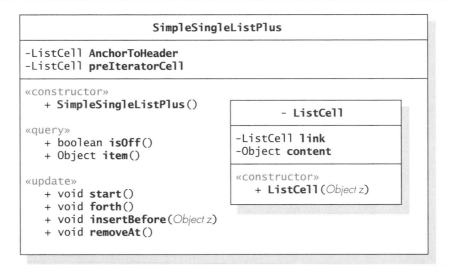

This basic form of the list is sufficient for many types of list processing. For example, suppose a club wishes to store its membership roll as an alphabetized list of names. A good design for this software might start with a more general-purpose concept: a `SortedList` ADT. Figure 6.2 contains the abstract specifications.

The `SortedList` design is as generic as possible. Even though the problem at hand requires sorting people's names, designing `SortedList` to sort various kinds of objects requires about the same amount of effort but produces a class that is generally more reusable in other programs.

`SortedList` cannot be completely generic (i.e., a sequence of `Object`) because `Object` data cannot be compared for less than or greater than. Declaring the content to conform to `Comparable` allows maximum genericity while still retaining the ability to compare for less than or greater than. (Recall that `Comparable` is a Java interface within the `java.lang` package.)

The class invariant for `SortedList` is used to specify the additional "sortedness" property as follows.

and forAll(p : 1 <= p < theSeq->*size*() | theSeq->*at*(p) <= theSeq->*at*(p+1))

Figure 6.2 SortedList specifications
....

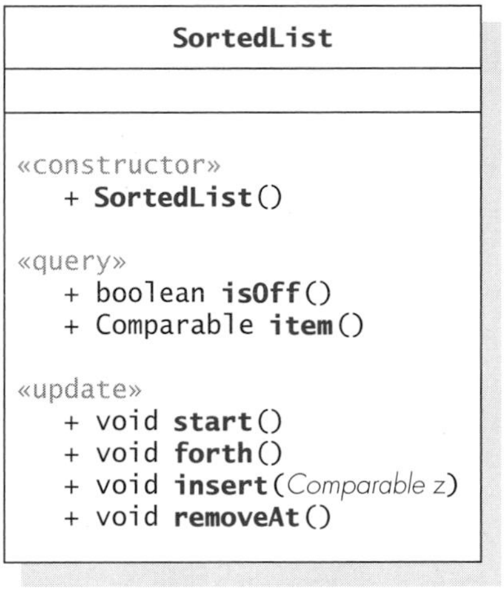

```
┌─────────────────────────────────────┐
│              SortedList               │
├─────────────────────────────────────┤
│                                       │
├─────────────────────────────────────┤
│  «constructor»                        │
│      + SortedList()                   │
│                                       │
│  «query»                              │
│      + boolean isOff()                │
│      + Comparable item()              │
│                                       │
│  «update»                             │
│      + void start()                   │
│      + void forth()                   │
│      + void insert(Comparable z)      │
│      + void removeAt()                │
│                                       │
└─────────────────────────────────────┘
```

SortedList ADT Specifications

Domain (Every SortedList object has the following components)

  sequence of Comparable **theSeq**;
  integer **iteratorPos**;

Invariant:

  $1 <= \text{iteratorPos} <= \text{theSeq->size()} + 1$

  and forAll$(p : 1 <= p < \text{theSeq->}size()$
    $| \text{theSeq->}at(p) <= \text{theSeq->}at(p+1))$

Constructor Method

public **SortedList**( )

  post: theSeq == *sequence*{}
   and iteratorPos == 1

Query Methods

public boolean **isOff**( )

  post: result == (iteratorPos > theSeq->*size*())

public Comparable **item**( )

  pre: !isOff() (throws java.util.NoSuchElementException)

  post: result == theSeq->*at*(iteratorPos)

Update Methods

public void **start**( )

  post: iteratorPos == 1

Continued on next page

```
public void forth( )
    post: !isOff()@pre implies iteratorPos == iteratorPos@pre + 1)
          and isOff()@pre implies iteratorPos == iteratorPos@pre
public void insert(Comparable z)
    post: theSeq == theSeq@pre with z inserted
          and iteratorPos == 1
public void removeAt( )
    post: iteratorPos <= theSeq@pre->size() implies
          theSeq == theSeq@pre with the item deleted from iteratorPos
          and iteratorPos > theSeq@pre->size()
          implies theSeq == theSeq@pre
```

This assertion states that every item in the list has lesser or equal value than its successor item. In other words, the items are sorted in ascending order (least to greatest).

All methods from SortedList have the same behavior as the corresponding methods from SimpleSingleListPlus with one exception: The insert method is the only way to add new items to a SortedList. Because the insert method, like all other methods, is obligated to maintain the class invariant, every newly inserted value must maintain the sorted nature of the list.

Figure 6.3 shows an implementation for SortedList. The proxy design pattern is used through the instance variable theList. The reasoning behind using the proxy design pattern, rather than inherit SimpleSingleListPlus, is that this solution avoids inheriting unwanted methods such as insertBefore. If a client were permitted to call insertBefore, there would be no guarantee that the list would remain sorted. The given implementation avoids this potential pitfall by giving a client no other way to add new items except by calling insert.

Figure 6.3 SortedList implementation

```
/* invariant: All items in theList are in ascending order with
              duplicate items permitted. */
public class SortedList extends SortedListADT {
    private SimpleSingleListPlus theList;

    /* post:  theList is empty */
    public SortedList() {
        theList = new SimpleSingleListPlus();
    }
    /* post:  result == theList.isOff() */
    public boolean isOff() {
        return theList.isOff();
    }
```

Continued on next page

```
/*  pre:     !isOff()
                    (throws java.util.NoSuchElementException)
    post:   result == theList.item() */
public Comparable item() {
    return (Comparable)(theList.item());
}
/*  post    theList's iterator is positioned at the front of the
            list */
public void start() {
    theList.start();
}
/*  post:    !isOff()@pre implies
                theList.iteratorPos == theList.iteratorPos@pre+1
             and isOff()@pre implies nothing changed */
public void forth() {
    theList.forth();
}
/*  pre:     !isOff() (throws java.util.NoSuchElementException)
    post:   theSeq == theSeq@pre with z inserted
            and theList.iteratorPos == 1 */
public void insert(Comparable z) {
    theList.start();
    while( !theList.isOff() && z.compareTo(theList.item())>0) {
        theList.forth();
    }
    theList.insertBefore(z);
    theList.start();
}
/*  post:   theList.iteratorPos <= theSeq@pre->size()
                implies theSeq == theSeq@pre with item deleted
                from theList.iteratorPos
            and theList.iteratorPos>theSeq@pre->size()
                implies theSeq==theSeq@pre */
public void removeAt() {
    theList.removeAt();
}
}
```

Most of the methods from the SortedList implementation are adapted from SimpleSingleListPlus by calling the corresponding method on the theList variable. The primary exception is the insert method. The insert method contains a *while* loop to search for the position where the new item should be inserted. The loop continues as long as the following condition is true:

```
!theList.isOff() && z.compareTo(theList.item()) > 0
```

The second clause in this condition is true as long as the value of z is greater than the item where the iterator is positioned. This condition ensures that the loop terminates when either all list items have been found to be less than z or when the item at the iterator position is greater than or equal to z. In either case, the proper action following the loop is expressed in the following statement:

```
theList.insertBefore(z);
```

The algorithm used by `insert` is essentially the same as the search portion of the well-known insertion sort algorithm (see Section 3.5). Each call to `insert` has a performance of O(*length of* `theList`).

Note that every call to the `insert` method alters the iterator that is built into `SimpleSingleListPlus`. To avoid confusion over the location of the iterator immediately after an insert, the `insert` method includes the following final statement. This positioning of the iterator is also reflected in the abstract specifications of `insert`.

```
theList.start();
```

Applying the `SortedList` class to solving the problem of maintaining a list of people's names requires a class such as the `PersonName` class shown in Figure 6.4.

Figure 6.4 PersonName class

```
public class PersonName implements Comparable {
    private String firstName;
    private char midInital;
    private String lastName;

    /* post:   firstName == f and midInital = m and lastName == n */
    public PersonName(String f, char m, String n) {
        firstName = f;
        midInital = m;
        lastName = n;
    }
    /* post:   this.equals(z) implies result == 0
                and this alphabetically precedes z
                    implies result ==-1
                and this follows z alphabetically
                    implies result == 1 */
    public int compareTo(Object z) {
        String zFirst = ((PersonName)z).firstName;
        char zMid = ((PersonName)z).midInital;
        String zLast = ((PersonName)z).lastName;
        if ( equals(z) )
            return 0;
        else if ( lastName.compareTo(zLast) < 0
                    || (lastName.equals(zLast) &&
                        firstName.compareTo(zFirst) < 0)
                    || (lastName.equals(zLast) &&
                        firstName.equals(zFirst) && midInital < zMid))
            return -1;
```

Continued on next page

```java
        else
            return 1;
    }
    /* post:  result == (firstName, lastName and middleInitial are
                         the same for this and z) */
    public boolean equals(Object z){
        if ( !(z instanceof PersonName) )
            return false;
        else
            return lastName.equals(((PersonName)z).firstName)
                    && midInital == ((PersonName)z).midInital
                    && firstName.equals(((PersonName)z).firstName);
    }
    /* post:  result == lastName, firstName, midInital. */
    public String toString() {
        return lastName + ", " + firstName + " " + midInital + ".";
    }
}
```

If `PersonName` is going to work in conjunction with the `SortedList` class, then `PersonName` must properly implement the `Comparable` interface. This is accomplished by

1. Appending an `implements Comparable` clause on the first line of the class
2. Including a `compareTo` method

The `compareTo` method in the `PersonName` class returns 0 if all three name parts are the same, returns –1 if `this` alphabetically precedes the parameter (z), and returns 1 if z precedes `this`. Alphabetization is determined by first checking the last names. The smaller last name is the one closer to the beginning of the alphabet. If the last names are the same, the first name is compared in the same way. If both the last and the first names are identical, the middle initial is used to determine the alphabetical order.

The effort of writing the client code to construct a sorted list of names is made relatively easy by the `SortedList` and `PersonName` classes. The following code inserts six names into a list of names and then displays the list.

```java
SortedList personList = new SortedList();
personList.insert(new PersonName("Kasandra", 'J', "Riley"));
personList.insert(new PersonName("Derek", 'D', "Riley"));
personList.insert(new PersonName("Sara", 'L', "Toufar"));
personList.insert(new PersonName("Timothy", 'D', "Hoege"));
personList.insert(new PersonName("Marion", 'L', "Roecker"));
personList.insert(new PersonName("Edwin", 'C', "Roecker"));
personList.start();
while (!personList.isOff()) {
    System.out.println(personList.item() );
    personList.forth();
}
```

6.2 MULTIPLE ITERATORS PER LIST

All the list ADTs examined so far (`SimpleSingleList`, `SimpleSingleListPlus`, and `SortedList`) use a single built-in iterator. Such containers are sufficient to solve many list problems, but a single iterator can be a limitation. (A built-in iterator is akin to an array with only one index variable.)

This single iterator restriction causes some awkwardness for the `insert` method of the `SortList` class. Because the `insert` method must use the iterator to perform its insertion, it will necessarily disturb the iterator's prior positioning. For example, consider the following client code:

```
// assert: list is of type SortList and contains one or more items
list.start();
list.forth();
list.insert( somePerson );
```

You might expect that the iterator is still positioned at the second list item (from the call to `start()` followed by `forth()`). However, the call to `insert`, like all calls to this method, has reset the iterator to the beginning of the list. An `insert` method that is adapted from `SimpleSingleListPlus` would be much more complicated if it needed to return the iterator to its position at the time the method is called.

In the absence of multiple iterators per list, some algorithms, such as those that restore an iterator position, become complicated or less efficient to implement, and other algorithms are impractical. For example, an algorithm that removes all duplicate list cells essentially demands at least two iterators.

Supporting multiple iterators raises design considerations beyond those of the lists presented so far. The most significant change is that iterators are best decoupled from (not encapsulated within) lists. This decoupling into separate classes lets you instantiate multiple iterators for a single list. Figure 6.5 shows two such ADTs.

Figure 6.5 points out that most of the operations previously included in the list belong in the iterator class. The `start`, `forth`, and `isOff` methods are obvious inclusions in an iterator, rather than a list, ADT. The remaining `SimpleSingleListPlus` methods also are allocated to `SingleIterator` because they all involve computations that must occur relative to the iterator position. The `item` method returns a value that is dependent on the iterator position, and list insertions and removals are always relative to the iterator.

Software Engineering Hint

Methods that rely directly on the position of an iterator belong to an iterator class more than a list class. In fact, most operations that are considered to be for list manipulation should be designed as iterator methods.

Even though `SingleList` is separated from `SingleIterator`, this does not mean that iterators are disassociated with lists. Implementing the `start` method is impossible unless the iterator is associated with some list. A good technique for associating an iterator with its list is to do so when the iterator is instantiated. You might use a constructor method such as this:

Potential Constructor Method

```
public SingleIterator(SingleList s )
```

> **post:** theSeq == s
> *and* iteratorPos == 1

Figure 6.5 Class diagrams and specifications for `SingleList` and
`SingleIterator`

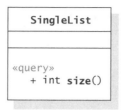

```
           SingleList

«query»
    + int size()
```

SingleList ADT Specifications

Domain Every SingleList object is a *sequence* of Object

Constructor Method

public **SingleList**( )
    post: this == *sequence*{}

Query Methods

public int **size**( )
    post: result == this->*size*()

```
            SingleIterator

«copy»
    + SingleIterator clonedIt()

«query»
    + boolean isOff()
    + Object item()

«update»
    + void start()
    + void forth()
    + void insertBefore(Object z)
    + void removeAt()
```

SingleIterator ADT Specifications

Domain (Every SingleIterator object consists of)
    sequence of Object **theSeq**;
    integer **iteratorPos**;

Copy Method

public SingleIterator **clonedIt**( )
    post: result.equals(this)

    All other methods are the same as SimpleSingleList (Figure 6.1)

This constructor is not the only way to connect an iterator to its class, as demonstrated later in this section when the implementation is presented.

Before proceeding to design strategies for SingleList and SingleIterator, you should be aware of the utility of multiple iterators. For this example, consider an algorithm to remove from a list all cells having duplicate content. In other words, the algorithm should leave one copy of each unique list cell and remove all others with the same content. Figure 6.6 contains a method to perform this algorithm on a SingleList object. This algorithm assumes the existence of the SingleIterator constructor shown earlier.

Figure 6.6 Method to remove duplicates from a SingleList

```
private void removeDuplicates( SingleList list ) {
    for (SingleIterator itA = new SingleIterator(list);
            !itA.isOff(); itA.forth())
    {
        SingleIterator itB = itA.clonedIt();
        itB.forth();
        while (!itB.isOff()) {
            if (itA.item().equals(itB.item()) ) {
                itB.removeAt();
            } else {
                itB.forth();
            }
        }
    }
}
```

The removeDuplicates method relies on two iterators. The first iterator, called itA, is advanced through the list from beginning to end by way of the outer *for* loop. Each time itA is assigned a new position, itB is positioned one cell beyond itA. This positioning of itB is accomplished by the following two statements.

```
SingleIterator itB = itA.clonedIt();
itB.forth();
```

The *while* loop of the removeDuplicates method advances itB through the remainder of the list. The content of each cell visited by itB is compared to the content of the itA cell. The itB cell is removed if it duplicates the itA cell's content. Notice that removing an item has the effect of advancing the iterator. Therefore, the *while* loop must not apply a forth method to itB when an item is removed.

Software Engineering Hint

Making implementation details visible is generally a poor programming practice. Sometimes such exposure permits data structure corruption. The design in Figure 6.7 is one such case.

Now it is time to examine how to implement SingleList and SingleIterator. There are at least two potential design strategies leading to an implementation. Figure 6.7 shows the class diagrams for the first of these designs.

Figure 6.7 Class diagram for a first potential `SingleList` design

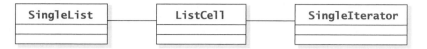

The Figure 6.7 design pictures the `SingleList` and `SingleIterator` classes. This design includes an additional `ListCell` class shared by both classes. The `ListCell` class is used by `SingleList` to maintain the list's anchor, and `ListCell` is needed by `SingleIterator` to provide the link and content attributes required in the various methods.

The shortcoming of this first design is that the `ListCell` class, and its members, must be public and therefore exposed. Because two other classes require access to `ListCell`, neither the class nor its members can be declared `private`, and this means that other classes may have access to `ListCell` and its members.

Figure 6.8 shows a second possible design. By making `ListCell` an inner class of `SingleList`, this design eliminates the need to expose `ListCell`. In this way, it is similar to the `SimpleSingleListPlus` implementation from Chapter 5.

Figure 6.8 Class diagram for `SingleList`

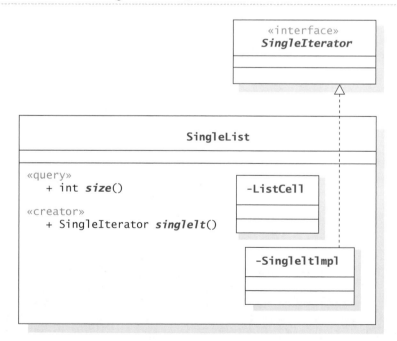

The key decision in this second design is to make `SingleItImpl` an inner class within `SingleList`. This inner placement permits `SingleItImpl` code to access `SingleList` members as well as access `ListCell` and its members. The `SingleIt` method is included in order to provide a public way to create new iterators. Figure 6.9 shows the declaration structure and new members of `SingleList`.

Figure 6.9 SingleList

```java
import java.util.NoSuchElementException;
public class SingleList {
    private class ListCell {
        public Object content;
        public ListCell link;
        /* post: content == z and link == null */
        public ListCell(Object z) {
            content = z;
            link = null;
        }
    }
    private ListCell anchorToHeader;
    private int length;
    /* post:   anchorToHeader != a newly instantiated cell
               and anchorToHeader.link == null
               and length == 0 */
    public SingleList() {
        anchorToHeader = new ListCell(null);
        length = 0;
    }
    /* post: result == length */
    public int size() {
        return length;
    }


    /* post:   result.preIteratorCell == anchorToHeader */
    public SingleIterator singleIt() {
        return new SingleItImpl(anchorToHeader);
    }

    private class SingleItImpl implements SingleIterator {
        private ListCell preIteratorCell;

        /* pre:    cell != null
           post:   preIteratorCell == cell */
        public SingleItImpl(ListCell cell) {
            preIteratorCell = cell;
        }

        /* post:   result.preIteratorCell == preIteratorCell */
        public SingleIterator clonedIt() {
            return new SingleItImpl(preIteratorCell);
        }
```

Continued on next page

```
        // Additional SingleItImpl methods are similar to those of
        // the  prior SimpleSingleList implementation with the
        //inclusion of attention to changes in length.
    }
}
```

The `SingleList` implementation shown in Figure 6.9 declares both local classes (`ListCell` and `SingleItImpl`) private, thereby insulating `ListCell` from access by external classes. This design also restricts access to `SingleItImpl` members, some of which should *not* be restricted. The solution to providing iterator access is to express `SingleIterator` in the form of a public Java interface and to provide a `SingleList` method (called `singleIt`) that returns a fresh iterator conforming to `SingleIterator`. The following code illustrates how client code can use this class to create a short list.

```
SingleList list = new SingleList();
SingleIterator it = list.singleIt();
it.insertBefore("eat.");
it.insertBefore("Goats");
```

6.3   ITERATOR INTEGRITY

You must avoid two potential pitfalls when implementing an iterator as a cell reference:

- Dereferencing an iterator that has been assigned `null`
- Permitting an iterator to reference a removed cell

Both pitfalls are appropriately viewed as threats to **iterator integrity**. To some extent, null pointer exceptions are always a consideration for programmers. However, iterator implementations pose an additional threat. Most list methods can throw null pointer exceptions when an iterator has a `null` value; and iterators are advanced by assigning the value from the link attribute, when the last cell in the list has a `null`-valued link. Such iterator advancement creates the potential of assigning `null` to an iterator. The `preIteratorCell` variable from earlier list implementations should never be assigned `null`. If `preIteratorCell == null`, then this iterator has lost its integrity.

Even small errors in methods that implement iterators can cause unwanted link attributes to become `null`-valued or an iterator to advance too far. Such logic errors can cause iterator variables to be assigned `null` prematurely, thus destroying the iterator's integrity.

Whereas dereferencing a `null`-valued iterator results from an erroneous implementation, you can encounter the second pitfall (removal of a referenced cell) while using a correct list implementation. This second snare is a potential danger whenever cells are removed from a list that involves multiple iterators. Consider the situation pictured by the object diagram in Figure 6.10.

Figure 6.10 Example SingleList object diagram

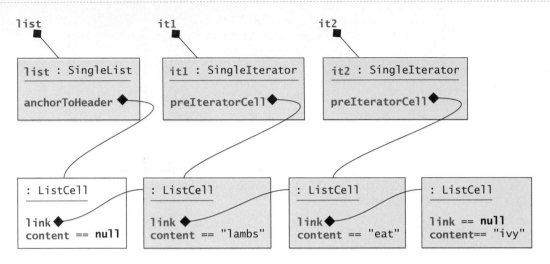

The state depicted in Figure 6.10 consists of a list, called list, and two associated iterators, called it1 and it2. Because this implementation uses prepointers, the actual position of it1 is the second ("eat") cell. Therefore, this second cell is the one to be removed by the following statement:

```
it1.removeAt();
```

Figure 6.11 shows the state resulting from this removal.

Figure 6.11 SingleList object diagram following it1.removeAt();

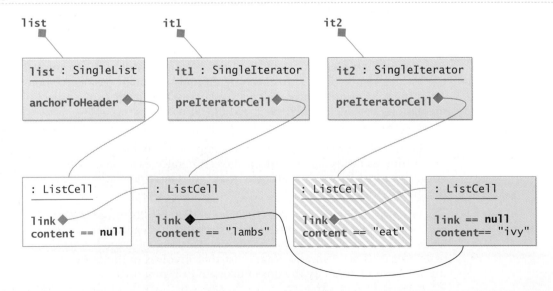

The value of it2 following this call to removeAt looks suspicious because it2 is positioned at the cell that has been removed. Despite this suspicious appearance, the code may proceed properly, depending on what occurs next. However, the it2 iterator integrity is clearly lost if the following statement executes next:

    it1.removeAt();

Figure 6.12 shows the state following this statement.

Figure 6.12   SingleList object diagram following it1.removeAt();

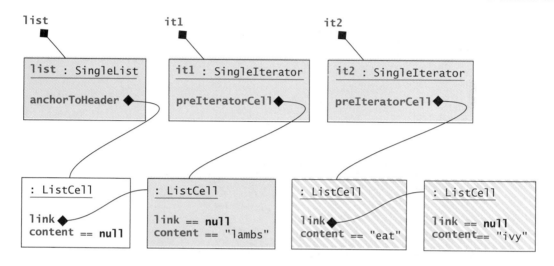

At this time the list is only one cell in length, and it1 is positioned off the end of the list. The problem is that it2 continues to be positioned on the portion of the list that was removed. A call to it2.item() returns the "ivy" value, and executing an insertion operation relative to it2 inserts into a portion of the list that was supposed to have been removed.

Software Engineering Hint

Many linked data structure implementations involving multiple iterators have the potential to corrupt iterators. When the list is manipulated (such as when a cell is removed), other iterators may become attached to improper cells. Programmers must take special care that changes involving one iterator do not corrupt other iterators over the same structure.

This potential pitfall is common among linked data structures that permit the use of multiple iterators. It is possible for the data structure implementation to ensure iterator integrity by maintaining a container of all of the object's iterators and checking each iterator whenever a remove operation occurs. However, such implementations of linked data structures are rarely used, mainly because the extra time for checking and repairing iterator integrity degrades performance. As a result, you must be aware of the potential loss of iterator integrity when performing remove operations.

6.4   CIRCULAR LISTS (OPTIONAL)

There are several common linear linked data structures in addition to singly linked lists; one such structure is called a circular linked list. As its name implies, a

circular linked list should be view abstractly as a sequence arranged around a circle. In a sense, there is no last item in the sequence.

Figure 6.13 pictures the difference between the abstract view of a linked list and that of a circular linked list. Both lists that contain the same three items: Kasandra, Sandra, and Derek.

Figure 6.13 A linked list and a circular list with the same three items

A Linked List of Names

< Sandra, Kasandra, Derek >

A Circular List of Names

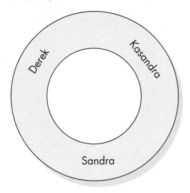

Even though there is no "last" item in a circular list, most versions include a start method and some way to test when an iterator has cycled completely around the list. Figure 6.14 shows a circular linked list iterator class.

Figure 6.14 Class diagram for CircularIterator

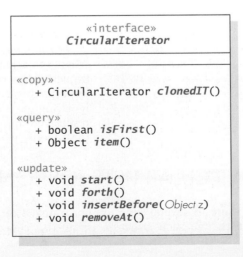

CircularIterator is almost identical to SingleIterator. The two key differences lie in the behavior of the forth method and the use of an alternative method: isOff.

The forth method for SingleIterator can advance only to the end of the list. However, there is no end to a circular linked list, so for CircularIterator the forth method can always advance.

The second difference between the two classes is that CircularIterator includes an isFirst method in place of the isOff method from SingleIterator. The isFirst method returns true exactly when the iterator is positioned at the first list item. An algorithm for visiting all the cells of a circular linked list is similar to that of a singly linked list if isFirst is used in place of isOff.

The representation of a circular linked list is analogous to that of a singly linked list. The most common implementation is one in which the link attribute of the last list cell references the first list cell. Figure 6.15 is a sample object diagram that illustrates such a representation.

Figure 6.15 Object diagram to demonstrate a circular list representation

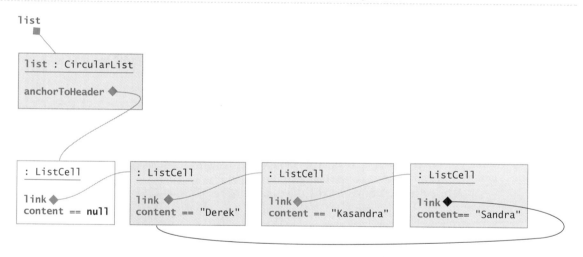

Circular lists are helpful for writing applications in which the container items are visited repeatedly. One example might be an aircraft guidance program that checks the values of all aircraft gauges. The gauges could be accessed through a circular list so that the program visits gauge after gauge without end.

A second circular list application can be found in the program (process) scheduling component of an operating system. Among other things, most computer operating systems are responsible for scheduling the execution of various simultaneously executing programs. For example, a word processor might be running in one window, a Java compiler translating a program in a second window, and a Web browser searching for an HTML page in a third window. Conceptually, all three programs are executing at the same time, but if the computer has only one processor, then only one of the programs can *actually* execute at any given time. One way to resolve the situation is to use a technique known as **round robin scheduling**, in which the programs take turns using the processor. The operating system treats programs as items in a circular list and visits all items in the list, allowing each item (program) to use the computer's processor for the duration of the visit. Each new program to begin executing must be inserted into the circular list, and a program is removed from the list when it completes execution.

Circular lists are best thought of as convenient, but not essential, data structures. Any task that can be accomplished with a circular list also can be accomplished with a one-way (singly linked) list. However, when the container is to be visited repeatedly in a continuous cycle and there is no clear need for a beginning or end, the circular list avoids the need to test for isOff and to reset iterators to the start of the list.

6.5 TWO-WAY LISTS AND DOUBLE LINKING

Iterators of singly linked lists are restricted in the sense that they always move in only one direction. This unidirectional iterator positioning is consistent with the name SingleList. But in many applications, a two-way linear container would make more sense. For example, consider a word processor storing a text document in the form of a list in which each item represents one line of text. A two-way list would be far more natural for permitting the user to scroll both forward and backward through the document's lines. A second kind of application that would be difficult to represent with a singly linked list is an electronic ROLODEX® of address information because the ROLODEX mechanism works on the concept of moving forward and backward through an address list. Such applications suggest the need for a linked list that supports two-way iterator traversal. Figure 6.16 proposes such a two-way ADT and the associated iterator.

The differences between a SingleList and a DoubleList are not so much differences in the containers themselves, because both are linear. However,

Figure 6.16 Class diagrams for DoubleList and DoubleIterator

DoubleList
«query»   + int **size**()   + DoubleIterator **doubleIt**()

«interface»   DoubleIterator
«copy»   + DoubleIterator **clonedIt**()   «query»   + boolean **isOffFront**()   + boolean **isOffRear**()   + Object **item**()   «update»   + void **start**()   + void **forth**()   + void **startAtRear**()   + void **back**()   + void **insertBefore**(Object z)   + void **removeAt**()

DoubleIterator includes two methods (startAtRear and back) that are not part of SingleIterator. This class also uses two query methods (isOffFront and isOffRear) in place of isOff. Figure 6.17 contains the specifications for these new methods.

Figure 6.17 Partial ADT specifications for DoubleIterator

DoubleIterator ADT Specifications

Domain (Every DoubleIterator object has the following components)

    sequence of Object **theSeq**;

    integer **iteratorPos**;

Invariant: $0 <= \text{iteratorPos} <= \text{theSeq->}size() + 1$

Query Methods

public boolean **isOffFront( )**

    post: result == (iteratorPos == 0)

public boolean **isOffRear( )**

    post: result == (iteratorPos == theSeq->*size*() + 1)

...

Update Methods

public void **startAtRear( )**

    post: iteratorPos == theSeq->*size*()

public void **back( )**

    post: !isOffFront()*@pre implies* iteratorPos == iteratorPos*@pre* - 1)

          and isOffFront()*@pre implies* iteratorPos == iteratorPos*@pre*)

...

The back method is the counterpart of forth. A call to back positions an iterator at the predecessor list item rather than the successor item. Similarly, the startAtRear method is analogous to start except that startAtRear positions an iterator at the last item in the list instead of the first.

The inclusion of a back method creates the potential for an iterator to be moved backward past the front of the list. Therefore, the isOff method from SingleIterator is split in two: an isOffRear method tests for an iterator that has been positioned beyond the last list item, and an isOffFront method tests for an iterator that has been positioned in front of the first item. Using these new methods lets you visit all list items from first to last or from last to first. The following loop shows the code pattern for visiting items from first to last:

```
// assert: it is a non-null DoubleIterator object
for (it.start(); !it.isOffRear(); it.forth()) {
    // visit it.item()
}
```

The loop to visit all items in the reverse order, from last to first, is coded as follows:

```
// assert: it is a non-null DoubleIterator object
for (it.startAtRear(); !it.isOffFront(); it.back()) {
    // visit it.item()
}
```

A linked data structure is a natural way to implement a two-way list. However, to maintain efficiency you must link the list's cells in both the forward and the backward direction, forming a structure known as a **doubly linked list**. Figure 6.18 shows the shell of such a DoubleList class in the style of SingleList.

Figure 6.18 The DoubleList class

```
import java.util.NoSuchElementException;
public class DoubleList {
    private class DoubleCell {
        public Object content;
        public DoubleCell nextLink;
        public DoubleCell prevLink;
        /* post:  content == z and nextLink == null
                  and prevLink == null */
        public DoubleCell(Object z) {
            content = z;
            nextLink = null;
            prevLink = null;
        }
    }
    private DoubleCell anchorToFrontHeader;
    private DoubleCell anchorToRearHeader;
    private int length;
    private class DoubleItImpl implements DoubleIterator {
        // DoubleItImpl methods are described in later figures.
    }
}
```

The DoubleCell class defines the type for the cells of DoubleList. Notice that DoubleCell contains two links: one link, called nextLink, to reference the successor cell, and a second link, called prevLink, to reference the predecessor cell. For any cell reference to a doubly linked list cell other than the first or last, cell.nextLink.prevLink should always reference the cell itself, as should cell.prevLink.nextLink. In other words, the cells of a doubly linked list form a linear structure with a chain of nextLink references in the forward direction and a chain of prevLink references in the backward direction. To illustrate such a two-way chain, Figure 6.19 pictures a particular DoubleList consisting of the following abstract sequence.

sequence{"fish", "speak"}

Figure 6.19 Object diagram of a DoubleList for *sequence*{"fish", "speak"}

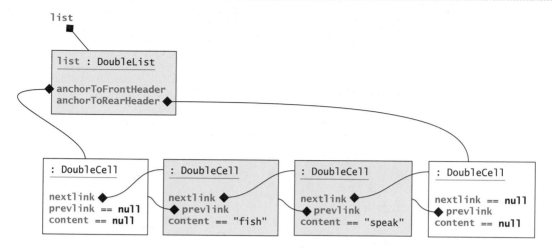

The prepointer implementation strategy is not required for a doubly linked list. Prepointers are helpful for locating the cell before the iterator cell, but with a DoubleList this cell can always be found by following the prevLink attribute.

Figure 6.19 points out that header cells are useful for implementing doubly linked lists. In fact, the preferred doubly linked list implementation includes not one, but two headers: one for the front of the list, and another one for the rear. For convenient implementations of the start and startAtRear methods, DoubleList contains instance variables to reference each header cell. These variables are called anchorToFrontHeader and anchorToRearHeader.

A doubly linked list effectively doubles the amount of link reconstruction that is needed for insertions and removals. The insertBefore method, shown in Figure 6.20, demonstrates.

Figure 6.20 insertBefore method for DoubleList

```
public void insertBefore(Object z) {
    if (isOffFront()) {
        throw new NoSuchElementException();
    } else {
        DoubleCell newCell = new DoubleCell(z);
        newCell.nextLink = iteratorCell;
        newCell.prevLink = iteratorCell.prevLink;
        iteratorCell.prevLink = newCell;
        newCell.prevLink.nextLink = newCell;
        length++;
    }
}
```

The insertBefore method must assign values to the prevLink and nextLink attributes of the newly-inserted cell. The method also must update the cells the neighboring cells. The cell previously preceding the iterator cell must have nextLink assigned to the new cell, and the cell previously following the iterator cell must have prevLink assigned to the new cell.

As suggested at the beginning of this section, a doubly linked list is useful for implementing such things as an electronic ROLODEX. Figure 6.21 pictures a user interface, created from javax.swing classes, for such a program.

Figure 6.21 User interface for ROLODEX program

The user interface has buttons to go forward (—>) and backward (<—) through the ROLODEX, as well as to clear the display fields, insert a new item into the ROLODEX from the display fields, and remove the displayed item from the ROLODEX. Each ROLODEX item can be stored as a separate object using the BizCard class shown in Figure 6.22.

Figure 6.22 BizCard class

```
public class BizCard {
    public String firstName;
    public String lastName;
    public String address;
    public String company;
    public BizCard(String f, String n, String a, String co) {
        firstName = f;
        lastName = n;
        address = a;
        company = co;
    }
}
```

A class called `RolodexApp` is shown in Figure 6.23. This program implements the electronic ROLODEX interface using both the `BizCard` and `DoubleList` classes.

Figure 6.23 RolodexApp class

```
import java.awt.event.*;
import javax.swing.*;
public class RolodexApp implements ActionListener {
    private JFrame window;
    private JButton addBtn, removeBtn,
                    forwardBtn, backBtn, clearBtn;
    private JTextField frstNameFld, lstNameFld, addrFld, coFld;

    private DoubleList addressList;
    private DoubleIterator listIt;
    /* note:  This method initiates program execution by
              instantiating this class. */
    public static void main(String args[]) {
        new RolodexApp();
    }

    /* post:  a user interface with five buttons and four fields
              has been displayed */
    public RolodexApp() {
        window = new JFrame();
        window.getContentPane().setLayout(null);
        window.setBounds(10, 10, 340, 300);
        makeLabeledFields();
        forwardBtn = newButton(80, 190, 100, 30, "->");
        backBtn = newButton(80, 230, 100, 30, "<-");
        clearBtn = newButton(250, 170, 80, 20, "Clear");
        addBtn = newButton(250, 200, 80, 20, "Insert");
        removeBtn = newButton(250, 230, 80, 20, "Remove");
        window.show();
        addressList = new DoubleList();
        listIt = addressList.doubleIt();
    }
    /* post:  event e was caused by the -> button
                    implies the rolodex displays the next
                      business card
                and event e was caused by the <- button
                    implies the rolodex displays the previous
                      business card
                and event e was caused by the Clear button
                    implies the rolodex display is cleared
                and event e was caused by the Insert button
                    implies the rolodex display is inserted after
                      the last card that was displayed
```

Continued on next page

```
                                    and event e was caused by the Remove button
                                    implies the business card last displayed is
                                        removed
                    note:   This method is called in response to all button
                            events */
        public void actionPerformed(ActionEvent e) {
            if (e.getSource() == forwardBtn) {
                if (!listIt.isOffRear())
                    listIt.forth();
                displayFieldsFromIteratorPosition();
            } else if (e.getSource() == backBtn) {
                if (!listIt.isOffFront())
                    listIt.back();
                displayFieldsFromIteratorPosition();
            } else if (e.getSource() == clearBtn) {
                clearAllFields();
            } else if (e.getSource() == addBtn) {
                insertNewAddressFromFields();
            } else { // RemoveBtn pressed
                if (!listIt.isOffFront() && !listIt.isOffRear())
                    listIt.removeAt();
                displayFieldsFromIteratorPosition();
            }
            window.repaint();
        }


        /* post:   All display fields are blank */
        private void clearAllFields() {
            frstNameFld.setText("");
            lstNameFld.setText("");
            addrFld.setText("");
            coFld.setText("");
        }


        /* pre:    listIt != null (throws nullPointerException)
           post:   addressList == addressList@pre with a new item
                        inserted after listIt@pre
                   and listIt is positioned at the newly inserted item
                   */
        private void insertNewAddressFromFields() {
            BizCard businessCard;
            businessCard = new BizCard( frstNameFld.getText(),
                lstNameFld.getText(), addrFld.getText(), coFld.getText());
            if (!listIt.isOffRear()) listIt.forth();
            listIt.insertBefore(businessCard);
            listIt.back();
        }
```

Continued on next page

```
/*  pre:    listIt != null (throws nullPointerException)
    post:   (listIt.isOffFront() || listIt.isOffRear())
                implies == the display is cleared
            and not (listIt.isOffFront() || listIt.isOffRear())
                implies == the listIt item is displayed */
private void displayFieldsFromIteratorPosition() {
    if (listIt.isOffFront() || listIt.isOffRear()) {
        clearAllFields();
    } else {
        BizCard businessCard = (BizCard)(listIt.item());
        frstNameFld.setText(businessCard.firstName);
        lstNameFld.setText(businessCard.lastName);
        addrFld.setText(businessCard.address);
        coFld.setText(businessCard.company);
    }
}


/*  post:   all display fields and labels are displayed */
private void makeLabeledFields() {
    ...
}
/*  post:   result == a button with upper left corner at (x,y)
                a width of w, height of h and displaying s
            and the result button delegates its events to this
            and the result button is displayed */
private JButton newButton(int x, int y, int w, int h, String s)
{
    ...
}
}
```

The key variable in the RolodexApp class is a DoubleIterator variable called listIt. The listIt variable maintains the "current" position within the electronic ROLODEX. To see how RolodexApp works, you should understand that each user button click causes the actionPerformed method to be called as an event handler. When the forward button is clicked, the following code executes:

```
if (!listIt.isOffRear())
    listIt.forth();
displayFieldsFromIteratorPosition();
```

This code causes the iterator to advance, as long as it is not already past the end of the ROLODEX cards (isOffRear). The call to displayFieldsFrom-IteratorPosition causes the display screen to be updated to the content of the new ROLODEX card. Similarly, when the backward button is clicked, the following code executes:

```
if (!listIt.isOffFront())
    listIt.back();
displayFieldsFromIteratorPosition();
```

The use of a doubly linked list ensures that both the forward and the backward button operations have performance of O(1). More importantly, you can conveniently implement both operations with similar code.

The following code is executed in response to clicking the Remove button:

```
if (!listIt.isOffFront() && !listIt.isOffRear())
    listIt.removeAt();
displayFieldsFromIteratorPosition();
```

Clicking the Insert button is slightly more complicated:

```
BizCard businessCard;
businessCard = new BizCard( frstNameFld.getText(),
    lstNameFld.getText(), addrFld.getText(), coFld.getText() );
if (!listIt.isOffRear()) listIt.forth();
listIt.insertBefore(businessCard);
listIt.back();
```

This code extracts address information from the display fields in order to instantiate an object called businessCard. The last three statements ensure that the businessCard object is inserted *after* listIt@pre and that the iterator is repositioned at the location of the newly inserted address.

6.6 JAVA.UTIL.LIST AND JAVA.UTIL.LINKEDLIST

Among the java.util package facilities are classes and interfaces for supporting linked lists. The most important such list interface is java.util.List. Figure 6.24 contains the interface diagram and specifications.

Figure 6.24 Interface diagram and specification for java.util.List (abridged)

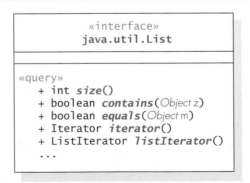

Continued on next page

java.util.List Specifications

Domain (Every List object has the following ittribute)
    sequence of Object `theSeq`;

Methods
`public int size( )`
    post: result == theSeq->*size*()
`public boolean contains( Object z )`
    post: result == theSeq->*includes*(z)
`public boolean equals( Object m )`
    post: result == (m.theSeq == theSeq)
`public Iterator iterator( )`
    post: result.position == 0
`public ListIterator listIterator( )`
    post: result.position == 0

. . .

Like `SingleList` and `DoubleList`, the `java.util.List` interface defines an ADT that specifies a basic container but allows iterators to provide much of the container's behavior. The `List` interface provides two methods for returning fresh iterator objects. The `iterator` method returns an iterator that conforms to the `java.util.Iterator` interface (described in Chapter 5). The `listIterator` method returns an iterator that conforms to the `java.util.ListIterator` interface.

Because `java.util.List` is an interface rather than a class, it provides a template that can be implemented for a variety of lists. The standard Java packages also provide implementations of this template. Most prominent among them is a class known as `java.util.LinkedList`. Figure 6.25 shows the key members of this class.

There are two `LinkedList` constructors. The parameterless constructor instantiates an empty linked list. The second constructor converts other containers into a `LinkedList` structure. This method accepts an argument conforming to `Collection`.[1]

Because the bulk of the behavior of `LinkedList` is provided by iterators, it is instructive to examine the `ListIterator` interface. Figure 6.26 contains the appropriate interface diagram and specifications.

The `ListIterator` and `Iterator` interfaces have many similarities and one primary difference. The difference is that `ListIterator` is designed for a two-way list, while `Iterator` is for one-way processing. `ListIterator` includes the `previous` method to reposition an iterator closer to the front of the list, and a `hasPrevious` method to test for more items in front of the iterator.

1. `Collection` refers to `java.util.Collection`, described in Chapter 5.

Figure 6.25 Class diagram for java.util.LinkedList (abridged)

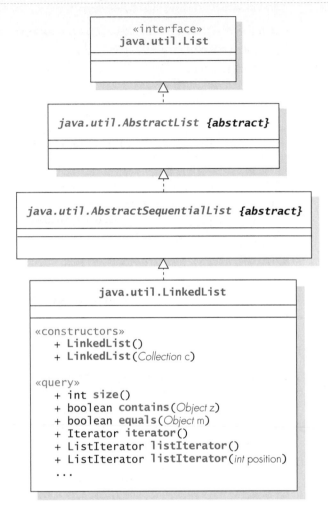

Figure 6.26 ListIterator interface diagram and specification

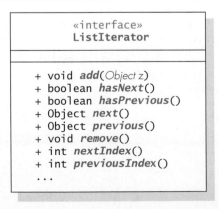

Continued on next page

ListIterator ADT Specifications

Domain (Every Iterator object has the following fields)

Sequence of Object `underlyingSeq`;

`int position`;

`boolean removeIsValid`;

Notes: The initial value of `position` should be zero (0). Any `add` or `remove` call upon one iterator invalidates other iterators of the same list. (ConcurrentModificationException is thrown for use of an invalidated iterator.)

Methods

`public Object add( Object z )`

post: underlyingSeq == underlyingSeq*@pre* with z inserted at
    position*@pre*
    and position == position*@pre* + 1
    and removeIsValid == false

`public boolean hasNext( )`

post: position < underlyingSeq->*size*()

`public boolean hasPrevious( )`

post: result == (position > 1)

`public Object next( )`

pre: position < underlyingSeq->*size*()
    (throws NoSuchElementException)

post: position == position*@pre* + 1
    and result == underlyingSeq->*at*(position)
    and removeIsValid == true

`public Object previous( )`

pre: position > 1 (throws NoSuchElementException)

post: position == position*@pre* − 1
    and result == underlyingSeq->*at*(position)
    and removeIsValid == true

`public int nextIndex( )`

post: result == position

`public int previousIndex( )`

post: result == position-1

`public void remove( )`

pre: removeIsValid == true   (throws IllegalStateException)

post: underlyingSeq == underlyingSeq*@pre* with item removed at
    position*@pre*
    and position == position*@pre* − 1
    and removeIsValid == false

ListIterator uses a style that is similar to that of the Iterator interface. Both include a next method that both returns and advances the iterator, and a hasNext method to test when the iterator has been advanced beyond the end of the list.

The java.util style of iterator is somewhat different from the iterators of the DoubleList class presented in Section 6.5. These differences lead to variations in the code that uses the iterators. For example, here are loops to visit all items of each list:

DoubleList algorithm

```
DoubleIterator it = list.doubleIt();
while (!it.isOffRear()) {
    // process it.item()
    it.forth();
}
```

LinkedList algorithm

```
ListIterator it = list.ListIterator();
while (it.hasNext()) {
    Object itemHolder = it.next();
    // process itemHolder
}
```

The primary distinction between these two algorithms stems from the next method, which combines the behavior of item and forth. The use of the itemHolder variable emphasizes that such an additional variable may be required if the value returned by next must be inspected more than once.

Just as there are two ways to instantiate a DoubleIterator from a DoubleList, there are two ways to instantiate a LinkedIterator from a LinkedList. The parameterless listIterator method returns a new iterator that is positioned at the front of the list. The second version of listIterator includes an int parameter that is used to assign the position of the newly instantiated iterator. The clonedIt method from DoubleList instantiates a new iterator positioned identically to a previous iterator in an statement such as this one:

```
DoubleIterator newIt = it.clonedIt();
```

You can achieve the same effect for a LinkedList iterator using this code:

```
ListIterator newIt = it.listIterator( it.previousIndex() );
```

The add method from ListIterator is analogous to the insertBefore method from DoubleList. No ListIterator method corresponds to insertAfter.

The ListIterator remove method is different from removeAt because remove deletes the item that was most recently returned by a call to next or previous. If neither next nor previous has been called since the last remove, a call to remove throws an IllegalStateException.

The ListIterator class takes a strict view of iterator integrity. When two iterators share the same list, any call to add or remove on one of these iterators invalidates the other. Any attempt to call next or previous on the other iterator results in a ConcurrentModificationException. This approach ensures the integrity of iterators, but it effectively requires that all other iterators of the same list must be reinstantiated following a call to add or remove.

6.7 IMPLEMENTING A LIST WITH AN ARRAY

Any linked structure can be implemented with an array. (After all, a computer's memory is nothing but one large array of storage cells.) Examining how to implement linking with an array provides insight into how dynamic memory is managed by computer operating systems and the Java virtual machine.

The fundamental concept for these implementations is to think of an array as a mechanism for emulating a list. An array cell plays the role of a list cell, and a list's link is represented as an array index. For purposes of this discussion, the array is called `cellSpace` and the type of `cellSpace` is an array of `ListArrayCell`, as shown in Figure 6.27.

Figure 6.27 `ListArrayCell` (the type of each item of the `cellSpace` array)

```
private class ListArrayCell {
    public Object content;
    public int linkIndex;
    public static final int nullLink = -1;
    /* post:    content == z and linkIndex == nullLink */
    public ListArrayCell(Object z) {
        content = z;
        linkIndex = nullLink;
    }
}
```

The difference between `ListArrayCell` and the inner cell classes of previous proposed linked-list implementations is that `ListArrayCell` uses an `int` attribute to store a link. The name of this attribute is `linkIndex` because it is used to store an index into the `cellSpace` array.

Figure 6.28 illustrates how the `cellSpace` array can be used to store a list of four cells: *sequence*{"bees", "play", "funk", "guitar"}. This particular `cellSpace` array contains seven items.

The anchor for the array is an `int` variable called `anchorIndex`. In this example, `anchorIndex` is 3, indicating that the first list item is stored in the array cell having index 3. The dashed arrow from `anchorIndex` points to the associated array cell object.

The list is linked together by `linkIndex` attributes, which store the indices of the subsequent list items. The `linkIndex` of `cellSpace[3]` stores the value 6, indicating that the second list item is stored in `cellSpace[6]`. Similarly, the third list item is at index 0 and the last item has an index of 1. A value of (–1) in the `linkIndex` attribute signifies the end of the list. The use of –1 is analogous to the use of `null` for the link attribute at the end of a dynamic linked list. The choice of –1 is based in part upon the observation that –1 is invalid as an array index, so this value cannot be confused with an actual index.

Figure 6.28 Object diagram of a `SingleListArray` for *sequence*{"bees", "play", "funk", "guitar"}

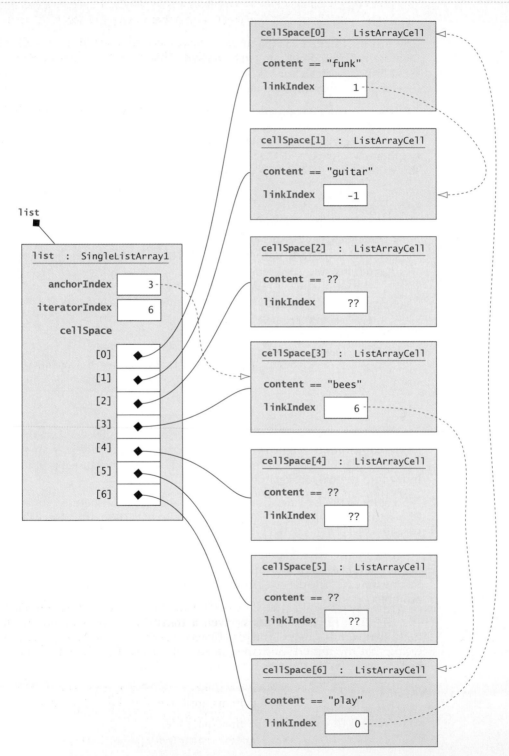

Figure 6.28 demonstrates that iterators also are represented by array indices for this implementation. The `iteratorIndex` value of 6 in this picture means that the iterator is positioned at `cellSpace[6]`—in other words, the second item in the list.

Figure 6.29 shows the code for some of the methods of the `SingleListArray` class associated with this implementation. This implementation represents a one-way list with a built-in iterator.

Figure 6.29 start, isOff, forth, and item methods for the array representation

```
/*  post:   iteratorIndex == anchorIndex */
public void start() {
    iteratorIndex = anchorIndex;
}
/*  post:   result == (iteratorIndex == nullIndex)
    note:   nullIndex == -1 */
public boolean isOff() {
    return (iteratorIndex == nullIndex);
}
/*  post:   !isOff()@pre implies
            iteratorIndex == cellSpace[iteratorIndex@pre].linkIndex
            */
public void forth() {
    if (!isOff()) {
        iteratorIndex = cellSpace[iteratorIndex].linkIndex;
    }
}


/*  pre:    !isOff() (throws java.util.NoSuchElementException)
    post:   result == cellSpace[iteratorIndex].content */
public Object item() {
    if (isOff()) {
        throw new NoSuchElementException();
    } else {
        return cellSpace[iteratorIndex].content;
    }
}
```

The `start` and `isOff` methods of the array implementation are similar to those of the linked implementations, given a translation from dynamic references to array indices. The `start` method resets `iteratorIndex` to the same value as `anchorIndex`. The `isOff` method returns true exactly when the iterator has a `nullIndex` (−1) value.

The `forth` method normally advances the iterator from its current position to the next list item. Because list items are linked by their `linkIndex` attribute, the statement to advance the iterator position is as follows:

```
iteratorIndex = cellSpace[iteratorIndex].linkIndex;
```

The `item` method must return the value of the cell associated with the iterator's position. Because this iterator is represented as an index, the following `return` statement returns the proper value:

```
return cellSpace[iteratorIndex].content;
```

Inserting a new item poses special difficulties for the array implementation. Which cells of `cellSpace` are unused and therefore available for insertion? What if all of the `cellSpace` becomes occupied? (These are the same difficulties that must have been solved by the creators of the Java virtual machine so that it would operate within its memory limitations.)

One solution to these problems is to keep a singly linked list of unused cells, often called **free space**. As a program begins to execute, the free space list consists of the entire `cellSpace` array. Each time `insertBefore` or `insertAfter` requires a new cell, one cell is removed from the front of the free space list to serve as the newly inserted item. Presumably, the implementation will throw an `OutOfMemoryError` exception when free space is exhausted and additional cells are requested.

A proper `remove` method also should cooperate with the free space list. When `removeAt` is called, the cell from `cellSpace` that is associated with the removed list item should be inserted into the free space list so that it can be repurposed for future insertions.

The Java virtual machine's management of memory is not quite so simple as suggested by this free space list. The JVM does maintain a list of free space. However, this space comes not only from one list but also from the many different ways that programs can create orphans. The JVM is not notified of the availability of removed cells, but rather it must go "looking" for them by way of its garbage collector algorithm. The work of the JVM is further complicated by the fact that the amount of dynamic memory allocation and deallocation varies.

6.8 LISTS AS RECURSIVE STRUCTURES

The discussion so far has taken the view that a list consists of a linear sequence of cells. However, there is a different approach that visualizes a list as something of a **recursive structure**. In this view, lists can have one of two forms:

a. A list can be empty.
b. A list is nonempty and consists of a first item and the rest of the list.

This is called "recursive" because part (a) is a base part of the definition and part (b) is the recursive part. The recursion stems from the fact that "the rest of the list" is a reference to another list. For example, consider the list described in the following sequence.

sequence{1, 2, 3}

The recursive structure approach would define this same list as follows.

$$sequence\{1, 2, 3\} == < 1 \text{ followed by } theRestOfList1 >$$

$$< 2 \text{ followed by } theRestOfList2 >$$

$$< 3 \text{ followed by } anEmptyList >$$

Figure 6.30 contains the ADT specifications for a `RecursiveList` ADT. Included in this ADT is a method to test for an empty list (`isEmpty`), two accessor methods to inspect the first item and the rest of any nonempty list (`first` and `tail`), two methods to assign a new first item and the `theRestOfList` (`setFirst`, `setTail`), and an `apply` method that is explained shortly.

Figure 6.30 RecursiveList specifications

RecursiveList ADT Specifications

Domain (Every RecursiveList object has one of the two following forms)

    a) an empty sequence

    b) a two-part sequence

```
        Object firstItem;
        RecursiveList theRestOfList;
```

Invariant

Every RecursiveList contains a finite number of other RecursiveLists

Query Methods

```
public boolean isEmpty( )
```
    post: result == (this is an empty list (Form a))
```
public Object first( )
```
    pre: !isEmpty() (throws UnsupportedOperationException)

    post: result == firstItem
```
public RecursiveList tail( )
```
    pre: !isEmpty() (throws UnsupportedOperationException)

    post: result == theRestOfList

Update Methods

```
public void setFirst(Object z)
```
    pre: !isEmpty() (throws UnsupportedOperationException)

    post: firstItem == z
```
public void setTail(RecursiveList list)
```
    pre: !isEmpty() (throws UnsupportedOperationException)

    post: theRestOfList == list
```
public void apply( )
```
    note: This method is included to be overridden for various list
           operations

The following code illustrates how these five methods can be used to manipulate lists.

```
RecursiveList theList, emptyList;

  . . .
/* assert: theList == sequence{"rain", "Spain", "plain"}
          and emptyList == sequence{} */
System.out.println( theList.first() );
// assert: "rain" was just displayed
theList = theList.tail();
// assert: theList == sequence{"Spain", "plain"}
theList.setFirst( "again" );
// assert: theList == sequence{"again", "plain"}
theList.setTail( emptyList );
/* assert: theList == sequence{"again"}
          and emptyList == sequence{} */
if (theList.isEmpty())
    System.out.println( "An empty list was encountered." );
```

The class diagram in Figure 6.31 illustrates one way to design RecursiveList. In this design RecursiveList is an abstract class. There are two different concrete implementations of RecursiveList—namely, NonemptyList and EmptyList. The NonemptyList class represents lists having one or more items, and EmptyList represents lists having no items. EmptyList not only inherits RecursiveList, but it is also an inner class. This arrangement hides the implementation of an empty list, and it is possible because the singleton design pattern has been used to provide a single emptyList variable (i.e., it is static and final) that is shared by all RecursiveList objects.

The code for the RecursiveList class is unveiled in Figure 6.32. This includes the EmptyList inner class. Notice that all EmptyList methods, except isEmpty and apply, throw UnsupportedOperationException.

The emptyList variable is initialized in its declaration to reference an object of type EmptyClass. This static final variable has public scope so that clients can use it to acquire a RecursiveList that is empty. For example, the following client statement declares a RecursiveList variable and sets it to reference an empty list:

```
RecursiveList myList = RecursiveList.emptyList;
```

The isEmpty method is not abstract because it can be conveniently implemented by simply testing to see whether the current (this) list is an empty list. The body of isEmpty consists of the following single statement:

```
return (this instanceof EmptyList);
```

Following is an alternative correct statement for the body of isEmpty:

```
return (this == emptyList);
```

This second implementation of isEmpty works because emptyList is static and final so there can be only one empty list.

Figure 6.33 shows an implementation of NonemptyList. This class inherits RecursiveList and implements the four abstract methods.

Figure 6.31 Class diagram for implementing RecursiveList

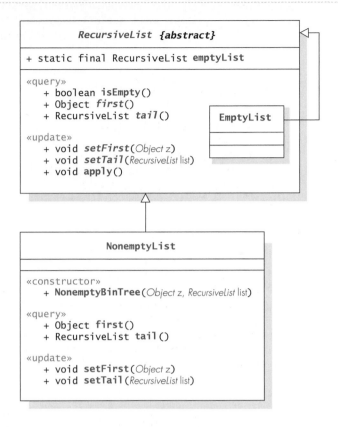

Figure 6.32 RecursiveList with inner EmptyList

```
/*  Domain (Every RecursiveList object has one of two forms)
        FORM a) The list is empty.
        FORM b) The list is nonempty and, therefore, has the
                following parts.
                    Object firstItem;
                    RecursiveList theRestOfList;
    invariant: moreList has finite length */
public abstract class RecursiveList {
    public static final RecursiveList emptyList = new EmptyList();
    private static class EmptyList extends RecursiveList {
        public EmptyList() {}
        public Object first()
          { throw new UnsupportedOperationException(); }
        public RecursiveList tail()
          { throw new UnsupportedOperationException(); }
```

Continued on next page

```
            public void setFirst(Object z)
              { throw new UnsupportedOperationException(); }
            public void setTail(RecursiveList list)
              {throw new UnsupportedOperationException(); }
    }
    /* post:   result == this is an empty list (Form a) */
    public boolean isEmpty() {
        return (this instanceof EmptyList);
    }
    /* pre:    !isEmpty() (throws UnsupportedOperationException)
       post:   result == firstItem */
    public abstract Object first();
    /* pre:    !isEmpty() (throws UnsupportedOperationException)
       post:   result == theRestOfList */
    public abstract RecursiveList tail();
    /* pre:    !isEmpty() (throws UnsupportedOperationException)
       post:   firstItem == z */
    public abstract void setFirst(Object z);
    /* pre:    !isEmpty() (throws UnsupportedOperationException)
       post:   theRestOfList == list */
    public abstract void setTail(RecursiveList list);
    /* note:   this method is intended to be overridden. */
    public void apply() {}
}
```

Figure 6.33 NonemptyList class

```
public class NonemptyList extends RecursiveList {
    protected RecursiveList moreList;
    protected Object content;
    /* pre:    rest is a valid RecursiveList
       post:   content == z and moreList == rest */
    public NonemptyList(Object z, RecursiveList rest) {
        moreList = rest;
        content = z;
    }
    /* post:   result == content */
    public Object first() {
        return content;
    }
    /* post:   result == moreList */
    public RecursiveList tail() {
        return moreList;
    }
```

Continued on next page

```
/* post:   content == z */
public void setFirst(Object z) {
    content = z;
}
/* post:   moreList == list */
public void setTail(RecursiveList list) {
    moreList = list;
}
}
```

The instance variables of NonemptyList parallel the ADT specifications. The content variable represents *firstItem*, and the moreList variable represents *theRestOfList*. This representation allows the four abstract methods to be implemented in one statement each.

The NonemptyList constructor is designed to support the construction of lists. NonemptyList accepts two arguments—an existing list and an Object—and it builds another list by prepending the object onto the parameter list. For example, the list *sequence*{"how", "now", "brown", "cow"} is built by prepending Strings from back to front as follows.

```
RecursiveList wordList = new NonemptyList("cow",
                             RecursiveList.emptyList);
wordList = new NonemptyList("brown", wordList);
wordList = new NonemptyList("now", wordList);
wordList = new NonemptyList("how", wordList);
/* assert: wordList == sequence{"how", "now", "brown", "cow"}
```

The apply method is included in RecursiveList to provide a template method for child classes to use in implementing operations that manipulate the list items. For example, Figure 6.34 shows a class, PrintList, for implementing a version of RecursiveList that can print the content of its list items from first through last. PrintList need only inherit NonemptyList and override apply to provide the desired functionality.

Figure 6.34 PrintList class

```
public class PrintList extends NonemptyList {
    /* pre:    rest is a valid PrintList
       post:   content == and moreList == rest */
    public PrintList(Object z, RecursiveList rest) {
        super(z, rest);
    }
    /* post:  All items in this list have been displayed from
              first through last */
    public void apply() {
        System.out.println(content);
        tail().apply();
    }
}
```

The PrintList implementation of apply is a recursive method. This method begins by displaying the value of the first item in the list (represented by content), and then it calls itself recursively on the remainder (tail) of the list. There is no check for the base step within the apply method. This omission of the nonrecursive base is possible only because of EmptyList. A call to this version of apply will eventually encounter an EmptyList object, and that object uses a version of apply that does nothing but return.

The following client code illustrates how to build a PrintList of three items, and then use the apply method to print the list.

```
RecursiveList theList;
theList = new PrintList("Richard", RecursiveList.emptyList);
theList = new PrintList("Sandra", theList);
theList = new PrintList("Beverly", theList);
theList.apply();
```

The apply template restricts each child class of RecursiveList to no more than one list manipulation method. The use of a technique, known as a **Command object design pattern**, provides more flexibility. A command object is an object whose only purpose is to supply a method implementation (a command). Figure 6.35 shows the small modification of RecursiveList needed to incorporate the use of a command object.

Figure 6.35 RecursiveList modified to include applyCommand

```
public abstract class RecursiveList {
    // The RecursiveList class code from Figure 6.32 remains here
    /* post:   the method d.applyCommand has been applied to this
                  list. */
    public void applyCommand(CommandTemplate d) {
        d.command(this);
    }
}
```

The applyCommand method has a single parameter that accepts an object of type CommandTemplate. It is this parameter that serves as the command object. When applyMethod executes, it calls the method that is implemented by the command object—namely, command. The argument this is passed to command so that it has access to the current list.

This use of a command object requires a template class (Java interface), called CommandTemplate, and child classes—one child for each different command object (i.e., each method to be applied to the list). Figure 6.36 shows an implementation of the CommandTemplate class along with two child classes: PrintCommand to display a list, and AppendPeriodCommand to append the character "." to every item in the list.

Figure 6.36 CommandTemplate and two child classes

```
public interface CommandTemplate {
    /* post:   This method is meant to be overridden. */
    public void command(RecursiveList list);
}
public class PrintCommand implements CommandTemplate {
    /* post:   list has been output. */
    public void command(RecursiveList list) {
        if (!(list.isEmpty())) {
            System.out.println(list.first());
            list.tail().applyCommand(this);
        }
    }
}
public class AppendPeriodCommand implements CommandTemplate {
    /* post:   Every item in list@pre has a period appended. */
    public void command(RecursiveList list) {
        if (!(list.isEmpty())) {
            list.setFirst( (String)(list.first()) + "." );
            list.tail().applyCommand(this);
        }
    }
}
```

Both the PrintCommand and the AppendPeriodCommand classes implement versions of command that are extended to every item in their list (passed via the list parameter). Both implementations of command must test for an empty list using the isEmpty method (the base step of the recursive method). (This test for an empty list assumes that the inner EmptyList class does *not* override the RecursiveList version of applyCommand.)

Using the command object pattern requires that the client code instantiate a separate object of appropriate type for every desired list operation. The following code illustrates how to apply both the PrintCommand and the AppendPeriodCommand versions of the command method to all items in theList.

```
theList.applyCommand(new AppendPeriodCommand());
theList.applyCommand(new PrintCommand());
```

Figure 6.37 summarizes the use of command objects in a commonly used pattern, known as the command design pattern.

Figure 6.37 Command design pattern

Intent

to provide a way to deliver different versions of a method via different objects

Structure (class diagram)

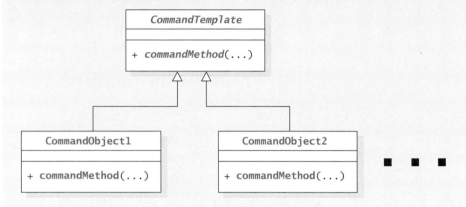

Key Client Method

```
public void performOperation(CommandTemplate z) {
    z.commandMethod(...);
}
```

Explanation

Each CommandObjectN provides its own implementation of commandMethod. The behavior of performOperation depends solely on which CommandObject is passed to it as an argument.

Example

The modified version of RecursiveList from Figures 6.35 and 6.36.

Following is a collection of hints on what to check when you examine a design or code that involves the concepts of this chapter.

✓ When you're using linked structures, it's often helpful to draw careful object diagrams, particularly for tracing run-time behavior.

✓ An insertion or removal from a doubly linked list requires twice as many links to be updated as for a singly linked list. An insertion requires update of four link attributes, and a removal requires that two links be altered.

✓ When you use code involving linked lists, it is a good idea to pay special attention to the front and rear of the list. Sometimes operations that occur at one end or the other must be handled as special cases.

✓ It's tempting to use multiple iterators but it increases the potential for loss of iterator integrity. When you're using multiple iterators, examine every insertion and deletion to be certain that iterators are not corrupted by these list alterations.

THE SOFTWARE INSPECTOR

EXERCISES

1. For each part, assume that the initial configurations of one or two SingleLists, called list1 and list2, are indicated by the initial assertion. Show the content of the container following the code's execution.

   a. ```
      // assert: list1 == sequence{"cat", "dog", "ant"}
      SingleIterator it = list1.singleIt();
      it.insertBefore("pig");
      it.forth();
      it.removeAt();
      it.forth();
      it.insertBefore("bug");
      ```

   b. ```
      // assert: list1 == sequence{"cat", "dog", "ant"}
      // assert: list2 == sequence{"bat", "frog", "gnat"}
      SingleIterator it1 = list1.singleIt();
      it1.start();
      SingleIterator it2 = list2.singleIt();
      it2.start();
      int k = 1;
      while (k < list1.size()) {
         it2.insertBefore( it1.item() );
         it2.forth();
         it1.forth();
         k++;
      }
      ```

c.
```
// assert: list1 == sequence{"cat", "dog", "ant"}
SingleIterator itA = list1.singleIt();
SingleIterator itB = list1.singleIt();
itB.start();
while (!itB.isOff()) {
   itB.forth();
}
itA.start();
while (!.itA.isOff()) {
   itB.insertBefore( itA.item() );
   itA.forth();
   itA.forth();
}
```

2. For each part assume that the initial configurations of one or two DoubleLists, called dlist1 and dlist2, are indicated by the initial assertion. Show the content of the container following the code's execution.

a)
```
// assert: dlist1 == sequence{"brick", "tick", "quick"}
DoubleIterator it = dlist1.doubleIt();
it.startAtRear();
it.insertBefore( "sick" );
it.back();
it.back();
it.insertBefore( "trick" );
```

b)
```
// assert: dlist1 == sequence{"brick", "tick", "quick"}
// assert: dlist2 == sequence{"can", "man", "fan"}
DoubleIterator it1 = dlist1.doubleIt();
it1.start();
DoubleIterator it2 = dlist2.doubleIt();
it2.startAtRear();
while (!it1.isOffRear()) {
   it1.insertBefore( it2.item() );
   it2.insertBefore( it1.item() );
   it1.forth();
   it2.back();
}
```

3. Assume that cit is an iterator for a circular linked list that contains the following sequence of items:

   sequence{"pepperoni", "mozzarella", "sausage"}

   Further assume that cit is positioned at the first item (pepperoni). Show the exact output that results from executing the following:

```
for (int k=1; k!=6; k++) {
   System.out.println( cit.item() );
   cit.forth();
}
```

4. Consider the array representation of a list, given in Section 6.7. This array uses the value –1 in place of null. What other integer values work just as well as –1 for this purpose?

5. Write code for each of the following methods.

a. Method name: `lastItem`
   Parameters: a DoubleList parameter called **dlist**
   pre: dlist.size() > 0
   post: result is the last object in dlist

b. Method name: `reverse`
   Parameters: a DoubleList parameter called **dlist**
   post: result has the same content as dlist except that all cells are reversed in order

c. Method name: `alternatingMerger`
   Parameters: two SingleList parameters called **listOdd** and **listEven**
   pre: listOdd.size() == listEven.size()
   post: result is a list that contains exactly the same cell content as the combined content of listOdd and listEven
           and the odd-numbered items of result taken in order match the items of listOdd
           and the even-numbered items of result taken in order match the items of listEven

d. Method name: `concatenatedLists`

   Parameters: two SingleList parameters called **listFront** and **listRear**
   post: result consists of the items of listFront followed by the items of listRear joined into a single list

6. Write code for the methods in Exercise 5, assuming that all lists are of type java.util.LinkedList.

1. Implement the ROLODEX program from Section 6.5 using the java.util.LinkedList class.

2. Implement a simple line-based text editor in which each line of text is a String and the lines are stored as a linked list. The user interface must allow for new lines to be inserted and removed and for the user to advance forward and backward through the lines.

3. Design, implement, and test a modified version of SingleList (from Section 6.2) that ensures iterator integrity. You can do this by including an additional container, an *iterator container*, in the SingleList class. Every time an iterator is instantiated for a SingleList, that iterator is added to the list's iterator container. You must also alter the removeAt method so that in addition to removing the item the method checks all the other iterators in the iterator container to ensure that no iterator is corrupted. Any iterator that is found to be referencing an invalid list cell should be reset to the front of the list.

4. Design, implement, and test a modified version of SingleArrayList that includes a full implementation of a free list and uses this list in conjunction with insert and remove methods. Modify the SortList class from Section 6.1 so that it is adapted from your implementation of SingleArrayList, and test this new version of SortedList.

5. Carry the Programming Exercise 4 one step further by implementing SortedList in three ways: as a SingleList, a DoubleList, and a java.util.LinkedList. Execute benchmarks to examine the relative performance of each implementation.

6. Programming Exercises 2 through 5 of Chapter 5 used other forms of lists. Design, implement, and test one a program for any of these exercises. Your program should be adapted from one of the following.

   a. the SingleList class presented in Section 6.2

   b. the DoubleList class presented in Section 6.5

   c. the java.util.LinkedList class presented in Section 6.6

   d. the SingleListArray class presented in Section 6.7

   e. the RecursiveList class presented in Section 6.8

STACKING AND QUEUEING

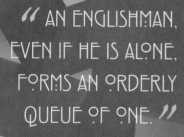

" AN ENGLISHMAN,
EVEN IF HE IS ALONE,
FORMS AN ORDERLY
QUEUE OF ONE. "

—George Mikes,
How to be an Alien

OBJECTIVES

- To examine the stack as an abstract LIFO container

- To present several software applications for stacks, including storing automatic data in run-time stacks, parsing expressions with nested parentheses, and evaluating RPN expressions

- To investigate representing a stack as a linked list

- To examine a bounded stack implementation using an array

- To compare and contrast `java.util.Stack` with a pure stack ADT

- To examine the queue as an abstract FIFO container

- To investigate representing a queue as a singly linked list with two iterators

- To explore a bounded queue implementation using a ring buffer

- To introduce the concept of priority queues and sketch three alternative representations

Two common eating utensils are the spoon and the fork. Spoons are effective dippers for eating liquids, such as soups. Forks are good for stabbing solid foods. The spork, a more general purpose single eating utensil, is something of a combined spoon and fork. A spork looks like a spoon with tines carved into the end.

Like most general-purpose devices, the spork represents a compromise that sacrifices some of the advantages of the more specialized devices in favor of broader utility. On a backpacking trip it might be handy to carry a single spork rather than both a spoon and a fork. However, a spork is not as effective for dipping as a spoon nor as good for stabbing as a fork.

When it comes to linear containers, arrays and lists are sporks—the general-purpose tools. An array doesn't prescribe the order in which its cells are assigned values. Neither does a list restrict the locations at which you can insert items. A virtually limitless number of algorithms are available for visiting the items of a list or array. However, other, more specialized containers have advantages that should not be overlooked.

This chapter examines two more specialized forms of linear containers: stacks and queues. Keep in mind that these special-purpose tools may seem more restrictive; but like spoons and forks, specialized tools are better utensils under many circumstances.

7.1   STACK AS A CONTAINER ADT

The first station in a cafeteria line is typically a stack of food trays. Each person entering the cafeteria removes a tray from the top of the stack and then proceeds through the remainder of the line. Periodically, a cafeteria employee brings out new trays to add to the stack. Each of the new trays is placed on top of the stack. A key feature of this stack is that all activity seems to take place on its top: New trays are added to the top of the tray stack, and customers also remove trays from the top.

The behavior of the stack of cafeteria trays demonstrates the distinguishing characteristics of the data structure commonly called a stack. A **stack** is a container in which new items are inserted and removed from the top. The stack insert and remove behavior is called LIFO (last in, first out) because the last (most recent) item placed in the stack will be the first (next) item to be taken out (removed).

This same stack behavior occurs elsewhere in real life. For example, a one-car driveway behaves like a stack. The last car to enter the driveway must be the first to leave because it blocks the path of all other cars in the drive. Similarly, the last person to enter a crowded elevator is likely to be the first to exit, even if it is only to allow others to pass.

The behavior of a stack container is typically defined by three methods.

- `push`: a method to insert a new item into the stack
- `pop`: a method to remove one item from the stack
- `top`: a non-void method to inspect a stack item

Each of these methods works on the top of the stack, as pictured in Figure 7.1. The `push` method places a new item on the stack's top. The `pop` method removes the top item from the stack. The `top` method returns the item from the stack's top.

Figure 7.1 A stack and its methods

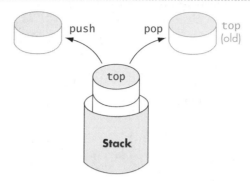

The picture in Figure 7.1 is an informal way to characterize the three stack methods. The content of the stack is pictured as a cylinder with a value exposed at the top. The stack methods can inspect this item (top), remove this item (pop), or add a new item on top (push). Figure 7.2 provides a more precise definition of this stack ADT in terms of an OCL *sequence*.

Figure 7.2 Stack ADT specifications

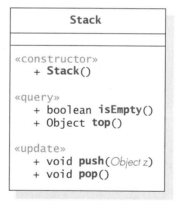

Stack Specifications

Domain Every Stack object consists of a *sequence* of Object

Constructor Method

```
public Stack()
```
    post: this == *sequence*{}

Query Methods

```
public boolean isEmpty()
```
    post: result == (this->*size*() == 0)

Continued on next page

```
public Object top()
    post: !isEmpty() (throws java.util.EmptyStackException)
    post: result == this->first()
```

Update Methods
```
public void push(Object z)
    post: this == this@pre->prepend(z)
public void pop()
    post: !isEmpty()@pre (throws java.util.EmptyStackException)
    post: this == this@pre->subSequence(2,this@pre->size())
```

The stack ADT is linear, so it is described in terms of a sequence. The front of the stack sequence serves as the top of the stack. Pushing a new item onto a stack is described by the following postcondition as concatenating that item onto the front of the sequence:

```
this == this@pre->prepend(z)
```

Similarly, popping a stack is described by the following postcondition as removing the front sequence:

```
this == this@pre->subSequence(2,this@pre->size())
```

In addition to push, pop, and top, the ADT specifications in Figure 7.2 include two other methods. The constructor method, Stack, instantiates a new stack—an empty stack. The second additional method, isEmpty, provides a way to test the stack size, returning true exactly when the stack is empty.

The following code illustrates the use of this stack by creating two stacks and manipulating their content. The assertions in the code explain the state resulting from code execution.

```
Stack furnitureStack, junkStack;
furnitureStack = new Stack();
furnitureStack.push( "chair" );
furnitureStack.push( "table" );
furnitureStack.push( "bed" );
/* assert: furnitureStack == sequence{"bed", "table", "chair"}
        and junkStack == null */
furnitureStack.pop();
/* assert: furnitureStack == sequence{"table", "chair"}
        and junkStack == null */
System.out.println( furnitureStack.top() ); //outputs "table"
furnitureStack.push( "desk" );
String myString = (String) furnitureStack.top();
/* assert: furnitureStack == sequence{"desk", "table", "chair"}
        and junkStack == null */
junkStack = new Stack();
junkStack.push( furnitureStack.top() ); //copy top
furnitureStack.pop();
```

```
/* assert: furnitureStack == sequence{"table", "chair"}
           and junkStack == sequence{"desk"} */
junkStack.push( furnitureStack.top() );
junkStack.push( "bike" );
junkStack.push( furnitureStack.top() );
/* assert: furnitureStack == sequence{"table", "chair"}
           and junkStack == sequence{"table", "bike", "table",
                                      "desk"} */
junkStack.pop();
junkStack.push( junkStack.top() ); //duplicate top
junkStack.push( junkStack.top() ); //duplicate top
/* assert: furnitureStack == sequence{"table", "chair"}
           and junkStack == sequence{"bike", "bike", "bike",
                                      "table", "desk"} */
```

This example illustrates, among other things, that you can copy the item from the top of one stack onto another by pushing onto one stack the top of another. (See the line labeled //copy top.) You also can duplicate the top item of a stack by pushing the top. (See the lines labeled //duplicate top.)

One of the limitations of the Stack ADT is that you can inspect only one stack item (the top item) without removing values from the stack. This means that to inspect all of the stack content you must empty the stack. The following code is an example; this loop displays the entire content of junkStack from top item through bottom.

```
Stack tempStack = new Stack();
while (!junkStack.isEmpty()) {
    System.out.println( junkStack.top() );
    tempStack.push( junkStack.top() );
    junkStack.pop();
}
```

Software Engineering Hint

When it will do the job, a stack is a better choice than a list. Stacks are simpler to use and can often be implemented more efficiently.

While this code empties junkStack, it also saves the complete content of junkStack by pushing each item onto tempStack. Notice, however, that the final content of tempStack is upside-down compared with the original junkStack content. This upside-down copy is a byproduct of the LIFO storage behavior of stacks.

7.2 SAMPLE STACK APPLICATIONS

Stacks are one of those concepts that are used in many fields of computer science. Theoreticians use a mathematical model of computation known as **push-down automata**. This model consists of a special kind of state machine augmented by a stack. (The name "push-down" comes from stack behavior.) In the 1970s, a new kind of computer hardware, known as a **stack architecture**, was invented. Stack architectures were designed to allow memory to be treated essentially as a giant stack. The top of the stack was used to evaluate expressions, and lower parts of the stack stored various variables from the executing program. Although the so-called stack computers of that era no longer exist, their legacy is the integration of hardware stacks as an integral part of today's microprocessors.

Another key computer application is the **run-time stack**, a mechanism used to implement program execution. The Java virtual machine relies on a run-time stack to provide for the automatic data required by the programs it interprets. Each method call causes the memory space associated with the method's automatic data (parameters and local variables) to be pushed on the run-time stack. While a method is executing, its automatic data is on top of the run-time stack. All the automatic data associated with the method is popped off the run-time stack at the time the method returns.

Suppose, for example, that method foo1 is executing and calls foo2. The foo2 method, in turn, calls foo3, and foo3 calls itself recursively. Figure 7.3 informally depicts the state of the Java virtual machine's run-time stack at this point in program execution.

Figure 7.3 Sample method calls and associated run-time stack content

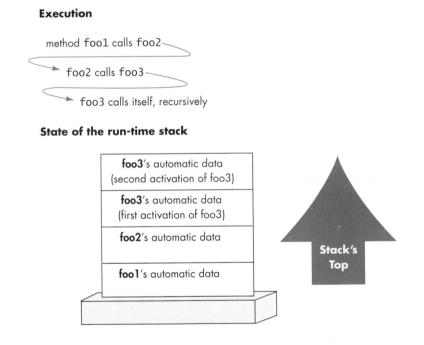

The applications of stacks go beyond run-time usage. Compilers also rely heavily on stacklike storage in analyzing program syntax. The **parser** is the compiler component that is responsible for such analysis, and the task performed by a parser is calling **parsing**. To illustrate parsing, consider the problem of checking for a properly parenthesized expression. For purposes of this discussion, it is assumed that there are three kinds of grouping symbols: braces {...}, brackets [...], and parentheses (...). A properly grouped expression is one in which all grouping symbols occur in pairs that are properly nested. For example, each of the following lines is a properly grouped expression. (Each α denotes an arbitrary string made from non-grouping symbols.)

Properly Grouped Expressions

α

(α)

(α (α) (α)) α (α)

(α [α]α {α} (α))

{α [α (α [α]α)α]α}

Each line that follows is improperly grouped. The nature of the improper grouping is indicated to the right of the expression.

Improperly Grouped Expressions

(α	Unmatched left paren
(α] α)	Right bracket without matching left bracket
(α)α) α (α	Left paren must occur prior to its matching right paren
(α [α}α)	Left bracket doesn't pair with the right brace

The algorithm to analyze an expression for proper grouping provides a glimpse of the kind of algorithms required for parsing. Figure 7.4 gives such an algorithm for parentheses, brackets, and braces.

Figure 7.4 Parsing algorithm to check for properly grouped expressions

```
Stack symbolStack = new Stack();
char inChar = nextExpressionSymbol();
while (expressionNotCompletelyProcessed()) {
    if (inChar == '(' || inChar == '[' || inChar == '{') {
        symbolStack.push( new Character(inChar) );
    } else if (inChar == ')' || inChar == ']' || inChar == '}') {
        if (symbolStack.isEmpty())
            throw new unmatchedRightGroupingSymbolException();
        else if ( ")}]".indexOf(inChar) ==
            "({[".indexOf((Character)symbolStack.top()).charValue()))
        {
            symbolStack.pop();
        } else {
            throw new unmatchedRightParenException();
        }
    }
    inChar = nextExpressionSymbol();
}
if (symbolStack.isEmpty())
    System.out.println("PROPERLY GROUPED!");
else
    throw new unmatchedLeftGroupingSymbolException();
```

The expression parser is formed from a loop that examines an expression symbol-by-symbol from left to right. The first call to the nextExpressionSymbol method is assumed to return the leftmost character of the expression, and each subsequent nextExpressionSymbol call must return the leftmost of the expression characters not previously returned. The loop terminates when all characters have been input and checked. The expressionNotCompletelyProcessed method returns false only when the rightmost character has been previously read and checked by the algorithm.

The inChar variable stores the next unprocessed expression character within the body of the *while* loop. If this character is one of the left grouping symbols—either (, [, or {—the symbol is pushed on top of symbolStack. Pushing the symbol in this way saves it for future checks of proper grouping.

If the inChar variable is one of the right grouping symbols—either),], or }—this symbol should match a corresponding left grouping symbol that has been previously processed. If the grouping symbols are properly nested in the expression, a matching left symbol must be on top of the stack. To match properly the algorithm checks for (when inChar is), [when inChar is], and { when inChar is }. If the algorithm detects an improperly matched symbol, an exception is thrown indicating the nature of the mismatch. When a right grouping symbol is encountered and a matching left symbol is found atop symbolStack, then symbolStack is popped, removing the matching symbol from further consideration. Therefore, at any time, symbolStack contains only those left grouping symbols that have not yet been paired with their corresponding right symbol.

When the parsing loop completes processing of all symbols in the expression, one last check must be performed to ensure the expression is properly grouped. At the time of loop completion, symbolStack must be empty because any remaining items can be only left grouping symbols for which there is no matching right symbol.

There are variations on this algorithm for matching grouping symbols. For example, HTML files, which are commonly used on the Internet, use tags that occur mostly in matched pairs. An <I> tag designates the beginning of a region of text to be italicized, and the matching </I> tag follows the last character in the italicized group. Similarly, a region of text to be boldfaced starts with a <B> tag and ends with </B>. Different pairs of tags follow the same rules for proper nesting as parentheses and can be checked with a similar algorithm. With minor modifications, you could use the algorithm from Figure 7.4 to check HTML files for proper tags nesting.

Another common use for a stack is to evaluate an arithmetic expression. One such algorithm evaluates expressions expressed in **Reverse Polish Notation** (**RPN**), also known as **postfix notation**. RPN has been used by mathematicians for centuries. The concept is also used in some calculators, most notably in those manufactured by Hewlett-Packard.

RPN expressions contain operands (numbers) and operations (such as "+" for addition and "*" for multiplication). The operands of an RPN expression must be ordered left-to-right in the same order they would occur in a normal (a so-called infix) arithmetic expression). The operation symbols are interspersed within the operands following a simple rule: An operation appears as soon as possible *following* its constituent subexpressions. Figure 7.5 contains several infix expressions and their corresponding RPN equivalent.

Figure 7.5 Arithmetic expressions in infix and RPN form

Ordinary Infix Expression	*Equivalent RPN Expression*
(1+2)*3	1,2,+,3,*
(1–2)*(3+4)	1,2,–,3,4,+,*
(((((1+2)*3)–4)/5)*6	1,2,+,3,*,4,–,5,/,6,*
((2+3)–(4*5))+6	2,3,+,4,5,*,–6,+
2*(3–(4+5))	2,3,4,5,+,–,*

Notice that an RPN subexpression made up from two constants and their operation is always expressed as the operation symbol followed immediately by its operand constants. So, for example, the infix expression (3*4) is written 3,4,* in RPN. An RPN operation involving more complex subexpressions requires that the entire subexpression occur to the left of the operation symbol that uses it. Therefore, the infix expression (8*9)+2 is written 8,9,*,2,+ in RPN. Similarly, the infix expression 7–(5*6) is written as follows in RPN: 7,5,6,*,– One of the unique characteristics of RPN is that arithmetic expressions are expressed unambiguously without the need for parentheses.

You can evaluate RPN expressions using a stack to hold operand values (including those operands from subexpression evaluations). The basic algorithm behaves according to the following rules.

1. The RPN expression is examined from left to right.
2. Whenever an operand is encountered, it is pushed on the operand stack.
3. Whenever an operation is encountered, its operands are popped from the stack and replaced by the value of the operation.

Consider the following RPN expression:

1,2,–

This can be roughly translated into the following stack operations, where operandStk refers to the stack.

```
operandStk.push( 1 );
operandStk.push( 2 );
rightOperand = operandStk.top();
operandStk.pop();
leftOperand = operandStk.top();
operandStk.pop();
operandStk.push( leftOperand - rightOperand );
```

The last five lines evaluate the subtraction operation: Two lines retrieve and remove the right operand, two lines retrieve and remove the left operand, and the last line evaluates the subexpression and pushes its resulting value. The LIFO nature of a stack means that the right operand is always popped off the stack before the left operand. After an RPN expression is evaluated in this way, the value of the expression remains on top of the stack.

Figure 7.6 contains the code for RPN expression evaluation, based on the following assumptions:

- Only four binary integer operations are permitted: + (addition), − (subtraction), * (multiplication), and / (integer division).
- All operands are single decimal digits (0 through 9).
- No symbols except the five operators and 10 digits should be included (although commas and blanks are ignored).

Figure 7.6 Algorithm for evaluating simple RPN strings

```
/*  pre:    s is an integer RPN expression consisting of single
            decimals digit operands and the following possible
            operators: +, -, *, /
    post:   result == numeric value of s (using integer arithmetic)
            */
public int evaluateRPN( String s ) {
    char token;
    int leftOperand, rightOperand;
    StackOfInt operands = new StackOfInt();
    for (int j=0; j<s.length(); j++) {
        token = s.charAt(j);
        if ('0' <= token && token <= '9') {
            operands.push( token - '0' );
        } else if (token=='-' || token=='+' || token=='*' ||
                   token=='/') {
            rightOperand = operands.topInt();
            operands.pop();
            leftOperand = operands.topInt();
            operands.pop();
            if (token=='-')
                operands.push(leftOperand - rightOperand);
            else if (token=='+')
                operands.push(leftOperand + rightOperand);
            else if (token=='*')
                operands.push(leftOperand * rightOperand);
            else // (token=='/')
                operands.push(leftOperand / rightOperand);
        } else if (token != ',' && token != ' ') {
            // ignore commas and blanks
            throw new IllegalArgumentException("invalid RPN char: "
                + token);
        }
    }
    return operands.topInt();
}
```

To trace `evaluateRPN`, assume that it is called as follows:

`System.out.println( evaluateRPN( "`**1 2 - 3 4 + ***`");`

This expression is equivalent to the following common infix expression: (1–2) * (3+4).

Each execution of the `evaluateRPN` *for* loop visits the next character in the string and assigns that character to a local variable called `token`. Therefore, the first loop iteration examines the first character, 1, from the string. Because this character is an operand, it is pushed onto the previously empty stack that is designed to store `int` values, as pictured next.

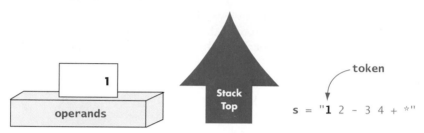

The second execution of the *for* loop assigns the second operand, 2, to `token`, and also pushes it onto the stack:

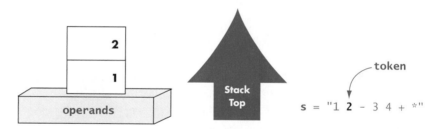

The next symbol in the expression string is the first operator, "-". The `evaluateRPN` algorithm pops two operands from the stack, causing `rightOperand` ==2, `leftOperand` ==1; then pushes the value of 1–2 or –1 onto the stack:

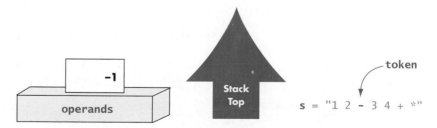

The algorithm proceeds to push the next two operands (3 and 4) onto the stack, as follows.

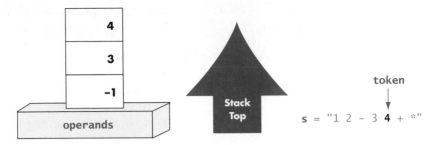

Next, the evaluation of the addition symbol (+) causes the two operands atop the stack (4 and 3) to be popped from the stack and replaced by their sum. At this time the bottom of the stack contains the value of the (1–2) subexpression and the top of the stack has the value of the (3+4) subexpression.

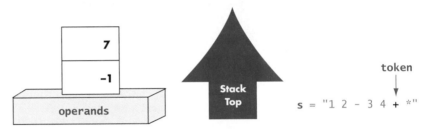

The final expression symbol is an asterisk that indicates the two subexpressions should be multiplied. The resulting stack is as follows.

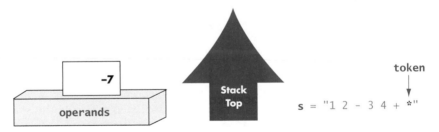

The `evaluateRPN` method completes by returning the value from on top of the stack—namely, –7.

7.3 LIST IMPLEMENTATIONS OF STACK

There are many ways to implement a stack. This section examines a list implementation, and Section 7.4 explores an implementation via arrays.

A stack can be viewed as a restricted kind of list—a list for which all insertions, removals, and item inspections occur at one end. This "business end" of the list corresponds to the stack's top. This view of a stack as a special kind of list leads to the design decision to implement a stack by inheriting a list.

The choice of which list to use when you implement a stack is of little consequence. Because a stack uses only one end of the list, double linking is not needed but also is not harmful. All stack manipulation occurs at the same point within the list, so no more than one iterator is required. Therefore, almost any linked list will suffice as a stack representation.

One of the simpler, and more efficient, list implementations from Chapter 5 is SimpleSingleListPlus. This class uses a singly linked list implementation with a single built-in iterator. As with any use of the adapter design pattern, adapting a stack from SimpleSingleListPlus involves two options: designing the stack class as a child class of SimpleSingleListPlus or using the proxy design pattern by virtue of a SimpleSingleListPlus instance variable. As is often the case, many of the SimpleSingleListPlus methods are not needed by a stack, so the proxy design pattern appears to be a better design alternative.

Figure 7.7 shows the class diagram for this implementation of the Stack class. Notice the typical picture for a proxy design pattern, in which an instance variable (theList) of the new class belongs to the class from which the new class is adapted.

Figure 7.7 Class diagram for Stack

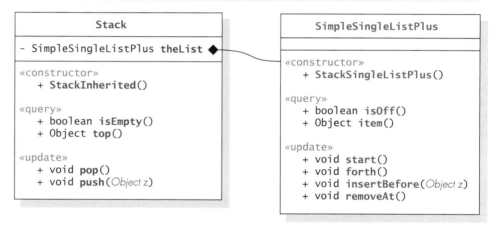

The only remaining decision for this representation is to decide which end of SimpleSingleListPlus should represent the top of the stack. The front of the list seems the best choice for the top of the stack, because of the convenience of iterator positioning. (A call to start places the iterator at the front of the list.) Figure 7.8 shows the code for this implementation.

This implementation of Stack utilizes a private SimpleSingleListPlus variable theList to encapsulate the list data structure. All Stack methods manipulate theList in place of this. The advantage of this proxy implementation is that it implements a pure stack, permitting calls only to isEmpty, push, pop, and top. By comparison, if the stack had been built by inheriting SimpleSingleListPlus, client code would be able to manipulate iterators and invoke methods such as insertBefore, insertAfter, removeBefore, and removeAt.

Figure 7.8 Stack implementation using the proxy design pattern

```java
import java.util.EmptyStackException;
public class Stack {
    private SimpleSingleListPlus theList;

    /* post:  theList is an empty list */
    public Stack() {
        theList = new SimpleSingleListPlus();
    }

    /* post:  result == (theList is an empty list) */
    public boolean isEmpty() {
        theList.start();
        return (theList.isOff());
    }

    /* pre:  !isEmpty() (throws java.util.EmptyStackException)
       post:  result == the first item from theList */
    public Object top() {
        if (isEmpty()) {
            throw new EmptyStackException();
        } else {
            theList.start();
            return theList.item();
        }
    }

    /* post:  theList == theList@pre with z appended to the front
              */
    public void push(Object z) {
        theList.start();
        theList.insertBefore(z);
    }
    /* pre:  !isEmpty() (throws java.util.EmptyStackException)
       post:  theList == theList@pre with the first item removed */
    public void pop() {
        if (isEmpty()) {
            throw new EmptyStackException();
        } else {
            theList.start();
            theList.removeAt();
        }
    }
}
```

7.4 AN ARRAY IMPLEMENTATION OF STACK

The restricted behavior of a stack that leads to convenient representation via a linked list also allows for array representation. The key observation is that representing a stack with an array requires only one index variable, which is used to maintain the cell location of the top of the stack. Figure 7.9 contains the code for such an implementation.

Figure 7.9 BoundedStack implementation

```java
import java.util.EmptyStackException;
public class BoundedStack {
    private Object[] theArray;
    private int topIndex;

    /* post:  theArray.length == m and topIndex == -1 */
    public BoundedStack( int m ) {
        theArray = new Object[m];
        topIndex = -1;
    }

    /* post:  result == (topIndex == -1) */
    public boolean isEmpty() {
        return (topIndex == -1);
    }
    /* pre:   !isEmpty() (throws java.util.EmptyStackException)
       post:  result == theArray[topIndex] */
    public Object top() {
        if (isEmpty()) {
            throw new EmptyStackException();
        } else {
            return theArray[topIndex];
        }
    }

    /* pre:   topIndex < theArray.length-1
                (throws IllegalStateException)
       post:  topIndex = topIndex@pre + 1
                and theArray[topIndex] == z */
    public void push(Object z) {
        if (topIndex < theArray.length-1) {
            topIndex++;
            theArray[topIndex] = z;
        } else {
            throw new IllegalStateException();
        }
    }
}
```

Continued on next page

```
        /*  pre:    !isEmpty() (throws java.util.EmptyStackException)
            post:   topIndex == topIndex@pre - 1 */
    public void pop() {
        if (isEmpty()) {
            throw new EmptyStackException();
        } else {
            topIndex-;
        }
    }
}
```

The representation used by BoundedStack uses two private instance variables: theArray and topIndex. The items of the stack are stored, one per array cell, from theArray[0] through theArray[topIndex]. Figure 7.10 illustrates this representation with a specific stack and the corresponding values of theArray and topIndex.

Figure 7.10 Sample of the BoundedStack representation

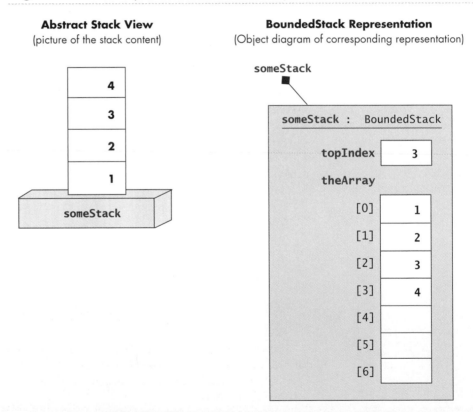

Figure 7.10 depicts a stack that stores four items: the numbers 1 through 4, increasing from the bottom of the stack to the top. The corresponding BoundedStack representation consists of an array, theArray, with four or more cells. (Figure 7.10 happens to show a seven-cell array.) The value of topIndex stores the

index where the top of the stack is represented. In this picture, the top of the stack is stored in `theArray[3]`, the second from the top item is `theArray[2]`, and so forth.

The implementation in Figure 7.10 follows directly from this representation. For example, the `top` method returns the top stack value by way of the following instruction:

```
return theArray[topIndex];
```

Pushing a new item onto the stack requires incrementing `topIndex` by 1, and popping the stack consists of decrementing `topIndex` by 1. You pop the stack by decrementing `topIndex`; you need not do anything to the cell containing the prior top-of-stack value because this cell will be reassigned by any future call to `push`.

As with all implementations based on array representations, the `BoundedStack` implementation imposes a fixed limit on the size of the implemented container. Because every item in the stack occupies a separate cell of `theArray`, the stack's **depth** (the number of items in the stack) can never exceed `theArray.length`. The `BoundedStack` implementation permits the client to establish the maximum array depth to be equal to the parameter `m` used in the `BoundedStack` constructor. The `Stack` constructor method presented earlier has no such parameter.

> ### Software Engineering Hint
>
> Even though a bounded container has a maximum size, you can gain some flexibility by allowing the client code to establish the maximum size (usually when the container is instantiated). `BoundedStack` illustrates.

The bounding property of `BoundedStack` requires that you give attention to any method that might attempt to increase the stack size beyond its bound. The only stack method capable of increasing the number of items in a stack is `push`. Therefore, the `push` method for `BoundedStack` is different from the push method of `Stack`. The `BoundedStack` push includes the additional potential for throwing an exception to protect against array index violations.

With the exception of the added parameter in the constructor method and the extra test to ensure the bounded property, a `BoundedStack` implementation is largely interchangeable with a `Stack` implementation. You can also expect both implementations to exhibit similar performance.

7.5   JAVA.UTIL.STACK

The `java.util` library contains a class called `Stack` that reflects a somewhat different abstraction for a stack from that presented thus far. Figure 7.11 contains the class diagram for `java.util.Stack`. The other class and interfaces shown in this figure—`Collection`, `List`, and `Vector`—are also part of the `java.util` library.

The greatest difference between `java.util.Stack` and previously presented stack implementations is that `java.util.Stack` is designed to be an extension of existing classes and interfaces. From its class diagram it is evident that `java.util.Stack` inherits `Vector` and implements two other data structure-related interfaces (`Collection` and `List`). All these inherited and implemented methods mean that `java.util.Stack` permits different kinds of operations than a so-called **pure stack**, which permits manipulations only to the top of the stack. The methods inherited from `Vector` allow any value within a stack to be updated directly. The methods implemented from `Collection` and `List` permit the free use of itera-

Figure 7.11 Class diagram for `java.util.Stack`

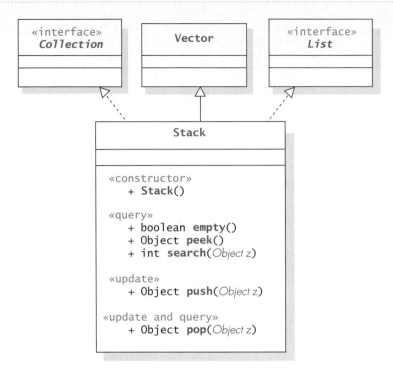

tors, both one-way and two-way, to move about a stack. The result is a kind of general-purpose linear data structure that can be treated as an array, a singly linked list, a doubly linked list, or a stack.

Because `java.util.Collection`, `java.util.List`, and `java.util.Vector` are examined earlier in this book, this section explores only those methods that are unique to `java.util.Stack`. Figure 7.12 expands on these methods in the form of a class specification.

Figure 7.12 `java.util.Stack` specifications

java.util.Stack Specifications

Domain

    Every Stack object consists of a *sequence* of Object

Constructor Method

`public Stack()`

    post: this == *sequence*{}

Query Methods

`public boolean empty()`

    post: result == (this->*size()* == 0)

Continued on next page

```
public Object peek()
```
> **pre:** !empty() (throws java.util.EmptyStackException)
>
> **post:** result == this->*first*()

```
public int search(Object z )
```
> **post:** result == 1 greater than the number of cells separating the top of
> this
> *and* the first occurrence of z within the stack

Update Methods

```
public Object push(Object z)
```
> **post:** this == this@*pre*->*prepend*(z)
> *and* result == z

Update & Query Methods

```
public Object pop()
```
> **pre:** !empty()@*pre* (throws java.util.EmptyStackException)
>
> **post:** this == this@*pre*->*subSequence*(2,this@*pre*->*size*())
> *and* result == this@*pre*->*first*()

Software Engineering Hint

A single method that serves both as a query and as an update method is said to contain a **side effect**. When such a method is called as a non-void method, it returns a value, but the method also has the byproduct, or side effect, of updating state. Avoiding side effects is generally considered to be better design. However, many developers continue to use the side effect version of pop.

Most of the java.util.Stack methods are similar to corresponding methods from the Stack ADT. Both constructors have identical abstract behavior. The behavior of empty is the same as isEmpty, and the peek method has the behavior of top. The push method from java.util.Stack adds an item to the top of the stack, just like prior push methods. However, this new version of push has a slight difference in the fact that it is non-void, always returning the item just pushed.

The method with the most significant difference is pop. The java.util.Stack version of pop performs two tasks: It removes one item from the top of the stack, and it returns the value of the removed item. This version of pop is sometimes called **pop with side effect** because it exhibits a dual purpose as a combined query and update method. Historically, the very earliest stacks used such side effect pop methods. These earlier stack versions often omitted the top or peek method so that the only way to inspect the top of the stack required popping it from the stack. The java.util.Stack design uses the side effect version of pop but also includes the peek method, permitting flexibility in stack usage style.

The search method from java.util.Stack is further evidence of the non-stacklike ways in which this data structure can be used. No method corresponds to search in the traditional stack abstraction, primarily because any search treats a stack more like an array. If stack items are arranged consecutively within an array so that the top stack item is in the first array cell, then search returns the position (1 greater than the index) of the first cell that equals the search value. For example, a search that finds the top of the stack returns 1, and a search that finds the second stack item returns 2. The search method uses content equality (equals) and not identity equality (==) to perform its search.

7.6 THE QUEUE AS A CONTAINER ADT

Stacks occur in everyday life, but not as frequently as another kind of linear container: the **queue**. People stand in queue to purchase a ticket for an athletic event, board a passenger train, pay the cashier at a retail store, or enter the theater for a concert. Automobiles are queued waiting for a traffic light to turn green, and aircraft are queued awaiting clearance for departure.

The defining characteristic of queue behavior is that items from the queue container are processed in the same order that they were previously added to the queue. This first-come-first-served behavior can also be called **FIFO** (First In First Out). In other words, the item that has been in the queue for the longest time will be the next item to be removed. Contrast this with stacks, in which the item to be removed next is the one that has been in the stack for the *shortest* time.

Queues also occur frequently in computer systems and are often referred to by other names. Input and output **streams** are queues for transferring data between a file and an executing program. A **buffer** is a container for accumulating data to be transferred as a group to or from a disk drive. When a document is sent to a shared printer, it is said to be **spooled** so that it will be printed in the proper (queuelike) order along with other documents awaiting print.

Figure 7.13 depicts a queue and its associated operations. Notice that the container is drawn so that individual items are lined up horizontally. This container can be thought of as a conduit, with new items being inserted at the right and items being removed from the left.

Figure 7.13 A queue and its methods

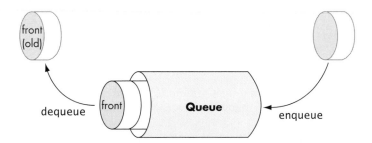

The behavior of a queue container is typically defined by three methods.

- enqueue: A method to insert a new item into the queue
- dequeue: A method to remove one item from the queue
- front: A nonvoid method to inspect a queue item

Conceptually, the dequeue and front methods operate on one end of the queue (pictured as the left end in Figure 7.13), and the enqueue operation inserts items into the opposite (right) end. Figure 7.14 provides a precise definition of a queue ADT in the form of a class diagram and specification.

Figure 7.14   Queue ADT specifications

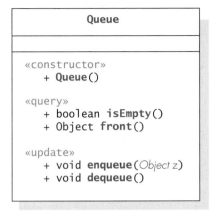

Queue Specifications

Domain

Every Queue object consists of a *sequence* of Object

Constructor Method

public Queue( )

post: this == *sequence*{}

Query Methods

public boolean isEmpty( )

post: result == (this->*size*() == 0)

public Object front( )

pre: !isEmpty() (throws java.util.NoSuchElementException)

post: result == this->*first*()

Update Methods

public void enqueue(Object z)

post: this == this@*pre*->*append*(z)

public void dequeue( )

pre: !isEmpty()@*pre* (throws java.util.NoSuchElementException)

post: this == this@*pre*->*subSequence*(2,this@*pre*->*size*())

The queue ADT bears a close resemblance to the stack ADT, with enqueue, front, and dequeue replacing push, top, and pop, respectively. The specifications of these three methods remain the same except for enqueue, which is defined to insert the new item at the opposite (rear) end of theSeq sequence.

The constructor method, `Queue`, instantiates a new, empty queue. The `isEmpty` method tests for an empty queue, returning true exactly when the queue is empty. The following code illustrates the use of this queue by creating two queues and manipulating their content. The assertions in the code explain the state resulting from code execution.

```
Queue furnitureQueue, junkQueue;
furnitureQueue = new Queue();
furnitureQueue.enqueue( "chair" );
furnitureQueue.enqueue( "table" );
furnitureQueue.enqueue( "bed" );
/* assert: furnitureQueue == sequence{"chair", "table", "bed"}
           and junkQueue == null */
furnitureQueue.dequeue();
/* assert: furnitureQueue == sequence{"table", "bed"}
           and junkQueue == null */
System.out.println( furnitureQueue.front() ); //output "table"
furnitureQueue.enqueue( "desk" );
/* assert: furnitureQueue == sequence{"table", "bed", "desk"}
           and junkQueue == null */
junkQueue = new Queue();
junkQueue.enqueue( furnitureQueue.front() ); //copy front
furnitureQueue.dequeue();
/* assert: furnitureQueue == sequence{"bed", "desk"}
           and junkQueue == sequence{"table"} */
junkQueue.enqueue ( junkQueue.front() ); //duplicate front
junkQueue.enqueue ( "bike" );
junkQueue.enqueue ( junkQueue.front() ); //duplicate front
/* assert: furnitureQueue == sequence{"bed", "desk"}
           and junkQueue == sequence{"table", "table", "bike",
                                      "table"} */
```

Visiting all items in a queue, like visiting all items of a stack, requires that the items be dequeued. However, unlike a stack, copying from one queue to another preserves the order of the content. The following algorithm illustrates.

```
Queue tempQueue = new Queue();
while (!junkQueue.isEmpty()) {
    System.out.println( junkQueue.front() );
    tempQueue.enqueue( junkQueue.front() );
    junkQueue.dequeue();
}
```

When this code is executed, all the items of `junkQueue` are output in order from the queue's front to its back. The code also saves the complete content of `junkQueue`, enqueueing each item onto `tempQueue`.

The FIFO nature of a queue and LIFO nature of a stack give rise to interesting behavioral differences. Suppose that each container is empty and then several items are inserted before all are removed. When the items are removed (popped) from the stack, they are removed in the *reverse* of the order of insertion. When the items are removed (dequeued) from the queue, they are removed in the *same order* as they were inserted.

Many algorithms exploit the property that stacks can be used to reverse order, but queues do not. For example, consider a program to check for palindromes. Figure 7.15 contains one such program.

Figure 7.15 CheckPalindromes class

```
/* This program checks to see whether or not strings are
   palindromes. */
public class CheckPalindromes {
    public static void main(String args[]) {
        printPalindromeMessage( "I prefer Pi." );
        printPalindromeMessage(
            "Did I draw Della too tall, Edward? I did?");
        printPalindromeMessage("This is not a palindrome.");
    }


    /*  post: (s is a palindrome)
                 implies "is a palindrome" is displayed
              and not (s is a palindrome)
                 implies "is NOT a palindrome" is displayed */
    public static void printPalindromeMessage(String s) {
        if (isPalindrome(s))
            System.out.println(s + " <- is a palindrome.");
        else
            System.out.println(s + " <- is NOT a palindrome.");
    }


    /*  post: result == (s is a palindrome)
        note: Palindromes are strings that whose alphanumeric
              characters have the same order when reversed.
              Blanks, punctuation,and capitalization are ignored. */
    public static boolean isPalindrome(String s) {
        char nextChar;
        String newS = s.toUpperCase();
        StackOfChar stk = new StackOfChar();
        QueueOfChar que = new QueueOfChar();
        for (int j=0; j<newS.length(); j++) {
            nextChar = newS.charAt(j);
            if (('A'<=nextChar && nextChar<='Z')
                || ('0'<=nextChar && nextChar<='9') )
            {
                stk.push( nextChar );
                que.enqueue( nextChar );
            }
        }
```

Continued on next page

```
            boolean charsMatch = true;
            while ( !que.isEmpty() ) {
                charsMatch = charsMatch
                    && (que.frontChar() == stk.topChar());
                que.dequeue();
                stk.pop();
            }
            return charsMatch;
        }
    }
```

Executing the `main` method of the `CheckPalindromes` class causes three strings to be tested to see whether they are palindromes:

```
"I prefer Pi."
"Did I draw Della too tall, Edward? I did?"
"This is not a palindrome."
```

The first two of these strings are palindromes because reversing their alphanumeric characters results in the same sequence. (Punctuation, blanks, and capitalization are all ignored when identifying palindromes.) The third string is obviously not a palindrome.

The algorithm to check whether a string is a palindrome takes the form of an `isPalindrome` method. Capitalization is ignored by shifting all lowercase alphabetic characters to uppercase via the following statement:

```
String newS = s.toUpperCase();
```

The remainder of `isPalindrome` is a two-part algorithm, corresponding to its two loops. The first part (the *for* loop portion) scans all the characters in `newS` from left to right. As each character is scanned, it is found to be alphabetic or numeric and then is both pushed onto `stk` and enqueued in `que`. On the completion of the *for* loop, all alphanumeric characters from `newS` have been placed (in order) within both the stack and the queue.

The second part of the `isPalindrome` algorithm (corresponding to the *while* loop) empties both `stk` and `que`. This second subalgorithm begins by assigning true to a `boolean` variable called `charsMatch`. One by one, the character atop `stk` is compared to the character at the front of `que`. If these characters are the same, `charsMatch` remains true and the two characters are removed from their respective containers; otherwise `charsMatch` is false. Because a stack returns content in the reverse order of a queue, `isPalindrome` will correctly recognize any palindrome.

7.7 A LIST IMPLEMENTATION OF QUEUE

A list is an effective data structure for representing a queue. The obvious representation is to use one end of the list as the front of the queue and to enqueue on the opposite end of the list. Unfortunately, such a representation does not work efficiently for a singly linked list with a built-in iterator (such as SimpleSingleListPlus). The inefficiency stems from the need to position the iterator at one end of the list to implement front and dequeue and to position the iterator at the other end to implement enqueue. More efficient implementations result from using a doubly linked list implementation or a singly linked list with two iterators. Figure 7.16. shows the latter.

Figure 7.16 Class diagram for Queue implementation

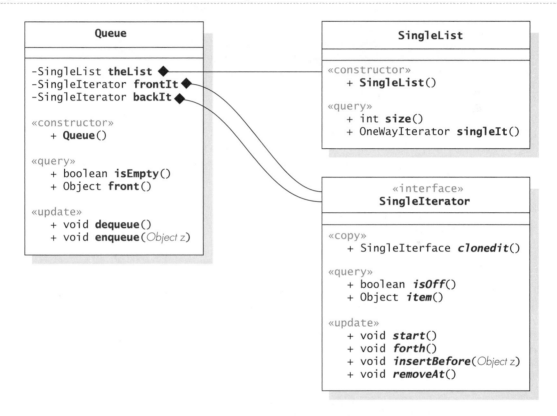

The class diagram shows that this implementation of Queue relies upon three instance variables.

- theList is a SingleList that stores one queue item per list cell.
- frontIt is an iterator positioned at the front of theList.
- backIt is an iterator positioned at the back of theList.

This solution uses the proxy design pattern by virtue of the theList variable. The other two variables in the representation are frontIt and backIt. Figure 7.17 shows the complete linked-list implementation of Queue.

Figure 7.17 Queue implementation using proxy design pattern

```java
import java.util.NoSuchElementException;
/* invariant:
        !isEmpty() implies backIt.isOff() */
public class Queue {
    private SingleList theList;
    private SingleIterator frontIt, backIt;

    /*  post:   theList is an empty list */
    public Queue() {
        theList = new SingleList();
        frontIt = theList.singleIt();
        backIt = theList.singleIt();
    }

    /*  post:   result == (theList is an empty list) */
    public boolean isEmpty() {
        return (frontIt.isOff());
    }

    /*  pre:    !isEmpty() (throws java.util.NoSuchElementException)
        post:   result == the first item from theList */
    public Object front() {
        frontIt.start();
        if (isEmpty()) {
            throw new NoSuchElementException();
        } else {
            return frontIt.item();
        }
    }

    /*  post:   theList == theList@pre with z appended to the rear */
    public void enqueue(Object z) {
        if (isEmpty()) {
            backIt.start();
            backIt.insertBefore(z);
            backIt.forth();
        } else {
            backIt.insertBefore(z);
            backIt.forth();
        }
    }
```

Continued on next page

```
/*  pre:      !isEmpty() (throws java.util.NoSuchElementException)
    post:     theList == theList@pre with an item removed from the
              front */
public void dequeue() {
    frontIt.start();
    if (isEmpty()) {
        throw new NoSuchElementException();
    } else {
        frontIt.removeAt();
    }
}
}
```

This Queue implementation must take care to properly maintain and use the frontIt and backIt iterators. Both the front method and the dequeue method use frontIt. Both methods begin by calling start to reset frontIt to the front of the list (queue). The enqueue method must work on the opposite end of the list, so it uses backIt. This enqueue algorithm is based on the assumption that backIt is positioned off the end of the list unless the list is empty. (This assumption is claimed by the class invariant.)

In the case of a nonempty queue, the enqueue method executes the following two statements.

```
backIt.insertBefore(z);
backIt.forth();
```

Because backIt must be positioned off the end of the list, the first statement appends z to the end of the list. The second statement is essential to ensure that backIt remains off the end of the list, consistent with the class invariant.

If enqueue is called on an empty queue (list), the following statements are executed.

```
backIt.start();
backIt.insertBefore(z);
backIt.forth();
```

Calling start on the backIt variable ensures that it is properly positioned off the end of the empty list. The last two statements perform the same functions as an enqueue on a nonempty queue.

7.8 RING BUFFER IMPLEMENTATION OF QUEUE

As you might expect, a bounded version of Queue can be implemented using an array to store the queue content. The preferred representation technique for such an implementation, called a **ring buffer**, is pictured in Figure 7.18.

This figure shows that a ring buffer is an array of cells. (In this case the array is named queueContent.) As with other arrays, the cell with index 0 immediately precedes the cell with index 1, and the cell with index 1 immediately precedes the cell with index 2. What is unique about a ring buffer is that the cell with index

Figure 7.18 A ring buffer

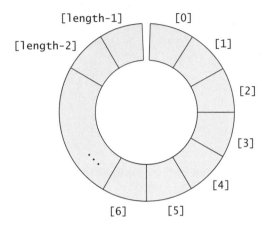

queueContent.length-1 (the last cell of the array) is treated as though it immediately precedes the cell with index 0. In other words, the array is treated as though it were circular, and hence the name "ring buffer."

When a queue is represented as a ring buffer, additional indices are used. The representation discussed here uses two such indices.

- newest is the index of the most recently enqueued item.
- oldest is the index of the item that has been in the queue the longest (the queue's front).

Suppose, for example, that the queue contains the following content. (The left end of the sequence is the front of the queue.)

sequence{ "flea", "gnat", "fly" }

You can store this content in the queueContent ring buffer in various ways. The only restriction for this representation is that the items of the queue be stored in consecutive array cells arranged from front to back in clockwise fashion. This usage of "consecutive cells" includes the ringlike arrangement that considers cell [queueContent.length-1] to be adjacent to cell [0]. Figure 7.19 illustrates four different ways to store the *sequence*{ "flea", "gnat", "fly" } queue. The bottom two pictures demonstrate how the queue content can span the end of the last cell of the array.

Figure 7.20 contains the complete ring buffer implementation. Notice that queueContent, newest, and oldest are instance variables of this BoundedQueue class.

Figure 7.19 Four ways to store *sequence*{"flea", "gnat", "fly"}

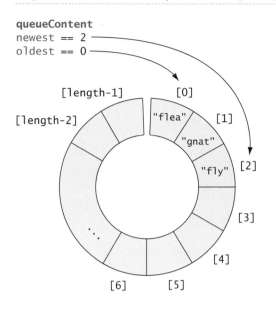

queueContent
newest == 2
oldest == 0

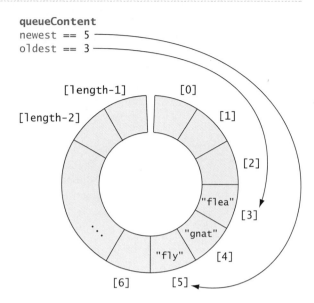

queueContent
newest == 5
oldest == 3

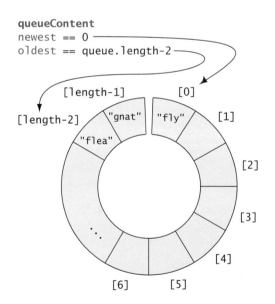

queueContent
newest == 0
oldest == queue.length-2

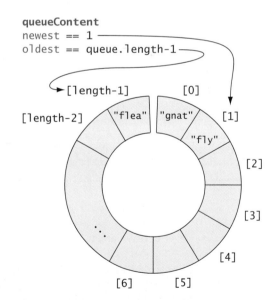

queueContent
newest == 1
oldest == queue.length-1

Figure 7.20 BoundedQueue implementation with ring buffer

```
import java.util.NoSuchElementException;
/*  invariant: 0 <= newest <= queueContent.length
               and 0 <= oldest <= queueContent.length */
public class BoundedQueue {
    private Object[] queueContent;
    private int newest;
    private int oldest;

    /*  post:   queueContent.length == m+1
                and newest == m and oldest == 0 */
    public BoundedQueue( int m ) {
        queueContent = new Object[m+1];
        newest = m;
        oldest = 0;
    }

    /*  post:   result == ((newest+1) % queueContent.length ==
                          oldest) */
    public boolean isEmpty() {
        return ((newest+1) % queueContent.length) == oldest;
    }
    /*  pre:    !isEmpty() (throws java.util.NoSuchElementException)
        post:   result == queueContent[oldest] */
    public Object front() {
        if (isEmpty()) {
            throw new NoSuchElementException();
        } else {
            return queueContent[oldest];
        }
    }

    /*  pre:    (newest+2) % queueContent.length != oldest
                  (throws IllegalStateException)
        post:   newest = (newest@pre + 1) % queueContent.length
                and queueContent[newest] == z */
    public void enqueue(Object z) {
        if ((newest+2) % queueContent.length != oldest) {
            newest = (newest + 1) % queueContent.length;
            queueContent[newest] = z;
        } else {
            throw new IllegalStateException();
        }
    }
```

Continued on next page

```
    /*  pre:    !isEmpty() (throws java.util.NoSuchElementException)
        post:   oldest = (oldest@pre + 1) % queueContent.length */
public void dequeue() {
    if (isEmpty()) {
        throw new NoSuchElementException();
    } else {
        oldest = (oldest + 1) % queueContent.length;
    }
}
}
```

The implementation of this ring buffer representation advances the value of newest around the ring clockwise. The following expression advances the value of the newest index to the "next" cell;

```
newest = (newest + 1) % queueContent.length;
```

For most potential values of newest, this expression merely increments the variable by 1. However, when newest == queue.length-1, executing this instruction causes newest to be assigned zero (the index of the next cell in the ring). The value of oldest trails newest, advancing in the same clockwise direction. A call to enqueue advances the value of newest, and each call to dequeue advances the value of oldest.

The implementation of isEmpty for this representation deserves examination. Normally, the value of newest leads oldest around the ring. However, when the queue is empty, the value of oldest will be one cell beyond newest. You can discover this fact by considering that a queue of length 1 means that oldest == newest. If the dequeue method is called on such a queue, the queue becomes empty by advancing oldest beyond newest.

This algorithm of testing for an empty queue by comparing oldest and newest imposes a minor constraint: The size of the ring buffer array must be 1 larger than the maximum queue length. The difficulty with permitting queue content to fill every array cell is that the resulting state will be indistinguishable from an empty queue. A slight modification of the representation—to include an additional instance variable maintaining the queue's length—eliminates the need to make the array one cell too large.

7.9 PRIORITY QUEUE

Most airlines begin boarding an aircraft with passengers "accompanying small children" or who "need extra time in boarding." The second group of individuals to board are the first-class passengers. First-class boarding is typically followed by general boarding. This boarding process has overtones of a queue, because passengers stand in a line and board the aircraft according to their position in the line. But it isn't a pure queue because some passengers have higher priority even though they haven't been standing in line.

The airline boarding process is an example of a **priority queue** because passengers are queued within priority groups. All passengers accompanying small children or needing extra assistance are a part of the highest-priority group. These highest-priority individuals leave the queue (board the plane) before others waiting in the queue. The first-class passengers have the second highest priority. Only when all the first-class passengers have left the queue is it time for those with lowest priority to board.

A priority queue, in general, is a container in which the next item to be removed is the item that

- Has highest priority of all container items
- Has been in the container the longest among items with equal priority

For example, consider the timeline of priority queue insertions shown in Figure 7.21. This picture depicts the passage of time from left to right. Along the timeline are events that signify the time at which an item is inserted into the priority queue. Each item is labeled with an alphabetic letter and a priority. Higher numbers mean greater priority.

Figure 7.21 Timeline of priority queue insertions

The first item inserted is item A, and it has a priority of 2. The second item inserted is B, and it has a higher priority (3). The first two insertions are followed by six additional insertions, labeled C though H; each item has the indicated priority (either 1, 2, or 3).

Assuming that the priority queue is empty when the timeline begins and that there are no intervening removals, at the end of the timeline the item at the front of the priority queue is item B. The three highest-priority items in the container are B, F, and H; and item B has been in the priority queue longer than F or H.

If item B is removed from the priority queue, item F is the front item. If item F is removed, item H is at the front. If item H is removed, item A is the front item. Continuing this algorithm of removing all the priority queue items reveals their position in the priority queue as follows.

Removal order (first to last): **B, F, H, A, E, C, D, G**

Figure 7.22 contains a class diagram and specifications for a priority queue ADT. Rather than specify fixed priorities, this ADT allows the prioritization to remain somewhat abstract. `PriorityQueue` objects must conform to the `Comparable` interface, and the ADT specifies that those objects having greater value (as determined by `compareTo`) have the greater priority.

Figure 7.22 PriorityQueue ADT specifications

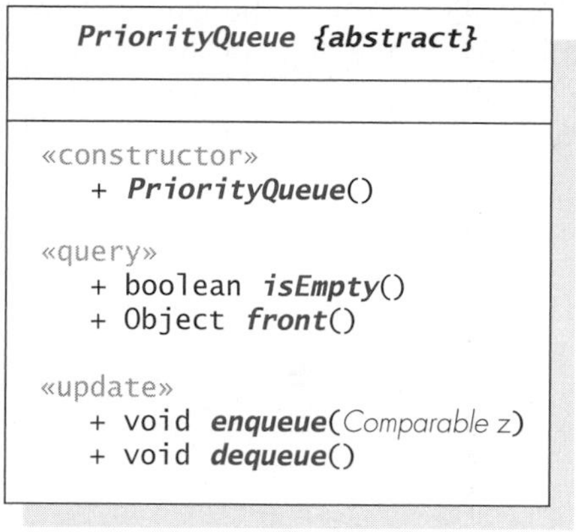

```
┌─────────────────────────────────────────┐
│         PriorityQueue {abstract}          │
├─────────────────────────────────────────┤
│                                           │
├─────────────────────────────────────────┤
│  «constructor»                            │
│      + PriorityQueue()                    │
│                                           │
│  «query»                                  │
│      + boolean isEmpty()                  │
│      + Object front()                     │
│                                           │
│  «update»                                 │
│      + void enqueue(Comparable z)         │
│      + void dequeue()                     │
│                                           │
└─────────────────────────────────────────┘
```

PriorityQueue Specifications

Domain

Every PriorityQueue consists of a *sequence* of Comparable

Constructor Method

public **PriorityQueue**()

> **post:** this == *sequence*{}

Query Methods

public boolean **isEmpty**()

> **post:** result == (this->*size*() == 0)

public Object **front**()

> **pre:** !isEmpty() (throws java.util.NoSuchElementException)

> **post:** result == the item in this that has greatest value (via compareTo) *and* has smallest seqeuence position if there are multiple greatest items

Update Methods

public void **enqueue**(Object z)

> **post:** this == this@*pre*->*append*(z)

public void **dequeue**()

> **pre:** !isEmpty() (throws java.util.NoSuchElementException)

> **post:** this == this@*pre* with the item removed that front() would return

There are many possible implementations of `PriorityQueue`. One possibility is to represent `PriorityQueue` with a linked list that stores items together with a double-valued priority in the same order in which they are enqueued. This implementation orders the items of the linked list in the same way as `theSeq` from the specifications in Figure 7.22. Using such a representation the insertion timeline from Figure 7.21 would result in the linked list depicted in Figure 7.23.

Figure 7.23 A first linked-list representation of the `PriorityQueue` timeline

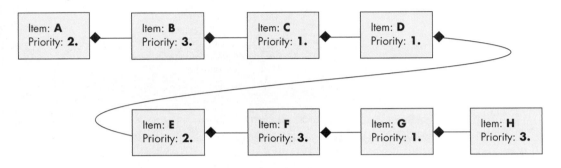

The implementation of the `enqueue` operation for this representation consists of merely inserting the new item at the end of the priority queue. The algorithms for implementing `front` and `dequeue` are more complicated. The `front` implementation begins by identifying the greatest priority of all priority queue items, and then finds the first queue item with such a greatest priority. At a minimum, this `front` implementation requires that each item be visited at least once (i.e., it performs in O(*list Length*) time). The implementation of `dequeue` is similar to that of `front` except that the item that is identified to be the front item must be removed from the list.

A second linked-list representation of `PriorityQueue` is to order the items in the list in the same order that they should be removed. This representation is pictured for the timeline example in Figure 7.24.

Figure 7.24 A second linked-list representation of the `PriorityQueue` timeline

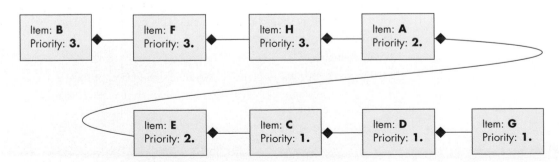

This second representation leads to more efficient—O(1)—implementations of front and dequeue because the front item of the priority queue is always the first item in the list. However, implementing the enqueue method is more complicated. The enqueue algorithm consists of visiting list items from front to back until the first item with lesser priority is encountered; the new item is inserted before this location.

If all the potential priority levels are known in advance, a third possible representation is to store a priority queue as an array of queues—one queue for each potential priority level. Figure 7.25 pictures this representation for the timeline example.

Figure 7.25 An array of queues representation of the PriorityQueue timeline

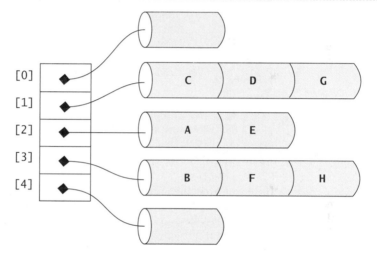

For the array of queues representation, the enqueue method is implemented by enqueueing into the queue with index matching the new item's priority. The front and dequeue methods must search the array from higher to lower indices for the first nonempty queue. The front of this first nonempty queue is the front of the priority queue.

The size of the array is determined by the range of potential priorities. When you can't predict this range of priorities or when the range is too large, you can't use the array of queues representation.

THE SOFTWARE INSPECTOR

Following is a collection of hints on what to check when you examine a design or code that involves the concepts of this chapter.

✓ Many of the stack and queue methods—including pop, top, peek, dequeue, and front—rely on nonempty containers. You should examine each call to one of these methods to ensure that it is applied to a nonempty container. Another option is to guard such calls by checking isEmpty.

✓ Some stack algorithms always remove items from the stack when the items are processed. To avoid bugs for such algorithms, always examine a call to front to look for the associated pop.

✓ The side effect of the pop method from java.util.Stack suggests caution. Programmers often call pop to inspect the top of the stack but forget that it also removes the value. You may need to replace the top of stack following a call to pop.

✓ The ring buffer implementation of a queue requires care in writing expressions to increment the queue front and rear indices. You should check these expressions to ensure that they always advance properly from one cell index to the next.

✓ Unless the queue representation includes a separate variable to store the queue size, a ring buffer must contain one more cell than the maximum queue size.

EXERCISES

1. Assume that before every part that follows, the state of ohStack can be pictured abstractly as follows.

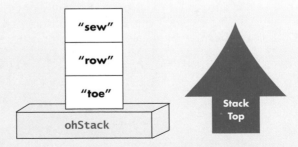

Redraw the picture to show the state of all stacks following the code segment.

a. ohStack.push("mo");
   ohStack.pop();
   ohStack.push("go");

b. ohStack.push(ohStack.top());
   ohStack.push("though");
   ohStack.push(ohStack.top());

c. Stack oStack = new Stack();
   oStack.push(ohStack.top());
   oStack.pop();
   oStack.pop();
   ohStack.push("snow");
   while(!ohStack.isEmpty()) {
       oStack.push("no");
       ohStack.pop();
   }

d. Stack oStack = new Stack();
   while(!ohStack.top().equals("toe")) {
       oStack.push(ohStack.top());
       ohStack.pop();
   }

2. Rewrite parts (a) through (d) of Exercise 1 to express the same algorithms, assuming that ohStack and oStack both belong to the java.util.Stack class.

3. Which of the following data structures are properly classified as LIFO because they can't be used in any other way?

   Array

   Singly linked list

   Stack

   Queue

4. Which one of the four ADTs from Exercise 3 is most closely associated with buffering and spooling?

5. Assume that before every part that follows, the state of the queue called iQueue can be pictured abstractly as follows.

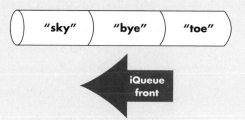

Redraw the picture to show the state of all queues following the code segment.

```
a. iQueue.enqueue("my");
   iQueue.enqueue("why");
   iQueue.dequeue();
   iQueue.dequeue();
```

```
b. iQueue.enqueue( iQueue.front() );
   iQueue.enqueue("sigh");
   iQueue.enqueue( iQueue.front() );
```

```
c. Queue iQ = new Queue();
   iQ.enqueue(iQueue.front());
   iQueue.dequeue();
   iQ.enqueue("eye");
   while( !iQueue.isEmpty() ) {
       iQ.enqueue("I");
       iQueue.dequeue();
   }
```

```
d. Queue iQ = new Queue();
   while( !iQueue.front().equals("high") ) {
       iQ.enqueue(iQueue.front());
       iQueue.dequeue();
   }
```

6. For each of the following ADTs and associated representation, explain whether it is bounded. If it is, in what sense is the representation bounded?

   a. A stack implemented via a list (see Figure 7.8)

   b. A stack implemented via an array (see Figure 7.9)

   c. A queue implemented via a list (see Figure 7.16)

   d. A queue implemented via a ring buffer (see Figure 7.20)

7. Assume that

   • In the midst of executing method m1, call is made to m2.

   • During the resulting execution of method m2, a call of m3 is made.

   • During the resulting execution of method m3, a call of m4 is made.

   • During the resulting execution of method m4, a call of m5 is made.

   • The m5 method returns.

   • During the subsequent execution of method m4, a call of m6 is made.

   • During the resulting execution of method m6, this method calls itself recursively.

Draw a picture of the state of the run-time stack at the time the last call has just occurred. Your picture should indicate all the groups of automatic data associated with each method call and should depict their order on the run-time stack.

8. Consider the algorithm for evaluating RPN expressions. Trace the algorithm for the following expression.

1, 2, 3, –, 4, *. 5. +, –, 2, *

9. Trace the execution of the following set of queue operations, assuming that the queue is implemented as a ring buffer and that it is initially empty. Show a picture of the final state of the queue picturing a ring buffer in the style of Figure 7.19. Also be certain to show the values of newest and oldest.

```
BoundedQueue queue = new BoundedQueue(4);
queue.enqueue("aa");
queue.enqueue("bb");
queue.enqueue("cc");
queue.dequeue();
queue.dequeue();
queue.enqueue("dd");
queue.enqueue("ee");
```

10. Write code for each of the following methods.

a) Method name: `stackCopyOfQueue`

Parameters: a Queue parameter called **q**

Post: result has the same content as q where bottom-to-top of the result stack corresponds to front-to-rear of the queue. (Note that q should remain unaltered by this method.)

b) Method name: `arrayCopyOfQueue`

Parameters: a Queue parameter called **q**

Pre: q.size() > 0

Post: result has the same content as q where lowest index to greatest of the result array corresponds to rear-to-front of the stack. (Note that q should remain unaltered by this method.)

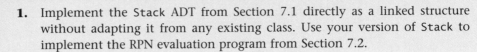

1. Implement the Stack ADT from Section 7.1 directly as a linked structure without adapting it from any existing class. Use your version of Stack to implement the RPN evaluation program from Section 7.2.

2. Make the modification to the ring buffer implementation that is suggested in Section 7.8 (represent a bounded queue with an array that is the same length as the maximum queue size by including one extra instance variable). Test your implementation to ensure correctness, and then use it to run the palindrome program (Figure 7.15).

3. Implement the Queue ADT from Section 7.6 by adapting DoubleList from Section 6.5. You should use only one iterator in your representation. Using your version of DoubleList, produce a working version of the palindrome program (Figure 7.15).

4. Design, implement, and test a program that can be used to analyze office printer needs. This program should simulate the behavior of a network printer that averages 10 pages per minute. Input to the program consists of a sequence of integers that represent the time delays (in seconds) between consecutive print jobs being sent to the printer. (For example, an input of 10, 3, 55 means that the second print job arrives 10 seconds after the first; the third arrives 3 seconds after the second; and the fourth arrives 55 seconds later.) You may assume that print jobs have a random size between 1 and 50 pages.

   Your program should simulate the activity of this printer in a loop that follows the passage of time. Each pending print job should remain in the print queue until it completes. The program should display the average length of time each print job was in the queue (the time from which is was sent until it started printing), the average time to print, and the average queue length.

5. Design, implement, and test a program to evaluate arbitrary parenthesized arithmetic expressions that include operands (integer constants) and binary operations, including + (addition), – (subtraction), * (multiplication), / (integer division), and ^ (exponentiation; 2^3 means 2^3). Use the following stack algorithm, sometimes called a shunting algorithm.

   Two stacks are needed: one for storing operands (oprndStk) and a second one for storing operators (oprStk). The shunting algorithm initializes oprStk to contain a special operator called BOS (short for "bottom of stack"). The oprndStk is empty initially.

   The operators, operands, and parentheses of the expression are scanned one at a time from left to right. The following actions are taken for each symbol:

   • When an operand (integer constant) is encountered, it is pushed on to oprndStk.

- When a left paren, "(", is encountered, it is pushed onto `oprtrStk`.
- When a right paren, ")", is encountered, *subexpressions are evaluated* until the top of `oprStk` is "(", and then the "(" is popped off `oprStk`.
- When an operator (+, −, *, /, or ^) is encountered, subexpressions are evaluated until the top of `oprStk` has lower precedence than the encountered operators, and then the encountered operator is pushed onthe `oprStk`.
- When the expression has been fully scanned, subexpressions are evaluated until the top of `oprStk` is BOS.

The *subexpressions are evaluated* portions of the algorithm that consist of using a technique somewhat like the RPN evaluation strategy for evaluating a small subexpression. In this case, the two operands involved in the subexpression are atop `oprndStk`, and the operation to be performed is atop `oprStk`. To evaluate the subexpression, the two operands must be popped. (The top value is the right operand, and the second value is the left operand.) The `oprStk` must also be popped to remove the operator. The subexpression is evaluated, and its value is pushed onto `oprndStk`.

The precedence relationship of the operators for this program is as follows.

Operator(s)	Precedence
^	High
/ * %	Mid
+ −	Low
(, BOS	Lowest

6. Implement a priority queue using all three techniques suggested in Section 7.9. Create a program to benchmark the three implementations, and compare the observed performance.

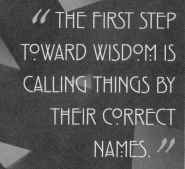

CONSULTING A MAP

> " THE FIRST STEP
> TOWARD WISDOM IS
> CALLING THINGS BY
> THEIR CORRECT
> NAMES. "
>
> —Ancient Chinese proverb

OBJECTIVES

- To examine the concept of a look-up table, also known as a map or a function

- To explore alternative map representations using lists and arrays

- To examine variations among maps (static maps versus dynamic maps, and one-way mapping versus two-way)

- To present the use of hash tables as a general-purpose set implementation strategy

- To introduce the issues relating to selection of hash functions

- To introduce various collision resolution strategies for hashing

- To explore the use of a hash table as an efficient implementation for a map

- To examine the `java.util.Map` interface and the `java.util.HashMap` class

Containers are defined largely in terms of the behavior of their methods, but certain kinds of methods are more important to some containers than others. Music CDs and MP3 players can be viewed as containers of songs. For both containers, the most important operation is the accessor method (i.e., the operation that plays a song). Despite their similarities, music CDs and MP3 players have important behavioral differences. Operations to add a new song or to remove a song are crucial for an MP3 player, whereas CD players rarely support ways to edit a playlist.

For many containers, such as the music CD, the behavioral focus is not insertions and removals but rather accessor methods. Dictionaries, telephone books, and income tax tables are all examples of containers in which the accessor operation (a look-up operation) is the dominant behavior. In fact, the look-up operation is so important that this style of container is commonly called a **look-up table**. This chapter focuses on abstractions and implementations of look-up tables as well as the closely related concept of a map.

8.1 MAP ADT

Look-up tables can be viewed as a collection of **key-value pairs**. A key-value pair consists of the key that is used to look up an item and the information (value) associated with the key. For example, the key for a pair within an English dictionary is an English word, and the value is the word's definition. A person's name together with an address form the key for a telephone book look-up, and the purpose of the look-up is to discover a telephone number (the value). The key for a tax table is an adjusted income (in dollars), and looking up the adjusted income yields the amount of tax to be paid for such income. Figure 8.1 lists additional containers that also consist of a collection of key-value pairs.

Figure 8.1 Containers and their key-value pairs

Container	*Key*	*Corresponding Value*
Glossary	A word ⟶	The word's meaning
Table of contents	Chapter or section title ⟶	Page number for beginning of chapter or section
Restaurant menu	Name of an entrée ⟶	The entrée's description and cost
Internet search engine	A search string ⟶	A collection of Web page "hits"
Grade book	A student's name ⟶	Examination scores for the student
Life expectancy table	Years of age ⟶	Expected life span
Club directory	Name of club member ⟶	Member's address, telephone, etc.
Collection of bank accounts	Account number ⟶	A record of all transactions for the account
Thesaurus	A word ⟶	A set of synonyms
National capitals	A country ⟶	The capital city

A look-up table is also called a **map** because such a table is used to map from a key to a value. A dictionary look-up supplies a key (an English word) in order to retrieve a value (the word's definition). A grade book look-up supplies a key (the name of a student) and maps to that student's examination scores. Figure 8.2 contains a class diagram and specification for MapADT.

Figure 8.2 MapADT Specifications

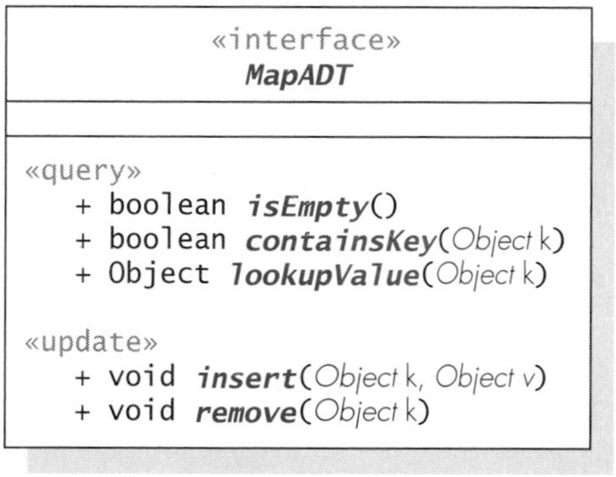

```
                  «interface»
                    MapADT


   «query»
       + boolean  isEmpty()
       + boolean  containsKey(Object k)
       + Object   lookupValue(Object k)


   «update»
       + void  insert(Object k, Object v)
       + void  remove(Object k)
```

MapADT Specifications

Domain

Every MapADT object consists of a *set* of KeyValuePair where KeyValuePair is the pair (Object **key**, Object **value**) (Note that **key** and **value** are inspected using functional notation, e.g., key(kv) refers to the key portion of a KeyValuePair called kv.)

Invariant

forAll(kv1, kv2 : KeyValuePair *and* `this`->*includes*(kv1)
    and `this` *includes*(kv2) | (kv1 (kv2)
    implies not key(kv1).equals(key(kv2)))

Query Methods

```
public boolean isEmpty( )
```
    post: result == (theMap == *set*{ })

```
public boolean containsKey(Object k)
```
    post: result == *exists*(kv : KeyValuePair *and* `this`->*includes*(kv)
                     | k.equals(key(kv)))

```
public Object lookupValue(Object k)
```
    pre: containsKey(k) (throws `java.util.NoSuchElementException`)

    post: *exists*(kv : KeyValuePair *and* `this`->*includes*(kv)
              and k.equals(key(kv)) | result == value(kv))

Update Methods

```
public void insert(Object k, Object v)
```
    post: theMap == theMap*@pre*
         − theMap*@pre*->*select*(kv | theMap*@pre*->*includes*(kv)
                           and k.equals(key(kv)))
                           ->*including*(KeyValuePair(k, v))

```
public void remove(Object k)
```
    pre: containsKey(k) (throws `java.util.NoSuchElementException`)

    post: theMap == theMap*@pre*
         − theMap*@pre*->*select*(kv | theMap*@pre*->*includes*(kv)
                         and k.equals(key(kv)))

The abstract specifications for MapADT define this ADT as the following.

set of KeyValuePair theMap;

The specifications go on to describe KeyValuePair as a pair consisting of a **key** part and a **value** part. Throughout the specification, the notation *key*(p) is used to denote the key portion of pair p, and the notation *value*(p) denotes the value portion of p.

As an example of a MapADT, consider a table that maps from the name of a planet to the planet's gravitational force relative to gravity on earth. Such a MapADT can be thought of as the following set of key-value pairs.

gravity == *set*{ ("Earth", 1), ("Venus", 0.90), ("Mars", 0.38),
      ("Mercury", 0.38), ("Jupiter", 2.36), ("Saturn", 0.92),
      ("Uranus", 0.89), ("Neptune", 1.13), ("Pluto", 0.07) }

Each of the nine items in this map is a pair consisting of the name of a planet and a real number representing the relative gravity of the planet. The MapADT specifications use the names "key" and "value" as though they were functions that yield the corresponding portion of a pair. Therefore, the following expression refers to the key portion of a pair:

key(("Venus",0.90))

The value of this expression is "Venus". Similarly, the following equality uses this functional notation to inspect the value part of a KeyValuePair.

value(("Saturn",0.92)) == 0.92

One fundamental characteristic of a map is that every key must be unique. In other words, each pair of the map must have a key that is different from all other keys in the same map. Mathematicians refer to such a mapping as a **function**. The MapADT invariant specifies this unique key restriction:

invariant: *forAll*(kv1, kv2 : KeyValuePair *and* this->*includes*(kv1)
      and this->*includes*(kv2) | (kv1 ≠ kv2)
      implies not key(kv1).equals(key(kv2)))

A literal translation of this invariant could be stated this way: "For any two different pairs (call the pairs kv1 and kv2) of the map, the key value of kv1 must be different from the key value of kv2." This allows multiple keys to be associated with the same value, but a single key cannot be associated with multiple values.

The method that defines the essence of MapADT behavior is called lookupValue. You call this method by passing a key as a parameter and the method responds by returning the value corresponding to the key. The following equalities illustrate three examples of get calls and the equivalent return value.

```
gravity.lookupValue( "Mars" ) == 0.38
gravity.lookupValue( "Mercury" ) == 0.38
gravity.lookupValue( "Pluto" ) == 0.07
```

MapADT uses generic keys (keys of type Object), and that allows for the following two choices for look-up.

- Look up an object with the identical key (==).
- Look up an object with a key of equal content (equals).

The lookupValue method uses the second (content equality) behavior. This means that *any* String variable, s, that stores "Pluto" will return 0.07 for the call gravity.lookupValue(s).

The precondition of lookupValue is expressed in terms of a closely related method, containsKey. This method returns true exactly when the map contains a pair with the specified key. A client program can call the containsKey method to test for this inclusion. According to its precondition, a call to lookupValue is valid only for a key that is found in the map.

Although the lookupValue and containsKey methods provide behavior essential to a look-up table, MapADT needs additional methods to serve as a general-purpose map. In particular there must be a way to initialize the look-up table with the appropriate mapping information. For this purpose, MapADT includes the insert method. (Note that a class constructor will also play a role in building the table. Because it is an interface, MapADT cannot include a constructor.)

A call to insert requires two parameters: *k* and *v*. The method inserts a new mapping pair into the container. This pair uses *k* as its key and *v* as its value. If MapADT already contains a pair with *k* as its key, a call of insert(k, v) will replace the prior pair with the (k, v) pair; this behavior preserves the invariant by eliminating the earlier pair that shared the same key.

MapADT also includes two other methods: isEmpty and remove. These methods aren't essential, but they provide additional utility and convenience to client code. For example, remove provides another mechanism to allow MapADT objects to be dynamic; that is, the look-up table can change as time passes.

To illustrate the use of MapADT, consider a look-up table to map from the name of a country to the name of its capital city. Figure 8.3 contains a table for countries whose names begin with the letter "I".

Figure 8.3   Look-up table of nations' capitals

Country	*Capital*
Iceland	Reykjavik
India	New Delhi
Indonesia	Jakarta
Iran	Tehran
Iraq	Baghdad
Ireland	Dublin
Israel	Jerusalem
Italy	Rome

As an example of the use of MapADT, the look-up table in Figure 8.3 is constructed and assigned to a `capitalsI` variable by the following code.

```
MapADT capitalsI = new MapAsList();
// MapAsList will be shown shortly as a MapADT constructor that
// instantiates an empty map.
capitalsI.insert( "Iceland", "Reykjavik" );
capitalsI.insert( "India", "New Delhi" );
capitalsI.insert( "Indonesia", "Jakarta" );
capitalsI.insert( "Iran", "Tehran" );
capitalsI.insert( "Iraq", "Baghdad" );
capitalsI.insert( "Ireland", "Dublin" );
capitalsI.insert( "Israel", "Jerusalem" );
capitalsI.insert( "Italy", "Rome" );
```

Because a MapADT object is fundamentally a set, the order in which pairs are inserted doesn't matter. This setlike behavior also means that inserting the same pair more than once has no effect. Therefore, the following code should construct the same abstract look-up table. Note that the order of insert calls is different, and the code inserts the pair for Italy twice.

```
MapADT capitalsI = new MapAsList();
// MapAsList will be shown shortly as a MapADT constructor that
// instantiates an empty map.
capitalsI.insert( "India", "New Delhi" );
capitalsI.insert( "Iceland", "Reykjavik" );
capitalsI.insert( "Iran", "Tehran" );
capitalsI.insert( "Iraq", "Baghdad" );
capitalsI.insert( "Indonesia", "Jakarta" );
capitalsI.insert( "Israel", "Jerusalem" );
capitalsI.insert( "Italy", "Rome" );
capitalsI.insert( "Italy", "Rome" );
capitalsI.insert( "Ireland", "Dublin" );
```

8.2 IMPLEMENTING MAP AS A LIST

Because MapADT is defined as a set, the alternatives for representing a MapADT are analogous to the representation strategies for sets. The use of singly linked lists provides for general-purpose representations.

Using a singly linked list as an implementation data structure still allows for various representations, as is indicated by the following questions.

- Should the representation use one list, or should there be one list for the keys and a separate list for the values?
- If the representation uses only one list, should each key-value pair be stored one pair per list cell, or should the key be stored in one list cell and the value in a separate cell?
- Should the list(s) be permitted to contain duplicate pairs, or should all duplicates be removed?

- Is there any additional constraint on the order of the list items (e.g., that they be sorted)?

Software Engineering Hint

Choosing a representation is one of the most important software design decisions. Questions such as those asked regarding the list representation of MapADT are typical design considerations.

Among the alternative representations, one good choice is to store one key-value pair per cell without duplicates. Figure 8.4 shows such an example.

Figure 8.4 MapAsList implementation of MapADT

```
/*  invariant: forAll(p1, p2 : is_in(this,p1) and is_in(this,p2)
                   | (p1 != p2) implies (not p1.key.equals(p2.key)) */
import java.util.NoSuchElementException;
public class MapAsList implements MapADT {
    private SingleList theList;
    private class KeyValuePair {
        public Object key;
        public Object value;

        public KeyValuePair(Object k, Object v) {
            key = k;
            value =v;
        }
    }

    /* post:  theList.isEmpty() */
    public MapAsList( ) {
        theList = new SingleList();
    }

    /* post:  result == (theList.singleIt().isOff()) */
    public boolean isEmpty(){
        return theList.singleIt().isOff();
    }
    /* post:  result == exists(kv : is_in(theList,kv)
                       | k.equals(key(kv))) */
    public boolean containsKey(Object k) {
        return (!iteratorAtKey(k).isOff());
    }

    /* pre:   containsKey(k)
                  (throws java.util.NoSuchElementException)
       post:  exists(kv : is_in(theList,kv) and k.equals(key(kv))
                       | result == kv.value) */
    public Object lookupValue(Object k) {
        SingleIterator it = iteratorAtKey(k);
```

Continued on next page

```
                if ( !it.isOff() ) {
                    return ( ((KeyValuePair)(it.item()))).value );
                } else {
                    throw new NoSuchElementException();
                }
            }


        /*  post:   the key-value pair (k,v) has been inserted in theList
                    and any item in theList@pre with key of k has been
                        deleted */
        public void insert(Object k, Object v) {
            SingleIterator it;
            it = iteratorAtKey(k);
            if (!it.isOff()) {
                it.removeAt();
            }
            it.start();
            it.insertBefore( new KeyValuePair(k, v) );
        }
        /*  pre:    containsKey(k)
                        (throws java.util.NoSuchElementException)
            post:   theList == theList@pre with the item with a key of k
                        deleted */
        public void remove(Object k) {
            SingleIterator it = iteratorAtKey(k);
            if ( !it.isOff() ) {
                it.removeAt();
            } else {
                throw new NoSuchElementException();
            }
        }
        /*  post:   (containsKey(k) implies
                        ((KeyValuePair)result.item()).key.equals(k))
                    and (!containsKey(k) implies result.isOff()) */
        private SingleIterator iteratorAtKey(Object k) {
            SingleIterator it = theList.singleIt();
            while (!it.isOff() &&
                    !k.equals((((KeyValuePair)(it.item()))).key)) {
                it.forth();
            }
            return it;
        }
    }
    /*  Specification Function
        is_in(MapADT m, KeyValuePair p) [a Boolean-valued function]
        DEFINITION
        is_in(m,p) == (p is the content of some cell in m) */
```

MapAsList provides a concrete implementation of
the abstract MapADT class, relying upon two classes: the
singly linked list class SingleList, and an internal class
called KeyValuePair. These class relationships are pictured in the class diagram in Figure 8.5.

Figure 8.5 Class diagram for MapAsList and related classes

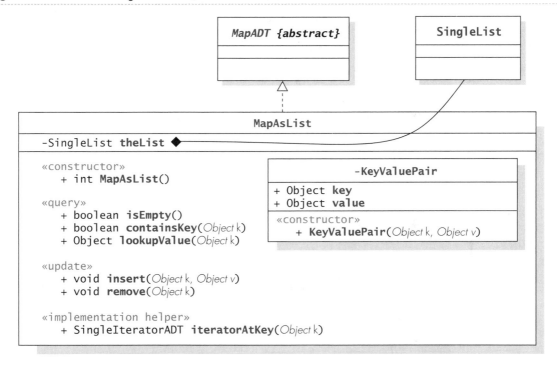

The KeyValuePair class provides an encapsulated form (inner class) for the
cells of the singly linked list. KeyValuePair contains two variables: one for the key
of the pair, and another one for its value. These variables are declared public, so
they can be directly inspected and updated by the surrounding MapAsList class.

Figure 8.6 shows an object diagram that results from constructing a MapAsList
object. Each table entry occupies one cell of a singly linked list.

Figure 8.6 Sample map instantiated as `MapAsList`

```
// MapAsList
MapADT capitals = new MapAsList();
capitals.insert( "Iceland", "Reykjavik" );
capitals.insert( "India", "New Delhi" );
capitals.insert( "Indonesia", "Jakarta" );
// Assert: the following object diagram results
```

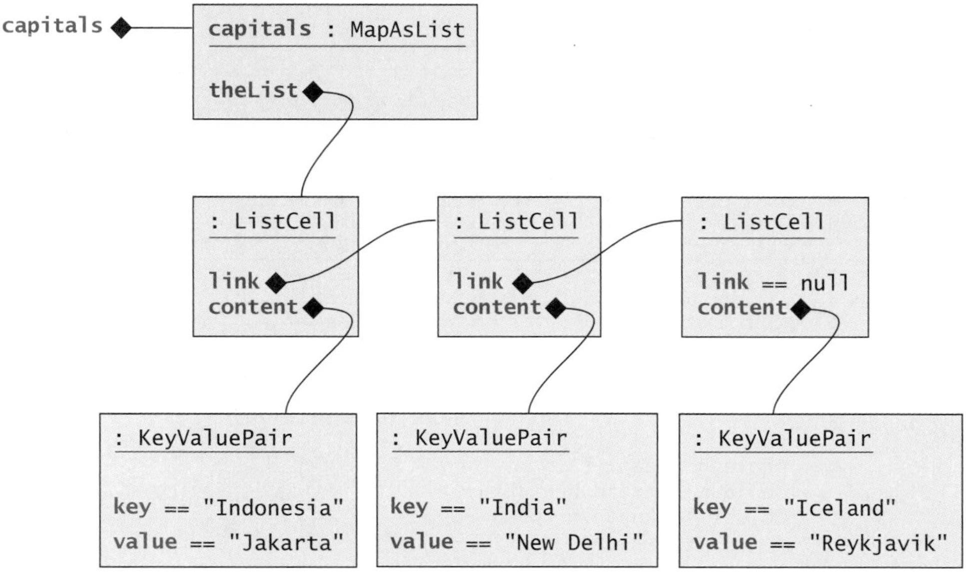

Many of the `MapAsList` methods share the same basic search algorithm. In particular, `containsKey`, `lookupValue`, `insert`, and `remove` all involve an algorithm that uses an iterator to search for an item with a matching key. This common algorithm is captured in the form of a private method called `iteratorAtKey`. This method performs a typical linear search, traversing `theList` until an item with a matching key is found or until all list items have been visited without a match (i.e., `isOff()` is true). When `iteratorAtKey` has completed execution, it returns the iterator that was used in the search; this iterator either is positioned at the desired item or is off the list.

Using `iteratorAtKey`, the `containsKey` method can be expressed with the following return statement:

```
return (!iteratorAtKey(k).isOff());
```

Similarly, the code from the `lookupValue` method uses `iteratorAtKey` to identify the location of the list item whose value needs to be returned. Here is the body of `lookupValue`:

```
SingleIterator it = iteratorAtKey(k);
if ( !it.isOff() ) {
    return ( ((KeyValuePair)(it.item())).value );
} else {
    throw new NoSuchElementException();
}
```

The common use of `iteratorAtKey` makes it obvious that `containsKey`, `lookupValue`, `insert`, and `remove` all have similar O(theList.size()) performance. Whenever any of these methods executes, `theList` must be searched for the indicated key. For most look-up tables, the performance of `MapAsList` is acceptable. However, for extremely large maps, you may prefer alternative implementations. The following sections explore techniques to improve map performance.

8.3 IMPLEMENTING A MAP AS AN ARRAY TABLE

The `MapAsList` implementation from Section 8.2 uses a singly linked list to represent MapADT. When the size of a map is limited, an obvious alternative representation is to use an array in place of the list. For such an implementation, each cell of the array stores a single key-value pair from MapADT. Unfortunately, such an array representation has no clear performance advantages over a list because array cells must be searched in the same way that `iteratorAtKey` searches list cells. Furthermore, this array representation is less dynamic because of its fixed size.

A general-purpose array implementation of MapADT may have similar performance to `MapAsList`. However, under special circumstances you can to improve MapADT performance using array representations. For example, consider a look-up table to map from a calendar month sequence number (1 through 12) to that month's English name. Such a table is pictured in Figure 8.7.

Figure 8.7 Look-up table for month names

#	*Month*
1	January
2	February
3	March
4	April
5	May
6	June
7	July
8	August
9	September
10	October
11	November
12	December

This month name mapping is best represented as an array of 12 `String` elements in which each array cell contains a month name and names are arranged in sequence from January to December. Following is the declaration for such an array.

```
String[] monthName
    = { "January", "February", "March", "April", "May", "June",
        "July", "August", "September", "October", "November",
        "December" };
```

A look-up operation for this representation is simple array access. For example, the name of month 5 is output by the following statement:

```
System.out.println( monthName[4] );
```

Notice that this statement accesses the array cell with index 4, not 5, because Java arrays have a lowest index of zero. It is straightforward to translate a month number of m into an array index of m–1.

Figure 8.8 shows slightly more cumbersome approach to implementing this array representation. The MonthNameMap class is written in the style of MapADT, and it is included to illustrate several characteristics of this kind of array table representation.

The MonthNameMap class is highly specialized. It implements only one kind of mapping—that from month number to month name. This specialization is so

Figure 8.8 MonthNameMap class

```
/*  invariant: monthName.length == 12
                and forAll(j : Integer
                            and 1 <=j <= 12 | monthName[j-1] ==
                            English name of the jth month */
// NOTE:   It might be better to implement this as an array within
//          the client code or as static members.
import java.util.NoSuchElementException;
public class MonthNameMap {
    private final String[] monthName = { "January", "February",
                    "March", "April", "May", "June", "July","August",
                    "September", "October", "November", "December" };

    public MonthNameMap( ) {
    }

    /*  post:   result == (1 <= k <= 12) */
    public boolean containsKey(int k) {
        return 1 <= k && k <= 12;
    }

    /*  pre:    containsKey(k)
                    (throws java.util.NoSuchElementException)
        post:   result == monthName[k-1] */
    public Object lookupValue(int k) {
        if ( containsKey(k) ) {
            return ( monthName[k-1] );
        } else {
            throw new NoSuchElementException();
        }
    }
}
```

extreme that the class cannot fully implement MapADT, so it does not attempt to implement the interface even though the methods of MonthNameMap use MapADT signatures.

The key data structure in the MonthNameMap class is the monthName array; it is declared as a private instance variable. This array is declared final because this happens to be a mapping that does not change over time. This constant nature of monthName also explains why the class omits the isEmpty, remove, and insert methods that are normally included in MapADT. In fact, the mapping of month names is so constant that it makes a good candidate for static translation. Figure 8.9 demonstrates a third representation for the month name mapping, with this one using a static final array.

Figure 8.9 CalendarStrings class

```
/*  invariant:  monthName.length == 12
                and forAll(m : Integer and 0 <= m <= 11
                | monthName[m] == English name of the (m+1)th month
                and dayName.length == 7
                and forAll(d : Integer and 0 <= d <= 6
                | dayName[d] == English name of the (d+1)th day */
public class CalendarStrings {
    public static final String[] monthName
            = { "January", "February", "March", "April", "May",
            "June", "July", "August", "September", "October",
            "November", "December" };
}
```

The monthName array, the MonthNameMap class, and the CalendarStrings class provide three alternative implementations that share the same underlying array representation. However, the client code is different for each alternative.

The first alternative is for the client code to create its own array:

```
String[] monthName
        = { "January", "February", "March", "April", "May", "June",
        "July", "August", "September", "October", "November",
        "December" };
```

Following such a declaration, the name of month 5 (May) is referenced by the following expression:

```
monthName[4] //denotes a look-up for the month of May
```

The second alternative implementation makes it easier for the client to create the table via instantiating an object with a statement such as the following.

```
MonthNameMap months = new MonthNameMap();
```

Following this instantiation, the name of month 5 (May) is referenced by the following expression:

```
months.lookupValue(5) //denotes a look-up for the month of May
```

The third (static array) alternative eliminates the need to declare or instantiate any structures. The name of month 5 (May) is referenced by the following expression:

```
CalendarStrings.monthName[4]
//denotes a look-up for the month of May
```

In addition to eliminating the need for declarations and instantiations, the **static** alternative also has advantages when the look-up table is accessed from classes of the same program. The static implementation is inherently shared among all classes without the need for parameter passage or multiple declarations.

All three of the alternative array implementations share a similar O(1) look-up performance. Array's direct access lets you perform a look-up by inspecting any array cell without the need to visit other cells. You can use this table look-up only when you have an efficient way to translate the map's keys into array indices. If the keys aren't consecutive integers, you need an efficient algorithm for converting keys into integer indices. For example, consider a look-up table to map from an alphabetic letter to its corresponding number on a telephone keypad. Such a map would be useful for converting from a telephone number such as "1-GHIJKLMNOP" into the corresponding "1-444-555-6667". Figure 8.10 shows a typical telephone keypad.

Figure 8.10 Telephone keypad

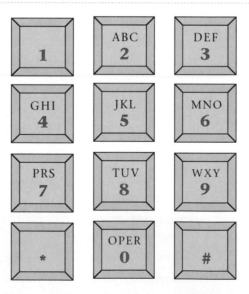

The characters "Q" and "Z" are not included on the keypad. Figure 8.11 demonstrates one way to represent this telephone keypad, taking advantage of direct access in an array. This representation uses a static array together with a static look-up method.

Figure 8.11 TeleMap class for mapping from telephone keypad letter to digit

```
import java.util.NoSuchElementException;
public class TeleMap {
    private static final int[] teleDigit
        /* 'A' 'B' 'C' 'D' 'E' 'F' 'G' 'H' 'I' 'J' 'K' 'L' 'M' */
        = {  2,  2,  2,  3,  3,  3,  4,  4,  4,  5,  5,  5,  6,
             6,  6,  7, -1,  7,  7,  8,  8,  8,  9,  9,  9, -1 };
        /* 'N' 'O' 'P' 'Q' 'R' 'S' 'T' 'U' 'V' 'W' 'X' 'Y' 'Z' */

    /* pre:    'A' <= c <= 'Z' and teleDigit[c-'A'] != -1
                    (throws java.util.NoSuchElementException)
       post:   result == monthName[k-1] */
    public static int lookupValue(char c) {
        if (c < 'A' || c > 'Z' || teleDigit[c - 'A'] == -1) {
            throw new NoSuchElementException();
        } else {
            return teleDigit[c - 'A'];
        }
    }
}
```

The TeleMap class supports mapping from a letter on the telephone keypad to its corresponding digit. For example, the digit for the letter "D" is referenced by the following expression:

```
TeleMap.lookupValue('D')
```

Including the lookupValue method, rather than simply using a public array offers two advantages. The first is that lookupValue relieves client code from the need to translate the char key into the proper array index. The lookupValue method translates its char parameter into the corresponding array index by subtracting the integer value of the character "A". (In other words the letter "A" maps to the index 'A' – 'A' == 0, the letter "B" maps to an index of 'B' – 'A' == 1, and so forth.) The second advantage is that lookupValue tests for invalid keys, throwing exceptions for any parameter that is outside the array index range and throwing exceptions for the letters "Q" and "Z".

The month name map and the telephone keypad map are examples in which the use of final arrays is effective because both maps are constant. However, using array tables as map representations also is advantageous for maps that change dynamically. For example, consider a small business of five employees that operates its own telephone switch. Because there are only five employees, each has a unique one-digit telephone extension. The software that operates the telephone switch uses a map with the extension number as a key and uses the corresponding employee's first name as a value. Figure 8.12 contains a TelephoneExtensions class that is designed for such mapping.

Figure 8.12 TelephoneExtensions class

```
import java.util.NoSuchElementException;
public class TelephoneExtensions {
    private String[] names;

    /*  post:   names.length == 10
                and forAll(j : 0<=j<=9 | names[j]==null) */
    public TelephoneExtensions( ) {
        names = new String[10];
    }
    /*  post:   (k<0 OR k>9) implies result == false
                and (0<=k<=9) implies result == names[k]!=null */
    public boolean containsExtension(int k) {
        if (k < 0 || k > 9) {
            return false;
        } else {
            return (names[k]!=null);
        }
    }
    /*  pre:    containsExtension(k)
                    (throws java.util.NoSuchElementException)
        post:   result == names[k] */
    public String lookupByExtension(int k) {
        if ( containsExtension(k) ) {
            return names[k];
        } else {
            throw new NoSuchElementException();
        }
    }


    /*  pre:    0 <= k <= 9
                    (throws java.util.NoSuchElementException)
        post:   names[k] == s */
    public void insert(int k, String s) {
        if (0 <= k && k <= 9) {
            names[k] = s;
        } else {
            throw new NoSuchElementException();
        }
    }
    /*  pre:    containsExtension(k)
                    (throws java.util.NoSuchElementException)
        post:   names[k] == null */
    public void remove(int k) {
        if ( containsExtension(k) ) {
            names[k] = null;
```

Continued on next page

```
        } else {
            throw new NoSuchElementException();
        }
    }

/*  pre:    exists(j : Integer and 0<=j<=9 | s.equals(names[j]))
                (throws java.util.NoSuchElementException)
    post:   exists(j : Integer and 0<=j<=9
                    | s.equals(names[j]) and result == j) */
    public int lookupByName(String s) {
        int m = 0;
        while (m <= 9 && !s.equals(names[m])) {
            m++;
        }
        if (m <= 9) {
            return m;
        } else {
            throw new NoSuchElementException();
        }
    }
}
```

The `TelephoneExtensions` class includes methods corresponding to all the MapADT methods except `isEmpty`. The following code uses this class to create a map for five employees:

```
TelephoneExtensions extensions = new TelephoneExtensions();
extensions.insert( 3, "Ed" );
extensions.insert( 1, "Marion" );
extensions.insert( 7, "Beverly" );
extensions.insert( 4, "Sandra" );
extensions.insert( 5, "Richard" );
```

This code declares, instantiates, and initializes a `TelephoneExtensions` map called `extensions`. The resulting look-up table is more pliable than the earlier maps in this section because of the inclusion of the `insert` and `remove` methods. If an employee leaves the company, that person's phone extension can be removed from the map by calling the `remove` method. Similarly, when a new employee joins the firm, an extension is added to the map by a call to `insert`.

The important thing to note about `TelephoneExtensions` is that the primary look-up method, `lookupByExtension`, is another of the highly efficient, O(1), algorithms resulting from a direct array access. Except for checking to ensure that the key k is valid, the essential code for `lookupByExtension` consists of the following return statement.

```
return names[k];
```

A byproduct of the array table implementation is that `insert` and `remove` methods also have the same O(1) performance. Both of these methods use a key in the same way as `lookupByExtension` to go directly to the proper array cell where the insertion or removal must occur.

Normally, a map is a one-way translation device, that permits a mapping from key to value. Sometimes, it is possible to map "in reverse" from value to key. The TelephoneExtensions method called lookupByName provides for this kind of reverse translation. A call to lookupByName supplies an employee name as argument and is designed to return the telephone extension corresponding to the employee name.

The implementation of lookupByName is not as efficient as lookupByExtension. The lookupByName method uses a linear search of the array, so its performance is O(*list length*), similar to MapAsList look-up performance. It also is important to notice that there is nothing to prohibit having two employees with the same first name. If this occurs, the lookupByExtension method still works properly, but lookupByName will always return the smaller of the two extensions. This underscores the importance of key uniqueness in look-up tables.

8.4   HASH TABLES

As explained in Section 8.3, the performance of the array look-up table depends on the ability to efficiently translate a key into the array index for the cell that stores the value corresponding to the key. Translating keys into indices is relatively easy when the set of potential keys is a contiguous collection of integers or characters. For other kinds of keys, such a translation may not be as convenient, or the potential range of possible indices may be impractically large. In such cases, a clever implementation strategy known as a **hash table** can often provide performance almost as good as that of the array table.

Section 8.5 examines how to use a hash table as a MapADT implementation. This section examines a more general-purpose view of a hash table as a set. For example, consider the task of implementing a set of decimal digits such as the following:

set{ 3, 1, 7, 0, 2, 5 }

You could represent this set using a list in which each digit is stored in a separate list cell. Figure 8.13 pictures this list representation.

Figure 8.13 A list that represents the set {3, 1, 7, 0, 2, 5}

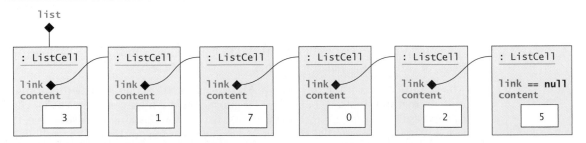

The list implementation of a set requires a linear search in order to test for set membership. For example, to discover the value 5 to be an element of the set represented in Figure 8.13, you traverse the list until you encounter a cell with the value 5. In this case you must visit all six cells.

A bit vector representation also is possible for sets of decimal digits. Figure 8.14 illustrates the bit vector representation of *set*{3, 1, 7, 0, 2, 5}.

Figure 8.14 A bit vector that represents the set {3, 1, 7, 0, 2, 5}

: boolean[]	
[0]	true
[1]	true
[2]	true
[3]	true
[4]	false
[5]	true
[6]	false
[7]	true
[8]	false
[9]	false

As is pointed out in Chapter 4, the advantage of the bit vector technique is that you can test to see whether 5 is a set member using a single array cell inspection (an O(1) operation) without visiting other items. The price you pay for the bit vector performance is the limitations that the bit vector imposes on potential set elements. For example, the list representation strategy works equally well for set of double as it does for set of decimal digits. Unfortunately, the bit vector implementation isn't practical for a set of double. The number of potential set elements (and therefore the number of array cells) is enormous, and it isn't clear how to translate from a double to an appropriate integer index. The intent of a hash table is to capture much of the performance advantage of a bit vector but, as with the list representation, allow for a wider range of possible set elements.

Like a bit vector, a hash table uses an array as its container. Unlike a bit vector, a hash table does not use boolean as its cell type. Instead, the hash table array is described as an array of **buckets**, where each bucket is can store multiple values. The complete content of a hash table is the collective content of all hash table buckets. For example, Figure 8.15 shows a hash table that consists of an array of 10 buckets.

This hash table has five null (empty) buckets and five nonempty buckets. The set content of this hash table is the collection of all values in the nonempty buckets. This hash table stores the following set:

set{14, 28, 31, 34, 44, 56, 80, 100}

Figure 8.15 A sample hash table and its buckets

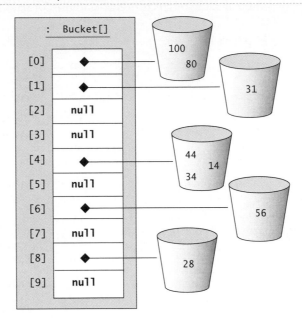

In Figure 8.15, the integers in each bucket share a common characteristic: Every integer has the same last digit as the other integers in the same bucket. Such a common characteristic is not an accident;, it is the way that the proper bucket is selected for an element. This characteristic is determined by something called a hash function. A valid hash function is any function that, when applied to a set element, yields the associated hash bucket index. In other words, applying a **hash function** to an element yields the number of the specific bucket into which that element should be placed. Following is the hash function, h, that would result in the hash bucket contents pictured in Figure 8.15:

h(e) == e % 10

Every item in a hash table is placed into the hash bucket, and its index is determined by applying the hash function to the element. For example, the element 31 is placed in hash bucket 1 because h(31) == 31 % 10 == 1. Similarly, the value 28 is placed in hash bucket 8 because h(28) == 28 % 10 == 8.

The insert method adds new items to a hash table by first applying the hash function to determine which bucket to place the value into. The look-up and remove methods also can take advantage of the separation into buckets. The first step in looking for an element is to apply the hash function to discover which bucket should contain the element. This narrows the search to a single bucket. If there are ten buckets in the hash table, applying the hash function eliminates the need to examine nine of them. In fact, if each hash bucket contains no more than one value, then the performance of a hash table is O(1), as with a bit vector.

In a bit vector, every array cell represents a single potential set element. Unfortunately, several values can share the same hash table bucket, and that degrades hash table performance. Two elements are placed in the same hash bucket by virtue of the fact that the hash function yields the same value for both. For example, 100 and 80 are in the zero (0) bucket because of the following applications of the hash function to these two elements.

h(100) == 100 % 10 == 0
h(80) == 80 % 10 == 0

When two elements hash to the same bucket, they are said to **collide**. In addition to the collision of 80 and 100, the Figure 8.15 example illustrates a collision among the 14, 34, and 44 elements in bucket 4.

You can use a number of techniques, called **collision resolution strategies**, to represent the content of a bucket that involves collisions. One reasonable approach is to store each bucket in the form of a list. Figure 8.16 pictures this representation for the same sample set.

Figure 8.16   A sample hash table with linked list buckets

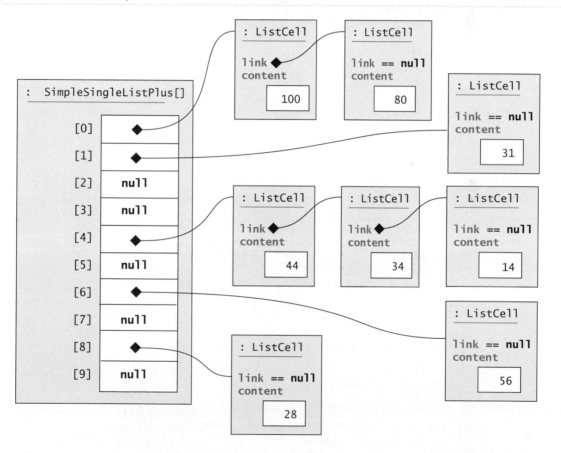

Using linked lists as a collision resolution strategy implies that every insertion into the hash table first hashes the element to the appropriate bucket, and then inserts the element into the list that represents the bucket. A look-up operation for this representation begins by applying the hash function and then searching the bucket (list) for the desired element. If the element is not in the list of the appropriate hash bucket, the element is not in the set represented by the hash table.

Figure 8.17 shows the class for such an implementation of a hash table. This implementation uses the same hash function and table size as the previous examples.

Figure 8.17 HashTableOfInt class

```
/*  invariant:
        forAll(e : e is wrapped within an item of some list from
               buckets[0...9] | e is wrapped within an item of the
               buckets[h(e)] list) */
public class HashTableOfInt {
    private SimpleSingleListPlus[] buckets;
    /* post:   buckets.length == 10
               and forAll(k : 0<=k<=9 | buckets[k] is empty) */
    public HashTableOfInt() {
        buckets = new SimpleSingleListPlus[10];
        for (int j=0; j!=10; j++) {
            buckets[j] = new SimpleSingleListPlus();
        }
    }

    /*  post:   result == e % 10
        note:   This is the hash function. */
    private int h(int e) {
        return e % 10;
    }
    /* post:   result == (z is wrapped within an item of
                          the list at buckets[h(z)]) */
    public boolean isIn(int z) {
        SimpleSingleListPlus searchList = buckets[ h(z) ];
        searchList.start();
        while (!searchList.isOff() &&
        ((Integer)(searchList.item())).intValue()!=z) {
            searchList.forth();
        }
        return !searchList.isOff();
    }
    /* post:   z is wrapped within some item of the list at
               buckets[h(z)] */
    public void add ( int z) {
        SimpleSingleListPlus insertList;
        if (!isIn(z)) {
            insertList = buckets[ h(z) ];
            insertList.start();
            insertList.insertBefore(new Integer(z));
        }
    }
}
```

HashTableOfInt implements an add method to insert int elements into the hash table and implements an isIn method as a look-up method. Both methods use the hash function, h, to select the particular list. The private instance variable buckets is the array of lists that forms the hash table. Each of these lists belongs to the SimpleSingleListPlus class.

One of the advantages of representing hash buckets as lists is that even at its worst, the hash table method implementation performs approximately like a list. Suppose that every element in a hash table collides to the same hash bucket. In that case the performance of the hash table is linear, similar to that of the list representation of the set.

Using linked lists as hash table buckets is often called **open** hashing because the hash table "opens" from an array into external data structures (i.e., linked lists). There are other collision resolution strategies that are **closed**. A closed hash table is one in which every element must be stored in the same array. This requires a strategy for calculating an alternative array index to the one that resulted in the collision.

A common form of closed hashing, using **linear probing**, consists of incrementing the array index by 1 for each collision. (Array indices are reset to zero when the incrementing would result in a value outside valid index boundaries.) To illustrate linear probing in conjunction with the hash function, consider inserting the following items into an empty hash table in the indicated order.

sequence{27, 14, 79, 24, 89, 94, 74}

Figure 8.18 traces the changes to the hash table array from this sequence of insertions.

Figure 8.18 Tracing the hash table insertions using linear probing

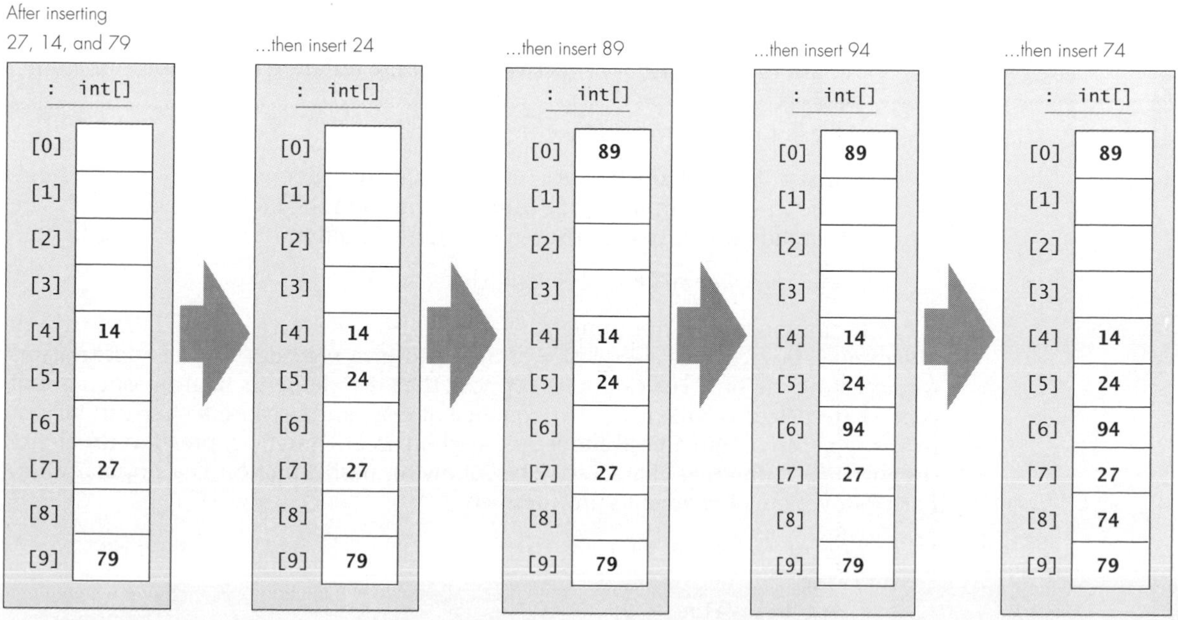

The leftmost array in the trace shows the result of inserting 27, 14, and 79. None of these elements collide. Next, the insertion of 24 collides with 14, which already occupies the hash table cell at index 4. The linear probing collision resolution strategy causes this collision to proceed from index 4 to the next index (5). Because the cell at index 5 is empty, 24 is inserted into this cell, as shown in the second array.

The next step is to insert 89. Again, a collision results because h(89) == 9, and 79 already occupies the cell at index 9. Because 9 is the index of the last array cell, linear probing, which treats the array as a ring, advances to an index of zero (0), and an empty cell is discovered. The third array shows the state of the hash table following the insertion of 89.

When 94 is inserted it collides with 14. Linear probing advances from an index of 4 to an index of 5, but this collides with the 24 element. Therefore, linear probing must be applied again to advance from an index of 5 to an index of 6. It is this empty cell with an index of 6 where the 94 value is assigned. This state is pictured in the second-to-last array.

The final step is to insert 74. This insertion collides with 14, and then linear probing collides with 24, then 94, and then 27. The first empty cell found by the linear probing is at index 8.

This example illustrates the greatest disadvantage of closed hash tables: Their collisions can **cluster** in such a way that a collision at one index can produce future collisions with elements having differing hash function values. Clustering collisions degrades the performance of all methods that use the hash table. Closed hashing collisions and clustering also make it difficult to remove elements from such hash tables.

The quality of the performance of all hash tables, whether they use open or closed hashing, is highly dependent on the success of the hash function. Three characteristics determine the success of a hash function.

- A hash function must yield a valid hash table index.
- A hash function should effectively distribute different elements to different buckets.
- A hash function should be efficient to calculate.

The first of these characteristics suggests that the value yielded by a hash function must be an integer in the range from zero through the table's cell count –1. The return of a valid array index is ensured by a hash function of the following form:

h(e) == *expression*(e) % buckets.length

A hash function for nonnumeric elements also poses no problem, because every object must be stored as a sequence of bits, and Java provides various mechanisms for accessing the bits. For example, suppose that the elements being hashed are of type String. Because a String is a sequence of char and because a char can be cast to int, you can design a hash function based on an arithmetic expression involving the String's individual characters. The following hash function is a popular alternative in which all characters are summed:

```
// Note: s.length must be small for the following to be effective
private int h( String s ) {
    int hashValue = 0;
```

```
      for (int j=0; j!=s.length(); j++) {
         hashValue = hashValue + (int)(s.charAt(j));
      }
      return hashValue % buckets.length;
   }
```

This hash function uses a common technique known as **folding**; it combines (folds) the individual parts of String (s) together into an integer. The operation that is used to fold characters in this case is addition. Another common version of folding uses an exclusive OR operation to fold. Folding is an effective technique for spreading out hash table values, because even if only one character differs between two strings, they are still likely to hash to different locations.

The third characteristic of an effective hash function is that a hash function should be efficient to calculate. The preceding folding hash function satisfies this characteristic as long as the length of the String, s, is short. The problem with a large s.length value is that the time taken to execute the loop becomes too great. The hash function is called for every isIn and add invocation, so the hash function algorithm must be efficient if the hash table is to be efficient.

Another hash function technique that satisfies all three characteristics of a good hash function is the **midsquare method**. A midsquare calculation consists of squaring a value and then selecting a central (mid) portion of the square. For example, hashing the value 721 begins by squaring the element (721^2 == 519841). If the middle part to be used consists of the third and fourth digits, then the value of the hash function yields 98. Therefore, h(721) == 98. Selecting a hash value from the "middle" digits or the center of a bit string is an important concept because the middle tends to be more random, thereby leading to hash functions less prone to collisions.

Perhaps the best hash function when you're using Java is a mechanism that is built into the programming language. The Object class includes a hashCode function that returns an arbitrary int associated with an object. This hashCode method provides a basis for designing excellent hash functions. The following is an obvious choice for the hash function.

```
h(e) == Math.abs(e.hashCode()) % buckets.length
```

The absolute value part of the calculation (Math.abs) is included because hashCode sometimes returns negative values.

The choice of hash function is not the only decision that impacts the performance of a hash table. Another important consideration is the size of the hash table. The measure that is most often applied to determine hash table size is called the **load factor**. The load factor of a hash table is calculated as follows. (The term "**capacity**," used in this equation, refers to the number of buckets in the hash table.)

load factor == *hash table cardinality / capacity*

A newly instantiated (empty) hash table has a load factor of 0.0. For closed hashing, a load factor of 1.0 means that every table cell is occupied. (Hash tables using open hashing can exhibit load factors greater than 1.0.) Generally speaking, lower load factors result in better performance because they result in fewer collisions. Load factors of no more than 0.6 to 0.75 generally offer a reasonable trade-off between performance and the memory space costs of the hash table.

8.5 IMPLEMENTING A MAP AS A HASH TABLE

Section 8.4 describes a hash table as a set of elements that uses a hash function that maps each element to its hash bucket index. With two slight alterations, you can use such a hash table to represent a map:

- Each hash table element is a key-value pair.
- The hash function is based solely on the key, not the value, of the pair.

Figure 8.19 contains a class for a generic hash table representation of MapADT.

Figure 8.19 MapAsHashTable class

```
/* invariant: forAll(p1, p2 : is_in(m, p1) and is_in(m, p2))
                  | (p1 != p2) implies not p1.key.equals(p2.key))
                  and forAll (p : is_in(m, p1)
                       implies is_in(buckets[h(p.key)], p) */
import java.util.NoSuchElementException;
public class MapAsHashTable implements MapADT {
    private SimpleSingleListPlus[] buckets;

    private class KeyValuePair {
        public Object key;
        public Object value;

        public KeyValuePair(Object k, Object v) {
            key = k;
            value =v;
        }
    }


    /* post:  buckets.length == n
            and forAll(k : 0<=k<=n-1 | buckets[k] is empty) */
    public MapAsHashTable(int n ) {
        buckets = new SimpleSingleListPlus[n];
        for (int j=0; j!=n; j++) {
            buckets[j] = new SimpleSingleListPlus();
        }
    }


    /* post:  result == (theList.singleIt().isOff()) */
    public boolean isEmpty(){
        SimpleSingleListPlus searchList;
        for (int j=0; j!=buckets.length; j++) {
            searchList = buckets[j];
            searchList.start();
```

Continued on next page

```
            if (!searchList.isOff()) {
                return false;
            }
        }
        return true;
    }


    /* post:   result == Math.abs(k).hashCode() % buckets.length
       note:   This is the hash function. */
    private int h(Object k) {
        return Math.abs(k.hashCode()) % buckets.length;
    }
    /* post:   result == exists(kv : KeyValuePair
                and is_in(buckets[h(k)],kv | k.equals(kv.key)) */
    public boolean containsKey(Object k) {
        SimpleSingleListPlus searchList = listWithIteratorAtKey(k);
        return !searchList.isOff();
    }


    /* pre:    containsKey(k)
                  (throws java.util.NoSuchElementException)
       post:   exists(kv : is_in(buckets[h(k)],kv
                and k.equals(kv.key) | result == kv.value) */
    public Object lookupValue(Object k) {
        SimpleSingleListPlus searchList = listWithIteratorAtKey(k);
        if ( !searchList.isOff() ) {
            return ( ((KeyValuePair)(searchList.item())).value );
        } else {
            throw new NoSuchElementException();
        }
    }


    /* post:   a KeyValuePair with key of k and value of v has been
                inserted in the list from buckets[h(k)] */
    public void insert(Object k, Object v) {
        SimpleSingleListPlus insertList = listWithIteratorAtKey(k);
        if ( !insertList.isOff() ) {
            insertList.removeAt();
        }
        insertList.start();
        insertList.insertBefore(new KeyValuePair(k, v));
    }
    /* post:   containsKey(k)
                  (throws java.util.NoSuchElementException)
       post:   buckets[h(k)] == buckets[h(k)]@pre with any
                KeyValuePair with key of k removed */
```

Continued on next page

```
public void remove(Object k) {
    SimpleSingleListPlus removeList = listWithIteratorAtKey(k);
    if ( !removeList.isOff() ) {
        removeList.removeAt();
    } else {
        throw new NoSuchElementException();
    }
}
/* post:  containsKey(k) implies
                ((KeyValuePair)result.item()).key.equals(k)
           and !containsKey(k) implies result.isOff() */
private SimpleSingleListPlus listWithIteratorAtKey(Object k) {
    SimpleSingleListPlus theList;
    theList = buckets[ h(k) ];
    theList.start();
    while (!theList.isOff() &&
    !k.equals(((KeyValuePair)(theList.item())).key)) {
        theList.forth();
    }
    return theList;
}
}
/* Specification Function
        is_in(Container c, KeyValuePair p)
            [a Boolean-valued function]
        DEFINITION
            is_in(m,p) == (p is contained within c) */
```

Software Engineering Hint

Localizing repeated code into a separate component can often make the software easier to modify. For example, the MapAsHashTable class includes a separate h method for a hash function, instead of merely performing this computation where it is applied. This separate method makes it convenient to change the hash function for the entire class by altering only one line of code.

The MapAsHashTable class uses a hash table, called buckets, that is an array of singly linked lists (of type SimpleSingleList). An internal KeyValuePair class provides the type for the items that are stored in the map. The hash function, h, relies on the hashCode function, and h is applied only to the key portion of a pair.

A private method called listWithIteratorAtKey is called by containsKey, lookup, insert, and remove. Each call to listWithIteratorAtKey searches the appropriate list (i.e., from buckets[h(k)]) for an item with a key part matching k. If such an item doesn't exist, then listWithIteratorAtKey returns a list with the iterator positioned off the list end. The code for the containsKey, lookup, insert, and remove methods is analogous to that of the corresponding methods from the HashAsList implementation.

The MapAsHashTable constructor method permits the client to specify the number of buckets in the hash table by passing this value as a parameter. This allows the client code to tailor the size of the hash table to the expected number of simultaneous map items. The result is to give the client better control over the hash table load factor.

8.6 JAVA.UTIL.MAP AND JAVA.UTIL.HASHMAP

The `java.util` package includes several facilities for supporting maps. Foremost among them is an interface called `java.util.Map`. This interface has many similarities to MapADT (described in Section 8.1). Figure 8.20 compares the two abstractions by listing the key methods of each and showing the corresponding methods.

Figure 8.20 Comparison of the MapADT and `java.util.Map` methods

MapADT	*java.util.Map*
containsKey	containsKey
	containsValue
	equals
	entrySet
insert	put *(optional, returns Object)*
isEmpty	isEmpty
	keySet
lookupValue	get
remove	remove *(optional, returns Object)*
	size
	values

Several of the `java.util.Map` methods have the identical abstract behavior as methods from MapADT. The `containsKey`, `isEmpty`, and `remove` methods have not only the same behavior, but also the same name and signatures, as their MapADT counterparts. One method is named differently between the two classes; the `get` method from `java.util.Map` has the same behavior as the `lookupValue` method.

The `put` method from `java.util.Map` is similar to `insert`. However, `put` is non-void, whereas `insert` is void. The `put` return value is intended to assist in identifying any previous map pair with the same key. The call `put(k,v)` returns `null` if there is no prior map entry for key k. If there is a prior pair—call it (k, v_{old})—with key of k and value of v_{old}, then the call `put(k,v))` returns v_{old}. The `java.util.Map` `remove` method is defined in a similar way to return the value of the removed entry, or `null`.

Two of the `java.util.Map` methods are considered "optional." An optional method may, or may not, be implemented by a class providing functionality for the interface. In particular, `put` and `remove` may not be implemented by some `java.util.Map` implementations.

A few other methods are included as conveniences in `java.util.Map`. Many, but not all, are listed in Figure 8.20.

- The `containsValue` method is analogous to `containsKey` except that `containsValue` returns true if a value, rather than a key, is present in the map.
- The `equals` method compares two Map objects for content equality.

- The size method returns the number of pairs in the map.
- The entrySet, keySet, and values methods return map information that has been translated into the form of another container. entrySet and keySet return, respectively, java.util.Set containers of the complete collection of pair mappings and the keys. The values method returns a java.util.Collection object that contains all the values from the key-value pairs.

The java.util.Map interface is a container of objects that belong to another interface, called java.util.Map.Entry, that defines the type of the pairs in the map container. This means, for example, that entrySet returns a set in which all the elements belong to java.util.Map.Entry. Figure 8.21 contains the interface specifications for the most important members of java.util.Map.Entry.

Figure 8.21 java.util.Map.Entry interface specifications

java.util.Map.Entry Interface Specifications

Domain (Every Map.Entry object consists of the following components)

    Object key;

    Object value;

Query Methods

public boolean **equals**(Object z)

    post: result == key.equals(z.getKey()) *and* value.equals(z.getValue())

public Object **getKey**()

    post: result == key

public Object **getValue**()

    post: result == value

The java.util.Map.Entry interface is a public interface that is declared in java.util.Map. This relationship is illustrated in the interface diagram in Figure 8.22. Using java.util.Map.Entry, you can supply the details of the java.util.Map interface as summarized in the interface specification in Figure 8.23.

Figure 8.22 java.util.Map interface diagram

Figure 8.23 java.util.Map interface specifications

java.util.Map Interface Specifications

Domain (Every Map object consists of the following component)

    set of java.util.Map.Entry

Invariant

    forAll(kv1, kv2 : this->*includes*(kv1)
        and this->*includes*(kv2) | (kv1 != kv2)
        implies not kv1.getKey().equals(kv2.getKey())

Query Methods

```
public boolean isEmpty( )
```
    post: result == (this == set{ })
```
public int size( )
```
    post: result == this->*size*()
```
public boolean equals(Object z)
```
    post: result == (this.equals(z))
```
public boolean containsKey(Object k)
```
    post: result == *exists*(kv : this->*includes*(kv) | k.equals(kv.getKey()))
```
public boolean containsValue(Object v)
```
    post: result == *exists*(kv : this->*includes*(kv) | v.equals(kv.getValue()))]

Continued on next page

```
public Object get(Object k)
    pre: containsKey(k) (throws java.util.NoSuchElementException)
    post: exists(kv : this->includes(kv) and k.equals(kv.getKey()))
                | result == kv.getValue())
public Set keySet( )
    post: result == this->select(k | containsKey(k))
public Set entrySet( )
    post: result == this
public Collection values( )
    post: result == this->select(v | containsValue(v))
```

Update Methods

```
public Object put(Object k, Object v)
    post: this == this@pre
                - this->select(kv | k.equals(kv.getKey()))
                ->including( (k, v) )
            and containsKey(k)@pre implies result == get(k)@pre
            and !containsKey(k)@pre implies result == null
public Object remove(Object k)
    post: this == this@pre
                - this->select(kv | k.equals(kv.getKey())
            and containsKey(k)@pre implies result == get(k)@pre
            and !containsKey(k)@pre implies result == null
```

The java.util package also includes several implementations of the java.util.Map interface. The most appropriate of these implementations for this discussion is called HashMap. This class is diagrammed in Figure 8.24.

The java.util.HashMap class provides a complete implementation of java.util.Map, including the optional put and remove methods. The clone method, also included in HashMap, provides an implementation of the Cloneable interface.

Four methods are provided as HashMap constructors. The m parameter is used to establish the initial capacity (the number of buckets) of the hash table. The HashMap implementation can adjust the hash table capacity to accommodate larger maps. When the load factor exceeds a maximum load factor, the HashMap capacity is enlarged. This maximum load factor is specified as the second parameter in the constructor method with two parameters. All other constructor methods use the default maximum load factor of 0.75. The behavior of the constructors is further illustrated in the following four sample statements.

```
Map myMap = new HashMap(int 10, .6f);
// instantiates myMap as an empty hash table with capacity of 10
// and load factor of 0.6

Map yourMap = new HashMap(int 99);
// instantiates yourMap as an empty hash table with capacity of 99
// and load factor of 0.75
```

Figure 8.24 java.util.HashMap class diagram

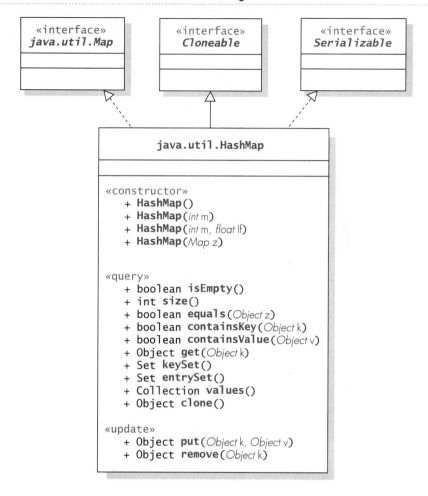

```
Map hisMap = new HashMap();
// instantiates hisMap as an empty hash table with unknown capacity
// and load factor of 0.75

Map herMap = new HashMap(someOtherMap);
// instantiates herMap as a map with the same content as
// someOtherMap, a load factor of 0.75
// and a capacity of the greater of 11 or 2*someOtherMap.size()
```

The alternative HashMap constructor methods demonstrate how data structure libraries for production programming should provide flexibility to meet the needs of various situations. Some programmers may know precisely how large their map will become, so they would prefer to control the capacity. Other programmers may have an application in which performance is far more important than memory, so they may wish to have the option of establishing an extremely low load factor. The priority

Software Engineering Hint

The **HashMap** method, and particularly its constructors, allows for a hash table implementation that can be tailored to the needs of the client. Such flexibility is an important consideration in the design of library classes of widespread applicability.

for still other programmers might be to save on software development time and allow the system defaults to establish capacity and load factor.

Figure 8.25 illustrates the abstract differences between the `MapAsHashTable` class described in Section 8.5 and the `java.util.HashMap` class. This figure repeats the look-up table for capitals of countries whose names begin with "I", together with client code for constructing and manipulating this table for each of the two hash table classes.

Figure 8.25 Sample client code for `MapAsHashTable` and `java.util.HashMap`

Country	*Capital*
Iceland	Reykjavik
India	New Delhi
Indonesia	Jakarta
Iran	Tehran
Iraq	Baghdad
Ireland	Dublin
Israel	Jerusalem
Italy	Rome

```
// MapAsHashTable
MapADT capitalsI = new MapAsHashTable(12);
capitalsI.insert( "Hungary", "Budapest" );
capitalsI.insert( "Iceland", "Reykjavik" );
capitalsI.insert( "India", "New Delhi" );
capitalsI.insert( "Indonesia", "Jakarta" );
capitalsI.insert( "Iran", "Tehran" );
capitalsI.insert( "Iraq", "Baghdad" );
capitalsI.insert( "Ireland", "Dublin" );
capitalsI.insert( "Israel", "Jerusalem" );
capitalsI.insert( "Italy", "Rome" );
capitalsI.remove( "Hungary" );
System.out.println("Italy's capital is " +
    (String)(capitalsI.lookupValue("Italy")));
// java.util.Map
java.util.Map capitals2 = new java.util.HashMap(12);
capitals2.put( "Hungary", "Budapest" );
capitals2.put( "Iceland", "Reykjavik" );
capitals2.put( "India", "New Delhi" );
capitals2.put( "Indonesia", "Jakarta" );
capitals2.put( "Iran", "Tehran" );
capitals2.put( "Iraq", "Baghdad" );
capitals2.put( "Ireland", "Dublin" );
capitals2.put( "Israel", "Jerusalem" );
capitals2.put( "Italy", "Rome" );
capitals2.remove( "Hungary" );
System.out.println("Italy's capital is " +
    (String)(capitals2.get("Italy")));
```

Java

THE SOFTWARE INSPECTOR

Following is a collection of hints on what to check when you examine a design or code that involves the concepts of this chapter.

✓ Because a map is a function, a map cannot contain duplicate keys. When you're using a map ADT, the first thing to explore is what happens when an attempt is made to insert a duplicate key. Is the previous key-value pair replaced? Is the new insertion ignored? Is an exception thrown?

✓ Implementing a map via an array makes sense only if there is an efficient way to translate from key to array index. If such a translation algorithm doesn't exist, perhaps it would be better to implement the map with a list or a hash table.

✓ Whenever the mapping is essentially constant, using a static final representation is worthy of consideration.

✓ Hash tables are only as efficient as the hash function is effective at spreading out bucket indices. Time is well spent investigating how the hash function works for typical hash table entries.

✓ Hash function values must not be allowed to extend beyond the index range of the representation array. Using % *arrayLength* is a good way to force indices to fall within the array bounds.

✓ When using a hash table, especially with closed hashing collision resolution, you must consider the load factor. As the load factor of a hash table approaches 1.0, the table becomes far less efficient.

EXERCISES

1. Show the precise output that results from executing the following code segment.

```java
MapADT ids = new MapAsList();
ids.insert( "Tom", "111" );
ids.insert( "Karen", "222" );
ids.insert( "Barb", "333" );
ids.insert( "Steve", "444" );
ids.insert( "Cherryl", "555" );
ids.remove( "Karen" );
ids.insert( "Tom", "777" );
if ( !ids.containsKey("Tom") ) {
    System.out.println( "NOT FOUND" );
} else {
    System.out.println( ids.lookupValue("Tom") );
}
```

```
if ( !ids.containsKey("Kenny") ) {
    System.out.println( "NOT FOUND" );
} else {
    System.out.println( ids.lookupValue("Kenny") );
}
if ( !ids.containsKey("Karen") ) {
    System.out.println( "NOT FOUND" );
} else {
    System.out.println( ids.lookupValue("Karen") );
}
```

2. Draw a picture of the state of a hash table in the style of Figure 8.13. Your hash table should have 8 buckets, the values inserted in the hash table should be as follows.

   {5, 8, 10, 16, 20, 3, 11, 19}

   Use the following hash function.

   $h(e) == (e + 2) \% 8$

3. Repeat Exercise 2, except use the style of Figure 8.15 to show the precise representation that results from inserting the hash table items in the order (left to right) that they are listed.

4. Show the precise output that results from executing the following code segment.

```
java.util.HashMap ids = new java.util.HashMap();
ids.put( "Kasi", "111" );
ids.put( "Mao", "222" );
ids.put( "Catherine", "333" );
ids.put( "Steve", "444" );
ids.put( "Mark", "555" );
ids.put( "Mao", "777" );
ids.put( "Steve", "888" );
if ( !ids.containsKey("Catherine") ) {
    System.out.println( "NOT FOUND" );
} else {
    System.out.println( ids.get("Catherine") );
}
if ( !ids.containsKey("Mike") ) {
    System.out.println( "NOT FOUND" );
} else {
    System.out.println( ids.get("Mike") );
}
if ( !ids.containsValue("777") ) {
    System.out.println( "NOT FOUND" );
} else {
    System.out.println( "FOUND" );
}
```

```
if ( !ids.containsValue("444") ) {
    System.out.println( "NOT FOUND" );
} else {
    System.out.println( "FOUND" );
}
```

5. Write a map class using an array representation in the style of Figure 8.8. Your class should map lowercase alphabetic characters ("a" through "z") to one of three strings. The characters "a", "e", "i", "o", and "u" should map to the string "vowel sounds". The characters "y" and "w" should map to the string "sometimes vowel sounds". All other characters should map to the string "consonants".

6. Answer the following questions regarding hash tables.

   a. What does a load factor of zero say about a hash table?

   b. When a container is represented by a hash table that uses closed hashing, is this container bounded? If it is bounded, in what sense is it bounded?

   c. When a container is represented by a hash table that uses open hashing, is this container bounded? If it is bounded, in what sense is it bounded?

PROGRAMMING EXERCISES

1. Design, implement, and test a spell checker. Use the Internet to download a list of words and store it in a text file that can be read by your program. The spell checker should use a hash table to store the dictionary as a set of properly spelled words. The hash table from Section 8.4 will work except that it must store words, not integers. Use the Java `hashCode` from the `Object` class as a hash value.

2. For Programming Exercise 1, the size of the hash table makes it extremely important that the hash function spread out items. Imagine that the hash function treats each character as an integer from 1 through 26 and folds (sums) the letters of the word. Even for a 10-letter word, such a hash function cannot produce an index greater than 10*26 == 260. This means that nearly all elements hash to the first 100 to 200 array cells.

   Design a hash function that spreads out words better than folding. Implement a spell checker like the one in Programming Exercise 1. Compare the number of collisions that result from building this spell checker dictionary, building a spell checker using simple folding for a hash function, and building a spell checker dictionary using your hash function. Be certain to build all three dictionaries from the same file of words.

3. Use the spell checker from either Programming Exercise 1 or Programming Exercise 2 to design, implement, and test a program to accept user input of nine or fewer letters and display all the English words that can be constructed from any subset of these letters.

4. Use the spell checker from either Programming Exercise 1 or Programming Exercise 2 to design, implement, and test a Boggle puzzle solver. A Boggle puzzle is a 4 by 4 grid of alphabetic characters. The purpose of the game is to identify every word in the grid. For purposes of the game, a word must be in a contiguous group of cells, where the order of the letters must follow cell neighborhoods. In other words, each letter must come from a cell that is a neighbor of the prior cell, where "neighbor" refers to any of the eight cells that surround a cell. (No cell can be used more than once in a word.) Your program should allow the user to input the puzzle configuration and then should print the valid words in the puzzle.

5. Design, implement, and test a program that deals and evaluates bridge hands. A bridge hand consists of 13 playing cards, and the standard technique for evaluating each hand is to total points for any of the following characteristics that are exhibited by the hand:

   4 points for each ace

   3 points for each king

   2 points for each queen

   1 point for each jack

   3 points for each void (no cards in an entire suit)

   2 points for each singleton (only one card in an entire suit)

   1 point for each doubleton (only two cards in an entire suit)

   N–5 points for each suit when holding N cards in one suit and N ≥ 6

   Your program should represent a bridge hand as a set implemented with an array of boolean in the style of the array representations shown in Section 8.3. The deck of cards from which cards are dealt is to be implemented as a hash table, using the hash table from Section 8.4. (Note that dealing cards at random will require selecting a random card, and then checking the deck (hash table) to be certain that the selected card has not been already dealt.)

6. Design, implement, and test a program to store a single-level index. The index should consist of an arbitrary number of unique words, and each word maps to its own sequence of one or more page numbers. The look-up operation must supply a word and return the associated sequence of page numbers.

7. Design, implement, and test a song organizer for maintaining an MP3 playlist. For each song, the following information should be maintained:
   • Name of the song
   • Name of the artist
   • Genre of the music
   • ID number

   The ID number of the song must be a unique number that can be used by the MP3 player to identify the song. Your program should use a hash table to map from song name and artist to the ID number. (Note that song name is not a sufficient key because many songs are recorded by multiple artists.) Possible variations on this program include the following.

a. Modify the hash table so that it has a second accessor method to look up a song title and return all the songs that share the same title. Try to design your hash table so that this operation is O(1) without significantly damaging the performance of the earlier look-up operation.

b. Add additional hash tables to permit accessing songs by artist or genre.

8. Repeat any of the prior programming exercises by using the `java.util.HashMap` class to implement your hash table.

TREES

OBJECTIVES

- To introduce tree terminology

- To survey a variety of tree applications

- To examine a binary tree ADT based on iterators

- To explore several tree traversal algorithms

- To examine the effect of various traversal algorithms when applied to expression trees

- To compare and contrast various linked and array representations for binary trees

- To present binary search trees as searchable containers

- To introduce the tree property known as balance and examine tree balancing algorithms

- To explore the heap container and demonstrate heap applications

- To examine a binary tree ADT that defines a tree recursively by subtrees

- To introduce the concept of a general tree and suggest related implementation issues

" THE ANALYTIC ENGINE WEAVES ALGEBRAIC PATTERNS JUST AS THE JACQUARD LOOM WEAVES FLOWERS AND LEAVES. "

—Ada Augusta,
Countess of Lovelace

Much has been said about linear data structures because they are the most widely used of all containers. But not all containers are linear. A genealogical database, for example, is not easily linearized because families have multiple children who create various separate lines from ancestors to descendants. Similarly, a reservation system for distributing reserved-seat tickets for an auditorium uses a nonlinear arrangement, often organized by section, row, and seat numbers.

Our society contains many other examples of systems in which the structure of the individual objects is nonlinear. The managerial structure of any company might begin with a chief operating officer who has several vice presidents, each responsible for a collection of directors who, in turn, manage a few employees. A biological classification system identifies an organism according to one of many kingdoms; each kingdom includes a separate set of potential phyla that are further subdivided into class, order, family, genus, species, and variety.

Many of these nonlinear structures are treelike because, like a tree, they have "trunks" that subdivide into "branches" and branches that subdivide into smaller branches. Not only is this treelike organization a characteristic of several real-life systems, but it also turns out to be a good way to organize program data.

9.1   TREE TERMINOLOGY

Mathematicians have long studied these so-called **trees**. They are defined as part of a field of mathematics known as **graph theory**. Graph theory includes the study of various kinds of graphs and trees. The kind of graph most often modeled by the trees used in computing is called a **directed graph**, or digraph. A directed graph consists of two parts:

- A set of **nodes** (also called **vertices**)
- A set of **arcs**

Each arc connects one node to another node. Nodes are often pictured as circles, and arcs as arrows. For example, the following arc goes from node n_1 to node n_2.

Directed graphs can be composed into the particular geometries known as trees, or more specifically, **rooted trees**. Informally, a directed graph is a rooted tree exactly when there is one node (the **root**) from which all other nodes can be reached by following one and only one sequence of arcs. This is a bit like a biological tree in which there is one trunk and all the other tree parts can be reached by only one path from the trunk. (Banyan-style trees qualify as a tree in the plant kingdom, but not as a model for mathematical trees!) Figure 9.1 pictures four sample trees.

The root node plays the role of "tree trunk" in a rooted tree. All the trees in Figure 9.1 label the root $\mathbf{n_1}$. A tree can be quite simple, such as the single node of tree 2. Trees can be more complicated, such as the nine-node tree 3. Trees can even have a linear form, like tree 4. Following is a more careful definition of a tree (rooted tree).

Rooted Tree

Definition

A rooted tree either is

an empty digraph (empty digraphs have no nodes and no arcs)

or all the following are true:

- The tree is a digraph with one node designated as the root.
- There is exactly one directed walk from the root to every other tree node.

Figure 9.1 Four sample trees

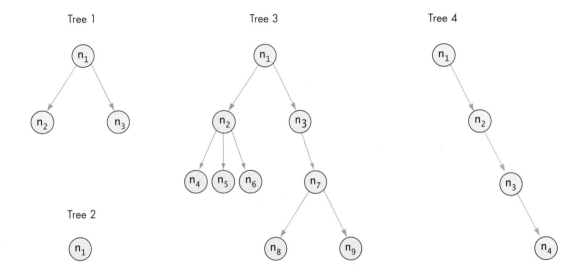

The term **directed walk** used in this definition refers to following the arc arrows from node to node. For example, the directed walk in tree 3 from n_1 to n_8 proceeds from n_1 to n_3 to n_7 to n_8, and there is no other directed walk from n_1 to n_8. To further illustrate the concept of a tree, Figure 9.2 contains three directed graphs that are *not* trees.

Digraph 1 is not a tree because one node, n_3, cannot be reached by any directed walk beginning at root n_1. Digraph 2 is not a tree because there are many directed walks from n_1 to n_3. Among these walks are the following.

n_1 *to* n_3
n_1 *to* n_3 *to* n_1 *to* n_3

Figure 9.2 Nontree digraphs

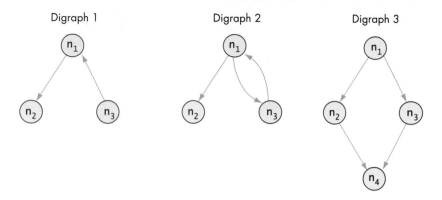

Digraph 1   Digraph 2   Digraph 3

There are directed walks from n_1 to every other node of digraph 3. However, digraph 3 fails to be a tree because not all these walks are unique. In particular, there are two directed walks from n_1 to n_4:

n_1 to n_2 to n_4
n_1 to n_3 to n_4

The definition of a rooted tree implies several interesting properties, including these:

1. A tree contains *no* cycles. (A **cycle** is a directed walk from a node to itself.)
2. The total number of arcs in a rooted tree is 1 less than the number of nodes.
3. The root node has no incoming arcs and all other nodes have only one incoming arc.

Digraph 1 violates the last of these properties (3) because it includes an arc from n_3 to the root (n_1). Digraph 3 violates properties (2) and (3). Property (2) fails because digraph 3 contains four nodes and four arcs. Property (3) fails because n4 has two incoming arcs. Digraph 2 violates all three of the properties.

Figure 9.3 pictures a tree with 10 nodes. The root node of this tree is labeled a. It is customary to draw rooted trees with the root at the top and to position nodes vertically according to their distance from the root to the node. These drawing conventions imply the direction of the arcs, so trees are usually drawn without arrowheads, like the one in this figure.

Several commonly used terms are associated with rooted trees. Figure 9.4 summarizes the most often used.

Some of the tree terminology, such as **root** and **leaf**, correspond to the biological notion of tree. The root of a tree is similar to its biological counterpart; every other part of the tree grows from the root. The root of the 10-node tree in Figure 9.3 is node a. A leaf of a rooted tree, like any leaf of a biological tree, has no other tree parts beyond it. The leaves of the 10-node tree are as follows: c, e, g, h, i, and j.

Some of the terminology related to rooted trees is more consistent with the concept of a family tree. For example, the root node of the 10-node tree (node a) has three **children**: b, c, and d. Node b is the parent of the single child, g. Node d has two children: nodes f and g. Node f has three children: nodes h, i, and j. Note that leaf nodes do not have any children.

Figure 9.3 A 10-node tree

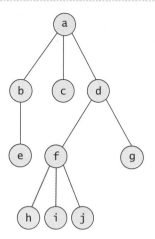

Figure 9.4 Terminology for rooted trees

Term	*Definition*
root	The only tree node with no incoming arcs.
leaf	Any tree node with no outgoing arcs.
parent	n_p is the parent node of n_c exactly when there is an arc from n_p *to* n_c.
child	n_c is a child node of n_p exactly when n_p is the parent of n_c.
ancestor	n_a is an ancestor node of n_d exactly when there is a directed walk from n_a to n_d.
descendant	v_d is descendant of v_a exactly when v_a is an ancestor of v_d.
sibling	Two nodes are siblings exactly when they have the same parent.
subtree	A subtree of a tree from node n_r consists of n_r together with all of its descendants and all of the connecting arcs.
level	The level of tree node is an integer value equal to the number of arcs traversed in the directed walk from the root to the node (the root's level is zero).
height	The height of a tree is equal to the maximum level of all tree nodes.

The notion of parent and child is extended to ancestor and descendant. Node a is the **ancestor** of all other nodes in the tree, and these other nodes are **descendants**. Similarly, node d is the ancestor of five descendants: f, g, h, i, and j. The root node is the only node in a tree without ancestors, and leaves have no descendants.

Sibling is another term that borrows its meaning from a family tree. Two nodes are siblings if and only if they share the same parent. For example, the nodes b, c, and d form a group of siblings in the 10-node tree.

A tree has the interesting property that any node, together with all its descendants and their connecting arcs, forms another tree. Because this second tree is contained within the original, it is called a **subtree**. For example, following is the subtree of the 10-node tree that is rooted at node d. Remember that a subtree must contain *every* descendant and *every* connecting arc from its root.

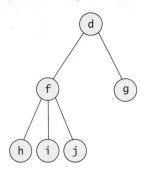

The **level** of a node is determined by the distance from the root to the node. (The term **distance** refers to the number of arcs that are traversed in a directed walk from root to node.) For the 10-node tree, the level of a is zero. Nodes b, c, and d all have a level of 1. Nodes e, f, and g have a level of 2, and nodes h, i, and j have a level of 3. One alternative definition for the root node is that it is the only node with a level of zero.

The tree **height** is defined to be equal to the maximum of all node levels. The height of the 10-node tree is 3—the level of nodes h, i, and j. A different, and equivalent, definition for the height of a tree is equal to the length of its longest directed walk. This definition means that a tree that consists of one node has a height of zero and a tree with no nodes has an effective height of –1.

9.2 TREE APPLICATIONS

There are countless ways to use trees in computer software. Many well-known algorithms are based on graph theory principles that involve tree-related concepts and theorems. Trees also serve as an organizational model for many data structures.

Some tree applications result from real-world uses of trees. For example, consider a program to store the management organization chart for a company. Figure 9.5 contains an example.

It is easy to imagine that a company might wish to store the information from its organization chart in its human resource database. The company's software might include such things as a method to retrieve any employee's direct manager.

```
public Employee managerOf( Employee e ) ...
```

The organization chart points out a common characteristic of the kind of trees that seem to be useful in most (but not all) software applications:

Each tree node has content (a value).

In the organization chart, the root of the tree is the CEO, and the children of each node represent those employees who report directly to the parent employee. Each node contains both the first name and the job classification of an employee.

Figure 9.5 Sample organization chart

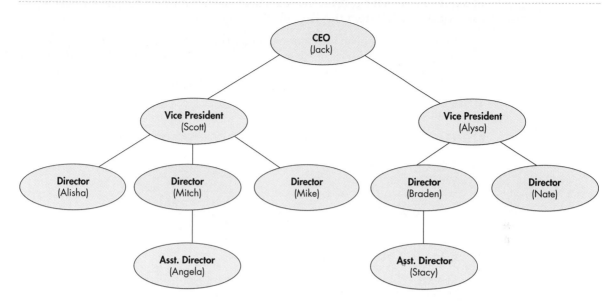

As a second tree application, consider the work of a program to draw class diagrams for programming languages, such as Java, that incorporate inheritance. Class systems using inheritance form **inheritance trees**. For example, Figure 9.6 pictures a portion of the inheritance tree from the java.util package.

Figure 9.6 A partial inheritance tree from java.util

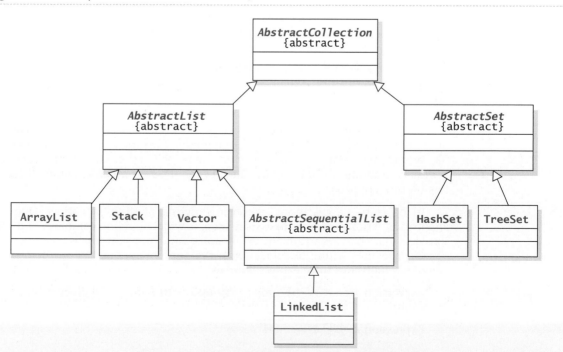

Again, inheritance hierarchies take the form of rooted trees. The class diagram in Figure 9.6 uses its nodes to represent the classes of the inheritance hierarchy of some of the classes from the java.util package.

A third example of an inherent tree organization that is used by many programs is a file system. Each folder or file can be viewed as a node identified by the folder or file name. Files are the leaves of the file system tree. The folder containing folder or file f can be thought of as f's parent. Figure 9.7 contains a sample collection of 10 files and their associated folders.

Figure 9.7 Sample collection of files and their folders

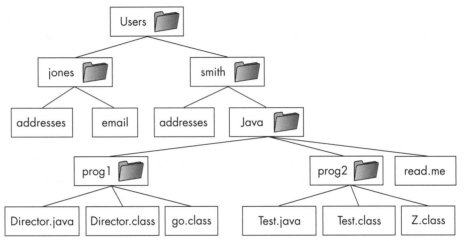

The notation used to specify complete path names for files follows the tree path from the root to the desired file or folder. For example, the Z.class file shown in Figure 9.7 is identified by the following path name:

/Users/smith/Java/prog2/Z.class

Because the file system forms a tree, this path (like all paths connecting two tree nodes) must be unique.

The order of siblings is of little or no consequence in the three examples of trees presented thus far (company organization charts, class inheritance hierarchies, and file system organizations). As shown in Figure 9.7, Test.java, Test.class, and Z.class are all files within a folder called prog2. There is no order among these sibling children of prog2.

In other tree applications, however, ordering of siblings matters. One such application, known as an **expression tree**, is widely used by compilers and other software that analyzes arithmetic expressions. An expression tree is constructed by placing operands within leaf nodes with the appropriate operator as their parent. Figure 9.8 illustrates three expression trees.

Expression tree A is the proper expression tree for the following arithmetic expression.

Expression A: 1 - 2

Figure 9.8 Three sample expression trees

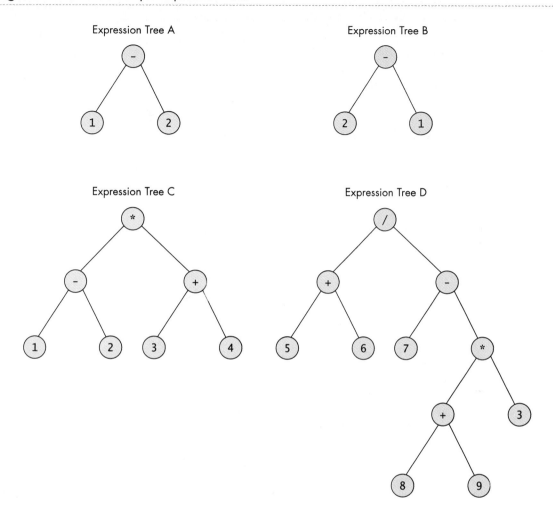

This expression tree consists of a node for each of its two operands (1 and 2) and a node for the operator (–). Furthermore, expression tree A follows the expression tree rules because the operator node is the parent of its operands. Even though expression tree B has the same root and children nodes, it represents a different expression than does expression tree A.

Expression B: 2 - 1

These two trees illustrate the importance of node ordering in an expression tree. It is significant that the leftmost child represents the leftmost operand. Reversing sibling nodes reverses the order of operands in the associated expression.

Any nonempty subtree can represent a subexpression. Expression trees C and D in Figure 9.8 demonstrate.

Expression C: (1-2) * (3+4)
Expression D: (5+6) / (7 - ((8+9)*3))

A second application in which sibling nodes are ordered is a **classification tree**. Classification trees are used to identify (classify) an item by following a path from a root to a leaf according to questions placed in the nonleaf nodes along the path. Figure 9.9 contains a classification tree for determining a kind of data container from among those discussed in this book.

Figure 9.9 Classification tree for various types of data containers

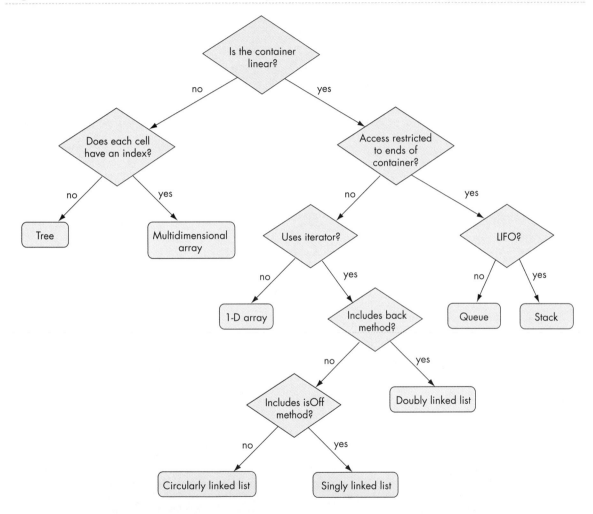

In a classification tree, each leaf node contains the value of some particular type, and the nonleaf nodes contain questions. To use Figure 9.9 to determine the type of a data container, the root question is considered first:

Is the container linear?

If the answer to this question is yes, the path of future questions proceeds to the root's right child, If the answer is no, the path to the left child is considered. Subtree questions are handled in the same manner. The arc labels shown in Figure 9.9 are unnecessary as long as the tree is understood to be ordered so that each left subtree corresponds to a no answer and each right subtree corresponds to a yes answer.

9.3 BINARY TREES

The most commonly used of all tree containers is a **binary tree**. Binary trees are rooted trees with two additional properties.

- Each node can have no more than two children.
- Children are designated *left* or *right*, and nodes can have at most one of each kind of child.

Taken together, these two properties imply that each node of a binary tree node must have either (i) no children nodes, *or* (ii) a left child only, *or* (iii) a right child only, *or* (iv) both a left child and a right child.

An expression tree (see Figure 9.8) is one example of a binary tree because each node has two or fewer children and the order of sibling children is significant. Classification trees that use yes/no questions, such as the one in Figure 9.9, also can be considered binary trees. For the classification tree, all left children are associated with no answers and right children are associated with yes answers.

There are various ways to define a tree ADT. Figure 9.10 shows the class diagrams for two Java interfaces that, taken together, provide a base abstraction for manipulating binary trees.

Figure 9.10 BinaryTree and BinTreeIterator diagram

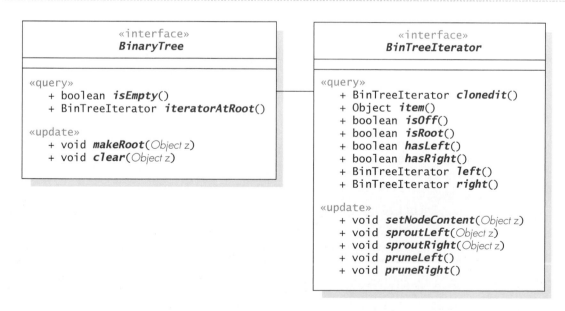

This first binary tree design separates the concept of a binary tree into two Java interfaces: `BinaryTree` and `BinTreeIterator`. This same separation strategy is often used to design linked lists as a list class or interface plus an iterator class or interface. Like a `SingleList` object, a `BinaryTree` object represents the structure (a binary tree). A `BinTreeIterator` object can be positioned at any node of the tree, similar to the way that `SingleIterator` objects are positioned within a list. Also like the list design, most of the tree methods are found in the iterator because most operations take place relative to a position (node).

`BinTreeIterator` differs from other iterators described in this book. The most obvious difference is the large number of methods of a tree iterator compared with linear structures. `BinTreeIterator` includes methods to change position from tree node to tree node (`left` and `right`), a method to access the content of the node at the iterator's position (`item`), methods to check properties of the node (`isRoot`, `hasLeft`, `hasRight`, and `isOff`), methods to update the node's content (`setNodeContent`), methods to append new children to the node (`sproutLeft` and `sproutRight`), and methods to eliminate a node's subtrees (`pruneLeft` and `pruneRight`).

Another thing that is unique about `BinTreeIterator` compared with to typical list iterators is that `BinTreeIterator` is **immutable** with respect to its position. List iterators often move an iterator via a mutator, such as `start()`, `forth()`, or `back()`. The two methods for `BinTreeIterator` don't alter the position of the iterator; rather, they return a new iterator. Calling `it.left()` returns a new iterator that is positioned at the node that is the left child of the node where `it` is positioned, whereas the `it` iterator remains unchanged. Similarly, a call to the `right` method returns a new iterator positioned at the right child.

Software Engineering Hint

Iterators that are immutable are convenient for expressing recursive algorithms. By not altering (mutating) an existing iterator, separate iterator positions are naturally maintained for separate recursive activations.

This immutable nature of `BinTreeIterator` makes it easier to express many recursive algorithms. This issue is significant because most tree processing algorithms are written recursively. Writing `left` and `right` in this way is also convenient for composing two consecutive calls. For example, the expression `it.left().left()` returns an iterator positioned at the leftmost grandchild of the node where `it` is positioned. Similarly, the following expression retrieves the content of the right child of the `it` position:

```
it.right().item()
```

The `BinaryTree` interface provides only minimal methods—those methods that apply to the whole tree or cannot be included conveniently in `BinTreeIterator`. Figure 9.11 contains the `BinaryTree` interface, including its abstract specifications. Figure 9.11 also includes the associated `BinaryTreeException` class.

Every tree has either an empty or a nonempty form. A `BinaryTree` exhibits this same characteristic. The `isEmpty` method permits querying a tree object's form.

The `iteratorAtRoot` method provides a means for instantiating an initial `BinTreeIterator` object. It is valid to call `iteratorAtRoot` only as long as the tree is nonempty. Each call to `iteratorAtRoot` returns a fresh iterator that is positioned at the root node of the tree. Given an iterator positioned at the tree's root, any other node of a tree can be "reached" by calling the proper sequence of `left` and `right` methods.

Figure 9.11 BinaryTree interface and BinaryTreeException class

```
/*  Domain (Every BinaryTree object has one of two forms)
        FORM 1: The tree is empty.
        FORM 2: The tree is nonempty and, therefore, has at least a
                root node.
    invariant: this tree contains no cycles */
public interface BinaryTree {
    /* post:   result == (this is an empty tree) */
    public boolean isEmpty();
    /* post:   not isEmpty() implies result identifies the root of
                this tree and isEmpty() implies result.isOff() */
    public BinTreeIterator iteratorAtRoot();
    /* pre:    isEmpty() (throw BinaryTreeException)
       post:   not isEmpty()
                and content of the tree's root == z
                and the tree's root is a leaf */
    public void makeRoot(Object z);
    /* post:   isEmpty() */
    public void clear();
}
public class BinaryTreeException extends RuntimeException {
    public BinaryTreeException( ) {super();}
    public BinaryTreeException( String s ) {super(s);}
}
```

A careful inspection of BinTreeIterator reveals that it is possible to append new children to existing nodes (via sproutLeft and sproutRight), but it is impossible to use these methods to construct a root node. The BinaryTree interface provides the needed functionality in the form of the makeRoot method. Calling makeRoot creates a new root node for the tree and assigns the new node's content. As the precondition indicates, calling makeRoot is possible only for an empty tree, and calling this method necessarily makes the tree nonempty.

The clear method of BinaryTree is used to turn a tree into an empty tree. A call to clear eliminates the root and all other tree nodes.

The BinaryTreeException class is a simple extension that supports unchecked exceptions for the BinaryTree and BinTreeIterator classes. Figure 9.12 shows the BinTreeIterator interface, including the abstract specifications for the corresponding ADT.

Figure 9.12 BinTreeIterator interface class

```
/*  Domain
        (Every BinTreeIterator is positioned at one node of a
        BinaryTree or it has been positioned off the tree.) */
```

Continued on next page

```
public interface BinTreeIterator {
    /* post:   result == another iterator positioned at the same
                node as this */
    public BinTreeIterator clonedIt();
    /* pre:    not isOff() (throw BinaryTreeException)
       post:   result == (the content of this node) */
    public Object item();
    /* post:   result == (this is positioned off the tree) */
    public boolean isOff();
    /* pre:    not isOff() (throw BinaryTreeException)
       post:   result == (this node is the tree's root) */
    public boolean isRoot();
    /* pre:    not isOff() (throw BinaryTreeException)
       post:   result == (a left child exists for this node) */
    public boolean hasLeft();
    /* pre:    not isOff() (throw BinaryTreeException)
       post:   result == (a right child exists for this node) */
    public boolean hasRight();
    /* pre:    not isOff() (throw BinaryTreeException)
       post:   hasLeft() implies result == the left child of this
                and !hasLeft() implies result.isOff() */
    public BinTreeIterator left();
    /* pre:    not isOff() (throw BinaryTreeException)
       post:   hasRight() implies result == the right child of this
                and !hasRight() implies result.isOff() */
    public BinTreeIterator right();
    /* pre:    not isOff() (throw BinaryTreeException)
       post:   the content of this node == z (i.e., item() == z) */
    public void setNodeContent(Object z);
    /* pre:    not isOff() and not hasLeft()
                (throw BinaryTreeException)
       post:   hasLeft() and left().item() == z
                and not left().hasLeft() and not left().hasRight() */
    public void sproutLeft(Object z);
    /* pre:    not isOff() and not hasRight()
                (throw BinaryTreeException)
       post:   hasRight() and right().item() == z
                and not right().hasLeft()
                and not right().hasRight() */
    public void sproutRight(Object z);
    /* pre:    not isOff() (throw BinaryTreeException)
       post:   not hasLeft() */
    public void pruneLeft();
    /* pre:    not isOff() (throw BinaryTreeException)
       post:   not hasRight() */
    public void pruneRight();
}
```

To illustrate how to construct a binary tree using the facilities of `BinaryTree` and `BinTreeIterator`, consider Figure 9.13. This figure includes a segment of code and a graph-style picture of the tree that results from executing the code.

Figure 9.13 Sample `BinaryTree` and `BinTreeIterator` code

```
/* assert: theTree is of type BinaryTree and theTree!=null */
theTree.clear();
theTree.makeRoot("8East");
BinTreeIterator treeIt = theTree.iteratorAtRoot();
treeIt.sproutLeft("Sandi");
treeIt.sproutRight("Jim");
treeIt = treeIt.right();
treeIt.sproutLeft("Lana");
treeIt.sproutRight("Jody");
/* assert: the resulting tree is
           shown to the right */
```

theTree

```
        8East
       /     \
   Sandi      Jim
             /    \
          Lana    Jodi
```

This example begins with the assumption that `theTree` is a variable of type `BinaryTree` and that it has already been instantiated to reference an object. Here are the first two statements of the sample code:

```
theTree.clear();
theTree.makeRoot("8East");
```

A call to the `clear` method will eliminate any root and other nodes from a tree. So after the first statement executes, `theTree` will be an empty tree, regardless of its prior state. Executing the second statement creates a new root node (the only node in the tree) while assigning the String `"8East"` as the node's content. The result of these two statements is pictured below.

theTree

Although a `BinaryTree` object is sufficient to build a root node, a `BinTreeIterator` object is required to build all other nodes. For this reason, the next statement is needed.

```
BinTreeIterator treeIt = theTree.iteratorAtRoot();
```

Executing this statement accomplishes two things:

1. A `treeIt` variable is declared to be of type `BinTreeIterator`.
2. `treeIt` is assigned to be positioned at the root node.

The picture below illustrates by showing `treeIt` in the form of a dashed arrow pointing to the node where the iterator is positioned.

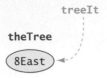

The next two statements follow:

```
treeIt.sproutLeft("Sandi");
treeIt.sproutRight("Jim");
```

Executing the first statement causes a left child to be appended to the node where `treeIt` is positioned. The argument, `"Sandi"`, will be the content of this new child. Similarly, the second statement causes a `"Jim"` node to be appended as the right child of the root.

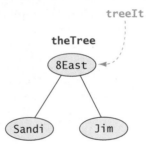

Next, the iterator is effectively "advanced" to the right child of its prior position by the following statement:

```
treeIt = treeIt.right();
```

Technically, calling the `right` method creates a new iterator object, and this iterator is positioned at the right child of the `treeIt` node. However, the preceding statement combines this call to `right` with an assignment to `treeIt`. The picture below demonstrates how `treeIt` has been repositioned.

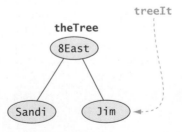

The last two statements of this example are as follows.

```
treeIt.sproutLeft("Lana");
treeIt.sproutRight("Jody");
```

Executing these statements adds two children to the new `treeIt` position (i.e., the `"Jim"` node). The new left child contains the string `"Lana"` and the new right child is `"Jody"`.

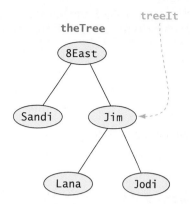

Traversing the nodes of a `BinaryTree` proceeds from parent nodes to their children, using the `left` and `right` `BinTreeIterator` methods. As an example, consider the following `printRightmost` method. When this method is called it displays the content of the nodes of tree t in order from the root of t to the right child of the root to the right child of the right child of the root, and so forth.

```
private void printRightmost(BinaryTree t) {
    if (!t.isEmpty()) {
        BinTreeIterator it = t.iteratorAtRoot();
        while (!it.isOff()) {
            System.out.println( it.item() );
            it = it.right();
        }
    }
}
```

A sample call such as `printRightmost(theTree)`, assuming the state of `theTree` depicted in Figure 9.13, will result in the following output.

```
8East
Jim
Jody
```

The `printRightmost` method uses a local `BinTreeIterator` variable, `it`, that is positioned at the right child of its prior position for each successive iteration of the loop. The last `System.out.println` is necessary to print the last node's content. The behavior of `printRightmost` also can be accomplished recursively, as shown in the `printRightmostR` and `printRightmostFromIt` methods:

```
private void printRightmostR(BinaryTree t) {
    printRightmostFromIt ( t.iteratorAtRoot() );
}
private void printRightmostFromIt(BinTreeIterator it) {
    if ( !it.isOff() ) {
        System.out.println( it.item() );
        printRightmostFromIt( it.right() );
    }
}
```

This recursive version is instructive because for many tree processing algorithms recursion is the only viable alternative. Recursive algorithms frequently rely on processing different tree nodes for different activations. You can do this by using a `BinTreeIterator` parameter, which explains the need for the helper method `printRightmostFromIt`.

Another common recursive tree algorithm determines the height of an arbitrary tree. Figure 9.14 contains a `height` method, along with a recursive helper method, to determine the height of any `BinaryTree` object.

Figure 9.14 Recursive height method for RecursiveBinaryTree

```
private int height(BinaryTree t) {
    return heightFromIt( t.iteratorAtRoot() );
}
private int heightFromIt(BinTreeIterator it) {
    if (it.isOff())
        return -1;
    else
        return 1 +
        Math.max(heightFromIt(it.right()),heightFromIt(it.left()));
}
```

Recursion is convenient for calculating the height of a binary tree by observing the following two properties:

- The height of an empty tree is –1. (This comes from the fact that the height of a single node is zero.)
- The height of a nonempty tree is 1 greater than the height of its highest subtree.

These two properties form the algorithm used by the `heightFromIt` method. This algorithm recursively examines the heights of both subtrees of a tree to determine the tree's height. The base step in the recursion corresponds to calculating the height of an empty tree.

9.4 TREE TRAVERSAL ALGORITHMS

Any algorithm that processes a tree for the purpose of visiting all the tree's nodes is called a **tree traversal algorithm**. The nonlinear nature of trees leads to various traversal algorithms. These algorithms can be classified as belonging one of two groups:

- breadth-first traversal
- depth-first traversal

The terms "breadth" and "depth" refer to the distance of a node from the root (i.e., the node's level). A node with greater level is considered to be "deeper" because it is farther from the root. A **breadth-first traversal** visits first the nodes with lesser level. To illustrate, consider the binary tree shown in Figure 9.15.

Figure 9.15 Sample binary tree

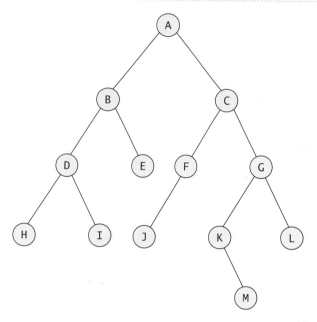

A breadth-first traversal of the Figure 9.15 tree would visit the root (level == 0) followed by the root's children (level == 1), then the root's grandchildren (level == 2), and so forth. Assuming that each level is visited from left to right, such a traversal would visit the sample tree in alphabetic order:

A, B, C, D, E, F, G, H, I, J, K, L, M

A typical breadth-first algorithm uses a queue to store nodes that have been visited but whose children have yet to be visited. Figure 9.16 contains both the algorithm and a picture illustrating with colored arrows the order in which nodes are visited by this algorithm.

As the `visitWithBreadth` method executes, every node that is visited will be enqueued immediately into que. The statements preceding the *while* loop cause the root node to be visited, and an iterator positioned at the root is placed as the only item in que. Each iteration of the *while* removes one item (an iterator) from the front of que, visits the removed iterator's two children, and enqueues an iterator positioned at each child node.

Although breadth-first traversals are possible, **depth-first traversals** are more popular. The reason for this popularity is that depth-first searches can often be expressed with brief recursive algorithms that do not require a separate container, such as que. One such depth-first traversal algorithm for binary trees is called a preorder traversal. Figure 9.17 shows a **preorder traversal** method for `BinTreeIterator`.

Figure 9.16 Breadth-first traversal of BinaryTree

```
private void visitWithBreadth(BinaryTree tree) {
    if (!tree.isEmpty()) {
        Queue que = new Queue();
        BinTreeIterator it = tree.iteratorAtRoot();
        // Visit the node at position: it
        que.enqueue(it);
        while ( !que.isEmpty() ) {
            it = (BinTreeIterator)(que.front());
            que.dequeue();
            if (it.hasLeft()) {
                // Visit the node at position: it.left()
                que.enqueue( it.left() );
            }
            if (it.hasRight()) {
                // Visit the node at position: it.right()
                que.enqueue( it.right() );
            }
        }
    }
}
```

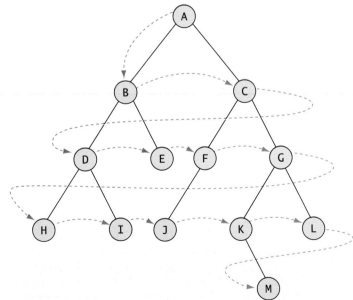

Figure 9.17 Preorder traversal of BinaryTree

```
private void preorder(BinTreeIterator it) {
    if (!it.isOff()) {
        // Visit the node at position: it
        preorder(it.left());
        preorder(it.right());
    }
}
```

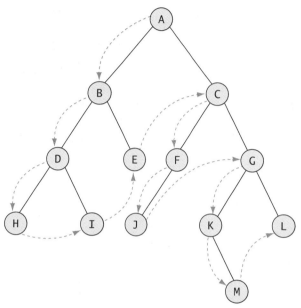

A preorder traversal begins by visiting the root. After visiting any node, pre-order calls itself recursively for iterators positioned at the two children of the visited node. Each call to preorder results in additional recursive calls unless the it parameter isOff(). If this preorder traversal algorithm is applied to the sample tree, the nodes are visited in this order:

A, B, D, H, I, E, C, F, J, G, K, M, L

Notice that this definition of "depth-first" does not require that all nodes with greatest level be visited before those with lesser level, but it does mean that the traversal proceeds to the extremities of the tree before backing up to consider all the alternative children of some nodes visited earlier.

The preorder traversal is one of a trio of binary tree traversal algorithms. The remaining two algorithms are **inorder traversal** and **postorder traversal**. Figure 9.18 shows the postorder and inorder algorithms.

Figure 9.18 Postorder and inorder traversals

```
private void postorder(BinTreeIterator
it) {
    if (!it.isOff()) {
        postorder(it.left());
        postorder(it.right());
        // Visit the node at position: it
    }
}
```

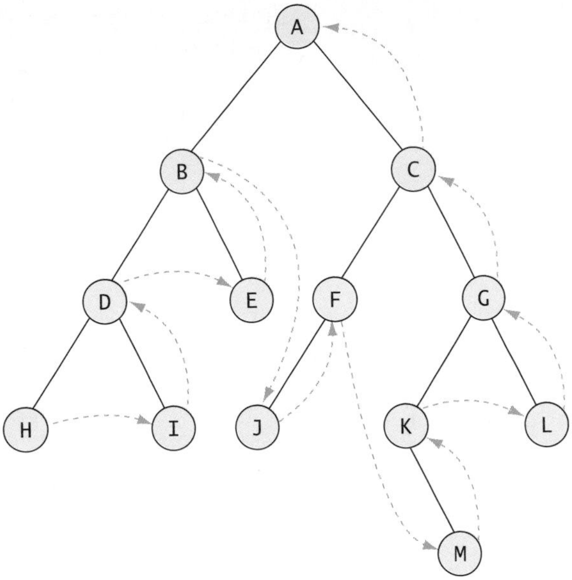

```
private void inorder(BinTreeIterator it)
{
    if (!it.isOff()) {
        inorder(it.left());
        // Visit the node at position: it
        inorder(it.right());
    }
}
```

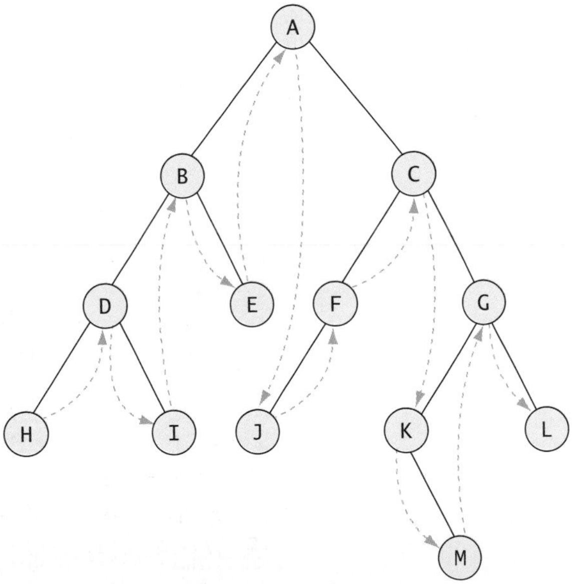

The only difference between the code for the three algorithms is the placement of the statement to visit the node. The preorder algorithm gets its name from the fact that the node at the iterator is visited *before* its left and right subtrees are traversed. As its name implies, the postorder algorithm causes a node to be visited only *after* it has completely traversed that node's left and right subtrees. The nodes of the sample tree are visited by a postorder traversal as follows:

H, I, D, E, B, J, F, M, K, L, G, C, A

An inorder algorithm traverses the left subtree of a node, visits the node, and then traverses the node's right subtree. Traversing the sample binary tree with an inorder traversal results in the following sequence of nodes:

H, D, I, B, E, A, J, F, C, K, M, G, L

There are several useful applications for the preorder, inorder, and postorder traversal algorithms. One of the more interesting applications involves performing such traversals on expression trees. For example, the visitation order that results from applying a postorder traversal to an expression tree is called the **postfix** expression form. The postfix form is such a common form of writing expressions that mathematicians call it Reverse Polish Notation. (A stack evaluation program for Reverse Polish Notation is given in Section 7.2.)

Figure 9.19 contains a sample expression tree. Following is the postfix expression that results from visiting the nodes of this sample expression tree via a preorder traversal:

3, 5, +, 4, 2, /, 7, –, *

Figure 9.19 Sample expression tree

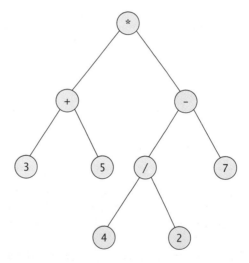

Postorder traversal is the best approach for deleting individual tree nodes. It works well for such deletion because it delays visiting (deleting) a node until the last possible instant of the traversal.

Applying a preorder traversal to an expression tree yields a **prefix** form of the expression. In this prefix form it is the operations that precede their associated operands. Following is the prefix form that results from a preorder traversal of the expression tree in Figure 9.19.

*, +, 3, 5, –, /, 4, 2, 7

Prefix expressions are referred to as **Polish Notation**. Like postfix expressions, prefix expressions need no parentheses to indicate the order in which operations are performed.

Another application for preorder traversal is cloning a tree—not only its content but also its structure. Preorder traversal is natural for cloning because each tree node is visited (and therefore can be duplicated) *before* any of its subtrees are traversed.

When an inorder traversal is applied to an expression tree, the resulting visitation sequence is called an **infix** expression, also known as an **algebraic** expression. The infix expression for Figure 9.19 is as follows:

3, +, 5, *, 4, /, 2, –, 7

The infix form of an expression is the form commonly used to express arithmetic expressions. Unfortunately, parentheses are required to provide proper semantics in an infix expression. For example, the sample expression tree represents the following infix expression.

(3 + 5) * ((4 / 2) – 7)

9.5 REFERENCE IMPLEMENTATION OF BINARYTREE

Linking (using references to join tree cells) seems to be a natural implementation for treelike structures. A typical binary tree implementation uses one object for each tree node, and each node object links to other nodes by way of instance variables. For example, Figure 9.20 pictures an abstract binary tree object on the left and an object diagram of the corresponding linked objects on the right.

The object diagram in Figure 9.20 is referenced by a rootNode variable of type BinTreeNode. Each BinTreeNode object contains rightLink and leftLink variables that reference the roots of the left and right subtrees. Each of these variables either references another BinTreeNode object or is null for a nonexistent child. This implementation is appropriate for the BinaryTree that was introduced in Section 9.3. Figure 9.21 supplies the details of this linked implementation by showing the entire BinaryLinkedTree class.

The BinTreeLinked implementation maintains a single variable, rootNode. A call to the BinaryLinkedTree constructor instantiates an empty tree by assigning null to rootNode. The isEmpty method identifies a tree as empty based on whether rootNode == null.

The BinTreeNode inner class declares the form of the individual tree nodes. In this case each node cell has a form consistent with those pictured in Figure 9.20. In other words, each node object contains a reference to the left child (leftLink), the right child (rightLink), and the node's content.

Software Engineering Hint

Sometimes only a single variable can change the potential of a data structure. For example, suppose that BinTreeNode included an additional parentLink variable used to reference the node's parent. Such a change would permit additional possibilities for iterator movement about a tree.

The makeRoot method must be called to create an initial (root) node for a tree. Calling makeRoot causes a new BinTreeNode cell to be instantiated. The content of the newly created cell is assigned z, and the node's left and right children are assigned null.

The BinaryLinkedTree implementation includes an implementation of BinTreeIterator in the form of an inner class, BTIterator. Figure 9.22 expands the code for BTIterator.

Figure 9.20 Sample `BinTree` object diagram

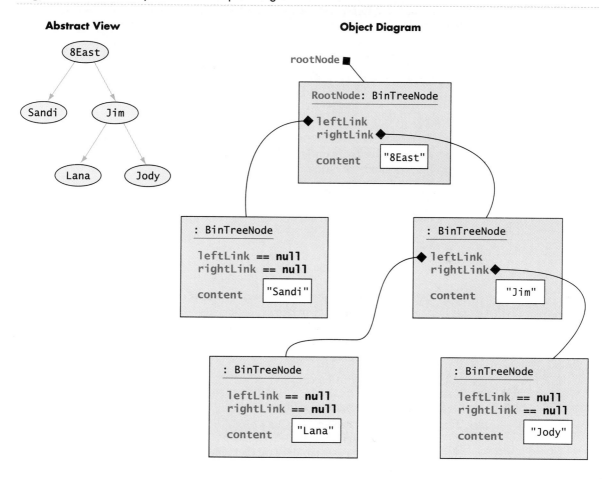

Figure 9.21 `BinaryLinkedTree` implementation

```
/* Domain (Every BinaryTree object has one of two forms)
     FORM 1: The tree is empty.
     FORM 2: The tree is nonempty and, therefore, has at least a
             root node.
   invariant: this tree contains no cycles */
public class BinaryLinkedTree implements BinaryTree {
    private class BinTreeNode {
        public Object content;
        public BinTreeNode leftLink;
        public BinTreeNode rightLink;
        public BinTreeNode(Object z) {
            content = z;
```

Continued on next page

```
            leftLink = null;
            rightLink = null;
        }
    }
    private class BTIterator implements BinTreeIterator {
        // This class is shown in Figure 9.22
    }
    private BinTreeNode rootNode;

    /* post:   rootNode == null */
    public BinaryLinkedTree() {
        rootNode = null;
    }
    /* post:  result == (rootNode == null) */
    public boolean isEmpty() {
        return (rootNode == null);
    }
    /* post:  !isEmpty() implies result is positioned at the root
               of this tree and isEmpty() implies result.isOff() */
    public BinTreeIterator iteratorAtRoot() {
        return new BTIterator(rootNode);
    }
    /* pre:   rootNode == null (throw BinaryTreeException)
       post:  not rootNode != null and rootNode.content == z
              and rootNode.leftLink==null
              and rootNode.rightLink==null */
    public void makeRoot(Object z) {
        if (!isEmpty())
            throw new BinaryTreeException
            ("Attempt to create 2nd root node.");
        else
            rootNode = new BinTreeNode(z);
    }
    /* post:  rootNode == null */
    public void clear() {
        rootNode = null;
    }
}
```

Figure 9.22 BTIterator implementation of BinTreeIterator

```
    // note:   The class below is an inner class of BinaryLinkedTree
    //         (Figure 9.21)
    private class BTIterator implements BinTreeIterator {
        public BinTreeNode theNode;
```

Continued on next page

```
/*  post:   theNode == n */
public BTIterator(BinTreeNode n) {
    theNode = n;
}
/*  post:   result.theNode == theNode and result != this */
public BinTreeIterator clonedIt() {
    return new BTIterator(theNode);
}
/*  post:   result == (theNode == null) */
public boolean isOff() {
    return (theNode == null);
}
/*  pre:    !isOff() (throws BinaryTreeException)
    post:   result == theNode.content */
public Object item() {
    if (isOff())
        throw new BinaryTreeException("iterator isOff()");
    else
        return theNode.content;
}
/*  pre:    !isOff() (throws BinaryTreeException)
    post:   result == (theNode == rootNode) */
public boolean isRoot() {
    if (isOff())
        throw new BinaryTreeException("iterator isOff()");
    else
        return (theNode == rootNode);
}
/*  pre:    !isOff() (throws BinaryTreeException)
    post:   result == (theNode.leftLink != null) */
public boolean hasLeft() {
    if (isOff())
        throw new BinaryTreeException("iterator isOff()");
    else
        return (theNode.leftLink != null);
}
/*  pre:    !isOff() (throws BinaryTreeException)
    post:   result == (theNode.rightLink != null) */
public boolean hasRight() {
    if (isOff())
        throw new BinaryTreeException("iterator isOff()");
    else
        return (theNode.rightLink != null);
}
/*  pre:    !isOff() (throw BinaryTreeException)
    post:   result.theNode == theNode.leftLink */
```

Continued on next page

```java
    public BinTreeIterator left() {
        if (isOff())
            throw new BinaryTreeException("iterator isOff()");
        else
            return new BTIterator(theNode.leftLink);
    }
/*  pre:    !isOff() (throw BinaryTreeException)
    post:   result.theNode == theNode.rightLink */
    public BinTreeIterator right() {
        if (isOff())
            throw new BinaryTreeException("iterator isOff()");
        else
            return new BTIterator(theNode.rightLink);
    }
/*  pre:    !isOff() (throw BinaryTreeException)
    post:   theNode.content == z */
    public void setNodeContent(Object z) {
        if (isOff())
            throw new BinaryTreeException("iterator isOff()");
        else
            theNode.content = z;
    }
/*  pre:    !isOff() and !hasLeft()
                (throw BinaryTreeException)
    post:   theNode.leftLink.content == z
            and theNode.leftLink.leftLink==null
            and theNode.leftLink.rightLink==null */
    public void sproutLeft(Object z) {
        if (isOff() || hasLeft())
            throw new BinaryTreeException(
                "Attempt to sprout second left child.");
        else
            theNode.leftLink = new BinTreeNode(z);
    }
/*  pre:    !isOff and !hasRight()
                (throw BinaryTreeException)
    post:   theNode.rightLink.content == z
            and theNode.rightLink.leftLink==null
            and theNode.rightLink.rightLink==null */
    public void sproutRight(Object z) {
        if (isOff() || hasRight())
            throw new BinaryTreeException(
                "Attempt to sprout second right child.");
        else
            theNode.rightLink = new BinTreeNode(z);
    }
```

Continued on next page

```
        /* pre:    !isOff() (throw BinaryTreeException)
           post:   theNode.leftLink == null */
        public void pruneLeft()
            if (isOff())
                throw new BinaryTreeException("iterator isOff()");
            else
                theNode.leftLink = null;
            }
        /* pre:    !isOff() (throw BinaryTreeException)
           post:   theNode.rightLink == null */
        public void pruneRight()
            if (isOff())
                throw new BinaryTreeException("iterator isOff()");
            else
                theNode.rightLink = null;
            }
        }
    }
```

The BTIterator class contains a single instance variable, theNode. At all times theNode represents the iterator's position. If theNode is null, the iterator is off the tree; otherwise, theNode references the node at which the iterator is positioned. When the BTIterator constructor is called, theNode is initialized to the method's parameter, n. This permits the iteratorAtRoot method from BinaryLinkedTree to return a properly positioned iterator in a single return instruction:

```
// method from BinaryLinkedTree
public BinTreeIterator iteratorAtRoot() {
    return new BTIterator(rootNode);
}
```

Implementing most of the BTIterator classes is straightforward. For example, if you remove the *if* checks for precondition violation, you can often express the essence of the methods in a single statement involving theNode:

isOff()
```
    return (theNode == null);
```
item()
```
    return theNode.content;
```
isRoot()
```
    return (theNode == rootNode);
```
hasLeft()
```
    return (theNode.leftLink != null);
```
hasRight()
```
    return (theNode.rightLink != null);
```
left()
```
    return new BTIterator(theNode.leftLink);
```
right()
```
    return new BTIterator(theNode.rightLink);
```

```
setNodeContent(Object z)
    theNode.content = z;
sproutLeft(Object z)
    theNode.leftLink = new BinTreeNode(z);
sproutRight(Object z)
    theNode.rightLink = new BinTreeNode(z);
pruneLeft()
    theNode.leftLink = null;
pruneRight()
    theNode.rightLink = null;
```

The immutability of the iterator is evident from the fact that none of the BTIterator methods, except the BTIterator constructor, assigns a value to theNode. The left and right methods, however, create new iterator objects at different positions.

9.6 AN ARRAY IMPLEMENTATION OF BINARYTREE

Binary trees can be represented not only as linked structures but also via arrays. The most often used array representation relies on using fixed array cells for specific tree cells. The root cell is represented by the first cell of the array, and each subsequent level is stored consecutively and left-to-right within a level. Figure 9.23 shows an example of this array representation for a six-node tree.

Figure 9.23 Sample BinaryArrayTree

Abstract View

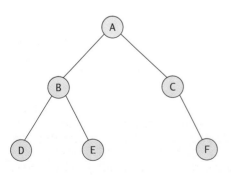

Object Diagram

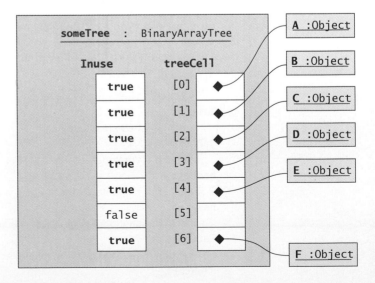

The `BinaryArrayTree` representation uses two parallel arrays. The `treeCell` array maintains the content of the tree nodes. `treeCell[0]` represents the root node (A); `treeCell[1]` represents the left child of the root (B); `treeCell[2]` represents the right child of the root (C); and `treeCell[3]` represents the leftmost grandchild of the root (D). This pattern continues by representing each level by increasing level numbers and representing the level's nodes left to right contiguously.

Notice that `treeCell[5]` is left blank. This signifies that a potential binary tree node is missing from the actual tree. In this case the missing node is the left child of the root's right child. Of course, the array cell is not really blank, but its value is unimportant, because this node is not part of the tree.

The `inUse` array is included in this representation for the purpose of keeping track of which potential nodes are actually contained within the tree. All `inUse` cells, except one, in this example have a value of `true` to signify that they represent actual nodes. The one exception is `inUse[5]`, which is `false`, indicating that this potential node is not part of the tree.

Absent potential nodes, such as the one with index 5, are common in array implementations. Figure 9.24 pictures a different tree with its array. This example contains far more absent nodes, as is evident from the many false-valued `inUse` cells.

An iterator for the array representation is naturally represented as an index (`int` variable). The index of an ancestor or descendant node is calculated by simple arithmetic expressions. For example, the following statement calculates the left child index for the node with index of `nodeNdx`.

```
leftChildNdx = nodeNdx*2 + 1;
```

Similarly, the right child of the `nodeNdx` node can be found via the following statement.

```
rightChildNdx = nodeNdx*2 + 2;
```

A parent's index can be calculated using integer division, as shown next. This statement works for both left and right children.

```
parentNdx = (nodeNdx-1) / 2;
```

Figure 9.25 shows a `BinArrayTree` class that uses this representation technique. This class includes `inUse` and `treeCell` arrays as instance variables, but it eliminates the need for an inner class to represent nodes, as used in the prior reference representation.

Like all array representations of containers, `BinaryArrayTree` must provide a mechanism for establishing the array size(s) (and the corresponding bound on the tree height). `BinaryArrayTree` uses the parameter of its constructor for this purpose. Calling `new BinaryArrayTree(m)` sets the `treeCell` and `inUse` arrays to a length of m. This limits the tree so that no cell can be included beyond an index of m–1.

Figure 9.24 A BinaryArrayTree with several absent potential nodes

Abstract View

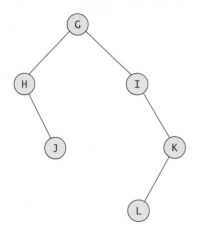

Object Diagram

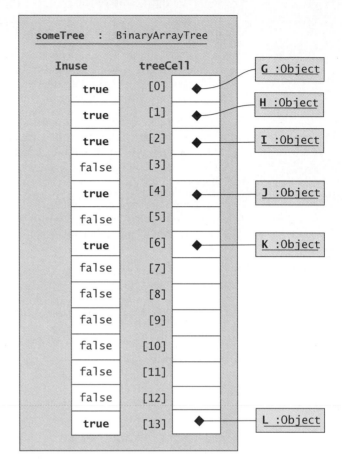

Figure 9.25 BinaryArrayTree implementation

```
/*  representation:
        the root cell has index of zero
        and for the vertex with index ndx, inUse[ndx] == true
        and the left child of node with index of ndx has index of
            ndx*2+1
        and the right child of node with index of ndx has index of
            ndx*2+2
        and inUse.length == treeCell.length */
public class BinaryArrayTree implements BinaryTree {
    private Object[] treeCell;
    private boolean[] inUse;
    private class ArrayIterator implements BinTreeIterator {
        // This class is shown in Figure 9.26
    }
```

Continued on next page

```
/* post:   treeCell.length == m and inUse.length == m
              and forAll(
                  j: 0<=j<=inUse.length-1 | inUse[j] == false)*/
public BinaryArrayTree(int m) {
    treeCell = new Object[m];
    inUse = new boolean[m];
    for (int j=0; j!=m; j++) {
        inUse[j] = false;
    }
}
/* post:   result == !inUse[0] */
public boolean isEmpty() {
    return !inUse[0];
}
/* post:   !isEmpty() implies result identifies the root of
              this tree
           and isEmpty() implies result.isOff() */
public BinTreeIterator iteratorAtRoot() {
    return new ArrayIterator(0);
}
/* pre:    isEmpty() (throw BinaryTreeException)
   post:   treeCell[0] == z and inUse[0] == true */
public void makeRoot(Object z) {
    if (!isEmpty())
        throw new BinaryTreeException(
            "Attempt to create 2nd root node.");
    else {
        treeCell[0] = z;
        inUse[0] = true;
    }
}
/* post:   forAll(j:0<=j<treeCell.length | inUse[j] == false)*/
public void clear() {
    for(int k=0; k<treeCell.length; k++)
        inUse[k] = false;
}
}
```

The `clear` operation is more involved for an array implementation than for a reference implementation. The `clear` method for `BinaryArrayTree` must ensure that the entire array is emptied, and not just that the link to the root of the tree has been eliminated. The resulting `clear` method for `BinaryArrayTree` is $O(\text{treeCell.length})$, whereas the clear method for `BinaryLinkedTree` is more efficient: $O(1)$.

The implementation of the iterator for a `BinaryArrayTree` has similar interesting differences from that of `BinaryLinkedTree`. This class is shown in Figure 9.26.

Figure 9.26 ArrayIterator implementation of BinTreeIterator

```
// note:   The class below is an inner class of BinaryArrayTree
//         (Figure 9.25)
private class ArrayIterator implements BinTreeIterator {
    public int nodeNdx;
    /* post:   result.nodeNdx == nodeNdx and result != this */
    public BinTreeIterator clonedIt() {
        return new ArrayIterator(nodeNdx);
    }
    public ArrayIterator(int j) {
        nodeNdx = j;
    }
    /* post:   result == (nodeNdx >= treeCell.length ||
                           !inUse[nodeNdx]) */
    public boolean isOff() {
        return (nodeNdx >= treeCell.length || !inUse[nodeNdx]);
    }
    /* pre:    !isOff() (throws BinaryTreeException)
       post:   result == treeCell[nodeNdx] */
    public Object item() {
        if (isOff())
            throw new BinaryTreeException("iterator isOff()");
        else
            return treeCell[nodeNdx];
    }
    /* pre:    !isOff() (throws BinaryTreeException)
       post:   result == (nodeNdx == 0) */
    public boolean isRoot() {
        if (isOff())
            throw new BinaryTreeException("iterator isOff()");
        else
            return (nodeNdx == 0);
    }
    /* pre:    !isOff() (throws BinaryTreeException)
       post:   result == (nodeNdx*2+1 < treeCell.length &&
                           inUse[nodeNdx*2+1]) */
    public boolean hasLeft() {
        if (isOff())
            throw new BinaryTreeException("iterator isOff()");
        else
            return (nodeNdx*2+1 < treeCell.length &&
                    inUse[nodeNdx*2+1]);
    }
    /* pre:    !isOff() (throws BinaryTreeException)
       post:   result == (nodeNdx*2+2 < treeCell.length &&
                           inUse[nodeNdx*2+2]) */
```

Continued on next page

```
public boolean hasRight() {
    if (isOff())
        throw new BinaryTreeException("iterator isOff()");
    else
        return (nodeNdx*2+2 < treeCell.length &&
                inUse[nodeNdx*2+2]);
}
/*  pre:    !isOff() (throw BinaryTreeException)
    post:   result.nodeNdx == nodeNdx*2+1 */
public BinTreeIterator left() {
    if (isOff())
        throw new BinaryTreeException("iterator isOff()");
    else
        return new ArrayIterator(nodeNdx*2+1);
}
/*  pre:    !isOff() (throw BinaryTreeException)
    post:   result.nodeNdx == nodeNdx*2+2 */
public BinTreeIterator right() {
    if (isOff())
        throw new BinaryTreeException("iterator isOff()");
    else
        return new ArrayIterator(nodeNdx*2+2);
}
/*  pre:    !isOff() (throw BinaryTreeException)
    post:   treeCell[nodeNdx] == z */
public void setNodeContent(Object z) {
    if (isOff())
        throw new BinaryTreeException("iterator isOff()");
    else
        treeCell[nodeNdx] = z;
}
/*  pre:    !isOff() and !hasLeft() (throw BinaryTreeException)
    post:   treeCell[nodeNdx*2+1] == z
            and inUse[nodeNdx*2+1] == true */
public void sproutLeft(Object z) {
    if (isOff() || hasLeft() || nodeNdx*2+1 >= treeCell.length)
        throw new BinaryTreeException("Attempt to sprout second
        left child.");
    else {
        treeCell[nodeNdx*2+1] = z;
        inUse[nodeNdx*2+1] = true;
    }
}
/*  pre:    !isOff and !hasRight() (throw BinaryTreeException)
    post:   treeCell[nodeNdx*2+2] == z
            and inUse[nodeNdx*2+2] ==true */
```

Continued on next page

```
    public void sproutRight(Object z) {
        if (isOff() || hasRight() || nodeNdx*2+2 >= treeCell.length)
            throw new BinaryTreeException(
                "Attempt to sprout second right child.");
        else {
            treeCell[nodeNdx*2+2] = z;
            inUse[nodeNdx*2+2] = true;
        }
    }
    /* pre:    !isOff() (throw BinaryTreeException)
       post:   inUse[nodeNdx*2+1] == false */
    public void pruneLeft() {
        if (isOff() || nodeNdx*2+1 >= treeCell.length)
            throw new BinaryTreeException("iterator isOff()");
        else
            pruneSubtree(nodeNdx*2+1);
    }
    /* pre:    !isOff() (throw BinaryTreeException)
       post:   inUse[nodeNdx*2+2] == false */
    public void pruneRight() {
        if (isOff() || nodeNdx*2+2 >= treeCell.length)
            throw new BinaryTreeException("iterator isOff()");
        else
            pruneSubtree(nodeNdx*2+2);
    }
    /* post:   forAll(j : r <= j <= treeCell.length |(j is an index
                   of a descendant node of r)
                       implies inUse[j] == false)) */
    private void pruneSubtree(int r) {
        if (r < treeCell.length) {
            inUse[r] = false;
            pruneSubtree(r*2+1);
            pruneSubtree(r*2+2);
        }
    }
}
```

The `ArrayIterator` class represents an iterator as a single `int` variable, `nodeNdx`. This variable is used to store the index for arrays `treeCell` and `inUse` of the node where the iterator is positioned. The `ArrayIterator` methods follow accordingly. For example, the following statement from the `item` method returns the content of the node at the iterator's position:

```
return treeCell[nodeNdx];
```

Similarly, the `isRoot` method checks whether the iterator is positioned at the root by way of the following statement:

```
return (nodeNdx == 0);
```

The bounded nature of arrays imposes some restrictions on the `BinaryArrayTree` implementation. For example, there are two ways that an iterator can be without a left child. One possibility is that `inUse[nodeNdx*2+1] == false`. The second possibility is that there is no space in the array for the left child (i.e., `nodeNdx*2+1 >= treeCell.length`). The `hasLeft` method handles these two cases with the following statement:

```
return (nodeNdx*2+1 < treeCell.length && inUse[nodeNdx*2+1]);
```

The `ArrayIterator` pruning methods (`pruneLeft` and `pruneRight`) are more involved than their linked counterparts. Each of these methods must remove *all* the nodes present in the subtree being pruned. This requires that all the `inUse` cells for the corresponding nodes be assigned `false`. The `ArrayIterator` implementation accomplishes this by way of a private method called `pruneSubtree`. This method is passed the index of the root node for a subtree, and the method removes all nodes from that index to the bottom of the tree (array). The `pruneLeft` method calls `pruneSubtree` with the following statement:

```
pruneSubtree( nodeNdx*2 + 1 );
```

Similarly, the `pruneRight` method calls `pruneSubtree` as follows:

```
pruneSubtree( nodeNdx*2 + 2 );
```

You must take care within `pruneSubtree` to remove only those nodes that are part of the subtree. (Some of the nodes in the later portions of the array may belong to other subtrees.) The solution is to use a tree traversal algorithm such as this pre-order traversal:

```
private void pruneSubtree(int r) {
    if (r < treeCell.length) {
        inUse[r] = false;
        pruneSubtree(r*2+1);
        pruneSubtree(r*2+2);
    }
}
```

The array implementation of a binary tree is an interesting possibility, but it is often inferior to the linked representations. `BinaryArrayTree` has three primary shortcomings.

- Absent potential nodes can "waste" computer storage space.
- `BinaryArrayTree` is bounded.
- Certain tree algorithms are less efficient for `BinaryArrayTree` than for `BinaryTree`.

The array utilization for a tree of n actual nodes and height of h is given by the following expression.

$$\frac{n}{2^h - 1}$$

If *h* is large and *n* is small, the array contains many cells that represent absent nodes. The cells for these absent nodes can be considered wasted space compared with a reference (linked) implementation that allocates space only for actual nodes. (Note also that reference implementations have their own potential for memory inefficiencies, usually resulting from frequent tree pruning that orphans nodes.)

Like all array implementations, `BinaryArrayTree` is bounded by the size of the array. This particular implementation bounds not only the number of nodes but also the height of the trees that can be represented.

An example of an algorithm that is less efficient for arrays than for linked representations is tree pruning. You can usually prune a subtree of a linked representation by altering one or two links. However, in the array implementation, every `inUse` cell of the subtree must be assigned a false value, as is performed by the `pruneSubtree` method.

9.7 HEAPS

One type of tree that is well suited for representation as an array is a **heap**. Heaps are binary trees with two properties:

- Every potential tree node is actually used.
- The greatest value in any subtree is stored in that subtree's root.

Another way of explaining the first property is that every level of the binary tree, except the bottom (highest) level, is completely filled, and the only missing nodes in the bottom level must be contiguous from the right side of the level.

The second property of a heap is what makes it useful for arranging the order of tree contents. This property requires that the node content of a heap be arranged so that the greatest value in every subtree is located in the root of that subtree.

Following is an informal algorithm to rearrange the items of an array binary tree representation so that the tree satisfies the second property of a heap. This algorithm assumes that all node content conforms to `Comparable` so that it can be compared using `compareTo`.

```
for every node, n, of tree t from root to last leaf {
    Promote the value of n up through the tree from parent to grandparent,
    to great-grandparent, etc.,
    demoting ancestors until an ancestor with value greater than n is found.
    (n remains the child of this greater-valued node.)
}
```

For purposes of this discussion **promotion** refers to moving a node value closer to the root. Similarly, **demoting** occurs when a node value is assigned to a child node. Consider the `treeCell` array from the array representation (Section 9.6). Assuming that `lastNdx` is the index of the last actual node in the array, the preceding algorithm translates into the following code.

```
// assert: treeCell[0] ... treeCell[lasNdx] represent actual tree
//         node content
for(int ndx=1; ndx<=lastNdx; ndx++) {
    Comparable promotable = treeCell[ndx];
```

```
    int promoNdx = ndx;
    int parentNdx = (promoNdx-1) / 2;
    while (promoNdx>0
            && promotable.compareTo(treeCell[parentNdx]) > 0) {
        treeCell[promoNdx] = treeCell[parentNdx];
        promoNdx = parentNdx;
        parentNdx = (promoNdx-1) / 2;
    }
    treeCell[promoNdx] = promotable;
}
// assert: treeCell[0] ... treeCell[lastNdx] forms a heap
```

Figure 9.27 traces this algorithm for a particular eight-node tree by showing the tree each time the exit test for the outer (*for*) loop is encountered.

This algorithm for creating an initial heap is O(NlogN), assuming N == lastNdx. The "N" in this performance is the result of promoting each of lastNdx–1 nodes (the root node need not be promoted). The "logN" comes from the algorithm to promote a single value because this is the path distance to the root.

Because the greatest value of any subtree is stored in the subtree's root, the greatest value in a heap must be in its root. This observation forms the foundation for several applications involving heaps. One of them is **heapsort**.

The heapsort algorithm is stated informally as follows.

```
// assert: treeCell[0]...treeCell[lastNode] forms a heap
for (int firstSorted=lastNdx; firstSorted >0; firstSorted--) {
    relocatable = treeCell[firstSorted];
    treeCell[firstSorted] = treeCell[0];
    Rebuild a heap by promoting node values until the proper location for
        relocatable is found.
    treeCell[vacantNdx] = relocatable;
}
```

This loop builds a sorted array by partitioning the array in two parts: The top part of the array is an unsorted binary tree (a heap), and the bottom part is the portion of the array already sorted. The variable firstSorted is one less than the smallest index of the sorted portion. Each time through the loop, the largest value in the unsorted part of the array is removed from the root of a heap (treeCell[0]) and is prepended to the sorted portion of the array. The next cell to be prepended is treeCell[firstSorted]. The value that was in treeCell[firstSorted] previously—call it relocatable—must be relocated in the unsorted portion. Such a relocation is a part of rebuilding a heap from the unsorted portion.

A key portion of this algorithm is rebuilding a heap from the remaining unsorted data. You could do this by performing the same algorithm that built the original heap, an O(NlogN) algorithm. However, there is a much more efficient O(logN) algorithm for rebuilding the heap. This algorithm relies on the fact that the unsorted structure is already a heap except for one location: the root whose value was just removed. There are three possible candidates for filling the root: the left and right children of the root and relocatable. The algorithm begins by identifying the index of the maximum of the root's two children; call this index maxNdx. If treeCell[maxNdx] > relocatable, then treeCell[maxNdx] should be promoted to the root. This promotion means that the tree is a heap except for the cell that contained the maximum child. The candidates for filling this cell are its two children and `relocatable`, and the process repeats. Eventually, either `relocatable` is greater than the cell's maximum child or the cell represents a leaf node of the unsorted tree. Figure 9.28 shows the complete code for a heapsort, including the portion for creating the initial heap.

Figure 9.27 Trace of the algorithm that creates a heap

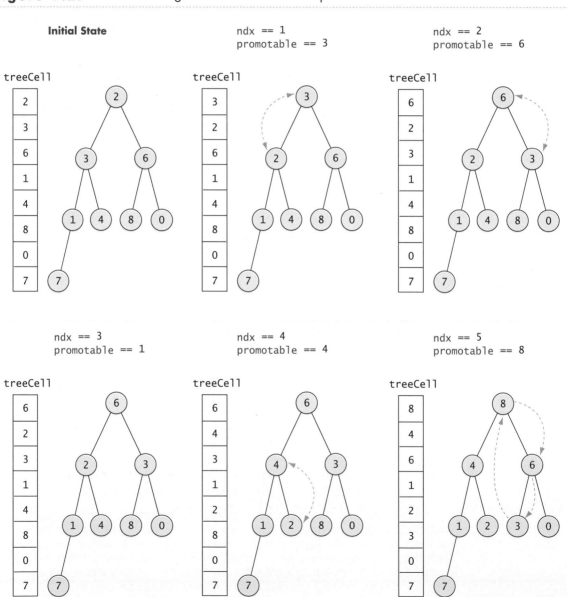

Continued on next page

Figure 9.27 Trace of the algorithm that creates a heap *(continued)*

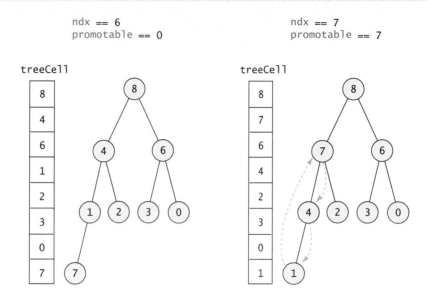

Figure 9.28 The heapSort method

```
/*  post:    forAll(j : 0<=j<lastNdx-1 | treeCell[j] <=
                      treeCell[j+1]) */
public void heapSort() {
    makeInitialHeap();
    for (int firstSorted=lastNdx; firstSorted>0; firstSorted--) {
        Comparable relocatable = treeCell[firstSorted];
        treeCell[firstSorted] = treeCell[0];
        int vacantNdx = 0;
        int maxNdx = indexOfMaxChild(vacantNdx,firstSorted);
        while (maxNdx<firstSorted &&
                relocatable.compareTo(treeCell[maxNdx])<0) {
            treeCell[vacantNdx] = treeCell[maxNdx];
            vacantNdx = maxNdx;
            maxNdx = indexOfMaxChild(vacantNdx,firstSorted);
        }
        treeCell[vacantNdx] = relocatable;
    }
}
/*  post:    treeCell[0] ... treeCell[lastNdx] forms a heap */
public void makeInitialHeap() {
    for(int ndx=1; ndx<=lastNdx; ndx++) {
        Comparable promotable = treeCell[ndx];
        int promoNdx = ndx;
```

Continued on next page

```
            int parentNdx = (promoNdx-1) / 2;
            while (promoNdx>0
                    && promotable.compareTo(treeCell[parentNdx]) > 0) {
                treeCell[promoNdx] = treeCell[parentNdx];
                promoNdx = parentNdx;
                parentNdx = (promoNdx-1) / 2;
            }
            treeCell[promoNdx] = promotable;
        }
    }
    /* post:  vacantNdx has no children implies result == firstSorted
              and vacantNdx has only a left child implies result ==
                  vacantNdx * 2 + 1
              and vacantNdx has two children
              and left greater than right implies result ==
                  vacantNdx * 2 + 1
              and vacantNdx has two children
              and left less than or equal to right implies result ==
                  vacantNdx * 2 + 2 */
    private int indexOfMaxChild(int vacantNdx, int firstSorted) {
        if (vacantNdx*2+1 >= firstSorted) // neither child exists
            return firstSorted;
        else if (vacantNdx*2+2 == firstSorted) // no right child exists
            return vacantNdx*2 + 1;
        else if
        (treeCell[vacantNdx*2+1].compareTo(treeCell[vacantNdx*2+2]) > 0)
            return vacantNdx*2 + 1;
        else
            return vacantNdx*2 + 2;
    }
```

A different application of heaps is based on rebuilding a heap by inserting a new value into an existing heap. Suppose that treeCell[0] ... treeCell[lastNdx] is already a heap and that another value needs to be inserted and the heap reconstructed. The preferred algorithm for this heap reconstruction is adapted from the inner loop of the makeInitialHeap method:

```
// assert: treeCell[0] ... treeCell[lastNdx] form a heap
Comparable promotable = value to be inserted;
    int promoNdx = lastNdx+1;
    int parentNdx = (promoNdx-1) / 2;
    while (promoNdx>0
            && promotable.compareTo(treeCell[parentNdx]) > 0) {
        treeCell[promoNdx] = treeCell[parentNdx];
        promoNdx = parentNdx;
        parentNdx = (promoNdx-1) / 2;
    }
treeCell[promoNdx] = promotable;
// assert: treeCell[0] ... treeCell[lastNdx+1] form a heap
```

These heap rebuilding algorithms are often applied to produce an efficient implementation of a priority queue. For this implementation compareTo must be defined so that greater queue items are those with greater priority, and for equal priorities a longer time in the queue means greater value. Given this definition of compareTo, the root value of a heap will always be the front item of the priority queue. When a new item arrives in the priority queue, the insertion algorithm rebuilds the queue in O(logN), and when the front item is removed, another O(logN) algorithm reconstructs the heap while refilling the vacancy.

9.8 BINARY SEARCH TREES

Heaps illustrate how to reorganize the content of a tree so that its nodes have a kind of sorted property. This section discusses a different kind of sorting, this one based on a different, and more commonly used, tree known as a **binary search tree**. Binary search trees are binary trees with an additional property:

- For any binary search tree node—call it N—the content of N is greater than all values in any node of N's left subtree, and the content of N is less than any node of N's right subtree.

Figure 9.29 pictures a sample binary search tree. This tree contains the integers from 0 through 9, except 1.

Figure 9.29 Sample binary search tree

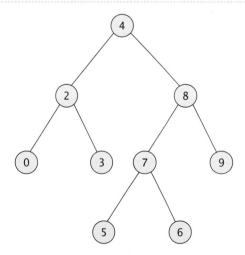

Arguing that a tree is a binary search tree requires that *every* node's value be compared to the values in its two subtrees. The root of the sample binary search tree contains 4, whereas the values in the left subtree are {0, 2, 3}—all less than 4—and the values in the right subtree are {5, 6, 7, 8, 9}, all greater than 4. Similarly, for the node containing 8, its left subtree contains only the lesser values {5, 6, 7}, and its right subtree contains the greater value {9}. This same "left subtree has smaller content and right subtree has greater content" property must hold for each one of the tree's nodes if the tree is to be a binary search tree. This requirement also means that a binary search tree cannot contain any duplicated content.

The advantages of using a binary search tree become obvious in a method—call it isIn—that searches a tree for a particular value. For a typical container (either a list, an array, or other kinds of trees), the isIn method can be expected to examine about half of the container values before it finds the look-up value. However, if the container happens to be a binary search tree, the algorithm for isIn can be written more efficiently.

Consider the execution of a call such as bst.isIn(3) for a binary search tree called bst. The associated look-up algorithm begins by comparing the search value 3 to the value in the root of the tree. If the search value is less than the root content, the entire right subtree can be ignored because all these values are greater than the root. Similarly, if the search value is greater than the root's value, the entire left subtree of the binary search tree can be eliminated from the search.

The complete search algorithm for a binary search tree consists of recursively comparing the search value to the root of the entire tree, then to a child of the root, then to a grandchild of the root, and so forth, until the desired value is found or the search has reached the end of the branch. Using the tree in Figure 9.29 as bst, the bst.isIn(3) call would proceed as follows.

1. Compare the search value (3) to the root node (4).
2. Because the search value is less than 4, proceed to the left and compare the search value (3) to the left child (2).
3. Because the search value is greater than 2, proceed to its right and compare the search value to node value (3).

This ability to eliminate an entire subtree in a single comparison resembles a binary search of an array. A binary search tree eliminates one of two subtrees of the remaining tree with every comparison, much as searching an array with a binary search eliminates half the remaining array with every comparison. Assuming that the two subtrees contain roughly equal numbers of nodes, searching a binary search tree, like a binary search, has an O(logN) performance, where N represents the number of nodes in the tree.

Figure 9.30 shows a class diagram and specifications for one version of BinarySearchTree. This ADT includes only three methods: a BinarySearchTree constructor, the isIn method, and an insert method to add new values.

The abstract specifications define BinarySearchTree as a set, with little hint of the internal ordering of the nodes. However, one key property cannot be hidden from the client: The items in a BinarySearchTree container must be orderable; it must be possible to distinguish between greater and lesser node values. The BinarySearchTree specifications demonstrate this by way of the required parameter types for the insert and the isIn methods. Both of these methods use the java.lang.Comparable interface for their parameter type. (Recall that any class that conforms to Comparable must implement the compareTo method, thereby defining greater than and less than.)

The true nature of a binary search tree is revealed in its implementation. Figure 9.31 shows one implementation of BinarySearchTree. This implementation is an adaptation of BinaryTree using BinTreeIterator.

Figure 9.30 BinarySearchTree class diagram and specifications

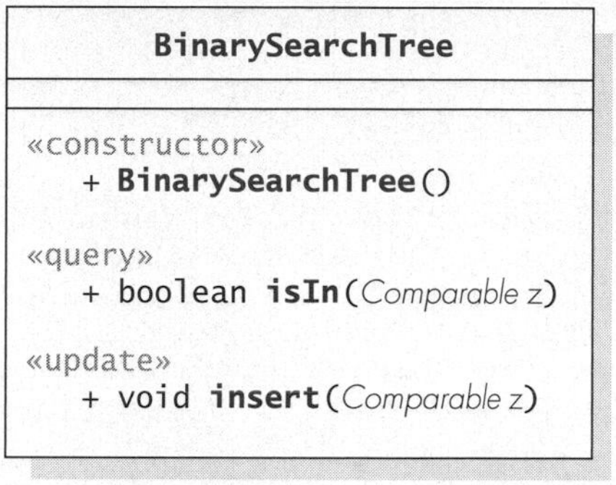

```
┌─────────────────────────────────────┐
│           BinarySearchTree           │
├─────────────────────────────────────┤
│ «constructor»                        │
│    + BinarySearchTree()              │
│                                      │
│ «query»                             │
│    + boolean isIn(Comparable z)      │
│                                      │
│ «update»                             │
│    + void insert(Comparable z)       │
└─────────────────────────────────────┘
```

BinarySearchTree Specifications

Domain

Every BinarySearchTree object consists of a *set* of Comparable

Constructor Method

public **BinarySearchTree**( )

> **post:** this == *set*{}

Query Method

public boolean **isIn**(Comparable z)

> **post:** result == this->*includes*(z)

Update Methods

public void **insert**(Comparable z)

> **post:** this == this@*pre*->*including*(z)

Figure 9.31 BinarySearchTree implementation using BinaryTree

```
/* invariant: this is a binary tree
            and forAll(st : a subtree of this | all content in
                the left subtree of st is < st
            and all content in the right subtree of st is > st)
public class BinarySearchTree {
    private BinaryTree bst;

    /* post:  bst.isEmpty() */
    public BinarySearchTree() {
        bst = new BinaryLinkedTree(); //BinaryArrayTree also works
    }
```

Continued on next page

```
/* post: isIn(z) */
public void insert(Comparable z) {
    if (bst.isEmpty()) {
        bst.makeRoot(z);
    } else {
        BinTreeIterator it = iteratorAt(z, bst.iteratorAtRoot());
        if (z.compareTo(it.item()) < 0) {
            it.sproutLeft(z);
        } else if (z.compareTo(it.item()) > 0) {
            it.sproutRight(z);
        }
    }
}


/* post:   result == z is equal to the content of one of the
                   bst nodes */
public boolean isIn(Comparable z) {
    if (bst.isEmpty()) {
        return false;
    } else {
        BinTreeIterator it = iteratorAt(z, bst.iteratorAtRoot());
        return (z.compareTo(it.item())==0);
    }
}
/* post:   isIn(z) implies result.item().equals(z)
           and !isIn(z) implies result == the tree node that
              would be the proper parent for z */
private BinTreeIterator iteratorAt(Comparable z,
                                   BinTreeIterator it)
{
    if ((z.compareTo(it.item()) < 0) && it.hasLeft())
        return iteratorAt(z, it.left());
    else if ((z.compareTo(it.item()) > 0) && it.hasRight())
        return iteratorAt(z, it.right());
    else
        return it;
}
}
```

This BinarySearchTree implementation is yet another example of the proxy
design pattern; it uses the private BinaryTreeADT object, called theBST, to represent
the tree. The BinarySearchTree constructor method instantiates theBST as an
empty tree.

The isIn method relies largely on a private method, iteratorAt. The
iteratorAt method is passed a search value and an iterator, and it performs the
look-up of the search value in the tree whose root is indicated by the iterator parameter. This method illustrates the proper recursive algorithm for searching through a

binary search tree. When `iteratorAt` locates a node that contains the search value, it returns an iterator positioned at this node.

When a search value is not contained in a binary search tree, `iteratorAt` returns an iterator that is positioned at the node where the missing search value is discovered. For example, searching for the value 1 in the following binary search tree will begin at the 4 node, and proceed to the 2 node, and then the 0 node, where it is discovered that the 0 node has no right child. Therefore, the `iteratorAt` method returns an iterator positioned at the 0 node.

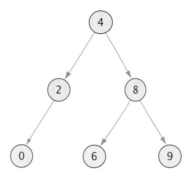

Similarly, a call to `iteratorAt` with a search value of 3 returns an iterator positioned at the 2 node, and a call to `iteratorAt` with a search value of either 5 or 7 returns the 6 node.

The specifications for the `BinarySearchTree` call the iterator value returned by an unsuccessful search a **proper parent**. This designation means that if the search value were to be inserted into the binary search tree, the proper parent would be the one node where the new value could be inserted as a left or right child.

The `insert` method uses this proper parent concept by calling the `iteratorAt` method to perform its search. If `iteratorAt` finds that the insertion value is not already within the tree, the proper parent is returned and `insert` selects between sprouting a left or a right child from this node.

Notice that different binary search trees can represent the same abstract set of values. For example, the three binary search trees in Figure 9.32 all represent the same *set*{1, 2, 3, 4, 5}. Binary search tree 1 results from inserting the values in the order *sequence*{3, 1, 2, 5, 4}. Binary search tree 2 is produced by inserting the values in the order *sequence*{4, 2, 1, 3, 5}. Binary search tree 3 results from inserting values in increasing order: *sequence*{1, 2, 3, 4, 5}

Binary search trees have a number of applications. One application is to store sets of any `Comparable` data. If properly implemented, a binary search tree can provide efficient `isIn` look-up. A slight modification to the concept of a binary search tree can be used as a technique for implementing a map. The modification is to store both the key and its associated value in the same node and organize the node content according to the keys. The binary search tree property for this kind of application can be restated this way: "Keys throughout the left subtree must be less than the key in the root, and the key values in the right must be greater than the root."

Figure 9.32 Three binary search trees with identical abstract content

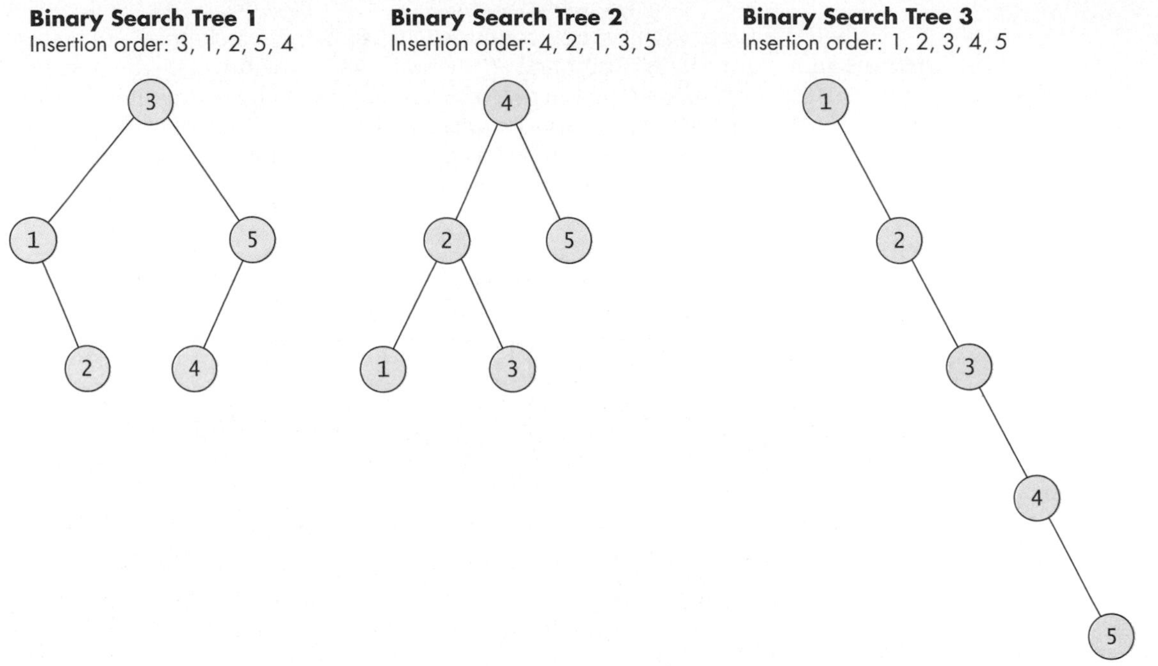

Binary Search Tree 1
Insertion order: 3, 1, 2, 5, 4

Binary Search Tree 2
Insertion order: 4, 2, 1, 3, 5

Binary Search Tree 3
Insertion order: 1, 2, 3, 4, 5

Binary search trees also form the key data structure in a sorting algorithm known as **treesort**. The treesort algorithm consists of repeated insertions into a binary search tree. To see that every binary search tree is sorted requires an important observation: *An inorder traversal of any binary search tree visits nodes in strictly ascending order.* This property means that every binary search tree is sorted. In the best case, treesort is an O(NlogN) sorting algorithm.

9.9 REMOVAL AND BALANCING IN A BINARY SEARCH TREE

Some algorithms that are important for binary search trees aren't as necessary for other binary trees. Two such algorithms are a removal algorithm capable of removing any node and algorithms for restructuring the tree content in a tree with lesser height. Both kinds of algorithms are introduced in this section.

The BinTreeIterator class provides two methods for removing tree nodes: pruneLeft and pruneRight. These methods have a characteristic that makes them useless for removing individual values from a binary search tree:

pruneLeft *and* pruneRight *cannot remove a node without removing its descendants.*

The pruneLeft and pruneRight methods aren't sufficient for removing an arbitrary value from a binary search tree, nor are they helpful in implementing such a removal operation. For the binary search tree, a different method, called remove in Figure 9.33, is appropriate.

Figure 9.33 BinarySearchTreeWithRemove class diagram and specifications

```
┌─────────────────────────────────────┐
│   BinarySearchTreeWithRemove         │
├─────────────────────────────────────┤
│                                      │
├─────────────────────────────────────┤
│ «constructor»                        │
│     + BinarySearchTree()             │
│                                      │
│ «query»                             │
│     + boolean isIn(Comparable z)     │
│                                      │
│ «update»                            │
│     + void insert(Comparable z)      │
│     + void remove(Comparable z)      │
│                                      │
└─────────────────────────────────────┘
```

BinarySearchTreeWithRemove Specifications

Domain

Every BinarySearchTreeWithRemove object consists of a set of Comparable

Constructor Method

public BinarySearchTreeWithRemove( )

    post: this == *set*{}

Query Method

public boolean isIn(Comparable z)

    post: result == this->*includes*(z)

Update Methods

public void insert(Comparable z)

    post: this == this@*pre*->*including*(z)

public void remove(Comparable z)

    post: this == this@*pre*->*excluding*(z)

Software Engineering Hint

There are always design trade-offs associated with the decision of how many methods to include in a container. The **BinTreeIterator** interface supplies only two methods to remove nodes: **pruneLeft** and **pruneRight**. This causes the **remove** method for **BinarySearchTree-WithRemove** to bypass iterators and work with the underlying representation. Another approach is to include more flexible removal and restructuring methods in the iterator interface, but this makes the interface more complicated to implement and adds to an already long list of methods.

A proper implementation of the remove method from BinarySearchTreeWithRemove demands access to the underlying representation. The design of the remove algorithm is built from three cases:

Case 1: The node to be removed is a leaf.

Case 2: The node to be removed has a left subtree but no right subtree.

Case 3: The node to be removed has a right subtree (i.e., any situation not covered in Case 1 or 2.)

These three cases are illustrated in the *Before* pictures in Figure 9.34. In each example in this figure, the value 3 must be removed from the binary search tree.

Figure 9.34 Three cases for removal from a binary search tree

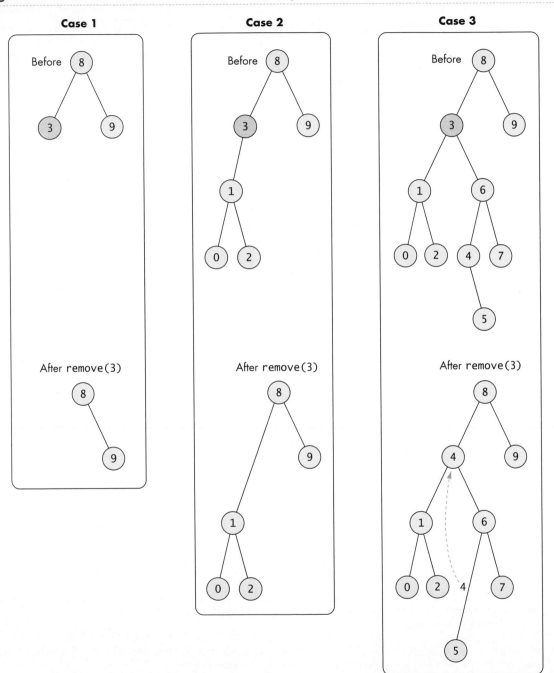

The most important thing to remember when you're designing a binary search tree removal method is that the tree resulting from the removal must preserve the binary search tree property (all values in the left tree are smaller, and all values in

the right tree are greater). This is not difficult in case 1, removing a leaf. The obvious solution in this case is simply to prune the removal node.

Case 2 (the removal node has a left subtree but no right subtree) is somewhat more complicated. The simplest solution is to restructure the tree by replacing the removal node with its left subtree. To do this, you execute one or two statements to update the proper links in a tree representation that relies on references (a linked tree). However, for an array representation, the Case 2 algorithm must relocate all the subtree contents to new array cells.

Case 3 is the most general case. The removal node has a right subtree and possibly a left subtree. The Case 3 algorithm has three steps:

Step 1: Search for the next larger tree value.
Step 2: Assign the next larger tree value (found in Step 1) to become the content of the removal node.
Step 3: Apply the Case 2 approach to restructure the tree by removing the next larger node.

The **next larger** concept comes from the observation that a binary tree is minimally disturbed by replacing the content of any node with the next closest tree value. If the removal node has a right subtree, the tree contains values that are greater than the value in the removal node. The smallest tree value that is still greater than the removal node is the next larger value.

Step 1 is to search for the next larger node. This search algorithm begins at the right child of the removal node and repeatedly moves from left child to left child until no left child exists. Using `BinTreeIterator` operations, the general case of the Step 1 search algorithm can be expressed as follows.

```
/* assert: removalIt is positioned at the node whose value is being
            removed.
          and removalIt.hasRight() */
BinTreeIterator nextLargerIt = removalIt.right();
while (nextLargerIt.hasLeft())
    nextLargerIt = nextLargerIt.left();
/* assert: nextLargerIt is positioned at the next larger node. */
```

Once the next larger node is identified, Step 2 is to assign the value from the next larger node to the removal node, using the following `BinTreeIterator` statement.

```
/* assert: removalIt is positioned at the node whose value is being
            removed.
          and nextLargerIt is positioned at the next larger */
removalIt.setNodeContent( nextLargerIt.item() );
```

Figure 9.34 illustrates Step 2 in the form of a dotted arrow showing that the next larger value (4) has effectively been moved from its prior node to the removal node. Following Step 2 the removal value is gone from the tree. However, the next larger value is still present in two places.

Step 3 eliminates the original node that contained the next larger value. The key observation for designing the Step 3 algorithm is to note that the next larger node will have no left child. (If it did have a left child, it couldn't be the next larger node!)

Because the next larger node has no left child, the easiest solution to eliminating this node is to replace the next larger node with its right child. This kind of restructuring uses the same restructuring algorithm as Case 2 except that it is the next larger node that is replaced instead of the removal node.

Some restructuring algorithms, like the one used in Case 2, are used to remove tree nodes. But other restructuring algorithms are useful for shifting tree content into differing tree geometries. These algorithms are especially useful for improving the **balance** of a binary search tree.

Informally speaking, one tree is said to be more balanced than another if it is "bushier." There are different types of balance, but they all share goals such as trees with less height and trees with more actual than potential children. Balance is important because the isIn search of a balanced binary search tree is more efficient. In the best case, the performance of isIn is O(NlogN), and in the worst case its performance is O(N^2). The best cases for isIn occur when you're searching the most balanced trees, and the worst cases stem from the least balanced trees.

One of the best known definitions of balance comes from the concept of an **AVL tree**. The name AVL comes from its three inventors: Adel'son, Vel'skii, and Landis. An AVL tree is a binary search tree in which the height of a left subtree never varies by more than 1 from its right subtree counterpart. To ensure that a binary search tree has this AVL height balance property, you must check every tree node to be certain that the node's left and right subtrees have the same height or differ in height by 1.

AVL trees, like many other kinds of balanced trees, rely on rebalancing algorithms to rearrange tree nodes to achieve better balance. Two of the most common rebalancing algorithms are known as a single rotation and a double rotation.

A **single rotation** is pictured in Figure 9.35. Consider a restructuring that begins with the tree on the left side of this figure. The two nodes involved in the rotation are labeled **P** (for parent) and **C** (for child). The entire left subtree of C is pictured as a triangle labeled CL. Similarly, the right subtree of C is labeled CR, and the right subtree of P is labeled PR. The dashed line at the top represents the potential connection to a parent as either a left or a right child.

Because this is a binary search tree, the following relationships must be true:

Every value in CL < C < every value in CR < P < every value in PR

Notice that these relationships hold for the tree on the left as well as the tree on the right. Because neither the number nor the content of the nodes is different, both trees represent the same abstract set, and their only difference is geometric. However, by rotating a binary search tree from one of these two forms to another, you can change the tree's balance.

For example, suppose that the tree on the left was previously an AVL tree before a new node was inserted into CL so that height(CL) == height(PR) + 1. In this case the left subtree of node P has a height that is 2 greater than that of the right subtree, so the tree is no longer an AVL tree. By performing a single rotation from the left picture to the one on the right, you restore the AVL property.

Single rotations involve two nodes and their three subtrees. A **double rotation** is slightly more complicated, involving three nodes and their four subtrees. Figure 9.36 illustrates.

Figure 9.35 Single rotation

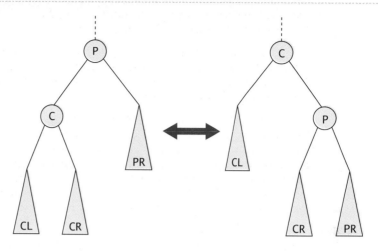

Figure 9.36 Double rotation

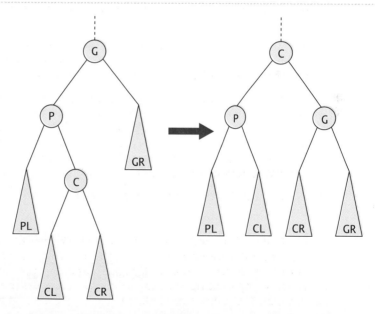

The left side Figure 9.36 illustrates a tree in which C is the right child of P, and P is the left child of G. The binary search tree order property ensures the following:

Every value in $PL < P <$ every value in $CL < C <$ every value in $CR < G <$ every value in GR

A careful examination of the tree at the right in Figure 9.36 reveals that these same order relations hold. The single rotation is used when it is a subtree on the edge of the substructure that is too tall. The double rotation is useful when it is an inner subtree that is too tall. The double rotation that is shown will correct an AVL when either *CL* or *CR* is 1 unit too high compared with GR.

There are actually two double rotations. One is pictured on the left side of Figure 9.36. The second possibility is the reflection of this picture. More specifically, the second form of a double rotation begins with a node *G* that has a right child called *P*, and *P* has a left child called *C*. The resulting rotation is analogous to the pictured double rotation with corrections consistent with the reflected nodes and their subtrees.

These rotation algorithms are further evidence of the advantages of reference representations of trees. Implementing single and double rotations is largely a matter of updating link values for a reference representation of a binary search tree. However, these same algorithms require complicated data rearrangement in an array representation of the tree.

9.10 A RECURSIVE TREE ADT

The binary tree ADTs you've seen thus far rely heavily upon tree nodes. Tree iterators are positioned at nodes, array implementations include a `treeCell` array to store nodes, and reference implementations consist of linked cells—one cell per tree node.

An alternative way to view trees focuses on subtrees rather than nodes. A subtree-based abstraction recursively views a tree as the composition of two subtrees, with those subtrees composed of still other subtrees, and so forth. Figure 9.37 contains this kind of tree specification.

RecursiveBinaryTree is unusual because it has two alternative forms (called Form 1 and Form 2 in the ADT specifications). These two forms stem from an inherent characteristic of all trees: A tree can be either empty or nonempty. The reason for treating an empty tree as a special case is that an empty tree has no nodes or arcs and therefore has no root node content, no left children and no right children. In contrast, every nonempty tree has a root node with content, has a left subtree (possibly empty), and has a right subtree (possibly empty).

Figure 9.37 RecursiveBinaryTree Specifications

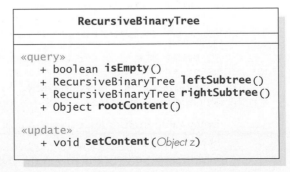

Continued on next page

RecursiveBinaryTree ADT Specifications

Domain (Every RecursiveBinaryTree object has one of two forms)

FORM 1: The tree is empty.

FORM 2: The tree is nonempty and therefore has the following parts.

Object **content**;
RecursiveBinaryTree **left**;
RecursiveBinaryTree **right**;

Invariant

all subtrees of this have finite height

and left and right share no common descendants

Query Methods

```
public boolean isEmpty( )
```
   post: result == this is an empty tree
```
public RecursiveBinaryTree leftSubtree( )
```
   pre: !isEmpty() (throws UnsupportedOperationException)
   post: result == left
```
public RecursiveBinaryTree rightSubtree( )
```
   pre: !isEmpty() (throws UnsupportedOperationException)
   post: result == right
```
public RecursiveBinaryTree rootContent( )
```
   pre: !isEmpty() (throws UnsupportedOperationException)
   post: result == content

Update Methods

```
public void setContent( Object z )
```
   pre: !isEmpty() (throws UnsupportedOperationException)
   post: content == z

Because trees come in two basic types (empty and nonempty), it is natural to implement this tree ADT using two alternative subclasses. Figure 9.38 shows the class diagram for this implementation.

This figure shows RecursiveBinaryTree as an abstract class with two child classes corresponding to the two forms of trees: EmptyBinTree and NonemptyBinTree. The EmptyBinTree is an inner class. The Java code for the abstract RecursiveBinaryTree class is shown in Figure 9.39. This class reflects the abstract specifications.

Figure 9.38 Class diagram for implementing RecursiveBinaryTree

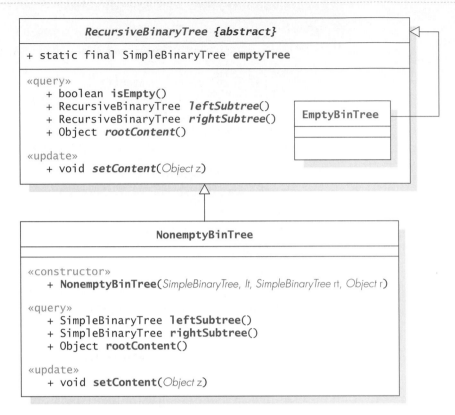

Figure 9.39 RecursiveBinaryTree abstract class

```
/*  Domain (Every RecursiveBinaryTree object has one of two forms)
    FORM 1: The tree is empty.
    FORM 2: The tree is nonempty with the following parts.
                Object content;
                RecursiveBinaryTree left;
                RecursiveBinaryTree right;
    invariant: all subtrees of this have finite height
                and left and right share no common descendants */
public abstract class RecursiveBinaryTree {
    public static final RecursiveBinaryTree emptyTree
        = new EmptyBinTree();
    public static class EmptyBinTree extends RecursiveBinaryTree {
        public EmptyBinTree() {
        }
```

Continued on next page

```java
    public RecursiveBinaryTree leftSubtree() {
        throw new UnsupportedOperationException();
    }
    public RecursiveBinaryTree rightSubtree() {
        throw new UnsupportedOperationException();
    }
    public Object rootContent() {
        throw new UnsupportedOperationException();
    }
    public void setContent(Object z) {
        throw new UnsupportedOperationException();
    }
}


/*  post:   result == this is an empty tree */
public boolean isEmpty() {
    return (this instanceof EmptyBinTree);
}
/*  pre:    !isEmpty() (throws UnsupportedOperationException)
    post:   result == left */
public abstract RecursiveBinaryTree leftSubtree();
/*  pre:    !isEmpty() (throws UnsupportedOperationException)
    post:   result == right */
public abstract RecursiveBinaryTree rightSubtree();
/*  pre:    !isEmpty() (throws UnsupportedOperationException)
    post:   result == content */
public abstract Object rootContent();
/*  pre:    !isEmpty() (throws UnsupportedOperationException)
    post:   content == z */
public abstract void setContent(Object z);
}
```

Software Engineering Hint

A few ADTs have two or more alternative forms (e.g., the empty and nonempty tree). One design for such cases is to create two subclasses and use dynamic dispatch to select the correct method implementations.

RecursiveBinaryTree has two noteworthy members: the isEmpty method and the emptyTree variable. The isEmpty method determines whether a tree is empty by using instanceof to check the type of the tree object; a tree object that is an instance of EmptyBinTree must be an empty tree. When you implement this method in the parent class, neither the EmptyBinTree class nor the NonemptyBinTree class need include this method.

The emptyTree variable demonstrates a use of the singleton design pattern. The emptyTree variable is both static and final, and this means that only one object is associated with emptyTree throughout run-time. This permits a client to access an empty tree using the following expression:

```java
RecursiveBinaryTree.emptyTree
```

In fact, this notation is the *only* means provided to access an empty list. This restriction is imposed by the fact that EmptyBinTree is declared private.

The EmptyBinTree class must include implementations of every abstract method, as required by Java. However, in the given implementation each of these methods does nothing more than throw an UnsupportedOperationException. This behavior is acceptable because the only two methods that make sense for an EmptyBinTree are its constructor and isEmpty.

The nonempty binary tree implementation is more interesting than EmptyBinTree. Figure 9.40 shows an implementation of the nonempty tree in the form of a class called NonemptyBinTree.

Figure 9.40 NonemptyBinTree class

```
public class NonemptyBinTree extends RecursiveBinaryTree {
    private RecursiveBinaryTree leftChild, rightChild;
    private Object content;
    /* pre:    left and right are binary trees
                and left is not a subtree of right and right is not
                    a subtree of left and left != right
        post:   this is a binary tree with left as its left subtree
                and rootContent() == z and leftSubtree() == left
                and rightSubtree() == right */
    public NonemptyBinTree( RecursiveBinaryTree left,
                            RecursiveBinaryTree right, Object z)
    {
        leftChild = left;
        rightChild = right;
        content = z;
    }
    /* post:   result == leftChild */
    public RecursiveBinaryTree leftSubtree() {
        return leftChild;
    }
    /* post:   result == rightChild */
    public RecursiveBinaryTree rightSubtree() {
        return rightChild;
    }
    /* post:   result == content */
    public Object rootContent() {
        return content;
    }

    /* post:   content == z */
    public void setContent(Object z) {
        content = z;
    }
}
```

`NonemptyBinTree` uses a linked data structure to represent `Recursive` `BinaryTree`. This class uses three variables: `leftChild` and `rightChild` are links to other `RecursiveBinaryTree` objects, and `content` references the value of the tree's root node. The `NonemptyBinTree` methods are easily implemented in terms of these three variables.

None of the methods of `NonemptyBinTree` has preconditions. This is because a `NonemptyBinTree`, by definition, is a nonempty tree, and the ADT specifies no restrictions for calling methods on nonempty trees.

Understanding the `NonemptyBinTree` constructor method is the key to understanding how to build binary trees using `NonemptyBinTree`. This constructor takes two existing trees and an object (to become the root content) and constructs a new tree; the existing trees become the left and right subtrees of the newly instantiated tree. For example, the following code constructs a tree with a singleton node.

```
RecursiveBinaryTree sandisTree;
sandisTree = new BinTree( RecursiveBinaryTree.emptyTree,
                          RecursiveBinaryTree.emptyTree "Sandi" );
```

This code instantiates a new tree with two empty trees as children. The empty trees are used as the left subtree and right subtree of the third tree (`sandisTree`). The content of the root of the resulting tree is "Sandi". The abstract tree that results from executing this code consists of the single node with content of "Sandi".

Constructing more complicated binary trees using the `BinTree` constructor follows the tree structure from the leaves toward the root. For example, executing the `buildTheTree` method in Figure 9.41 instantiates two trees—`lanasTree` and `jodysTree`—and then uses them as subtrees of a third tree, `jimsTree`. Subsequently, a `theTree` is constructed from `sandisTree` and `jimsTree`. The resulting structure is pictured in Figure 9.41.

The example in Figure 9.41 illustrates one advantage of the singleton design pattern with respect to handling empty trees. The approach used to implement `RecursiveBinaryTree` demands that each "nonexistent" child be represented by an object of type `EmptyBinTree`. For the small tree in Figure 9.41, this means that six empty tree objects are required (for both children of the *Sandi*, *Lana*, and *Jody* nodes). By declaring the `emptyTree` variable to be `static` and `final`, the code has created a single object that is shared by all the empty trees.

The methods of `RecursiveBinaryTree` permit four operations for inspecting tree properties.

- `isEmpty` can be called to check for an empty tree.
- `rootContent` can be called to inspect the value of the tree's root.
- `leftSubtree` can be called to access the left subtree.
- `rightSubtree` can be called to access the right subtree.

Visiting the several nodes of a `RecursiveBinaryTree` proceeds from parent node to its children. For example, the following `printRightmost` method displays the content of the following nodes in order: the root of `t`, the right child of `t`, the right child of the right child of `t`, and so on.

```
private void printRightmost( RecursiveBinaryTree t) {
    RecursiveBinaryTree tmpTree;
    tmpTree = t;
    while ( !tmpTree.isEmpty() ) {
        System.out.println( tmpTree.rootContent() );
        tmpTree = tmpTree.rightSubtree();
    }
}
```

A sample call such as printRightmost(theTree), assuming the state of theTree depicted in Figure 9.41, will result in the following output:

```
8East
Jim
Jody
```

The printRightmost method uses a local variable, tmpTree, that is assigned the right subtree of its prior value for each successive iteration of the loop. The task performed by printRightmost also can be implemented recursively, as shown in the following printRightmostR at the top of the next page.

Figure 9.41   Sample tree built via the NonemptyBinTree constructor

```
/* post:   theTree is the tree pictured
            to the right */
```

```
public void buildTheTree() {
    RecursiveBinaryTree lanasTree, jodysTree, jimsTree, sandisTree;
    RecursiveBinaryTree theTree;
    lanasTree = new NonemptyBinTree( RecursiveBinaryTree.emptyTree,
                                     RecursiveBinaryTree.emptyTree,
                                     "Lana" );
    jodysTree = new NonemptyBinTree( RecursiveBinaryTree.emptyTree,
                                     RecursiveBinaryTree.emptyTree,
                                     "Jody" );
    jimsTree = new NonemptyBinTree( lanasTree, jodysTree, "Jim" );
    sandisTree = new NonemptyBinTree( RecursiveBinaryTree.emptyTree,
                                      RecursiveBinaryTree.emptyTree,
                                      "Sandi" );
    theTree = new NonemptyBinTree( sandisTree, jimsTree, "8East" );
}
```

```
private void printRightmostR( RecursiveBinaryTree t) {
    if ( !t.isEmpty() ) {
        System.out.println( t.rootContent() );
        printRightmost( t.rightSubtree() );
    }
}
```

This recursive version is instructive because it illustrates a recursive algorithm for this type of tree. Figure 9.42 contains another recursive method that returns the height of any RecursiveBinaryTree object.

Figure 9.42 Recursive height method for RecursiveBinaryTree

```
private int height(RecursiveBinaryTree t) {
    if ( t.isEmpty() ) {
        return -1;
    } else {
        return 1 + Math.max(height(t.leftSubtree()),
                height(t.rightSubtree()));
    }
}
```

This algorithm recursively examines the heights of both subtrees of a tree to determine the tree's height. The base step in the recursion corresponds to calculating the height of an empty tree.

9.11 GENERAL TREES

This chapter concentrates on binary trees, rather than other types of trees, primarily because binary trees have less complicated implementations. Furthermore, binary tree algorithms generally exhibit better performance than corresponding general tree algorithms. On the other hand, for a few applications, a general tree is the preferred abstraction.

Fortunately, most of the issues regarding binary trees have an analog in general trees. For example, general trees can be, and usually are, rooted. Similarly, general trees can use an ordering of children. Instead of simply left and right, a general tree's children might be considered to be the *first* child, the *second* child, and so forth.

The representation of a truly general tree must allow for more or fewer children per node. One reasonable representation is to include a linked list within each node object with one list cell per child. Figure 9.43 pictures such a representation for a general tree.

Figure 9.43 Sample general tree representation

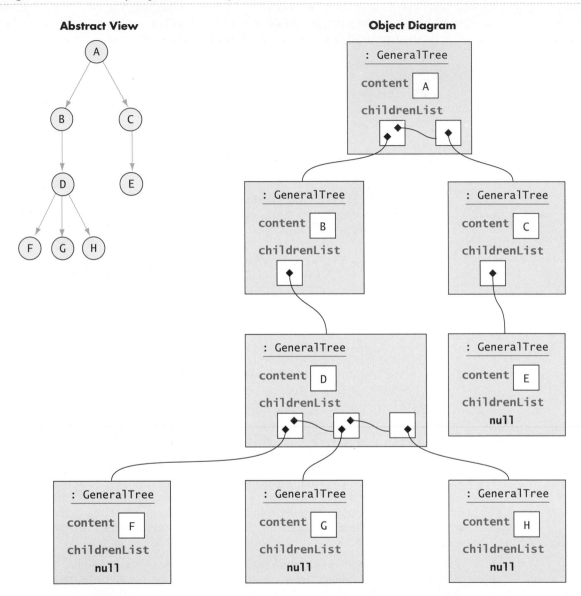

THE SOFTWARE INSPECTOR

Following is a collection of hints on what to check when you examine a design or code that involves the concepts of this chapter.

✓ A common source of errors in tree implementations is empty trees. Any testing for correctness of a tree-related algorithm should therefore include sufficient testing of empty trees.

✓ Appending to the bottom of a tree creates the potential for creation of a graph with repeated subtrees (i.e., the structure is no longer a tree). You must take care that this does not occur.

✓ Tree iterators have two potential pitfalls: Pruning a tree can remove a subtree where another iterator is positioned, and cloning the iterator is essential for recursive algorithms, except those that are tail recursive. When using a tree with iterators, it is best to look for these bugs.

✓ An array implementation of a binary tree is efficient and straightforward, but only if the tree height is predictable.

EXERCISES

1. Which of the following four trees can properly be called *binary* trees?

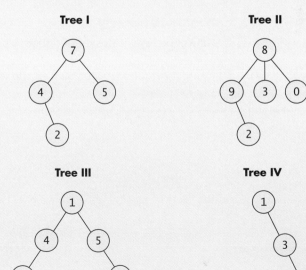

2. Use the following rooted tree to complete parts (a) through (f).

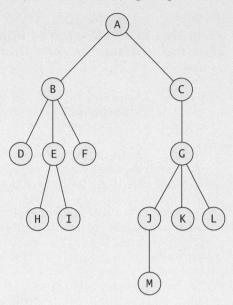

a. List all the leaf nodes of this tree.

b. Give the level each tree node.

c. List all of the descendants of node C.

d. List all of the ancestors of node J.

e. What is the height of this tree?

f. Draw a picture of the subtree that has node B as a root.

3. Draw an expression tree for each of the following expressions.

a. 1 + 2 * 3 − 4

b. 1 + 2 + 3 + 4 + 5 + 6

c. (1.0 + 2.0) * ((3.0 + 4.0) / (5.0 + 6.0))

4. Use the following binary tree to complete parts (a) through (g).

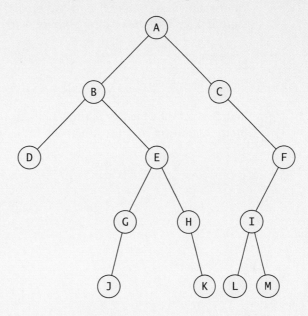

a. List every node that is a right child of its parent.

b. List the order in which these nodes would be visited in a preorder traversal.

c. List the order in which these nodes would be visited in an inorder traversal.

d. List the order in which these nodes would be visited in a postorder traversal.

e. Write a complete code segment to properly create this tree as a `BinaryLinkedTree` (Section 9.3) variable and assign it the tree shown. (You may assume that each node name is a `String`.)

f. Write a complete code segment to properly declare a `BinaryArrayTree` (Section 9.6) variable and assign it the tree shown. (You may assume that each node name is a `String`.)

g. Give a complete code segment to properly declare a `RecursiveBinaryTree` (Section 9.10) variable and assign it the tree shown above. (You may assume that each node name is a `String`.)

5. Which, if any, of the three binary trees in Exercise 1 are binary search trees?

6. Which, if any, of the three binary trees in Exercise 1 could be a heap?

7. Which, if any, of the three binary trees in Exercise 1 are AVL trees?

8. For each part, assume that a binary search tree is initially empty and that the values shown are inserted into the binary search tree in the order shown. Draw a picture of the resulting binary search tree.

a. 1, 3, 5, 7, 9

b. 5, 3, 1, 7, 9

c. 2, 1, 4, 3, 5, 8, 7, 9, 3, 0

9. Redraw the following tree to show how the node values have been rearranged by the algorithm that constructs the initial heap as shown in Section 9.7.

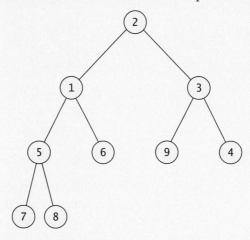

10. Beginning with the binary tree from Exercise 4, redraw the tree as it would appear after each of the following.

a. An application of a single rotation to nodes C and F

b. An application of a double rotation to nodes A, B, and E

11. Section 9.9 discusses a second double rotation algorithm for rebalancing binary search trees. In the style of Figure 9.36, draw a before and after picture for this alternative double rotation.

12. Write code for each of the following methods that could be added to the `BinaryTree` class. (See Section 9.3.)

a. Method name: **nodeCount**

   post: result is the count of all nodes in this tree

b. Method name: **isAtRoot**

   Parameters: a `BinTreeIterator` called **it**

   pre: !isEmpty() *and* it is positioned somewhere within bt

   post: result is true exactly when it is positioned at the tree's root

c. Method name: `isLeftChild`

Parameters: a BinTreeIterator called **it**

pre: !isEmpty() *and* it is positioned somewhere within this tree

post: result is true exactly when it is positioned at a node that is a left child of its parent

d. Method name: `level`

Parameters: a BinTreeIterator called **it**

pre: !isEmpty() *and* it is positioned somewhere within this tree

post: result is the level of the node where it is positioned

e. Method name: `printAncestors`

Parameters: a BinTreeIterator called **it**

pre: isEmpty() *and* it is positioned somewhere within this tree

post: All of the ancestors of it are output beginning with the it's parent and ending at the root.

PROGRAMMING EXERCISES

1. Using the `BinaryLinkedTree` representation from Section 9.3, design, implement, and test a program that provides a useful classification system, such as the one shown in Figure 9.9. Your program should traverse an existing tree from the root, asking the user yes/no questions until a leaf node is encountered. The program issues a "guess" that the leaf node contains the correct answer. If the user agrees with this guess, the program returns to begin another classification. On the other hand, if the user disagrees with the guess, the program should request from the user a yes/no question that distinguishes the correct answer from the guess. This information, along with the correct answer, is appended to the tree so that the program "learns" how to classify additional objects. You can write such a program to classify animals, famous people, or any other collection of distinguishable categories.

Make the minor modifications that are necessary for this same program to use `BinaryArrayTree` in place of `BinaryLinkedTree`, and test the resulting program.

2. This chapter discusses two sorting algorithms: treesort (based on binary search trees) and heapsort. Write a program that implements both algorithms to sort the same array. Use this program to compare the run-time performance of both algorithms for arrays of randomly chosen `double` values.

3. The `BinaryLinkedTree` representation from Section 9.3 uses a cell that contains only two links (`leftLink` and `rightLink`). Design, implement, and test a different version of this class, along with a modified `BinTreeIterator` that also includes a `parentLink` in the node cell. Your revised `BinTreeIterator` should support two new methods—hasParent and parent—that are analogous to hasLeft and left.

4. The BinTreeIterator class is constructed from iterators that are immutable. Design, implement, and test a MutableBinTreeIterator class so that the left and right methods are replaced with the following two mutator methods. Write preorder and postorder traversal algorithms to test these iterators.

    ```
    /* pre:   not isOff() (throw BinaryTreeException)
       post:  hasLeft() implies this == the left child of this@pre
              and !hasLeft() implies isOff() */
    public void goToLeft();
    /* pre:   not isOff() (throw BinaryTreeException)
       post:  hasRight() implies this == the right child of this@pre
              and !hasRight() implies isOff() */
    public void goToRight();
    ```

5. Design, implement, and test a program to store a single-level index. The index should consist of an arbitrary number of unique words, with each word mapping to its own sequence of one or more page numbers. The look-up operation must supply a word and return the associated sequence of page numbers. The container in which the index is stored must use a binary search tree style of storage and retrieval.

6. Design, implement, and test a program that implements a binary search tree with the following modifications.

    a. It includes a removal method to remove an arbitrary value.

    b. The insert method is modified to rebalance the tree into an AVL tree for each insertion. (You may assume there are no removals.)

PART 2

Core Concepts: Review and Reference

OBJECT-
ORIENTED
PROGRAMMING

> *" SIMPLE THINGS*
> *SHOULD BE SIMPLE.*
> *COMPLEX THINGS*
> *SHOULD BE*
> *POSSIBLE. "*
>
> —Alan Kay

OBJECTIVES

- To define objects as entities having state and behavior

- To present the connection, and the differences, between objects and their classes

- To review Java instance variables, methods (constructor, void, and nonvoid) and object instantiation

- To present program initiation in the form of a Java application and a Java applet

- To introduce object-oriented design

- To demonstrate object diagrams, a UML notation

- To provide an overview of software testing concepts

In recent years the shortage of skilled programmers and the corresponding high cost of software have placed increased emphasis on software development techniques that are reliable and efficient. The software industry demands software that is reusable, extensible, and

441

conveniently ported to multiple environments. **Object-oriented programming (OOP)** has proven to be a software development approach that is most effective for addressing these needs.

The **Java** programming language, a product of Sun Microsystems (www.java.sun.com), was designed, among other things, to support OOP. This book uses the Java 2 (SDK1.4) language definition throughout.

O1.1 OBJECTS AND CLASSES

Every software object is defined by two things: its state and its behavior. The **state** of an object consists of the value of its attributes, and **behavior** is determined by the methods that can be performed on it.

Every software object belongs to a **class** that determines its potential state and behavior. Object-oriented programming consists of writing software classes. For example, the software for maintaining the inventory of a retail sales operation can be expected to use objects to record the sales for specific products sold by the store. Figure O1.1 contains a Java class to define such objects.

Figure O1.1   OneProduct class

```java
public class OneProduct {
    private String name;
    private double sellingPrice;
    private double totalCost, totalSales;
    private int onHand, sold;
    /*  post:   name == n and sellingPrice == p
                and totalCost == 0 and totalSales == 0
                and onHand == 0 and sold == 0 */
    public OneProduct(String n, double p) {
        name = n;
        sellingPrice = p;
        totalCost = 0.0;
        totalSales = 0.0;
        onHand = 0;
        sold = 0;
    }
    /*  post:   onHand == onHand@pre + q
                and totalCost == totalCost@pre + q*c */
    public void receiveProduct(int q, double c) {
        onHand = onHand + q;
        totalCost = totalCost + q * c;
    }
    /*  post:   sellingPrice == p */
    public void setSellingPrice(double p) {
        sellingPrice = p;
    }
```

Continued on next page

```
/*  post:   onHand == onHand@pre - q
            and sold == sold@pre + q
            and totalSales == totalSales@pre + q*sellingPrice */
public void makeSale(int q) {
    onHand = onHand - q;
    sold = sold + q;
    totalSales = totalSales + (q * sellingPrice);
}
/*  post:   result == name */
public String productName() {
    return name;
}


/*  post:   result == onHand */
public int quantityOnHand() {
    return onHand;
}
/*  post:   result == sold */
public int quantitySold() {
    return sold;
}
/*  post:   result == totalSales - totalCost */
public double netProfitToDate() {
    return totalSales - totalCost;
}


/*  pre:    sold != 0
    post:   result == totalSales / sold */
public double averageSellingPrice() {
    return totalSales / sold;
}
}
```

The `OneProduct` class defines a type for objects that represent individual products. The state of each `OneProduct` object is determined by its instance variables:

- `name` maintains the title of the product.
- `sellingPrice` stores the retail price per unit.
- `onHand` maintains the quantity of such items that are currently in stock.
- `sold` maintains the total number of such items that have been sold.
- `totalCost` maintains the total amount of money that has been spent to purchase this product.
- `totalSales` stores the total amount of money that has been collected by sales of the product.

The potential behavior of the objects belonging to any class is determined by the **methods** included in the class. Some methods are classified as **update** methods because their purpose is to alter (update) an object's state. Another common name for an update method is **mutator** because it mutates (alters) the object's state. The OneProduct class includes the following update methods:

- OneProduct is a constructor that initializes all instance variables.
- receiveProduct is called to receive additional quantities of the product.
- setSellingPrice alters the retail price of the product.
- makeSale is used to record a sale of q items of a product.

Other methods are nonvoid (i.e., they return a value). Such methods are often classified as **query** methods or **accessor** methods because they are used to access (query) information about the state of objects. The OneProduct class includes the following query methods:

- productName returns the name of the product.
- quantityOnHand returns the quantity in stock.
- quantitySold returns the quantity that has been sold.
- netProfitToDate returns the total income from selling this product minus the purchase costs.
- averageSellingPrice returns the total sales income divided by the number of items sold.

Java requires that every object be **instantiated** (created) before performing any methods on the object. The following Java statement shows the notation for instantiating a single OneProduct object.

```
bobsBeans = new OneProduct("Bob's Baked Beans", 1.25);
```

A **constructor** is a special kind of method that is a required part of any instantiation used to initialize the state of the object. In this case the object is initialized so that its name is Bob's Baked Beans, its sellingPrice is 1.25, and all other instance variables of the object are zero.

It is common to refer to an object using a **variable**. The previously instantiated object uses a variable called bobsBeans. The same program might include other objects, referenced by their own variables. For example, the following statement instantiates a second OneProduct object, and this object is referred to by the name pamsPizza.

```
pamsPizza = new OneProduct("Pams Pepperoni Pizza", 5.99);
```

Java requires that all variables be declared before being instantiated. These **declarations** define the association between objects and the classes to which they belong. The following declaration declares the prior two local variables so that they can be used to reference objects that belong to the OneProduct class.

```
OneProduct bobsBeans, pamsPizza;
```

The preferred way to view the execution of an object-oriented program is as a sequence of method calls that is being performed on objects. The following segment of a Java program illustrates.

```
OneProduct bobsBeans, pamsPizza;
bobsBeans = new OneProduct("Bob's Baked Beans", 1.25);
pamsPizza = new OneProduct("Pam's Pepperoni Pizza", 5.99);
bobsBeans.receiveProduct(100, 0.98);
bobsBeans.makeSale(3);
```

```
bobsBeans.makeSale(8);
pamsPizza.receiveProduct(5, 4.25);
pamsPizza.makeSale(1);
bobsBeans.makeSale(2);
pamsPizza.receiveProduct(20, 4.30);
System.out.println( "Remaining inventory of "
                + bobsBeans.productName() + " is "
                + bobsBeans.quantityOnHand() );
```

Following the declaration and instantiation statements, this code will perform various methods on the bobsBeans and pamsPizza objects. When this code segment executes, the bobsBeans object is updated by a receiveProduct method call, followed by two makeSale calls. Subsequently, pamsPizza is updated by a call to receiveProduct, two calls to makeSale, and another call to receiveProduct. The final statement of this code segment uses two query methods: productName and quantityOnHand. Both are applied to the bobsBeans object when the code executes.

O1.2 JAVA APPLICATIONS

Initiating the execution of an object-oriented program is reminiscent of an ancient paradox: Which came first—the chicken or the egg? If every program consists of objects and if program execution consists exclusively of executing methods, where does a program begin its execution? Fortunately, Java provides two solutions to this problem.

One solution is to write a program in the form of an **application**. Every Java application must include one class that initiates program execution. A method within the class must meet the following four qualifications:

1. It must be named main.
2. It must be public and void.
3. It must be static.
4. It must have a single parameter of type String[].

The third restriction imposes several constraints. A **static** method is one that belongs to the class and is not associated with any particular object. Therefore, a static method cannot reference any instance variables from its own class, nor can it call any nonstatic methods from the same class. Figure O1.2 shows a sample class that contains an appropriate main method.

The most common way to execute a Java application is to use the **java command** from the Sun Microsystems development environment. For example, the specific java command to execute the application from Figure O1.2 is as follows:

```
java GroceryProgram
```

When this command is issued, the program executes the main method in the GroceryProgram class, thereby initiating program execution.

Figure O1.2 The GroceryProgram class

```
public class GroceryProgram {
    public static void main(String args[]) {
        OneProduct bobsBeans, pamsPizza;
        bobsBeans = new OneProduct("Bob's Baked Beans", 1.25);
        pamsPizza = new OneProduct("Pam's Pepperoni Pizza", 5.99);
        bobsBeans.receiveProduct(100, 0.98);
        bobsBeans.makeSale(3);
        bobsBeans.makeSale(8);
        pamsPizza.receiveProduct(5, 4.25);
        pamsPizza.makeSale(1);
        bobsBeans.makeSale(2);
        pamsPizza.receiveProduct(20, 4.30);
        System.out.println( "Remaining inventory of "
                        + bobsBeans.productName() + " is "
                        + bobsBeans.quantityOnHand() );
    }
}
```

01.3 OBJECT-ORIENTED DESIGN

Good engineering relies on effective planning. Software engineering is no different. The planning process for software development is commonly referred to as **software design**, and object-oriented programming relies on planning in the form of **object-oriented design (OOD)**. Figure O1.3 describes OOD as a three-step process.

Figure O1.3 A three-step OOD procedure

Step 1. Identify the objects.
Step 2. Group objects into classes.
Step 3. Locate or design the necessary classes, establishing necessary relationships.

The first step, identifying the objects, demonstrates that OOD begins with an examination of the program requirements in an attempt to extract objects. Listing all the unique objects that appear to be present in the requirements gives you essential insight into the problem, as well as potential solutions.

Not every object belongs to a different class. The second step in OOD is to group similar objects. Each

Software Engineering Hint

A simple technique for locating objects and methods is to look for nouns and verbs in the program requirements. Nouns are good candidates for objects, and verbs generally correspond to methods.

group of objects will result in a class (or perhaps a group of classes). Step 3 uses the information gathered in the previous two steps to define each class by exploring its state, its behavior, and its relationship to other classes. Sometimes this third step involves locating an existing software class, and other times you must design a new class.

As an example of OOD, consider a program to create a window containing an icon for a school bus, as shown in Figure O1.4. The requirements for this program are to draw a black and white icon of the front of a black school bus. The body of the bus must have rounded top corners, with square corners on the bottom. The bus icon contains two windows, two headlights, and a grille made from two white horizontal bars. Two tires protrude from the bus's bottom.

Figure O1.4 A window containing a school bus icon

The first design step results in a list of objects such as the following.

- Background window on which the bus is displayed
- Body of the bus
- Left front bus window
- Right front bus window
- Left headlight
- Right headlight
- Top grille bar
- Bottom grille bar
- Left front tire
- Right front tire

Each of these objects must come from a class, but sometimes you can group several objects to share a common class. To group the objects (Step 2 of OOD), you must look for similarities among them. Obviously, the left front bus window and right front bus window are similar, differing only in the location where they are drawn. If you think in terms of geometric figures, you can also include the two grille parts and the two tires in the same class as the bus windows. All six of these objects are rectangular solids. The differences between them could be attributed to state differences for rectangles with differing dimensions, locations, and colors. Continuing this geometric shape grouping, the two headlights belong together as circular solids.

Designing the bus body is not so simple. One method is to split this single object into two objects: a rectangular solid with rounded corners and an overlapping rectangular solid with square corners, as diagrammed in Figure O1.5. This design essentially splits one object in two. You can discover this kind of need for additional objects any time during design, but it is best to identify objects as early as possible.

Figure O1.5 Two rectangular solids composed to make the bus body

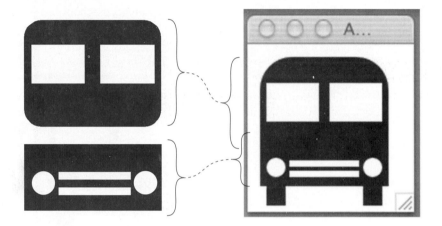

At this point you have the following four groups of objects. Each of these groups is unique, because it will need a unique constructor, a unique class name, and possible unique methods.

1. Rectangular solid group (with square corners)
   - Left front bus window
   - Right front bus window
   - Top grille bar
   - Bottom grille bar
   - Left front tire
   - Right front tire
   - Bottom portion of bus body

2. Rectangular solid group (with rounded corners)
   - Top portion of bus body

3. Circular solid group
   - Left headlight
   - Right headlight

4. Display window group
   - Background window upon which the bus is displayed

A key part of Design Step 3 (locating or designing the class) is to seek out possibilities for reuse. The Java programming language includes a rich collection of existing classes called the **Software Development Kit (SDK)**, and often referred to informally as "the standard Java packages." Most programming environments also add their own software class libraries. (Another name for the SDK is **Java Development Kit—JDK**) Reusing these existing classes often reduces software development time and can improve software reliability because frequently used classes are more likely to be correct.

> ### Software Engineering Hint
>
> Software reuse is one of the most important benefits of OOP. The wise software developer is always looking for ways to reuse existing code.

For the school bus program, SDK includes several classes that can be used as a background window. One of the best choices is a class called JFrame, which is part of the `javax.swing` package. Although SDK contains classes that can assist in drawing rectangular and circular solids, there are no SDK classes that are perfectly suited to the objects in the school bus program. Therefore, you're likely to design three classes: one for rectangular solids with square corners, one for rectangular solids with round corners, and one for circular solids.

These three geometric solid classes can use the same five state attributes (x, y, *width*, *height*, and *color*) to maintain the location, size, and color of the solid. Figure O1.6 shows one way to use the state attributes for position and size.

Figure O1.6 The meaning of x, y, width and height in graphical placement

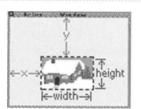

A simple design is to pass values for all five of these state attributes in the constructor for the solid classes. In other words, executing the following statement will instantiate a `RectangularSolid` object called `leftWindow` with x, y, width, height, and color values of 5, 20, 41, 30, and `Color.white`, respectively.

```
RectangularSolid leftWindow = new RectangularSolid(5, 20, 41, 30,
Color.white);
```

In addition to selecting state attributes, Step 3 of the OOD process also includes selecting methods for the newly designed classes. The methods of the three geometric solid classes must include those that cause the parts of the bus icon to display properly. The choice of the Java `javax.swing` package suggests using a method called `place`, which permits one solid to be "stuck on" another. The placed object will appear to be in front of its underlying object when it is displayed, and the placed object will use x and y values that are relative to those of the underlying object. Using such a method call, the following statement causes a `leftHeadlight` object to be placed on top of the underlying `busBodyBottom` object.

```
leftHeadlight.place(busBodyBottom);
```

Figure O1.7 summarizes the resulting class design for a `RectangularSolid` class. This diagram shows the five state attributes and two methods of the class.

Classes for circular solids (CircularSolid) and rectangular solids with round corners (RoundRectangularSolid) can use the same design, differing only in the name of the class and constructor.

Figure O1.7 RectangularSolid class diagram

RectangularSolid
- int *x*   - int *y*   - int *width*   - int *height*   - Color *color*

«constructor»
   + **RectangularSolid**(*int* x, *int* y, *int* w, *int* h, *Color* c)
 	
 «update»
   + void **place**(*Component* c)

O1.4 IMPLEMENTING A DESIGN

The product of software design is a kind of blueprint for the program. This blueprint must be **implemented** by writing the code for all necessary classes. For example, the class diagram in Figure O1.7 is a blueprint for the programmer who writes the Java code that will implement the RectangularSolid class.

It is easy to overlook an object that is needed for most programs. This "hidden" object is sometimes called a **driver** because it plays a key role in getting the program started, often creating and manipulating other key objects. In many programs the driver object also supplies public methods that are shared by other objects, providing mechanisms for cooperation among objects. The need for a driver object is evident in the school bus program. This object will provide the essential code to instantiate the display window and all the bus parts.

Sometimes you can implement the role of the driver object, and its associated class, in the main method of a Java application. However, this approach is often impractical because as a static method, the main method has no access to instance variables and nonstatic methods.

Figure O1.8 illustrates another approach for the class that contains the main method. The main method includes only a single statement, and this statement instantiates a single local object, schoolBus. The schoolBus object is the driver object for the application.

Software Engineering Hint

The technique of writing a **main** method whose sole purpose is to create a driver object by calling its constructor is a common technique in Java OOP.

Figure O1.8 BusApplication class

```java
public class BusApplication {
    public static void main(String args[]) {
        SchoolBus schoolBus = new SchoolBus();
    }
}
```

The main method of the BusApplication class calls only one method: the SchoolBus constructor. Therefore, a key portion of the implementation of this program is the code for this constructor, as shown in Figure O1.9.

Figure O1.9 SchoolBus class

```java
import java.awt.Color;
import javax.swing.*;
public class SchoolBus {
    private JFrame window;
    private RoundRectangularSolid busBodyTop;
    private RectangularSolid busBodyBottom;
    private RectangularSolid leftWindow, rightWindow, topGrill,
                            bottomGrill, leftTire, rightTire;
    private CircularSolid leftHeadlight, rightHeadlight;
    /* post:  a window is constructed and the icon of a school bus
              displayed. */
    public SchoolBus() {
        window = new JFrame();
        window.setBounds(10, 10, 130, 150);
        window.getContentPane().setLayout(null);
        busBodyTop = new RoundRectangularSolid(10, 10, 100, 80,
                                               Color.black);
        busBodyTop.place(window);
        leftWindow = new RectangularSolid(5, 20, 41, 30,
                                          Color.white);
        leftWindow.place(busBodyTop);
        rightWindow = new RectangularSolid(54, 20, 41, 30,
                                           Color.white);
        rightWindow.place(busBodyTop);
        busBodyBottom = new RectangularSolid(10, 80, 100, 30,
                                             Color.black);
        busBodyBottom.place(window);
        leftHeadlight = new CircularSolid(5, 8, 15, 15,
                                          Color.white);
        leftHeadlight.place(busBodyBottom);
```

Continued on next page

```
                    rightHeadlight = new CircularSolid(80, 8, 15, 15,
                                                   Color.white);
                    rightHeadlight.place(busBodyBottom);
                    topGrill = new RectangularSolid(23, 10, 54, 5, Color.white);
                    topGrill.place(busBodyBottom);
                    bottomGrill = new RectangularSolid(23, 18, 54, 5,
                                                   Color.white);
                    bottomGrill.place(busBodyBottom);
                    leftTire = new RectangularSolid(15, 110, 15, 15,
                                                   Color.black);
                    leftTire.place(window);
                    rightTire = new RectangularSolid(90, 110, 15, 15,
                                                   Color.black);
                    rightTire.place(window);
                    window.show();
                }
        }
```

The SchoolBus class includes instance variables for the display window (window), the body of the bus (busBodyTop and busBodyBottom), the windows (leftWindow and rightWindow), the tires (leftTire and rightTire), the grille (topGrill and bottomGrill), and the headlights (leftHeadlight and rightHeadlight). Most of the code in the SchoolBus constructor is devoted to instantiating the various objects and placing them on the proper background objects. The prior design work was essential so that the programmer knows such things as the behavior of the place method and the order of the parameters of the various constructors.

For example, the school bus coordinates must be understood and matched to the proper parameters. Figure O1.10 gives better insight into the correct coordinates by showing the school bus image on top of a grid of squares are drawn 10 units apart.

Figure O1.10 School bus image on a 10-unit grid

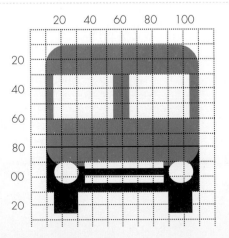

The SchoolBus class also underscores the importance of library classes. In an object-oriented environment, software developers need to be aware of software classes that are already available. The window object is of type JFrame, and the program calls the following JFrame methods:

- JFrame is a parameterless constructor.
- setBounds establishes, respectively, x, y, width, and height of the position and dimensions.
- getContentPane returns the inner drawing region of a JFrame, and setLayout establishes a layout manager for drawing.
- show causes the JFrame to become visible on the computer screen.

The SchoolBus constructor uses another standard class, called Color, to provide color constants. The Color.black and Color.white expressions represent their corresponding color values.

Java permits the use of **import declarations** to make it more convenient to use library classes from Java packages. The following import declaration is found at the beginning of the SchoolBus class:

```
import java.awt.Color;
```

This import declaration indicates to the compiler that all the classes from the java.awt package should be available throughout the SchoolBus class. One such class is Color. Similarly, the following declaration declares the availability of all classes from the javax.swing package, including JFrame.

```
import javax.swing.*;
```

O1.5 PROGRAM EXECUTION: OBJECT DIAGRAMS

Once a Java application is fully implemented and all classes are compiled, the resulting *.class* files are encoded in bytecode format so that they can be executed by a **Java virtual machine**. The virtual machine executes a program by executing each statement in the order that is dictated by the code. A class defines the *potential* state and behavior of objects, but it isn't until execution time that the actual state and behavior are realized.

Suppose that the following command is issued to begin the execution of the school bus application:

```
java BusApplication
```

This command causes the main method of the *BusApplication.class* file to begin executing. Recall that there is one and only one statement in this main method:

```
SchoolBus schoolBus = new SchoolBus();
```

The execution of this statement causes an object of type SchoolBus to be instantiated, and the local variable, called schoolBus, to reference the object. The resulting execution-time state can be pictured as shown in Figure O1.11.

Figure O1.11 An early object diagram for the school bus application

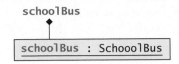

An **object diagram** depicts objects as shaded rectangles. Underlined inside the rectangle is the name of the variable for this object, followed by a colon, followed by the name of the object's class. To further illustrate the connection between variable and object, a line extends from the variable name to the object's rectangle. This line has a diamond on the variable end.

The object diagram notation shown in Figure O1.11 is part of a much larger collection of diagrammatic notations known as the **Unified Modeling Language (UML)**. UML is the most widely used among all graphical techniques for visualizing software artifacts. Rather than a single graphical form, UML contains many forms for various purposes. The notation for object diagrams is one such graphical form, as is the class diagram notation used in Figure O1.7.

Object diagrams capture the state of objects at one instant in time. As execution proceeds, the resulting object diagrams can, and usually do, change. When the SchoolBus constructor is called, the following two statements are executed:

```
window = new JFrame();
window.setBounds(10, 10, 130, 150);
```

These statements instantiate an instance variable, called window, and assign it a position and dimensions. Figure O1.12 shows the proper object diagram to illustrate the state of computation immediately following the execution of these two statements.

Figure O1.12 Object diagram following two statements from SchoolBus

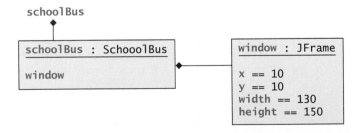

Figure O1.12 shows that a second object (window) has been created. The word window in the schoolBus rectangle denotes that window is an instance variable of the schoolBus object. The line connecting the two objects symbolizes the fact that the window variable references the object to its right. When instance variables are primitive, it is common to show their value within the object, as shown with the x, y, width, and height values of the window object.

The SchoolBus method continues to execute the following statements. These four statements create two more objects as pictured in the object diagram in Figure O1.13.

```
busBodyTop = new RoundRectangularSolid(10, 10, 100, 100,
                                Color.black);
busBodyTop.place(window);
leftWindow = new RectangularSolid(5, 20, 41, 30, Color.white);
leftWindow.place(busBodyTop);
```

Figure O1.13 Object diagram following four statements from `SchoolBus`

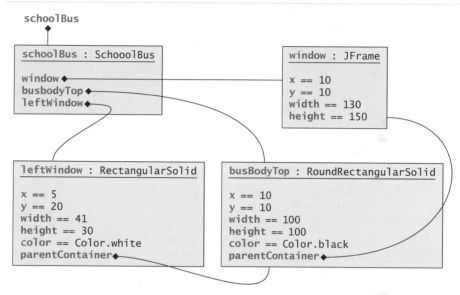

This last object diagram reveals the `leftWindow` and `busBodyTop` objects, which are referenced by instance variables from `schoolBus`. The `color` attribute of these new objects is not a primitive data type, but it is still conveniently symbolized in the containing object's rectangle. The two solid objects in Figure O1.14 also include a new variable called `parentContainer`, which denotes the background object on which each is placed. Placing the diamond end of a line segment immediately after a variable name, such as `parentContainer`, helps to clarify the particular variable associated with the reference line.

O1.6 TESTING AND DEBUGGING

Software that does not perform as desired is of little or no value. A program **fault** is an error (bug) in the code that causes the program to misbehave under certain circumstances. Software faults range in importance from annoying (such as a chess program that cannot recognize when a checkmate has occurred) to costly (such as a banking program that miscalculates interest) to life-threatening (such as mal-functioning airplane guidance software).

Software testing is the process of identifying software faults. The competent programmer tries to craft code that works, and the competent tester tries to make the code fail. Of course, the reason for finding failures is to correct the errors. The complete process of testing and correcting is commonly referred to as **debugging**.

Software testing is performed throughout the software development process. As they are produced, software design documents are typically tested by way of a **design review**. In this test, several software developers review the design to look for such things as missing objects, incomplete classes, design inconsistencies, and additional possibilities for reuse.

Component testing is a kind of testing that seeks to debug a single software unit, such as a class, in isolation from the remainder of the program. The programmer typically writes a separate software driver, called a **test harness**, that is intended to exercise the tested software in as many ways as is prudent.

Once the individual software components are fully debugged, it is time to proceed to **integration testing**. As its name implies, integration testing involves combining the separate software classes into the intended software program and testing the complete program.

> ### Software Engineering Hint
>
> One way to provide a simple test harness for a class is to include a main method of the following form.
>
> ```
> public class MyClass {
>     public static void main(String[]
>                             args) {
>
>         new MyClass();
>     }
>     ...
> }
> ```
>
> This allows the class to be instantiated as though it were an application.

Tests in the form of design reviews, component testing, and integration testing are generally performed by the company responsible for the software development. In large software projects, these forms of testing are often followed by **beta testing**, which is performed by software users. Software beta testing is similar to sneak previews of movies in that it gives the software company a way to assess customer reaction. However, the purpose of beta testing extends beyond that of movie previews. A good beta test program helps to uncover software faults or poor design decisions before final release of the program.

Many people play key roles in the complete testing process. Design reviews are often directed by the designer, but several other individuals are included. Individual programmers often perform **desk checks** of their software to informally investigate possible errors even before the software executes. One type of desk check is to use object diagrams to visually trace the execution of a small segment of code, as shown in Section O1.5.

Component testing may be the responsibility of the programmer who wrote the component, or separate testers may perform component testing. Integration testing typically involves programmers who did not write the code, although the writers also may be involved. Most beta testers aren't software developers because the goal of beta testing is to gain the perspective of the end user.

Testing also involves varying levels of formality. Desk checks and design reviews may involve ad hoc approaches. Component testing can be either **functional testing** (also known as **black box testing**) or **structure testing** (also known as **white box testing**). Functional testing relies on specifications of software behavior; the tester tries to exercise various behaviors (functions) of the software under as many different circumstances (states) as possible. Structure testing, on the other hand, focuses on exercising the various code structures. For example, a structure test is likely to test each *if* statement to ensure that the *then* clause and the *else* clause have been exercised.

Maintaining careful records of what has been tested is important for functional testing as well as structure testing. Each separate **test case** should be recorded along with the various behaviors or structures being exercised. Testers often store all software and files associated with their test cases so that these tests can be reapplied after future program modifications. This reapplication of software tests is so common that it has its own name: **regression testing**.

Sometimes test cases are collected into a group known as a **test suite**. For example, a customer who is purchasing software might construct a test suite. The process of checking a program to see whether it passes (properly executes) a test suite is called software **validation**.

Software Engineering Hint

Good software testing is a crucial part of good software development. Programmers must never assume that their code is correct. Instead, a good software engineer knows that it is essential to test software from the beginning and throughout the development process using many test cases.

An even more rigorous approach to software validation is **verification**. A careful program verification is similar to a mathematical proof. The verification is constructed from formal arguments using axioms and theorems that define programming language semantics. Program verification relies on precise software specifications.

O1.7 JAVA APPLETS

Section O1.2 mentions that Java supports two methods for initiating program execution and, correspondingly, two different kinds of programs. Thus far, program examples have taken the form of Java applications. Applications are quite similar in form to programs written in non-object-oriented programming languages—so much so that the C and C++ programming languages even use the same main method to initiate program execution.

The developers of Java felt that a different kind of program was important for delivering programs across a network. The so-called **applet** is a program that is specifically intended to be executed by a Web browser such as Netscape Navigator or Internet Explorer.

Web browsers are programs that display Web pages within a browser window on a computer display. Web pages are encoded in a kind of typesetting notation known as **Hypertext Mark-up Language (HTML)**.

HTML uses special symbols, known as **tags**, to control the page layout. (This text does not include a complete discussion of HTML tags.) The applet tag that begins the execution of an applet is written as follows:

```
<APPLET CODE = "XYZ.class" WIDTH=someInteger HEIGHT=someInteger>
</APPLET>
```

These lines cause the browser to execute an applet called *XYZ*. Typically, this applet file is in the same folder as the HTML file with the associated applet tag. If the applet file is elsewhere, then *XYZ* must include the complete file directory path name for the applet file. Figure O1.14 contains the text of an HTML file that will initiate the execution of the AppletStarter applet, assuming both files are in the same folder.

Figure O1.14 go.html

go.html:

```
<HTML>
<HEAD>
<TITLE>Example of how to use a Java Applet</TITLE>
</HEAD>
<BODY>
<APPLET CODE = "AppletStarter.class" WIDTH=120 HEIGHT=125>
</APPLET>
</BODY>
</HTML>
```

When the *go.html* file is displayed by a Web browser, the result is to activate the execution of the AppletStarter applet, where AppletStarter is a separate Java class that obeys the rules for a Java applet. Many of the applet rules are restrictions imposed by the nature of Web browser usage. Because a Web browser receives Web pages from remote servers, certain precautions must be observed so that the servers are not permitted to deliver pages that could corrupt the **client** (receiving) computer. For these kinds of security reasons, an applet is not permitted to perform such tasks as storing data on the disk drive of the client computer.

Another difference between an applet and an application is that every applet is implicitly associated with a graphical region. When the applet executes, this region is displayed in the browser window. The WIDTH and HEIGHT options in the APPLET tag establish the initial dimensions for this applet window. For example, Figure O1.14 specifies that the applet's graphical region is 120 pixels wide and 125 pixels high.

The applet class (AppletStarter in this example) is required to inherit a standard Java class called Applet from the java.applet package. You control the execution of an applet by including some or all of four parameterless, void methods within the applet class:

- init() is called when the browser first loads the HTML page with the applet tag.
- start() is called each time the applet's HTML page is displayed.
- stop() is called each time the Web browser stops displaying the applet's HTML page.
- destroy() is called each time the Web browser is no longer maintaining the applet's HTML page.

If a newly selected HTML page contains an applet tag, the applet's constructor is called, followed by its init method, followed by its start method. If the user subsequently selects a different Web page, the running applet's stop method is automatically called to notify the applet that it is no longer displayed in the Web browser.

Web browsers often maintain recently displayed pages in cache (a kind of quick-reference storage). As long as an applet's HTML page is maintained in cache, the start method will be called each time the user reselects the page. At some time the browser will be finished maintaining the applet's HTML page—perhaps because the page isn't recent enough to qualify for caching or because the browser is about to quit executing. When this occurs, the browser calls the applet's `destroy` method to notify the applet that it should complete its execution.

Programmers use the `init`, `start`, `stop`, and `destroy` methods to synchronize an applet's behavior with the Web browser. The `init` method should provide the code necessary to initiate applet execution. The `stop` method should perform tasks, such as closing external windows created by the applet. A `start` method might need to reopen external windows that were closed by a prior call to `stop`. The `destroy` method must perform any necessary final cleanup.

Figure O1.15 contains an `AppletStarter` class for the school bus program. The code in `AppletStarter` is similar to that of the `SchoolBus` class in Figure O1.9. The differences between these two classes point out key differences between applications and applets. The `AppletStarter` class includes `extends Applet` at the end of its "class line" in order to inherit `Applet`. The `AppletStarter` class also includes `init` and `start` methods to initiate the applet's execution. These two methods replace the `main` method used by applications. In this case the `init` method constructs and places all the school bus objects so that the `start` method needs only to call `repaint` to display them.

Another key difference between the classes is that unlike `SchoolBus`, the `AppletStarter` class includes no separate `JFrame` variable (`window`). Instead, the program uses of the window that is built into every applet. This built-in window is evident from statements such as

```
resize(120, 125);
```

This statement applies the `resize` method to the built-in window. Similarly, the following statement causes the `busBodyTop` object to be placed on the applet's built-in window.

```
busBodyTop.place(this);
```

Figure O1.15 AppletStarter class

```
import java.applet.*;
import java.awt.*;
public class AppletStarter extends Applet {
    private CircularSolid leftHeadlight, rightHeadlight;
    private RoundRectangularSolid busBodyTop;
    private RectangularSolid leftWindow, rightWindow, topGrill,
    bottomGrill, leftTire, rightTire;
    private RectangularSolid busBodyBottom;
    /* post: a window is constructed and the icon of a school bus
            displayed. */
    public void init() {
        resize(120, 125);
        setLayout(null);
        busBodyTop = new RoundRectangularSolid(10, 10, 100, 100,
                                        Color.black);
        busBodyTop.place(this);
```

Continued on next page

```
        leftWindow = new RectangularSolid(5, 20, 41, 30,
                                        Color.white);
        leftWindow.place(busBodyTop);
        rightWindow = new RectangularSolid(54, 20, 41, 30,
                                        Color.white);
        rightWindow.place(busBodyTop);
        busBodyBottom = new RectangularSolid(10, 80, 100, 30,
                                        Color.black);
        busBodyBottom.place(this);
        leftHeadlight = new CircularSolid(5, 8, 15, 15,
                                        Color.white);
        leftHeadlight.place(busBodyBottom);
        rightHeadlight = new CircularSolid(80, 8, 15, 15,
                                        Color.white);
        rightHeadlight.place(busBodyBottom);
        topGrill = new RectangularSolid(23, 10, 54, 5, Color.white);
        topGrill.place(busBodyBottom);
        bottomGrill = new RectangularSolid(23, 18, 54, 5,
                                        Color.white);
        bottomGrill.place(busBodyBottom);
        leftTire = new RectangularSolid(15, 110, 15, 15,
                                        Color.black);
        leftTire.place(this);
        rightTire = new RectangularSolid(90, 110, 15, 15,
                                        Color.black);
        rightTire.place(this);
    }
    public void start() {
        repaint();
    }
}
```

A couple of additional minor differences between SchoolBus and AppletStarter stem from the fact that SchoolBus uses an object of type JFrame from the javax.swing package, whereas the built-in graphics region of an applet is based on the Frame class from the java.awt package. AppletStarter calls repaint rather than show, and there is no need for getContentPane in AppletStarter.

One word of caution is in order regarding Java applets. Web browsers are designed to receive Web pages from external servers. Most Web browsers can display Web pages directly from a local file system, but sometimes they cannot do so properly for Java applets. An SDK tool called **appletviewer** provides one reliable way to execute an applet directly from a shell/command line. For example, the following command will properly execute the previously examined school bus applet.

```
appletviewer go.html
```

This command assumes that the compiled version (i.e., the *.class* files) for AppletStarter, CircularSolid, RectangularSolid, and RoundRectangularSolid are all included in the same directory with the go.html file.

THE SOFTWARE INSPECTOR

Software engineering teaches that the most productive way to improve code quality is to perform frequent and thorough **desk checks**. A desk check consists of manually scrutinizing various program-related documents, including specifications, design documents and code. This section offers a checklist of items (related to the chapter) worth considering when you're making a desk check.

✓ Software development begins with a statement of the program's requirements. Before you try to craft a program, you should scrutinize your requirements documents for completeness and precision.

✓ For most software projects, design should be separated from implementation. Devoting serious attention to design reduces both the time spent implementing and the overall development time.

✓ Reviewing OOD Step 1 consists of comparing the list of objects to the software requirements. The goal of this review is to uncover any forgotten objects.

✓ During design reviews, remember to check for the need for a separate object to serve as driver.

✓ Reviewing OOD Step 2 consists of checking for more ways to group objects. Combining more objects reduces the number of classes and often leads to a better design.

✓ During design reviews, you should look for opportunities to reuse existing classes.

✓ Reviewing OOD Step 3 consists of examining class diagrams. All the following are appropraite considerations for this stage of design review:

- Has every class been designed?
- Is the list of each class's attributes (instance variables) sufficient to describe all possible states?
- Is each class's method list sufficient to provide for the necessary object behavior?

✓ Every design review should include a search for objects not yet considered. The sooner you discover hidden objects, the better.

✓ When you're reviewing an implementation, object diagrams are a good tool for exploring run-time scenarios.

✓ You should perform testing often at all stages of software development:

- Component testing examines the individual parts of an implementation, and integration testing exercises the connections between the parts.

Core Concepts O1

- Black-box testing explores correctness in terms of external behavior, and white-box testing explores more thorough testing of the code innards.

- Informal testing, such as design reviews, can be performed more quickly and frequently; and formal verification is costly but yields more confidence regarding the correctness of the code.

- Testing by software developers is more rigorous and comprehensive, and beta testing tends to uncover issues that concern the end user.

EXERCISES

1. Suppose that you have been asked to create a program that draws an image of a camera like the one shown below. Perform all three steps of the OOD process given in Figure O1.3. Show the objects and classes that are required in your solution, and discuss which library classes might be helpful.

2. For each of the following parts, identify the type of testing that best pertains from the following choices: *component test*, *integration test*, *black-box test*, *white-box test*, and *design review*.

   a. This type of testing might ensure that every statement is exercised in at least one test case.

   b. The test cases for such a test do not require knowledge of the code, so they can be written in parallel with the implementation.

   c. This type of testing occurs when a programmer writes test cases to ensure that his or her software class is working before releasing the code for use by other classes in the project.

   d. This type of testing is often performed before program implementation begins.

Core Concepts 01

3. Use the following Java class to complete parts (a) through (e).

```java
public class Money {
    /* invariant:A MoneyUSA object maintains a monetary amount as
       an integer count of dollars, quarters, dimes, nickels,
       and pennies and dollars>=0 and quarters>=0 and dimes>=0
       and nickels>=0 and pennies>=0 */
    private int dollars;
    private int quarters;
    private int dimes;
    private int nickels;
    private int pennies;

    /* pre:   dol>=0 and q>=0 and di>=0 and n>=0 and p>=0
       post:  dollars == dol and quarters == q and dimes == di
              and nickels == n and pennies == p */
    public Money(int dol, int q, int di, int n, int p) {
        dollars = dol;
        quarters = q;
        dimes = di;
        nickels = n;
        pennies = p;
    }
    /* post:  result == dollars*100+quarters*25+dimes*10
                        +nickels*5+pennies */
    public int valueInCents() {
        return dollars*100+quarters*25+dimes*10+nickels*5+pennies;

    }
    /* post:  result == (dollars*100+quarters*25+dimes*10
                        +nickels*5+pennies)/100 */
    public double valueInDollars() {
        return valueInCents() / 100.0;
    }
    /* post:  valueInCents() == valueInCents()@pre
              and 0<=pennies<=4 and 0<=nickels<=1
              and 0<=dimes<=2
              and 0<=quarters<=3 */
    public void consolidate() {
        int remainingCents = valueInCents();
        dollars = remainingCents / 100;
        remainingCents = remainingCents % 100;
        quarters = remainingCents / 25;
        remainingCents = remainingCents % 25;
        dimes = remainingCents / 10;
        remainingCents = remainingCents % 10;
```

Continued on next page

```
        nickels = remainingCents / 5;
        pennies = remainingCents % 5;
    }


    /* post:   The amount of each denomination (dollars through
                cents) has been appended to the standard output
                stream, one line per denomination. */
    public void printByDenomination() {
        System.out.println( "Dollars: " + dollars );
        System.out.println( "Quarters: " + quarters );
        System.out.println( "Dimes: " + dimes );
        System.out.println( "Nickels: " + nickels );
        System.out.println( "Pennies: " + pennies );
    }


    /* post:   result == $dd.cc where dd is valueInCents()/100
                and cc is valueInCents() % 100 */
    public String toString() {
        return "$" + valueInCents()/100 + "." + valueInCents() %
        100;
    }
}
```

a. List all the instance variables from this class.

b. List all the methods from this class.

c. Select the best classification for each method from the following list: *constructor*, *query*, or *update*.

d. Write another class that can be used as a Java application that uses Money. Your class should do the following:

   • Declare and instantiate a Money object consisting of one dollar, five quarters, one dime, four nickels, and one penny.

   • Output the value of this Money object.

   • Call the consolidate method on the Money object.

   • Output the final value of this Money object.

e. Write a class that turns the application written in part (d) into an applet.

4. Using the Money class from Exercise 3, draw an object diagram that pictures the result of executing the following code.

```
Money sarasCash, joesCash;
joesCash = new Money(1, 2, 3, 4, 5);
sarasCash = new Money(6, 7, 8, 9, 0);
```

5. List and describe all the different instances of objects of type Money that can be identified in a typical grocery store operation.

PROGRAMMING EXERCISES

1. Design, implement, and test a program to draw a skyscraper of user-specified height. Your skyscraper must have a roof that appears as follows.

The first story of the building has the following appearance.

All intermediate floors have the following form.

The user specifies the number of stories (one or more) in the skyscraper, and the program draws the picture in response. For example, a five-story building should appear as follows.

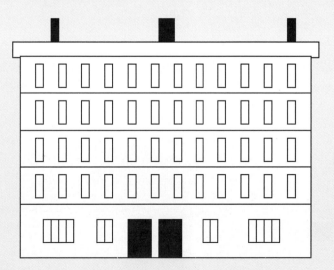

2. Design, implement, and test a program that implements an electronic checkbook. This checkbook accepts user input in the form of checks and deposits.

Every deposit includes a date and an amount. Every check includes a date, a description, the check identification number, and an amount. The checkbook must maintain a running balance along with a deposit balance and a withdrawal balance (total of checks). Use OOP techniques to design appropriate classes to support this effort.

3. Design, implement, and test a program that implements a four-function integer calculator. The calculator must allow the user to type numbers one digit at a time. For example, the user types 1, followed by 2, followed by 7 to specify the number 127. The user can also press an operation key (either +, –, *, or /). In addition, the user can press C for clear and = to perform operations, as in an ordinary calculator. For example, the user enters the following to add 25 and 17.

2, 5, +, 1, 7, =

The calculator must output the same thing that an ordinary calculator would display. If you know how to use javax.swing, you can implement this program with JButtons and a graphical display window.

SOFTWARE SPECIFICATIONS

OBJECTIVES

- To survey various types of software specifications, including requirements, user manuals, online help, object diagrams, class diagrams, and method specifications, examining the different applications for each type

- To present the UML notation for class diagrams, including notation for aggregation, inheritance, and association connections

- To summarize a notation for expression assertions that is based on Object Constraint Language notation

- To introduce the Java `assert` statement

- To examine programming by contract using assertions

- To explore several patterns that describe common assertion forms

- To present a format for method specifications based on method signatures, preconditions, postconditions, and *modifies* clauses

- To present a notation for detailed class specifications based on method specifications and class invariants

- To propose the use of specification functions to modularize class specifications

- To propose a notation for integrating exception potential into method specifications

By itself, a command in a language such as English is neither "correct" nor "incorrect." The command "Sweep the floor" attempts to invoke a particular action, and it wouldn't make sense to find fault with the command. To evaluate a command as correct or incorrect requires a context. When you're building a model ship, the command, "Glue the propeller to the end of the propeller shaft" would seem to be a correct action, whereas the command "Glue the propeller to the end of the mast" is most likely an incorrect action.

Computer software has this same characteristic: By itself, a computer program is neither correct nor incorrect. A program is merely a collection of statements. There is nothing either right or wrong with a program that draws a red circle. The only way that we can conclude that the program is correct or incorrect is to know what behavior was intended. If the intended behavior is to draw a red circle, the program behaves correctly. If the intended behavior is to draw a green triangle, the program is faulty.

02.1 WHY SPECIFY?

Any statement that defines the intended behavior of software is called a **software specification**. Such statements as the following are informal software specifications:

- This class maintains a balanced checkbook.
- This method alphabetizes a list of employees by their names.

Both statements are valid software specifications because they apply to a particular piece of software (either a class or a method) and define what constitutes proper behavior for that software.

A software specification can be thought of as a measuring stick for the associated software in the sense that the correctness of the software is measured by its specifications. If the software class fails to maintain a balanced checkbook, it is incorrect with respect to the above specification. Similarly, if the method intended to alphabetize employees leaves one or more employees out of order, it is faulty.

Software specifications take many forms corresponding to how and when they are used during development. All the following are examples of different kinds of software specifications.

- A program requirements document
- A user manual
- Online help files
- A collection of object diagrams
- A class diagram
- A method's behavioral specification

Useful software development doesn't result from randomly rearranging the order of statements until the resulting program does something interesting. Instead, programming is performed in response to a need for software with certain desired behavior. A **requirements document** defines the overall intent of a program. Typically, the very earliest stages of a software project are devoted to discussion between the customer and various software developers in order to define software requirements. It may seem obvious that programmers cannot proceed without clear requirements, but ill-conceived requirements are still among the most common complaints by software engineers.

Just as a requirements document defines program behavior at the beginning of the software development cycle, a **user manual** often defines program behavior upon program completion. The audience is also different. Whereas requirements documents are most often read by software developers, user manuals are written for the person who will use the program (the **user**). The purpose of a user manual is to explain how the software is used (i.e., which buttons to click or menu entries to select in order to accomplish desired tasks). **Online help** contains information similar to a user manual but is designed to be displayed on a computer screen and is intended for use while the program is running.

Object diagrams, as described in Section O1.5, are quite different from requirements documents, user manuals, or online help. The most significant difference is that object diagrams are intended to describe the innards of an executing program, as opposed to its outward behavior.

If these specification techniques were applied to an automobile, the requirements documents would describe such things as the car's capacity, its maximum speed, its fuel economy, and its outward appearance. The user manual for an automobile might explain how to start the car, set the cruise control, and so forth. An object diagram for an automobile could be used to illustrate the corresponding states of spark plug, fuel injector, and piston objects.

Object diagrams also have the unique characteristic of providing a snapshot view that is time relative. Each object diagram captures a snapshot of the state of computation at a particular instant during program execution. As the program continues to execute, the snapshots change, much as a motion picture can be constructed from a sequence of individual snapshots. Their snapshot nature makes object diagrams impractical for overall software specifications, but they are useful in tracing program execution.

You can overcome the inability of an object diagram to capture more than a fleeting moment by using a **class diagram**. Class diagrams, described more fully in Section O2.2, specify key information about the attributes and methods of classes along with relationships among classes, thereby providing a specification for all objects belonging to each specified class.

Because the behavior of any class depends upon the class's methods, **method specifications** are a popular way to describe methods. Each method specification focuses on the behavior of a single method, as shown in Section O2.6.

Software specifications are used to communicate among the various players in a software development project. A requirements document communicates the necessary specifications from the customer to software developers. User manuals and online help communicate information that the programmers wish to convey to users. An object diagram is a good way for programmers to communicate with themselves in a desk check or for an instructor to describe a programming technique to a student. Class diagrams and method specifications are used by designers wishing to communicate software specifications to implementers, or by implementers sharing specifications with each other. Figure O2.1 summarizes communication possibilities by listing who typically creates each kind of specification and who typically reads them.

Figure O2.1 Six different styles of specifications

Specification	Creator	Readers	Purpose
Requirements document	Customer (possibly with assistance)	Software developers	Convey the customer's wishes for behavior of the program
User manual	Software developers	Users	Explain how to properly use the program
Online help	Software developers	Users	Provide assistance for anyone running the program
Object diagram	Software developers	Software developers	Provide a visual image of a single state of computation (i.e., a snapshot of object state)
Class diagram	Designer or implementer	Software developers	Illustrate key features of classes and their relations to other classes
Method specification	Designer or implementer	Software developers	Specify detailed expectations for the run-time behavior of the method

This book explores various software design and implementation techniques. Therefore, object diagrams, class diagrams, method specifications, and the associated concept of class specifications are all used throughout the presentation. Other specification techniques, such as requirements documents, user manuals, and online help, are largely outside the scope of this book.

O2.2 CLASS DIAGRAMS

The adage "A picture is worth a thousand words" explains why many specifications take pictorial form. Two of the most common pictorial specification forms—object diagrams and class diagrams—are part of the Unified Modeling Language (UML). (See *The Unified Modeling Language Reference Manual*, Rumbaugh, Jacobson, and Booch, Addison-Wesley.) This section examines the UML notation for class diagrams. (An introduction to object diagrams is given in Chapter O1.)

Figure O2.2 contains a class diagram for the Point class from the standard java.awt package. A **class diagram** is drawn as a rectangle containing three compartments, separated by horizontal lines. The top compartment contains the name of the class—in this case Point. The middle compartment contains the attributes (instance variables) of the class. The bottom compartment lists the methods of the class.

Figure O2.2 java.awt.Point class diagram

```
                          Point

        + int x
        + int y

    «constructor»
        + Point()
        + Point(int x, int y)
        + Point(Point p)

    «query»
        + boolean equals(Object p)
        + double getX()
        + double getY()
        + Point getLocation()
        + String toString()

    «update»
        + void setLocation(int x, int y)
        + void setLocation(double x, double y)
        + void place( Container )
        + void translate(int x, int y)
        ...
```

Each class member (i.e., each instance variable or method) included in a class diagram is written on a separate line along with its type and parameter list, using the same notation as a Java program. The "+" symbol in front of each member indicates its scope. ("+" denotes public, "−" denotes private, and "#" denotes protected scope.) It is common to group methods into classifications in a class diagram. The most commonly used group headings are «constructor», «query», and «update».

Class diagrams can be incomplete. The Point class diagram is incomplete in the sense that it fails to include all the methods of the class. The three dots (...) at the bottom of the diagram emphasize the fact that some of the class methods have been omitted. (Incomplete class diagrams sometimes do not include the three-dot notation.)

UML class diagram notation also includes symbols to indicate relationships among classes. Figure O2.3 illustrates the three most common relationships. This diagram describes a standard class called Polygon that is found in the java.awt package.

The line segments that connect Polygon to the other four classes mean that Polygon is related in some way to each of these classes. The three types of line segments indicate three different kinds of relationships.

A line with a diamond on the end denotes **aggregation**. A class is said to be an aggregate when it includes instance variables, and the aggregate line connects

Figure O2.3 java.awt.Polygon class diagram including class relationships

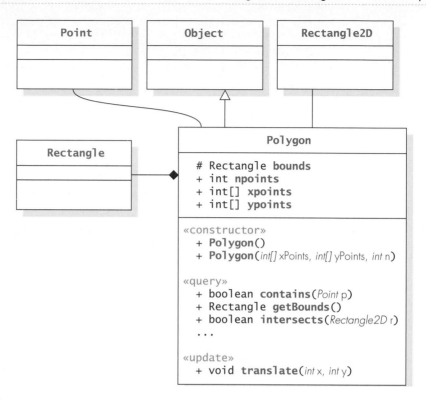

the aggregate class with the variable's class (with the diamond end on the aggregate class). Figure O2.3 uses this notation to indicate that Polygon contains a variable (bounds) that is of type Rectangle. A similar diamond-ended aggregate line notation is used in object diagrams.

An arrow in a class diagram denotes an **inheritance relation**. The arrow must always point from the subclass to its superclass. Figure O2.3 shows that Polygon inherits the Object class. (Inheritance is explored in Chapter O3.)

Although aggregation and inheritance are the two closest relationships between two classes, sometimes one class requires another class without aggregation or inheritance. For example, the Polygon class uses the Point class and the Rectangle2D class as parameter types. Therefore, Polygon is related to these two classes. Any relation other than aggregation and inheritance can be called an **association relation** and is symbolized as a simple line segment.

Figure O2.3 shows the somewhat informal nature of class diagrams. The Point class included in Figure O2.3 is the same class from Figure O2.2. In the later class diagram, the author has chosen to omit all the instance variables and methods of this class. This kind of abbreviation is acceptable in order to emphasize selected other software characteristics.

At first it may seem that class diagrams are somewhat similar to object diagrams. However, about the only thing the two notations have in common is that they both include instance variables and they both diagram aggregation. The key differences stem from the fact that object diagrams picture **dynamic** characteristics, whereas class diagrams picture characteristics that are **static**. Object diagrams are called *dynamic* because their information is transient; an object diagram must be redrawn to match changes resulting from software execution. Class diagrams are said to be *static* because their information is fixed (i.e., not altered during program execution).

Class diagrams contain only the name and type of a variable, as opposed to object diagrams, which show the value of the variable. The variable's name and type are static information, whereas the variable's value is dynamic. Class diagrams also picture methods, inheritance relationships and association relationships, which are static and are not included in object diagrams. In addition to the extra information within class diagrams, the other advantage of a static specification is that it is applicable to *all* executions of the software and not only to one possible instant during program execution.

Even though class diagrams contain more information than object diagrams, they still omit considerable information. A class diagram specifies the names and types of instance variables, but it doesn't indicate how the variables will be used nor provide limits on the potential values of variables. A class diagram contains the method's parameter list and return type but never explains the method's behavior. This incompleteness is analogous to an architectural blueprint that omits measurements. It isn't possible to construct the building from the blueprint without more information.

Even an incomplete blueprint, however, is useful for demonstrating basic structure and key relationships. Similarly, class diagrams, incomplete as they may be, are still useful, especially during software design. The relationship lines in a class diagram indicate key interdependencies. The methods listed for each class specify how various run-time responsibilities have been parceled to various classes. The attributes of each class strongly indicate how the class maintains its state. The scope symbols indicate which class members are available to other program components.

Class diagrams are best considered to be partial specifications. A class diagram shows useful "big picture" information to programmers. However, in practice, class diagrams must be augmented with considerable detail in order to be considered complete specifications. Section O2.7 suggests such an augmentation technique.

O2.3 A LANGUAGE FOR EXPRESSING SPECIFICATIONS

Class diagrams and object diagrams are useful software development tools, but as Section O2.2 explains, these two notations are insufficient to produce complete software specifications. But what notation should you use in order to be more comprehensive? To investigate this question it is best to begin by identifying the necessary qualities of a good specification.

Section O2.1 describes software specifications as both a measuring stick and a tool for communication. These two perspectives give rise to the two primary qualities of specifications. A good software specification must be both precise and readable. An imprecise measuring stick is of little utility, and an unreadable document doesn't support effective communication.

Often programmers resort to natural languages, such as English, to express software specifications. Natural languages should meet the need for readability, because these languages were created so that humans can communicate. Unfortunately, natural language specifications are rarely precise. For example, consider the specifications included with the Sun Microsystems' SDK documentation for a method called getChars from the standard java.lang.String class (shown in Figure O2.4).

Figure O2.4 The getChars specifications from Sun documentation

getChars
```
    public void getChars( int srcBegin,
                          int srcEnd,
                          char[] dst,
                          int dstBegin)
```
Copies characters from this string into the destination character array.

The first character to be copied is at index srcBegin; the last character to be copied is at index srcEnd-1 (thus the total number of characters to be copied is srcEnd-srcBegin). The characters are copied into the subarray of dst starting at index dstBegin and ending at index:

```
    dstBegin + (srcEnd-srcBegin) - 1
```

(END OF SPECIFICATION)

The specification continues to indicate that all of the following are erroneous calls to getChar:

- srcBegin is negative
- srcBegin is greater than srcEnd
- srcEnd is greater than the length of this string
- dstBegin is negative
- dstBegin+(srcEnd-srcBegin) is larger than dst.length
- dst is null

Like most of the Sun documentation, the getChars specification is reasonably good. However, it can still be criticized for lacking precise definitions of key terminology and containing ambiguities. Terms such as "index" and "subarray" are used without adequate definition. The reader must be aware that "index" refers to a sequence number of constituent String characters, that the leftmost character has an index of zero, and that each String character position has an index 1 greater than the position to its left. The term "subarray" also can lead to confusion unless the reader knows that it refers to a contiguous sequence of cells from another array.

The specification states that getChars "copies characters from this string into the destination character array." However, this can lead to ambiguities regarding the exact placement of the copied characters. Even though the later part of the definition explains clearly where the first and last characters are copied, it is not so clear about the characters that lie between the first and the last characters. Arguably, the definition also lacks clarity for the situation when srcBegin == srcEnd.

These criticisms of the `getChars` specification may seem unnecessarily fussy, but they illustrate how even a fairly simple method can be difficult to specify in a natural language. Imagine how much more difficult it is to be precise in a natural language specification for a complicated program!

As further evidence of the deficiencies of specifications expressed in natural languages, consider their use in expressing legal documents. Legal documents typically are verbose and often require interpretation by a court of law. Clearly, software specifications will not be useful if they share these characteristics of legal documents.

It is also tempting to ask a program to serve as its own specifications. Programming languages are precise by their very nature; otherwise, they would be useless for expressing computer algorithms. In a sense, a program is the ultimate authority for its own behavior. One way to ascertain the behavior of a program is to execute it and discover its behavior through a series of experiments.

The first problem with using a program as its own specification is that you lose the utility of the specification as a measuring stick. You cannot determine whether code is correct unless there is a separate specification to define correctness. (Measuring the length of a yardstick with the same yardstick isn't very productive.)

The second deficiency of expressing specifications in the notation of a programming language can be illustrated by an example. Figure O2.5 contains the code for a method that is part of a class called `Fraction`. The `Fraction` class is fully specified in later sections of this chapter.

Figure O2.5   The sum method

```
public Fraction sum(Fraction f) {
    Fraction result;
    int newNumerator = numerator*f.denom() + f.numer()*denominator;
    int newDenominator = denominator * f.denom();
    if (newDenominator >= 0) {
        result = new Fraction(newNumerator, newDenominator);
    } else {
        result = new Fraction(-newNumerator, -newDenominator);
    }
    result.simplify();
    return result;
}
```

As with all nontrivial software, the code for the `sum` method isn't easy to read. It would take longer for even a knowledgeable Java programmer to fully comprehend these 12 lines of code than it would to read a 12-line paragraph. The name of the method, `sum`, along with the use of `Fraction`, `denominator`, and `numerator` provide strong clues to the behavior of `sum`. However, the reason for the *if* statement may be unclear. The `sum` method's readability is further impaired by a lack of context. It simply isn't possible to fully understand `sum` without understanding the `numer`, `denom`, and `simplify` methods that it uses.

Because programs aren't suitable as their own specification and because reading code can be tedious, computer scientists have turned elsewhere for specification languages. The precision of various mathematical notations has served as a common basis for most popular software specification languages such as Z (pronounced "zed"), Object Z, Larch, and VDM. These and similar languages are called **formal specification languages** because of their precise (i.e., formal) symbolism. Formal specification languages can be excellent tools for design. However, they have yet to find widespread acceptance, in part because of a lack of standardization.

The **Object Constraint Language (OCL)** is another form of formalized specifications. OCL is a collection of notations first included in the Unified Modeling Language in 1997. Even though a complete presentation of OCL is beyond the scope of this book, care has been taken to use specification notation that is consistent with OCL.

It must be stated at the outset that formal notations, such as OCL, are a noble goal for expression specifications. OCL should be used as much as possible for its precision. However, sometimes a precise formal specification is too intricate to be truly readable. In such cases, a carefully structured natural language such as English is acceptable. This book uses primarily OCL with occasional English.

Software Engineering Hint

Specifications must be *both* precise and readable. The hazard of using a natural language to express specifications is lack of precision. The potential hazard of OCL is lack of readability. As a rule, it is best to use OCL unless the expression can be stated better in a natural language. Furthermore, expressing specifications in a natural language requires great care.

Many of the notations and concepts of formal specification languages have found their way into another specification form that has become widely accepted: the **assertion**. Assertions are logical statements that borrow certain notations from programming languages. OCL can be thought of as a language for expressing assertions. For example, the following assertion borrows variables a, b, and c, along with the relational less than (<) operation.

```
a < b and a < c
```

As a logical statement, each assertion can be either true or false. As a specification, an assertion is expected (asserted) to be true. This means that each assertion describes a specific desired state of computation. The preceding assertion, for example, defines a state in which the value of variable a is less than the value of both variable b and variable c.

Throughout this textbook, assertions are expressed using four operations from prepositional logic (and also included in OCL): *and*, *or*, *not*, and *implies*. Mathematicians often use alternative symbols for these operations.

$\land$ denotes *and*

$\lor$ denotes *or*

$\lnot$ denotes *not* (alternative notations include primed expressions, horizontal lines, and ~)

$\rightarrow$ denotes *implies*

Using English words in place of the mathematical symbols lets you embed the logical operations into the simple text of most programming language comments.

The semantics of these four logical operations is reviewed in truth-table form in Figure O2.6. Assuming that P and Q refer to arbitrary subassertions, another way to interpret these tables is that a specification of the form

```
P and Q
```

means that *both* P must be true and Q must be true, as with the Java && operator. Similarly, any assertion of the logical form

P *or* Q

means that either P is true or Q is true, or both are true. This definition of *or* is like the Java || operator.

Figure O2.6 Truth tables for NOT, AND, OR, and IMPLIES

Logical Negation (assuming logical expression P)

P	*not* P
true	false
false	true

Logical Conjunction (assuming logical expressions P and Q)

P	Q	P *and* Q
true	true	true
true	false	false
false	true	false
false	false	false

Logical Disjunction (assuming logical expressions P and Q)

P	Q	P *or* Q
true	true	true
true	false	true
false	true	true
false	false	false

Logical Implication (assuming logical expressions P and Q)

P	Q	P *implies* Q
true	true	true
true	false	false
false	true	true
false	false	true

The implication (*implies*) operation deserves more explanation. Implication defines a causal relationship between its two subassertions. If the first subassertion (P) is true, then the second (Q) also must be true. However, there is a second way for an implication to be true—namely, whenever its first subassertion is false. Some people say that when P is false, the expression P *implies* Q is **vacuously true** because the causal relationship doesn't exist. In other words, when P is false, the assertion specifies nothing regarding Q. For example, consider the following assertion regarding int variables a and b.

a >= 0 *implies* a > b

This assertion is satisfied (true-valued) whenever a is nonnegative and also greater than b, as well as whenever a is negative.

Some assertions include another notation, known as **quantification**, that is borrowed from logic. There are two types of quantification: *forAll* and *exists*. The mathematical symbols are as follows:

> ∀   denotes *forAll*
> ∃   denotes *exists*

This book uses the following notation for **universal quantification** (*forAll*):

forAll (quantifiedVar : type | quantifiedExpression)

The *quantifiedVar* is called a **quantified variable** and is a mathematical variable, *not a program variable*. The inclusion of *type* is optional and is used to specify the type of the quantified variable. Often the *type* includes a restriction to a particular range of values. The *quantifiedExpression* is an assertion that includes the use of the quantified variable.

As an example of universal quantification, consider the following English specification regarding the program variable n.

n is a prime number.

The following equivalent quantified expression is more precise:

*forAll (**j** : Integer and 2 ≤ j ≤ n–1 | n % j != 0)*

As *forAll* suggests, a universally quantified expression has a value of true only when the quantified expression is true for *every* potential value of the quantified variable. Note that the *type* of the quantified variable, j, includes both the fact that it is an *Integer* and its range (from 2 through n–1).

Informally, universal quantification can be understood as a sequence of subassertions, all *and*ed together, in which each subassertion is the quantified assertion with the quantified variable replaced by one of its potential values. For example, the same assertion

*forAll (**j** : Integer and 2 ≤ j ≤ n–1 | n % j != 0)*

expands into the following sequence of subassertions:

(n % 2 != 0) *and* (n % 3 != 0) *and* (n % 4 != 0) *and* ... *and* (n % (n–1) != 0)

Existential quantification (*exists*) is used somewhat less often in assertions than universal quantification. The notation used in this text for existential quantification is similar to that of universal quantification.

exists (quantifiedVar : type | quantifiedExpression)

The meaning of such an expression is indicated by the word *exists*, which is alternatively called "there exists." As an example of existential quantification, consider the following English specification regarding the program variables a and b.

a and b share a common factor.

The equivalent, and more precise, quantified expression is as follows:

*exists (**j** : Integer and 2 ≤ j ≤ a | a% j == 0 and b % j == 0)*

An existentially quantified expression has a value of true whenever the quantified expression is true for *any* potential value of the quantified variable. Informally, existential quantification can be understood as a sequence of subassertions, all *or*ed together in which each subassertion is the quantified assertion with the quantified variable replaced by one of its potential values. This reasoning is useful for interpreting the following expression.

exists (**j** : *Integer and* $2 \leq j \leq a$ | a% j == 0 *and* b % j == 0)

This expression can be expanded into the following sequence of subassertions.

(a % 2 == 0 *and* b % 2 == 0)
or (a % 3 == 0 *and* b % 3 == 0)
or (a % 4 == 0 *and* b % 4 == 0)
or ... *or* (a % a == 0 *and* b % a == 0)

Quantified expressions are particularly helpful in expressing properties of data structures such as arrays. For example, the following assertion states that every cell of the array called `arr` stores the value 3.

forAll (**k** : *Integer and* $0 \leq k <$ arr.length | arr[k] == 3)

Similarly, the following assertion states that at least one cell of `arr` stores the value 15.

exists (**k** : *Integer and* $0 \leq k <$ arr.length | arr[k] == 15)

Often, you can omit the explicit typing information for a quantified variable. In the preceding example it is clear that k must refer to an integer because it is used as an array index. Therefore, the expression can be abbreviated as follows.

exists (**k** : $0 \leq k <$ arr.length | arr[k] == 15)

Using such an abbreviation, you can write the specification for an array that is sorted in ascending order as follows.

forAll (**k** : $0 \leq k <$ arr.length–1 | arr[k] <= arr[k+1])

To specify that the variable `max` stores the largest value of all values in `arr`, it is best to use a two-part definition: (1) max stores one of the values from the array `arr`, and (2) every value within a cell of `arr` is less than or equal to `max`. The complete assertion is as follows.

exists (**j** : $0 \leq j <$ arr.length | arr[j] == max)
and forAll (**k** : $0 \leq k <$ arr.length | arr[k] <= max)

In much the same way as implication, quantified expressions have so-called vacuous cases. These cases occur whenever it is impossible to satisfy the restrictions on the value of the quantified variable. Consider the following expression.

forAll (**k** : $n1 \leq k \leq n2$ | arr[k] < 0)

This specification can be understood to mean

arr[n1]<0 *and* arr[n1+1]<0 *and* ... *and* arr[n2]<0

But what if n1 > n2? The correct interpretation is to understand universal quantification to be *true* for such vacuous situations. Informally, it can be said that the quantified expression is true for "all" potential values of the quantified variable because there are no potential values.

On the other hand, existential quantification is correctly interpreted to be *false* in its vacuous case. The informal reasoning for this interpretation is that "there exists" cannot be true if there is no potential value for the quantified variable.

Like class diagrams, assertions are static specifications. However, each assertion has a run-time context in the sense that the assertion specifies an appropriate state for one (or sometimes more than one) run-time location within the code.

Figure O2.7 contains a segment of Java code that illustrates assertion placement. Each assertion in this figure is written in the form of a comment that begins with assert.

Figure O2.7 Two assertions within code

```
int dereksHeight, kasandrasHeight, averageHeight;
dereksHeight = 74;
kasandrasHeight = 66;
// assert: dereksHeight == 74 and kasandrasHeight == 66
averageHeight = (dereksHeight + kasandrasHeight) / 2;
// assert: averageHeight == 70
```

The first assertion in this example is placed following the three Java statements, indicating that this assertion is presumed to be true at the precise time when these statements have just completed execution. In other words, this first assertion describes the state of computation just after the variables dereksHeight and kasandrasHeight have been assigned values. The second assertion is located last, indicating that it is asserted to be true immediately after all statements have been executed.

As of SDK Version 1.4, Java includes limited language support for assertion checking. The **assert** statement includes a boolean expression that can be tested each time that the statement is encountered at run-time. For example, the Figure O2.7 code can use the assert statement as follows.

```
int dereksHeight, kasandrasHeight, averageHeight;
dereksHeight = 74;
kasandrasHeight = 66;
assert dereksHeight == 74 && kasandrasHeight == 66;
averageHeight = (dereksHeight + kasandrasHeight) / 2;
assert averageHeight == 70: "Incorrect average height";
```

This example illustrates two important characteristics of the assert statement. First, the syntax of an assert requires that its initial expression be written in the form of a boolean expression. Notice that the OCL *and* operation from Figure O2.7 is replaced with the Java && operator in the assert statement. Many OCL assertions, such as those involving quantification, do not translate conveniently into boolean expressions.

The second observation about the assert statement is that it can include an additional expression preceded by a colon. The second assert statement in the preceding example has the following additional expression: **"Incorrect average height"**. This additional (second) expression is optional, and if included it should indicate something that distinguishes this assertion from others in the program.

Software Engineering Hint

The Java assert statement can be useful for expressing testable assertions. However, its utility is limited to those expressions that can be written using Java boolean notation.

Execution of an `assert` statement begins with evaluating the initial (`boolean`) expression. If this expression is true, as expected, execution proceeds to the next statement, and the `assert` statement has had virtually no effect on program execution. However, if the initial `assert` statement is found to be false, program execution is halted with an `AssertionError` and the second expression is displayed.

The `assert` statement is designed so that programs can be executed with, and without, assertion checking. By default a program is executed without any assertion checking, and this means that at run-time all `assert` statements are ignored as though they were comments. To activate assertion checking, you must include the `-enableassertions` or the `-ea` flag. For example, to run an application *with assertion checking* from the `Driver.class`, you use by the following shell command.

```
java -ea Driver
```

Also note that for some Java compilers it may be necessary to include a `-source` `1.4` flag in the compiler command. For example, the following command ensures that the `Driver.java` file is compiled including the possibility of run-time assertion checking:

```
javac -source 1.4 Driver.java
```

Assertions, whether they are expressed as OCL comments or Java assert statements, are useful for specifying code behavior, but there is an important difference between an assertion and the code it specifies. As a logical statement, an assertion specifies *what* must be true but not *how* to make the assertion true. Code is different because the whole purpose of software is to express *how* to execute. How an assertion becomes true is a software implementation decision. There are an infinite number of code segments that will satisfy the first assertion in Figure O2.7. For example, the following code segment satisfies the same first assertion as Figure O2.7.

> ### Software Engineering Hint
>
> An assertion must define the *what* and not the *how*. In other words, every assertion must be a logical statement. The responsibility for the *how* is left to the code.

```
int dereksHeight, kasandrasHeight, averageHeight;
kasandrasHeight = 66;
dereksHeight = 74;
// assert: dereksHeight == 74 and kasandrasHeight == 66
```

This difference between assertions and code is part of the reason that assertions make good specifications. Assertions are able to suppress unnecessary details of how the program execution proceeds. The last assertion in Figure O2.7 fails to mention the values of `dereksHeight` and `kasandrasHeight`. Apparently, the values of these variables are unimportant details of how the code attains the desired specification—namely, that `averageHeight == 70`. Similarly, a software specification for a method that sorts an array need only state that the array is sorted; it does not, and often should not, indicate which sorting algorithm accomplishes the task.

O2.4 COMMON ASSERTION PATTERNS

A few patterns (forms) recur frequently in assertions. Recognizing these patterns makes it easier to express specifications in assertion form. Becoming proficient in using these patterns also leads to better-written assertions and improves assertion readability. Most of these patterns correspond to commonly used algorithms. These patterns serve as useful specification templates for both OCL and English notations, although they have their origins in logic.

> **Software Engineering Hint**
>
> The outer structure of virtually every assertion is best expressed using the fundamental assertion pattern.

The most basic pattern for assertions is known by mathematicians as **conjunctive normal form**. Figure O2.8 shows the **fundamental assertion pattern**; it consists of one or more subassertions that are conjoined (i.e., joined via the *and* operation).

Figure O2.8 Fundamental assertion pattern

Assertion Pattern Name: Fundamental Assertion Pattern

Form

    SubAssertion1 **and** *SubAssertion2* **and** *SubassertionN*

Use

    This assertion specifies that *all* of the *SubAssertions* must be true.

Note

    The pattern includes one or more *SubAssertions*, each of which is a separate assertion.

The fundamental assertion pattern occurs most frequently as a result of executing a sequence of statements that perform separate subtasks, and the assertion includes a subassertion to specify the elements of the state resulting from each subtask. For example, the following sequence of three assignments is followed by an appropriate assertion exhibiting the fundamental assertion pattern.

```
int managerCount, clerkCount, custodialCount;
managerCount = 5;
clerkCount = 100;
custodialCount = 32;
/* assert: managerCount == 5
           and clerkCount == 100
           and custodialCount == 32 */
```

The three subassertions directly parallel the three assignment statements. The correspondence between code and assertion is not always so obvious as in this example.

Because assertions are static, they must specify *every* possible outcome. As a result, subassertions frequently follow the **one option assertion pattern**, shown in Figure O2.9.

For example, suppose that a payroll program is designed to give a salesperson a bonus of $20 whenever monthly sales exceed 100 units. This situation can be specified as follows, using the integer variables monthlySales and bonusDollars.

```
// assert: monthlySales > 100 implies bonusDollars == 20
```

This assertion specifies what the software must accomplish when monthlySales is greater than 100.

Figure O2.9 One option assertion pattern

Assertion Pattern Name: One Option Assertion Pattern

Form

> *Cause* **implies** *Effect*

Use

> This assertion specifies one cause and effect relationship and is often used for sub-assertions. Each occurrence of the one option assertion pattern specifies a particular situation, *Cause*, and the state of computation that results from the situation, *Effect*.

Note

> Both *Cause* and *Effect* denote individual assertions.

The one option assertion pattern corresponds closely to the semantics of the *if-then* statement. The *Cause* subassertion corresponds to the condition of the *if-then*, and the *Effect* subassertion corresponds to the state following *the* execution of the then clause. Here is the assertion along with a corresponding *if-then*.

```
if (monthlySales > 100) {
    bonusDollars = 20;
}
// assert: monthlySales > 100 implies bonusDollars == 20
```

The behavior of an implication in the so-called vacuous case can be problematic when you use the one option assertion pattern. For example, the assertion specifies the appropriate value for bonusDollars in the event that monthlySales exceed 100, but this assertion fails to give any information about the value of bonusDollars for lesser monthlySales. There is nothing inherently wrong with the assertion, but it does appear to leave an important question unanswered. This characteristic of implication leads to a related pattern called **both options assertion pattern**. Figure O2.10 explains this pattern.

Figure O2.10 Both options assertion pattern

Assertion Pattern Name: Both Options Assertion Pattern

Form

> *Cause* **implies** *Effect1*
> **and** (**not** *Cause*) **implies** *Effect2*

Use

> This assertion specifies both options of a cause and effect relationship and is often used for subassertions. Each occurrence of the both options assertion pattern specifies a particular situation, *Cause*, and the state of computation that results from the situation, *Effect1*, along with the state of computation, *Effect2*, that results from anything except the situation characterized by *Cause*.

Note

> *Cause*, *Effect1*, and *Effect2* denote individual assertions.

Following is an example of the both options assertion pattern, along with an appropriate segment of code, both using variables a, b, and min. The relationship between the both options assertion pattern and an *if-then-else* statement is apparent in this example.

```
if (a < b) {
    min = a;
} else {
    min = b;
}
/* assert: a < b implies min == a
        and a >= b implies min == b */
```

Software developers take liberties with logic in certain cases. The both options assertions pattern demonstrates a situation in which parentheses would normally be required, or suggested, to clarify the order of logical operations. In other words, the assertion would be properly parenthesized as follows.

```
/* assert: (a < b implies min == a)
        and (a >= b implies min == b) */
```

It is acceptable to include these parentheses, but they have been omitted in this case because this is an obvious instance of the fundamental assertion pattern, and both the indentation scheme and the placement of subassertions on separate lines give clear visual clues to the intended semantics.

The **many options assertion pattern** is a natural extension of the both options assertion pattern. This new pattern is used to specify more than two alternatives. Figure O2.11 explains the pattern.

Figure O2.11 Many options assertion pattern

Assertion Pattern Name: Many Options Assertion Pattern

Form

Cause1 **implies** Effect1
and (Cause2) **implies** Effect2

. . .

and (CauseN) **implies** EffectN
and (not Cause1 **and not** Cause2 **and** ... **and not** CauseN) **implies** EffectN1

Use

This assertion specifies all options of a cause and effect relationship and is often used for subassertions. Each line, except the last, of the many options assertion pattern specifies a particular situation, CauseK, and the state of computation that results from the situation, EffectK. The final line of the assertion specifies that in the situation where none of the CauseK expressions is true, the resulting state of computation should be EffectN1

Note

Cause1, Cause2, ..., CauseN, Effect1, Effect2, ..., EffectN and EffecN1 denote individual assertions.

The many options assertion pattern corresponds to multiway selection. The following example assumes an `int` variable called `examScore` and a `char` variable called `grade`:

```
if (examScore >= 90) {
    grade = 'A';
} else if (examScore >= 80) {
    grade = 'B';
} else if (examScore >= 70) {
    grade = 'C';
} else if (examScore >= 60) {
    grade = 'D';
} else {
    grade = 'F';
}
/* assert: 90 <= examScore implies grade == 'A'
       and 80 <= examScore < 90 implies grade == 'B'
       and 70 <= examScore < 80 implies grade == 'C'
       and 60 <= examScore < 70 implies grade == 'D'
       and examScore < 60 implies grade == 'F' */
```

Quantification is often used to specify things about data structures. Arguably, the most common assertion pattern involving quantification is the subarray property assertion pattern shown in Figure O2.12.

Figure O2.12 Subarray property assertion pattern

Assertion Pattern Name: Subarray Property Assertion Pattern

Form

> **forAll**(j : *Integer* **and** lowestNdx <= j <= highestNdx | Property)

Use

This assertion specifies some *Property* that must hold for each cell in the contiguous portion of an array from the index of *lowestNdx* through *highestNdx*. Usually, *Property* refers to the jth array cell.

Note

Property denotes an assertion, and *lowestNdx* and *highestNdx* are integer expressions.

For example, consider an array to maintain the inventory of magazines for a bookstore. The following assertion specifies a situation in which there is at least one copy of every magazine in stock.

```
/* assert: forAll(j : 0 <= j <= magazineStock.length-1
                | magazineStock[j] > 0 ) */
```

The subarray property assertion pattern often corresponds to the work of a loop. For example, consider the following code, and resulting assertion, for calculating the cell-wise difference between two parallel `double` arrays called `costPerItem` and `sellingPrice`.

```
for (int m = 0; m!=11; m++) {
    profitPerItem[m] = sellingPrice[m] - costPerItem[m]
}
/* assert: forAll(k : 0 <= k <= 10 | profitPerItem[k]
                    == sellingPrice[k]-costPerItem[k]) */
```

O2.5 DESIGNING AND PROGRAMMING BY CONTRACT

Sections O2.3 and O2.4 repeatedly demonstrate the close association of assertions and software. In fact, this association is so strong that it has been termed **contractual**. The technique of using assertions to formulate software specifications is called **design by contract**, and using these assertions to guide programming is called **programming by contract**. This section examines the basics of programming by contract, and Sections O2.6 and O2.7 explore design by contract issues.

A **software contract** is expressed as two assertions: a **preliminary assertion** and a **trailing assertion**. (When used in the context of methods, it is more common to refer to the preliminary assertion as a **precondition** and the trailing assertion as a **postcondition**.) Figure O2.13 describes this contract.

Figure O2.13 The software contract

Form of the code and specifications

```
// assert: PreliminaryAssertion

CodeSegment
// assert: TrailingAssertion
```

The Software Contract

If

the preliminary assertion (precondition) is true immediately before executing the code segment,

then

the trailing assertion (postcondition) is guaranteed to be true immediately after executing the code segment (method).

Legal contracts define the responsibilities of the parties entering into the contract, and software contracts do the same. The software contract assigns responsibility for ensuring that the trailing assertion is true to the code segment (or, more properly, to the programmer who wrote the code). However, this responsibility has a crucial condition: The code need satisfy its commitment only if the preliminary assertion is true just prior to execution. In other words, from a contractual point of view, the code segment behavior doesn't matter in the event that the preliminary assertion is false.

The software contract is the way in which assertions serve the role of a measuring stick. Code can be examined for correctness by applying the software contract. Any code that violates the contract is considered to be incorrect. If a test case is executed for a true-valued preliminary assertion and the trailing assertion can be shown to be false, then the code is demonstrated to be incorrect. You can even apply certain software axioms to formally argue the correctness of a segment of code based on the software contract concept.

Following is a simple example of a segment of code that is correct with respect to the indicated preliminary and trailing assertions.

```
// assert: s1 == "cat" and s2 == "dog"
String tmp = s1;
s1 = s2;
s2 = tmp;
// assert: s1 == "dog" and s2 == "cat"
```

The code in this example is the common swap algorithm that interchanges the values of the String variables s1 and s2. The trailing assertion specifies the exact values of these two variables—"dog" and "cat"—respectively. The swap algorithm can ensure such a trailing assertion only if the variables have opposite values immediately before swapping. Fortunately, the preliminary assertion specifies this precise situation.

Recall that correctness relies on specifications. Therefore, the following code is correct with respect to its specifications, even though it looks like an improper attempt at a swap algorithm and even though the second assignment statement is redundant.

```
// assert: s1 == "cat" and s2 == "dog"
s1 = s2;
s2 = s1;
// assert: s1 == "dog" and s2 == "dog"
```

If the first set of preliminary and trailing assertions is used as shown next, this second algorithm would be considered incorrect.

```
// INCORRECT CODE:
// assert: s1 == "cat" and s2 == "dog"
s1 = s2;
s2 = s1;
// assert: s1 == "dog" and s2 == "cat"
```

Similarly, if the second trailing assertion were used as shown next, the swap algorithm would be incorrect.

```
// INCORRECT CODE:
// assert: s1 == "cat" and s2 == "dog"
String tmp = s1;
s1 = s2;
s2 = tmp;
// assert: s1 == "dog" and s2 == "dog"
```

According to the software contract, the code has the responsibility to ensure the correctness of the trailing assertion. Furthermore, this responsibility is contin-

Core Concepts O2

gent on the preliminary assertion. But who is responsible for ensuring that the preliminary assertion is true? Actually, the software contract doesn't specifically assign such a responsibility. However, because programs execute sequentially, the preliminary assertion for one code segment usually is the trailing assertion for another. Therefore, the software contract code can be applied to suggest that whatever code executes before the preliminary assertion is responsible.

O2.6 PRECONDITIONS AND POSTCONDITIONS

A common form for expressing method specifications is a form of software contract in which the preliminary assertion is a precondition, and the trailing assertion is a postcondition. These two assertions are relative to the method's body.

The precondition is an assertion that defines the expected state of computation at the time of every method call. In a contract, the responsibility for ensuring the truth of the precondition lies with the code that calls the method. A postcondition is an assertion that specifies the computational state at the time the method returns. The responsibility for ensuring the postcondition belongs to the method body.

> ### Software Engineering Hint
>
> Preconditions and postconditions are the preferred way for a designer to specify the desired behavior of methods. They are also an effective way for one programmer to define the behavior of a method that is to be called from code written by other programmers.

Preconditions and postconditions are effective tools for providing code specifications via the concept of programming by contract. However, preconditions and postconditions are also effective design tools. A software designer can use a precondition–postcondition pair to specify the detailed behavior of each method. The phrase *design by contract* refers to using preconditions and postconditions in this way.

Figure O2.14 contains a specification for fillPowersOfTwo10 using a precondition and a postcondition. By convention in Java, these two assertions are placed before the name of the method. OCL notation uses the prefixes **pre:** and **post:** for these two assertions.

Figure O2.14 fillPowersOfTwo10 method specifications and code

```
/* pre:    arr.length >= 11
   post:   forAll (j : 0<=j<=10 | arr[j] == 2^j) */
   // Note that 2^j denotes 2 raised to the jth power.
public void fillPowersOfTwo10(int[] arr) {
    for (int k=0; k!=11; k++) {
        arr[k] = (int)Math.pow(2, k);
    }
}
```

The fillPowersOfTwo10 method has a single parameter, arr, that is declared as an array of int. According to the method's precondition, the calling code is obligated to pass an arr parameter that contains 11 or more cells. The postcondition stipulates that each of the first 11 cells of arr contain 2 raised to the power of its index (i.e., arr[0]==2^0, arr[1]==2^1, ... arr[10]==2^{10}).

The code of the method body for fillPowersOfTwo10 is included only to illustrate a correct solution and to demonstrate the need for preconditions. This method body relies on a parameter arr of sufficient length. If this method is called with an actual parameter array of length 10 or less, the method's execution is considered erroneous.

It is also possible to design a different set of specifications that does not restrict the size of the array parameter. This second version, called fillPowersOfTwo, is shown in Figure O2.15.

Figure O2.15 fillPowersOfTwo method specifications and code

```
/* post:   forAll (j : 0<=j<= arr.length-1 | arr[j] == 2^j) */
           // Note that 2^j denotes 2 raised to the jth power.
public void fillPowersOfTwo(int[] arr) {
    for (int k=0; k!=arr.length; k++) {
        arr[k] = (int)Math.pow(2, k);
    }
}
```

Software Engineering Hint

A method that can be called under all circumstances has a precondition of *true*. It is best to eliminate such preconditions from the specifications.

The fillPowersOfTwo method omits the precondition altogether. This common practice indicates that the caller has no contractual responsibilities before calling the method. Technically, there is always a precondition; an omitted precondition is the same as the precondition *true*. Note that *true* is always true.

Two kinds of assumptions are commonly made by the precondition/postcondition notation: one for preconditions, and one for postconditions.

- **Precondition assumption:** It is assumed that all reference parameters are nonnull.
- **Postcondition assumption:** It is generally assumed that the method doesn't alter state except as specified.

Software Engineering Hint

When you write a precondition, don't bother to state that reference parameters are nonnull. This is assumed.

When you write a postcondition, don't bother to list all the things that don't change when the method executes.

The reasoning behind the precondition assumption is that a null-valued parameter serves no useful purpose in Java. If an object is not first assigned to such a parameter, any attempt to use it raises a null pointer exception, and assigning an object to the parameter has no effect following the method's return.

Making the assumption that all reference parameters are nonnull simplifies the specifications by eliminating the obvious. Figure O2.15 illustrates a typical use of this precondition assumption because the fillPowersOfTwo method will fail with a null pointer exception if arr is null at call time.

The postcondition assumption also is used to abbreviate specifications. Suppose that a method is passed five parameters but alters the state of only one of the five. The postcondition would become cluttered and less readable if it included four sub-assertions to specify the parameters that do not change. It is preferable to use the postcondition only to specify those things that can potentially change as a result of calling the method.

The relationship of local variables (declared inside a method) and the method's specifications deserves special mention. Preconditions are asserted true only at the instant that the method is called. A precondition cannot include any local variable because local variables do not exist until the method has begun to execute. Neither can a postcondition include local variables; a postcondition defines state at the time the method returns, and at return time all local variables have been deallocated.

The program entities that *are* permitted within preconditions, and also post-conditions, include any instance variable that is accessible to the method and any method parameter. Two additional notations are useful for postconditions: the previous value notation and return value notation.

You use **previous value notation** whenever you need to refer to a prior state of computation, in particular, the state of computation at the time the method was called. The OCL convention to denote a previous value is to suffix an expression with *@pre*. Figure O2.16 illustrates the previous value notation for a method that reverses the order of the content of its array parameter.

Figure O2.16 reverse method specifications and code

```
/*  post:    forAll (j: 0<=j<=arr.length-1
                       | arr[j] == arr[arr.length-1-j]@pre) */
public void reverse(char[] arr) {
    char temp;
    for (int m=0; m!=arr.length/2; m++) {
        temp = arr[m];
        arr[m] = arr[arr.length-1-m];
        arr[arr.length-m-1] = temp;
    }
}
```

Software Engineering Hint

Use the previous value (@pre) notation only when absolutely necessary. For example, a nonvoid method that returns a value without altering any object's state has no need to refer to previous values.

Using the informal semantics of universal quantification, the reverse method's postcondition can be translated into the following expression.

```
arr[0] == arr[arr.length-1]@pre
and arr[1] == arr[arr.length-2]@pre
and arr[2] == arr[arr.length-3]@pre
. . .
and arr[arr.length-1] == arr[0]@pre
```

The first line of this translated expression specifies that at the time the method returns, arr[0] must have the same value that arr[arr.length-1] had at the time the method was called. Similarly, the second line stipulates that the value of arr[1] at return time must be the same as `arr[arr.length-2]` at call time. The remaining lines are analogous.

The previous value notation is essential whenever the postcondition must specify that the state of some variable or parameter has been altered in a way that depends on its prior value. Such is the case with the `reverse` method. It is impossible to precisely specify the concept of rearranging the content of array cells without referencing their previous content, so the `reverse` method's postcondition cannot be properly expressed without the use of a previous value notation.

The **return value notation** is required by postconditions for all nonvoid methods. Because the primary purpose of any nonvoid method is to return an object or value, the postcondition needs a way to refer to the value that is returned. This text uses the convention that the identifier `result` refers to the return value of any nonvoid method. Figure O2.17 contains a sample method called `parenthesizedString`.

Figure O2.17 `parenthesizedString` method specifications and code

```
/*  post:   result == '(' + s + ')' */
public void parenthesizedString(String s) {
    return '(' + s + ')';
}
```

When the nonvoid method returns data of reference type, the `result` notation can be thought of as a reference to an object—namely, the object returned by the method. Figure O2.18 illustrates with a method called `first5Cells`.

Figure O2.18 `first5Cells` method specifications and code

```
/*  pre:    arr.length >= 5
    post:   result.length == 5
            and forAll(j : 0<=j<=4 | result[j] == arr[j]) */
public int[] first5Cells(int[] arr) {
    int[] result;
    result = new int[5];
    for (int k=0; k!=5; k++) {
        result[k] = arr[k];
    }
    return result;
}
```

Software Engineering Hint

Using the identifier **result** to name any local variable that serves as a method's return value is a good idea because it is consistent with the use of **result** in postconditions. Figure O2.18 illustrates.

The postcondition of `first5Cells` specifies the return value by defining its properties. The first line of the postcondition states that the return value must be an array containing five cells. The notation `result.length` makes this possible by treating `result` as though it were an array of integer. The last line of the postcondition specifies that each cell of the return value array has the same value as the corresponding cell of arr.

Figure O2.19 summarizes the permissible notations that can be included in preconditions and postconditions. This figure also includes any restrictions on using the expressions.

Figure O2.19 Permissible precondition/postcondition notations

Symbol	*Permissible Use*	*Restrictions*
Parameter name	Precondition and postcondition	Parameter must be from the same method as the precondition or postcondition.
Instance variable name	Precondition and postcondition	Variable must be accessible within the class to which the method belongs.
@pre	Postconditions only	• *@pre* can suffix any object reference. • *@pre* should be used only when necessary. • Avoid using *@pre* in nonvoid methods.
result	Postconditions only	• result behaves like an object of the type returned by the method. • Don't use result in void methods.

In addition to preconditions and postconditions, one other clause is sometimes integrated into a set of method specifications. Unlike preconditions and postconditions, which are assertions, the **modifies clause** contains only a list of objects or variables. This list should include everything that might change state as a result of the method's execution.

A *modifies* clause is most useful in two situations: when the method is complicated and alters the state of many variables, and when the method's postcondition might otherwise be ambiguous. Figure O2.20 demonstrates the inclusion of a *modifies* clause to eliminate ambiguity.

Figure O2.20 copyArray method specifications and code

```
/* pre:      destination.length >= source.length
   modifies: destination
   post:     forAll(j: 0<=j<=source.length-1
                    | source[j] == destination[j]) */
public void copyArray(double[] source, double[] destination) {
    for (int k=0; k!=source.length; k++) {
        destination[k] = source[k];
    }
}
```

A *modifies* clause is best placed between the associated precondition and the postcondition, as shown in Figure O2.20. In this case, the postcondition states that the initial portion of the destination array has the same content as the source array. By itself, this postcondition is ambiguous because the postcondition could be satisfied by a loop that copied destination to source:

Software Engineering Hint

The use of *modifies* clauses is optional. A *modifies* clause should be included to remove ambiguities or add clarity to the specifications.

```
for (int k=0; k!=source.length; k++) {
    source[k] = destination[k];
}
```

The postcondition even allows the code to assign new values to *both* arrays, as long as corresponding array cells are assigned the same values. Following is a sample loop for this algorithm.

```
for (int k=0; k!=source.length; k++) {
    source[k] = 0.0;
    destination[k] = 0.0;
}
```

Software Engineering Hint

Something not included in the *modifies* clause may be most important. Any variable or parameter not included in a method's *modifies* clause can be assumed to be unaltered by the method.

The copyArray code and the most recent two loops perform different algorithms, but each of these three code segments is correct with respect to the method's precondition and postcondition. Including the *modifies* clause makes it clear that these last two loops are incorrect because they alter the state of source, which is not listed and therefore cannot validly be modified by copyArray.

O2.7   CLASS SPECIFICATIONS

Section O2.2 examines the use of class diagrams and concludes that although a class diagram serves as an overview specification, it lacks precise behavioral information. This deficiency of class diagrams is particularly problematic in the later stages of design, often called **detailed design**, when the designer must specify the particulars of the behavior of each method and class.

This section explores a technique for expressing the missing behavioral details as a means to augment class specifications. This technique, based on many of the concepts presented in the past few sections, is commonly called a **class specification**. The basic concept of a class specification is to gather all the assertion constraints for the class's methods, such as preconditions and postconditions, into a single collection. To illustrate this concept, we'll use a class, called Fraction. The class diagram for Fraction is shown in Figure O2.21.

Figure O2.21 Fraction class diagram

```
┌─────────────────────────────────────────┐
│                 Fraction                  │
├─────────────────────────────────────────┤
│  + int numerator                          │
│  + int denominator                        │
├─────────────────────────────────────────┤
│  «constructor»                            │
│    + Faction(int n, int d)                │
│                                           │
│  «query»                                  │
│    + boolean numer()                      │
│    + double denom()                       │
│    + String toString()                    │
│                                           │
│  «update»                                 │
│    + void invert()                        │
│    + void negate()                        │
│                                           │
│  «binary operation»                       │
│    + Fraction sum(Fraction f)             │
│    + Fraction product(Fraction f)         │
└─────────────────────────────────────────┘
```

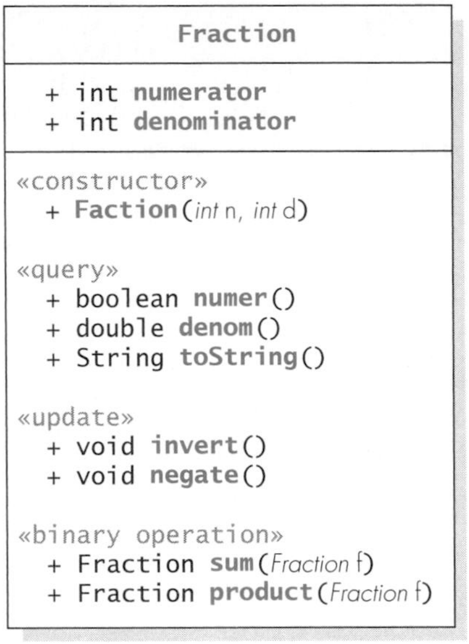

The Fraction class includes two private instance variables and eight public methods. The class member names, along with the name Fraction, give strong clues regarding class behavior. However, class diagrams can often raise as many questions as they answer. Among the questions left unanswered by the Fraction class diagram are these:

- What happens if the denominator of a Fraction is zero?
- Is a Fraction always stored in normalized form?
- What is returned by numer, denom, and toString?
- Are there any restrictions (preconditions) in calling sum or product?

To provide complete behavioral information, a class specification must answer such questions. Class specifications do this by providing details in the following three parts:

- A class invariant
- Method specifications for all public methods
- Specification function definitions

Figure O2.22 contains a class specification for the Fraction class. This specification places the class invariant first, followed by the method specifications and the specification function definitions.

Figure O2.22 Fraction class specification

Fraction Class Specification

Invariant (For every Fraction object)

   denominator > 0
   and gcd(numerator, denominator) == 1 (i.e., the fraction is normalized)

Core Concepts O2

Constructor Method

```
public Fraction( int n, int d )
```
    pre: d != 0
    post: *real_value_of*(this) == n / d

Query Methods

```
public int numer()
```
    post: result == numerator
```
public int denom()
```
    post: result == denominator
```
public String toString()
```
    post: result == numerator + "/" + denominator

Update Methods

```
public void invert()
```
    pre: numerator != 0
    modifies: numerator, denominator
    post: *real_value_of*(this) == 1 / *real_value_of*(this@pre)
```
public void negate()
```
    modifies: numerator
    post: *real_value_of*(this) == – *real_value_of*(this@pre)

Binary Operations

```
public Fraction sum(Fraction f )
```
    modifies: numerator, denominator
    post: *real_value_of*(result) == *real_value_of*(this) + *real_value_of*(f)
```
public Fraction product(Fraction f )
```
    modifies: numerator, denominator
    post: *real_value_of*(result) == *real_value_of*(this) * *real_value_of*(f)

Specification Functions

real_value_of(Fraction f) [a Real-valued function]

      Definition

            real_value_of(f) == f.numerator / f.denominator

      Informally

            real_value_of(f) is the numeric value from dividing the
                     numerator of f by its denominator.

gcd(int a, int b) [an Integer-valued function]

      Definition

            gcd(a, b) > 0
            and a % *gcd*(a, b) == 0
            and b % *gcd*(a, b) == 0
            and forAll (**j** : Integer *and* j > *gcd*(a, b) | a % j != 0 *or* b % j != 0)

      Informally

            gcd(a, b) is the greatest common divisor of a and b

The **class invariant** specifies those properties that are shared by all the class's nonprivate methods. The class invariant for Fraction requires that denominator be positive, thereby eliminating the mathematical problem of a denominator that is zero. The Fraction class invariant also indicates that a fraction is always maintained in normalized form.

A class invariant can be thought of as an implicit addendum to the postcondition of every nonprivate method in its class. In other words, public Fraction methods are responsible for ensuring that denominator > 0. Because methods ensure its truth when the method returns, the class invariant also can be assumed to be an implicit addendum to the precondition of every nonconstructor method. (A constructor is responsible for properly initializing an object, and the class invariant cannot be presumed true until after such initialization.)

The class invariant often reflects a key design decision. For example, by design, the Fraction class cannot store a negative-valued denominator.

Each method specification is expressed in the form of a precondition, a postcondition, a method signature, and possibly a *modifies* clause, as described in Section O2.6. **Method signatures** (the name, scope, return type, and parameter list of the method) are included as headings for their respective method specifications.

The method specifications for the Fraction constructor clarify that a Fraction with a negative denominator will be stored as an equivalent value. In other words, the fraction $-\frac{1}{3}$ is stored as numerator== −1 and denominator==3. Similarly, the fraction $\frac{2}{3}$ is stored as numerator==2 and denominator==3.

The designer of the invert method had to consider another issue. The intention of invert is to turn a fraction upside-down in the sense that the new numerator becomes the denominator *@pre* and the new denominator becomes the numerator *@pre*. The designer has to be careful not to allow the resulting fraction to have a zero-valued denominator. Fraction prohibits such a difficulty by including the following precondition on the invert method.

    numerator != 0

A **specification function** is a technique for modularizing specifications. Designers sometimes use specification functions to improve the readability of class specifications. For example, it's complicated to explain the addition of two fractions. However, by using a specification function called *real_value_of*, the postcondition of the sum method can be expressed in the following single line.

$$real\_value\_of(\text{result}) == real\_value\_of(\text{this}) + real\_value\_of(\text{f})$$

Assuming that, as its name indicates, *real_value_of* yields the equivalent numeric value of a Fraction object, the preceding expression states that the numeric value of result is the sum of the numeric value of this and the numeric value of f. With the aid of the *real_value_of* function, it is equally convenient to specify the postcondition for the invert and product methods.

A specification function is a mathematical function that assists in expressing specifications; usually, it is not an executable method. Therefore, a complete class specification also must include definitions for any specification functions used. Figure O2.22 illustrates by placing the definition of specification functions at the end of the class specification and underneath the word "Definition" and using a mathlike functional definition.

The Fraction class includes a second specification function, called *gcd*. Its definition clarifies that *gcd*(a, b) is the largest integer that divides into a with a remainder of zero and also divides into b with a remainder of zero. (Mathematicians commonly refer to this as the "greatest common divisor" of a and b.)

The class invariant use *gcd* by including the following subassertion.

$$gcd(\text{result.numerator, result.denominator}) == 1$$

Software Engineering Hint

Frequently, designers struggle with a trade-off between readability and precision. The "Definition" section of a specification function is intended to be reasonably precise. On the other hand, including an "Informally" section often improves readability.

This subassertion defines a result Fraction that is in normalized form. Both the sum and the product methods return only Fraction objects that are in normalized form.

Often, you can enhance the readability of a specification function by including an extra informal explanation for every specification function. Figure O2.22 demonstrates this option under the "Informally" headings.

A few kinds of execution-time behavior are extremely difficult to explain using standard mathematical expressions. One such behavior is exhibited by a statement that outputs a value to be printed on a display or terminal (e.g., the behavior of the System.out.println method). You should use specification functions in such cases, even if the "Definition" part is omitted in favor of the "Informally" part.

O2.8   SPECIFYING EXCEPTIONS

Previous sections have concentrated on designing and implementing programs that are correct. However, programmers must not ignore potential run-time problems. This issue is so important that software engineers use the term **robust** to refer to software that exhibits reasonable behavior under unanticipated circumstances. Sometimes robust software is a convenience, as with an operating system that doesn't turn into a useless blue screen. Other times, robust software is essential, as with the guidance program for an airplane.

Exceptions play a key role in facilitating robustness. (Exceptions are examined in Chapter O4.) A code segment can include an **exception handler** to recover from certain exceptions that might otherwise impair robustness.

Software Engineering Hint

The top priority for software developers is to write code that is correct. However, software can be totally correct and still not respond well to unexpected circumstances. In other words, robustness is also an important characteristic of a good program.

The concept of robustness is closely related to the notion of a precondition or preassertion. Violating a precondition is the kind of unexpected run-time situation to which robust programs respond. Therefore, one way to augment software specifications is to include comments regarding a method's response when preconditions are violated. Usually, such situations result in thrown exceptions, so this text adopts the convention of indicating a thrown exception parenthetically following a precondition clause. Figure O2.23 contains a sample method implementing the earlier Fraction specification. (Fraction is specified in Figure O2.22.)

Figure O2.23 invert method (from Fraction) specifications and code

```
/*  pre:     numerator != 0 (throws IllegalStateException)
    modifies: numerator, denominator
    post:    real_value_of(this) == 1 / (real_value_of(this@pre)) */
public void invert() {
    if (numerator == 0) {
        throw new IllegalStateException();
    }
    int temp = numerator;
    numerator = denominator;
    denominator = temp;
    if (denominator < 0) {
        denominator = denominator * -1;
        numerator = numerator * -1;
    }
}
```

The precondition states that it is improper to call the invert method whenever numerator has a value of zero. Appending the phrase throws IllegalStateException to the precondition explains the method's behavior when such a precondition violation occurs: The method throws the violation back to the calling code in the form of an exception of type IllegalStateException.

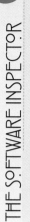

THE SOFTWARE INSPECTOR

Following is a collection of hints on what to check when you examine a design or code that involves the concepts of this chapter.

✔ It is natural for a software developer to eagerly pursue design and implementation, but countless studies have shown that time spent reviewing, correcting, and questioning requirements documents invariably reduces the cost of software.

✔ Class diagrams reveal considerable information regarding the class members and the class's relationships with other classes. Designers should seek to produce complete class diagrams for each class they design, reviewing them carefully.

✔ In a design review of a class diagram, you should search for missing methods, ways to provide better information hiding (e.g., `private` or `protected` members rather than `public`), and unnecessarily complicated relationships with other classes.

✔ It is a good idea to create and carefully review class diagrams before proceeding to detailed design.

✔ Detailed design of a class often begins with the class invariant as a way to discover the key properties of the associated objects.

✔ Each assertion should be examined for form. Does it use the proper patterns, especially the fundamental assertion pattern? Does the formatting (indentation and parentheses) enhance readability? Can you use specification functions to simplify a complicated assertion?

✔ Assertions also must be scrutinized for completeness and for sensibleness. Has every potential behavior been defined? Are the vacuous cases sensible? Is it possible to satisfy the assertion?

✔ When you review method specifications, it is wise to look for potential ambiguities. Often, a *modifies* clause can eliminate such problems.

✔ In a design review of a method specification, you should look for improper notations, such as the inclusion of local variables or misplaced previous-value notation.

✔ You should examine method specifications within a class to identify common subassertions. This is a good way to discover additional parts of the class invariant.

✔ Every precondition should be considered a candidate for exception handling to improve robustness.

EXERCISES

1. For each of the following class diagrams, supply as much of the correspon-
    ding Java class's code as is specified by the class diagram.

    a)

PhoneAnsweringMachine
+ Button playButton + Button eraseButton - Counter messageCount
+ PhoneAnsweringMachine() + void playNextMessage() + void rewind() + String eraseAll()

    b)

    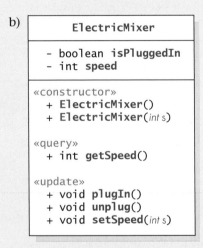

2. Draw a class diagram for the OneProduct class found in Figure O1.1.

3. Each of the following notations has a particular meaning within a UML class
    diagram. Explain what each notation means and how it is used.

    a) ⟶◆

    b) ⟶▷

    c) +

    d) -

4. Assume that `myInt` and `yourInt` are instance variables of type `int` and are declared within the same class as the methods discussed in parts (a) and (b).

   a) Write the code for the `doSomething` method so that it behaves according to its postcondition.
```
/* post:  yourInt == myInt * k
          and myInt == myInt@pre + 5 */
public doSomething( int k )
```

   b) What is the proper postcondition for the following method?
```
/* post:  ?? */
   public getMyInt() {
      return myInt;
}
```

5. Draw a picture (an object diagram) to illustrate the state of the array `arr` that is specified by each of the following assertions. (You should assume that `arr` is an array of 10 cells, each of type `double`.)

   a) *forAll*(**j** : $2 \le j \le 9$ | arr[j] == 22)

   b) arr[2] == 22 *and* arr[4] == 44 *and exists*(**j** : $2 \le j \le 4$ | arr[j] == 33)

   c) arr[0] == 2 *and* arr[1] == 3
      and forAll(**k** : $2 \le k \le 9$ | arr[k] == arr[k–1] + arr[k–2])

   d) *forAll*(**j** : $0 \le j \le 4$ | arr[j] == j)
      and forAll(**k** : $5 \le k \le 9$ | arr[k] == arr[9–k])

   e) *forAll*(**j** : $0 \le j \le 4$ | arr[j] == j
      and exists(**k** : $9–j \le k \le 9$ | arr[k] == arr[j]))

6. Express each of the following as an assertion, using the quantified expression notations presented in Section O2.3. You should assume that `a` and `b` are both arrays of 10 `double` cells.

   a) At least one of the cells of array `a` stores a positive number.

   b) Exactly one of the cells of array `a` stores a positive number.

   c) Every cell in array `a` stores the same value as the corresponding cell of array `b`.

   d) Every cell in array `a` stores a value that is larger than any cell of array `b`.

   e) Every value stored in a cell of array `a` also is stored somewhere in array `b`.

7. Write a method signature (method name, parameter list, and return type) together with a precondition and postcondition for each of the following.

   a) This method has three integer parameters and returns the largest value from the parameters.

   b) This method has an array of `double` as a parameter. The method permutes the array content so that the smallest value has been moved to the first array cell.

c) Write the specifications for the average method that returns the arithmetic mean of two int parameters.

d) This method has a single parameter of type array of String. The method is designed to swap the first and last cells of this array. If the array is only one cell long, the method throws an IllegalStateException.

e) This method has a single parameter that is an array of int. If the array contains at least one cell with the value zero, all array cells are assigned zero; otherwise, all array cells are assigned 25.

8. Assertions can be ambiguous if not written carefully. The following specifications are ambiguous because it isn't clear which parameter is altered. Assume that the method is designed to copy the state of the first parameter into the second.

```
/*  postcondition
        a.equals(b) */
public void copy(SomeType a, SomeType b) {
```

a) Add a *modifies* clause that removes the ambiguity.

b) Without a *modifies* clause, show how to modify the postcondition to remove the ambiguity.

9. Which of the following should never be included in a precondition?

a) A formal parameter

b) An actual argument

c) An instance variable

d) A local variable

e) The previous value (*@pre*) notation

10. Which of the following should never be included in a postcondition?

a) A formal parameter

b) An actual argument

c) An instance variable

d) A local variable

e) The previous value (*@pre*) notation

11. List all the specific times during a program's execution when a class invariant for the class called MyClass must be true.

PROGRAMMING EXERCISES

1. Figure O2.22 describes a class called Fraction. Design, implement, and test a program that extends the functionality of Fraction to include a method for dividing one fraction by another and a method for subtracting one fraction from another. Be certain to use design by contract techniques.

2. Rewrite your favorite programming project using design by contract and programming by contract methodology. Use the Java assert statement as much as possible, and exercise the statements by seeding one or two assertion violations; observe the run-time behavior of these errors.

3. Figure O2.2 shows a class diagram for a Point class. Write the proper preconditions and postconditions for all these class methods, and incorporate them into a working class so that points can be displayed as small dots on a javax.swing.JFrame. Create a user interface that allows the user to input coordinates for the points.

4. Using the Point class from the Programming Exercise 3, design, implement, and test a class that draws triangles. Each triangle should be defined by its three vertices (of type Point).

INHERITANCE

OBJECTIVES

- To examine the concept of inheritance and explain how one Java class inherits another

- To explore is_a and has_a relations as a means for making design decisions regarding inheritance or aggregation

- To review Java scope modifiers, including private, public, protected, and package

- To explore the Java rules for type conformance, including the `instanceof` operation

- To review dynamic dispatch and polymorphism in Java

- To explore the use of Java `abstract` classes, including class diagram notation

> " OF ALL ISSUES IN OBJECT TECHNOLOGY, NONE CAUSES AS MUCH DISCUSSION AS THE QUESTION OF WHEN AND HOW TO USE INHERITANCE. "
>
> —Bertrand Meyer,
> *Object-oriented Software Construction*

If asked to name the single thing that differentiates object-oriented programming from early approaches to software development, most computer scientists would answer with a single word: **inheritance**. Inheritance supports the reuse of software through the techniques of extension and specialization.

O3.1 EXTENSION AND SPECIALIZATION

Suppose a young company manufactures its first product—a solar-powered lawn mower. This mower is powered by an electric engine that is supplied electricity from a special solar panel located on top of the mower. The mower rolls on four wheels and has an aluminum deck that is a half meter square. The company has spent a great deal of money designing this mower and has purchased the necessary machinery to manufacture every mower component.

Like most good businesses, this company wants to take advantage of its sizable investment in product design and manufacturing. One of the most effective ways to accomplish this goal is to extend the product line. The most desirable kinds of extensions are those that can reuse existing components. For example, the mower design can be extended to apply to a self-propelled model by the addition of a gear and drive-shaft mechanism that links the motor to a rear wheel. An additional lever on the mower handle is required to turn the propulsion gears on and off.

A few potential customers live in heavily wooded areas, where the level of sunlight will not allow the solar panel to operate properly. In response to this need, the company might design a *specialized* version of its mower that includes supplemental power from an automobile battery. The battery supplies the additional power needed in shaded areas, and the battery is recharged by the solar panel when sunlight is sufficient.

This lawn mower example illustrates two key concepts that are used extensively by engineers:

- extension
- specialization

Engineers often seek to extend a design to satisfy broader needs or to specialize a design to satisfy more particular needs. As Figure O3.1 illustrates for this lawn mower example, an initial design is extended to design a self-propelled unit that does everything that the original mower does and more. The figure labels the mower with the battery supplement as *specialization* because this mower was designed to meet the special needs of those using their mower under extremely low light situations; other customers are unlikely to purchase the mower with the battery supplement.

The key to the utility of extension and specialization is the concept of **reuse**. The self-propelled mower can reuse the same motor, solar panel, deck, wheel, handle, and blade designs that were used for the original mower. Similarly, the battery supplement unit reuses most of the parts that were designed for the original mower. Reuse of engineering design through extension and specialization provides considerable business advantages. Companies even market a new product as the "new, improved" version (designed via extension) or one that is "tailored to meet your particular needs" (designed via specialization).

Figure O3.1 Extension and specialization in mower design

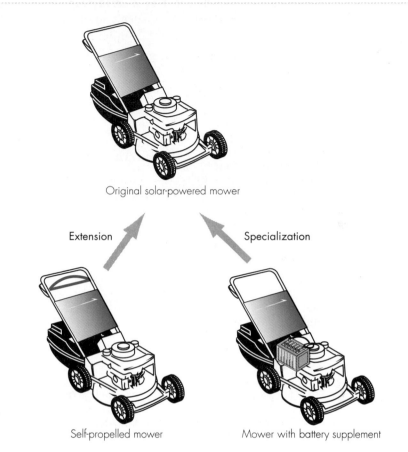

Original solar-powered mower

Extension

Specialization

Self-propelled mower

Mower with battery supplement

O3.2 IS_A RELATIONSHIPS

Extension and specialization are important concepts in software design. Just as in the design of lawn mowers, extension and specialization promote reuse when applied to software. Such software reuse can save time, reduce costs, and improve software reliability.

An understanding of **is_a relationships** is a good place to begin to recognize opportunities for extension and specialization. Consider the following is_a relations.

- A <u>self-propelled mower</u> is a <u>mower</u>.
- A <u>mower with battery supplement</u> is a <u>mower</u>.
- An <u>automobile</u> is a specialization of a <u>transportation vehicle</u>.
- A <u>word processor</u> is an extension of a <u>text editor</u>.
- A <u>shirt</u> is a particular kind of <u>clothing</u>.
- <u>Bald eagle</u> is a species of <u>bird</u>.
- <u>Triangle</u> is a type of <u>polygon</u>.

Not all relationships between two classes are is_a relations. Another common relationship is called a **has_a relation**. (This is alternatively known as a **contains_a relation**.) As the name implies, a has_a or contains_a relation occurs when an instance of one class is contained within another class:

- An <u>automobile</u> has a <u>steering wheel</u>.
- A <u>shirt</u> contains a <u>pocket</u>.
- A <u>bald eagle</u> has a <u>wing</u>.
- A <u>triangle</u> contains a <u>vertex</u>.

Software Engineering Hint

When you create a new class it is important to search for is_a and has_a relationships with existing classes. An is_a relation is best implemented via inheritance, and a has_a relation is implemented via aggregation.

A has_a relation leads to aggregation in which the containing class is an aggregate containing one or more instance variables.

The use of a programming construct called **inheritance** is suggested when two software classes are related by an is_a relation. A secondary design is_a specialized or extended version of the original design.

    secondary is_a original

An is_a relationship suggests that the class for the secondary design might inherit the original class.

    secondary inherits original

For example, Figure O3.2 shows a class diagram for a class designed to maintain information about an issue of common stock. Each stock has a unique ticker symbol, such as SUNW for Sun Microsystems or IBM for International Business Machines Corporation. The CommonStock class provides a variable called symbol to store the ticker symbol and a getSymbol method that returns the ticker symbol. Each stock also has its own selling price. The double variable called price stores the stock's price per share, and getPrice can be called to inspect this value. The CommonStock constructor method assigns initial values to symbol and price, and assignNewPrice has the behavior that its name implies. The "#" prefix indicates that the instance variables have protected scope, and the "+" denotes public scope for the methods.

The CommonStock class is sufficient for some applications, but it supplies fairly limited information (only the stock's ticker symbol and its price per share). It might be useful to include additional information about the stock. For example, the StockWithDividend class, shown in Figure O3.3, includes all the same information as CommonStock with the addition of an annualDividend variable and a method to retrieve this value.

The StockWithDividend class is an extension of the CommonStock class because StockWithDividend extends both the state and the behavior of CommonStock. (Extending either state or behavior is sufficient to constitute extension.) It is proper to say that a StockWithDividend object is_a CommonStock object with extra members. This is_a relationship suggests that StockWithDividend should inherit CommonStock, thereby reusing CommonStock members. Such inheritance is diagrammed in a UML class diagram as shown in Figure O3.4.

Figure O3.2 Class diagram for CommonStock

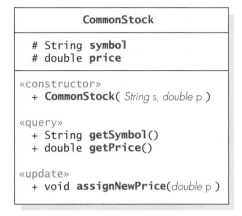

Figure O3.3 Class diagram for StockWithDividend

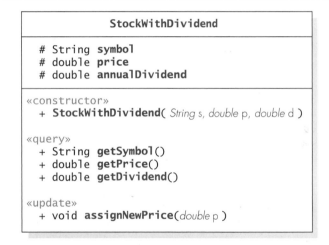

An inheritance arrow is always pointed *from* the inheriting class, also known as the **child class** or **subclass**, and pointing *toward* the inherited class, more properly called the **parent class** or **superclass**. Because the members of the parent class are reused by the child, they are not repeated within the child class rectangle.

An *over-the-counter* stock trades a bit differently than the common stocks considered so far. An over-the-counter stock has two prices: a *selling price*, which represents the price per share of the last stock sale, and an *asking price*, which is a price per share at which a current stockholder has agreed to sell. The selling price is slightly less than the asking price. An over-the-counter stock is a common stock. Such specialization suggests that you might design a class such as OverTheCounterStock by inheriting CommonStock.

Figure O3.4 illustrates an OverTheCounterStock class that is another child of the CommonStock class. Notice that OverTheCounterStock includes only one addi-

Figure O3.4 Class diagram showing inheritance of CommonStock

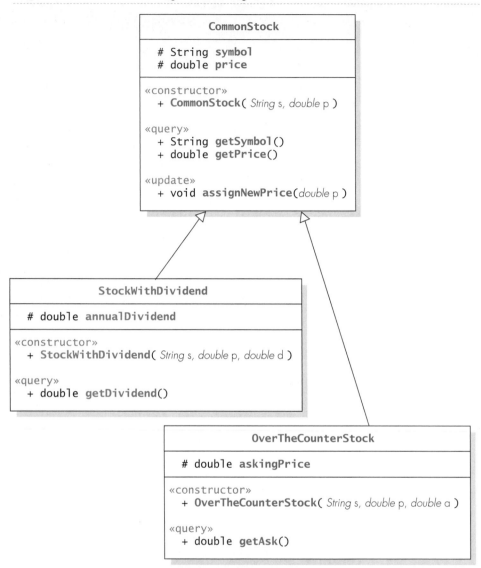

tional instance variable, askingPrice, presumably because the price variable is being reused to store the stock's selling price.

Design decisions can be difficult, and inheritance decisions are not always easy. Consider the task of designing two classes—Fraction and CompoundNumber—where a Fraction object stores a single numeric fraction and a CompoundNumber stores a number in terms of an integer (its whole part) plus a fraction (its fractional remainder). For example, the fraction 7/3 would be stored as 2⅓ as a CompoundNumber. The following three conclusions are all correct interpretations of these two classes.

- A CompoundNumber is_a Fraction because every compound number can be represented as a fraction.
- A Fraction is_a CompoundNumber because every fractional value can be represented as a compound number.
- A CompoundNumber has_a Fraction because every compound number is made from a fraction and an integer.

This analysis reveals that there are at least three ways to implement these two classes: The CompoundNumber class could be implemented as a child of Fraction; the Fraction class could be implemented as a child of CompoundNumber; or the CompoundNumber class could be an aggregate that contains an instance variable of type Fraction. Without careful consideration it isn't clear which of these three alternatives is preferable. However, combining more than one of the alternatives is almost certainly a poor choice.

O3.3 INHERITANCE IN JAVA

Figure O3.5 shows a Java implementation of the CommonStock class. CommonStock contains the members described in Section O3.2. This figure illustrates that no special inheritance notation is necessary within a parent class. Instead, it is the child class that must denote inheritance. This is shown in the StockWithDividend class in Figure O3.6.

Figure O3.5 The CommonStock class

```java
public class CommonStock {
protected String symbol;
    protected double price;
    /*  post:   symbol == s
                and price == p */
    public CommonStock(String s, double p) {
        symbol = s;
        price = p;
    }
    /*  post:   result == symbol */
    public String getSymbol() {
        return symbol;
    }
    /*  post:   result == price */
    public double getPrice() {
        return price;
    }
    /*  post:   price == p */
    public void assignNewPrice(double p) {
        price = p;
    }
}
```

Core Concepts O3

Figure O3.6 The StockWithDividend class

```
public class StockWithDividend extends CommonStock {
    protected double annualDividend;
    /* post:    symbol == s
                and price == p
                and annualDividend == d */
    public StockWithDividend(String s, double p, double d) {
        super(s, p);
        annualDividend = d;
    }
    /* post:   result == annualDividend */
    public double getDividend() {
        return annualDividend;
    }
}
```

The Java notation for inheritance consists of inserting, immediately after the child class's name, the keyword *extends* followed by the parent class name. The StockWithDividend class becomes a child class of CommonStock using the notation extends CommonStock found on the first line of the class.

A child class inherits (reuses) the members of its parent class. Therefore, the StockWithDividend class inherits the symbol and price variables—along with the getSymbol, getPrice, and assignNewPrice methods—from CommonStock. The following Java application illustrates a driver class that uses a StockWithDividend variable called stock.

```
public class Driver {
    public static void main(String[] args) {
        StockWithDividend stock;
        stock = new StockWithDividend("IBM", 78.5, 1.5);
        stock.assignNewPrice(79.6);
        System.out.println( stock.getSymbol()
            + " Price: " + stock.getPrice()
            + " Div: " + stock.getDividend() );
    }
}
```

Notice that this code segment is permitted to call assignNewPrice, getSymbol, and getPrice even though the StockWithDividend class never mentions these methods. These methods are all inherited from CommonStock, so the behavior of these method calls is determined by the CommonStock code.

Constructors are treated differently than other inherited methods. Constructors are unique because every parent class necessarily has a different name from those of its children, and constructors must use their class's name; therefore, a child class cannot obtain a constructor merely by inheritance. Strictly speaking, no constructor method is inherited by name. However, every child class constructor is required, either explicitly or implicitly, to call a constructor from its parent before executing any other statement. This latter requirement is made possible by a special notation: Java allows the reserved word `super` to be used to name a parent (superclass) constructor method as the first statement (and only the first statement) of a child class constructor. The `StockWithDividend` method illustrates the use of this notation by way of the following statement:

```
super(s, p);
```

This statement is actually a call to the `CommonStock` constructor method, which assigns s to the `symbol` variable and p to the `price` variable.

This use of `super` to call a constructor is unique in two ways. First, this constructor notation is permitted only as the first statement of a constructor. Any attempt to call a parent class constructor from a later statement within the child class constructor or from some other child class method will result in a compile-time error. The second unique thing about a child class constructor is that if `super` is not called as the first statement, an implicit call to the parameterless parent class constructor, `super()`, is made instead.

To illustrate a few more issues of inheritance, consider a class called `StudentInfo` and a child class called `UndergradStudentInfo`. Figure O3.7 pictures the class diagram for these two classes.

Figure O3.7 Class diagram for `StudentInfo` and `UndergradStudentInfo`

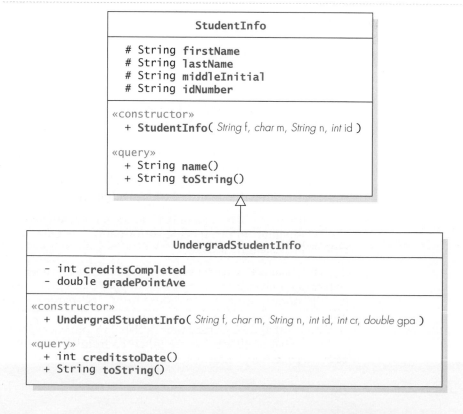

The StudentInfo class is designed to store information for any student. This information includes only a name and an ID number. Figure O3.8 contains code for StudentInfo.

Figure O3.8 The StudentInfo class

```java
public class StudentInfo {
    protected String firstName;
    protected String lastName;
    protected char middleInitial;
    protected int idNumber;
    /*  post:   firstName == f and middleInitial == m
                and lastName == n and idNummber == id */
    public StudentInfo(String f, char m, String n, int id) {
        firstName = f;
        middleInitial = m;
        lastName = n;
        idNumber = id;
    }
    /*  post:   result == lastName + ", " + firstName + " "
                            + middleInitial + "." */
    public String name() {
        return lastName + ", " + firstName + " "
                + middleInitial + ".";
    }
    /*  post:   result == info regarding the state of this student */
    public String toString() {
        return "Student Name: " + name()
                + "\n ID: " + idNumber;
    }
}
```

The StudentInfo class includes four variables for the student's first name, last name, middle initial and ID number. The three methods from StudentInfo are a constructor; a method, name, that returns the complete student name; and a toString method that returns all information regarding the student in String form.

An undergraduate student is a specific kind of student, and that makes it possible to include more specific information. Figure O3.9 demonstrates the UndergradStudentInfo class.

The UndergradStudentInfo class inherits StudentInfo. So as a result, UndergradStudentInfo has access to all public and protected instance variables and to all nonconstructor methods from its parent class. In other words, UndergradStudentInfo inherits access to firstName, lastName, middleInitial, and idNumber just as though they were declared within UndergradStudentInfo. The name and toString methods also are inherited from the parent class. The body of the toString method within UndergradStudentInfo illustrates that the notation for

Figure O3.9 The UndergradStudentInfo class

```
/* invariant:
      0 <= this.creditsCompleted
      and 0.0 <= this.gradePointAve <= 4.0 */
public class UndergradStudentInfo extends StudentInfo {
    private int creditsCompleted;
    private double gradePointAve;
    /* pre:   1 <= r <= s (throws IllegalStateException)
       post:  firstName == f
              and middleInitial == m and lastName == n
              and idNummber == id and creditsCompleted == cr
              and gradePointAve == gpa */
    public UndergradStudentInfo(String f, char m, String n,
                                int id, int cr, double gpa) {
        super(f, m, n, id);
        creditsCompleted = cr;
        gradePointAve = gpa;
    }
    /* post:  result == creditsCompleted */
    public int creditsToDate() {
        return creditsCompleted;
    }
    /* post:  result == info regarding the state of this student
       */
    public String toString() {
        return "Student Name: " + name()
               + "\n ID: " + idNumber
               + "\n Credits: " + creditsCompleted
               + "\n GPA: " + gradePointAve;
    }
}
```

accessing inherited instance variables, such as idNumber, and calling inherited methods, such as name, is the same a child class as in its parent.

A child class is free to add new instance variables and new methods to those that are inherited. The UndergradStudentInfo class includes two additional instance variables. creditsCompleted and gradePointAve maintain the total number of credits that the student has accumulated by successful course completion and the resulting grade point average (GPA), assuming a 4-point scale. UndergradStudentInfo also includes its own constructor method and a new method, called creditsToDate, that returns the value of creditsCompleted. Collectively, any object of type UndergradStudentInfo will contain all the following instance variables.

Variable	*Origin*
firstName	Inherited from StudentInfo
lastName	Inherited from StudentInfo
middleInitial	Inherited from StudentInfo
idNumber	Inherited from StudentInfo
creditsCompleted	Declared in UndergradStudentInfo
GradePointAve	Declared in UndergradStudentInfo

Similarly, the following collection of all methods is available within the UndergradStudentInfo class.

Method	*Origin*	*Special Child Class Notation*
name	Inherited from StudentInfo	
toString	Inherited from StudentInfo	super.toString()
UndergradStudentInfo	Declared in UndergradStudentInfo	
creditsToDate	Declared in UndergradStudentInfo	
toString	Declared in UndergradStudentInfo	

Often, a parent class's version of a method doesn't quite meet the needs of a child. For example, the toString method from StudentInfo returns the student's name and ID number, but it cannot include the course credit total or GPA.

Any child class is free to create its own version of an inherited method. Such method redefinition is called **overriding** because for the child class's objects the child's definition takes precedence over the parent's version. The UndergradStudentInfo class overrides the toString method by including a method with the identical name and parameter list as the method inherited from its parent class. This overriding version of toString appends credit count and GPA to the earlier toString output.

The type of the object always determines which method will be used. Calling toString on a StudentInfo object returns a string with only the name and ID, but calling toString on an UndergradStudentInfo object causes the credit count and GPA to be included in the return string. For example, suppose the following client code is executed.

```
StudentInfo stu;
stu = new StudentInfo("Della", 'O', "Ware", 112233);
System.out.println( stu.toString() ); //toString() is redundant

UndergradStudentInfo underStu;
underStu = new UndergradStudentInfo("Mare", 'E', "Land", 778899,
                                    95, 3.8);
System.out.println( underStu.toString() ); //toString() is redundant
```

The resulting output is shown next. This output is produced by two calls to toString; the first call uses the StudentInfo version of toString, and the second call uses the UndergradStudentInfo version.

```
Student Name: Ware, Della O.
    ID: 112233
Student Name: Land, Mare E.
    ID: 778899
    Credits: 95
    GPA: 3.8
```

The fact that a method is overridden does not mean that the parent's version isn't inherited. Again, Java uses the reserved word super to allow access to a super-class method that is otherwise inaccessible. Following is the precise syntax for use within the child class to refer to its parent version of an overridden method.

```
super.methodName( argumentList );
```

Without the super. prefix, any call to methodName invokes the method that is proper for the class containing the call statement. When the super. prefix is included, the inherited version is invoked. In other words, the following alternative version of toString can be used within UndergradStudentInfo without changing the method's behavior.

```java
public String toString() {
    return super.toString()
            + "\n Credits: " + creditsCompleted
            + "\n GPA: " + gradePointAve;
}
```

Software Engineering Hint

When you create a child class, avoid unintentionally declaring instance variables that have the same names as instance variables of the parent class. Such redeclaration causes the parent's variable to be "hidden" within the child.

Software Engineering Hint

When you implement a subclass, take care to obey the specifications of the superclass. Among other things, the subclass must abide by the class invariant of the superclass (although additional restrictions can be added to the subclass invariant). The subclass should also maintain the intent of all superclass methods in the subclass context.

Overriding is generally applied to methods, not instance variables. With some restrictions it is possible to reuse an inherited instance variable name to declare a new instance variable of a child class, but such reuse of instance variable names is best avoided because it results in a hidden variable.

One important rule for any descendant class is to obey the specifications of its ancestors. This means that if the parent class has a class invariant, its children also should maintain that invariant. The child is free, however, to include additional restrictions in its invariant, because child classes are often more specialized than their parents. The UndergradStudentInfo class includes restrictions, specified by the class invariant, that aren't present in StudentInfo.

Obeying the parent class specifications also means that the child has an obligation to make each inherited method satisfy the specifications from the parent, but in the child's context. This is the reason for overriding the toString method. By overriding toString, the UndergradStudentInfo class can include additional information in the return value, making this return information more comprehensive.

O3.4 SCOPE AND INHERITANCE

Scope is the region of a program in which a variable or method is accessible. Software developers know that proper scope choices enhance software robustness by restricting unwanted access. For example, the scope of a local variable is restricted to the method in which the variable is declared. Therefore, the local variable is hidden from external code and cannot be altered except within the declaring method.

Java supports four types of scope declaration that can be applied to methods and instance variables. Each member must have one of these four scopes, and the scope is established by the member's declaration.

- Private scope
- Public scope
- Protected scope
- Package scope

Most class members have one of the first three scopes. Syntactically, these scopes are declared by prefixing the member's declaration with the appropriate word: `private`, `public`, or `protected`. Below are a few sample declarations taken from prior sections of this chapter.

```
protected String firstName;
private int classSize;
public void paint(Graphics g) { ... }
```

Software Engineering Hint

Restriction is considered to be a good idea when scope is declared, because less access means more protection from unwanted usage. Scope possibilities from most restrictive to least are as follows.

1) Local scope
2) Private scope
3) Protected scope
4) Package scope
5) Public scope

Private scope is the most restrictive of the three options. A private variable can be assigned a value, and the value of the variable can be inspected from code within the declaring class. However, the private variable is not directly accessible outside the class. Similarly, a private method cannot be called from any statement that is outside the class that declares the method.

Java scope rules follow class boundaries, not object boundaries. It is therefore possible for an object to access a private member of a different object, as long as both objects belong to the same class. For example, consider the following Bunch class and its associated munge method.

```
public class Bunch {
    private int size;
    public void munge(Bunch b) {
        // b.size is accessible here
        ...
    }
}
```

The `size` variable is a private instance variable of Bunch. However, when the `munge` method is called on an object of type Bunch—namely, the `this` object—it still has access to the `size` variable of its parameter. Of course, if the b parameter were of a type not conforming to Bunch, then accessing a private member would be impossible.

Public scope is the least restrictive alternative. A public instance variable can be accessed (assigned or inspected) from any class that has access to an object belonging to the declaring class. Similarly, a public method can be called from a statement in any class.

If it were not for inheritance, a selection of three alternative scopes (local, private, and public) would most likely be sufficient. Private members and local variables provide protection for those features that are used to implement the design, and public members provide the class's public interface. However, a child class implementation often requires access to the same hidden members that were used to implement its ancestors. For such cases, Java includes another scope option, called protected scope. **Protected scope** is like private scope except that access is extended to all descendant classes. Figure O3.10 summarizes the access rules for private, public, and protected scope.

Figure O3.10 Scope of private, protected, and public members

Member (except constructors)	Available within A?	Available within descendants of A?	Available elsewhere?
private member of class A	Yes	No	No
protected member of class A	Yes	Yes	No
public member of class A	Yes	Yes	Yes
Package member of class A	Yes	Yes	Yes, in same package

The fourth Java scope option is package scope. Java supports facilities for grouping software classes into libraries, called **packages**. When a class member is declared to have **package scope**, that member is accessible to every class in the same package but is not available outside the package. Syntactically, any member that is declared without a scope prefix has package scope.

Inheritance has the potential to complicate scope issues. However, Java avoids most of the possible complications with a simple rule:

Every inherited member inherits its scope from its parent class.

This rule means that all the public methods of the parent class must remain public methods in its descendants, even if they are overridden. This rule also means that protected instance variables cannot be made private or public by any child class. (If a child class declares another variable with the same name, it creates a parallel variable not modifying the inherited variable; such redeclaration is discouraged because the parent's variable is hidden within the child.)

O3.5 TYPE CONFORMANCE

Java, like most modern programming languages, is known as a **strongly typed** language. Strongly typed languages use compilers that enforce strict rules on data types. For example, a Java `int` expression cannot be assigned to a variable of type `StudentInfo`. Similarly, a compiler error results from an attempt to pass an argument of type `Bunch` for a parameter that is declared to be of type `StockWithDividend`.

The Java data type restrictions are defined via a concept called **type conformance**. Figure O3.11 contains a definition of type conformance and the associated usage rule.

Figure O3.11 Type conformance rules for reference types

Definition
An expression type *conforms* to its own class, as well as any ancestor class.

Usage Rule
An expression can be used anywhere that its type conforms to the required class type.

The definition of conformance states that the type of any object *conforms to* any and all ancestor classes. According to this definition, the type of the box variable declared next conforms to `java.awt.Container` because the type of box (`javax.swing.JComponent`) is a descendant of `java.awt.Container`. According to the class diagram in Figure O3.12, the type of box also conforms to `java.lang.Object`, `java.awt.Component`, and `javax.swing.JComponent`.

```
javax.swing.JComponent box;
```

The usage rule from Figure O3.11 points out that it is acceptable to use an expression as long as its type conforms to the required type. Therefore, box can be passed as an argument when the required parameter type is `java.lang.Object`.

Type conformance adds pliability to methods. The add method that is defined in the standard `java.awt.Container` class is declared to support a parameter of type `java.awt.Component`. The following statement is acceptable because the type of box conforms.

```
window.getContentPane().add( box );
```

Type conformance is **directional**. In other words, for any two different types, if *type1* conforms to *type2*, then *type2* does not necessarily conform to *type1*. To illustrate the directionality of type conformance consider, the proper classification of the following set of geometric figures.

Hexagon
Polygon
Quadrilateral
Square
Triangle

Figure O3.12 Class diagram of ancestor classes for javax.swing.JComponent

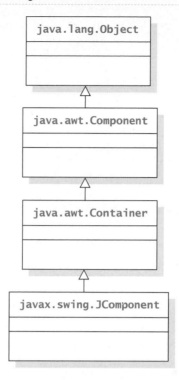

The following statements summarize the usual definitions of these figures.

- A hexagon is a six-sided polygon.
- A quadrilateral is a four-sided polygon.
- A square is a quadrilateral with four sides of equal length and corners forming right angles.
- A triangle is a three-sided polygon.

Figure O3.13 diagrams the appropriate inheritance hierarchy for the is_a relations from these definitions.

The directional nature of conformance means that it is acceptable to pass an actual argument of type Square or Triangle or Hexagon or Quadrilateral or Polygon when the corresponding formal parameter is of type Polygon. However, a Polygon expression cannot be passed when a Triangle parameter is required. Neither can a variable of type Quadrilateral be passed when the formal parameter type is Square.

The same type conformance rules that apply to parameter passage also apply to assignment statements. For example, suppose that myPolygon, myTriangle, myQuadrilateral, myHexagon, and mySquare are all variables with the type indicated by their name. The rules of type conformance permit assignments such as the following.

```
myPolygon = myTriangle;
myQuadrilateral = mySquare;
myPolygon = mySquare;
```

Figure O3.13 Inheritance hierarchy for selected closed polygons

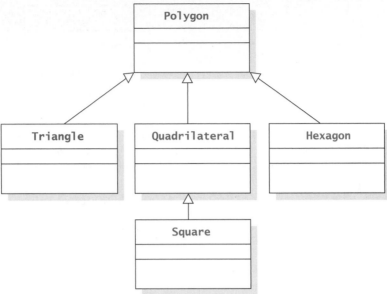

However, the following statements produce compile-time errors as a result of conformance violations.

```
// The statements below all violate type conformance rules.
myTriangle = myPolygon;
mySquare = myTriangle;
myTriangle = myHexagon;
```

Again, the is_a relation is the key to understanding how type conformance works in assignment statements. Because Triangle, Quadrilateral, Hexagon, and Square all have an is_a relation with Polygon, it is sensible to allow a Polygon variable to name any of these kinds of objects. (The object is_a instance of the variable's type.) On the other hand, it does not make sense to allow a Square variable to name a Polygon nor a Triangle nor a Quadrilateral nor a Hexagon object because none of these objects is necessarily a square.

Because a variable can be assigned an object of a different type, it is useful to have a programmatic means of checking the actual type of the variable's object. Java provides for such a check in the form of a relational operator called **instanceof**. The instanceof operator compares an expression to a class and is true-valued exactly when the object referenced by the expression conforms to the class.

For example, consider the need to check for the type of object assigned to the myPolygon variable. The following *if* statement performs such a test and prints a message that is appropriate for each possible type.

```
if (myPolygon instanceof Triangle) {
    System.out.println( "myPolygon references a Triangle." );
} else if (myPolygon instanceof Quadrilateral) {
    System.out.println( "myPolygon references a Quadrilateral." );
```

```
    } else if (myPolygon instanceof Square) {
        System.out.println( "myPolygon references a Square." );
    } else if (myPolygon instanceof Hexagon) {
        System.out.println( "myPolygon references a Hexagon." );
    }
```

O3.6 POLYMORPHISM

Type conformance rules coupled with the ability of a child class to override methods gives rise to questions regarding which version of a method is called. For example, Figure O3.14 contains two classes: Parent and Child.

Figure O3.14 Parent and Child classes

```
public class Parent {
    public Parent() {
    }
    public void printMessage() {
        System.out.println("This is the parent's message.");
    }
}
public class Child extends Parent {
    public Child() {
        super();
    }
    public void printMessage() {
        System.out.println("This is the child's message.");
    }
}
```

The Child class inherits Parent and overrides its printMessage method. Now suppose that the following four statements are executed.

```
Parent parentVariable;
Child childVariable = new Child();
parentVariable = childVariable;
parentVariable.printMessage();
```

Which version of printMessage is called by the last statement? The answer lies in a concept called **dynamic dispatch**. Java executes (dispatches) the version of the method that is associated with an object's type, not necessarily the variable's type. In this situation parentVariable is bound to an object of type Child. Therefore, according to the dynamic dispatch policies, the version of printMessage that is executed is the one from the Child class, and the following message is displayed.

```
This is the child's message.
```

Dynamic dispatch is an effective implementation tool when used as a part of **polymorphism** (more properly called "subtype polymorphism." The word "polymorphism" comes from the Greek words "poly," meaning *many*, and "morph," meaning *structure* or *shape*. When used in programming, polymorphism refers to the ability of a variable to reference objects of varying types throughout program execution. This occurs when a variable is reassigned to objects belonging to different descendant classes at various times during program execution. Such reassignment is also known as **dynamic binding**.

As an example of polymorphism consider a collection of classes used to store geometric solids. Figure O3.15 sketches three such classes, along with their parent class, GeometricSolid.

Figure O3.15 GeometricSolid, Cube, Sphere, and Cylinder classes

```
public class GeometricSolid {
    /* post:   result == the total surface area for this solid */
    public double area() {
        return 0.0;
    }
        . . .
}
public class Cube extends GeometricSolid {
    private double side;
    /* post:   side == s */
    public Cube(double s) {
        side = s;
    }
    /* post:   result == 6 * side * side */
    public double area() {
        return 6 * side * side;
    }
        . . .
}
public class Sphere extends GeometricSolid {
    private double radius;

    /* post:   radius == r */
    public Sphere(double r) {
        radius = r;
    }

    /* post:   result == 4 * Math.PI * radius * radius */
    public double area() {
        return 4 * Math.PI * radius * radius;
    }
        . . .
}
```

Continued on next page

```java
public class Cylinder extends GeometricSolid {
    private double height;
    private double radius;
    /* post:  height == h and radius == r */
    public Cylinder(double h, double r) {
        height = h;
        radius = r;
    }

    /* post:  result == 2 * Math.PI * height * radius
                      + 2 * Math.PI * radius * radius */
    public double area() {
        return 2 * Math.PI * height * radius + 2 * oneEndCap();
    }

    /* post:  result == Math.PI * radius * radius */
    private double oneEndCap() {
        return Math.PI * radius * radius;
    }
    . . .
}
```

Each of the geometric solid classes includes its own version of the area method to return a surface area that is calculated appropriately for that type of solid. The surface area of a cube is the total area of its six faces, whereas the area of a cylinder is the sum of the area of its curved exterior plus the area of its two circular end caps.

The following method takes advantage of polymorphism to calculate the cost of painting any geometric solid.

```java
public int costToPaint(GeometricSolid g, int centsPerUnitArea) {
    return (int)(g.area() * centsPerUnitArea);
}
```

The first parameter of the costToPaint method is a geometric solid, and the second parameter is the cost, in cents, to paint one square unit of surface area. The costToPaint method works properly for Cube, Sphere, and Cylinder objects because the call to g.area() will dynamically dispatch the version of area that is consistent with the class of g. Note that two things are necessary for this polymorphism to work properly:

- GeometricSolid (the parent class) must include an area method.
- Cube, Sphere, and Cylinder (the children classes) must inherit GeometricSolid and override area.

O3.7 ABSTRACT CLASSES

Often there is no reason to implement the parent's version of a method. The `area` method from `GeometricSolid` (Figure O3.15) illustrates. It makes sense to provide implementations of `area` in child classes such as `Cube` and `Sphere`, but `GeometricSolid` has indeterminant surface area. Similarly, the `Object` class does not provide any implementation of the `clone` method. (The `clone` method is provided to permit child classes an operation for duplicating objects.) In both of these cases, the methods are included as templates; the important implementations are expected to occur when child classes override these methods.

Java provides an alternative mechanism, called an **abstract method**, for declaring methods such as `area` and `clone`. An abstract method has no body because its implementation is deferred to child classes. Syntactically, an abstract method includes the reserved word `abstract` immediately before the method's return type, and a semicolon (;) is substituted for the method's code and enclosing braces. Figure O3.16 shows a second version of `GeometricSolid` that uses abstract methods for area and volume.

Figure O3.16 An abstract class version of `GeometricSolid`

```
public abstract class GeometricSolid {
    public GeometricSolid() {
    }
    /* post:  result == the total surface area for this solid */
    public abstract double area();
    /* post:  result == the volume enclosed by this solid */
    public abstract double volume();
}
```

Software Engineering Hint

When a class is needed solely to provide method templates (i.e., it will never be instantiated), then it should be written as an abstract class. Abstract classes are still able to supply code and can be inherited, making them useful within a class hierarchy.

Whenever a class includes one or more abstract methods, it is called an **abstract class**. The new version of `GeometricSolid` is an abstract class because it contains two abstract methods—namely, `area` and `volume`. Abstract classes are virtual entities because it is impossible to instantiate an object belonging to an abstract class. Abstract classes, however, are still quite useful, because they can be used as the type for variables and parameters. Abstract classes also can be inherited, and their protected and public instance variables and methods are available for use by descendant classes.

In Java, classes are called **concrete classes** unless they are declared to be abstract. You declare a class to be abstract by inserting the word `abstract` before the word `class`. Any class containing one or more abstract methods cannot be concrete and must include the `abstract` modifier. The `Cube`, `Sphere`, and `Cylinder` classes are concrete, assuming they include implementations for both `area` and `volume`.

Child classes of an abstract class are also abstract classes unless they implement every abstract method. This is one of the benefits of an abstract class: Abstract classes force the child classes to provide implementations for template (abstract) methods, or else they cannot be instantiated.

Class diagrams use a special notation for abstract classes and methods. An abstract class is denoted by the inclusion of the property **abstract** in curly braces following the class name. Methods are identified as abstract by italicizing their names. Figure O3.17 illustrates the class diagram for the abstract GeometricSolid class and child classes.

Figure O3.17 Class diagram for abstract GeometricSolid and child classes

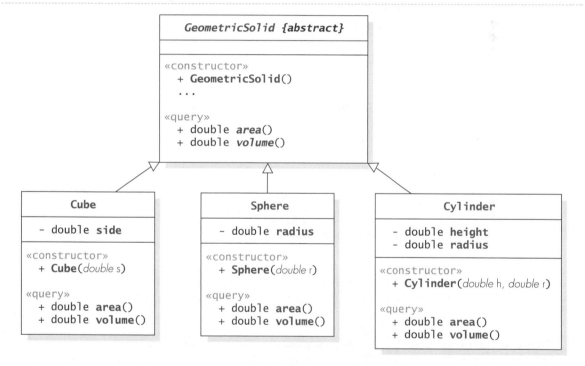

As a second example of the use of abstract classes and methods, consider the problem of storing and printing calendar date information. The Gregorian calendar is widely recognized around the world as a way to keep track of a date in terms of a year number (A.D.), a month within that year, and a day within the month. There is far less agreement about precisely how to represent a date. In personal letters, many people represent a date in this form:

Mar. 27, 1951

Around the time of the American Revolution, the English language was written in more formal notations. In those days the sample date might well have been written as follows.

Day 27 during the month of March in the year of our Lord, 1951

Today, Americans tend to abbreviate dates in the form *month/day/year*, often representing the month as a number and using only the last two digits of the year. Using this notation, the sample date would be denoted as follows.

3/27/51

In Europe it is more common to use an abbreviated form such as *day.month.year*, which leads to the following representation.

27.3.51

This variation in the way that dates are represented suggests that an abstract class—call it `Date`—might be a good design strategy. Figure O3.18 contains a class diagram for `Date`, together with three concrete children. The key abstract method in `Date` is `dateString`, which is expected to return the desired form of the date representation.

Figure O3.18 Class diagram for `Date` classes

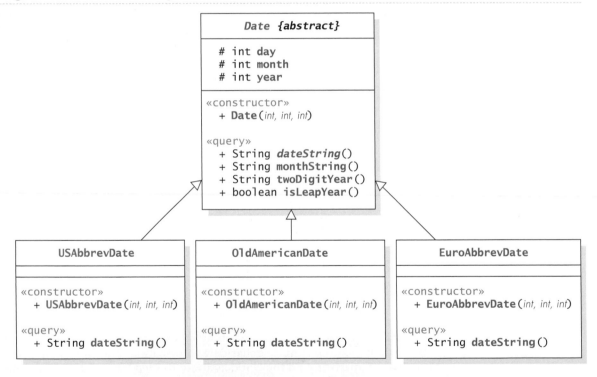

The code for the `Date` class is shown in Figure O3.19. The `Date` class contains three `protected` instance variables, two `private` arrays, and five methods.

Figure O3.19 The `Date` class

```
/* invariant:  1 <= month <= 12
              and 1 <= day <= number of days in month
              and 1 <= year (A.D.) */
```

Continued on next page

```java
public abstract class Date {
    protected int day;
    protected int month;
    protected int year; // full calendar year (A.D.)
    private int[] monthLength
            = {31, 28, 31, 30, 31, 30, 31, 31, 30, 31, 30, 31};
    private String[] monthName
            = {"January", "February", "March", "April", "May",
               "June", "July", "August", "September", "October",
               "November", "December"};
    /*  pre:   1 <= y (throw IllegalArgumentException)
               and 1 <= m <= 12 (throw IllegalArgumentException)
               and d is a valid day for month, and year
                   (throw IllegalArgumentException)
        post:   day == d and month == m and year == y */
    public Date( int d, int m, int y ) {
        if (y > 1) {
            year = y;
            if (1 <= m && m <= 12) {
                month = m;
                if (m==2 && d==29 && isLeapYear()) {
                    day = d;
                } else if (1 <= d && d <= monthLength[month-1]) {
                    day = d;
                } else {
                    throw new IllegalArgumentException(
                        "Day number invalid");
                }
            } else {
                throw new IllegalArgumentException(
                    "Month number invalid");
            }
        } else {
            throw new IllegalArgumentException(
                "Year number invalid");
        }
    }
    /* post:   result is the English name for month */
    public String monthString() {
        return monthName[month-1];
    }
    /* post:   result is the last two digits of year */
    public String twoDigitYear() {
        return "" + year % 100;
    }
```

Continued on next page

```
        /* post:    result == year is a leap year */
        public boolean isLeapYear() {
            return (year % 4 == 0)
                    && ((year % 100 != 0) || (year % 400 == 0));
        }
        /* post:    result is some appropriate string form of the date */
        public abstract String dateString();
    }
```

Abstract classes frequently include non-abstract (concrete) methods as a potential aid to child classes. The monthString and twoDigitYear methods are examples. The Date class stores each month as a number. The monthString method returns that month as a String representation of the English word for the month. Similarly, the Date class stores a year as a four-digit number. Many date abbreviations depict only the last two digits of the year, so the twoDigitYear method is included to return such a value.

Figure O3.20 shows the code for three possible concrete children: USAbbrevDate, EuroAbbrevDate, and OldAmericanDate. Each of these classes is designed for a different form of date representation.

Figure O3.20 USAbbrevDate, EuroAbbrevDate, and OldAmericanDate

```
public class USAbbrevDate extends Date {
    /* pre:     1 <= y (throw IllegalArgumentException)
                and 1 <= m <= 12 (throw IllegalArgumentException)
                and d is a valid day for month, and year
                     (throw IllegalArgumentException)
        post:    day == d and month == m and year == y */
    public USAbbrevDate( int d, int m, int y ) {
        super(d, m, y);
    }

    /* post:    result is a string in the form "<m>/<d>/<y2>"
                where <m> is the month number, <d> is the day number
                and <y2> is the last two digits of the year. */
    public String dateString() {
        return "" + month + "/" + day + "/" + twoDigitYear();
    }
}
public class EuroAbbrevDate extends Date {
    /* pre:     1 <= y (throw IllegalArgumentException)
                and 1 <= m <= 12 (throw IllegalArgumentException)
                and d is a valid day for month, and year
                     (throw IllegalArgumentException)
        post:    day == d and month == m and year == y */
```

Continued on next page

```
    public EuroAbbrevDate( int d, int m, int y ) {
        super(d, m, y);
    }


    /* post:   result is a string in the form "<d>.<m>.<y2>"
               where <d> is the day number, <m> is the month number
               and <y2> is the last two digits of the year. */
    public String dateString() {
        return "" + day + "." + month + "." + twoDigitYear();
    }
}
public class OldAmericanDate extends Date {
    /* pre: 1 <= y (throw IllegalArgumentException)
               and 1 <= m <= 12 (throw IllegalArgumentException)
               and d is a valid day for month, and year
                                   (throw IllegalArgumentException)
       post:   day == d and month == m and year == y */
    public OldAmericanDate( int d, int m, int y ) {
        super(d, m, y);
    }
    /* post:   result is a string in the form
               "day <d> during the month of <m> in the year of our
               Lord, <y>" where <d>, <m> and <y> are, respectively,
               day, month & year. */
    public String dateString() {
        return "day " + day + " during the month of " +
            monthString() + " in the year of our Lord, " + year;
    }
}
```

The following code can be used to test the four date classes. This code illustrates the use of type conformance and polymorphism by declaring its three local variables to belong to the abstract Date class, and then assigning them objects from the concrete children.

```
Date sandiBirthday;
Date derekBirthday;
Date kasBirthday;
sandiBirthday = new OldAmericanDate(27, 3, 1951);
System.out.println( sandiBirthday.dateString() );
derekBirthday = new USAbbrevDate(17, 11, 1981);
System.out.println( derekBirthday.dateString() );
kasBirthday = new EuroAbbrevDate(9, 10, 1979);
System.out.println( kasBirthday.dateString() );
```

THE SOFTWARE INSPECTOR

Following is a collection of hints on what to check when you examine a design or code that involves concepts of this chapter.

✔ In early stages of software design, as well as early design reviews, you should search for is_a and has_a relationships among newly designed classes and available library classes. The is_a relationships can often use inheritance, and has_a relationships suggest aggregation.

✔ Every scope modifier should be scrutinized. Generally speaking, local scope is preferable to private; private scope is preferable to protected; and protected scope is preferable to public. Public scope should be reserved for those class members that are discovered to be a part of the fundamental public view of a class.

✔ You should examine every method inherited by a child class to see whether the inherited version makes sense in the child's context. Sometimes the child needs to override an inherited method.

✔ If an abstract class contains no concrete methods, perhaps it should be written as an interface.

EXERCISES

1. Show the complete code for a class called GradStudentInfo. This class should inherit StudentInfo (from Figure O3.8) and add a private String variable to store the student's undergraduate degree.

2. Draw a class diagram for the GradStudentInfo class (from Exercise 1) along with its parent class.

3. For each part that follows, two classes of real-world objects are given. For each pair of objects, select the best of the following five possibilities.

    (1) Left class is_a right class

    (2) Right class is_a left class

    (3) Left class has_a right class

    (4) Left class has_a left class

    (5) None of these relations seems appropriate

    a) **furniture** and **table**

    b) **airplane** and **wing**

    c) **roll of tape** and **tape dispenser**

d) **roll of tape** and **paper**

e) **car** and **sedan**

f) **northern pike** and **freshwater fish**

g) **instrument** and **oboe**

h) **oboe** and **brass instrument**

i) **oboe** and **tuba**

j) **rowboat** and **oar**

k) **blouse** and **button**

l) **blouse** and **clothing**

m) **blouse** and **clothing store**

n) **retail establishment** and **clothing store**

o) **plant** and **flower**

p) **plate** and **spoon**

q) **spoon** and **silverware**

r) **dictionary** and **book**

s) **book** and **library**

t) **beverage** and **soda pop**

u) **chemical compound** and **beverage**

v) **beverage** and **coffee**

w) **animal** and **giraffe**

x) **giraffe** and **neck**

y) **animal** and **monkey**

z) **monkey** and **giraffe**

Use the following classes to complete Exercises 4 through 10.

```
public class Animal {
    protected int legCount;
    public double age;
    private String name;
    public Animal(String s) {
        name = s;
    }
    public void setAge(double d) {
        age = d;
    }
    public void setLegCount(int j) {
        legCount = j;
    }
}
```

```
public class Dog extends Animal {
    private double tailLength;
        public String hairColor;
        public Dog() {
        // Dog statement here
    }
    public void setLegCount(int j) {
        legCount = 4;
    }
}
public class TwoDogs {
    public Animal theBeast;
    public Dog fido;

    public TwoDogs() {
        theBeast = new Animal("Beast");
        fido = new Dog();
        // TwoDogs statement here
    }
}
```

4. For each of the following parts, suppose that this statement were inserted in place of // TwoDogs statement here in the TwoDogs class. Which of the following best explains the result of this code insertion?

1. The statement references an instance variable or method that is outside its scope.

2. The statement compiles and executes without error.

    a) fido.tailLength = .67;

    b) fido.hairColor = "spotted";

    c) fido.legCount = 4;

    d) fido.age = 3.2;

    e) fido.name = "dalmation";

    f) fido.setAge(3.2);

5. For each part that follows, suppose that this statement were inserted in place of // Dog statement here in the Dog class. Which of the following best explains the result of this code insertion?

1. The statement references an instance variable or method that is outside its scope.

2. The statement compiles and executes without error.

    a) legCount = 3;

    b) age = 7;

    c) name = "beagle";

d) `tailLength = .67;`

e) `hairColor = "blackAndBrown";`

f) `setAge(1.2);`

g) `setLegCount(3);`

h) `setLegCount();`

i) `super("canine");`

6. Draw a class diagram that shows all the aggregation and inheritance relationships from the Animal, Dog, and TwoDogs classes.

7. Suppose that the statement that is shown below is inserted in place of `// Dog statement here` in the Dog class. Precisely what value is assigned to the object's `legCount` attribute as a result of executing this code?

`setLegCount( 2 );`

8. Suppose that the statement that is shown below is inserted in place of `// Dog statement here` in the Dog class. Precisely what value is assigned to the object's `legCount` attribute as a result of executing this code?

`super.setLegCount( 2 );`

9. Suppose that the statements that are shown below are inserted in place of `// TwoDogs statement here` in the Dog class. Precisely what value is assigned to the object's `legCount` attribute as a result of executing this code?

```
theBeast.setLegCount(3);
theBeast = fido;
theBeast.setLegCount(5);
```

10. There is one statement that should be first in the Dog constructor method. What is it?

Use the following classes to complete Exercises 11 and 12.

```
public class Weather {
    // other methods omitted
    public void report() {
        System.out.println( "No Warnings or watches." );
    }
}
public class HighWind extends Weather {
    // other methods omitted
    public void report() {
        System.out.println( "Wind Advisory." );
    }
}
```

Continued on next page

```
public class StormWatch extends Weather {
    // other methods omitted
}
public class TornadoWarning extends StormWatch {
    // other methods omitted
    public void report() {
        System.out.println( "TORNADO WARNING!!" );
    }
}
public class MyWarning {
    public TornadoWarning bigWind;
    // other methods omitted
    }
}
```

11. Using the preceding five classes, assume the following instance variable declarations.

```
public Weather w;
public HighWind hw ;
public StormWatch sWatch;
public TornadoWarning tWarn;
public MyWarning warn;
```

Which of the following assignment statements are valid according to the type conformance rules of Java?

a) w = hw;

b) w = sWatch;

c) sWatch = warn;

d) warn = tWarn;

e) tWarn = hw;

f) warn.bigWind = tWarn;

g) tWarn = warn.bigWind;

h) w = warn.bigWind;

12. Assuming that all variables from Exercise 11 have been attached to objects of the same type, give the output that results from executing the following code segment.

```
w.report();
w = tWarn;
w.report();
w = sWatch;
w.report();
```

13. Consider the following three classes.

```java
public class Bumper {
    public int theNum;

    public Bumper() {
        theNum = 1;
    }
    public void bumpIt() {
        theNum = theNum + 1;
    }
    public void printTheNum() {
        System.out.println( theNum );
    }
}


public class Bumper20 extends Bumper {
    public Bumper20() {
        theNum = 100;
    }
    public void bumpIt() {
        theNum = theNum + 20;
    }
}


public class Bumper300 extends Bumper20 {
    public Bumper300() {
        super();
    }
    public void bumpIt() {
        the_num = the_num + 300;
    }
}
```

Assume the following instance variable declarations use the classes just declared.

```java
public Bumper bumped;
public Bumper20 lumped;
public Bumper300 gumped;
```

Precisely what is output when the following code segment executes?

```java
lumped = new Bumper20();
gumped = new Bumper300();
gumped.printTheNum();
lumped.bumpIt();
lumped.printTheNum();
bumped = lumped;
```

```
bumped.bumpIt();
bumped.printTheNum();
bumped = new Bumper300();
bumped.bumpIt();
bumped.printTheNum();
```

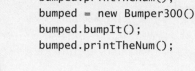

PROGRAMMING EXERCISES

1. Sections O3.6 and O3.7 describe a GeometricSolid class and subclasses. Redesign this software as follows:

    a) GeometricSolid must provide facilities to maintain volume and weight. Specifically, a method must be included to store and report the volume (in cubic meters), to set the density (in kilograms/meter3), and to calculate the weight (in kilograms) based on the volume and density. All children of GeometricSolid must provide for the calculation of volume.

    b) Write two more classes—Cone and RectangularSolid—that are children of GeometricSolid. These classes must fully implement the surface area, volume, and weight features. Redesign the Cube class to take advantage of these new classes.

2. Design, implement, and test a collection of classes to store employees. An abstract class, Employee, is the parent class for the collection, and must include facilities to maintain an employee's name, address, job title, and date of hire, along with methods to print the next weekly paycheck and increase wages by p percent (where p is a double parameter). Your program must include two children classes, HourlyEmployee—for storing any employee whose salary is a fixed dollar amount per hour, and FixedWageEmployee—for storing any employee whose salary is a set dollar amount per week. HourlyEmployee must include methods to set both the hourly wage and the number of hours worked in a recent week. FixedWageEmployee must include a method to assign the weekly wage. Demonstrate how to use these three classes in a polymorphic way.

3. Design, implement, and test a CompoundNumber class, as introduced in Section O3.2. Your class must include methods to assign any valid compound number, to perform basic arithmetic operations, and to output CompoundNumber in normalized form. (Define normalized form to mean that the fractional part is less than 1.) Using the Fraction class from Section O2.7, implement CompoundNumber in two ways: One implementation inherits Fraction, and the second implementation is based on an aggregate of Fraction and int.

4. Design, implement, and test a one-line text editor. Your editor maintains a single line of characters and provides functionality through a menu. The menu must include objects from a MenuEntry class, which has two basic methods—performAction and undoAction—with the implied behavior. Utilize children classes of MenuEntry to provide the following user operations:

- Set cursor to beginning of the line

- Move the cursor forward by one character

- Cut the character immediately after the cursor from the line and into a paste buffer

- Copy the character immediately after the cursor into a past buffer

- Paste the character from the paste buffer immediately before the cursor

EXCEPTIONS

OBJECTIVES

- To introduce robustness as a software property and examine its relationship to exceptions

- To examine the `try` statement for handling exceptions

- To explore the possibilities for handling and recovering from Java exceptions

- To introduce several standard Java exceptions

- To examine the distinction between checked and unchecked exceptions and explain why Java includes three exception categories: `Exception`, `Error`, and `RuntimeException`

- To demonstrate how to create and use your own exception classes

" COMPUTERS ARE GOOD AT FOLLOWING INSTRUCTIONS, BUT NOT READING YOUR MIND "

—Donald Knuth, *Tex*

Sometimes during program execution something goes wrong. Perhaps the program has attempted to store data on a disk that is full. Perhaps the code has attempted to inspect the value of an array cell using an index that is larger than the length of the array. Perhaps a method has been called on an object not yet instantiated. These and many similar problems can occur at run-time. The compiler can't predict such errors, leaving the situation to be resolved by the executing program.

Java provides facilities for detecting, handling, and recovering from run-time errors. This chapter explores these features of the language and the role they play in software design.

O4.1 ROBUSTNESS AND EXCEPTIONS

Anyone who has ever used a program for any length of time has no doubt experienced a run-time error. Sometimes your word processor simply quits and disappears from the screen without properly storing your work. At other times an entire operating system stops with the infamous "blue screen of death," making you restart the computer. Names such as "crash" and "hang" are used to describe these kinds of severe program failures.

Software Engineering Hint

Robustness occurs not in black and white but in shades of gray. The more immune a program is to severe failure and the better the program deals with run-time errors, the more robust it is. Programmers should always strive to find ways to improve their software's robustness.

The existence of these failures and the frequency with which they occur are evidence that the software industry should pay more attention to run-time errors. The term most often used for software that handles run-time errors gracefully is **robustness**. A program that warns the user that a laptop's battery is dangerously low is more robust than a program that simply halts without notice when the battery expires. A Web browser that pops up a "bad URL" window is more robust than a Web browser that crashes in response to an invalid Web page address.

Software developers seeking to improve robustness need to be aware of two basic kinds of potential run-time errors:

- Undetected common logic errors
- Exceptions

An **undetected common logic error** is the result of an incorrect program. Such errors may not halt program execution, but they are likely to result in incorrect behavior. For example, a common logic error results when a program adds two values instead of subtracting them as stipulated in the specifications. The best way to avoid logic errors is sound software engineering practices.

Java is one of several programming languages that include the exception, a mechanism for detecting and responding to run-time errors. An exception is any one of several kinds of detectable run-time errors. Following are four common kinds of exceptions.

- Attempting to apply a method to a null-valued variable
- Attempting a division by zero
- Attempting to access an array cell using an index less than zero or greater than the array length
- Attempting to read from a nonexistent file

When an exception is **thrown** (the error is detected), normal program execution is interrupted. An exception can be thrown for many reasons and from many locations in the program. To assist in identifying the type and location of the exception, an object is always thrown with the exception. These exception objects belong to various classes, but the class of every exception object must be a descendant of `Throwable` (`java.lang.Throwable`). Figure O4.1 contains a class diagram and specification for `Throwable`.

Figure O4.1 Throwable class diagram and specification

```
        java.lang.Throwable

«constructor»
  + Throwable()
  + Throwable(String s)

«query»
  + String getMessage()
  + String toString()

«update»
  + void printStackTrace()
```

Throwable Class Specification

Domain (Every Throwable object has the following components)

String **detailedMsg**;

Constructor Methods

public **Throwable** ( )

   post: detailedMsg == ""

public **Throwable** (String s)

   post: detailedMsg == s

Query Method

public String **getMessage**( )

   post: result == detailedMsg

public String **toString**( )

   post: result == the name of the class + ":" + detailedMsg

Update Method

public void **printStackTrace**( )

   post: the traceback (like the one for an uncaught exception) has been appended to the standard error stream.

Figure O4.2 shows several of the predefined exception classes. Each of these classes is a descendant of Throwable. (All these classes, except IOException, are part of the java.lang package; IOException is in the java.io package.)

Figure O4.2   Selected exception classes from `java.lang`

Exception Name	*Potential Causes*
ArithmeticException	Performing an invalid numeric calculation e.g., `int divisor = 0;` `System.out.println( 5 / divisor );`
ArrayIndexOutOfBoundsException	Accessing an array cell with a negative index or an index greater than or equal to the array length e.g., `int[] arr = new int[3]` `System.out.println( arr[3] );`
ClassCastException	Performing an invalid cast e.g., `Object oneChar = new Character('a');` `System.out.println( (String) oneChar );`
IllegalArgumentException	Calling a method with an invalid argument for some parameter (this is appropriate for some pre-condition violations)
IllegalStateException	Calling a method from an improper state of computation (this is appropriate when a precondition is violated)
IOException	Performing an invalid input or output method (this represents a whole category of exceptions)
NegativeArraySizeException	Constructing an array with a negative length e.g., `int[] arr = new int[-3]`
NullPointerException	Calling a method or referencing an instance variable of a variable that is null-valued e.g., `String s;` `System.out.println( s.length() );`
OutOfMemoryError	Instantiating a new object or calling a method when all computer memory is consumed

A thrown exception is said to be either **uncaught** or **caught**. An uncaught exception is handled by the Java virtual machine and results in the termination of the executing program with an error message to the standard output stream, something like the one following.

```
Exception in thread "main" java.lang.IllegalStateException:
too much data
    at Director.doSomething(Director.java:8)
    at Director.<init>(Director.java:4)
    at Driver.main(Driver.java:5)
```

Software Engineering Hint

The several lines of an uncaught exception report portray a single exception, not many. The lines in the report follow the complete traceback of method calls that were active at the time the exception was thrown.

The first line of the message indicates the kind of exception that occurred (`IllegalStateException`) and (optionally) a detailed message regarding the exception. The remaining lines consist of a **traceback** through the methods that are active at the time of the exception. Each line of the traceback lists first the name of the method, followed in parentheses by the method's class and the line number that was executing at the time the exception was thrown. The second line of the traceback indicates the method that was active when the exception occurred. Each subsequent line indicates the method that called the method one line above. Figure O4.3 dissects this sample traceback.

Figure O4.3   Information from a typical exception traceback

A traceback lists each active method from the most recent one back through the call chain. Reading the traceback from bottom to top reveals the sequence of active method calls leading to the exception. In Figure O4.3, the main method from a class called Driver has called the Director constructor. (The exact line of Driver that caused the call is line 5.) This traceback also shows that line 4 of the Director method has called the doSomething method within the same class, and the exception is thrown from line 8, a statement within doSomething.

Most exceptions are thrown unintentionally. But Java includes a **throws** statement to allow exceptions to be thrown explicitly. The syntax of the throws statement consists of the word throw followed by an expression that references the object to be thrown. For example, executing the following statement causes an exception object of type IllegalStateException to be thrown.

```
throw new IllegalStateException("too much data");
```

This statement both instantiates and throws an IllegalStateException object. The String argument for the constructor supplies the detailed message referred to in Figure 4.3. This argument lets you supply a unique message for each separate throw instruction, independent of the type of the exception. All the predefined exceptions from the standard Java library include a constructor method for supplying this sort of detailed message.

Core Concepts O4

O4.2 EXCEPTION HANDLING

Throwing an exception is preferable to allowing a logic error to go undetected. Even uncaught exceptions report information regarding the nature and location of the error. However, truly robust software relies on taking more care to catch exceptions.

Each caught exception uses a special piece of code known as an **exception handler**. Java notation for exception handlers uses `try` statements. The **try** statement's syntax is described in Figure O4.4.

Figure O4.4 Syntax of the `try` statement

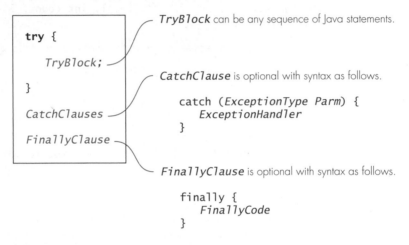

Notes

- *ExceptionHandler* and *FinallyCode* can be any sequence of Java statements.
- *ExceptionType* is the name of a valid exception class (i.e., any class descending from `Throwable`).
- If multiple catch clauses are used, they must have unique *ExceptionTypes*.
- *Parm* is an identifier.

A `try` statement defines both a collection of exception handlers and a region over which those exception handlers are active, sometimes called the **try block**. The `try` statement's exception handling capabilities extend to the `try` block and possibly to methods called from within the `try` block.

Each `try` statement includes one or more exception handlers, called *CatchClauses* in Figure O4.4. (Technically, it is possible for a `try` statement to have no exception handlers, but such a statement would be impractical.) By allowing multiple *catch* clauses a single `try` statement can include different exception handlers for different types of exceptions. The name of the type of exception to be handled is specified by *ExceptionType*, and the *Parm* acts much like a parameter for receiving the thrown object. When an exception is thrown while executing the `try` block, then the *ExceptionHandler* code of the *catch* clause with the conforming *ExceptionType* will execute. No more than one exception handler is invoked for any thrown exception.

As an illustration of exception handling, Figure O4.5 contains a method called average. The body of the average method consists of a try statement followed by a return statement.

Figure O4.5   The average method, an example of the try statement

```
public double average(double total, int count, String msg) {
    double result = 0;
    try {
        if (msg == null) {
            throw new IllegalStateException();
        }
        result = total / count;
    }
    catch (IllegalStateException e) {
        System.out.println( "ERROR: attempt to pass msg == null" );
        result = -1;
    }
    catch(ArithmeticException e) {
        System.out.println( "ERROR: division by zero (count) " );
        e.printStackTrace();
        result = 0;
    }
    return result;
}
```

The try statement in this average method includes two *catch* clauses. If average is called with a third argument (msg) that is null-valued, the throw statement executes and the exception is caught by the first of the two *catch* clauses. If the method is called when the third parameter (msg) is not null but the second parameter (count) has a value of zero, an attempt to divide by zero is caught by the second *catch* clause. Notice that the first *catch* clause can handle only exception objects that conform to IllegalStateException. Similarly, the second *catch* clause catches only exception objects that conform to ArithmeticException.

The rules of conformance imply that a *catch* clause catches not only the specified exception type but also those from all descendant exception classes. The Java compiler reduces potential confusion by insisting that within a single try statement, a *catch* clause for any descendant exception must always precede any *catch* clause for an ancestor exception. For example, the following try instruction is permissible.

```
try {
    ...
}
catch (IllegalStateException e) {
    System.out.println( "ERROR: IllegalStateException object" );
}
catch(Throwable e) {
    System.out.println( "ERROR: Throwable object" );
}
```

If this try block throws an exception conforming to IllegalStateException, the exception is handled by the first *catch* clause. All other exceptions that are thrown within the try block are caught by the second *catch* clause. Even though IllegalStateException is a descendant of Throwable, listing the descendant first is allowed—and useful. Reversing the two *catch* clauses of this instruction, as shown next, is not allowed.

```
// The code below results in a compiler error
try {
    ...
}
catch(Throwable e) {
    System.out.println( "ERROR: Throwable object" );
}
catch (IllegalStateException e) {
    System.out.println( "ERROR: IllegalStateException object" );
}
```

The problem with this try statement is that Throwable is an ancestor of IllegalStateException. Because Java catches exceptions with the first conforming *catch* clause, the second *catch* clause can never be used. For this reason the Java compiler reports the following error in response to this try statement.

```
Driver.java:11: exception java.lang.IllegalStateException has
already been caught
    catch (IllegalStateException e) {
    ^
1 error
```

Catch clauses always receive the thrown object as though it were a parameter. The examples thus far refer to this object as e. This parameter can be used by an exception handler to extract information regarding the exception. The methods for extracting this information are primarily those inherited from Throwable. (See Figure O4.1.) For example, an exception handler could call getMessage() to access the detailed message for an exception, or it could call printStackTrace() to write traceback information. The ArithmeticException *catch* clause from the average method illustrates.

O4.3   EXCEPTION RECOVERY

Throwing an exception within a `try` block causes the remainder of the `try` block to abort (i.e., none of the remaining statements within the `try` block will execute at this time). This means that if `msg == null` at the time average is called, the `result = total/count;` statement will not execute. Both exception handlers assign a value to `result` because the assignment within average will not be executed in the event of either type of exception.

This interruption of normal program execution leads to questions regarding exception **recovery**: How and where does the program resume (recover) its execution following exception handling? Java recovers as follows: At the completion of the execution of any exception handler, execution resumes with the statement that would normally have executed following the `try` block. In other words, for the average method (Figure O4.5) the `return` statement will execute regardless of which *catch* clause is used.

Software Engineering Hint

The *finally* clause provides a way to include code that must be executed regardless of whether or not an exception is thrown in the **try** block.

Java recovery also includes another portion of the `try` statement: the **finally clause**. A *finally* clause is an optional portion of `try` statements and is frequently omitted, as seen in the average method. When a *finally* clause is included, the body of this clause *always* executes after the `try` block and any exception handling code. If the average method had included a *finally* clause, its body would execute immediately before the execution of the `return result;` statement. Note that *finally* clauses execute when an exception is caught, when an exception is *not* caught, and also when no exception is thrown within the `try` block.

The rules for exception handling and recovering become more complicated when there is no local *catch* clause matching the exception type. Figure O4.6 explains this and all other possible situations that can occur when an exception is thrown.

The immediately enclosing code can behave in three possible ways in response to a thrown exception. If the exception occurs within an immediately surrounding `try` block that includes a conforming *catch* clause, it is handled as described previously.

The second possible outcome results from a `try` with no conforming *catch* clause; the remainder of the `try` block is aborted, and the aborted `try`'s *finally* clause (if included) is executed. Next, the exception is thrown to the statement that would normally execute immediately following the `try`. Throwing the exception in this way is like "forwarding" the problem to another location in the code. Once an exception is thrown forward, the same three responses are possible. For example, if one `try` statement is nested within another and if the outer statement contains a *catch* clause for `NullPointerException` but the inner does not, then any `NullPointerException` that is thrown within the inner `try` will ultimately be caught by the outer `try`.

Figure O4.6 The sequence of events following an exception

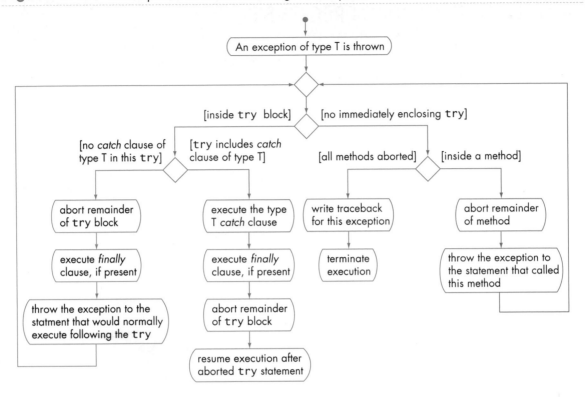

The third possible outcome to a thrown exception occurs when there is no surrounding `try` within the method where the exception is thrown. In this case the remainder of the method must abort and throw (forward) the exception. However, this time the message is thrown forward to the statement that called the method.

If an exception has been thrown forward to every active method and none has an appropriate exception handler, the exception is considered uncaught. As described previously, uncaught exceptions are handled by the Java virtual machine, which outputs the traceback and terminates program execution.

O4.4 VARIETIES OF EXCEPTIONS

The standard Java exceptions are partitioned into two categories:

- Checked exceptions
- Unchecked exceptions

All the exceptions discussed thus far, except `IOException`, are unchecked exceptions; `IOException` is a checked exception. The class diagram in Figure O4.7 shows that the distinction between checked and unchecked exceptions is determined by the exception's ancestry.

Figure O4.7 Inheritance hierarchy for typical exceptions

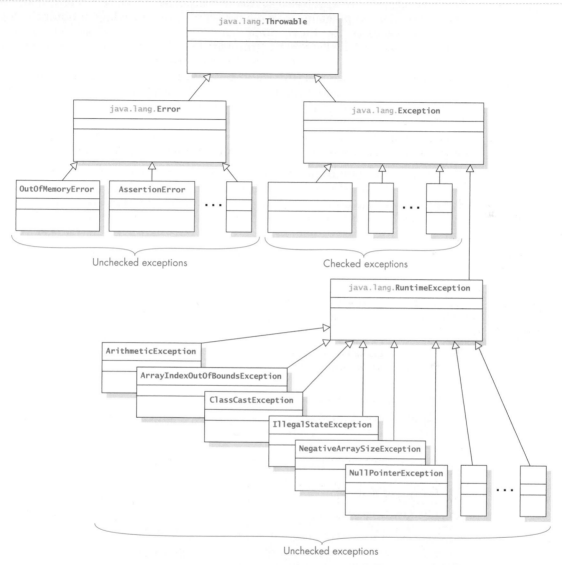

The unchecked exceptions fall into two categories: those that descend from Error, and those that descend from RuntimeException. The Error exceptions are associated with the most severe and unpredictable errors that occur within the Java virtual machine. These Error exceptions include such things as OutOfMemoryError, LinkageError, ThreadDeath, and VirtualMachineError. Java programs rarely catch Error exceptions and should never throw one.

One interesting exception among the Error descendants is AssertionError. This exception is thrown whenever an assert statement detects a false assertion. Like other Error exceptions, an AssertionError is considered to be so severe that the software should not be expected to recover but merely to halt execution with an appropriate error message and traceback.

The other group of unchecked exceptions are those that inherit RuntimeException. A RuntimeException is considered to be less severe than an Error exception, so programs have the option of either including or not including exception handlers for them. Some sample RuntimeExceptions include the following: ArithmeticException (thrown for things such as dividing by zero), ClassCastException (thrown in response to an invalid type cast), IndexOutOfBoundsException (thrown in response to an attempt to access an array cell with an invalid index), SecurityException (thrown to prohibit invalid resource access such as accessing a file without proper permissions), and the ubiquitous NullPointerException. It is often difficult to predict where RuntimeExceptions might occur, so they are sometimes left uncaught. However, RuntimeExceptions are often caught within software regions where robustness is a high priority.

Checked exceptions are treated differently at compile time than unchecked exceptions. The intention of the language designers is to force code to provide exception handling code for any potential occurrence of a checked exception. This intent is enforced by a Java compiler that generates a compiler error for any unhandled potential checked exception. There are two ways to avoid such compiler errors.

- The method containing the statements with potential to throw a checked exception includes a *throws* clause for this exception.
- The statements with potential to throw a checked exception are enclosed in a try block with a *catch* clause for this type of exception.

A *throws* clause is a signal to the compiler that the associated method has the potential to throw an exception of specified type(s). A *throws* clause is placed immediately following the method's parameter list and consists of the word throws followed by a list of exception class names, separated by commas. For example, the following method contains a *throws* clause that indicates the potential to throw a checked exception (IOException).

```
public void readFromFile() throws IOException {
    // The body of this method may contain code that
    // can throw exceptions of type IOException
}
```

Every call statement to a method containing a *throws* clause for a checked exception must be considered a potential site for throwing a checked exception. Therefore, such call statements are subject to the compiler restrictions regarding checked exceptions. This restriction means that any call to readFromFile must either be enclosed by a method that has a throws clause or located within a try block with a *catch* clause for IOException.

Unchecked exceptions are exempted from the mandatory exception handling of checked exceptions for one of two reasons: It is difficult to predict the site where an unchecked exception might be thrown, or useful recovery from an unchecked exception is often impossible. An exception of type OutOfMemoryError can potentially be thrown by almost any statement. A program would be cluttered with *throws* clauses and try statements if OutOfMemoryError were treated as a checked exception. Although the ArithmeticException exception that is thrown as a result of division by zero is more predictable, the program termination that occurs automatically is often the best response to division by zero.

O4.5   PROGRAMMER-DEFINED EXCEPTIONS

Many times a software developer would like to throw exceptions that don't fit well into any of the predefined exceptions in the standard Java libraries. Figure O4.8 contains code for a programmer-defined exception called FractionException.

Figure O4.8   FractionException class

```
/* This type of exception is associated with methods applied to the
      Fraction class. */
public class FractionException extends Exception {
    public FractionException() {
        super();
    }
    public FractionException(String s) {
        super(s);
    }
}
```

To implement a programmer-defined method, all you need is a class that inherits a Throwable descendant (usually Exception or RuntimeException). The class should include constructors that invoke their corresponding parent constructions. The FractionException class illustrates.

The choice of whether to inherit Exception or RuntimeException corresponds to a design decision of whether exceptions should be checked or unchecked. Because FractionException inherits Exception, this class defines exception objects for checked exceptions. Here, Figure O4.9 shows a Fraction class that uses FractionException.

Figure O4.9   Fraction class implementation with exceptions

```
/* class invariant (For every Fraction object, f)
        f.denominator > 0
        and gcd(f.numerator, f.denominator) == 1
                (i.e., this fraction is normalized) */
public class Fraction {
    private int numerator;
    private int denominator;
    /* pre:    d != 0 (throws FractionException)
       post:   real_valueOf(this) == n / d */
    public Fraction(int n, int d) throws FractionException {
        if (d == 0)
            throw new FractionException("denominator cannot be zero");
```

Continued on next page

```
        if (d < 0) {
            numerator = -n;
            denominator = -d;
        } else {
            numerator = n;
            denominator = d;
        }
        simplify();
    }
    /* post:   result == numerator */
    public int numer() {
        return numerator;
    }
    /* post:   result == denominator */
    public int denom() {
        return denominator;
    }
    /* post:   result == numerator + "/" + denominator */
    public String toString() {
        return numerator + "/" + denominator;
    }
    /* pre:    numerator != 0 (throws FractionException)
       modifies:  numerator, denominator
       post:   real_value_of(this) == 1 / (real_value_of(this@pre))
               */
    public void invert() throws FractionException {
        if (numerator == 0)
            throw new FractionException(
                "can't invert fraction with 0 numerator");
        int temp = numerator;
        numerator = denominator;
        denominator = temp;
        if (denominator < 0) {
            denominator = -denominator;
            numerator = -numerator;
        }
    }
    /* modifies:  numerator
       post:   real_value_of(this) == -real_value_of(this@pre) */
    public void negate() {
        numerator = -numerator;
    }
    /* pre:    f != null (throws FractionException)
       post:   real_value_of(result) ==
               real_value_of(this) + real_value_of(f) */
    public Fraction sum(Fraction f) throws FractionException {
        if (f == null) throw new FractionException(
            "null-valued argument");
```

```
        Fraction result;
        int newNumerator = numerator*f.denom() +
            f.numer()*denominator;
        int newDenominator = denominator * f.denom();
        if (newDenominator >= 0) {
            result = new Fraction(newNumerator, newDenominator);
        } else {
            result = new Fraction(-newNumerator, -newDenominator);
        }
        result.simplify();
        return result;
    }
    /*  pre:    f != null (throws FractionException)
        post:   real_value_of(result) == real_value_of(this) *
                                        real_value_of(f) */
    public Fraction product(Fraction f) throws FractionException {
        if (f == null)
            throw new FractionException("null-valued argument");
        Fraction result = new Fraction(numerator*f.numer(),
                                    denominator*f.denom());
        result.simplify();
        return result;
    }
    /* post:    real_value_of(this) = real_value_of(this@pre)
                and gcd(numerator,denominator) == 1 */
    private void simplify() {
        int div = 2;
        while ( div <= min(Math.abs(numerator), denominator) ) {
            if ( (numerator % div == 0) &&
                 (denominator % div == 0) ) {
                numerator = numerator / div;
                denominator = denominator / div;
            } else {
                div++;
            }
        }
    }
    /* post:    a < b implies result == a
                and a >=b implies result == b */
    private int min(int a, int b) {
        if (a < b) {
            return a;
        } else {
            return b;
        }
    }
}
```

Continued on next page

```
/*  Specification Functions
    real_value_of(Fraction f) [a Real-valued function]
        DEFINITION
            real_value_of(f) == f.numerator / f.denominator
        INFORMALLY
            real_value_of(f) is the numeric value from dividing the
            numerator of f by its denominator.
    gcd(int a, int b) [an Integer-valued function]
        DEFINITION
            gcd(a, b) > 0
            and a % gcd(a, b) == 0
            and b % gcd(a, b) == 0
            and forAll (j : Integer and j > gcd(a, b)
                | a % j != 0 or b % j != 0)
        INFORMALLY
            gcd(a, b) is the greatest common divisor of a and b */
```

The Fraction class includes four methods that can throw FractionExceptions—namely, Fraction, invert, sum, and product. These four classes follow a similar form, as shown in the following portion of the invert class:

```
public void invert() throws FractionException {
    if (numerator == 0)
        throw new FractionException(
            "can't invert fraction with 0 numerator");
    . . .
```

Software Engineering Hint

Generally, it is preferable for programmer-defined exceptions to be of the checked variety. However, in cases such as **Fraction**, where these exceptions are precondition violations, an unchecked exception is also permissible.

The throw statement is designed to throw an exception object that is instantiated with its own detailed message ("can't invert fraction with 0 numerator"). The *throws* clause is required in the first line of this method because FractionException is a checked exception.

Every client class of Fraction is obligated to provide exception handlers for any statement that calls one of the four methods capable of throwing a FractionException. Figure O4.10 demonstrates such a segment of code.

Figure O4.10 Client code of the Fraction class

```
try {
    Fraction f1, f2, f3;
    f1 = new Fraction(1,3);
    f2 = new Fraction(3,5);
    System.out.println("1/3 + 3/5 is " + f1.sum(f2));
    System.out.println("1/3 * 3/5 is " + f1.product(f2));
    f2.invert();
```

Continued on next page

Core Concepts O4

```
        System.out.println("1/3 / 3/5 is " + f1.product(f2));
        f3 = new Fraction(-15,30);
        System.out.println("1/3 + -15/30 is " + f1.sum(f3));
        System.out.println("1/3 * -15/30 is " + f1.product(f3));
    }
    catch (FractionException e) {
        System.out.println( e );
    }
```

This client code fulfills its obligation regarding the checked exceptions by wrapping a try block around all the statements that have potential to throw a FractionException. Technically, the first line declaring the three variables could be relocated to a position prior to the try block, but this isn't done because the declaration seems to belong naturally with the code that follows, and there is no harm in this grouping.

Checked exceptions are generally preferred for programmer-defined exceptions because they ensure that the code cannot ignore the possibility of a thrown exception. However, unchecked exceptions are simpler to implement and are considered acceptable for precondition violations, such as those in the Fraction class. For Fraction to use unchecked exceptions involves three changes:

1. FractionException inherits RuntimeException rather than Exception:

```
public class FractionException extends RuntimeException {...
```

2. All throws clauses should be removed from Fraction methods.

```
public void invert() {...
```

3. Client code needs *no* try block.

```
Fraction f1, f2, f3;
f1 = new Fraction(1,3);
f2 = new Fraction(3,5);
...
```

The remaining code in Figures O4.8, O4.9, and O4.10 would not require any changes to use unchecked exceptions rather than checked.

Core Concepts O4

THE SOFTWARE INSPECTOR

Following is a collection of hints on what to check when you examine a design or code that involves the concepts of this chapter.

✔ Software should always be perused for potential run-time errors. Is it ever possible that the program code would try to use an array index that is negative or greater than the maximum index? Could division by zero occur? Can a method be applied to a variable that has never been instantiated? Any potential run-time error is a weakness in the robustness of the code.

✔ try blocks improve robustness by allowing the program to detect, and sometimes recover from, unexpected behavior.

✔ Check for methods that impose preconditions. These methods are best implemented by throwing an exception in response to precondition violations. (These exceptions should either be of a programmer-defined type or `AssertionException`.)

✔ All checked exceptions must be enclosed in a try block with an appropriate *catch* clause, or else their enclosing method must include a *throws* clause.

✔ When multiple *catch* clauses are included in a single try, they must be ordered so that any descendant exception classes precede their ancestors.

EXERCISES

1. Rewrite the Fraction class (from Figure O4.9) so that it throws `AssertionException` errors rather than `FractionExceptions`. Also show how the code from Figure O4.10 would change for this new implementation.

2. Name the Java exception that is thrown when each of the following code segments executes.

   a) `int[] arr = null;`
      `System.out.println( arr[3] );`

   b) `int[] arr = new int[3];`
      `System.out.println( arr[3] );`

   c) `int[] arr = new int[3];`
      `System.out.println( arr[-1] );`

   d) `String s = null;`
      `s = s.toUpperCase();`

e) ```
int n, d;
n = 0;
d = 4 / n;
```

f) ```
int j = 3;
assert j == 0;
```

g) ```
// Assume that Child1 and Child2 both inherit Parent
Parent p = new Child1();
Child2 c = (Child2)p;
```

h) ```
//Assume the following method is called
private void repeatUntilCrash() {
   int j;
   repeatUntilCrash();
}
```

3. List all the following exceptions that can be caught by the given *catch* clause in each part.

   ```
   AssertionError
   Error
   Exception
   FractionException (See Figure O4.8)
   IOException
   NullPointerException
   RuntimeException
   ```

   a) ```
   catch(Throwable e) {
      . . .
   }
   ```

   b) ```
   catch(Exception e) {
      . . .
   }
   ```

   c) ```
   catch(FractionException e) {
      . . .
   }
   ```

   d) ```
   catch(RuntimeException e) {
      . . .
   }
   ```

4. Which of the exception types listed in Exercise 3 are checked exceptions, and which are unchecked?

5. Modify the following `trimEnds` method so that it uses exception handling mechanisms to print the message "NULL" if the first line of the precondition is violated, and the message "String parameter too short" if the second precondition line is violated.

```
/*  pre:    s != null
            and s.length > 1
    post:   result == str@pre without the first and last
                      characters */
public String trimEnds(String str) {
    return str.substr(1,s.length-1);
}
```

6. Show the precise lines of output that result when the following program begins executing with the bull method.

```
public void bull() {
    heifer();
    System.out.println( "bull1" );
    calf();
    System.out.println( "bull2" );
}
public void heifer() {
    try {
        yearling();
        System.out.println( "heifer1" );
        calf();
        System.out.println( "heifer2" );
    }
    catch ( NullPointerException e ) {
        System.out.println( "exception handled by heifer" );
    }
}
public void yearling() {
    try {
        String s=null; // note that s is null.
        System.out.println( s.charAt(1) );
        System.out.println( "yearling1" );
    }
    catch ( NullPointerException e ) {
        System.out.println( "exception handled by yearling" );
    }
}
```

```
        public void calf() {
            try {
                String s=null; // note that s is null.
                System.out.println( "calf1" );
                System.out.println( s.charAt(1) );
                System.out.println( "calf2" );
            }
            catch ( NullPointerException e ) {
                System.out.println( "exception handled by calf" );
            }
        }
```

7. Use the classes that follow to determine the exact output that results from calling each of the following methods.

    a) slicePepperoni();

    b) sliceMozzarella();

```
    public void slicePepperoni() {
        try {
            System.out.println("PEPPERONI - 1");
            continuePizza();
            System.out.println("PEPPERONI - 2");
        } catch (IllegalArgumentException e) {
            System.out.println("exception handled by PEPPERONI");
        }
    }
    public void sliceMozzarella() {
        try {
            System.out.println("MOZZARELLA - 1");
            startPizza();
            System.out.println("MOZZARELLA - 2");
        } catch (IllegalArgumentException e) {
            System.out.println("exception handled by MOZZARELLA");
        }
    }
    public void startPizza() {
        try {
            System.out.println("START - 1");
            continuePizza();
            System.out.println("START - 2");
        } catch (NullPointerException e) {
            System.out.println("exception handled by start - A");
        } catch (IllegalArgumentException e) {
            System.out.println("exception handled by start - B");
        }
        System.out.println("START - 3");
    }
```

Continued on next page

```
        public void continuePizza() {
            try {
                System.out.println("CONTINUE - 1");
                if (true) throw( new IllegalArgumentException() );
                System.out.println("CONTINUE - 2");
            } catch (ArithmeticException e) {
                System.out.println("exception handled by continue");
                }
            System.out.println("CONTINUE - 3");
        }
```

PROGRAMMING EXERCISES

1. Design, implement, and test a program to input and analyze a name. The program begins by retrieving a user input string. This string is intended to be the user's name and is expected to have the following format.

   lastName, firstName middleInitial.

   lastName and *firstName* are sequences of one or more alphabetic characters, *middleInitial* is a single alphabetic character followed by a period, and one or more blanks must follow the comma and *firstName*. Your program must analyze the input to look for the following format errors.

   • No comma following last name
   • No blanks after comma
   • Non-alphabetic characters in name or initial
   • No period after initial
   • Initial more than one character

   Each of these errors must be thrown as an uncaught exception. All exceptions must belong to a programmer-defined class called NameException. Each exception should use a detailed message to differentiate among the five types of errors.

2. Design, implement, and test a program that inputs names, using facilities from the Exercise 1 class, and outputs every name so that the first name precedes the middle initial, which precedes the last name. The comma following the last name is omitted in this output. Your client code must supply appropriate exception handlers to catch every NameException and recover without halting the program's execution.

3. Design, implement, and test a program to read and evaluate single operation integer expressions. The user input must consist of three things: two strings that represent integers, and an operator (the character +, −, *, or /). The program should output the integer result of evaluating the expression.

The program must be as robust as possible; no potential exceptions should go uncaught, and no expression evaluation should yield incorrect results. All potential errors should be handled as exceptions of type `IntegerExpressionException` (a programmer-defined checked exception). You must assume that all calculations are performed within the constraints of the `int` data type, but that the user may try to enter expressions or integers or both that cannot be performed within the constraints of `int` and are therefore erroneous.

FILES AND STREAMS

OBJECTIVES

- To introduce the concept of a file system and the use of files and directories

- To examine the `File` class as a way to manage files and file systems programmatically

- To explore the Java concepts of streams, readers, and writers and examine the way such objects are used to read from and write to files

- To suggest general-purpose algorithms for file input and file output

- To explore binary file I/O using `DataInputStream` and `DataOutputStream`

- To examine the concept of an end of file condition and the many ways in which it is detected

- To explore text file I/O using `PrintWriter` and `BufferedStream`

- To introduce terminal-style file I/O using `System.in` and `System.out`

- To explore persistent object implementation using `ObjectInputStream` and `ObjectOutputStream`

- To introduce the use of `JFileChooser` as a means to allow the user to specify file names

Software is designed to store and manipulate information in the form of data. Many applications create their own data, process it, and report the results of these computations. In such cases you can represent data in the form of internal program data structures, perhaps using arrays, other objects, and primitive variables. These data can be considered transient in the sense that when the program completes executing, none of its internal data exists any longer.

Other software problems require data to be less transient. For example, an insurance company is likely to have many programs to manipulate its customer data. These several programs are probably designed to form a single coherent software system. There might be one program to enter new clients, another to generate notices for premium invoices, and a third to process insurance claims. The data for the company's customers cannot disappear at the end of each program execution because it is probably required by a subsequent program.

O5.1 FILES

The need to retain data between program executions is supported by a construct called a file. Files are categorized as **persistent**, rather than transient, because the data of the file persists even when programs are not executing. This unique property of files means that they play an important role in software that requires persistence.

If you've ever written and executed a Java program, you have used at least two files. A Java program consists of one or more source code files. Suppose you author a new class called MyClass. This class is stored in the source code file called *MyClass.java*. Some type of text editor program is used to create the MyClass.java file. When the MyClass class is compiled, a second bytecode file, called *MyClass.class*, results. This *MyClass.class* file is used by the Java VM during program execution. In other words, the *MyClass.java* file is shared by the text editor and the Java compiler, whereas the *MyClass.class* file is shared by the Java compiler and the Java VM. Both files must be persistent in order to be shared in this way.

Another difference between transient program variable data and file data is the physical devices where they are stored. The data referenced by program variables and parameters are stored within computer memory (sometimes called the **main memory** or **RAM**)[1]. The transient nature of this kind of data is underscored by the fact that turning off the power to most computers causes main memory to be erased.

Files are retained by devices other than main memory. Hard disks, floppy disks, compact disks, various forms of computer tapes, and DVDs can all store files. The name **secondary storage** is commonly used to refer to the type of storage used for files. Because data stored in secondary storage must be persistent, secondary storage devices do not automatically erase their content when power to the computer is lost.

Computer systems use **file systems** to organize secondary storage. Modern file systems organize their storage in terms of files and directories.

---

[1]In computer systems with virtual memory, program data may be stored outside the main computer memory. However, such situations do not alter the behavior of this data.

The file is the basic unit of secondary storage. Data must first be collected into a file before it can be stored within secondary storage.

A **directory** is a mechanism for cataloging files. Files can be grouped into a single directory, and directories, and possibly other files, can be grouped into larger directories. Many computer systems refer to directories as **folders** because of the similarity between a computer directory and a file folder. Just as paper documents can be grouped in file folders, computer files can be grouped in computer folders.

Figure O5.1 pictures a small segment of a typical file system. Each rectangle in this picture depicts a separate file or directory. The rectangles with folder icons are directories, and those without the icon are files.

Figure O5.1 Sample file system

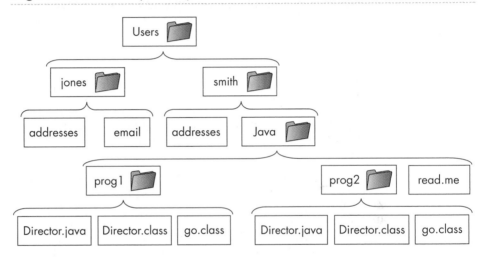

The **root directory**, or **master directory**, of the file system shown in Figure O5.1 is named *Users*. The *Users* directory contains two other directories: *jones* and *smith*. The *jones* directory consists of two files: one called *addresses* and one called *email*. The *smith* directory contains one file, called *addresses*, and one directory, called *Java*.

Figure O5.1 also illustrates that each file and each directory has its own name. These **file names** and **directory names** follow a syntax that is defined by the file system. In general, these names can include alphabetic letters and periods. Also, two files or directories (or a mixture of files and directories) share the same name as long as they are not in the same immediate directory.

The file system provides two ways to identify a particular file. The first technique uses a **path name**. The complete path name for a file is formed by joining all the containing directories (from most distant to immediate) followed by the file name. Each directory or file name is separated from adjacent names using a separator symbol ("/" for UNIX and Apple file systems and "\" for Windows file systems). The path name for the *read.me* file would be as follows for a UNIX or Apple file system.

```
/Users/smith/Java/read.me
```

Following is the path name for this same file in a Windows file system:

```
\Users\smith\Java\read.me
```

The first symbol in each of these names is a file separator that signifies that the path name begins with the master directory for the entire device.

The second way to identify a file uses a **current directory** (also called a **working directory**). Many programs and operating systems keep track of such a working directory, and it is generally possible to change the working directory from one folder to another. For example, UNIX shells and DOS both use the **cd** command to allow the user to type a new current directory.

The purpose of a current directory is to simplify the identification of files. When a current directory is established, a file can be identified by a **relative path name**, which consists of the substring of the complete path name that omits the names up to and including the current directory. For example, here is the complete path name for the *go.class* file that is within *prog2*:

```
/Users/smith/Java/prog2/go.class   (in UNIX/Apple notation)
```

or

```
\Users\smith\Java\prog2\go.class   (in Windows notation)
```

However, if the current directory is set to the *prog2* folder, the following relative path name will uniquely identify the same file.

```
go.class
```

Notice that complete path names begin with a file separator symbol and relative path names omit this character. A Java virtual machine and the Java compiler typically treat the directory of the class that initiates program execution as its current directory.

Unfortunately, an executing Java program cannot rely on a current directory because it is possible to execute Java programs from foreign directories or as applets, which have no current directory. Therefore, a program that uses relative file names for existing files should translate them into complete path names. Figure O5.2 shows a method to perform this translation.

The `completePath` method has a single `String` parameter that represents the relative path name for a file (relative to the class file that is executing). The `String` that is returned by `completePath` is expected to be the complete path name for the corresponding file. If a file with the relative name doesn't exist or is inaccessible, `completePath` throws a `FileNotFoundException`. The details of the methods used by `completePath` are not important to this presentation, but the method is used in many of this chapter's examples.

> ### Software Engineering Hint
>
> Existing files should not be accessed with relative path names in Java. The `completePath` method shows how to translate relative to complete path names to avoid potential difficulties.

Figure O5.2 The `completePath` method

```
/*  pre:    relativePath is a file name for a file relative to the
            folder that contains this class (throws
            FileNotFoundException)
```

Continued on next page

```
        post:   result is the complete path name associated with
                relativePath */
private String completePath(String relativePath)
    throws FileNotFoundException
{
    java.net.URL url = getClass().getResource(relativePath);
    if (url == null)
        throw new FileNotFoundException(
            "invalid relative file name");
    else
        return url.getPath();
}
```

O5.2 THE JAVA FILE CLASS

Java includes many file-related classes in a package called java.io. Some of these classes are used to build objects to extract data from files, and others are used to place data within files.

Still another of the classes from the java.io package provides Java programs with a mechanism for interacting with the file system. This class is called File (java.io.File). Figure O5.3 contains a class diagram and class specification for some of the most commonly used methods of the File class.

Figure O5.3 File class diagram and specifications

```
┌─────────────────────────────────┐
│              File               │
├─────────────────────────────────┤
│  – String FileName              │
├─────────────────────────────────┤
│ «constructor»                   │
│    + File(String )              │
│    ...                          │
│                                 │
│ «query»                         │
│    + boolean canRead()          │
│    + boolean canWrite()         │
│    + boolean exists()           │
│    + String getAbsolutePath()   │
│    + boolean isFile()           │
│    + boolean isDirectory()      │
│    + long length()              │
│    ...                          │
│                                 │
│ «update»                        │
│    + boolean createNewFile()    │
│    + boolean delete()           │
│    + void deleteOnExit()        │
│    + boolean mkdir()            │
│    ...                          │
└─────────────────────────────────┘
```

Continued on next page

File Class Specifications

Invariant

A File object represents the file with the name given by *FileName*.

Constructor Method

public **File** (String s)

> **post:** A new File object is created and, if possible, associated with a file
> named s.
> *and FileName* == s (a complete path name for an existing file or a
> relative name for a new file)

Query Methods

public boolean **canRead( )**

> **pre:** the executing program has permission to access the file or directory
> identified by *FileName* (throws SecurityException)

> **post:** result == true if and only if the file exists and it is permissible
> for the program to read from this file

public boolean **canWrite( )**

> **pre:** the executing program has permission to access the file or directory
> identified by *FileName* (throws SecurityException)

> **post:** result == true if and only if the file exists and it is permissible
> for the program to write to this file

public boolean **exists( )**

> **pre:** the executing program has permission to access the file or directory
> identified by *FileName* (throws SecurityException)

> **post:** result == true if and only if the file or directory identified by
> *FileName* already exists

public boolean **getAbsolutePath( )**

> **post:** result == the complete path name associated with *FileName*
> (even if the file doesn't exist)

public boolean **isFile( )**

> **pre:** the executing program has permission to access the file or directory
> identified by *FileName* (throws SecurityException)

> **post:** result == true if and only if a file identified by *FileName* already
> exists

public boolean **isDirectory( )**

> **pre:** the executing program has permission to access the file or directory
> identified by *FileName* (throws SecurityException)

> **post:** result == true if and only if a directory identified by *FileName*
> already exists

Continued on next page

```
public long length( )
```

> **pre:** the executing program has permission to access the file or
>   directory identified by *FileName* (throws `SecurityException`)
>
> **post:** (exists() *implies* `result` == the number of bytes occupied by the
>   file or directory)
>   *and not* exists() *implies* `result` == 0)

Update Methods

```
public boolean createNewFile( )
```

> **pre:** the executing program has permission to access the file or
>   directory identified by *FileName* (throws `SecurityException`)
>   *and* the secondary storage system is prepared to create a new
>   file (throws `IOException`)
>
> **post:** A new, empty file called *FileName* was created. (Note that any
>   existing file with the same name was lost.)
>   *and* `result` == the file creation was properly performed

```
public boolean delete( )
```

> **pre:** the executing program has permission to access the file or
>   directory identified by *FileName* (throws `SecurityException`)
>
> **post:** The file identified by *FileName* has been deleted from the file
>   system.
>   *and* `result` == the deletion was properly performed

```
public void deleteOnExit( )
```

> **pre:** the executing program has permission to access the file or
>   directory identified by *FileName* (throws `SecurityException`)
>
> **post:** At the time that the currently executing program terminates, the
>   file identified by *FileName* will be deleted from the file system.
>   If no such program exists, then this method has no effect.

```
public boolean mkdir( )
```

> **pre:** the executing program has permission to access the file or
>   directory identified by *FileName* (throws `SecurityException`)
>
> **post:** An empty directory identified by *FileName* has been constructed.
>   *and* `result` == the directory creation was properly performed

```
public void setReadOnly( )
```

> **pre:** the executing program has permission to access the file or
>   directory identified by *FileName* (throws `SecurityException`)
>
> **post:** The file identified by *FileName* has permissions that prohibit
>   writing new values into the file.

Using the standard `File`, you can check whether *EXAMPLE* is the relative name for a file or a directory as follows.

```
// Note that the code below requires exception handling (see
//  Section 05.3)
File file = new File( completePath("EXAMPLE") );
if (file.isFile()) {
    System.out.println( "A file with name EXAMPLE exists." );
} else if (file.isDirectory()) {
    System.out.println( "A directory with name EXAMPLE exists." );
}
```

This code demonstrates how you can use an object of type `File` to examine a file system by checking to see whether the relative path name represents a file (`isFile`) or a directory (`isDirectory`). You can also use `File` to ascertain the complete path name (by calling `getAbsolutePath`) or to check a file's size (by calling `length`).

To illustrate how a `File` object can be used to create a new file, consider the following code.

```
// Note that the code below requires exception handling (see
//  Section 05.3)
File file = new File( "myFile.fil" );
boolean operationOK;
if ( !file.exists() ) {
    operationOK = file.createNewFile();
} else {
    System.out.println( "A file/directory with name myFile.fil
    exists." );
}
```

Software Engineering Hint

When you manipulate the file system from a program, take care regarding the unexpected cases. For example, don't attempt to create a new file without first checking to see whether one already exists. Don't attempt to delete a file unless it is known to be a file and not a directory. Don't attempt to make a new directory without first checking for a previous file or directory of the same name. Fortunately, the Java `File` class provides ample methods to test for these unexpected conditions.

When the `file` variable is instantiated, it is associated with the relative name of *myFile.fil*. If a file with this name already exists, the *else* clause executes, displaying a suitable message. If no file named *myFile.fil* exists, the *then* clause will execute. The resulting call to `createNewFile` in this example performs two functions. This method attempts to create a new file with the given name. Second, the `createNewFile` method returns a true or false, indicating whether or not such a creation was properly performed.

To maintain file privacy, computer file systems assign various **file permissions** to their files. A file's permissions typically grant access to some of the computer system's users and deny access to others. These access permissions for a user also must extend to the programs the user might execute. A Java applet that is delivered via the Internet must abide by even stricter file access permissions.

Java uses an exception from the `java.lang` package to enforce access permissions. Whenever an executing program attempts to violate the permissions of the executing user, a `SecurityException` is raised. Many of the methods involved in file manipulation can throw such exceptions. The File class specifications demonstrate. Because this potential is ubiquitous, the remaining class specifications in this chapter don't bother to include the potential for SecurityException, considering it to be implicit.

O5.3 IOEXCEPTION

The creators of Java felt that most of the exceptions associated with files are sufficiently important that the programmer must handle them as checked exceptions. Therefore, all I/O exceptions descend from the IOException class found in the java.io library. Because they involve potential checked exceptions, calling I/O methods must be enclosed either by a try block or a method with a *throws* clause. Figure O5.4 demonstrates the try statement solution.

Figure O5.4 Form of the try statement needed for file-related methods

```
try {
    // Code with potential to throw exceptions goes here.
}
catch ( IOException e) {
    // Code to handle the exception goes here.
}
```

Software Engineering Hint

The entire collection of related code that would be impacted by an exception should be collected together within a **try** block. For file-related code, this usually means that all the code for a single algorithm performed on the same file should be kept together.

When you're writing programs that manipulate files, it is best to collect statements associated with one file within a single try block. This grouping ensures that any remaining file access is aborted when an exception occurs. Typically, an exception thrown by the file-related methods is not recoverable. Therefore, the exception handling code of the *catch* clause can do little more than print an error message.

Figure O5.5 contains a code segment that attempts a new file creation and reports on the outcome. This class includes an import declaration of java.io in order to import both the File class and the IOException class.

If this program executes without an exception being thrown, it first instantiates a File object for a file named *example.txt*. The first instantiation of the file object calls completePath. If an exception results, the *catch* clause instantiates file using a relative file name. The outer *if* statement tests whether this file or directory already exists. If exists() returns true, the program proceeds to check whether the existing entity is a file or a directory. If it is a directory, the program displays a message without attempting to replace this with a file. If, however, it is an existing file, that file is first deleted and a new file is created. The Boolean values returned by these delete and create operations are assigned, respectively, to the deleteOK and createOK variables. These variables are used to print an appropriate message. If the file doesn't exist in the first place, a new file is created and an appropriate message displayed.

Figure O5.5 Code segment to attempt to create a new file

```java
File file;
boolean createOK;
try {
    file = new File( completePath("example.txt") );
}
catch (FileNotFoundException e) {
    file = new File("example.txt");
}
try {
    if ( file.exists() ) {
        if ( file.isDirectory() ) {
            System.out.println( file.getAbsolutePath()
                                + " is a directory. No file
                                created.");
        } else {
            boolean deleteOK = file.delete();
            if ( deleteOK ) {
                System.out.println("Existing file deleted.");
                createOK = file.createNewFile();
                if ( createOK ) {
                    System.out.println("File created. ");
                } else {
                    System.out.println( "Unable to create file "
                                        + file.getAbsolutePath() );
                }
            } else {
                System.out.println( "Unable to delete file "
                                    + file.getAbsolutePath() );
            }
        }
    } else { // file doesn't exist
        createOK = file.createNewFile();
        if ( createOK ) {
            System.out.println("File created. ");
        } else {
            System.out.println( "Unable to create file "
                                + file.getAbsolutePath() );
        }
    }
}
catch (IOException e) {
    System.out.println( "I/O error occurred");
}
```

O5.4 INPUT AND OUTPUT

Computer scientists use the term **I/O** (**input/output**) to refer to the transfer of data between a program and an external device, such as a secondary storage device. The operation of sending data to a device is called **writing**, and the data are program **output**. The operation of retrieving data from a device is called **reading**, and the data are program **input**.

The File class includes methods for creating new files and deleting existing files. However, a File object alone cannot read from or write to a file. Fortunately, the java.io package includes a rich collection of classes to support I/O. Various classes provide for various ways for programs to organize and retrieve data. These classes accommodate the differences between I/O devices.

The notion of a **stream** is fundamental to Java I/O. Java programs do not communicate directly with external devices. Instead, a program creates a stream object to connect the program to a device. Each stream functions as a conduit for the data to flow between the program and the I/O device. Figure O5.6 illustrates this connection. It shows an executing program with an input stream to serve as a conduit for reading data from a file, and an output stream to serve as a conduit for writing data to a file.

Figure O5.6 Using streams with readers and writers

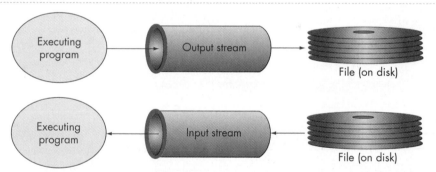

This book examines **sequential files**. An essential requirement of every sequential file is that data be processed from the beginning. An input stream supplies the data from the file in precisely the order in which that data is stored, starting with the first data item. An output stream writes data to the file in the order that write methods are executed.

Figure O5.7 diagrams some of the most commonly used Java stream classes. Arrows depict the inheritance relations among these classes.

Stream classes are subdivided into two categories: those that are used for input, and those that are used for output. The FileInputStream and FileOutputStream classes are not very useful by themselves because these kinds of streams support data flow only in the form of bytes. The DataInputStream and DataOutputStream classes are more useful because they provide methods for reading and writing data of any primitive data type, as well as String data. The ObjectInputStream and ObjectOutputStream classes include methods for reading and writing whole

Core Concepts O5

objects. Section O5.5 discusses `DataInputStream` and `DataOutputStream`, and Section O5.7 examines `ObjectInputStream` and `ObjectOutputStream`.

Figure O5.7 Inheritance relations for selected stream classes

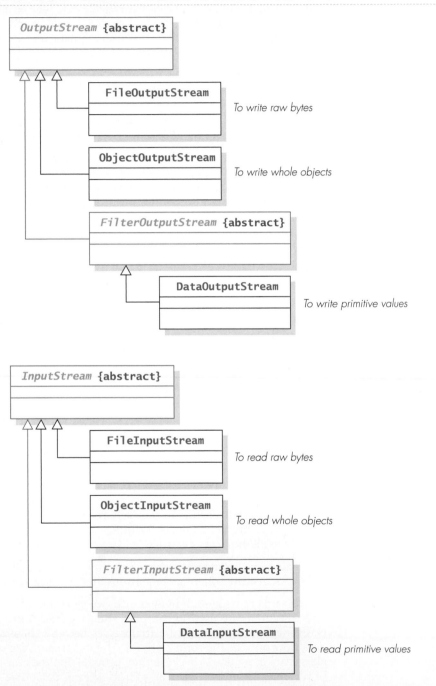

Before exploring the particulars of each of these streams, it is instructive to explore the basic algorithms employed by programs that perform I/O. Figure O5.8 contains a basic algorithm for reading from a file.

Figure O5.8 General algorithm for reading from a file

1. Open the file for input, instantiating associated stream objects.
2. Call read methods to retrieve the stream's content.
3. Close the file or stream.

Software Engineering Hint

Streams are closed automatically when the program completes with or without a call to a `close` method. However, it is still best to explicitly call `close` for several reasons.

- An explicit `close` makes it clear when the programmer expects to be finished performing I/O.
- Once a file is closed, it is possible to reopen the file.
- The run-time environment has a finite set of resources. Failing to close files consumes resources unnecessarily, potentially resulting in program failure.
- Many run-time environments fail to properly close files for certain types of program "crashes."

This algorithm shows that files must be **opened** before they can be read. Opening a file for input consists of associating a file from the file system with the appropriate input stream object(s). Opening a file generally positions the file data so that it is read from the beginning of the file. The Java stream objects include constructor methods that are used to open files.

After a program is finished reading from a file, it is wise to close the file. Most streams include a parameterless `close` method for this purpose.

The basic algorithm for writing to a file is similar to the reading algorithm. Figure O5.9 contains the writing algorithm.

The additional requirement of the writing algorithm is to flush the stream, which is usually done by calling a parameterless `flush` method on the appropriate output stream. Flushing ensures that no data is left in the stream conduit.

Figure O5.9 General algorithm for writing to a file

1. Open the file for output, instantiating associated stream objects.
2. Call write methods to write data into the stream.
3. Flush the stream.
4. Close the file or stream.

Another difference between input and output algorithms is the behavior of their open operations. When a file is opened for input, it is expected that the file already exists. The stream for the newly opened input file begins to supply the first data item that is stored in the file. When a file is opened for output, it is because the program intends to place data into it. For all except certain specialized streams, the program will place *all* the data into the file. Therefore, the process of opening a file for output typically creates a new file. Even if the file already exists, opening an output stream on a file should be expected to create a new file.

The stream class constructors in Java are designed in a curious way. Only two of the java.io streams—namely, FileInputStream and FileOutputStream—can be connected directly to a file. No other java.io stream class includes the proper constructor methods to allow the program to specify a file name or to use a File object. This unique property of FileInputStream and FileOutputStream gives these two classes special importance. Figure O5.10 contains a class diagram and class specifications for FileInputStream.

Figure O5.10 FileInputStream class diagram and specifications

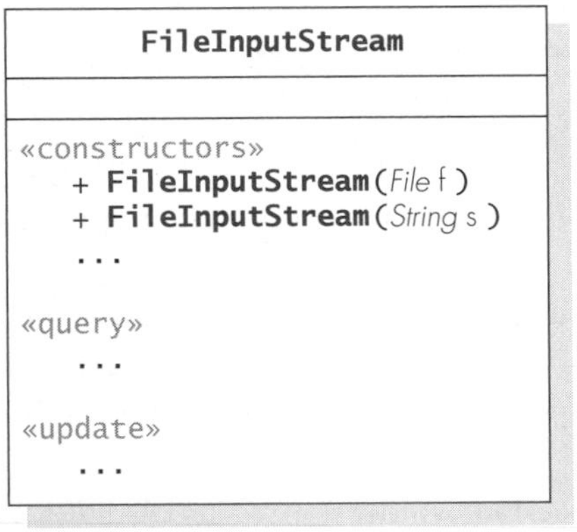

```
┌─────────────────────────────────────┐
│           FileInputStream            │
├─────────────────────────────────────┤
│                                      │
├─────────────────────────────────────┤
│ «constructors»                       │
│    + FileInputStream(File f )        │
│    + FileInputStream(String s )      │
│    ...                               │
│                                      │
│ «query»                              │
│    ...                               │
│                                      │
│ «update»                             │
│    ...                               │
└─────────────────────────────────────┘
```

FileInputStream Class Specifications

Invariant

A FileInputStream object...
serves as a conduit for input from a file specified at the time this object is instantiated.

Constructor Methods

public **FileInputStream** (File f)

pre: *f*.isFile() (throws *FileNotFoundException*)

post: A new FileInputStream object is created and, if possible, associated with a file named *f*.
and the file is positioned to begin reading from the beginning.

public **FileInputStream** (String s)

pre: s is a path name for an existing file (throws *FileNotFoundException*)

post: A new FileInputStream object is created and, if possible, associated with a file named *s*. (*s* should be a complete path name)
and the file is positioned to begin reading from the beginning.

Only two FileInputStream methods are of interest to this discussion: the two constructor methods. These are the methods that make FileInputStream unique. The first constructor instantiates a stream object and connects it to the file from a File object. The following code segment illustrates how to open a file using this constructor.

```
try{
    File file;
    FileInputStream inStream;
    file = new File( completePath("sampleFile") );
    inStream = new FileInputStream( file );
}
catch (FileNotFoundException e) {
    System.out.println(
        "Unable to locate a file named sampleFile.");
}
// The code to read the file and close it belongs here.
```

When this code executes, a file object is instantiated and connected to a file with the relative path name *sampleFile*. Next, a FileInputStream object, inStream, is instantiated and connected to the same file by passing file as an argument to the constructor method. The try statement captures the potential FileNotFoundException that might occur.

This first example of opening a stream via a File object is useful whenever the program needs to check other file properties using File queries such as isDirectory(), exists(), or length(). However, if the program doesn't require such tests, using the second constructor method leads to abbreviated code for opening the same file:

```
try{
    FileInputStream inStream;
    inStream = new FileInputStream( completePath("sampleFile") );
}
catch (FileNotFoundException e) {
    System.out.println(
        "Unable to locate a file named sampleFile.");
}
// The code to read the file and close it belongs here.
```

The FileOutputStream class includes two constructor methods that parallel those from FileInputStream. Figure O5.11 contains their specifications.

Figure O5.11 FileOutputStream constructor specifications

FileOutputStream Constructor Specifications

public FileOutputStream (File f)

> **pre:** *not f*.isDirectory() (throws *FileNotFoundException*)

> **post:** A new FileOutputStream object is created and, if possible, associated with an empty file named *f*.
> *and* the file is positioned to begin writing from the beginning.

Continued on next page

```
public FileOutputStream ( String s )
```

> **pre:** *s* is not the path name for an existing directory
> (throws *FileNotFoundException*)
>
> **post:** A new `FileOutputStream` object is created and, if possible,
> associated with an empty file named *s*. (*s* may be either a
> complete or relative path name)
> *and* the file is positioned to begin writing from the beginning.

O5.5 DATAINPUTSTREAM AND DATAOUTPUTSTREAM

As mentioned previously, the `DataInputStream` and `DataOutputStream` classes are well suited for reading and writing data of primitive type. Figure O5.12 illustrates this by showing that `DataOutputStream` includes a separate method to output each primitive type.

Figure O5.12 `DataOutputStream` class diagram

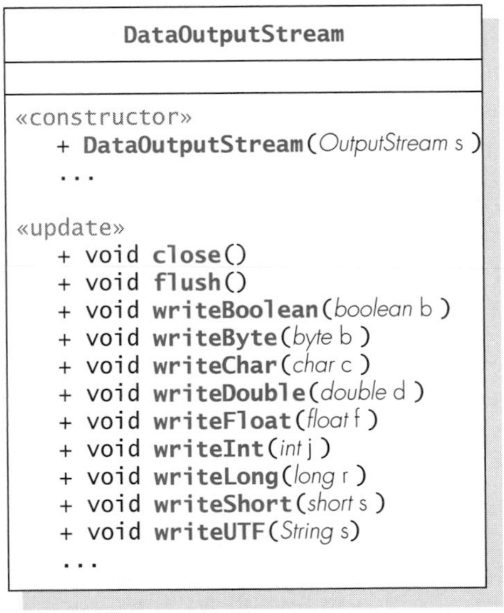

```
┌─────────────────────────────────────────────┐
│             DataOutputStream                  │
├─────────────────────────────────────────────┤
│                                               │
├─────────────────────────────────────────────┤
│ «constructor»                                 │
│     + DataOutputStream(OutputStream s )       │
│     ...                                        │
│                                               │
│ «update»                                      │
│     + void close()                            │
│     + void flush()                            │
│     + void writeBoolean(boolean b )           │
│     + void writeByte(byte b )                 │
│     + void writeChar(char c )                 │
│     + void writeDouble(double d )             │
│     + void writeFloat(float f )               │
│     + void writeInt(int j )                   │
│     + void writeLong(long r )                 │
│     + void writeShort(short s )               │
│     + void writeUTF(String s)                 │
│     ...                                        │
└─────────────────────────────────────────────┘
```

Opening a `DataOutputStream` is complicated by the fact that the constructor method has a parameter of type `OutputStream` rather than `File` or `String` (for the file's name). However, `FileOutputStream` is a subclass of `OutputStream`. In this way, you can open a `DataOutputStream` by first instantiating a `FileOutputStream` object, and then passing this object as an argument to instantiate a `DataOutputStream`. The resulting situation is pictured in Figure O5.13.

Figure O5.13 Connecting a DataOutputStream to a file

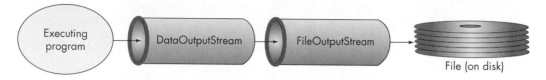

Figure O5.14 shows sample code to open a file in this way. It also illustrates how to write, flush, and close such a file.

Figure O5.14 Code segment to write to a binary file

```
try{
    FileOutputStream outStream;
    DataOutputStream dataStream;
    outStream = new FileOutputStream( "example.bin" );
    dataStream = new DataOutputStream( outStream );
    dataStream.writeInt( 12 );
    dataStream.writeBoolean( true );
    dataStream.writeDouble( 98.7 );
    dataStream.writeUTF( "hello world" );
    dataStream.writeChar('Z');
    dataStream.flush();
    dataStream.close();
}
catch (IOException e) {
    System.out.println("ERROR writing." );
}
```

The first four statements in the body of the try statement open the stream for a file named *example.bin*. The third statement instantiates a FileOutputStream object called outStream, and the fourth statement uses outStream as an argument to instantiate dataStream. All subsequent method calls are appropriately directed to dataStream, not outStream.

The DataOutputStream and DataInputStream classes are designed to perform I/O using a storage format that essentially matches the format used to store data in memory. So the content of *example.bin* following the execution of the code from Figure O5.14 can be pictured as follows.

Content of the *example.bin* file:

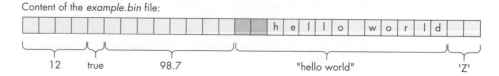

Each of the small squares in the picture represents one byte of the file. The first four bytes store the int value 12 because this is what was output by the first write statement of the program. The fifth byte stores the boolean value. When the writeDouble method is called, eight bytes are written to store the value 98.7.

You might be wondering why DataOutputStream has no writeString method. As is evident in this example, the writeUTF method[2] plays this role. UTF refers to a technique for storing String data efficiently. A single Unicode character occupies two bytes of storage. However, a UTF encoding reduces this to one byte for most commonly used symbols. This example shows each character in the "hello world" string stored in a single byte. The two bytes preceding this string are also part of the overhead required for UTF encoding.

The methods of DataInputStream parallel those of DataOutputStream. Figure O5.15 shows a class diagram for DataInputStream.

Figure O5.15 DataInputStream class diagram

The most significant differences between DataOutputStream and DataInputStream are that (1) DataInputStream has no flush method and (2) the void write methods from DataOutputStream are replaced by nonvoid, parameterless read methods in DataInputStream. Figure O5.16 illustrates how to use DataInputStream to read the file that was created by the code in Figure O5.14.

The code segment in Figure O5.16 opens the file for input using a FileInputStream object in the same way that FileOutputStream was used for opening an output stream. Each of the values is read from the input file and assigned to a separate variable. The method uses System.out.println to display each of these variables.

---

[2]UTF stands for Unicode Transformation Format.

Figure O5.16 Code to read and print the binary file created in Figure O5.14

```
try {
    int inInt;
    boolean inBool;
    double inDouble;
    String inStr;
    char inCh;
    FileInputStream inStream;
    DataInputStream dataStream;
    inStream = new FileInputStream( completePath("example.bin") );
    dataStream = new DataInputStream( inStream );

    inInt = dataStream.readInt();
    inBool = dataStream.readBoolean();
    inDouble = dataStream.readDouble();
    inStr = dataStream.readUTF();
    inCh = dataStream.readChar();
    dataStream.close();

    System.out.println( inInt );
    System.out.println( inBool );
    System.out.println( inDouble );
    System.out.println( inStr );
    System.out.println( inCh );
}
catch (IOException e) {
    System.out.println("ERROR reading." );
}
```

The most important thing to remember when you use `DataInputStream` is that *data must be read (by type) in the same order it was written*. The order used to write the *example.bin* file is as follows.

an int → a boolean → a double → a String → a char

Therefore, it must be read with the following order of calls:

`readInt, readBoolean, readDouble, readUTF, readChar`

Reading data in the wrong order from a `DataInputStream` can produce extremely unusual behavior. Consider the following code segment (a variation on the Figure O5.16 code).

```
inStream = new FileInputStream( completePath("example.bin") );
dataStream = new DataInputStream( inStream );
inBool = dataStream.readBoolean();
inInt = dataStream.readInt();
```

When `readBoolean` is called, it will consume the first byte in the file. Unfortunately, the file's first byte was one-fourth of an `int` value. When the `readInt` method is called, it consumes the next four bytes from the file. The result is that `inInt` is assigned a value formed from three-fourths of an `int` value appended to a `boolean` value. The values assigned to `inBool` and `inInt` resulting from the execution of this code are simply not sensible, but no error will be reported.

Sometimes the author of the input program does not know the exact amount of data in a file. In such cases the program must test for a condition known as **end of file**. An end of file condition becomes true when all data from an input file has been read.

`DataInputStream` handles an end of file condition by throwing an `EOFException` when any read method is called that would retrieve more bytes of data than remain unread in the stream. This condition can be caught by a separate *catch* clause. For example, suppose that *fileOfInts* is a file that is known to contain exclusively int values. The following code reads every value from this file and prints it using System.out.println.

```
try {
    FileInputStream inStream;
    DataInputStream dataStream;
    inStream = new FileInputStream( completePath("fileOfInts") );
    dataStream = new DataInputStream( inStream );

    while (true) {
        System.out.println( dataStream.readInt() );
    }
}
catch (EOFException e) {
    // This occurs normally when reading past the last int.
}
catch (IOException e) {
    System.out.println("ERROR reading." );
}
```

The loop in this program may appear to be infinite, but remember that each time through the loop another `int` value is read from the stream. When `readInt` is called after all values from the stream have been read, an `EOFException` is thrown. The exception is handled by its own *catch* clause, which does nothing.

O5.6 TEXT FILES

A file that contains exclusively `char` data is said to be a **text file**. Memos, letters, and manuals are often stored in the computer in the form of text files. Your source code (*.java*) files also are stored as text files. **Text editors** are programs that are used to create and modify text files.

Not all files are in text file format. For example, any file created using `DataOutputStream` is not a text file unless only `writeChar` methods are used.

Nontext files are referred to collectively as **binary files**. When a binary file is opened by a text editor, it tends to appear as a random collection of symbols.

Because many humans prefer text separated into separate lines, text files use a special character (written '\n' in Java) to separate consecutive lines. Figure O5.17 shows three lines of text the way they would be viewed by humans, and the corresponding characters as they would be stored in a text file.

Figure O5.17   Text file storage format for lines

Three lines of text:

    This
    is a
    test

Content of a text file storing three lines:

T	h	i	s	\n	i	s		a	\n	t	e	s	t

The java.io package includes several classes to manipulate text files. Many of these classes use the concepts of **reader** and **writer** objects to massage stream data.

In a sense, the data that comes from a stream is like crude oil. It is possible to use crude oil in its natural form. However, it is useful in a wider variety of applications after it has been refined and repackaged. Readers and writers give you tools to refine and repackage data.

Figure O5.18 pictures a typical way to use readers and writers for I/O. To write to a file, a program creates two objects: a writer object and an output stream. The actual output methods are performed on the writer. Similarly, a program can input from a file by way of a reader object that is connected to an input stream object.

Figure O5.18   Using streams with readers and writers

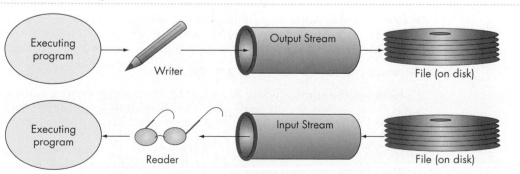

Figure O5.19 contains a class diagram for a writer class called PrintWriter, an output class that produces only text files.

Figure O5.19 PrintWriter class diagram

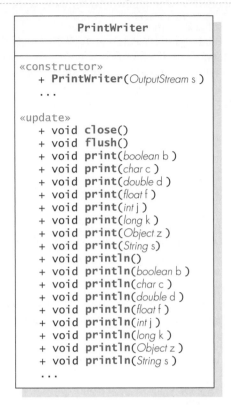

On the surface, the PrintWriter class looks somewhat similar to DataOutputStream. Both classes use the same close and flush methods. Both classes include separate methods for most of the primitive data types, although PrintWriter does so by overloading its print and println methods. The constructor method of the two classes even uses the same type of stream parameter.

The primary difference between DataOutputStream and PrintWriter is that DataOutputStream writes data in binary form, whereas PrintWriter transforms all data into a textual form before writing. For example, the following DataOutputStream method call writes its data in the form of an 8-byte double.

```
dataStream.writeDouble( 1234567890.1 );
```

However, the corresponding PrintWriter method call writes a sequence of 12 characters, including the decimal point, to represent the same output data in textual form.

```
printWriterObject.print( 1234567890.1 );
```

The PrintWriter class includes println methods to make the insertion of end of line separations more convenient. Each call to the parameterless version of println writes a single end of line character into the output stream. In other words, a call to the method

```
println();
```

performs the same function as the following statement.

```
print('\n');
```

When an argument is passed to println, an end of line character is appended to the stream *following* the textual representation of the argument.

Figure O5.20 contains sample code that uses PrintWriter to create a text file by writing the same program data as given in Figure O5.14. Figure O5.20 also shows the content of the resulting text file.

Figure O5.20 Code using PrintWriter

```
try {
    FileOutputStream outStream;
    PrintWriter printWriter;

    outStream = new FileOutputStream( "example.txt" );
    printWriter = new PrintWriter( outStream );
    printWriter.print( 12 );
    printWriter.print( true );
    printWriter.println( 98.7 );
    printWriter.print( "hello world" );
    printWriter.print('Z');
    printWriter.flush();
    printWriter.close();
}
catch (IOException e) {
    System.out.println("ERROR writing." );
}
```

Content of the resulting *example.txt* file:

| 1 | 2 | t | r | u | e | 9 | 8 | . | 7 | \n | h | e | l | l | o | | w | o | r | l | d | Z |

You can read from a text file in many ways. One way is to read one character at a time. Another way is to read an entire line in a single method call. The BufferedReader class provides both options. Figure O5.21 contains a class diagram for BufferedReader.

The constructor method of BufferedReader differs from previously presented input classes in that it cannot accept an argument of type FileInputStream. However, another java.io class, FileReader, is a subclass of Reader and can be used in the same way as FileInputStream.

Each call to the BufferedReader readLine method returns the next unread line as a String value. There are two important things when you call readLine.

- The String returned by readLine does *not* include the end of line character ('/n'), but the end of line is consumed by the method call.
- When readLine is called after reaching the end of file, null is returned.

Figure O5.21 BufferedReader class diagram

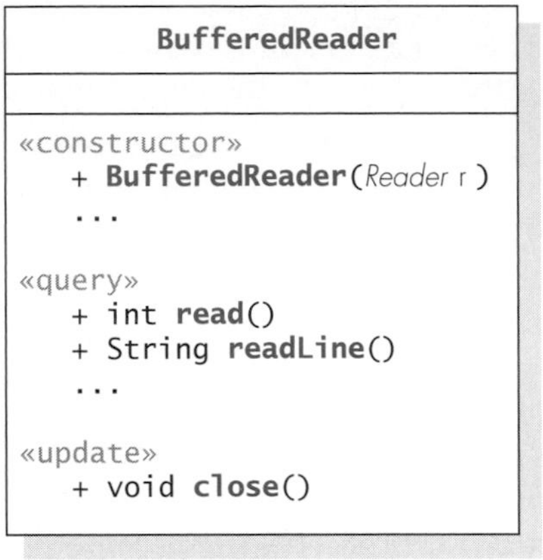

Figure O5.22 shows a class with a main method that invokes the Driver constructor. When Driver executes, it opens the *example.txt* file and reads its contents line by line. The lines are then output double-spaced to the standard output stream.

Figure O5.22 Program to read and print a text file

```
import java.io.*;
public class Driver {

    /* pre:   The "example.txt" file exists (throw IOException)
       post:  The text lines from "example.txt" have been output
              double-spaced to the standard output stream. */
    public Driver() {
        try {
            String inStr;
            FileReader inReader;
            BufferedReader bReader;
            inReader = new FileReader( completePath("example.txt") );
            bReader = new BufferedReader( inReader );

            inStr = bReader.readLine();
            while ( inStr != null ) {
                System.out.println(inStr);
                System.out.println();
                inStr = bReader.readLine();
            }
            bReader.close();
        }
        catch (IOException e) {
            System.out.println("ERROR reading." );
        }
```

Continued on next page

```
    }
    public static void main(String[] args) {
        new Driver();
    }
    /* pre:    relativePath is a file name for a file relative to
                the folder that contains this class (throws
                FileNotFoundException)
       post:   result is the complete path name associated with
                relativePath */
    private static String completePath(String relativePath)
                          throws FileNotFoundException
    {
        java.net.URL url = getClass().getResource(relativePath);
        if (url == null)
            throw new FileNotFoundException("invalid relative file
            name");
        else
            return url.getPath();
    }
}
```

To read a file character by character, `BufferedReader` provides a method called read. This method is a bit unusual because it returns an int value rather than a char. A cast is required before the read method's value can be used as a char. Another characteristic of the read method is that it returns the value –1 to indicate any attempt to read past the end of file. The following code is an example of reading an entire text file character by character while checking for end of file.

```
try {
    int inInt;
    char inChar;
    FileReader inReader;
    BufferedReader bReader;
    inReader = new FileReader( completePath("example.txt") );
    bReader = new BufferedReader( inReader );

    inInt = bReader.read();
    while ( inInt != -1 ) {
        inChar = (char) inInt;
        System.out.println(inChar);
        inInt = bReader.read();
    }
    bReader.close();
}
catch (IOException e) {
    System.out.println("ERROR reading." );
}
```

O5.7 TERMINAL-STYLE I/O (OPTIONAL)

Before the use of graphical user interfaces, the most common form of I/O between an executing program and the user was **terminal-style I/O**, also known as **console I/O**. This type of I/O is so named because it behaves like an old-fashioned computer terminal: a keyboard and an output device (either a video screen or a printer). An executing program typically communicates with the terminal in a kind of dialog. The program might display several lines of output and then request input from the user. Typically, an input request causes the program to suspend execution until the user supplies input in the form of keystrokes. Even though textual computer terminals are largely devices from the past, terminal-style I/O is still used in many places. For example, the DOS prompt in the Windows operating system and UNIX shell programs operate on terminal-style I/O.

The creators of Java felt that terminal-style I/O was sufficiently important that they included two objects to provide programs convenient access to a standard way of emulating computer terminal-like I/O.

- The System.out object is an output stream, analogous to a computer terminal display.
- The System.in object is an input stream for the computer keyboard.

The System.out object is of type PrintStream and can be used directly without initialization by calling the print and println methods. Executing either of these methods displays the argument in the standard output stream (usually a window of textual display).

The System.in object is of type InputStream, so using System.in requires a bit of initialization to accomplish terminal-style I/O. In particular, because computer terminals typically read data one line at a time, it is best to use BufferedReader to process the input from System.in. Figure O5.23 illustrates.

Figure O5.23 Example of terminal-style I/O

```
try {
    String userInput;
    InputStreamReader inReader;
    BufferedReader bReader;

    inReader = new InputStreamReader( System.in );
    bReader = new BufferedReader( inReader );

    System.out.print("Type your message: ");
    userInput = bReader.readLine();
    System.out.println("Your message is as follows. " + userInput);
}
catch (IOException e) {
    System.out.println("ERROR reading." );
}
```

The code in Figure O5.23 connects to System.in with two other objects: inReader (of type InputStreamReader) and bReader (of type BufferedReader). The inReader object is instantiated and attached to System.in via the following statement:

```
inReader = new InputStreamReader( System.in );
```

The bReader object is instantiated and attached to inReader via the following statement:

```
bReader = new BufferedReader( inReader );
```

These two statements properly initialize System.in so that all subsequent input can be processed through bReader.

Terminal-style I/O usually begins when the program displays a prompt. The following statement is an example of how to produce such a user prompt.

```
System.out.print("Type your message: ");
```

Next, the program executes the following statement:

```
userInput = bReader.readLine();
```

Because this bReader is reading from System.in, the execution of this statement causes the program to delay further execution until the user has typed an input line terminated by striking the *return* key. The string that represents this line of keystrokes is returned by the readLine method and assigned to userInput.

The delay that is a part of any readLine from System.in is unlike event-driven code. Such a readLine suspends execution until the user has supplied the proper input.

O5.8   PERSISTENT OBJECTS

Sometimes whole objects must be retained from one program execution to the next. Such persistent objects require that a program store the complete state of the object in a file. This object and its state can be restored later by reading the data back from the file.

One situation that calls for persistent objects is a program that keeps track of its final state to use as the initial state the next time the program is executed. For example, consider a computer program that plays the game of chess against the user. You might want to write this program so that the user can suspend a game and turn off the computer to resume the same game later. Such a program can be written by making the game board, along with its associated chess piece objects, persistent.

You can use java.io streams, such as DataOutputStream and DataInputStream, as a crude mechanism for implementing persistent objects. This technique requires that all the key individual attributes of the persistent object be written and read. For complicated objects, this approach is tedious.

A better technique for implementing persistent objects is provided by way of the ObjectOutputStream and ObjectInputStream classes. These classes include methods to read or write an entire object at once.

Figure O5.24 contains a sample use of ObjectOutputStream. Executing this class writes two objects (from window and dot[3]) to a binary file.

Figure O5.24 Writing objects with ObjectOutputStream

```java
import java.io.*;
import java.awt.*;
public class MakeObjFile {
    public MakeObjFile() {
        Frame window;
        BlueDot dot;
        window = new Frame();
        window.setBounds(10, 10, 300, 200);
        window.setLayout(null);
        dot = new BlueDot(125, 75, 50);
        window.add(dot);
        window.show();
        try{
            FileOutputStream outStream;
            ObjectOutputStream objStream;
            outStream = new FileOutputStream( "example.obj" );
            objStream = new ObjectOutputStream( outStream );
            objStream.writeObject( window );
            objStream.writeObject( dot );
            objStream.flush();
            objStream.close();
        }
        catch (IOException e) {
            System.out.println("ERROR writing." );
        }
    }
    public static void main(String[] args) {
        new MakeObjFile();
    }
}
```

The method used to write persistent objects to an ObjectOutputStream is writeObject. Executing writeObject outputs the complete state of its argument object. If the object is an aggregate, the state of its instance variables also is written. This inclusion of referenced objects is applied transitively so that the complete state of the object can be retained.

One requirement of the use of ObjectOutputStream is that any argument to the writeObject method must be serializable. You make a class serializable simply by

---

[3]The *Java.awt* library is used in place of *javax.swing* for this example because *swing* objects are lightweight and may not work properly with ObjectStream. The BlueDot clas is a subclass of *java.awt*.component.

implementing the Serializable interface included in the java.lang package. (Note that implementing Serializable does not require providing any additional code.) In other words, both the Frame class and the BlueDot class that are used for the types of the persistent objects in the MakeObjFile class example must implement Serializable.

If a persistent object is stored using ObjectOutputStream, it should be restored using ObjectInputStream and its readObject method. Figure O5.25 uses a ReloadObjFile class to restore the objects written by the Figure O5.24 code.

Figure O5.25 Reading objects using ObjectInputStream

```
import java.io.*;
import java.awt.*;
public class ReloadObjFile {
    public ReloadObjFile() {
        Frame window;
        BlueDot dot;
        try{
            FileInputStream inStream;
            ObjectInputStream objStream;

            inStream = new FileInputStream(
                completePath("example.obj") );
            objStream = new ObjectInputStream( inStream );
            window = (Frame) objStream.readObject();
            dot = (BlueDot) objStream.readObject();
            objStream.close();
            window.show();
            dot.setForeground( Color.red );
            dot.repaint();
        }
        catch (Exception e) {
            System.out.println("ERROR reloading object." );
        }
    }
    public static void main(String[] args) {
        new ReloadObjFile();
    }
    /*  pre:    relativePath is a file name for a file relative to
                the folder that contains this class (throws
                FileNotFoundException)
        post:   result is the complete path name associated with
                relativePath */
    private String completePath(String relativePath)
        throws FileNotFoundException
```

Continued on next page

```
            {
                java.net.URL url = getClass().getResource(relativePath);
                if (url == null)
                    throw new FileNotFoundException(
                        "invalid relative file name");
                else
                    return url.getPath();
            }
        }
```

You must observe these three requirements to input objects using `ObjectInputStream`.

- Objects must be read in the same order they were written.
- The value returned by `readObject` is of type `Object` and must be cast to the proper type.
- A call to `readObject` may throw various exceptions, requiring a different *catch* clause.

The code in Figure O5.24 observes all three requirements. The first object read is assumed to be a `Frame`, and the second is a `BlueDot`. Both calls to `readObject` are immediately cast to the proper type. The *catch* clause uses a parameter of type `Exception`, which is a superclass of `IOException` and includes all the required types of exceptions that must be handled by this code.

Files created by `writeObject` are sometimes called **serialized files**. Serialization plays an important role in many Java applications because serialized files are portable across platforms and operating systems. Such portability could permit, for example, one program to share its objects across the Internet with another program even though the two programs are executing on separate computers.

O5.9 JFILECHOOSER (OPTIONAL)

Most modern operating systems include graphical file browser windows to make it easier for the user to select a file from the file directory. Many applications also permit the user to select an input file or an output file using a similar file browser.

The *swing* package includes a graphical file browser class for just this purpose. Figure O5.26 contains a class diagram for this `JFileChooser` class, along with a picture of a typical `JFileChooser` window.

A `JFileChooser` object can be instantiated from a parameterless constructor. Such an object becomes visible by executing either of two methods.

- `showOpenDialog` is called to display a `JFileChooser` that is appropriate for selecting an input file.
- `showSaveDialog` is called to display a `JFileChooser` that is appropriate for selecting a new output file.

Note that `null` can be used as an argument for both `showOpenDialog` and `showSaveDialog`.

Figure O5.26 JFileChooser class diagram and sample image

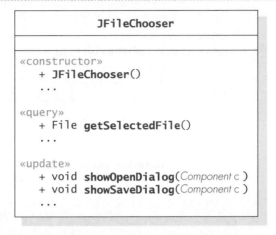

After having called showOpenDialog or showSaveDialog to display the file finder, the program should call getSelectedFile. This method performs three tasks:

- Execution is suspended until the user selects a file or cancels the action in the JFileChooser window.
- A File object is returned for the user-selected file (null is returned if the user canceled this action or selected an invalid file.)
- If a valid file is selected, it is opened for input or output from the beginning of the file.

Figure O5.27 illustrates how to use a JFileChooser object to open a file for input. The code in this example reads all characters from a user-specified text file, writing them to System.out.

Figure O5.27 Using `JFileChooser` to read from a file

```java
import java.io.*;
import javax.swing.*;
public class EchoChooserFile {
    public static void main(String[] args) {
        try {
            JFileChooser chooser = new JFileChooser();
            int tmp = chooser.showOpenDialog( null );
            File file = chooser.getSelectedFile();
            if (file != null) {
                FileInputStream inStream;
                InputStreamReader reader;
                int inInt;
                inStream = new FileInputStream(file);
                reader = new InputStreamReader( inStream );
                inInt = reader.read();
                while (inInt != -1) {
                    System.out.print( (char)inInt );
                    inInt = reader.read();
                }
                reader.close();
            } else {
                System.out.println("No file name selected.");
            }
        }
        catch (FileNotFoundException e) {
            System.out.println("ERROR opening input stream." );
        }
        catch (IOException e) {
            System.out.println("ERROR reading." );
        }
    }
}
```

The following three lines display a `JFileChooser` and open the specified file:

```java
JFileChooser chooser = new JFileChooser();
int tmp = chooser.showOpenDialog( null );
File file = chooser.getSelectedFile();
```

Executing the first of these three lines instantiates a `JFileChooser` object called `chooser`. The second statement displays `chooser` in a form that is proper for opening an existing file. The call to `getSelectedFile` suspends execution until the user has selected a file or canceled the selection via the `chooser` window. If the user selects a valid file name, the associated file is opened and assigned to the `file` variable. If the user makes an invalid selection or cancels the selection, `file` is assigned `null`.

THE SOFTWARE INSPECTOR

Following is a collection of hints on what to check when you examine code that involves the concepts of this chapter.

✔ The standard Java I/O packages are located together in the *java.io* folder. It is best to include a declaration such as the following when using these libraries:

```
import java.io.*;
```

✔ When a program opens a file with its path name, take care to ensure that the file's name and directory match the file system on which the program executes.

✔ Because relative path names depend on how a Java program is initiated, it is best to translate relative paths for existing files into complete paths using code such as `completePath` (Figure O5.2).

✔ Always check to be certain that the file is properly opened before attempting to read from it or write to it.

✔ Opening a file for output generally deletes any existing file having the same path name. If you don't want this deletion, then use a `File` object to check for its existence before executing the opening code.

✔ Always ensure that a file is closed after the I/O is complete. Output files usually require the additional step of calling `flush` before closing.

✔ Most I/O operations throw checked exceptions. You must handle these exceptions by enclosing your I/O code within a *try* statement and catching the appropriate type of exceptions. (`IOException` is the superclass for most exceptions that occur during I/O.)

✔ Java contains many classes for I/O. You must select classes carefully to perform I/O properly. Following is a list of the classes associated with certain types of I/O.

- To read *bytes* from a binary file, connect a `FileInputStream` object to the file.

- To write *bytes* to a binary file, connect a `FileOutputStream` object to the file.

- To read *primitive values* or *Strings* from a binary file, connect a `DataInputStream` object to a `FileInputStream` object connected to the file.

- To write *primitive values* or *Strings* to a binary file, connect a `DataOutputStream` object to a `FileOutputStream` object connected to the file.

Core Concepts O5

- To read *chars* and/or *Strings* from a text file, connect a `BufferedReader` object to a `FileReader` object connected to the file.

- To write *primitive values* or *Strings* to a text file, connect a `PrintWriter` object to a `FileOutputStream` object connected to the file.

- To read persistent *objects* from a binary file, connect an `ObjectInputStream` object to a `FileInputStream` object connected to the file.

- To write persistent *objects* to a binary file, connect an `ObjectOutputStream` object to a `FileOutputStream` object connected to the file.

- To read *lines* terminal-style from the standard input stream, connect a `BufferedReader` object to an `InputStreamReader` object connected to `System.in`.

- To write *primitive values* or *Strings* to the standard output stream, use `PrintWriter` methods on `System.out`. (No additional objects are required.)

✔ When you read from a file, you must be familiar with the type of data stored in the file. If it is a binary file, it must be read as a binary file. If there are different types of data in the file, the data must be read in the order (by type) that they were written. Failure to read in the proper order results in meaningless input or thrown exceptions.

✔ Always check input code to ensure proper handling of the end of file condition. Java provides various ways to check for end of file. An attempt to read past end of file on a `DataInputStream` object throws an `EOFException`. When you're reading reference data (such as a `readLine` applied to a `BufferedReader` object), an attempt to read past end of file returns `null`. A call to `read` that normally returns the next character from a `BufferedReader` object returns –1 when reading beyond the end of file.

✔ Objects that are made persistent via `ObjectInputStream` and `ObjectOutputStream` must belong to classes that implement `Serializable`.

EXERCISES

1. Figure O5.1 contains a sample file directory. Using this directory, specify the names for each of the following files.
   a) The complete path name for the *email* file
   b) The complete path name for the *Director.java* file from *prog1*
   c) The complete path name for the *Director.class* file from *prog2*
   d) The relative path name for the *email* file if the current directory is /Users

e) The relative path name for the *Director.class* file from *prog2* file if the current directory is `/Users/smith`

f) The relative path name for the *Director.class* file from *prog2* file if the current directory is `/Users/smith/prog2`

2. Figure O5.13 depicts the connections that are used to write to a file called *example.bin*. This figure names the classes involved in this output and shows the proper connection sequence. For each of the following parts, draw a picture in this same style that describes the indicated example.

   a) The objects used to read from *example.bin* in the code in Figure O5.16

   b) The objects used to write to *example.txt* in the code in Figure O5.20

   c) The objects used to read from *example.obj* in the code in Figure O5.24

3. Label each of the following standard Java I/O classes with the best choice from the following:

   (1) Writes data in binary form

   (2) Reads data in binary form

   (3) Writes data in textual form

   (4) Reads data in textual form

   a) `BufferedReader`

   b) `DataInputStream`

   c) `DataOutputStream`

   d) `PrintWriter`

   e) `ObjectInputStream`

   f) `ObjectOutputStream`

4. Suppose that following code segment is executed.

```
try{
    FileOutputStream outStream;
    DataOutputStream dataStream;
    outStream = new FileOutputStream( "Ex4File" );
    dataStream = new DataOutputStream( outStream );
    dataStream.writeInt( 34 );
    dataStream.writeLong( 644 );
    dataStream.writeFloat( 7.3f );
    dataStream.writeDouble( 12.345 );
    dataStream.writeFloat( 9.87f );
    dataStream.flush();
    dataStream.close();
}
catch (IOException e) {
    System.out.println("ERROR writing." );
}
```

a) Assuming that no file named *Ex4File* exists before this code executes, how many bytes in total are written to *Ex4File* after the code finishes execution?

b) How does your answer to part (a) change if a file with the name *Ex4File* already exists before this code executes?

c) Diagram the content of the *Ex4File* created by this code, depicting the number of bytes devoted to each output value.

5. Suppose that following code segment is executed.

```
try{
    FileOutputStream outStream;
    PrintWriter printWriter;
    outStream = new FileOutputStream( "Ex5File" );
    printWriter = new PrintWriter( outStream );
    printWriter.print( 34 );
    printWriter.println( 644 );
    printWriter.print( 7.3f );
    printWriter.print( 12.345 );
    printWriter.print( 9.87f );
    printWriter.flush();
    printWriter.close();
}
catch (IOException e) {
    System.out.println("ERROR writing." );
}
```

a) Assuming that no file named *Ex5File* exists before this code executes, how many bytes in total are written to *Ex5File* after the code finishes execution?

b) Diagram the content of the *Ex5File* created by this code, depicting the actual characters devoted to each output value.

6. Assume that the following code has just executed.

```
try {
    FileOutputStream outStream;
    DataOutputStream dataStream;
    outStream = new FileOutputStream( "sample" );
    dataStream = new DataOutputStream( outStream );
    dataStream.writeInt( 101 );
    dataStream.writeDouble( 102.0 );
    dataStream.writeInt( 103 );
    dataStream.writeInt( 104 );
    dataStream.writeInt( 105 );
    dataStream.flush();
    dataStream.close();
    outStream = new FileOutputStream( "sample" );
```

```
                   dataStream = new DataOutputStream( outStream );
                   dataStream.writeInt( 201 );
                   dataStream.writeDouble( 202.0 );
                   dataStream.writeInt( 203 );
                   dataStream.writeInt( 204 );
                   dataStream.writeInt( 205 );
                   dataStream.flush();
                   dataStream.close();
                   outStream = new FileOutputStream( "sample2" );
                   dataStream = new DataOutputStream( outStream );
                   dataStream.writeUTF( "Cows R not us" );
                   dataStream.writeUTF( "Cows R them" );
                   dataStream.flush();
                   dataStream.close();

                   int j1, j2, j3, j4;
                   String str;
                   FileInputStream inStream;
                   DataInputStream dataInStream;
                   inStream = new FileInputStream( completePath("sample") );
                   dataInStream = new DataInputStream( inStream );
                   j1 = dataInStream.readInt();
                   j2 = dataInStream.readInt();
                   j2 = dataInStream.readInt();
                   j2 = dataInStream.readInt();
                   dataInStream.close();
                   inStream = new FileInputStream( completePath("sample") );
                   dataInStream = new DataInputStream( inStream );
                   j3 = dataInStream.readInt();
                   dataInStream.close();
                   inStream = new FileInputStream( completePath("sample2") );
                   dataInStream = new DataInputStream( inStream );
                   str = dataInStream.readUTF();
                   dataStream.close();
                   // variable values from HERE.
          }
          catch (IOException e) {
                   System.out.println("ERROR in I/O." );
          }
```

a) Is the first output file created a binary file or a text file?

b) What values are assigned to the following variables by the end of this second code segment?

```
    j1
    j2
    j3
    str
```

PROGRAMMING EXERCISES

1. For this assignment you must write a program that copies text files in a peculiar manner. When your program executes it accepts input from a file called *source.txt*. The program creates a new text file called *copyOfSource.txt* that contains the same lines as *source.txt* except that the order of the lines has been reversed. Note that keeping both files in the same folder as your code is easiest. Also note that you can use a text editor to create text files for *source.txt*.

2. Using your favorite program that uses javax.swing or java.awt classes to construct a graphical display, modify the program so that the objects of the display are made persistent. The program must "remember" the state of the display each time it quits and must reload this state each time it starts. You may use a separate SAVE button to save the state and assume that the user clicks this button before terminating the program's execution.

3. Modify Programming Exercise 1 to allow the user to select the name of the output file by using a JFileChooser object.

RECURSION

OBJECTIVES

- To explore the concept of recursive definition and examine how it leads naturally to recursive methods

- To introduce recursion as a form of control

- To examine the run-time behavior of recursion in the form of activation records

- To compare and contrast loops and recursion

- To examine more complicated forms of recursion, including multiple recursive calls from a single method and indirect recursion

- To introduce Backus-Naur Form as a recursive language for the definition of syntax

Programs are particularly effective for performing repetitive tasks. Looping control mechanisms, such as the *while* statement, support repetition, but loops are not the only way to express algorithms involving repeated tasks. This chapter explores a way to use control abstraction to produce a repetitionlike form of control. The result is a sufficiently different form of control to deserve its own name: **recursion**.

O6.1 RECURSIVE DEFINITION

Long before computer programs made use of recursion as a form of control flow, people were using recursion as a definitional tool. In fact, mathematicians have long accepted recursion as a sound method for defining properties.

Informally, a **recursive definition** is the definition of a property that is self-referential. In other words, a property is defined in terms of itself. For example, consider a definition of the **factorial** function, commonly used in analyzing mathematical combinatorics and probability. The factorial function is symbolized as a nonnegative integer followed by an exclamation point (e.g., 4! is read *four factorial*). Following is a list of factorial values.

```
0! == 1
1! == 1
2! == 2 * 1 == 2
3! == 3 * 2 * 1 == 6
4! == 4 * 3 * 2 * 1 == 24
5! == 5 * 4 * 3 * 2 * 1 == 120
o o o
```

From these few examples it is easy to see how to calculate the factorial function for larger integers. However, it is not so easy to express a precise definition for the value of the factorial function for an arbitrary integer—call it N. The following expression is one attempt to do so.

N! == N * (N–1) * (N–2) * ... * 1

The problem with this definition is that "..." is not mathematically precise. Furthermore, the definition is unclear with regard to the value of 0! or 1!.

A more careful definition for factorial is possible through the use of recursion. Figure O6.1 shows such a recursive definition.

Figure O6.1 Recursive definition of factorial

Base Clause
N! == 1 for N == 0

Recursive Clause
N! == N * (N–1)! for integer N > 0

This definition, like all recursive definitions, is separated into two parts: a base clause and a recursive clause.

The **base clause** defines the property for a few (one or more) situations that can be defined nonrecursively. The base clause can be thought of as defining the property for the simplest case(s). In the definition of N!, the base clause defines the situation when N==0. In other words, the base clause defines the value of 0!, which can be considered the "simplest" case because zero is the smallest of the nonnegative integers and 0! is understood to have a value of 1.

Recursive clauses must extend the definition to the more general cases; in other words, a recursive clause must define the property for all valid situations that are not defined in the base clause. For the definition of N! the recursive clause applies to any integer N that is greater than zero.

A recursive clause is characterized by the fact that it defines a property in terms of itself. Indeed, the name "recursive" comes from the fact that a property *recurs* in its own definition. The recursive clause in Figure O6.1 defines a factorial (!) by using another factorial in the recursive clause:

$$N! == N * (N{-}1)!$$

To understand this definition, consider how it can be applied to ascertain the value of 4!. Because N == 4 is an integer greater than zero, the recursive clause of the definition is applicable. This leads to the following conclusion.

$$4! == 4 * 3! \quad \textbf{(a)}$$

To calculate this value, it is essential to know the value of 3!. Again, the definition of factorial can be applied. Because 3 > 0, the recursive clause leads to the following conclusion.

$$3! == 3 * 2! \quad \textbf{(b)}$$

Similarly, the recursive clause is applied a third and a fourth time to conclude the following two equations.

$$2! == 2 * 1! \quad \textbf{(c)}$$
$$1! == 1 * 0! \quad \textbf{(d)}$$

Equation (d) defines the value of 1! in terms of 0!, so the base clause of the recursive definition is useful. The base clause defines 0! == 1. Therefore, using the base clause and equation (d) leads to the following conclusion.

$$1! == 1 * 0! == 1 * 1 == 1$$

By substituting the value of 1! into equation (c), the value of 2! is calculated as follows.

$$2! == 2 * 1! \quad == 2 * 1 == 2$$

Similarly, the value of 2! can be substituted into equation (b) to calculate 3! as follows.

$$3! == 3 * 2! \quad == 3 * 2 == 6$$

Finally, the value of 3! can be substituted into equation (a) to calculate 4! as follows.

$$4! == 4 * 3! \quad == 4 * 6 == 24$$

All recursive definitions share two characteristics:

- The base clause is a nonrecursive definition for the "first" situation.
- The recursive clause is crafted so that repeated applications lead toward the base clause.

To discover the value of 4! it was necessary to apply the recursive clause repeatedly for 4!, for 3!, for 2!, and for 1!. It was also necessary to use the base clause to discover that 0! == 1. Applying the base clause once and the recursive clause four times leads to a precise definition for the value of 4!.

As a second example, consider the concept of the odd positive integers. Figure 06.2 contains a recursive definition for **odd positive integer**.

Figure 06.2 Recursive definition of *odd positive integer*

Base Clause

K is an *odd positive integer* for K == 1

Recursive Clause

K is an *odd positive integer* if K–2 is an odd positive integer

Again, the base clause defines the meaning of the property (odd positive integer) for a specific value: the smallest odd positive integer (1). Again, the recursive clause can be applied repeatedly to move toward the base. For example, applying the recursive clause results in the conclusion that 7 is an odd positive integer if 5 is an odd positive integer; 5 is an odd positive integer if 3 is, and 3 is if 1 is. Because 1 is an odd positive integer by the base clause, this definition allows the conclusions that 3, 5, and 7, among others, are also odd positive integers.

Software Engineering Hint

Using recursion in programming begins with **recursive thinking**. Studying recursive definitions is a good way to learn recursive thinking.

Every recursive definition (and every recursive Java method) has both a base and a recursive part. The base must work for the first or simplest situation(s). The recursive part is self-referential in such a way that it makes progress toward the base.

A recursive definition is useful only if the base and recursive clauses of a recursive definition work in concert with one another. The recursive clause must be written so that repeated applications of this clause will eventually lead to the base clause, and the base clause must define the property for some small number of elements. Figure 06.3 shows two attempts at recursive definitions for odd positive integer that fail.

Figure 06.3 Two incorrect definitions of *odd positive integer*

Incorrect Attempt A

Base Clause

K is an *odd positive integer* for K == 7

Recursive Clause

K is an *odd positive integer* if K–2 is an odd positive integer

Continued on next page

Incorrect Attempt B

Base Clause

K is an *odd positive integer* for K == 1

Recursive Clause

K is an *odd positive integer* if K+2 is an odd positive integer

Incorrect Attempt A fails to maintain the key characteristic of the base clause: that it must provide the "first" occurrence(s) of the definition. This base step may be a correct statement regarding the number 7. However, such a base makes it impossible to conclude that 1, 3, and 5 are odd positive integers, and that is contrary to the usual notion of odd positives.

Incorrect Attempt B fails to observe a key characteristic of a proper recursive clause: that it provides a way to make progress toward the base clause. This new recursive clause may be a correct statement mathematically, but it isn't useful in a recursive definition. For example, consider applying this recursive clause to determine whether the value 11 is an odd positive integer. The recursive clause can be translated into the following by substituting 11 for K.

11 is an odd positive integer if 13 is an odd positive integer.

This statement may be consistent with our understanding of numbers, but it isn't helpful in the sense that 13 is farther from 1, which is defined in the base clause.

Technically, every recursive definition also includes a third clause, known as an **extremal clause**. The extremal clause defines the situations in which the property is *not* true. Figure O6.4 adds an extremal clause for the definition of odd positive integer. Frequently, extremal clauses are not included in definitions because they are taken for granted. In the case of odd positive integers it is reasonable to assume that any number that satisfies neither the base nor the recursive clause must *not* be an odd positive integer.

Figure O6.4 Recursive definition of *odd positive integer* with extremal

Base Clause

K is an *odd positive integer* for K == 1

Recursive Clause

K is an *odd positive integer* if K–2 is an odd positive integer

Extremal Clause

Anything that cannot satisfy the base clause and cannot satisfy the recursive clause is *not* an *odd positive integer*.

Core Concepts O6

Some recursive definitions contain multiple base or recursive clauses. For example, Figure O6.5 contains a definition of **even integer**.

Figure O6.5 Recursive definition of *even integer*

Base Clause

K is an *even integer* for K == 0

Recursive Clause

(Option 1)

    K is an *even integer* if K–2 is an even integer

(Option 2)

    K is an *even integer* if K+2 is an even integer

This definition contains two recursive clauses labeled "Option 1" and "Option 2." Both options are true, and both can be used independently when applying the definition. Option 1 must be applied repeatedly in order to reason that a value greater than zero is an even integer. Option 2 must be applied repeatedly for reasoning about negative numbers.

The base clause of the definition of *even integer* is also interesting. The value zero really isn't the "simplest" or the "first" even integer. The even integer property is a somewhat unusual situation in which any even number can be selected for the base and still lead to an equivalent workable definition.

O6.2 BNF (OPTIONAL)

Recursive definitions also can be an effective tool for defining programming language syntax. In the 1960s, John Backus and Peter Naur, well-known computer scientists, invented and applied a recursion-based notation for such definitions. This notation, called **Backus-Naur Form (BNF)**, remains as one of the most widely used languages for detailing the syntactic structure of programming languages.

A BNF definition consists of a set of **rules**, sometimes called **productions**. Each rule defines the potential syntax of a single entity. A separate **nonterminal** is used to name each rule. The form of a rule consists of a nonterminal followed by "::=", followed by an expression for the syntax of the nonterminal. For example, the following rule defines the nonterminal <radioAlert> to be the sentence that is often broadcast for tests of the Emergency Broadcast System.

<radioAlert> ::= This is a test.

Nonterminals are labels that refer to a piece of text. The <radioAlert> nonterminal refers to the single sentence "This is a test." Once a nonterminal is so defined, it can be used in rules defining other nonterminals. For example, consider the following BNF rule.

<biggerAlert> ::= <radioAlert> <radioAlert> This is only a test.

This second rule defines the form of a second nonterminal, <biggerAlert>. The <biggerAlert> nonterminal refers to three consecutive sentences: "This is a test. This is a test. This is only a test." The first two sentences are represented by the <radioAlert> nonterminal that was defined by the first rule.

The right side of a BNF rule (i.e., the portion defining the nonterminal's syntax that is found to the right of the "::=" symbol) can include symbols from the actual syntax, nonterminals, parentheses, and/or "|" symbols. This text adopts the commonly used notation of enclosing each nonterminal within less than and greater than brackets, <...>, to distinguish nonterminals from other syntax.

The "|" symbol is used in a BNF rule to separate alternative syntax options. For example, the following rule defines <uppercaseVowel> to be any of seven possible strings, each one character long: "A", "E", "I", "O", or "U".

<uppercaseVowel> ::= A | E | I | O | U

The following three rules use the preceding one.

<b-vowel> ::= B <uppercaseVowel>

<twoVowels> ::= <uppercaseVowel> <uppercaseVowel>

<twoOrThreeVowels> ::= <twoVowels>
                     | (<uppercaseVowel> <uppercaseVowel>
                     <uppercaseVowel>)

The first of these three rules defines the syntax of <b-vowel> to have seven two-letter possibilities: "BA", "BE", "BI", "BO", or "BU". The second rule defines the <twoVowels> nonterminal as one <uppercaseVowel> followed by another. In other words, <twoVowels> can be any two consecutive uppercase vowel symbols; there are a total of 5*5=25 possible strings.

The nonterminal <twoOrThreeVowels> is defined to be either two consecutive uppercase vowels or three consecutive uppercase vowels. Therefore, "AI" is a syntactically valid option for <twoOrThreeVowels>, as is "AIE". Notice that the parentheses are used in this last rule as a grouping device and are not intended to be part of the actual syntax.

Nothing prohibits a BNF rule from including the nonterminal from the left of the "::=" within its own definition on the right side of the rule. Such a self-referential nonterminal rule is recursive. The following BNF rule illustrates.

<manyQuestions> ::= ?
                    | ? <manyQuestions>

This rule specifies that one option for <manyQuestions> is the single character "?". Using this single-character syntax and the second alternative, this rule allows "??" to be valid syntax for <manyQuestions>. Because "??" is valid, so is "???", and because "???" is valid, so is "????". This reasoning leads to the conclusion that this rule defines <manyQuestions> to be any string of one or more consecutive "?" symbols.

To illustrate how BNF is used to define programming language syntax, consider the collection of BNF rules in Figure O6.6. These rules are intended to define the syntax of a Java-like Boolean expression. It is the <BooleanExpression> nonterminal that represents the expression. (Note that the quotations around the parentheses denote that parentheses *are* part of the syntax.)

Figure O6.6 BNF definition of *Boolean expression syntax*

```
<BooleanExpression> ::= <BooleanConstant>
                      | "(" <BooleanExpression> ")"
                      | ! <BooleanExpression>
                      | <BooleanExpression> && <BooleanExpression>
                      | <BooleanExpression> || <BooleanExpression>
<BooleanConstant> ::= true | false
```

Using the definition from Figure O6.6, it is possible to conclude that each of the following lines, and many others, represent valid syntax for a Boolean expression.

```
true
! true
( false )
false && ( true )
!( false || (true && !false))
```

Recursion in BNF parallels recursion in other definitions. Like other forms of recursion, recursive BNF rules require a nonrecursive (base) alternative. The base for the Boolean expression BNF is the first line of the definition:

```
<BooleanExpression> ::= <BooleanConstant>
```

Also, like other forms of recursive definition, BNF includes an implicit extremal clause that indicates "...and no other strings are syntactically valid." This extremal clause permits the conclusion that none of the following lines are valid Boolean expressions because there is no way to compose the rules to formulate them.

```
true !
( )
false && || ( true )
```

It takes many BNF rules and many nonterminals to define a complete programming language.

O6.3 FROM RECURSIVE DEFINITION TO METHOD

The Fibonacci number sequence, originally invented to model population growth patterns, is an example of an inherently recursive concept. Figure O6.7 supplies a definition for the "jth" value in the Fibonacci number sequence.

The recursive clause of the Fibonacci definition indicates that the fourth Fibonacci number is the sum of the third Fibonacci plus the second. The recursive clause also indicates that the third Fibonacci is the sum of the second plus the first Fibonacci numbers. Because the base clause states that the first and second Fibonacci numbers are 0 and 1, respectively, it can be concluded that the third Fibonacci is 0+1 ==1, and the fourth Fibonacci is 1+1==2, the fifth Fibonacci is 1+2 == 3, the sixth Fibonacci is 2+3 == 5, the seventh Fibonacci is 3+5 == 8, and so forth.

Figure O6.7 Recursive definition of *jth Fibonacci number*

Base Clause

(Option 1)

   0 is the *first Fibonacci number.*

(Option 2)

   1 is the *second Fibonacci number.*

Recursive Clause

If *J1* is the (j–1)st Fibonacci number and *J2* is the (j–2)nd Fibonacci number, then *J1 + J2* is the *jth Fibonacci number.*

This definition for the jth Fibonacci number can be transformed into a recursive method. Figure O6.8 contains this code.

Figure O6.8 jthFibonacci method

```
/*  pre:    j >= 1 (throws AssertionError)
    post:   result == the jth number in the Fibonacci sequence */
private int jthFibonacci( int j ) {
    if (j < 1) {
        throw new AssertionError("Argument must be > 0");
    } else if (j == 1) {
        return 0;
    } else if (j == 2) {
        return 1;
    } else {
        return jthFibonacci(j-1) + jthFibonacci(j-2);
    }
}
```

The jthFibonacci method uses its parameter to indicate the position of the value within the Fibonacci sequence (1 for the first Fibonacci, 2 for the second, and so on). Whenever the j parameter is 1, the method returns 0, and when j is 1, the method returns 1. This corresponds to the two options of the base clause in the Fibonacci definition. Whenever the j parameter value is greater than 2, jthFibonacci returns the sum of the (j–1)st and (j–2)nd Fibonacci numbers. This is consistent with the recursive clause of the Fibonacci number definition. The situation in which j is less than or equal to zero corresponds to the implicit extremal clause and throws an exception.

The thought of a method calling itself may seem unusual, but it is perfectly acceptable Java code. A method that calls itself is known as a **recursive method**. Figure O6.9 explains the values returned by this method for arguments 1 through 6. The source of the values of the later calls can be found in the earlier ones.

Figure 06.9 Values returned by `jthFibonacci` method for arguments 1 to 6

```
jth_Fibonacci(1)

        return 0


jth_Fibonacci(2)

        return 1


jth_Fibonacci(3)

            return jth_Fibonacci(2) + jth_Fibonacci(1) == 1 + 0 = 1


jth_Fibonacci(4)

            return jth_Fibonacci(3) + jth_Fibonacci(2) == 1 + 1 = 2


jth_Fibonacci(5)

            return jth_Fibonacci(4) + jth_Fibonacci(3) == 2 + 1 = 3


jth_Fibonacci(6)

            return jth_Fibonacci(5) + jth_Fibonacci(4) == 3 + 2 = 5
```

As a second example of a recursive method, consider the problem of printing all the names of the ancestor classes of a particular object. A class called `java.lang.Class` provides two methods to permit programs to investigate object classes and their names. Figure 06.10 illustrates.

As explained in these specifications, the `Object` class provides a method called `getClass` that returns the `Class` to which an object belongs. Calling `getName` on such a `class` object retrieves the class's name, and calling `getSuperclass` retrieves its `superclass` (or `null` if no `superclass` exists). For example, the first of the two following statements instantiates a `kq` object of type `Kumquat`.

```
Kumquat kq = new Kumquat();
Class kqClass = kq.getClass();
```

The second statement assigns the `Class`-type object for `kq` to the `kqClass` variable. Executing the following instruction upon `kqClass` outputs the name of the class, *Kumquat*.

```
System.out.println( kqClass.getName() ); //Output: Kumquat
```

The `getSuperclass` method can also be applied to a class object:

```
Class kqParentClass = kqClass.getSuperclass();
System.out.println( kqParentClass.getName() );
```

Figure O6.10 java.lang.Class class specifications

```
┌─────────────────────────────────┐
│         java.lang.Class          │
├─────────────────────────────────┤
│                                  │
├─────────────────────────────────┤
│ «query»                          │
│   + Class getSuperclass()        │
│   + String getName()             │
│   ...                            │
└─────────────────────────────────┘
```

Class Specifications

Note

The Class of any instantiated object (z) is returned by calling z.getClass().
The method getClass is in the java.lang.Object class.

Query Methods

public String **getName** ( )

    post: result == the class name associated with this class

public Class **getSuperclass** ( )

    post: (this object is a class that inherits another)
           implies result == the class for the parent of this
        and (this object has no parent class) *implies* result == null

Assuming that the Kumquat class has no explicit parent class, it still has the implicit parent class of java.lang.Object. In this case, executing the second statement outputs the following line.

    java.lang.Object

Figure O6.11 shows a recursive method based on the getSuperclass and getName methods. The printAllAncestorClasses method is passed a parameter, c, of type java.lang.Class, and it outputs the names of all ancestor classes of c from most distant (java.lang.Object) through c.

Figure O6.11 printAllAncestorClasses

```
/* post:   ancestors from Object through c have been output one per
            line */
private void printAllAncestorClasses( Class c ) {
    if (c.getSuperclass() != null) {
        printAllAncestorClasses( c.getSuperclass() );
    }
    System.out.println(c.getName());
}
```

Careful inspection shows that `printAllAncestorClasses` includes base and recursive clauses just like any other recursive method. The base clause for `printAllAncestorClasses` occurs when `c==null`. In this base case, the method outputs the name of `c` and returns without further recursion.

Any nonnull parameter `c` results in recursion. In these recursive cases, the *if* statement causes `printAllAncestorClasses` to be called recursively on the parent class of `c` before the output of `c`'s name. Whether or not a method is recursive has no impact on call syntax. Figure O6.12 contains a class that uses the recursive `printAllAncestorClasses` method.

Figure O6.12 Driver class for `printAllAncestorClasses`

```
public class Director {
    public static void main(String[] args) {
        new Director();
    }
    /* post:  The names of ancestor classes of Child from
                java.lang.Object through Child have been output one
                per line. */
    public Director() {
        Child exampleObject = new Child();
        printAllAncestorClasses( exampleObject.getClass() );
    }
    /* pre:    c != null
       post:   all ancestors from Object thru c have been output one
                per line */
    private void printAllAncestorClasses( Class c ) {
        if (c.getSuperclass() != null) {
            printAllAncestorClasses( c.getSuperclass() );
        }
        System.out.println(c.getName());
    }
}
```

Executing the `Director` class as an application causes the `Director` constructor to execute. The `Director` constructor instantiates an `exampleObject` variable of type `Child`, and then calls the `printAllAncestorClasses` via the following statement.

```
printAllAncestorClasses( exampleObject.getClass() );
```

The argument for this method call is the `Class` object associated with `exampleObject`. Executing the preceding statement outputs all class names for the `Child` class and its ancestor classes, as examined in Section O6.4.

O6.4 RECURSIVE EXECUTION

Tracing the execution of a recursive method reveals the run-time behavior of recursion. To demonstrate, consider the recursive method call in Figure O6.12. Tracing this recursion relies on the specific inheritance hierarchy for a class called `Child`. Figure O6.13 diagrams a potential inheritance hierarchy that is assumed in the trace that follows.

Figure O6.13 Sample inheritance tree for `Child` class

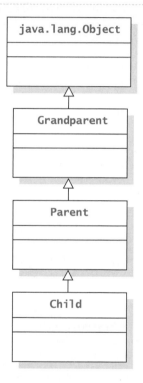

To trace recursion, it is important to keep track of all **activations**. A method activation is defined to be a separate, single call to that method. Each activation has its own copy of all parameters and local variables, which is collectively called an **activation record**. This activation record also includes the location of the currently executing statement. Consider a trace of the `printAllAncestorClasses` method shown in Figure O6.12, assuming the inheritance structure in Figure O6.13. When `printAllAncestorClasses` is called with `exampleObject.getClass` as an argument, its activation record can be pictured as shown in Figure O6.14.

This activation record shows that the c parameter is bound to the object for the `Child` class (i.e., the class to which `exampleObject` belongs). The activation also records the point of execution within the method's code (pictured as an arrow). This arrow points to the area just before the *if* statement to indicate that execution is about to begin the *if* statement.

Core Concepts O6

Figure 06.14 Initial activation of `printAllAncestorClasses`

```
Activation 1 for printAllAncestorClasses

Parameter
              Child class
    c

Method code (arrow indicates point of execution)

  ➤   if (c.getSuperclass() != null)    {
          printAllAncestorClasses( c.getSuperclass() );
      }
      System.out.println( c.getName() );
```

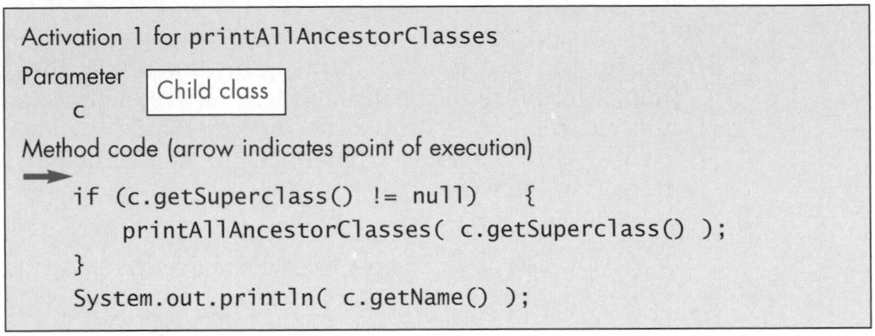

As this first activation proceeds to execute, it is discovered that the superclass of c is not `null`. Therefore, the `printAllAncestorClasses` method is called recursively, and the superclass of c (the Parent class) is passed as the argument. This second call produces Activation 2, as shown in Figure 06.15.

Figure 06.15 Two activations of `printAllAncestorClasses`

```
Activation 1 for printAllAncestorClasses

Parameter
              Child class
    c

Method code (a│   Activation 2 for printAllAncestorClasses
             │
  if (c.get  │   Parameter
  ➤ print    │                 Parent Class
             │       c
  }          │
  System.ou  │➤  Method code (arrow indicates point of execution)
             │
             │   ➤   if (c.getSuperclass() != null)    {
             │           printAllAncestorClasses( c.getSuperclass() );
             │       }
             │       System.out.println( c.getName() );
```

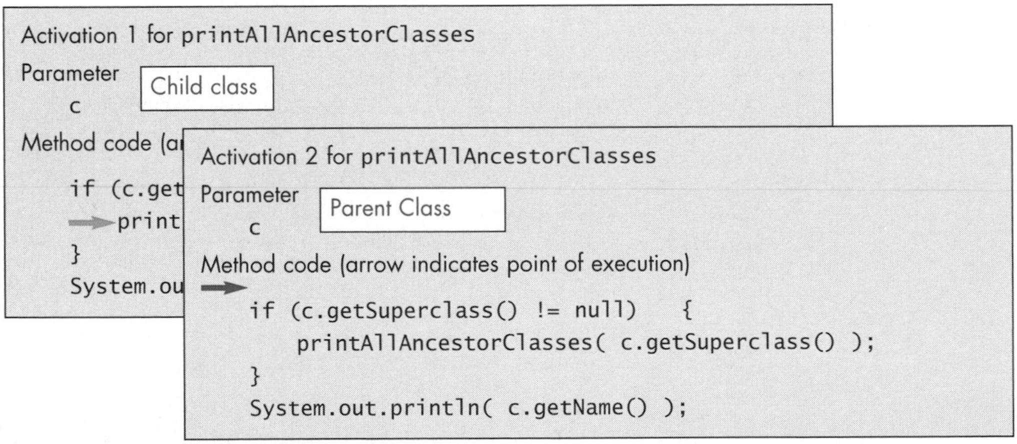

This second activation is superimposed on top of the first activation to illustrate that both activations are in progress at the time of this execution snapshot. The first activation is "on hold" in the sense that it has performed a recursive call. The location of the statement that caused this call is indicated by the light blue arrow. The second activation is beginning to execute at the darker blue arrow.

Notice that both activations have their own c parameters. The c parameter of the first activation continues to bind to the Child class, whereas the c parameter of the second activation is bound to the Parent class.

As the execution of this second activation proceeds, it will call printAllAncestorClasses a third time, passing the superclass of Parent (the Grandparent class). The recursive second activation results in yet a third activation of the method that passes the background window. Similarly, the third activation results in a fourth because the Object class is an implicit superclass of Grandparent. Figure O6.16 illustrates the state of the four activation records as this fourth call begins.

Figure O6.16 Four activations of printAllAncestorClasses

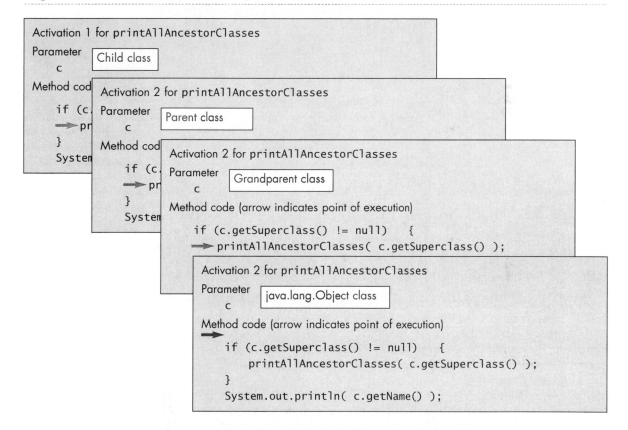

The execution snapshot in Figure O6.16 shows the different values for each c parameter. The first three activations are executing in the midst of their call statement. The fourth activation is about to begin executing. When c is bound to the java.lang.Object class, c.getSuperclass() returns null. Therefore, the fourth activation skips the *then* clause and proceeds to output java.lang.Object. Next, the fourth activation returns to the third, as pictured in Figure O6.17.

Returning to the third activation, the output statement executes and displays the name of its c parameter, Grandparent. Next, this third activation returns to the second, as shown in Figure O6.18.

Figure 06.17 After return from the fourth activation of printAllAncestorClasses

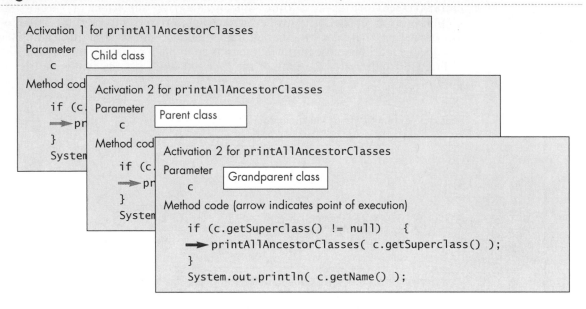

Figure 06.18 After return from the third activation of printAllAncestorClasses

Activation 1 for printAllAncestorClasses

Parameter | Child class
c

Method code (a

```
if (c !=
    print
}
System.ou
```

Activation 2 for printAllAncestorClasses

Parameter | Parent Class
c

Method code (arrow indicates point of execution)

```
    if (c.getSuperclass() != null)   {
        printAllAncestorClasses( c.getSuperclass() );
➡ }
    System.out.println( c.getName() );
```

The second activation proceeds to display the name of its c parameter (Parent). Then the second activation returns to the first. Finally, the first activation displays the name of its c parameter (Child) and returns to the site of the original call. Following is the complete output that results from these four activations.

```
java.lang.Object
Grandparent
Parent
Child
```

Figure O6.19 summarizes this entire execution trace of the `printAllAncestorClasses`. This figure lists each call, output statement, and return. Each recursive activation is indented from the activation that calls it.

Figure O6.19 Summarized trace of `printAllAncestorClasses`

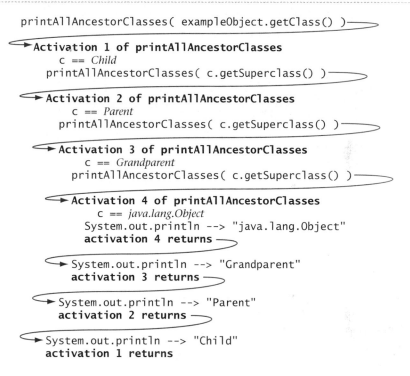

O6.5 THINKING RECURSIVELY

Tracing recursion by examining a sequence of activations gives you insight into the run-time behavior of recursive methods. However, writing recursive methods requires that you learn to think recursively.

Recursive thinking relies on a **divide-and-conquer** strategy. Recursive methods are made up of one or more base clauses and one or more recursive clauses. Each of these clauses can be thought of as a subalgorithm to the complete recursive method. A divide-and-conquer strategy begins by dividing the entire algorithm into the separate cases and then conquering each case by writing the subalgorithm for the corresponding clause.

For example, consider the calculation of the **greatest common divisor** of two positive numbers. The greatest common divisor of two positive integers—call them *a* and *b*—is defined to be the largest integer that divides *a* with a remainder of zero and *b* with a remainder of zero. Following are four examples of greatest common divisors, symbolized *gcd(a, b)*.

$$gcd(12, 9) == 3$$
$$gcd(12, 24) == 12$$
$$gcd(121, 22) == 11$$
$$gcd(25, 32) == 1$$

Euclid, an ancient Greek mathematician, observed two rules that help in the divide-and-conquer process. These rules are as follows for positive integers a and b.

gcd(a, b) == b, if a ≥ b and (a % b) == 0   **(1)**
gcd(a, b) == gcd(a%b, b), if a ≥ b and (a % b) != 0   **(2)**

Software Engineering Hint

The "divide" referred to in "divide and conquer" means that an algorithm must be partitioned into all possible cases.

These relationships describe a means to calculate the greatest common divisor whenever the first parameter, a, is greater than or equal to the second parameter, b. However, these two rules fail to consider all possible cases because they do not apply when a < b. Fortunately, the order of parameters doesn't matter in gcd, and that leads to the following third rule.

gcd(a, b) == gcd(b, a), if a < b   **(3)**

Rules (1), (2), and (3) collectively partition the computation of greatest common divisor by considering all possible cases. These rules lead to the recursive gcd method shown in Figure O6.20.

Figure O6.20 gcd method

```
/*  pre:    a > 0 AND b > 0
    post:   result == greatest common divisor of a and b */
private int gcd(int a, int b) {
    if (a >= b && a%b == 0) {
        return b;
    } else if (a >= b && a%b != 0) {
        return gcd(a%b, b);
    } else { // a<b
        return gcd(b, a);
    }
}
```

The first *then* clause corresponds to rule (1); the second *then* clause corresponds to rule (2); and the else clause corresponds to rule (3). The last two clauses are recursive.

Once the "divide" portion of the divide-and-conquer has produced a recursive algorithm, three conditions remain that must be guaranteed.

1) All potential cases must be accounted for in the algorithm.
2) Every base clause and every recursive clause must correctly handle its case.
3) Every recursive clause must ensure progress toward completion via a base clause.

The gcd method satisfies the first condition because every possible state that satisfies the precondition is handled by one of the three clauses. We can also assume the second condition because Euclid's rules have stood the test of time and the scrutiny of countless mathematicians.

Software Engineering Hint

Every recursive clause must make progress toward completion.

The final condition, demanding progress toward completion, is more difficult to show. The first *then* clause serves as the base clause for gcd; this clause is nonrecursive. The second *then* clause is executed only when a > b > 1. (If a == b or b == 1, the first *then* clause is selected, not the second.) These relations between a and b ensure that (a % b) has a value from 1 through b–1, and this means that the recursive call has a first parameter with a smaller value. Progress toward completion is guaranteed by successive activations with smaller parameter values.

The last recursive call to gcd (in the *else* clause) also can be shown to make progress toward completion. Each such call swaps the value of the a and b parameters, ensuring that the subsequent activations must use either of the other two clauses, which are guaranteed to reach completion.

Euclid's rules for computing greatest common divisor lead to an obvious way to divide and conquer the gcd method. For other algorithms it is often wise to begin the divide-and-conquer strategy by searching for the base cases because they tend to be the simpler options to identify and to code.

For example, consider writing a recursive method that identifies strings that are palindromes. (A palindrome is any string that consists of the same sequence of characters when it is reversed. The following words are all palindromes: "level", "racecar", "deed".) Figure O6.21 shows the specifications for the method.

Figure O6.21   Specifications for the isPalindrome method

```
/* post:   result == (s is a palindrome) */
private boolean isPalindrome(String s)
```

Software Engineering Hint

Divide and conquer often begins by considering the simplest cases. These usually lead to ensuring the existence of base clauses that are required for recursion.

Two base cases can be identified for isPalindrome. When String s is the empty string, it is a palindrome. When String s has a length of 1, it is also a palindrome. Figure O6.22 shows the isPalindrome method with the two base clauses combined into a single *then* clause.

The more general recursive clause requires progress toward the base clauses. Recursive calls to isPalindrome are guaranteed to make proper progress as long as they shorten the string with each successive activation. One way to accomplish this is to compare the first and last characters in the string. If these characters are the same, then only the string between these two characters must be considered further. Figure O6.23 uses this algorithm to complete the isPalindrome method.

Figure O6.22 The `isPalindrome` method with base clauses

```
/* post:   result == (s is a palindrome) */
private boolean isPalindrome(String s) {
    if (s.length() <= 1) {
        return true;
    } else {
        // recursive clause
    }
}
```

Figure O6.23 The finished `isPalindrome` method

```
/* post:   result == (s is a palindrome) */
private boolean isPalindrome(String s) {
    if (s.length() <= 1) {
        return true;
    } else {
        if (s.charAt(0) == s.charAt(s.length()-1))
            return isPalindrome(s.substring(1, s.length()-1));
        else
            return false;
    }
}
```

The *else* clause that returns `false` is an important part of the `isPalindrome` method. This clause executes as a result of a string with unequal first and last characters.

As a third example of designing a recursive method, consider a method to return the number of combinations of n objects taken r at a time, often symbolized C(n, r). By definition, C(n, r) is the number of different sets of size r that can be made using n distinguishable objects. For C(4, 3), if the four different objects are called *a*, *b*, *c*, and *d*, all the possible sets of size 3 can be enumerated as follows.

{a, b, c} {a, b, d} {a, c, d} {b, c, d}

This leads to the conclusion that C(4, 3) == 4. Similarly, the following enumerated sets demonstrate that C(5, 2) == 10.

{a, b} {a, c} {a, d} {a, e} {b, c} {b, d} {b, e} {c, d} {c, e} {d, e}

Two cases seem to be obvious for C(n, r):

C(n, r) == n, if r == 1
C(n, r) == 1, if n == r

Both cases can be developed into recursive clauses for a recursive `combinations` method, as shown in Figure O6.24.

Figure O6.24 The combinations method with incomplete recursive clause

```
/*  pre:    n >= r >= 1
    post:   result == the number of combinations of n items
            taken r at a time */
private int combinations(int n, int r) {
    if (r == 1) {
        return n;
    } else if (r == n) {
        return 1;
    } else {
        // recursive clause
    }
}
```

You can design the recursive clause of the `combinations` method by recognizing that the total number of combinations includes all combinations that contain item *a* plus the number of combinations that do not include item *a*. This relationship is restated in the following equation.

C(n, r) == Number of combinations with item *a* +
Number of combinations without item *a*   **(4)**

Notice that all sets of length r that include item *a* can be found by forming the union of {*a*} and one of the possible sets of length r–1 that are made from any of the original objects except *a*. In other words, the following equation defines the number of combinations including *a*.

Number of combinations with item *a* == C(n–1, r–1)   **(5)**

The number of original combinations that do *not* include item *a* is the same as the number of combinations with *a* removed from the possible items, which can be restated as follows.

Number of combinations without item *a* == C(n–1, r)   **(6)**

Substituting equations (5) and (6) into equation (4) leads to the following conclusion.

C(n, r) == C(n–1, r–1) + C(n–1, r)

Software Engineering Hint

Programmers often can discover and debug a recursive method faster than a loop that performs the same task. There are nonrecursive algorithms for the **combinations** method, but none so succinct.

This final equation supplies the necessary recursive clause for the `combinations` method, as shown in Figure O6.25.

Core Concepts O6

Figure O6.25 The completed combinations method

```
/*  pre:    n >= r >= 1
    post:   result == the number of combinations of n items
            taken r at a time */
private int combinations(int n, int r) {
    if (r == 1) {
        return n;
    } else if (r == n) {
        return 1;
    } else {
        return combinations(n-1, r-1) + combinations(n-1, r);
    }
}
```

The recursive clause for the combinations method ensures that one or both parameters decrease for recurring activations. The combinations(n-1,r-1) call clearly leads to the base clause with a condition of (r==1). Repeated calls to combinations(n-1,r) lead toward the base clause with the condition (r==n). Both base clauses are necessary to ensure the method's correctness.

Software Engineering Hint

Recursive methods amplify the importance of data sharing choices because each recursive activation needs appropriate facilities for communicating with its preceding and subsequent activation(s). Parameter passage, return values, and shared instance variables are three possible choices for communicating such data.

Like all methods, recursive methods exchange data in three ways: through parameter passage, through shared instance variables, and by return values (for nonvoid methods). This data exchange applies not only to different methods but also to different activations of the same method. When one activation of isPalindrome calls the method recursively, the calling activation shares a new String with the new activation (a String that is two characters shorter than the caller's parameter). Similarly, recursive calls to combinations share new arguments for the n and r parameters. A return from isPalindrome or combinations communicates some results to its caller. (isPalindrome returns true or false, and combinations returns an integer value.) The communication of data between recursive activations is crucial to the correctness of the method.

As a more complex example of how activations share data, consider the problem of finding a path through a maze. In this example, the maze is considered to be a Grid object. The class diagram for Grid is shown in Figure O6.26.

A Grid should be thought of as a rectangular collection of cells. The Grid constructor has two parameters to initialize the number of rows and the number of columns. Figure O6.27 shows an image of a Grid. Notice that rows and columns are numbered. (In the figure, row and column numbers are shown in blue with row numbers on the left and column numbers across the top.) The rowMax and columnMax methods are designed to return the highest row and column numbers, respectively.

Figure O6.26 Grid and MazeGrid class diagram

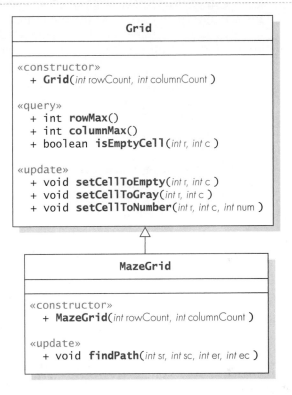

Figure O6.27 Sample image of Grid

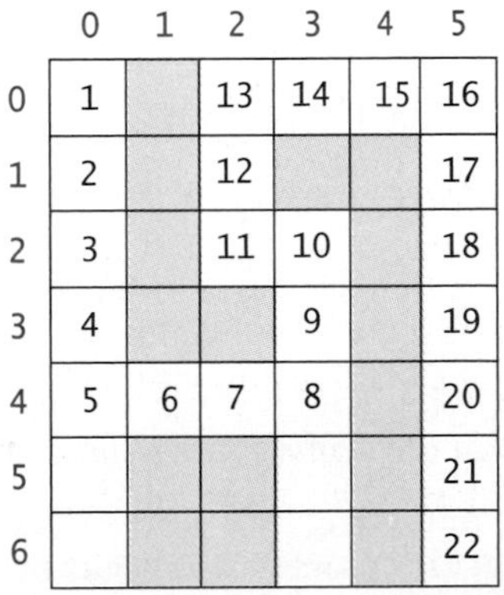

A cell can be empty (pictured as a white square in Figure O6.27), or it can be a wall (pictured as a gray filled square). The isEmptyCell method permits the client to check this state. Three methods (setCellToEmpty, setCellToGray, and setCellToNumber) can be called to alter cells. Calling setCellToEmpty turns any valid grid cell into an empty cell. Calling setCellToGray makes a cell into a wall by coloring it gray. Calling setCellToNumber also makes a cell nonempty but does so while assigning the cell a visible number.

A path through a maze results from following a sequence of previously empty neighboring cells that extend from a start cell to an end cell without encountering any cell more than once. For this kind of path, any two cells that share a common side are considered to be neighbors. Figure O6.27 illustrates by numbering the cells from a start cell in the upper left to an end cell in the lower right.

The MazeGrid class, diagrammed in Figure O6.26, extends Grid to include the desired findPath method. A call to findPath checks for a valid path from the start cell (the cell in row sr and column sc) through the end cell (the cell in row er and column ec). If such a path exists, it is numbered with consecutively increasing integers as shown in the figure. If no such path exists, then calling findPath leaves the grid unchanged.

The obvious choice for a recursive algorithm to find a maze path involves considering one cell at a time: each activation considers only one cell along some potential, relying on other activations to consider other cells. This algorithm can be sketched approximately as follows.

Recursive algorithm for finding a path given one particular cell
If the grid cell is invalid or is valid but nonempty,
>   then this attempt to find a path has failed.

If the grid cell is the end cell and is empty,
>   then the path is found successfully.

If the grid cell is empty but is not the end cell,
>   then number the cell and check neighboring cells recursively.

This algorithm identifies two base clauses: one when the given state can't lead to a successful path, and a second for the end of a successful path search. Many of the data sharing issues among activations can be drawn from this somewhat sketchy algorithm. These data are as follows:

- endRow: the row number of the end cell of the search path
- endColumn: the row number of the end cell of the search path
- row: the row of the particular cell examined by a single activation
- column: the column of the particular cell examined by a single activation
- this: the Grid object used to call such things as isEmptyCell and setCellToNumber
- counter: the integer number to use as a label for this cell

Actually, there is one more datum that isn't quite so obvious but can be revealed by a more careful examination of the following portion of the algorithm:

"check neighboring cells recursively"

Without going into all the details of implementing this subalgorithm, it is still clear that this process will begin by checking one neighbor and then proceed to a different neighbor if the *first attempt fails*. But discovering whether the first attempt fails requires that one activation communicate success or failure with another, and that leads to the need for the following seventh piece of shared data.

- pathExists: a Boolean value used to identify whether or not a path has yet been discovered

As with any method design, it is a good idea to identify which shared data are never altered by the method, because these data make good candidates for instance variables, as opposed to parameters. Of the seven pieces of shared data, two of them fall into this category (endRow and endColumn). The this item can also be removed from consideration as a parameter or return object because this is automatically available within any class. The four remaining data items can be partitioned into two groups: those that must be communicated *to* an activation at call time (row, column, and counter), and those that are communicated *from* the activation at return time (pathExists).

The data to be communicated requires the use of parameters because activations must keep track of different cell addresses and different counter values. However, the findPath command does not include these parameters. In such cases in which the public method has an insufficient parameter list, the usual solution is to use a **helper** method. A helper method is a private method called by the public method to perform some of the public method's behavior. In this case the helper method will be recursive, but it includes the parameters needed to support recursion. Figure O6.28 shows the complete MazeGrid class, including a helper method called checkAndNumberPath.

Figure O6.28 The complete MazeGrid class

```
/* invariant:  this is a rectangular grid of 20 pixel by 20 pixel
               square cells that displays upon a background canvas.
               and forAll (c : a cell of this | c.isEmptyCell()
                  implies c displays as a white square with a
                  black border
               and forAll (c : a cell of this | not
                  c.isEmptyCell()) == c displays as a non-white
                  square or a numbered square */
import java.awt.event.*;
public class MazeGrid extends Grid {
    private boolean pathExists;
    private int endRow, endCol;


/*  post:   this is a rectangular array of rowNum rows and colNum
            columns and forAll (c : a cell from this |
            c.isEmptyCell()) */
public MazeGrid(int rowNum, int colNum) {
    super(rowNum, colNum, "Run the Maze");
}


/*  post:   exists(a path of previously empty squares from
            (startRow, startCol) thru (endRow,endCol)) implies such
            a path is numbered sequentially
```

Continued on next page

```
                          and not exists (a path of previously empty squares from
                             (startRow, startCol) thru (endRow,endCol))
                             implies (this == this@pre) */
          public void findPath(int sr, int sc, int er, int ec) {
                endRow = er;
                endCol = ec;
                pathExists = false;
                checkAndNumberPath(sr, sc, 0);
          }


          /* pre:    The path from (startRow,startCol) to (r,c) has been num-
                     bered through counter.
             post:   exists(a path of previously empty squares from (r, c)
                         thru (endRow,endCol)) if and only if pathExists
                     and pathExists implies an empty path is numbered
                         sequentially
                     and not pathExists implies (this == this@pre) */
          private void checkAndNumberPath(int r, int c, int counter) {
              if (0<=r && r<=rowMax() && 0<=c && c<=columnMax()
                      && isEmptyCell(r,c)) {
                  counter++;
                  setCellToNumber(r,c, counter);
                  if (r == endRow && c == endCol) {
                      pathExists = true;
                  } else {
                      checkAndNumberPath(r+1, c, counter);
                      if (!pathExists) {
                          checkAndNumberPath(r, c+1, counter);
                      }
                      if (!pathExists) {
                          checkAndNumberPath(r-1, c, counter);
                      }
                      if (!pathExists) {
                          checkAndNumberPath(r, c-1, counter);
                      }
                      if (!pathExists) {
                          setCellToEmpty(r, c);
                      }
                  }
              }
          }
      }
```

Figure O6.28 demonstrates that a call to findPath consists primarily of an initial value assignment to the endRow and endColumn variables, and it calls checkAndNumberPath to do the remainder of the work. The pathExists data is also implemented as an instance variable, and findPath assigns this variable an initial value of false to signify that the path has not been found prior to a call to checkAndNumberPath. (Another alternative is to change the type of the method to Boolean and return whether or not a path exists.)

The recursive clause of checkAndNumberPath is designed to check each of the cell's four neighbors, if necessary. A recursive call to

```
checkAndNumberPath(r+1, c, counter);
```

checks for a path by proceeding to the neighboring cell having the next greater row number. If this recursive activation succeeds, pathExists will be true and no further recursive activations are made. If this recursive activation does not find a path, then pathExists will remain false and the algorithm performs the same kind of check on the neighboring cell having the next greater column number.

The return that occurs between any two consecutive recursive calls issued from the same activation is often referred to as **backtracking**. The algorithm has tried to find a path by a recursive call on a neighboring cell, but because that attempt failed to discover a path, the algorithm backtracks to the same activation to look for a path from an alternative neighboring cell. If an activation cannot find a path from any of its four neighbors, then it, too, backtracks to its caller and the pathExists variable remains false.

O6.6 RECURSION AND REPETITION

Recursion resembles looping (repetition) in many ways. Like looping, recursion is used to perform repetitive tasks. Both forms of control require attention to initialization and making progress, and both have the potential for seemingly endless execution.

It is always possible to replace repetition with recursion. To illustrate, Figure O6.29 contains a pattern for translating any *while* loop into a recursive method that performs the same algorithm.

Figure O6.29 A *while* loop and the corresponding recursive method

A while algorithm

```
while ( theCondition ) {
    loopBody;
}
```

The corresponding recursive method

```
private void recWhile() {
    if ( theCondition ) {
        loopBody;
        recWhile;
    }
}
```

Calling the `recWhile` method results in the same basic behavior as the while algorithm of Figure O6.26. The execution of `recWhile` begins by checking the value of *theCondition*. If this boolean condition is false, `recWhile` returns in the same way that the *while* loop algorithm completes execution whenever *theCondition* is found to be false. Whenever the test finds *theCondition* to be true, `recWhile` executes *loopBody* and calls itself recursively. This is the same behavior as the *while* algorithm that executes *loopBody* whenever *theCondition* is true.

Translating from a recursive method into a loop is not so simple, nor is it always feasible. Part of the difficulty stems from the fact that recursive methods often incorporate parameter passage, something that is not easily mimicked by a loop.

Despite the difficulties in translating from recursion to loops, there is one category of recursion, **tail recursion**, that can be routinely translated into repetition. Tail recursion is a category of recursive methods in which the recursive call is the last statement to be executed by an activation. For example, `isPalindrome`, repeated below, uses tail recursion.

```
private boolean isPalindrome(String s) {
    if (s.length() <= 1) {
        return true;
    } else {
        if (s.charAt(0) == s.charAt(s.length()-1))
            return isPalindrome(s.substring(1, s.length()-1));
        else
            return false;
    }
}
```

The only recursive call in `isPalindrome` occurs in its sixth line. This line may not be the last one of the method, but it is the last statement of an activation to execute in the event of recursion.

Tail recursion can be eliminated by using a loop that captures the recursive work within the loop body and uses a loop condition(s) corresponding to the base step of the recursion.

For example, Figure O6.30 shows a nonrecursive version of `isPalindrome`. This new version uses a local variable, `newS`, to play the same role that the `s` parameter plays in the recursive method.

Figure O6.30 Nonrecursive version of `isPalindrome`

```
private boolean isPalindrome (String s) {
    String newS = s;
    while ( newS.length() > 1
            && newS.charAt(0) == newS.charAt(newS.length()-1)) {
        newS = newS.substring(1, newS.length()-1);
    }
    return (newS.length() <= 1);
}
```

Software Engineering Hint

Recursion is generally less efficient than repetition because of the time required to manage the multiple environments of the recursive activations. Therefore, eliminating tail recursion tends to improve algorithm efficiency.

Some optimizing compilers can eliminate tail recursion, freeing the programmer from worrying about the inefficiencies of recursion.

In contrast to isPalindrome, the printAllAncestor Classes method, which is repeated below, is not tail recursive. The reason for this is because the System.out.println is called after the recursive call. Typically, it is difficult to translate non-tail-recursive code into loops. A loop to do the work of printAllAncestorClasses would need to progress through all parent classes, somehow "remembering" them for subsequent output.

```java
private void printAllAncestorClasses( Class c ) {
    if (c.getSuperclass() != null) {
        printAllAncestorClasses( c.getSuperclass() );
    }
    System.out.println(c.getName());
}
```

A final similarity between recursion and loops is that both have the potential for infinite execution. A method that calls itself without making progress toward the base clause is similar to an infinite loop. The only difference is that such "infinite recursion" throws a **stack overflow** exception.

Software Engineering Hint

A stack overflow exception usually means that a recursive method has recurred too deeply.

The name "stack overflow" comes from the fact that the Java VM stores each activation record within a so-called **run-time stack**. When a method is called recursively without end, the Java VM will eventually exhaust all the available space for method activations, and the exception results.

06.7 MORE COMPLICATED FORMS OF RECURSION (OPTIONAL)

Nontail recursion is more complicated than tail recursion in the sense that nontail recursion is not easily translated into an equivalent loop. Another way in which one algorithm can be more complicated than another is to perform multiple recursive calls per activation. The jthFibonacci method from Section O6.3 is such an example of a method that calls itself twice for each recursive activation. Furthermore, the checkAndNumberPath method from Section O6.5 can produce up to four recursive activations per call.

Many **fractal** algorithms also require multiple recursive calls. Fractals are visualized as drawing patterns that repeat in varying scales. For example, the **Sierpinski gasket**—a fractal created by Waclaw Sierpinski, a famous Polish mathematician (1882–1969)—appears within an equilateral triangle with the apex pointing directly up. (Call this outer gray triangle the **bounding triangle**.) The recursive pattern used to draw a Sierpinski gasket is to draw a second equilateral triangle

Core Concepts O6

inside the bounding triangle, as shown in Figure O6.31. In this picture the bounding triangle is a solid gray and the second triangle is the white center triangle. The white triangle is half the width and height of the bounding triangle, and perfectly centered from left to right. A Sierpinski gasket is formed by applying this drawing pattern recursively using the remaining gray triangles as bounding triangles.

Figure O6.31 The Sierpinski gasket pattern

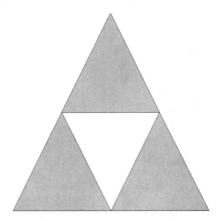

Fractals, such as the Sierpinski gasket, are drawn recursively by levels. A level N+1 fractal consists of a level N fractal with the next smaller copy of the pattern included. For the Sierpinski gasket, a level N+1 fractal is formed by drawing half-sized triangles in the center of every solid gray (bounding) triangle of a level N gasket. Figure O6.32 illustrates.

Figure O6.32 Level 1 through Level 4 Sierpinski gasket fractals

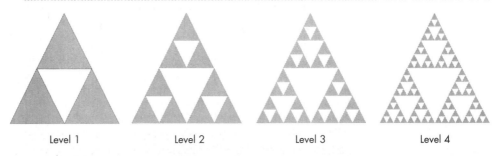

| Level 1 | Level 2 | Level 3 | Level 4 |

Figure O6.33 shows a class, DownTriangle, that creates an appropriate triangle for use in a Sierpinski gasket fractal. The DownTriangle constructor is a nonrecursive method that is passed the apex (x,y) and height (h) of a bounding triangle. DownTriangle draws a downward-pointing triangle within the specified bounding triangle.

Figure O6.33 DownTriangle class

```java
import javax.swing.*;
import java.awt.Graphics;
public class DownTriangle extends JComponent {

    /* post:   boundingX == x-h/4 and boundingY == y+h/2
                and boundingWidth == h/2 and boundingHeight == h/2 */
    public DownTriangle(int x, int y, int h) {
        super();
        setBounds(x-h/4, y+h/2, h/2, h/2);
    }
    /* post:   an equilateral triangle is drawn with its base on
                the top of this bounding rectangle and apex at
                (getWidth()/2, getHeight()) */
    public void paint(Graphics g) {
        g.setColor( getForeground() );
        g.setClip(0, 0, getWidth()+1, getHeight()+1);
        g.drawLine(0, 0, getWidth(), 0);
        g.drawLine(0, 0, getWidth()/2, getHeight());
        g.drawLine(getWidth(), 0, getWidth()/2, getHeight());
    }
}
```

Figure O6.34 diagrams the bounding triangle as a dashed gray line and the triangle to be drawn in solid black. After the black triangle is drawn, its three surrounding triangles are potential bounding triangles for other DownTriangle objects. As shown in Figure O6.34, the height of each of these three new bounding triangles is h/2, and the apex of each is (x, y), (x–h/4, y+h/2), and (x+h/4, y+h/2).

Figure O6.34 DownTriangle drawing

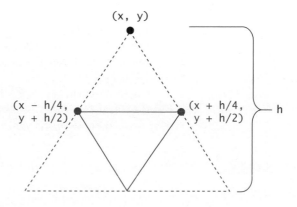

Figure O6.35 contains the code for a `displayGaskets` method that recursively draws Sierpinski gaskets. Each call to `displayGaskets` draws a single triangle. The first three parameters to `displayGaskets` are the x and y coordinates of the bounding triangle's apex along with the height of the bounding triangle. The fourth parameter is the level of the drawing. Each activation of `displayGaskets` begins by constructing a `DownTriangle`. Assuming that an activation has a `level` parameter greater than 1, it will result in three more activations—one for each of the surrounding triangles. Notice that the height argument for the recursive calls is half the height of the method's own height parameter. Progress is made toward completion because each recursive call uses a level argument that is 1 less than its calling activation.

The `displayGaskets` method requires three recursive calls to accomplish its task. This leads to a more complicated form of recursion—one that is impossible to implement nonrecursively unless additional data structures are used.

Figure O6.35 Sierpinski gasket program

```
import java.awt.*;
import javax.swing.*;
public class Director {
    private JFrame win;
    public Director() {
        win = new JFrame();
        win.setBounds(10, 10, 600, 600);
        win.getContentPane().setLayout(null);
        displayGaskets(300, 0, 600, 5);
        win.show();
    }

    /*  pre:    lev > 0
        post:   Sierpinski gaskets of level lev are drawn on win
                within a triangle with upper apex at (x, y)
                and height of h */
    private void displayGaskets( int x, int y, int h, int lev ) {
        DownTriangle gasket;
        gasket = new DownTriangle(x, y, h);
        win.getContentPane().add(gasket);
        if (lev > 1) {
            displayGaskets(x, y, h/2, lev-1);
            displayGaskets(x-h/4, y+h/2, h/2, lev-1);
            displayGaskets(x+h/4, y+h/2, h/2, lev-1);
        }
    }
}
```

Another form of recursion is known as **indirect recursion**. Indirect recursion occurs when a method can produce simultaneous activations of itself without calling itself directly. Such a situation occurs only when a method calls a sequence of other methods that eventually result in another call to the original method. Figure O6.36 shows a variation on the Sierpinski gasket program that is accomplished by indirect recursion.

Figure O6.36 `displayDownTriangle` and `displayUpTriangle`

```
private void displayDownTriangle( int x, int y, int h, int lev ) {
    DownTriangle triangle;
    triangle = new DownTriangle(x, y, h);
    win.getContentPane().add(triangle);
    if (lev > 1) {
        displayUpTriangle(x, y+h, h/2, lev-1);
    }
}

private void displayUpTriangle( int x, int y, int h, int lev ) {
    UpTriangle triangle;
    triangle = new UpTriangle(x, y, h);
    win.getContentPane().add(triangle);
    if (lev > 1) {
        displayDownTriangle(x, y-h, h/2, lev-1);
    }
}
```

The `displayDownTriangle` method is similar to the method by the same name from the Sierpinski gasket program. This method draws a `DownTriangle` in the same way as before. However, this new method does not call itself but instead calls `displayUpTriangle`. The `displayUpTriangle` method mirrors the behavior of `displayDownTriangle`. The `displayUpTriangle` method uses a bounding triangle with its apex at the bottom. A call to one of these methods draws a triangle and passes the newly drawn triangle to the other method, where it will be used as a bounding triangle. `displayUpTriangle` calls `displayDownTriangle`, and `displayDownTriangle` calls `displayUpTriangle`. The indirect recursion terminates when the `lev` parameter is no longer greater than 1. The picture drawn by calling these methods is a collection of triangles nested inside each other as shown in Figure O6.37.

Multiple recursive calls and indirect recursion contribute to algorithm complexity. Both can be difficult to replace with loops.

Figure O6.37 Image from `displayDownTriangle` and `displayUpTriangle`

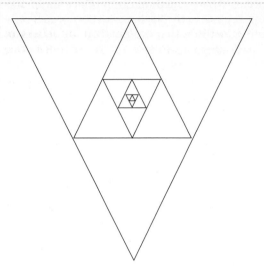

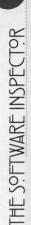

Following is a collection of hints on what to check when you examine code that involves the concepts of this chapter.

✔ Every recursive method needs a base clause that terminates the recursion. Checking for the presence of such a clause is always helpful.

✔ When a recursive method calls itself, it must be making progress toward the base clause. Checking for such progress can often eliminate stack overflow errors.

✔ Because recursive algorithms are generally based on divide-and-conquer strategies, it is wise to check to see that all possible cases have been properly accounted for in the method.

✔ Look for missing extremal clauses. The counterpart of the extremal clause for a recursive method tends to be a situation for which the method was not really intended.

1. Write a recursive definition for each of the following.
   a) Define what it means for one positive expression to be greater than (>) another positive expression. This should be defined in terms of + and ==.
   b) Define what it means for an airline to fly from A to B. Note that flying from A to B may require several individual connecting flights.

2. Consider the following method.

```java
private void munge( int x ) {
    System.out.println( x );
    if ( x != 10 ) {
        munge( x+3 );
    }
    System.out.println( x );
}
```

   a) What output results from the following call?
      ```java
      munge(10);
      ```
   b) What output results from the following call?
      ```java
      munge(1);
      ```
   c) What output results from the following call?
      ```java
      munge(11);
      ```
   d) What output results from the following call?
      ```java
      munge(0);
      ```

3. Consider the following method.

```java
private int times( int k, int m ) {
    if ( k != 0 ) {
        return m + times( k-1, m );
    } else {
        return 0;
    }
}
```

a) What output results from the following statement?

```java
System.out.println( times(3, 2) );
```

b) What output results from the following statement?

```java
System.out.println( times(2, 3) );
```

c) What output results from the following statement?

```java
System.out.println( times(100, 75) );
```

d) What output results from the following statement?

```java
System.out.println( times(-1, 2) );
```

e) Write a precondition and a postcondition to describe the behavior of this times method.

4. Following is a Java version of a famous algorithm known as Ackermann's function. What value is output for the statements in parts (a) through (c)?

```java
public int ack( int m, int n) {
    if (m == 0) {
        return n + 1;
    } else if (n == 0) {
        return ack(m-1, 1);
    } else {
        return ack( m-1, ack(m, n-1) );
    }
}
```

a) ack(2, 3)

b) ack(2, 4)

c) ack(3, 3)

5. Show how to replace each of the following methods with a recursive method that produces the same output without a loop.

a)
```java
private void printProducts( int j, int k ) {
    while (j < k) {
        System.out.println( j*k );
        j++;
        k = k - 2;
    }
}
```

```
b) private void printOtoN( int n ) {
       for (int k=0; k!=n+1; k++) {
          System.out.println( k );
       }
    }
```

6. Rewrite the code for the jthFibonacci function so that it performs the same task as the method in Figure O6.8. Do not use recursion in your method.

7. Show how to replace the following method with a recursive method that returns the same values when executed.

```
private int sum1ThruN( int n ) {
    int sum = 1;
    int k = 1;
    while (sum <= n) {
        sum = sum + k;
        k++;
    }
    return sum;
}
```

8. Figure O6.29 shows a recursive method that mimics the execution of a *while* loop.

   a) Supply a similar recursive method to mimic the behavior of the following *do* loop pattern.

```
do {
    loopBody;
} while ( theCondition );
```

   b) Supply a similar recursive method to mimic the behavior of the following *for* loop pattern.

```
for ( ; theCondition; progressStatement) {
    loopBody;
}
```

1. Write a recursive method for making change. When passed an amount of money, the method should print all the combinations of pennies, nickels, dimes, and quarters that equate to this amount.

2. The game Boggle is played on a 4 by 4 grid of letters. The object is to find English words within the grid. These words must be formed from a sequence of neighboring cells, where a neighbor is defined to include all cells with a common border *and* those with a common vertex (i.e., the diagonal cells). For example, the word "recur" is highlighted in the following Boggle puzzle.

I	A	K	A
S	Q	T	R
H	E	E	W
R	U	C	X

   Write a recursive program to randomly generate a Boggle puzzle, along with a recursive method to search for the occurrence of any word (passed as a String parameter).

3. Write a program to draw a Sierpinski carpet fractal pattern. This Sierpinski carpet begins with a black background square. The drawing pattern is a black square with a filled white square centered within the black square. The side length of the white square is one-third the side length of the black square on which it is placed.

   The fractal pattern is repeated on the eight black squares that surround the white center square. Dashed lines in the following image show the location of these eight squares.

Your program must be capable of drawing Sierpinski carpets to different levels. Following is an illustration of the repeated pattern.

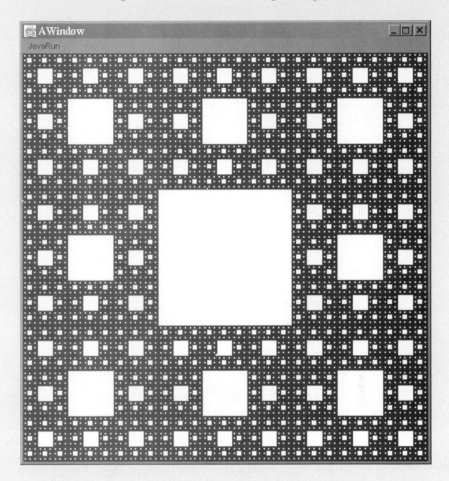

4. Write a program to produce fractal images based on a regular hexagon. A level 0 image consists of a hexagon with the following form.

The repeated pattern is to draw six more hexagons at the corners of the larger hexagon. These six new hexagons have side length that is half of that of their predecessor. The following level 1 picture illustrates.

The following picture shows a level 4 version of this fractal pattern.

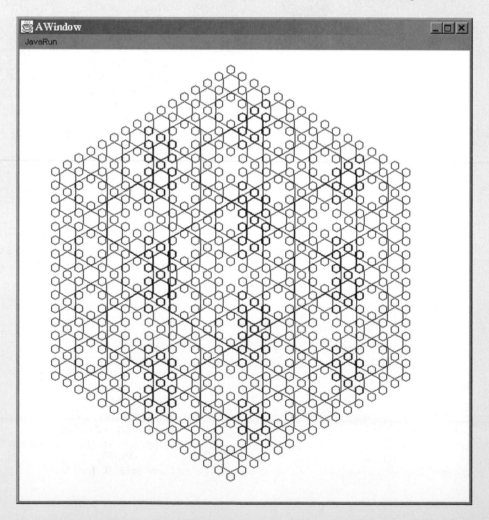

INDEX